GRECO-ROMAN WRESTLING

William A. Martell, MS
Diablo Valley College
Pleasant Hill, CA

Human Kinetics Publishers

Library of Congress Cataloging-in-Publication Data

Martell, Bill.
   Greco-Roman wrestling / William A. Martell.
     p.   cm.
   Includes index.
   ISBN 0-87322-408-6
   1. Wrestling. I. Title.
   GV1195.M327 1993   92-28782
                              CIP

ISBN: 0-87322-408-6

Acquisitions Editor: Brian Holding
Developmental Editors: Mary E. Fowler and Lori Garrett
Assistant Editors: Dawn Roselund, Julie Swadener, and John Wentworth
Copyeditor: Barbara Walsh
Proofreader: Tom Rice
Indexer: Theresa J. Schaefer
Production Director: Ernie Noa
Typesetter: Julie Overholt
Text Design: Keith Blomberg
Text Layout: Tara Welsch, Denise Lowry
Cover Design: Jack Davis
Cover Photo: Dave Black
Interior Photos: Keith Simonian and Steve Brown/USA Wrestler
Models: Randy Takahashi, Scott Osterholt, and Eustacio Torres. Anthony Amado, Gogi Parseghian, and Andy Seras appear courtesy of *USA Wrestler*.
Printer: United Graphics

Human Kinetics books are available at special discounts for bulk purchase. Special editions or book excerpts can also be created to specification. For details, contact the Special Sales Manager at Human Kinetics.

Printed in the United States of America   10 9 8 7 6 5 4 3

Human Kinetics
Web site: http://www.humankinetics.com/

United States: Human Kinetics, P.O. Box 5076, Champaign, IL 61825-5076
1-800-747-4457

Canada: Human Kinetics, Box 24040, Windsor, ON N8Y 4Y9
1-800-465-7301 (in Canada only)

Europe: Human Kinetics, P.O. Box IW14, Leeds LS16 6TR, United Kingdom
(44) 1132 781708

Australia: Human Kinetics, 57A Price Avenue, Lower Mitcham, South Australia 5062
(08) 277 1555

New Zealand: Human Kinetics, P.O. Box 105-231, Auckland 1
(09) 523 3462

Dedication

To my wife, Betty, who has wholeheartedly supported my wrestling adventures for 40 years. Her enthusiastic involvement and hard work in helping develop American wrestlers and wrestling have made the wrestling journey our adventure.

Contents

About the Author

Bill Martell has experienced success at every level of coaching. He guided junior wrestlers to national and world championships and high school wrestlers in Oregon and California to state championships. His 13 years as a member of the United States national coaching staff provided him the opportunity to coach national, world, Pan American, and Olympic champions.

During his tenure at the University of California-Berkeley, Bill Martell served for 27 years as supervisor of physical education and 15 years as wrestling coach. He was also a team leader and assistant coach of the 1992 United States Olympic Greco-Roman wrestling team.

He actively coaches wrestling at Diablo Valley Community College and the Concord Wrestling Club.

Bill Martell also has directed youth and Olympic training camps and has led coaching accreditation programs at the national and local levels. He has served as president of the National Collegiate Athletic Association coaches' association and chairman of the National Greco-Roman Sports Committee. He is also chairman of USA Wrestling's development committee and a member of its executive committee and board of directors.

Preface

Greco-Roman Wrestling will not only create more experts in this unique wrestling style, but also will allow folkstyle and freestyle competitors and coaches to enjoy their sport more as their knowledge increases. Greco-Roman wrestling offers additional techniques to the freestyle or folkstyle wrestler, and any serious student of wrestling should explore the Greco-Roman refinements.

Folkstyle wrestling, on the other hand, adds an aggressive element to Greco-Roman competition that is changing the complexion of the international sport. In the 1984 and 1988 Olympiads, for example, the United States Greco-Roman team blended the upper body Olympic-style techniques with their traditional style; they earned both medals, and, for the first time, international respect for their efforts. The unique style of the U.S. team is rooted itself in the aggressiveness of freestyle and folkstyle techniques as taught by American high schools and colleges. This book recognizes these accomplishments and encourages continued growth.

Every coach and wrestler, no matter what your style preference, can use the skills I present in *Greco-Roman Wrestling* to expand and develop your understanding of wrestling. Your experience and level of expertise will determine how and when you apply this expanded knowledge.

I have prepared tried and true techniques for you to use in your coaching or wrestling development, and more than 550 photographs illustrate these points. The techniques in *Greco-Roman Wrestling* are the actual scoring moves used at the Olympic Games. Some techniques will seem to naturally fit your style better than others. Start with these. If you are constantly aware of sound position, and you understand how and why a move works, your execution and application of the technique also will be sound. Remember, it takes years of training to excel in wrestling. Be patient. Don't give up if a particular move doesn't work the first time, or the second, or the third. Wrestling takes years to master.

The first step in becoming a complete wrestler is learning the basics of the sport. The first three chapters of the book provide this background. In chapter 1, you'll learn how the moves and techniques common to Greco-Roman wrestling can be used in other styles of wrestling. You'll learn in chapter 2 the fundamentals of Greco-Roman wrestling that can be used to strengthen your performance as a freestyle or folkstyle wrestler. In chapter 3 you'll learn how to attack your opponent and discover ways to select effective counterattacks that can put you back into control of a match.

The techniques that you should develop first appear in chapters 4 through 6. All attacks to the body are in chapter 4, arm attacks are found in chapter 5, and a discussion of attacks to the head and arm follows in chapter 6.

Chapter 7 on par terre wrestling, or wrestling on the mat, helps you bring together all you've learned and prepares you for actual Greco-Roman competition. You'll learn how to read your opponent's moves and discover when techniques such as the gut wrench and the reverse lift will lead you to a score. You'll also find out how to counter those moves and turn them into scoring opportunities.

To complement your skills, you'll need an effective training program. Chapter 8 outlines the components of a quality program, from warm-up and flexibility to practicing techniques, cross-training, and cool down. I've also included sample workout calendars that have been used to train some of America's best wrestlers in their quest to reach the Olympic Games. Sample workouts appear for 7-day intervals, both during the developmental phase of the year and leading up to a competition, and for 9-day, 5-month, and 1-year periods. A special 4-year calendar outlines the road to making it to the Olympics.

The skills you'll learn by combining Greco-Roman techniques with those used in folkstyle and freestyle will help you achieve your highest goals, whether you're pursuing a gold medal or a championship in your weight class. Use the sound wrestling techniques you have learned and weave them with the upper body techniques presented in *Greco-Roman Wrestling* to develop a more complete style of wrestling. The broader your frame of reference, the wider your field of understanding becomes. By knowing the broadest scope of wrestling, you can be able to select the specific path you want to follow.

Acknowledgment

I'd like to gratefully acknowledge the coaches and athletes who taught me wrestling and allowed me to teach them wrestling.

CHAPTER 1

Refining Wrestling Using Greco-Roman Techniques

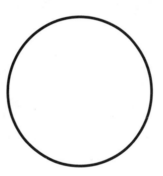

When they hear the term ''Greco-Roman wrestling,'' most freestyle and folkstyle wrestlers and coaches picture a wrestler being lifted from the mat and thrown backward onto his head. Most people don't consider this a pleasant experience, so it is understandable that they may be reluctant to learn this international style of wrestling.

Greco-Roman refers to one of the two styles of wrestling used in the Olympic Games and is known in Europe as the ''classic'' style of wrestling. It is a throwing sport that employs upper body locks. Very simply, it is upper body wrestling; attacks to an opponent's head, trunk, and arms are fundamental. It differs from freestyle (the other Olympic style of wrestling) in that it does not allow the use of the legs in holds nor the application of any holds below the waist. By the same token it differs from American folkstyle wrestling, which has traditionally focused on attacks that occur from the waist down.

Because Greco-Roman is limited to upper body attacks, the refinement of technique is much greater than in folkstyle and freestyle wrestling. By applying the techniques used in Greco-Roman wrestling to these other styles, however, wrestlers using any style can improve their abilities and refine their skills.

Greco-Roman Wrestling in the United States

When the U.S. fielded its first Greco-Roman Olympic wrestling team in 1952, about the only requirement for participation was showing up. Not until 1968 did the U.S. win a place at an international championship, taking fourth at the World Championships. The predominant regions producing Greco-Roman wrestlers in the U.S.

1

have changed little since 1968. New York, Michigan, Minnesota, and California provide most of our Greco-Roman wrestlers because most coaches experienced in Greco-Roman have established clubs in these states. The number of youth wrestlers participating in Greco-Roman at the national junior championships has increased to about 500 annually. The number of participants in the senior national championships has remained the same or decreased slightly over the past years. The senior tournament usually fields between 150 and 180 entries. The quality of our senior wrestlers has improved, but the number has not.The number of our junior wrestlers has increased, but the quality, in terms of world competition, has not improved. The experience and technical knowledge of a small number of senior-level coaches has improved, but the number of Greco-Roman coaches has increased only slightly.

Because the Greco-Roman expertise seems to be available and athletes and coaches seem interested, we must find a way to bring them together to arrange a structured, orderly program of Greco-Roman development. This means wrestling people active in folkstyle, freestyle, and Greco-Roman must share their knowledge and enthusiasm for wrestling. The numerous wrestling organizations to which these people belong must be directed by their membership to take part in the development of a unique American style of Greco-Roman wrestling. The uniqueness of style will come from the application of folkstyle philosophy and technique to the philosophy and technique of today's Greco-Roman wrestling. Each individual, club, and school should seize the opportunity to broaden and improve American wrestling.

Folkstyle Tactics

In attempting to nurture an American style of international Greco-Roman wrestling, we must determine the sound characteristics of folkstyle wrestling that can be applied to international wrestling and eliminate emphasis on training that is not applicable or might even be detrimental to effective international wrestling. For example, in folkstyle wrestling, the desire to win the escape point leads to movement for movement's sake alone. This tactic may be effective in folkstyle wrestling because the top man is not permitted to lock his hands around the defensive man's trunk or legs. One of the top

man's main concerns then becomes controlling his opponent and keeping him on the mat in an inferior wrestling position. The man in the advantage position now becomes a defender in that he must do things to counter his opponent's escape threat. The rules recognize this situation by allowing a wrestler to gain a point for holding his opponent on the mat for a minute more than the opponent holds him down.

Because a wrestler can win a match by escaping, riding, or both, these two endeavors enter the category of wrestling tactics. As a result, every folkstyle wrestler spends time in daily practice on escaping and riding. The time and energy allotted to these two wrestling tactics is specific to a style of wrestling practiced only in the U.S. and having limited application to international wrestling.

Current sound physiological, psychological, and biomechanical principles should guide our selection of techniques and tactics. Folkstyle wrestling develops athletes who must be in top physical condition. This is mainly because in folkstyle, a wrestler spends a large portion of the match on the mat. He therefore is always in *direct contact* with his opponent. This means that the defensive wrestler is continually being held down by the offensive wrestler who is striving to accumulate riding time. Because an escape by the defensive wrestler results in a point being scored, the activity by both wrestlers is intense. The level of endurance required for this type of wrestling ensures that both wrestlers remain in top shape.

The *constant attacking* of the opponent's legs forces a folkstyle wrestler to *focus* on one area of the body in his attempts to score. This allows the opponent to focus his defense on one area of attack. So to succeed, a wrestler must be very strong and have a well-developed sense of *stubborn determination*.

In addition to an open style of leg attack, folkstyle wrestlers learn to *scramble from all positions* in the constant sequences of escape and counter, stand up, takedown and sit out, and follow.

Applying Folkstyle to Greco-Roman

Upper body wrestling, as it might be defined in folkstyle, usually means arm drags, duck unders, bear hugs, side whizzers, lateral drops, front head and arms, and headlock hip throws. All are legitimate wrestling moves used in

Greco-Roman to score and win matches. But in folkstyle, more often than not these moves are used as defensive tactics to counter a leg attack or as a last-ditch maneuver when a wrestler is behind, running out of time, and needing big points.

The use of upper body position and control has not been developed enough in the United States to allow wrestlers and coaches the opportunity to study and understand *standing* wrestling.

The techniques employed to take an opponent down (below-the-waist leg attack) and the positions adopted to keep him down (ride him) put both wrestlers in a position that causes the long axis of the body (the back) to be parallel to the surface of the mat. Generally this leads wrestlers to become accustomed to wrestling on their knees with their heads close to the mat. They become comfortable wrestling in positions that limit their usable techniques and provide their opponents with a variety of defensive tactics and scoring opportunities. The wrestling maneuvers that best fit the folkstyle rules force individuals to wrestle from a very difficult and inefficient wrestling position.

A wrestler with a limited area of attack (from the waist down) is easily defended against. In addition, because of the inferior position of attack he is often scored against with countermoves by an opponent in a position of better leverage that offers greater mobility with less energy expended. The semi-erect posture and higher level of attack used in Greco-Roman offer a valid alternative to the low attack. Familiarity with some simple principles and techniques will allow a wrestler to develop a style, sequence, and coordination of upper and lower body holds into a plan for total body wrestling.

The folkstyle wrestler's initial involvement with upper body wrestling might well begin by applying skills he has developed in folkstyle to Greco-Roman. For example, in folkstyle wrestling, the arm drag is a secondary technique. In Greco-Roman, it is a highly developed attack series. Any attack or defense that concerns any part of the body from the waist up in any style of wrestling is applicable to Greco-Roman. All of the techniques of Greco-Roman apply to other styles of wrestling as well. The depth of study done on upper body control, balance, and throwing in Greco-Roman has occurred simply because the area of attack is limited by the rules. The variety and nuances of Greco-Roman enrich the other styles. Adding a sophisticated up-

per body attack to a leg attack–oriented wrestler requires the time, practice, and patience needed to alter a subconscious conditioned reflex. The examples that follow provide an idea of how wrestlers can use folkstyle skills in Greco-Roman wrestling.

• Though direct attacks on the legs of an opponent that require use of the arms or legs are not used in Greco-Roman wrestling, proper foot and leg positioning is crucial. The wrestler's foot and leg position provides the base from which all upper body wrestling emanates. Correct positioning of hips and legs makes lifting and throwing an opponent not only possible, but also more efficient.

• The direct frontal attack learned from the double-leg attack in folkstyle can readily be adjusted to a high double leg aimed at and above the waist. Likewise, the body movement learned in a high-crotch single leg can very easily become a duck under. The up-and-down, in-and-out movement so familiar to folkstyle wrestlers can be used effectively in changing level and flanking movements in Greco-Roman. The value of these movements is increased because the wrestler's legs need not be defended.

• The contact or locked positions seen in folkstyle are few. Most attacks start from a no-contact position. However, the locks used can be developed readily and expanded upon in Greco-Roman.

• The collar-elbow lock commonly used in folkstyle can be adjusted to a head and arm headlock position in Greco-Roman. The two-on-one armlock (controlling an opponent's arm with both of your arms) and the over-under arm position are common in Greco-Roman.

The folkstyle wrestler will have to adjust his stance and positioning to facilitate wrestling in a chest-to-chest contact position. He also must develop confidence in his ability to arch and throw back. Most throws come from a pulling and turning motion. These movements are in direct opposition to the drive-and-push action taught in folkstyle. Adjusting to this difference takes effort and time. The ability to scramble from any position learned in folkstyle is a valuable asset in Greco-Roman. Many Greco-Roman flurries that result from throws and near throws offer the scrambler a chance to score and use an opponent's action against him.

Scrambling can be effective in mat wrestling if it is not defined as movement for the sake of movement alone. In folkstyle, continual movement is used by the bottom man because he can score points by escaping, and his opponent can score by riding him. Careless movement on the mat can offer easy opportunities for one's opponent to score. Well-thought-out movement and constant adjustment are essential to good mat defense.

In certain circumstances, a stand-up to a neutral position is a wise tactic, even in Greco-Roman wrestling. Side rolls and switch actions can score points for the bottom man when the situation is right. However, they usually are not the first move on the bottom. The prime concern for the bottom man is defense. If he is successful in his defense, the referee will return both wrestlers to a neutral position. Remember that any sound wrestling maneuver can be effective in the correct situation, no matter what the style. The only limitation comes from rule restrictions or tactical concerns.

CHAPTER 2

Fundamentals of Greco-Roman Wrestling

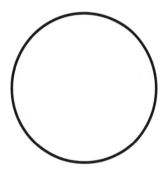

In all sports, certain body positions and movement patterns are essential to the successful execution of the techniques of that sport. This is especially true in wrestling. In a wrestling match, not only must you execute the skill correctly, but you also must allow for an opponent who may be in direct physical contact with you and does not want you to succeed in executing your maneuver. You must be concerned with the position and movement of your opponent's body as well as your own. The goal is to start your technique from a biomechanically correct position, execute the technique with a biomechanically correct movement pattern, and finish the technique in a position of advantage.

Center of Gravity

Because Greco-Roman begins and occurs primarily with wrestlers in a standing position, the position of the body in relation to its center of gravity is extremely important. An efficient, functional biomechanical position that allows the body to move and exert maximum force in a desired direction is essential. This position must allow you to control not only your center of gravity but that of your opponent as well. Therefore, the position of your body in relation to that of your opponent is very important. Pummeling, or fighting to secure a position from which a scoring maneuver will be successful, precedes the scoring move. Your center of gravity must always be a little lower than or directly under your opponent's when you are defending, pummeling for position, or throwing your opponent.

Wedge Position and Centering

The basic body position from which wrestling begins is the *wedge*. In this position your weight is directly over a point just behind the heel of your front foot (see Figure 2.1a). Your back foot supports a little less of your weight and is freer to move than the front foot. The knees are flexed and the long axis of your body (your back) is essentially upright and almost perpendicular to the floor. The head is up and in a direct line with the spine. The shoulders are parallel to the floor. The upper arm is held close to the body and slightly to the front (see Figure 2.1b). The forearm is parallel to the floor and extended out from the center of gravity.

When assuming the wedge position, a wrestler must always *center*. Centering is simply focusing on your center of gravity. To maintain a correct position, focus your thoughts on a point in your body immediately behind and slightly lower than your belly button. Breathe down into your belly, and relax your shoulders and upper body as you exhale. This will allow you to maintain the proper body position and relax your upper body. Breathing up into your chest and tensing your upper body will tend to raise your center of gravity.

Off-Balancing and the Throw

Although you must always strive for and maintain a stable position for defense and pummeling, you must do just the opposite to throw your opponent. One of three things must occur:

1. Your opponent must put himself in an off-balance position.
2. You must move him to an off-balance position.
3. You must secure a lock (position) in which his body must go where your body goes.

When you secure a lock, your opponent will immediately adjust his balance to defend against

Figure 2.1, a and b   Side and front views of the wedge position.

the locked position. At this point you must shift your center of gravity, breaking your opponent's balance and taking him with you to an off-balance position. This creates the opportunity for you to throw him. As the throw occurs, you must be conscious of ending the throw on the mat with you in control. Make this adjustment as you are throwing him.

Taking your opponent off balance without securing a lock or having strong control of some part of his body presents opportunities for one-point takedowns. By consciously creating situations of equal unbalance in training, you can learn to recognize by feel when the instant of mutual unbalance occurs. At that precise moment, action and/or counteraction must occur. The instant you feel the position of mutual off-balance is the time to throw and the time to counter the throw.

Thus we see that a wrestler must apply force and velocity when he is in optimum position. Your opponent will waste much energy if you force him to wrestle from less than optimum body positions. Creating such situations can become an important part of match strategy.

Maintaining correct body position, centering, and off-balancing your opponent are fundamental to maintaining control of the center of the mat. Keeping your opponent wrestling from the zone (the edge of the mat) is tactically sound and keeps you in a position on the mat where passivity calls from the judges are more likely to go in your favor. We can begin bringing all of these factors into focus and creating our own personal style of Greco-Roman wrestling by first examining your opponent and his vulnerable areas.

Attack Areas

As we examine the various methods of controlling, moving, off-balancing, and throwing an opponent to the mat, it becomes apparent that it is essential for you to control specific areas of your opponent's body by pummeling (battling to secure a position of advantage)—fighting for the best position of hips, legs, arms, and head.

The five primary attack areas are shown in Figure 2.2. They are as follows:

1. The area between your opponent's feet and directly under his center of gravity
2 and 3. The areas immediately under your opponent's left (2) and right (3) shoulders
4. Your opponent's center
5. Your opponent's head

Controlling the Attack Areas

Gaining control of one or more of the attack areas will help you create proper leg and hip position. Good control of two or more of the primary attack areas almost ensures success of a technique if you time the execution correctly.

The fight to control an attack area below the waist is carried out with your hips, knees, and feet in proper positioning. Your shoulder, head,

Figure 2.2 The five primary attack areas.

hands, and arms attack the areas above the waist. Proper hip and leg placement aids the attacks on your opponent's upper body.

Fighting for control of attack area 1 is fierce, important, and a constant battle between the two wrestlers, involving the legs and hips. To control this area, get one or both of your legs deep in the attack area. Securing a leg position between your opponent's knees and tight to his hips will put your center of gravity under his and facilitate lifting him from the mat (see Figure 2.3).

Figure 2.3 The lifting position.

This position also will allow you to off-balance your opponent by pulling and turning his upper body, as in Figure 2.4.

Figure 2.4 Positioning for the throw.

If you can pull your opponent over your center of gravity and lift him from the mat even one inch, you can throw him, as shown in Figure 2.5, a-c. As stated earlier, at the precise time that you feel the position of mutual off-balance you must make the throw. Your opponent will feel the bad position he is in and attempt to recover to a safe position quickly.

As the fight for area 1 is going on, each wrestler will be working for control of positions 2, 3, and 4 with both arms, both shoulders, and the head. The areas to be controlled here are at the shoulder joint and your opponent's center of gravity.

Control of attack areas 2 and 3 is dependent upon getting one arm, two arms, or your head in the attack area close to your opponent's body and controlling his shoulder (see Figure 2.6, a and b). From this position, you can gain a high locked position that can lead to a score (see Figure 2.7, a and b).

You can control area 4 by getting one or both arms around your opponent's waist from the front, side, or back (see Figure 2.8).

Controlling primary attack area 5 is particularly important. The head is a very heavy part that is attached to the long axis (the backbone) of the human body. Where the head goes, the

Figure 2.5, a-c Pulling, lifting, and completing the throw.

Figure 2.6, a and b   Attacking areas 2 and 3.

Figure 2.7, a and b   The high lock puts you in position to score.

rest of the body will follow (see Figure 2.9a). Control of your opponent's head means control of his body. The muscles of the torso essentially are designed to function when the vertebrae are in line and erect. The efficiency of these muscles in your opponent can be severely limited if you twist or move his head (see Figure 2.9b). Head position and movement are closely related to correct timing in the execution of moves.

Secondary Attack Areas

Very often you can work into control of a primary attack area by controlling a secondary attack area, such as the wrist, as shown in Figure 2.10. Having control of the primary attack areas allows you to secure and maintain a dominant body position. Having control of the secondary

attack areas makes it possible for you to control and overcome an opponent without a chest-to-chest confrontation. Controlling both secondary and primary attack areas makes for scoring opportunities. If you control your opponent's head and hands, you will be able to move your opponent and achieve proper foot placement and positioning.

The five secondary attack areas are shown in Figure 2.11. They are as follows:

6. The waist
7. The wrist
8. The elbow
9. The shoulder
10. The neck

Figure 2.8 Creating a bodylock by controlling attack areas 1 and 4.

Figure 2.10 Controlling a primary attack area at the shoulder and a secondary attack area at the wrist.

Figure 2.9, a and b Adjusting your opponent's head by controlling it with your hands or your arms.

Figure 2.11 The five secondary attack areas.

Every movable part of the body has a particular set of muscles that give it a specific and limited range of motion. Setting up a position that will allow a joint and its muscles to function at maximum strength and efficiency will greatly assist you in controlling and off-balancing an opponent. Off-balancing will in turn keep your opponent's joints and muscles from functioning normally. Your primary goal is to attack your opponent's center of gravity by attacking and controlling his limbs.

For example, a person's arm has three movable joints—the shoulder, the elbow, and the wrist. Isolating and controlling the shoulder will give you the best opportunity to attack your opponent's center of gravity (see Figure 2.12, a-c).

Figure 2.12 Controlling the shoulder (a and b); a bodylock at the waist (c).

This position, however, will not give you control of the other two joints of the limb. At this point you must attack the trunk or head. Isolating and controlling all three of the joints of a limb (see Figure 2.13) will give you complete control of the limb. Achieving this degree of control obviously dictates that you use techniques, such as the two-on-one fireman's carry, to attack your opponent's limbs. Pull your opponent in a circle to a position where attack areas 2 or 3 are exposed (see Figure 2.14a). Place your head in the attack area and lower your center of gravity (see Figure 2.14b). Lift and pull your opponent off the mat and arch your back to the side (see Figure 2.14c). The power to complete the throw

Figure 2.13 Controlling the arm.

comes from the position of your legs and body. Having strong control of a limb will present opportunities to utilize techniques involving your opponent's arm and neck, and arm and trunk. You can gain a front head- and armlock by controlling the arm. Lift your opponent by the arm (see Figure 2.15a). As you turn in a right circle away from him, pull his shoulder to his hip (see Figure 2.15b). Go over his head with your underhook and secure a front head and arm position (see Figure 2.15c). You can also gain a bodylock by controlling the arm. Place your leg deep in attack area 1 (see Figure 2.15d). Work your opponent's shoulder and pull him up on your hip (see Figure 2.15e). Push the controlled arm across his chest and under his other arm (see Figure 2.15f). From this position you can lift your opponent from the mat or drive through his hips to the mat (see Figure 2.15g).

Figure 2.14, a-c   The two-on-one fireman's carry.

Figure 2.15, a-c   The two-on-one to a front head- and armlock.

(continued)

Figure 2.15, d-g *(continued)*

Figure 2.15, d-g The two-on-one to a bodylock.

Positioning

All wrestlers must know the word *position* and must learn to use position to their advantage. Your body position, your opponent's body position, and the relationship of each to the other is extremely important.

Properly positioning your own body and maintaining that position as it relates to your opponent, the mat, and your center of gravity is the base from which you develop control of your opponent. You must maintain this position when attacking or defending.

Getting into the preferred positions is not easy and requires tenacity as well as technique. Whenever you venture from the sound basic positions, it must be to attack. Your attack must be immediate and without hesitation.

You can create strong positions by moving either your opponent or yourself to the desired position. If you are tactically accomplished, you can create situations where your opponent will unknowingly and voluntarily move himself into the position you desire. Very often you must take a risk and present him with bait that he cannot refuse. You must be prepared to instantly recognize your advantage and attack.

Positions that put your shoulder at the midline of your opponent's body and one leg in primary attack area 1 while your total body position is a wedge will keep your center of gravity below your opponent's and give you an advantage (see Figure 2.16, a and b). Pulling and turn-

Figure 2.16, a and b   The wedge position provides the base from which control of your opponent develops.

Figure 2.17   Pulling an opponent out of his wedge position.

Figure 2.18   Maintaining a strong position.

ing your opponent are effective methods to use in getting your opponent out of his wedge and thereby creating opportunities for you to score points (see Figure 2.17). In maintaining a strong position, you must constantly pull your opponent and force all of your weight down on the area of your opponent's body that you are controlling (see Figure 2.18).

When you are forced into a bad position, your counter or block also must be immediate and without hesitation. To recover from a weak position, you must get to the wedge position by making your opponent move his legs. Often, you can do this by controlling your opponent's

head and forcing him into a nonfunctional position (see Figure 2.19). Facilitate your recovery by moving your legs to the inside or outside of your opponent's legs. When you are close to a position where you can be scored upon, immediately lower your center of gravity and position your legs to re-create the wedge position.

Figure 2.19 Countering a bear hug.

Pummeling

The concept of total body pummeling is important in wrestling. The idea is to position your head, arms, legs, and body to provide a position of advantage from which you can off-balance your opponent, throw him, or both. It is easy for beginning wrestlers to perceive pummeling as strictly a hand and arm function. A wrestler's hands and arms are his most mobile and versatile weapons. To best utilize these assets, you must remember that they must not function independent of the body. They are most effective when used as hooks to hold your opponent tightly to your body. Hands and arms also provide a first line of defense to keep your opponent out of scoring positions.

When working for the advantage of an underhook, extending your arms out from your body will give your opponent scoring opportunities and will take you out of a sound body position (see Figure 2.20, a and b). Pulling and turning with the underhook will break your opponent's balance (see Figure 2.21).

The moment your opponent is off balance, position your underhook shoulder under his shoulder. This will create space between your bodies that will allow you to move your overhook hand to his wrist, and drive your hand, arm, and shoulder down to facilitate a double underhook (see Figure 2.22a). You are now in a position to use your leg strength to lift your arm and hook your opponent at the shoulder joint (see Figure 2.22b) or secure a double underhook (see Figure 2.22c).

Figure 2.20, a and b Improper arm extension opens an attack area.

Figure 2.21 The underhook can break your opponent's balance.

Figure 2.22, a-c   Securing the double underhook.

If you achieve a double underhook position, attack areas 1 through 4 of your opponent are vulnerable to many techniques. Keep your opponent out of his wedge by pulling him tightly to you (see Figure 2.23a) and twisting his trunk (see Figure 2.23b).

Figure 2.23, a and b   Keeping your opponent out of his wedge.

You must constantly use your whole body to off-balance your opponent. You must pull and turn the overhooked arm as you strike your opponent's chest with your shoulder (see Figure 2.24a), pull your opponent toward your hips as you drive your forearm down on his forearm (see Figure 2.24b), lift your opponent's elbows by dipping your shoulder and driving it up

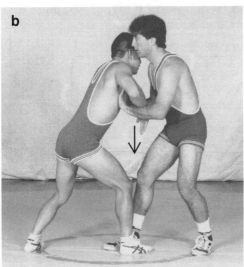

Figure 2.24, a-e *(continued)*

under your opponent's shoulder (see Figure 2.24c), pull and pummel his head (see Figure 2.24c), and use leg and head position to keep him constantly adjusting (see Figure 2.24, d and e).

(continued)

Figure 2.24, a-e Off-balancing techniques.

Scoring Points

Any time you can gain two-on-one control of a limb or control of two of the primary attack areas, you should score points.

As you learn the attack areas, you will begin to recognize the basic scoring positions in Greco-Roman wrestling that are shown and discussed in subsequent chapters. The scoring positions on your feet are the double underhook, the over-and-under arm position, the single underhook, the single overhook, the outside two-on-one armlock, the inside two-on-one armlock, the front head- and armlock, the pinch headlock, and the bodylock around one arm and the body.

The scoring positions on the mat are the bodylock, the reverse bodylock, the armlock, the head-and armlock, and the nelson series of arm- and headlocks.

What is the common element that allows a technique to be effective in several wrestling styles? The areas of vulnerability of the human body are the same regardless of style. Only the particular rules make one area of vulnerability more promising in one style than in another. The basic positions of advantage discussed in this chapter provide each wrestler with a sound base from which he may create personal variations of known and successful techniques and perhaps create a new maneuver.

CHAPTER 3

Active Wrestling:
Attack and Counterattack

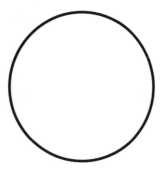

A wrestler can take three courses of action in a match: attack, counterattack, or block. Attack and counterattack are considered active wrestling. Blocking is considered passive and can be classified as stalling. It is neither an attack nor a counterattack, but rather defensive pummeling, the sole intent of which is to prevent your opponent from scoring. It is used when the score, time of the match, or strategic situation dictates that a wrestler maintain a passive posture to preserve a lead. To be effective in blocking, you must close all attack areas to your opponent. This means that your opportunities to score will become negligible. You must be able to pummel and maintain mat position in a manner that will prevent the official from penalizing you for passivity before you want him to.

Because the rules of wrestling clearly encourage active wrestling, this chapter will focus on the principles of attack and counterattack.

Attacking Your Opponent

When attacking an opponent, you may choose to react to your opponent's moves or make him react to yours.

Reacting to your opponent's moves makes you dependent on your opponent's creating opportunities for you and on your ability to recognize and take advantage of these opportunities. You need to have considerable experience to be able to direct your opponent's moves.

When you plan to score by making your opponent react to your moves, you must create positions that allow you to execute scoring techniques. In doing so, you must be conscious of beginning the action from a sound position, moving through a sound position, and finishing in a sound position.

Gaining Control

You must gain control of one of your opponent's primary or secondary attack areas (see pages 7, 9, and 10 in chapter 2) before voluntarily moving out of the wedge position to begin your attack. You then work for control of a second attack area. The instant you have control of the second area, execute the technique for which you were working. For example, when working to off-balance your opponent, gain control of his wrist (a secondary attack area) with an overhook (see Figure 3.1a) or with an underhook, and use your hips to off-balance him (see Figure 3.1b). Or duck under your opponent from a pinch headlock position (see Figure 3.2a). An outside leg position head pull to off-balance him is also very effective (see Figure 3.2b).

If you do not get control of two attack areas, recover to your wedge position and keep your opponent out of your vulnerable areas by using defensive pummeling. When your position is secure, immediately begin probing for new openings.

Weakening Your Opponent

It is to your advantage to be able to recognize weaknesses in your opponent's style. You also must be able to create weaknesses. Creating a weakness gives you opportunities to score.

Tiring your opponent is an obvious way to weaken him. The most active body parts in pummeling are the arms. If you tire his arms, you break down his first line of defense. Putting constant pressure on his arms forces him to constantly carry your weight and lift from a weak position. Pummeling his head with your arms and his body with your shoulders will take its toll on his trunk. Every time your opponent tries to lift from a weak position, he loses valuable energy.

You also can weaken your opponent by making him wrestle at a tempo to which he is unaccustomed. Having to wrestle faster or slower

Figure 3.1, a and b   Positioning below the waist to break your opponent's balance.

than he desires takes him out of the tempo for which he has trained and gives you control of the match.

In addition to tiring your opponent, you can gain an advantage by using positions and locks that are not to your opponent's liking. Wrestling from positions at which you are most adept not only puts your opponent at a disadvantage, but also allows you to wrestle from a familiar position of strength.

If you have an opportunity to scout your opponent before your match, make sure to observe the physical and technical aspects of his style as well as his intellectual approach (tactics). You also must get a sense of his emotional approach (intensity). Observe him closely for any subconscious habits that you might be able to use to your advantage. For example, if he always under-

Figure 3.2, a and b   Positioning above the waist to break your opponent's balance.

hooks with his right arm or always moves in the same direction in the zone, you can predict his actions and make plans to take advantage of the situation.

Selecting an Effective Counterattack

If you observe technical errors or habitual movement patterns in your opponent, your next step is to select an effective counterattack. Counterattacking takes place only when there is an attack. If you can predetermine what that attack

will be, you have the advantage. Your counterattack must be swift and properly timed. If the attack is not the one you anticipated, you must be able to maintain good position, block to achieve a momentary draw, and return to a neutral position.

Understanding what is necessary for a technique to be successful helps you know what you must prevent to block the move. It also helps you recognize the opportunities for counterattack.

When you are in a weak position, attacking secondary attack areas usually is all you can do. Securing control of your opponent's head, shoulder, or elbow, coupled with pulling and turning him around his center of gravity or yours, will very likely off-balance him enough for you to recover to a stronger position (see Figure 3.2b).

The following discussions offer counterattacking techniques for specific situations.

When Lifted From the Mat

When you are lifted free of the mat, arch your back (see Figure 3.3a) as your opponent begins his throw. Then attempt to swing your upper and lower body around the pivot point formed by his lock (see Figure 3.3b). Finish by covering him as you fall to the mat (see Figure 3.3c).

When Hitting the Mat

If you hit the mat before you can make any countermove, recover to a safe position by immediately turning your belly to the mat in a defensive position.

When Your Arm Is Controlled

In a position where your opponent has control of your arm (see Figure 3.4a), do not allow the joints of your arm to be locked or put in a weak position. Bend your arm and secure your opponent's elbow with your free hand (see Figure 3.4b). Pull up on his elbow and drive the shoulder of your controlled arm down toward the mat (see Figure 3.4c). Forcing your arm down to the mat will make it hard for your opponent to maintain control of your arm, and it will limit his movement, possibly presenting you with a chance to score.

Figure 3.3, a-c Body control in the air.

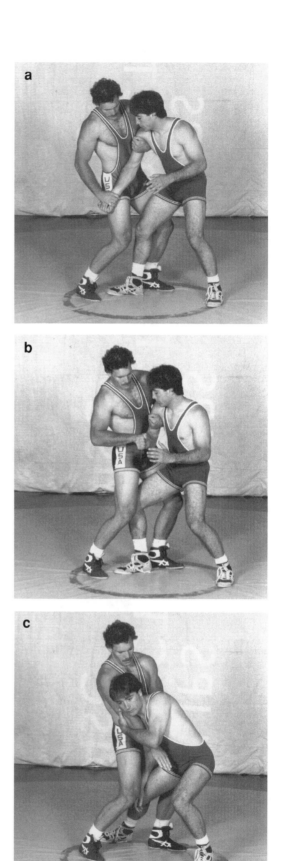

Figure 3.4, a-c Countering a two-on-one armlock.

When Your Back Is Parallel to the Mat

When your opponent has his back parallel to the mat (see Figure 3.5a), you can achieve a most effective control position by locking your arms around your opponent's head and one arm (see Figure 3.5b). A tight lock enables you to direct your opponent around the mat. This position is so strong that it warrants a good deal of training in countermoves. One such move is to duck under your opponent, putting your head to one side of your opponent's body as you drop your hips down and in toward him (see Figure 3.5c), and counter by lifting him off the mat, using the high dive or "snake" counter to the front head- and armlock (see Figure 3.5d). Your back must be perpendicular to the mat, with your hips under your shoulders. Drive up and into your opponent with your legs.

Figure 3.5, a-d   *(continued)*

(continued)

Figure 3.5, a-d   Countering a front head- and armlock.

When your back is parallel to the mat, your opponent may be in the same position (see Figure 3.5a). If so, he will have no balance to the side and can be tipped to his back. To tip your opponent, start a duck under to get your opponent's hips back (see Figure 3.6a). Step outside your opponent's heel and lower your center of gravity (see Figure 3.6b). Lower your inside shoulder and swing your arm over his back as you push with your head and bring your trailing leg around (see Figure 3.6c). Finish the move and cover your opponent on the mat (see Figure 3.6d).

Another way to counterattack when your opponent has your back parallel to the mat is by using the arm drag. Position the shoulder of your free arm on the outside and above your opponent's shoulder (see Figure 3.7a) and pull him forward, loosening his lock. Then pull yourself

Figure 3.6, a-d Executing the duck under.

Figure 3.7, a-c The arm drag counter to the front head and arm lock.

around with an arm drag (see Figure 3.7b) and finish the arm drag, taking your opponent to the mat (see Figure 3.7c). Remember, if your shoulder is in front of his, you will not be able to pull around him and force him down to complete the move.

When Your Body Is Attacked

To counter an attack to your body, getting into the wedge position with control of one major attack area is your first move. Constant off-balancing and pummeling will keep your opponent reacting to you.

If you are caught on your back, keep your free shoulder off the mat (see Figure 3.8a) and position your free arm under your opponent's shoulder and between your bodies so that you can drive your hand between your body and your opponent's (see Figure 3.8b). Then turn to a defensive position on your stomach (see Figure 3.8c).

Counterthrows are possible but depend on planning and luring your opponent into a throw for which you are ready. You must then turn his throwing action into your throwing action.

For example, if your opponent starts a headlock, lower your hips and lock around his body (see Figure 3.9, a and b). Step in front of your opponent, tighten your lock, and lower your hips to achieve a lifting position (see Figure 3.9,

(continued)

Figure 3.9, a-f The step-around counter to the headlock.

c and d). Then lift him, throw him back, and cover him (see Figure 3.9, e and f). Anytime your opponent moves his hips in front of yours, lower your center of gravity (hips) and step around in front of him.

Figure 3.8, a-c   Countering a head and arm attack on the mat.

(continued)

Figure 3.9, a-f

Figure 3.9, a-f *(continued)*

Putting It All Together

As you train and experiment with the ideas presented here, logical combinations of techniques and countertechniques based on your preferred style will emerge as you create your own unique method of wrestling. The longer you wrestle, the more you will expand your knowledge and abilities. Always keep in mind the fundamental positions on which all successful techniques are based.

Controlling the attack areas allows you to move your opponent to a vulnerable position or to keep him under control while you move to a position of advantage. Attacks to control your opponent's head, shoulder, elbow, hand, trunk, or hips prepare you to score. Pummeling can create an opening for you to score, making your opponent put himself in a position from which you can either score or fight to maintain your wedge and gain a draw.

All these options have a place in a well-thought-out game plan as you work not only to control your opponent's body but also to direct his efforts into areas where you are superior and most comfortable. In doing so, you may take your opponent out of his best positions and create frustrations that lead to careless mistakes. If you dictate the tempo of wrestling, you can take your opponent out of his functional comfort zone. Because you will be determining the speed of the match, you will always be prepared for the intensity level you select.

CHAPTER 4

Attacks to the Body

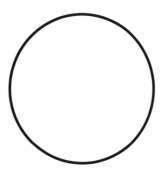

Scoring big in Greco-Roman wrestling means throwing your opponent. Throwing your opponent requires that you control his center of gravity, which you do by controlling his trunk. To control his trunk you must lock your arms around his body. Thus we see that attacks to the body are not only fundamental but also essential to scoring big and creating opportunities for arm and head throws.

To attack the body effectively, you must be reasonably close to your opponent's center of gravity. Thus, pummeling, pulling, and turning are important actions and allow you to penetrate and control vulnerable attack areas. This control creates opportunities for scoring and provides control related to defense and counter-wrestling.

Bodylocks

Securing control of primary attack areas gives you the opportunity to score with a bodylock. Locking your hands around some part of your opponent's body is essential for control. In general, the greatest force can be exerted in the direction in which the palms of your hands are facing. When the palms of your hands face each other in a lock, the greatest force can be exerted in a side-to-side movement.

There are many ways to lock your hands. Each method has strengths and weaknesses. This naturally means that particular locks are better for some holds than for others.

Figure 4.1   The hook lock.

The Hook Lock

The hook lock (see Figure 4.1) is best for pulling side to side and lifting from the mat. By simply bending your fingers and hooking your hands together, you form the hook lock.

The Butterfly Lock

The butterfly lock is best for pulling, twisting, and lifting your opponent in a standing position. It is also best for the gut wrench because you can pull your opponent tightly to your body and make the lock tighter by moving your hands up your arms toward your elbows (see Figure 4.2a).

To execute the butterfly lock, cross your arms in front of your body, placing the inside of one wrist against the other. Bend the fingers of each hand to form two hooks and force your elbows out as you move your hands closer to your body. Each hand will lock naturally on the opposite wrist (see Figure 4.2b).

The Hand-to-Hand Lock

A hand-to-hand lock (palms down) is best for bear hugs from a double underhook. A strength of this lock is that it enables you to pull down and toward your body. Securing a double underhook position with the hand-to-hand lock gives you control of three major attack areas and presents several scoring options. As your arms go around your opponent, keep the palms of your hands toward the mat and hook one hand over the top of the opposite wrist (see Figure 4.3).

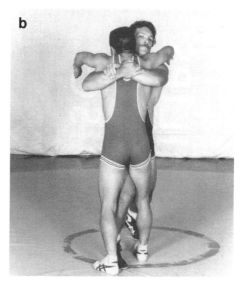

Figure 4.2, a and b   The butterfly lock.

Figure 4.3   The palms-down lock.

Slide-Bys

A slide-by allows you to move to the side of your opponent while in contact with him and slide around him to a position of advantage. A slide-by is a type of duck under used when you have a lock on your opponent's body or are in a pinch headlock position.

Using a hook lock, you can do a one-point slide-by. Pull your opponent toward you (see Figure 4.4a), and work your lock to a position to one side of the midline of your opponent's body. Pull and twist your opponent's trunk until you position your shoulder in your opponent's armpit (see Figure 4.4b). As you turn your head to face in the direction in which you are pulling, shuck your opponent's arm over your head and step to a rear bodylock position (see Figure 4.4c). If possible, regrip and throw your opponent back or to the side (see Figure 4.4d). If your opponent goes to the mat, immediately gut wrench or lift (see Figure 4.4e).

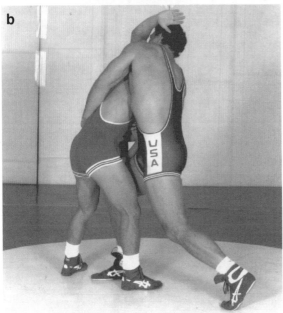

Figure 4.4, a-e *(continued)*

(continued)

Figure 4.4, a-e Executing the slide-by.

From an over-and-under bodylock position, you can do another type of slide-by that is particularly effective late in a match when both wrestlers are perspiring. Again with a hook lock, start the action by pulling your opponent toward you as you lower your center of gravity by stepping with the foot on your overhook side to a position outside and behind your opponent's heel on your underhook side (see Figure 4.5, a

(continued)

Figure 4.5, a-d　The bodylock slide-by.

Figure 4.5, a-d　*(continued)*

and b). Shuck his shoulder by as you swing your free leg to a position behind your opponent (see Figure 4.5c). Continue pulling down and toward you as you snap your hips and shoulders around your opponent. Your other foot will follow, and you will end up on top of your opponent on the mat (see Figure 4.5d).

The slide-by also can be effective from a pinch headlock position (see Figure 4.6, a-d). Swing your outside leg around and behind your opponent as you shuck his shoulder by (see Figure 4.6, a and b). From this position you can lift and throw your opponent (see Figure 4.6c). Your opponent will probably choose to go to the mat (see Figure 4.6d). Be ready to gut wrench him. When you do not have a lock around your opponent's body, several variations of the slide-by can be effective. With one arm underhooked and with control of your opponent's other hand (to con-

(continued)

Figure 4.6, a-d　The head-and-arm slide-by.

b

a

c

b

d

c

Figure 4.6, a-d *(continued)*

trol your opponent's arm, your lock must be at or slightly below the wrist), twist his hand and pull it down and away from his body (see Figure 4.7a). Lower your center of gravity so that your head is outside your opponent's elbow (see Figure 4.7b).

(continued)

Figure 4.7, a-d The head-under slide-by.

Figure 4.7, a-d *(continued)*

Push against his elbow with your ear and turn your head so it comes between his elbow and hip (see Figure 4.7c). As you do this, release your grip on his wrist and move that hand around his waist. Drop your other hand from his shoulder and catch his arm (see Figure 4.7d).

Figure 4.8, a and b The head-under slide-by on the mat.

You can also do this by dropping to the mat (changing levels) and sliding your head to a position outside and behind your opponent's elbow as you drop your other hand to his hip (see Figure 4.8, a and b).

Positioning your head outside and behind your opponent's elbow gives you additional options.

1. Hold onto your opponent's hand and lower your center of gravity (see Figure 4.9a). As you push on his hand, pull his hip toward you (see Figure 4.9b) and turn in a tight circle to the mat (see Figure 4.9c; notice the position of the attacker's right knee).
2. Instead of pulling and turning your opponent to the mat, pull down on your opponent's arm, freezing his near foot, and drive laterally through his hips (center of gravity) (see Figure 4.10a). Then step in front and to the outside of your opponent's far leg (see Figure 4.10b; note the leg positions and the direction of force) and guide him to the mat (see Figure 4.10c).

If your slide-by gets you to a position at your opponent's side, you have a great opportunity to throw. If you immediately change levels (see Figure 4.11, a and b), you are positioned to lock your hands at your opponent's hips (see Figure 4.11c). Your body will be to the side of your opponent's knee and ankle. Pull his hips to you and backpedal. As you lift him up on your hips, look back to begin your back arch (see Figure 4.11d). Throw back with a turn in the direction that will put your opponent on his back.

Double Underhook Position

The double underhook bear hug position allows you to lift, twist your opponent's trunk, or snap down on his hips, causing him to lose his balance.

A palms-down lock will facilitate a snap-down bear hug. After securing the lock, move your opponent from side to side. With the lock high on his body, pull and turn him so that his body comes to an erect position (see Figure 4.12a). As soon as he is close to your body and standing tall, tighten your lock, lift him free from the mat, and allow his leg muscles to relax (see Figure 4.12b).

Then change levels quickly by moving your hands from the high lock to a very tight lock on your opponent's hips. Your hands should move away from your opponent's back (see Figure

Figure 4.9, a-c The turning slide-by.

Figure 4.10, a-c The step-across slide-by.

(continued)

Figure 4.11, a-d   The slide-by to a bodylock.

Figure 4.11, a-d   *(continued)*

(continued)

Figure 4.12, a-e   The double underhook to a high double leg.

4.12c) and strike at the small of his back as you place one leg between your opponent's legs and tighten your lock (see Figure 4.12d). Pull down and drive him to the mat (see Figure 4.12e).

Figure 4.12, a-e *(continued)*

Once your hands are at the small of your opponent's back, you can drop to a position where both of your knees are between your opponent's legs (see Figure 4.13a). Then spread your knees

apart as you drop to provide a sound base from which to drive your opponent to the mat (see Figure 4.13b). Pull his hips tight to your chest as you bend forward to the mat.

Figure 4.13, a-c A variation of the high double leg.

When you have secured a high hook lock and your opponent lowers his center of gravity and moves away from you, you will find it hard to drop to his waist or slide by (see Figure 4.14, a and b).

Figure 4.14, a and b Your opponent can limit you from sliding by or dropping your high hook to his waist by lowering his center of gravity and pulling away.

In this situation, place one foot deep between your opponent's legs, slide your lock to a position close to his armpit on one side, and work your shoulder under his arm on the opposite side (see Figure 4.15a). Pull him tightly to your body and twist his body toward the mat. Move your penetration leg deeper under his center of gravity and turn the toe of your penetration foot in the direction you are turning your opponent (see Figure 4.15b). Your back leg must move in

a circle away from the direction in which you are twisting him. You must maintain contact between your hip and your opponent's belly to keep your center of gravity under his. As you pull, twist, and turn in a tight circle, your opponent's back will turn toward the mat as he lifts his free leg above your hip (see Figure 4.15c). Keep your hips lower than and under your opponent's. Continue turning until your opponent is taken to the mat (see Figure 4.15d).

To throw your opponent back from a double underhook in a belly-to-belly position, use a high butterfly lock. As you backpedal to create the throwing posture, remember that your opponent's arms and legs are free. Your arch must be high and straight back. Your opponent must hit the mat on his back.

When you are in a double underhook and your opponent goes to a double overhook (salto

(continued)

Figure 4.15, a-d Gaining a twisting bodylock from a double underhook.

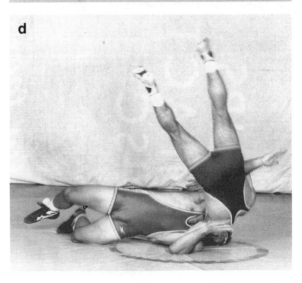

Figure 4.15, a-d *(continued)*

position), a high lock on your part will make a salto more convenient for your opponent. If you are in this position, pull your opponent to you and backpedal (see Figure 4.16a). When your opponent comes to a position with one foot forward and one foot back (see Figure 4.16b), plant both of your feet close together, with the heels of your feet becoming your throwing base. As you pull your opponent to you, swing him in the direction of his trailing foot in a lateral drop motion to his back (see Figure 4.16, c and d).

(continued)

Figure 4.16, a-d The double underhook lateral drop.

Figure 4.16, a-d *(continued)*

Changing levels and pulling, twisting, and turning your opponent are actions that set up double underhook moves.

After you pull and turn your opponent to get him in an erect posture, a quick change of level to his hips allows you to lift him from the mat (see Figure 4.17a). When he is free of the mat, hold him tightly to your body as you turn slowly. Gradually move his hips so that the midline of his body is on your side. When you get to this position, stop turning and pull his hips past your body (see Figure 4.17b). As his hips pass your body, drop to one knee and bend forward. This will put your opponent's back to the mat (see Figure 4.17c).

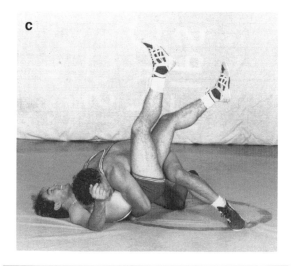

Figure 4.17, a-c   *(continued)*

(continued)

Figure 4.17, a-c   The high double leg hip swing.

Over-Under Chest-to-Chest Position

A very common position in classic Greco-Roman wrestling is the over-under chest-to-chest position. This is the position from which pummeling for an advantage has traditionally begun.

It is possible to make many different attacks from this position. The over-under chest-to-chest position requires constant centering and maintaining a good wedge. You must keep your center of gravity lower than your opponent's and keep your overhook-side leg forward. Your shoulder should be at the midline of your opponent's body and your head outside his shoulder.

Your underhook should not be deep and should be at your opponent's hip or shoulder. All of your weight must be centered and used to pull your opponent down. Stand on your own points of support; do not lean on your opponent (see Figure 4.18). To attack the body from this position, you must secure control of at least two attack areas. You can do this with your overhook arm, your legs or hips, or your head.

Figure 4.18   The over-and-under bodylock.

Step-Around Bodylock

One of the classic throws from the over-under chest-to-chest position is the step-around body-lock. Once you are in the correct position, start the throw by pulling your opponent's shoulder to you with your underhook hand. As you pull and turn, position your overhook-side foot between your opponent's feet in attack area 1 (see Figure 4.19a). As his body comes close to yours, change levels and lock your hands in a butter-fly grip at his hips (see Figure 4.19b). When his arm is encircled, press tightly to his body. Step around with the leg further from your opponent to a position that would place your foot behind your opponent if you were not lifting him from the mat as you turn (see Figure 4.19c)

Keep turning into a back arch position, throw-ing your opponent in an arc that will take him over your overhook arm's shoulder (see Figure 4.19, d and e). He will turn 360 degrees and land on his back (see Figure 4.19f). Finish the throw to a bodylock pin position.

You can create a different throw by altering your foot position after preparing your upper body for the step-around bodylock. When you have secured the bodylock position, put your underhook foot between your opponent's legs and bring the overhook leg to a position to the side of your opponent's underhook leg. Twist his upper body toward your underhook (see Figure 4.20, a and b). You will be in an arched position under your opponent. As you begin to

(continued)

Figure 4.19, a-f   The step-around bodylock.

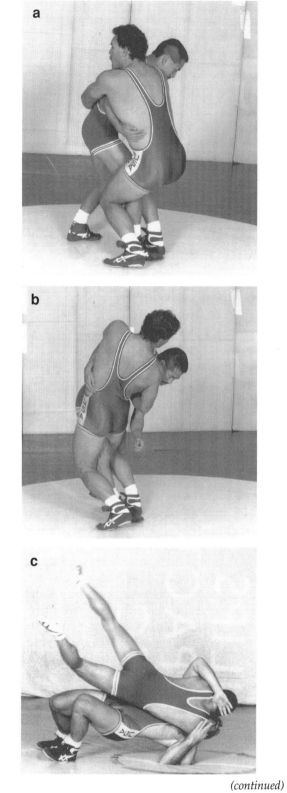

Figure 4.19, a-f *(continued)*

(continued)

Figure 4.20, a-d The side-sagging bodylock.

Figure 4.20, a-d *(continued)*

arch your back, look over your overhook shoulder and pop your hips toward the ceiling (see Figure 4.20c). Throw your opponent over your overhook shoulder in a line that would be a continuation of the long axis of your body (your backbone) (see Figure 4.20d). Finish the throw to a sagging bodylock.

Chances are your opponent will pull back or step around you as you step around him to prevent the throw (see Figure 4.21a). If he does, pull him in tight and keep both of your bodies in a vertical position (see Figure 4.21b). Then bend your upper body forward and step past your opponent's overhook leg (see Figure 4.21c). Force down with your weight, freezing his heel to the mat and making him lose his balance (see Figure 4.21d).

Figure 4.21, a-d *(continued)*

(continued)

Figure 4.21, a-d The step-by bodylock.

Sagging Bodylock

The sagging bodylock throw is a favorite of Olympian and national champion Andy Seras. The preparation for this throw is identical to that of the step-around bodylock.

The throw begins when your penetration leg is between your opponent's legs, before the step-around (see Figure 4.22a). Assume an arched position with your hands locked and encircling your opponent's body and one arm (see Figure 4.22b). Both of your feet should be committed to a full body arch. Pull your opponent directly over your body (see Figure 4.22c). Thrust your hips up and hold them in tight contact with your opponent. Keep the leg that is between his pressed against the inside of his thigh on the side of his free arm. Your body position will put all of your weight on your opponent's foot (see Figure 4.22d).

Your opponent might now believe that he can put his free arm to the mat and land on top of you. At this critical position, a change of direction must occur.

Thrust your hips toward the ceiling, creating a high arch (see Figure 4.23a). Look over your shoulder (of the tied-up arm) and throw your opponent over your shoulder in the direction in line with your backbone (see Figure 4.23b).

If you catch your opponent off guard, sometimes twisting his upper body and placing all your weight over the heel of the foot on the side of his tied-up arm can make him simply fall to his side (see Figure 4.24, a-c).

a

(continued)

Figure 4.22, a-d The classic sagging bodylock.

b

c

d

Figure 4.22, a-d *(continued)*

It is important to remember that any movement that makes your opponent try to support himself on one of his heels presents you an effective takedown opportunity from many different tie-up positions. The following unbalancing principle also makes head and heel takedowns work in freestyle. You can apply this technique

a

b

Figure 4.23, a and b Completing the throw.

a

b

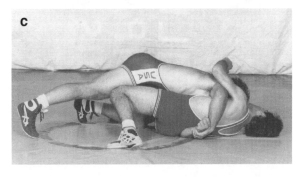

c

Figure 4.24, a-c Off balancing from the sagging bodylock.

from a front head-and-arm position, a two-on-one arm position, and as many other positions as you can develop.

To unbalance your opponent when both wrestlers are in an over-under tie-up, pull him in a circle that makes his underhook foot come forward (see Figure 4.25a). Lower your center of gravity and pull his arm down and to the side with your overhook and body. Your body should form an angle into your opponent (see Figure 4.25b). His center of gravity must be directly over or to the outside of his heel to prevent him from moving his foot. Drive your opponent over his trapped heel and set him on the mat (see Figure 4.25, c and d). Remember, forcing down strongly will keep his foot planted, and nominal force from your legs should make him lose his balance. Finish the throw with an over-under pin position.

(continued)

Figure 4.25, a-d   The heel trap lateral drop.

Figure 4.25, a-d   *(continued)*

Duck Under

The duck under is an important part of Greco-Roman wrestling. This technique is widely used in freestyle and American folkstyle wrestling and is one of the natural bridges between the styles. As we continue to develop our presentation of Greco-Roman wrestling, other bridges will appear as well.

To execute the duck under, you need enough space between your opponent's body and upper arm to allow your head to penetrate the attack area. In Greco-Roman, the erect stance and upper body contact tend to make a wrestler keep his upper arms close to his sides. This also is an obvious defensive position. As the upper body inclines forward, the functional position of the upper arm changes. To keep his balance and engage in hand contact, your opponent will move his elbows away from his trunk as he bends forward (see Figure 4.26a). From this position, simply changing levels will allow you to place your head in the attack area or duck under (see Figure 4.26b).

You may not get the opportunity to execute the duck under when wrestling a conservative and basically upright wrestler. So, when fighting for the underhook is fierce, keep your opponent's arm out of your armpit (see Figure 4.27a). As he becomes intent on driving his hand under your arm, pull his arm by your body and turn your head as if to look at your own armpit (see Figure 4.27b). This action will place his arm over your head (see Figure 4.27, c and d). To secure a scoring position, lift your head as it gets under your opponent's shoulder.

Figure 4.26, a and b Creating an opening for an underhook-side duck under.

(continued)

Figure 4.27, a-d A duck under variation.

Figure 4.27, a-d *(continued)*

Turning your opponent also can bring his elbow away from his body. First, get into the duck under position as previously described. As your head enters the attack area, the rest of your body must continue to wrestle. You may place your feet in any of several areas that facilitate a body attack. Your foot on the duck under side may move to a position directly behind your opponent (see Figure 4.28, a-d).

(continued)

Figure 4.28, a-d Using the duck under to go behind your opponent.

The same foot can move to a position between your opponent's legs (see Figure 4.29a). It also is effective to move your other foot to a position in front of and to the far side of your opponent (see Figure 4.29b). From these positions, a one-point move to the mat is likely and a throw is a good possibility.

Figure 4.28, a-d *(continued)*

Arm Drag

The arm drag is another universal technique that allows you to control your opponent's body. Out of a pummel or any other action, it is possible to reach across your body and hook your opponent's arm above the elbow. In other words, grab your opponent's right arm above the elbow with your right hand, or grab his left arm with your left hand. Hook his triceps and pull his shoulder across the front of your body. Your chest will come to a position above your opponent's shoulder (see Figure 4.30, a-c). The same foot positions used with the duck under are effective with the arm drag.

Over-Under Tie-Up

Folkstyle wrestlers will recognize the over-under tie-up as the lateral drop position. In Greco-

Figure 4.29, a and b   Alternative foot positions.

Roman wrestling the simplest throw comes from the over-under tie-up when your opponent is pushing into you.

As you feel pressure on your back foot as a result of a strong push by your opponent, move your back foot forward to a position close to your front foot. As your opponent's force pushes you toward your back, look back to your overhook side, thrust your hips toward the ceiling, and turn 180 degrees as you snap your shoulders toward the mat so that you will land on the mat belly down. This will put your opponent on his back between you and the mat. Remember, this move can work only when your opponent is pushing into you. The overhook is very impor-

Figure 4.30, a-c   The shoulder snap over.

tant in this position. Make sure that your overhook secures your opponent's arm high in your armpit and that your arm is locked tightly above his elbow.

Using Your Opponent's Position

Lateral drops are extremely effective if you select the correct throw for your opponent's body position. You must learn to "feel" your opponent's position and force. Selecting the throw that matches the situation is a matter of training.

You can laterally drop an opponent who is in an erect stance by placing your lead leg deep in attack area 1 (see Figure 4.31a). As you do this, a pull and twist of your opponent's upper body with your underhook arm will off-balance him. A push from your overhook arm on your opponent's elbow will add force to the twisting action. To make the twisting action more effective, swing your trailing leg back to clear a path to the mat (see Figure 4.31b). Make sure to twist

your opponent's shoulders from as near a vertical standing position as possible. Do not bend his trunk to the side.

An opponent who keeps his hips low and somewhat back will make the use of lateral drops difficult. It might be necessary to lead your opponent in a circular movement toward your overhooked arm. Gentle pressure sometimes will move a person as well as strong force will. As you move smoothly in the direction in which you want to throw your opponent, allow his head to move from above your underhook to the other side of your head (see Figure 4.32a). As his head clears yours and is on your overhook side, turn your back to him as you drop to both knees in front of and under his center of gravity (see Figure 4.32b). Pull down and across your chest with the overhook and up and over with the underhook as you bend your head to the mat.

From a very tight pummeling position, you will have difficulty getting an underhook on your opponent. In this situation, move your

Figure 4.31, a and b The inside leg position lateral drop.

Figure 4.32, a and b The lateral drop from your knees.

overhook shoulder to a position outside of your opponent's shoulder (see Figure 4.33a). As your overhook arm pulls down on your opponent's upper arm above the elbow, move your under-hook arm to a "shake hands" position on the controlled arm (see Figure 4.33b). Clasp hand to hand and twist his wrist as you pull his hand to your hip (see Figure 4.33c). Lift with your other arm under his shoulder and pull him over your hip as you position your overhook side leg deep between his legs (see Figure 4.33d). Work the joints of his arm by lifting and pulling to your body.

From the position shown in Figure 4.33d, you will have many opportunities to attack your opponent's body, arm, or head. You can pull his arm up, attack his body (see Figure 4.34, a and b), or pull down toward you so his back becomes parallel to the mat (see Figure 4.34). You then can swing your underhook arm around his waist

Figure 4.33, a-d *(continued)*

(continued)

Figure 4.33, a-d Creating an opening for a two-on-one armlock.

(continued)

Figure 4.34, a-e Attacking the body from a two-on-one armlock.

and take him to the mat (see Figure 4.34, d and e). Very often, attacks to the head and arm will be possible (see Figure 4.35, a and b). You can even develop an effective arm throw from this position (see Figure 4.35, c and d).

Another position that allows several sound body or head and arm attacks begins from a very tight bodylock with one arm and shoulder in a position to control the neck and head. Your

(continued)

Figure 4.34, a-e *(continued)*

Figure 4.35, a-d Attacking the head and the arm.

Figure 4.35, a-d *(continued)*

Figure 4.36   Positioning for a body or a head and arm attack.

penetration leg should be deep under your opponent's center of gravity, and your hands should be locked as close to his hip as possible (see Figure 4.36).

You can achieve a head-and-arm takedown to a danger position if you keep a tight lock and run to the side of your opponent as you lower your center of gravity (see Figure 4.37, a-d). From this position, you can use a sagging-type body lock (see Figure 4.38, a-d).

(continued)

Figure 4.37, a-d   A head and arm takedown.

d

Figure 4.37, a-d   *(continued)*

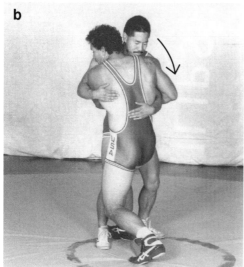

Figure 4.38, a-d   *(continued)*

(continued)

Figure 4.38, a-d   A sagging-type bodylock.

The body attacks that are unique to Greco-Roman wrestling serve to distinguish it from folkstyle and freestyle. Developing the body attack and making it just as equally crucial to folkstyle wrestling not only would open up a new and exciting area of wrestling, but also would create a valid threat to opponents and a logical reason for the changing levels of attack that are currently popular in folkstyle and freestyle wrestling.

It also would increase the effectiveness of leg attacks, because as the threat of upper body scoring techniques becomes a reality, the nature and complexity of defense changes. A leg attack is specific to one area of the body. This dictates that the defense can be specific, also. A leg attack most often results in a one-point takedown, and no danger of a fall occurs.

Upper body wrestling creates a position where you are closer to your opponent's center of gravity and therefore closer to his legs. A throw from standing can result in one, three, or five points, with a fall always imminent.

The chance to create scoring opportunities is greater when you have contact with your opponent. Wrestling from a noncontact position depends on speed, determination, and catching your opponent off guard. Very often, you end up wrestling from an inferior mechanical position.

To be more than a "half-body" wrestler, you must have a working knowledge of both upper and lower body techniques.

CHAPTER 5

Arm Attacks

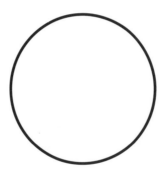

In many cases, the first contact you have with your opponent will be with his hands and arms. It is most certainly to your advantage to be able to use your opponent's hands and arms to gain an advantage that can create opportunities for you to score while limiting his chances of scoring.

Because our arms can move rapidly and in many directions, arm control is difficult. It will be to the attacker's advantage to have two arms on one, or three arms on one whenever possible—that is, using your body, your head, or your shoulder as a third ''arm'' is essential to complete control of an opponent's arm. Again, remember that each arm has three movable joints—the shoulder, the elbow, and the wrist. Isolating and positioning these joints to limit both their range of motion and the complete use of their attached muscle groups will give you better control of the limb.

Exposing the Arm

The further away from one's center of gravity a limb is extended, the lesser the person's strength and control of that limb. Extending an arm not only weakens the limb but also exposes critical attack areas. Begin the attack on the arms with correct arm pummeling along with good body position that off-balances your opponent.

Moving your opponent's center of gravity or causing him to move it for you will expose his arms to attack. Many successful arm throws begin with a body attack, and vice versa. Changing the level of your center of gravity and turning to outflank your opponent also can open up the attack areas of his arm.

One of the objectives of the pummel is to off-balance your opponent. You can do this by pulling and controlling his head (see Figure 5.1). You

Figure 5.1 Controlling your opponent's head.

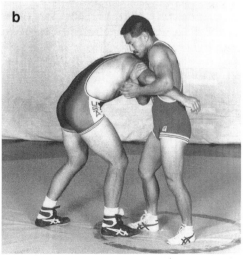

Figure 5.2, a and b Off-balancing your opponent by controlling his shoulder.

also can achieve it by lifting or pulling down on his shoulder (see Figure 5.2, a and b). All three techniques should be done with a pulling and turning motion. It is to your advantage to make your opponent reposition his feet. This is done by your leg, foot, and hip positions that take your opponent out of position. Your getting control of his elbow and hands also will make him readjust his arm position, offering you openings for attack.

Types of Arm Throws

There are many individual variations of arm throws. All seem to fall into one of four general categories: arm spin, hip throw, flying mare, and shoulder throw.

Arm Spin Throw

The arm spin throw requires good body control and gymnastic ability. It occurs high on your opponent's arm and is effective on an opponent who is in a relatively erect posture. You must direct your opponent's arm to an extended position that exposes the underarm attack area (see Figure 5.3a). Begin the throw by bringing your back leg between your bodies to begin the spin. Drive your throwing arm under your opponent's armpit and thrust directly toward the ceiling (see Figure 5.3b). This action will place your opponent's shoulder on yours and against your neck (see Figure 5.3c). Pull your throwing hand in a large arc as your body spins in a tight circle as high into your opponent's armpit as possible (see Figure 5.3d).

Look into your opponent's chest and press your nose into him as his arm is tightly wound around your neck. Keep your head and near shoulder in front of your opponent, and turn it up and into him (see Figure 5.3e). As the spin brings him over, extend your spin leg back to allow you to land and stay on your stomach (see Figure 5.3f). Kick over your opponent and pin him with an armlock (see Figure 5.3g), and put force against your opponent's hip with your knee as you pull his hand to his side (see Figure 5.3h).

You can also use the arm spin from a two-on-one armlock. Start the spin, keep your head tight in your opponent's armpit, and complete the throw into the mat in the same manner as the inside arm spin (see Figure 5.4, a-d).

(continued)

Figure 5.3, a-h

(continued)

Figure 5.3, a-h Executing the arm spin.

Figure 5.3, a-h *(continued)*

(continued)

Figure 5.4, a-d The outside arm spin.

Figure 5.4, a-d *(continued)*

The Armlock Hip Throw

The armlock hip throw is dependent on your getting to a position where your hips (center of gravity) are in front of and lower than your opponent's. Your hips provide the fulcrum that enables you to lift your opponent from the mat. As is the case in all wrestling, correct foot position is essential. Achieve proper hip position by using a back-step maneuver (see Figure 5.5, a and b) or by stepping around the front foot and using it as a pivot point for a 300+ degree turn. You can make the step-around movement from the overhook side (see Figure 5.6a) or the underhook side (see Figure 5.6b). Be sure that your front foot does not move.

The armlock hip throw is effective against an opponent in a semi-erect position. Begin the throw with the foot position and hip action just

Figure 5.6, a and b   The step-around.

Figure 5.5, a and b   The back step.

described to move your opponent into position. Do not step toward him. Pull your opponent's arm up and into you to prepare space for your hips (see Figure 5.7a). At the instant that your hips are past the center of your opponent's body, bend your knees to keep your center of gravity below his (see Figure 5.7b). Move your throwing arm to a position that locks your opponent's upper arm in the crook of your elbow (see Figure 5.7c). In this position, your hips punch up as you pull your opponent over. As he comes over, thrust back the leg closer to him to keep you on your belly as you land. This keeps your opponent between you and the mat (see Figure 5.7d). Finish by using the arm-over-waist pin (see Figure 5.7e).

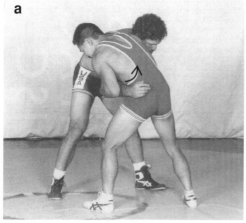

(continued)

Figure 5.7, a-e   The armlock hip throw.

Figure 5.7, a-e   *(continued)*

Flying Mare

Use the flying mare arm throw when your opponent is pushing into you, is bent forward at the waist, or both. This throw must be done as a swift, compact, one-action move. As your opponent pushes into you, place your shoulder under his opposite armpit (see Figure 5.8, a and b). Grasp his upper arm, lift both of your feet from the mat as you turn 180 degrees, and drop to a position directly under his center of gravity on both your knees (see Figure 5.8, c-e). If you do not penetrate a second attack area between his legs with your body, it will be hard to make this move successful. Pull down on his arm and touch your forehead to the mat (see Figure 5.8f). He should be coming over your shoulder just before your knees touch the mat. Keep your weight on his shoulder as you work for a pin position.

The flying mare also may be used from an outside armlock. Again, place your shoulder under your opponent's opposite armpit and grasp his arm (see Figure 5.9a). Turn and bend your knees to drop to a position directly under his center of gravity. Drive your throwing arm under your opponent's armpit and thrust it toward the ceiling (see Figure 5.9b). Pull down on his arm and touch your forehead to the mat (see Figure 5.9c), and finish off the throw (see Figure 5.9d).

Figure 5.8, a-f (continued)

(continued)

Figure 5.8, a-f The flying mare.

(continued)

Figure 5.9, a-d   *(continued)*

Shoulder Throw

An effective shoulder throw can be used as a single technique or as a variation of one of the previously mentioned arm throws. In one type of shoulder throw, you can combine attack area control and base foot off-balancing. To do this, place your shoulder in your opponent's armpit. You must pull his arm down and away from his center of gravity to freeze his foot to the mat (see Figure 5.10a). From your base foot, deliver force in a direction that will drive your opponent over his base foot and to the mat (see Figure 5.10, b and c).

A shoulder throw variation of the arm spin is feasible in several situations. One is a combination of arm spin, shoulder throw, and hip throw. As you drop your shoulder under your opponent's armpit, adopt a modified arm spin foot position (see Figure 5.11a). By pivoting on the balls of both feet, you turn your back to your opponent (see Figure 5.11b). From here you can take him to the mat by spinning, hip throwing, or dropping to both knees.

When you are attempting an arm spin or other arm throw, very often it becomes apparent that the original technique you intended is not going to work. This situation dictates a change in direction of force. A shoulder throw can do this and keep your chance of scoring alive. When your opponent counters the arm spin (see Figure 5.12a), the direction of force is changed, and the arm spin becomes an arm throw (see Figure 5.12b).

Figure 5.9, a-d   The outside flying mare.

Figure 5.10, a-c   The shoulder throw.

Figure 5.11, a and b   The modified foot position (a) and throwing position (b).

A missed step-around bodylock can turn into a shoulder throw. If you start the bodylock (Figure 5.13a) and your opponent counters by pulling out or stepping around you (see Figure 5.13b), an opening for the arm spin throw is created (see Figure 5.13c).

A missed headlock can turn into a scoring arm throw hiplock. If your opponent's head slips out of your lock (see Figure 5.14a), you can easily secure the correct hip position for the arm throw (see Figure 5.14b). Keep a tight lock on your opponent's arm and make the throw (see Figure 5.14c).

As you can see, a myriad of combinations exist, providing you with enough individual creative opportunities to last you a lifetime of wrestling.

Figure 5.12, a and b Change of direction.

Figure 5.13, a-c An arm throw opportunity when your opponent has a bodylock.

Figure 5.14, a-c The arm throw hiplock.

Body and Arm Attack

A good example of attack area control is the combination body and arm attack. From the classic over-under position, let your hand and head control your opponent's underhook elbow (see Figure 5.15a). Move your opponent's elbow away from his body and pull down, keeping your grip on his elbow or lowered to his wrist (see Figure 5.15b).

Drive your underhook arm and corresponding leg deep past your opponent's center of gravity (see Figure 5.15c). Keep the crest of your ilium (hipbone) as tight to your opponent's underside as possible. Hold your opponent's hips tightly to yours with the elbow of your penetrating arm (see Figure 5.15d). Reach your penetration leg as far as you can between your opponent's legs. This will hold his foot in position on the mat, and he will be unbalanced to the rear and sit down (see Figure 5.15e).

(continued)

Figure 5.15, a-e Creating an opening (a), hand control (b), and the drive shoulder throw (c-e).

Figure 5.15, a-e   *(continued)*

Figure 5.16, a-c   A variation of the drive position to a flying mare.

Salto Position

Occasionally, you may have the opportunity or may find it necessary to attack both arms. The double-over armlock or salto position can be an effective offensive or defensive scoring tactic. The word salto is used to describe this technique because your opponent will likely do a forward somersault as the move is completed. This action is known as the full salto.

When your opponent has secured a bear hug position, immediately lower your center of gravity, get the double overhook armlock, and work to get one or both feet between your opponent's knees and in the attack area (see Figure 5.17a).

If your opponent is not knocked off his feet, you will be in perfect position for the shoulder throw. For example, if he moves his hips back (see Figure 5.16a), note the increasing space between your bodies, and immediately drop to a flying mare position (see Figure 5.16b). Then complete the throw to the mat (see Figure 5.16c).

To tighten your armlock, push both of your hands up toward your opponent's chin and pull your elbows together. Pull your opponent toward you, backpedal, and begin your arch by looking straight back (see Figure 5.17b).

When both of your knees are between your opponent's legs, spread your knees apart to weaken his base. Look back right or left and try to see the mat behind you. Arch your back and make the throw over your shoulder (see Figure 5.17c). As your body approaches the back arch position, thrust your hips toward the ceiling and pull your opponent over and to one side of the midline of your body (see Figure 5.17d). Then follow your opponent to a pin position (see Figure 5.17e).

If you are able to get only one leg in the primary attack area, place the other in the secondary attack area beside your opponent's leg. Prepare the same as for the full salto. As you feel the proper position, look to the side of your outside leg and arch and throw to that side, executing a three-quarters salto—that is, an arching throw not straight back but to the side. When your opponent has a bear hug, you can use a partial arch back to a headlock if you do not achieve a strong double lock.

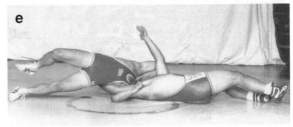

(continued)

Figure 5.17, a-e The salto.

Figure 5.17, a-e *(continued)*

Controlling the Arms and Hands

Your opponent's arms and hands are his first and most mobile line of defense. His arms and hands are like the pawns, knights, and bishops of a chess game; they probe for weaknesses and create openings for attack. It will benefit you to control your opponent's arms and hands. Furthermore, it is tactically sound to develop the ability to direct your opponent's arm and hand movement so that he voluntarily uses and positions them in a manner for which you are prepared. In essence, he will present to you the opportunity to use your planning and training to your best advantage. Good fortune occurs when preparation meets opportunity.

Having sound control of your opponent's head, hands, or both will limit him and create opportunities for you. Very often an opponent will attempt to control your head, giving you an opening to control his arm and hand. When he places his hand on your neck, for example, look away from him as you shrug your shoulder to free your neck (see Figure 5.18a).

Catch his upper arm with your outside hand as you catch his hand with yours (see Figure 5.18b). Use both hands as hooks and pull his arm to your chest (a "third hand") (see Figure 5.18c). Bend forward as you pull away from your opponent and roll his arm until the palm of his hand is against your chest. From this position it is possible to move behind your opponent (see Figure 5.18d).

Opportunities to execute all of the arm throws previously discussed also arise when you control the arms and hands. For example, if you have gained two-on-one arm control (see Figure 5.19a) and your opponent battles to free his arm or neutralize your control, you may choose to swing him and open the underarm attack area.

You can choose to execute a head-under arm throw. Keep both your arms on his, position your head under his arm, turn in close to his body, and lower your center of gravity (see Figure 5.19, b and c). Keep your feet on the mat, arch back to a two-on-one arm throw, and take him to the mat (see Figure 5.19d).

Having strong control of one arm will allow you to move your opponent up, down, back, or around. You can move him into a duck under bodylock, headlock, or front head- and armlock where you have his arm tightly locked to the side of his head with both your arms. Securing a two-on-one armlock from any position is desirable.

Figure 5.18, a-d Controlling the hand.

Figure 5.19, a-d Two-on-one fireman's throw.

When your opponent has an overhook (see Figure 5.20a), a circular motion with your underhook arm will move his arm to a position that will allow you to "shake hands" with him with your other hand (see Figre 5.20b). Swing your arm out from the underhook and move it into an overhook (see Figure 5.20c). You then can move into a two-on-one armlock (see Figure 5.20d).

(continued)

Figure 5.20, a-d Getting a two-on-one armlock.

Figure 5.20, a-d *(continued)*

Figure 5.21, a-c Shake hands two-on-one.

The "shake hands" approach is effective in helping you execute a two-on-one armlock when your opponent keeps his elbows in close to his body (see Figure 5.21, a-c).

If you move your hips back and circle away from your overhook, reach across with your underhook arm and hook your opponent's wrist to a two-on-one. You should immediately pull your opponent to you and position yourself to work his shoulder.

If he comes close to you, attack his body. If he pulls away, equalize the pulling action by circling (keeping control of his arm and around his center of gravity). Very often this action will allow you to slip your head under his armpit from the side and armthrow him with your body action in a manner similar to a fireman's carry without the leg hold.

When your opponent is working to get a two-on-one on you, take the opportunity to get a two-on-one on him. To counter a two-on-one, do not lift your arm or pull away. Stay close to your opponent, grab his elbow (see Figure 5.22a), and force the arm he is attempting to control down to the mat (see Figure 5.22b). His arm will become extended. You will be able to attack him with an arm throw or a bodylock. Drop to a flying mare arm throw (see Figure 5.22c) and complete the throw (see Figure 5.22d).

Figure 5.22, a-d *(continued)*

(continued)

Figure 5.22, a-d The arm throw counter to the two-on-one armlock.

Remember that to control a limb you must isolate the movable joints and position them to inhibit normal muscle function. The same principle applies to the trunk, head, and legs. You achieve off-balancing when your opponent is in a position from which he cannot adjust his support points to accommodate movement of his center of gravity, or when he cannot adjust his center of gravity to accommodate movement of his head or limbs. Position, force, and velocity combine for positive control of your opponent.

As we have seen, there are a variety of arm attacks. This number is expanded by your ability to attack either side of your opponent's body with one or two arms from numerous positions. And because the limbs are attached to the body (center of gravity), the opportunities for you to off-balance your opponent and create weakness in his defense are literally at your (or his) fingertips.

CHAPTER 6

Attacking the Head and Arm

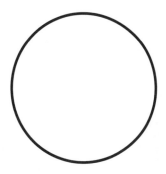

Control of an opponent's head and arm will give you a position of major control. It also is one of the highest percentage scoring moves from both an offensive attacking position and a counter-attacking front headlock position. That's why attacking the head and arm is one of the most popular moves in all styles of wrestling. Even beginning wrestlers, without any instruction, will naturally attack the head and arm.

Never pass up the opportunity to lock your arms around one of your opponent's arms and his head. From this position, you can control your opponent's movement and put him in a weak wrestling posture. This presents many scoring situations.

Front Head and Arm Positions

Several front head and arm positions are effective, and the front head- and armlock is a favorite

among wrestlers. When an opponent keeps his head lower than yours, it is convenient to pull and move him in a circle. This action will bring his shoulders ahead of his hips and place his back parallel to the mat.

When setting up the opportunity for a front head- and armlock, begin by pulling your opponent's shoulder using a two-on-one shoulder pull, and step in toward your opponent (see Figure 6.1a). Turn your opponent, lower your hips, and begin the arm drag (see Figure 6.1b). Pull in a circle and snap his shoulder down (see Figure 6.1c).

You are now prepared to wrestle for a head- and armlock. As you pull and turn your opponent, grab his chin and move away from him. Place the biceps of your arm holding his chin on the back of his neck. You now should be shoulder to shoulder with him (see Figure 6.2a). With the inside of the forearm of your other arm, pull his elbow tight to the side of his head. Move

Figure 6.1, a-c Setting up the head and arm.

your hand holding his chin to meet your other hand, and lock in a hook lock with the palm of your outside hand facing up (see Figure 6.2b). Squeeze your elbows together. Put your head to your opponent's side and position it under his latissimus dorsi (large back muscle) (see Figure 6.2c). Stay off of your knees and lift with

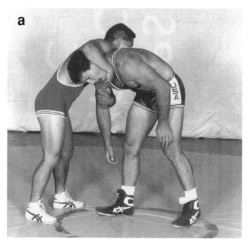

(continued)

Figure 6.2, a-d The head- and armlock.

Figure 6.2, a-d   *(continued)*

(continued)

Figure 6.3, a-g   The bridge over (a-e) and head shuck (f-g).

your head as you tighten your arms (see Figure 6.2d).

This lock is very effective for dragging your opponent to the mat and for executing bridge over moves to the side and shuck-bys. (When using a bridge over move, remember that a bridge over to the side is not a sit-through. You must move from a front bridge position to a back bridge position, keeping your body arched and off the mat to facilitate the spin through, and turn your opponent with you.)

To continue from the position shown in Figure 6.2d, pull your opponent's head to the mat (see Figure 6.3a) and place your forehead on the mat in a front bridge position (see Figure 6.3b). Kick over into a back bridge—do not sit through—and do not put your hip on the mat (see Figure 6.3c). Pull your opponent over your clavicle (not your chest) from the back bridge position (see Figure 6.3d) and complete the roll through (see Figure 6.3e). If your opponent is moving and your lock is not secure enough for a bridge over (see Figure 6.3f), move him in a circle and shuck his head by with your forearm that is under his chin (see Figure 6.3g).

You can use the same shoulder-to-shoulder position with one hand controlling your opponent's chin and the other holding his wrist for bridge overs to the side, head under arm bridge backs, and fireman's carry throws. In bridge back throws, having firm control of your opponent's chin is essential to making your bridge back effective. This also is true when you drop under his center of gravity for a Greco-Roman (no leg hold) fireman's carry.

Figure 6.3, a-g *(continued)*

Use a bridge over to the side when you are on the mat and have control of your opponent's chin and wrist (see Figure 6.4a). Kick back for the bridge over, keeping your control (see Figure 6.4b), and roll through to complete the move (see Figure 6.4c).

Begin the head under arm bridge back move from a standing hand- and chinlock position (see Figure 6.5a). Open the attack area by extending your opponent's arm horizontally (see Figure 6.5b). Put your head into the attack area (see Figure 6.5c) and bridge back to complete the throw (see Figure 6.5d).

You can execute the fireman's throw from the position shown in Figure 6.5a. Drop to your knees under your opponent to get into the fireman's throw position. Pull down on his head and push up on his trunk (see Figure 6.6a). Then lift your opponent's hips and complete the throw (see Figure 6.6b).

Figure 6.4, a-c Front bridge over to the side with a chin and hand position.

(continued)

Figure 6.5, a-d A bridge back.

Figure 6.6, a and b   The fireman's carry.

Figure 6.5, a-d   *(continued)*

Front Head and Shoulder Position

When your front head- and armlock is really a front head- and shoulderlock, the effective control position is slightly different. To limit your opponent's movement and establish control, you must work to a position where the crown of your opponent's head is slightly lower than the nape of his neck (see Figure 6.7).

The front head and arm throwback is a favorite of 1988 Olympian and national champion Anthony Amado. Anthony is shown making the throw in Figure 6.8, a-h.

To begin the throw, position your head outside of your opponent's shoulder (see Figure 6.8a). Pulling your opponent in a circle with your underhook arm will help you to get into the proper position (see Figure 6.8b). Force his shoulder down and under your chest with your overhook arm (see Figure 6.8c).

Figure 6.7   Correct head position.

Keep your opponent's head down and in front of your body. Do not allow his head to penetrate the attack area under your arm. As your opponent's head comes to a position even with or lower than his hips, you may effectively secure a front head and shoulder lock (see Figure 6.8d).

From this lock you can exert a great deal of pressure to keep your opponent's head down and his shoulders turned. As you force his head down with your lock and body position, your arm that is around his shoulder will lift his other shoulder (see Figure 6.8e). Throwing him to his back from this position should be easy. If he is able to keep his hips lower than his head, pull him in a circle. As he moves his foot forward and places it on the mat, move his center of gravity over the advanced foot and execute a bridge over throw over the base foot (see Figure 6.8, f-h). Move your hips into him and arch (see Figure 6.8f). Snap your shoulders (see Figure 6.8g) and turn to your stomach on the mat (see Figure 6.8h).

If your opponent is able to loosen the lock, catch his chin with one hand and his upper arm with the other (see Figure 6.9). Pull him in a circle away from the chinlock and put his head in a weak position.

a

b

c

(continued)

Figure 6.8, a-h   Front head and arm throwback.

(continued)

Figure 6.8, a-h

Figure 6.8, a-h *(continued)*

Figure 6.9 Positioning the head.

Pull his upper arm toward your hand that holds his chin, and make a one-quarter nelson lock by placing your underarm hand on the forearm of the chinlock hand (see Figure 6.10, a and b). Test how strong his neck is. From here you may pop him to his back by pulling on his chin,

Figure 6.10, a-d The quarter nelson.

snapping his shoulder over, and turning his back to the mat (see Figure 6.10, c and d).

You also may choose to move to a head-to-head position and do a bridge over with the one-quarter nelson grip (see Figure 6.11, a and b).

If your opponent is able to get his head under your arm, turn and pull his head to keep him from bringing his hips under his shoulders. Thrust your other arm across his body and in front of his hips to keep them back. Your arm under his body very often is in position to grasp the back of his upper arm.

Lock the hand of your arm that is around his head on the forearm of your arm that is across his chest. From this position you can throw back or bridge over.

Head- and armlocks are fundamental to Greco-Roman wrestling. No repertoire of Greco-Roman techniques is complete unless it includes several variations.

Figure 6.11, a and b The quarter nelson bridge over.

Over-Under Position

From the over-under position, you can achieve a very fast and effective headlock. Position yourself and present resistance (see Figure 6.12a). Then allow your opponent to begin to gain a position inside your underhook. As he attempts to get the underhook, allow his head to move to your overhook side.

Pivot on the foot of your lead leg as if your leg were a corkscrew drilling down into the mat (see Figure 6.12b). This will make your center of gravity lower than his. Pull his underhook arm tight to your body. It will be wound tightly around your trunk as you twist. At the same time, release your other arm and allow it to follow the rotation of your trunk. Turn the palm of your hand that is moving to his head up toward the ceiling (see Figure 6.12c). This rotation will allow you to strike the side of your opponent's head with the triceps and armpit of your headlocking arm (see Figure 6.12d). This arm must force down toward the mat so that your opponent's neck will be turned to a nonfunctional position (see Figure 6.12e).

This headlock is fast and powerful. It can be used from open or locked-up positions. It is usually most effective when your opponent has his head below yours and is leaning toward you.

If your opponent is in an erect stance, it is more efficient to employ a hip throw headlock; you will need the fulcrum provided by your hips to lift him from the mat and throw him.

If you have positioned your overhook-side foot in the attack area and are in a pinch headlock position, a back-step hip punch is most effective. Back-step hip punch refers to the foot and hip movement that precedes a hip throw. Position your right foot toe-to-toe with his left foot. Pivot 180 degrees on the toe of your right foot as you place your left foot at the heel of your right foot. At this point your back is turned to your opponent, allowing you to lever him over your hip.

(continued)

Figure 6.12, a-e The corkscrew headlock.

Figure 6.12, a-e *(continued)*

For example, from a pinch headlock position (see Figure 6.13a), use one quick movement that positions your hips under your opponent's center of gravity (see Figure 6.13, b and c). You must bend your knees and place your hips past the midline of his body. At this point your hips punch up into your opponent, and he will be lifted from the mat. You then can complete the throw to the mat (see Figure 6.13, d and e).

The headlock can be effective from an open position also. Figure 6.14, a-f, shows Gogi Parseghian, a Greco-Roman national champion, executing from an open position the headlock technique just discussed.

Foot, leg, and hip position is fundamental to correct technique selection and execution. For hip throws, you may not always use the back-step foot movement. For example, if the situation dictates a hip throw and your forward foot will not allow the back step, use the foot in the attack area as a pivot point. By pivoting more than 270 degrees, your hips will come to the proper position to complete a successful hip throw.

(continued)

Figure 6.13, a-e   The hip punch headlock.

Figure 6.13, a-e   *(continued)*

(continued)

Figure 6.14, a-f   The hip punch headlock from an open position.

Figure 6.14, a-f   *(continued)*

Collar-Elbow Position

From a collar-elbow position, your overhook arm pulls your opponent's arm tightly to your chest. As you execute your step-around, the headlocking arm will follow your hips and strike your opponent's neck with your armpit. The rotation continues in a circular pattern down to the mat as your hips bump his hips up. You achieve the hip punch by bending your upper body down toward the mat and casting your body forward from your toes. As your opponent comes to the mat, move your foot that was in the attack area back to allow you to land on your stomach and prevent a roll through (see Figure 6.15, a and b; note hip and foot position).

Figure 6.15, a and b The step-around headlock.

Pinch Headlock

When you are in a position where your hips are deep under your opponent's center of gravity, and he is extended close to your body, simply rotating your hips and lowering your center of gravity by dropping to one knee will effectively take your opponent to the mat (see Figure 6.16, a-c). Your lead leg must be deep in the attack area. Pivot on the balls of your feet.

Figure 6.16, a-c The hip rotation headlock.

Upright Position

Securing a lock in which you control your opponent's head and arm in an upright position can offer you several head and arm opportunities (see Figure 6.17a). In this pinch lock, the elbow of your arm around his head should be on the midline of his body. Your other arm should be positioned so that your shoulder is under his armpit (see Figure 6.17b).

Your hands should be in a hook lock on the side of his head. Pull his head tightly to your chest. Your underhook-side leg is deep in the attack area. From this position you can pull and turn him to the mat with a headlock, or move to a rear bodylock position (see Figure 6.17, c and d).

Figure 6.17, a-d *(continued)*

(continued)

Figure 6.17, a-d The offside head- and armlock.

If your head gets caught by his arm, look away from your opponent and change levels, freeing your head (see Figure 6.18, a and b).

If it happens that you cannot get your shoulder under his armpit and your lock is behind his head, move your head to the other side of his head. Squeeze his head and arm together. You are now in position for a hip throw (see Figure 6.19).

This head and arm position also can create an opening for a duck under that can open up your opponent's body (see Figure 6.20, a-c). Pull your opponent's arm toward your left shoulder and look under your armpit (see Figure 6.20b). Position your hips close to his and attack his body (see Figure 6.20c).

Figure 6.18, a and b   Freeing your head.

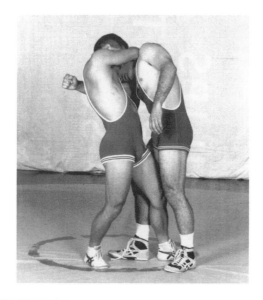

Figure 6.19   Positioning for a hip throw.

Figure 6.20, a-c   Positioning for a duck under.

Control of the head and arm is fundamental in directing your opponent into positions from which you can score. It also is an effective position for limiting your opponent's movement and scoring opportunities. You must allot practice time for developing both a head and arm attack and counters to the head- and armlocks. When an opponent ties up with you, he presents himself as a willing subject for the head and arm series. Be ready to take advantage of the situation and score.

CHAPTER 7

Par Terre Wrestling

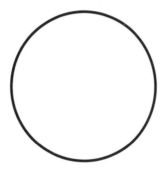

Par terre wrestling, or wrestling on the mat, is of special concern to the international wrestler. By nature of the par terre starting position, the top man is the attacker and the bottom man is the defender. Here the defensive wrestler is truly at a disadvantage. His movement is limited because the top man has a distinct leverage and mobility edge.

It is possible for the bottom man to score a one-point reversal or a two-point back exposure on the top man. However, in attempting such moves he very likely will open himself up for two-point exposures, three-point lifts, and even a five-point lift. Because the top man is in position to score big points, the most common tactic the bottom man employs is to assume a defensive strategy until it is apparent that the top man is unable to score in a reasonable amount of time (15–20 seconds) and the referee returns the wrestlers to a standing neutral position.

Every wrestler must master both top and bottom wrestling techniques.

American folkstyle wrestling has historically been on the mat. It would seem, then, that American wrestlers would be strong in mat wrestling. In international wrestling, however, Americans have been weak in par terre. They have been scored on and have not been able to score on the mat. Certainly a wrestling technique that is legal and effective in folkstyle will work in international-style wrestling. Why then have Americans been weak in par terre?

The problem begins with the philosophy of constant control on the mat—holding your opponent down and his constant movement to escape. American rules give points for riding an opponent and escaping from his control to a neutral position. Neither of these actions work directly toward the fall—the ultimate goal of all wrestling. A wrestler can be very successful, even win titles, without being concerned about putting his opponent's shoulders toward the mat. As a result, the rules tolerate many actions that are not directed toward securing a fall but are designed to keep your opponent from scoring points. Many wrestlers play it safe by moving out of bounds when in danger.

We most certainly need to teach our wrestlers the international techniques of turning, lifting, and defending on the mat simply because the international rules dictate those techniques that are the most effective scoring maneuvers. It is equally important to teach our wrestlers a philosophy that is focused on turning the opponent's back to the mat and always seeking the fall.

As physical techniques become subconsciously recalled movement patterns, as they must to be effective, the wrestler's mind is freed to perceive the competition between wills and intellects. In this perception a philosophy is needed. Your body will sustain the guidance of the intellect. Your willingness to creatively seek out a solution to the problem at hand will fully utilize your physical training, your philosophical direction, and your emotional commitment. If all three are not compatible with each other, your chances of beating a great opponent are minuscule.

International Versus Folkstyle

The international starting position on the mat is familiar to most American folkstyle coaches and wrestlers. It is basically the same as the optional start employed in American high schools and colleges. However, the intent and actions of the top and bottom from the starting position in international wrestling differ considerably from those in folkstyle.

In folkstyle, the bottom man's first movement is usually up, his intent being to escape to a neutral position. In international wrestling, the bottom man's first movement is usually down to a defensive position with his belly on the mat. His intent is defense. If the bottom man is not scored upon in a short time, the match is stopped, and both wrestlers come to a standing neutral position to continue the match.

In folkstyle the top man's main effort when the whistle blows is to contain his opponent on the mat and prevent an escape. If he does this, wrestling continues on the mat.

International rules allow the top man a limited time to score on the bottom man. He must work directly on locks that will turn his opponent. Because no points are given for holding

the man down or escaping from his lock, the top man's entire focus is on turning and pinning his opponent. The bottom man's main focus is to prevent his opponent from scoring. Note that the bottom man is not limited to defense. He can score if he exposes the top man's back to the mat or reverses the position of advantage, in which case wrestling continues.

Defensive Position

The defensive position on the mat is designed to prevent turns and lifts from the mat. When you are the bottom man and you drop to the mat, you should drop in a direction that will put you a small distance forward, back, left, or right of the original starting position. Your belly, hips, and legs are pressed tightly to the mat. Your back is arched and your head is up. Both arms are extended in a direction 45 degrees from the long axis of the body. Your fingers are curled under, and the weight of your upper body is on the heels of each hand. Your legs are extended out at a 45 degree angle from the long axis of the body (see Figure 7.1, a and b).

Maintain this position. As the top man secures a lock and begins to move you around the mat or lift you, *constant adjustment* to maintain your defensive posture is required. Any break in your concentration will allow your proper defensive position to be altered, and the top man will score. Figure 7.2, a and b, shows adjustments

a

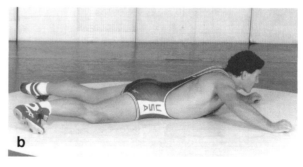

b

Figure 7.1, a and b The defensive mat position.

Figure 7.2, a and b Making adjustments to maintain defensive mat position.

you should use to maintain your defensive posture.

The Gut Wrench

The most commonly used scoring move on the mat is the gut wrench. This is a very tight lock around your opponent's trunk that allows you to bridge over and expose his back to the mat to score points. Any hold locked around the body that turns the opponent in a bridging action is a gut wrench. You can use the gut wrench from a high lock around an opponent's upper body, a middle lock around the bottom of the rib cage, and a low lock at your opponent's hips. The hold is so popular that rule adjustments are made periodically to increase the scoring opportunities and create an environment where the many throws of Greco-Roman wrestling can be more readily displayed.

The Lock

It is fundamental to all gut wrenches that you hold your opponent's body as tightly to yours as possible. Two bodies must become as one. It will be very difficult to turn your opponent if his body position keeps his shoulders above his hips and his back arched. For the gut wrench to work, your opponent's hips must be even with or above his shoulders. This means you

must force his shoulders down, lift hips, or both. It also is difficult to secure a proper lock if your opponent is moving around on the mat. Keep him still by having one knee on the back of his knee or exerting sufficient pressure down into him with your shoulder to keep him from moving around.

You must move your opponent to allow your body to be between his and the mat. You do not pull him over your body so much as move under his. The power for the turn comes mainly from your legs as they push your hips up into an arched position. The direction of the force is along the line of your backbone toward your head.

After your opponent drops to the mat, he will try to prevent you from locking your hands around his trunk. Place one hand palm down beside your opponent's body at his armpit. The other hand can hook his shoulder from the front at the pectoris major and lift his chest up, allowing you to lock your hands (see Figure 7.3). You also can secure a lock by reaching under his arm-

Figures 7.3 and 7.4 Creating an opening to lock your hands around your opponent for a gut wrench.

pit to the other side of his neck and lift his upper body over the hand on the mat to secure a lock (see Figure 7.4).

Hooking both hands under your opponent's shoulders and lifting his upper body from the mat also will clear a path to lock your hands (see Figure 7.5, a and b).

a

b

Figure 7.5, a and b   Clearing a path for your hands to lock for a gut wrench.

Figure 7.6   The butterfly lock.

You should hold your opponent as tight to your body as possible. Therefore, the best lock is a butterfly lock to an elbow-to-elbow lock (see Figure 7.6).

The Low Gut Wrench

When your hands are locked, place one knee on the mat between his legs and the other to one side (see Figure 7.7a). Pull and lift as you move your lock down his body to his hips. Your lock should now be around his hipbones (see Figure 7.7b).

Place your shoulder in the small of his back below his rib cage. From this position, you begin a low gut wrench (see figure 7.7c). Pull his hips back toward you and lift as you keep the pressure on his lower back with your shoulder. This will break his back's arch and allow you to get your knee between his hips and the mat (see Figure 7.7d).

You can move from side to side to see how your opponent moves. This will disguise which side you plan to attack. When you decide from which direction you are going to take him, place your knee against his hip on that side. Pull his hips back toward your lap and force down with your shoulder in his back as you lift his hips up (see Figure 7.8a). Hold him tight to your body as you begin to pull him into your lap. When his far hip comes off the mat, tighten your grip to an elbowlock (see Figure 7.8b).

Pull him to your body and move to a position under his hips. Once you begin the pull, do not release the pressure on his hips. Destroy his defensive leg position (see Figure 7.8c). Thrust from the heels of your feet into an arched position, and turn your opponent over to expose his back. When your bridge over is complete, do not go flat on your belly but follow him around to a position in which you are ready to lift him (see Figure 7.8d).

Middle Gut Wrench

The lock for the middle gut wrench is around your opponent's body at the bottom of the rib cage (see Figure 7.9a). All of the locking, bridging, and turning skills are the same as in the low gut wrench. With your lock at the middle of his body, the opportunity to lift your opponent from the mat and then move to a gut wrench offers a variation that may confuse your opponent

Figure 7.7, a-d Preparing for the low gut wrench.

Figure 7.8, a-d Completing the low gut wrench.

momentarily. The lift will create a space between your opponent's body and the mat into which you can slip your leg (see Figure 7.9, b and c). From here you can complete the gut wrench.

a

b

c

Figure 7.9, a-c   The middle gut wrench.

High Gut Wrench

The lock for the high gut wrench is as high on the trunk as you can get (see Figure 7.10, a and b). Try to force your opponent's arms forward and narrow his front support base. Several attack options are open to you from this position.

You may choose to rock from elbow to elbow. As your opponent's hand comes off the mat, inch your lock on that side up and tighten it (see

Figure 7.10, c and d). This should move his arm forward and destroy his base (see Figure 7.10e).

When you feel that your lock is tight enough, pull your opponent's back tight to your chest, pull him into your lap, and place your near leg deep under his body (see Figure 7.10, f and g). Push from your heels into a bridge and turn him (see Figure 7.10h).

a

b

c

d

(continued)

Figure 7.10, a-h   The high gut wrench.

Figure 7.10, a-h *(continued)*

Figure 7.11, a-c A high gut wrench variation.

A high lock also will enable you to straddle your opponent with both of your feet on the mat. Lift his upper body from the mat, pulling him tight to your body. Keep his hips below his shoulders (see Figure 7.11, a and b).

Regrip to tighten your lock around his chest. Place one foot on the mat under your opponent and past the midline of his body. Turn into and through a back arch position. Your opponent will turn with you (see Figure 7.11c).

Another option is to lock your hands at your opponent's middle (see Figure 7.12a). With one knee between his legs, swing your other leg forward to a lifting position. Push from your front leg and pull his hips up and into your lap. Start to lift. At this point, your opponent must begin to counter a lift.

As his hips come away from the mat, hold him tight in your lap, tighten your lock, and move your front foot under him toward his hips (see Figure 7.12b). From this position, he can be bridged over (see Figure 7.12, c and d).

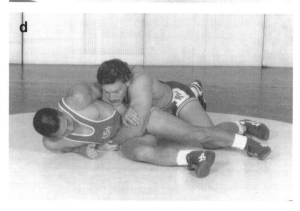

Figure 7.12, a-d   The fake lift gut wrench.

Defending Against the Gut Wrench

Countering the gut wrench requires intense focus, ribs of iron, and a will of steel. Your opponent clearly has a dominant position on the mat, and you surely will be required to defend on the mat.

Your basic position on the mat is arched with your head and shoulders off the mat. Your limbs are extended and forcing in toward your center to keep your hips glued to the mat (see Figure 7.13a). As your opponent commits to a direction of attack, look toward your arm on the side being attacked and place your head close to this shoulder (see Figure 7.13b).

Push from the palm of your hand through your arm toward your opposite hip. This action will keep your back arched and your hips on the mat because it focuses your force on the point your opponent is trying to lift. Move your hips away from your opponent and stay off his lap. Constant adjustment is necessary.

If your opponent relaxes the pressure momentarily, do not relax and become overconfident. He will change directions, and you will have to change your defensive position from side to side and also be ready to counter lifts. You must be ready to resist one more time than your opponent tries to turn you.

Figure 7.13, a and b   The gut wrench counter.

The Lift

When lifting an opponent from the mat, you must create a lifting position that most nearly approximates the proper body posture and movement that weight lifters use. Your opponent will be resisting, of course—moving and trying to put you in a position from which you cannot lift him. Therefore, you must disguise as much as possible your intent to lift. You must move to the lifting posture and get your opponent off the mat with as much speed and force as you can.

A hook lock of the hands is best to begin the lift. Place your lock at the midpont of your opponent's body. One knee is on the mat between your opponent's legs at his knees. The other leg is back and to his side (see Figure 7.14a).

Swing your extended leg forward and place your foot past your lock with the toes of your foot pointing toward your opponent's body (see Figure 7.14, b and c). As your foot swings forward, pivot on the foot that is between your opponent's legs, raising his hips to your lap, placing your opponent's thigh on the thigh of your leg that is between his (see Figure 7.14, d and e). As your opponent comes off of the mat, immediately squat and position your back perpendicular to the mat.

Push from your front foot and pull your opponent to your lap as you lower your hips and then lift with your legs (see Figure 7.14, f and g). Regrip to tighten your lock if needed.

Keep your head up and your back as perpendicular to the mat as possible. You can go from this position into a back arch, throwing him across your body (see Figure 7.14, h and i).

After securing the lock around your opponent's body, you can place your head in the middle of your opponent's back and use it as a pivot

(continued)

Figure 7.14, a-i A basic lift from the mat.

(continued)

Figure 7.14, a-i

point as you jump from one side of your opponent to the other. This disguises which side you plan to attack. The lifting technique for this tactic differs slightly from the one described previously. When you decide which side you are

(continued)

Figure 7.30, a-i

Figure 7.14, a-i   *(continued)*

going to attack, proper foot placement is essential. If you plan to lift your opponent from his right side, as you jump to that side your left foot must make contact with the mat at the point next to your opponent's hip bone. It will touch the mat before your right foot swings into lifting position. The lifting action begins by sliding your opponent up the side of your left leg as your right leg comes into lifting position. As your opponent comes off the mat, lower your hips and tighten your lock.

When you have partially completed the lift, with one of your opponent's legs between yours (at the point shown in Figure 7.14f), you may choose to move your knee between his legs to a position outside of the thigh of his free leg. From here you can execute a gut wrench to the far side (see Figure 7.15, a and b).

You can execute another form of the gut wrench when your opponent's leg that is between yours is raised, and you find yourself with your hips close to his. Pull his hips back as you lower your hips to a sitting position to place your center of gravity lower than his (see Figure 7.16, a and b). Then turn your body to pull him back and over you, thrusting up from your heels into an arch and popping your hips up to complete the gut wrench (see Figure 7.16, c and d). Your opponent may keep his leg between yours and lower his chest to the mat as a countering position (see Figure 7.17, a and b). From here you still can throw your opponent.

Tighten your lock around his waist and pull his hips tight to yours. Position your outside foot directly under his hips. The thigh of your inside leg will come to a point close to your opponent's

a

b

Figure 7.15, a and b   The far side gut wrench.

center of gravity and against the inside of his thigh as you slowly move his hips toward his free leg (see Figure 7.17c).

As your shoulders bend forward and turn toward the mat, kick your leg that is against the inside of his thigh over into a back bridge position, and twist his hips to expose his back. Stay as tight to his hips as possible (see Figure 7.17, d and e).

a

(continued)

Figure 7.16, a-d   The sit-down gut wrench.

b

c

d

Figure 7.16, a-d   *(continued)*

a

b

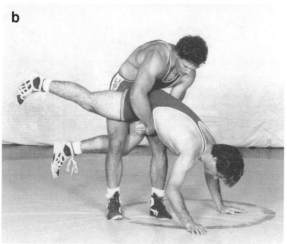

c

(continued)

Figure 7.17, a-e   Achieving a throw when defense is made against the lift.

d

e

Figure 7.17, a-e   *(continued)*

The Reverse Lift

When you are stymied at the half-lift position, many times you can place your front foot under your opponent's center of gravity and hold him up while you change to a reverse bodylock.

Pull your opponent's hips tight into your lap, and hold him against your lap with your right arm as you move your left arm over to a reverse bodylock position (see Figure 7.18, a and b).

Hold him in your lap with your left arm as you switch your right arm and secure a reverse bodylock (see Figure 7.18c). Look up and back in the direction of the throw, and complete the throw (see Figure 7.18d).

The reverse bodylock is a very strong lift from the mat. To get a reverse lock, position yourself to your opponent's side with your front knee on the mat against his side immediately below his armpit. Keep this arm outside your leg. Your other knee is against his hip. Place one hand in front of your opponent's far shoulder and the other on the far side of his body under his hip-

(continued)

Figure 7.18, a-d Changing to a reverse bodylock.

Figure 7.18, a-d *(continued)*

bone. Pull and lift him onto your lap. Move your hand from his shoulder to a position around his waist and secure the reverse bodylock. (see Figure 7.19, a and b).

Place your front arm as far around his body as possible. Pull his inside hip up with your other hand, and lock your hands around his waist. From this position, pull his hips to your lap as you rotate your back knee up and off the mat. His hips are directly over your raised knee (see Figure 7.19, c and d).

Come to a standing position by turning your body in a circle, raising and positioning his hips for the throw. His hips must be even with or above your hips for an efficient throw (see Figure 7.19, e and f). Turn toward his head as you begin the throw and throw him over your shoulder.

Often it will be to your advantage to adjust your lock to the side of your opponent's body, away from you. The usual counter to a reverse bodylock is to turn into your opponent, position your inside arm between him and your body, and push away from him as you keep the hip further from him pressed to the mat. When this occurs, drive your arm (pictured in Figure 7.20a as the right arm) under his body. This will put your lock at the side of his body away from you. Your arm under his body is in a lifting position. The elbow of your other arm is on your opponent's back. Keep your front knee in his armpit, forcing against his chest to possibly expose his shoulders to the mat (see Figure 7.20a). Place your other foot on the mat, lift your opponent, and come to a standing position. Turn his hips to expose his back, and complete the throw (see Figure 7.20, b and c).

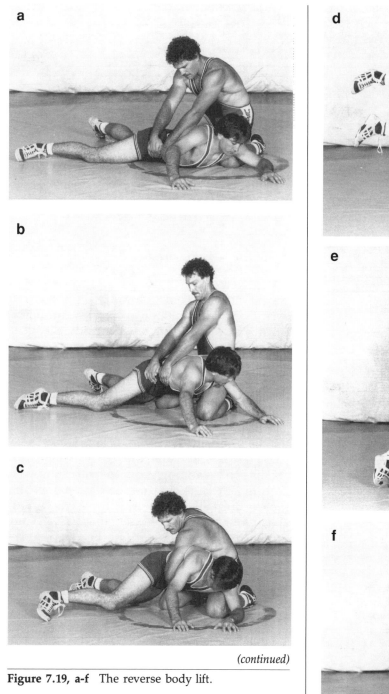

(continued)

Figure 7.19, a-f   The reverse body lift.

Figure 7.19, a-f   *(continued)*

Figure 7.20, a-c A reverse body lift variation.

On occasion you will be able to use this lock and come up to a throwing position by lifting your knee that is at your opponent's armpit and placing your foot on the mat under his chest. Turn toward his hips as you prepare for the throw (see Figure 7.21).

Figure 7.21 Foot variation on the lift.

As your opponent attempts to counter the reverse lift, he may move away from you and fight to a body position that presents an opening for you to do a front head- and armlock (see Figure 7.22a). Release the bodylock and quickly move to a front head- and armlock position, with the lock at the side of his head (see Figure 7.22b). Come to a squat in front of your opponent and lift his upper body from the mat. As he comes up, push into him with your hips (see Figure 7.22, c and d). From here you may do a bridge over or throw him back (see Figure 7.22e).

The reverse body lift is a very effective technique that will score big points. Every Greco-Roman wrestler must master this hold.

Many matches are won by the wrestler who has the advantage in par terre. It follows, then, that when you are in the defensive par terre position, you must be able to effectively prevent being lifted from the mat. You will find that being lifted from the mat and thrown for a five-point score is almost as exhilarating as lifting and throwing your opponent. But to win, you must defend against the lift.

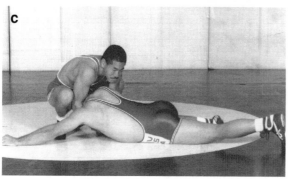

(continued)

Figure 7.22, a-e   Change to a front head and arm.

Figure 7.22, a-e   *(continued)*

Defending Against the Lift

Have you ever tried to pick up a child who did not want to be picked up? He will wiggle, twist, slide, push, pull, and do anything else he can to stay on the floor. To prevent being lifted from the mat, you must have the same degree of determination and intensity. Your opponent must secure a good lifting base, so your job is to move and fight to keep him off balance. You cannot relax or stop fighting for even an instant. Do not allow him to secure a lifting position.

If your opponent gets his hands locked and starts to work for a lift, keep your back arched and your limbs extended. Stay as close to the mat as possible, and launch your center of gravity forward, backward (see Figure 7.23a), into him, or away from him, breaking his lifting position (see Figure 7.23b).

Put one or both legs between his and move back (see Figure 7.23c). Place your knee directly behind your opponent's knee (see Figure 7.23d). Move your other leg between his legs and push your body back between his legs. Beware of a gut wrench if you do not break his balance to his rear.

Use his lock as a pivot point to swing your upper and lower body in circular patterns on the mat (see Figure 7.23, e and f).

If he manages to raise your hips, put one leg between his and get your chest close to the mat (refer to Figure 7.17, a and b). Keep your arms extended and your back arched, and move away from your opponent, swinging your shoulders from side to side to break his balance.

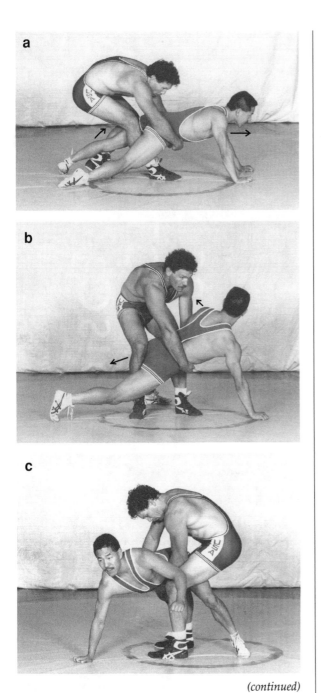

(continued)

Figure 7.23, a-f Countering the lift.

Figure 7.23, a-f (continued)

As a temporary restraint, you may reach back and push on your opponent's shoulder. If your arm is there too long, he can hook it with his chin and gut wrench to that side (see Figure 7.24, a-e) or change to a reverse bodylock.

a

b

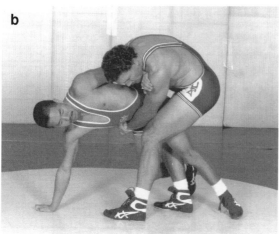

c

d

e

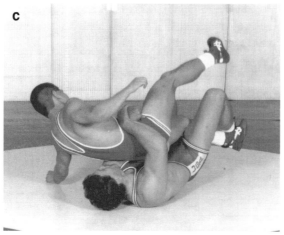

(continued)

Figure 7.24, a-e Temporary restraint can result in a gut wrench.

Figure 7.24, a-e (continued)

If you get lifted up to his hips, keep your hips square to the mat and raise the shoulder closer to your opponent, turn your chest toward him, and wiggle energetically (see Figure 7.25, a and b). Arch your back to put all of your weight on his lock. Be ready to change the position of your shoulders if your opponent attempts to snap your hips over to the mat away from his body.

Countering a reverse body lift is slightly different. As your opponent positions himself and seeks to secure a reverse bodylock, you must not allow him to keep your body elongated by placing his knee behind your armpit (see Figure 7.26a). Turn toward your opponent, bringing your inside arm between your bodies. Place the elbow of your inside arm under the knee of your inside leg (see Figure 7.26, b and c).

Turn and push away from your opponent. Keep his arms straight and your hips away from his lifting base. Stay as close to the mat as possible (see Figure 7.26d). Be very active. Do not allow him to place his knee or foot against your shoulder. He could stabilize your upper body and lift your hips over your shoulders.

Figure 7.25, a and b Wiggle to help counter the lift.

Figure 7.26, a-d *(continued)*

(continued)

Figure 7.26, a-d Countering the reverse body lift.

If your opponent gets your hips off the mat, arch your back and raise your shoulders higher than your hips. Raise your shoulders and come to a standing position facing your opponent (see Figure 7.27, a and b). You may secure a reverse bodylock on him (see Figure 7.27, c and d), get a double overhook (see Figure 7.27e), or simply break away (see Figure 7.27f).

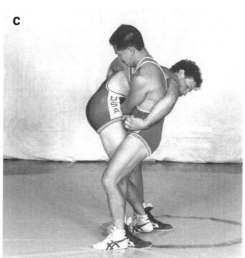

(continued)

Figure 7.27, a-f   Countering the lift and gaining several attack options.

Figure 7.27, a-f   *(continued)*

Attacking the Arms

Very often the defensive wrestler will be so concerned about defending against an attack to his trunk that he will leave his arms in a vulnerable position. When you are attacking your opponent's arms in the par terre position, it is to your advantage to arrange to have two arms against one.

Securing the Arm

Having two arms against one is a situation that creates obvious strength and leverage advantages. When you are attempting to turn an opponent with an armlock, the strength of your arm muscles is not nearly as crucial as the correct application and use of your arms as levers. You must be conscious of isolating the secondary attack areas of the arms. Proper positioning will impair the bottom man's strength. As you focus your attack on one of your opponent's arms, you should control his hand and elbow. This position will neutralize his shoulder strength.

An opponent who is very strong in the arms and shoulders can make it difficult for you to control an arm. You can get help from the muscles of your body if you use the right lock. If you make your armlock deep and move from the front rather than the side, you can anchor your hand on your own shoulder and bring more than your arm muscles into play when controlling an arm (see Figure 7.28, a and b).

Another effective method of securing an arm is to lock your hands around your opponent's arm and use your elbow to hold him still as your two arms lever his one arm away from his body. His arm now will be in a position for you to use it as a lever to turn him over (see Figure 7.29a).

From this position, isolate your opponent's elbow with your elbow and body, and his head and shoulder with your other arm (see Figure 7.29b). Force down through his arm into the mat. Place your free hand on the mat at the side of his head to keep him from moving away (see Figure 7.29c). Move your hips into his armpit and move around his head. As he turns, put your free hand around his head to secure a fall (see Figure 7.29, d and e).

Figure 7.28, a and b   Using your body's muscles to secure an arm.

(continued)

Figure 7.29, a-e   Securing an arm bar.

c

d

e

Figure 7.29, a-e *(continued)*

In the mat position you also can gain control of an arm by placing both hands under your opponent's armpits from the rear and forcing his shoulders to one side so that the elbow of your arm on that side comes in contact with the mat (see Figure 7.30a). Reach under and secure a lock over the back of your opponent's hand (see Figure 7.30b).

Use your forearm as a lever and push forward as you turn your elbow to a position on the back of your opponent's shoulder (see Figure 7.30c). Your body will move beside your opponent, with all your weight focused on his shoulder joint. Both your hands should be on your opponent's hand and wrist (see Figure 7.30d). Place his hand in the small of his back (see Figure 7.30e).

Pull your opponent's arm toward your lap as you pivot your body around his shoulder. Move in front of your opponent with your hip on the side of his head and your back arched. Pull his arm to your chest with both hands, slip your out-

side arm around his, and place your shoulder in his armpit (see Figure 7.30, f and g). Rotate your hips toward the mat then open up your hips so that your stomach is toward the ceiling to allow your other arm to secure a chinlock on your opponent's head (see Figure 7.30, h and i). Close your hips by turning your stomach back to the mat. Lift and drive your opponent to his back (see Figure 7.30j).

a

b

c

d

(continued)

Figure 7.30, a-j   Gaining a two-on-one arm bar.

e

f

g

h

i

(continued)

Figure 7.30, a-i

j

Figure 7.30, a-i *(continued)*

The Half Nelson

The half nelson is an effective turning hold when applied properly. Attack one of your opponent's arms with both of yours. Extend his arm and get his elbow as close to his head as possible (see Figure 7.31, a and b).

From here move your hand from your wrist to the crown of your opponent's head. Place his elbow behind his head before you turn him (see Figure 7.31, c and d). Move to the side and turn him with the half nelson. As he turns to his back, move your half nelson deep around his neck (see Figure 7.31, e and f). Raise his head, tighten the lock, and touch his shoulders to the mat.

a

b

(continued)

Figure 7.31, a-f The half nelson.

Figure 7.31, a-f   *(continued)*

If you are not successful in controlling the arm you attacked, reach to the opposite hand with your arm that is under your opponent's shoulder. Lift and pull his hand toward his armpit (see Figure 7.32, a-c).

Place your other shoulder on your opponent's scapula and force into him as your free hand

moves to control the elbow of the arm you have pulled under his shoulder (see Figure 7.32d). Move your hips around your opponent's head, and turn his back to the mat (see Figure 7.32, e and f). Tie up both arms to secure a fall.

(continued)

Figure 7.32, a-f   A half nelson variation.

Figure 7.32, a-f *(continued)*

The Crossface

Very often when you are working for a half nelson, your opponent will raise his head. This offers you an opportunity for a reverse crossface (see Figure 7.33a). Place your triceps against the side of your opponent's face. Push and lift so that you can reach back and hook his other arm above the elbow (see Figure 7.33, b and c). Use your arm as a lever to turn him toward his back. Lock both arms for the fall (see Figure 7.33, d and e).

When you have a crossface and see that it is not going to be effective, reach under your opponent's far shoulder with your free hand (see Figure 7.34a). Lock that hand on the wrist of your crossface hand (see Figure 7.34b). Move your inside leg tight behind your opponent's near shoulder (see Figure 7.34c). You are now in a position to get your leg under his shoulder. As soon as you do this, lift his far shoulder, and pull and turn your opponent to expose his back (see Figure 7.34, d and e).

You can do the same technique in the opposite direction. When you secure the lock, jump to the opposite side of your opponent, drive your inside knee under his armpit, arch back, and turn him (see Figure 7.35).

Another effective way to improve a loose crossface is to make it a double crossface. If you have a loose crossface position with your right hand, move on top of your opponent and reach around his head with your other arm. Place your left hand on his right shoulder (see Figure 7.36, a and b). Jump to the left side of your opponent as you release the loose crossface and turn him with your left arm (see Figure 7.36, c and d). Secure both arms for a fall.

Figure 7.33, a-e The reverse crossface.

Figure 7.34, a-e A crossface whipover.

Figure 7.35 The crossface whipover from a different direction.

Figure 7.36, a-d The double crossface.

In par terre wrestling, it is important to be ready to defend or attack immediately. Indecision on top will result in the referee returning both wrestlers to a standing position, and a scoring opportunity will be lost. Indecision when you are on the bottom will result in your opponent scoring on you.

To the top man, par terre is a great chance to score. The gut wrench and the opportunity to lift your opponent from the mat provide avenues to score big points. These skills, coupled with the correct use of arm levers, provide a formidable attack.

When you are the bottom man, maintaining correct defensive posture and movement is essential to neutralizing the top man's attack. Pay special attention to countering the lift. You must master correct body position designed to thwart the mechanical advantage that the top position provides to your opponent.

CHAPTER 8

Training Exercises and Activities

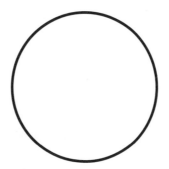

The act of wrestling requires control of all of one's senses; a sharp intellect; and the subconscious, pretrained movement patterns of numerous physical techniques.

Whenever wrestlers engage in repeated live throwing, the use of a crash pad is advisable. This is particularly important if you are a beginner. As you become adept at the throwing maneuvers, and after all wrestlers have been instructed in safe falling, you should do the throws on a regular legal wrestling mat. As you develop mastery of wrestling techniques, your practice situations should duplicate actual wrestling conditions as often as is practical.

Using gymnastic crash pads will help alleviate the stress on a live partner and will give beginners a safe, soft landing area (see Figure 8.1).

Figure 8.1 Using a crash pad.

Warm-Up

A wrestler needs a pretraining warm-up to prepare the body for the wrestling activity planned for each day's training session. The general goals of the warm-up are to raise your heart rate to 70% of working heart rate, to increase circulation of synovial fluids in your joints, to increase circulation to your muscles, and to prepare your muscles for the planned activity.

Phase 1

Each warm-up session should include three phases of activity with varying degrees of intensity. In the first phase, you will raise your heart rate by doing activities that fall within an easily available range of motion. Circulation in your joints and muscles will increase. This phase should last 6 to 10 minutes. At the conclusion of this phase, your pulse rate should be checked and should show an increase to 70% of age-adjusted maximum heart rate.

Some activities that will accommodate the goals of phase 1 of the warm-up are the following:

Light jogging
Skipping
Sliding sideways
Hopping
Walking and striding
Arm circles
Trunk rotation
Shadow wrestling
Wrestling movements without a partner
Joint rotation

Phase 2

Phase 2 of the warm-up sequence will increase circulation to your entire skeletal muscles and joint system as you concentrate on a larger range of motion for the joints and muscles. This phase should be 6 to 8 minutes long.

Some activities that fit phase 2 are the following:

Pulling your knees to your chest
Hurdlers' stretch
Crab stretching and rotation of joints
Upper body press-up with hips on the mat
Back arches on hands and feet

Isometric neck exercises with a partner
Partner joint stretches for the shoulders, hips, and trunk

After you finish phase 2, you will be ready to begin preparing your body for the demands of the wrestling practice.

Phase 3

Phase 3 of the warm-up consists of activities that let your body make contact with the mat and another body. Tumbling exercises such as forward rolls, dive rolls, backward rolls, and cartwheels fit here. You can do these singly and in series. Exercises in which you work with another person should follow the tumbling. "Buddy" exercises may be used here. Some buddy exercises follow:

Reverse body lifts
Front bodylock lifting and turning
Buddy squats with partner on your shoulders
Cooperative pummeling for position
Head and arm position countered by a dip and lift "snake" action
Cooperative "mirror" techniques on your feet

Review defensive par terre position by doing gut wrenches, exercising correct form with 50% resistance. Work on lifting and countering the lift in the same manner.

This phase of the warm-up should last 10 to 12 minutes.

Mirror Techniques

As you begin to master your techniques, partners may warm up and train by doing "mirror techniques." For a given time (e.g., 5 minutes), you execute techniques with your partner, giving only the amount of resistance necessary to make sure that each technique is executed correctly. It proceeds like this: Wrestler A executes a move. Wrestler B does the same technique; then wrestler B does a technique and wrestler A must do the same thing. As the wrestlers run through their repertoire of set-ups and techniques, both wrestlers have the opportunity to suggest new variations to each other and coach each other. This practice should be encouraged and required so that both wrestlers can analyze and better understand how, why, and when various techniques are effective.

Flexibility

Body flexibility is essential to effective wrestling. Every day, you must do exercises that are specific to positions you will assume in the act of wrestling with another person.

The Back Arch

The back arch is fundamental to many Greco-Roman throws. Exercises that increase back flexibility and help reduce one's natural fear of arching backward should be part of the teaching sequence.

Begin the individual back flexibility exercise sequence by lying on your back; place your hands and feet on the mat, and arch so that your belly is thrust toward the ceiling as high as possible.

Skill level: All wrestlers

Basic skill: None

Purpose: To develop the ability to arch

Prerequisite: None

Two exercises that will help with back flexibility utilize a wall. Stand 2 feet from the wall with your back to it. Twist your trunk so that you can touch the wall with both hands. Your feet should remain in the original position. You must turn both left and right.

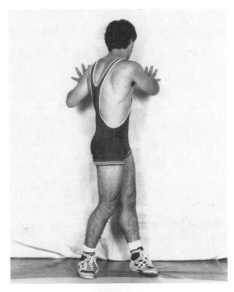

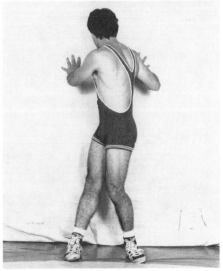

Skill level: All wrestlers

Basic skill: None

Purpose: To develop trunk rotation and get the wrestler accustomed to using the wall

Prerequisite: None

Now use the wall to help develop an arch from a standing position. Assuming the same position as for the previous exercise, look straight back and touch the wall with both hands. Then move your hands alternately and progressively

down the wall. This will put you into a back arch position. When you believe you have reached your limit of flexibility, walk your hands back up the wall.

Skill level: All wrestlers

Basic skill: Back arch

Purpose: Lead-up activity to doing a back arch from a standing position

Prerequisite: Arching exercises from the mat

A little more body movement associated with arching is now needed. Your partner is placed on his hands and knees on the mat. You do a handstand at your partner's side, arching over his back so that your feet touch the mat on the other side of the wrestler on the mat.

The wrestler doing the arching finishes the exercise by coming to a standing position on the side opposite the starting point.

As your body control improves, you will be able to bridge over your partner and kick back to the original starting position. This exercise may be done from a handstand to the feet or from standing to a back arch over.

Skill level: All wrestlers

Basic skill: Back arch

Purpose: To introduce arching from a standing position

Prerequisite: Wall walking

At this point, we can introduce arching from a standing position with the help of a partner. You and your partner stand side by side facing opposite directions. Lock hands by each grasping the other's wrist. Arch back toward the mat. Your descent is controlled by your partner, who assists in making sure the arching action is correct.

Skill level: All wrestlers

Basic skill: Back arch

Purpose: To simulate arching back from a standing position

Prerequisite: Bridge over drills with a partner

Wrestlers should repeat this action daily to develop and maintain back flexibility and body control.

Spatial Awareness

In arching back to throw, you must always know exactly where you are in relation to the mat. When you arch back you must not land on your head. You will turn just before you touch the mat so that you complete the throw with your opponent between you and the mat.

Touching your head to the mat is acceptable when you are learning the arch. Your body weight is partially supported by your partner, and you are not supporting the weight of an opponent. Landing on your head with an opponent's weight on top of you may cause injury. The object of the arching is to pull your opponent to an extended body position where he has no supports (feet) on the mat. From here you can easily move his body in the direction and to the position you desire.

Arching with your head on the mat is fundamental to defense when you are in danger of being pinned and must keep your shoulders off the mat.

A drill to help develop spatial awareness is to have you and your partner stand facing the same direction with one—the catcher—3 feet behind the other—the archer. The archer begins a straight-back arch, looking back to see the catcher. The catcher will stop the arch back by placing both hands on the back of the archer's neck as he comes to him. You should do this many times. Each time, the catcher allows his partner to fall a little more, and the archer progressively assumes a more fully arched position. When the archer has achieved a full arch fallback, he will then turn quickly and land on the mat belly down.

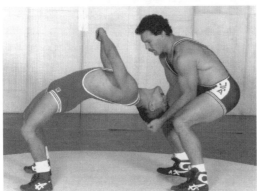

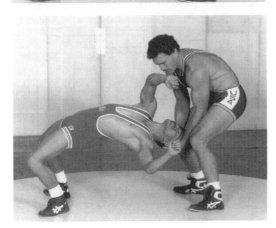

Skill level: All wrestlers

Basic skill: Back arch without restraining assistance

Purpose: To help wrestlers become accustomed to arching back without assistance, to increase spacial awareness, and to help the wrestler develop confidence in his ability to turn before touching his head to the mat

Prerequisite: Back arching with assistance

Practicing Techniques

Wrestling involves two live bodies. Every wrestler must become accustomed to controlling and moving a live body that does not want to be controlled or moved. Exercises and drills that help you become familiar with this situation can be an important part of daily practice.

To make sure that you cover all important phases of wrestling, you can prearrange drills and live wrestling situations to simulate the problems of actual competition. Start in the particular lock, mat position, tactical situation, or emotional and psychological climate that you will encounter in competition. Be specific as to what you are doing, how you are doing it, and when it is to be done.

Lifting Drills

Lifting your opponent is a very important part of Greco-Roman wrestling. You must incorporate lifting exercises into your daily practice plan to develop your lifting ability. You can use cooperative bodylock lifting drills to develop lifting techniques, the backpedal into the beginning of the back arch, the arch into a side throw into a crash pad, and correct defensive posture for the bottom man. Emphasize only one of these in each drill sequence. In each case, the lifting and movement pattern necessary to complete a successful lift and throw should be emphasized. Incorporate each of the following drills into live wrestling sequences with full resistance.

In the standing position you must pummel and adjust your body to secure a lifting position so you can throw your opponent. On the mat, bodylock your opponent and lift him so you can handle his body more easily in the gut wrench and, most importantly, lift him to where you can arch and throw him.

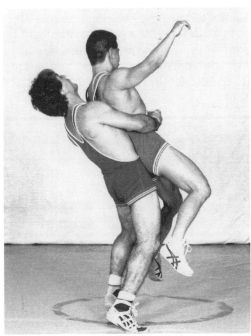

Variation: By assuming a reverse bodylock position with a partner, you can make cooperative lifting exercises that emphasize correct lifting posture specific to a particular technique part of a daily warm-up sequence.

Skill level: Junior high and above

Basic skill: Lifting

Purpose: To teach correct body position and lifting technique

Prerequisite: Instruction in proper body position when lifting and why the position of your back is important to safe and efficient lifting

Practice the turning, arching action of the step-around bodylock by assuming identical body-lock positions. As you step around, lift, and swing your partner, you allow him to land on his feet, and he in turn duplicates the action.

Wedge Position Drills

To develop the wedge position and centering, have your partner assume a bear hug lock and you an over-arm lock. From this position each wrestler tries to get himself in the control posture.

Skill level: All wrestlers

Basic skill: Knowledge of the wedge position

Purpose: To teach the wedge position and body pummeling

Prerequisite: None

Skill level: High school and above

Basic skill: Moving into an arched throwing position

Purpose: Lead-up drill to the step-around bodylock

Prerequisite: Mastery of correct lifting and arching movement

Hip Throwing

Making your opponent come over your hips or shoulders also is a fundamental position-movement sequence. Each wrestler assumes identical over-under lock positions. From this lock each wrestler will execute an arm throw or a hiplock. You and your partner do the actions alternately, with the emphasis on correct form.

Skill level: All wrestlers

Basic skill: Arm throw

Purpose: To teach the arm throw

Prerequisite: Basic arm throw skills

Use of Throwing Dummies

Throwing dummies come in various sizes and weights. A lightweight wrestler should not be expected to train with the same size dummy as a heavyweight wrestler any more than he should be expected to wrestle with a heavyweight. Likewise, bigger wrestlers should train with bigger dummies.

Virtually all standing and mat techniques can be simulated with a dummy. Note that this type of activity is a simulation and does not replace live wrestling.

Simulated Competition

Proper development requires that you focus your skills and the simulated situations into an effective game plan. You can do this by allowing yourself to have actual competition-type matches in practice. The matches should last as long as those in actual competition, and you should keep score. Require each wrestler to referee and judge his teammates' matches. This forces each wrestler to know the rules and, perhaps even more important, to look at the application of the rules from an official's perspective.

You should instruct wrestlers that the emphasis in these matches should be on analyzing an opponent, analyzing yourself, creating a game plan to win, and sticking to the game plan. You must have enough confidence in your training and focus that you can just let the match happen. These practice sessions are needed to test your preparation, to focus on broad and specific goals, and to improvise as well as carry out a plan.

Cross-Training Activities

Developing confidence in your ability to wrestle effectively may begin with the confidence that comes from the ability to direct your body to do various physical tasks not associated with normal daily movement. In selecting and organizing supplemental training that differs physically from the act of wrestling, you must be aware of the value of dissimilar physical movement as well as the opportunity to present intellectual and emotional challenges that can strengthen your ability to cope with unfamiliar problems and stress. This development can take place in an environment apart from wrestling. Lessons learned can be readily applied. For example, problem solving and stress management are universally applicable.

The integration into the total wrestling plan of activities other than wrestling that develop strength, coordination, flexibility, cardiovascular endurance, and total body awareness can be of significant value. A wrestler who develops physical abilities that may not be sufficiently emphasized and isolated in wrestling may then be able to overcome related technical movements that have previously stymied him. In addition, allowing wrestlers to perform a new activity that embraces movement patterns foreign to wrestling helps them ease the emotional and intellectual intensity associated with serious high-level training.

Gymnastic Activities

The flexibility and strength required by the unusual body positions associated with gymnastics also play a role in the unusual positions that occur in wrestling. Balance, body control, and awareness of the precise position of your body in relation to your center of gravity and the floor is essential to tumbling events in gymnastics. This is also true in wrestling.

When you lift your opponent or you are lifted from the mat, you must be able to anticipate and accommodate any landing so that you will end up in a good wrestling position. Simple gymnastic activities can help you get a feel for your position as you move through the air and can serve as part of the daily warm-up.

Forward and backward rolls help to develop body control and also serve to get the body accustomed to contacting the mat before practice. Cartwheels and dive rolls over your partner who is on his hands and knees can get you used to knowing where the mat is when your feet are above your head. Front handsprings are also valuable in helping athletes to develop spatial awareness.

Simple gymnastics will help you; you do not need to engage in complex, difficult gymnastic activities. The time and skill required to do more advanced gymnastics will quickly become counterproductive to the development of wrestling.

Weight Training

Today, all athletes are involved in some form of weight training designed to enhance performance. Weight training for wrestling is most effective when the program features exercises that are as close to the actual wrestling movements as possible. In a program of this nature, free weights and dumbbells seem to fit best.

Wrestling requires constant adjustment of position. Your opponent is very rarely stationary. Constant awareness of your optimal biomechanical position in relation to your opponent and your own center of gravity is essential to effective technique execution. Being able to maintain proper position and combat the bad position your opponent forces upon you requires strength. This is where weight training comes into play.

To build strength, the activity must overload the muscle to the point of failure. This means a very demanding and intense exercise program. The weights used must stress the muscles to exhaustion.

Small Muscle Groups

Wrestling uses most of the body's muscles at some time or another. The small muscle groups of the arms almost always are constantly active. The arms must be trained for strength and endurance. Sets of exercises that utilize heavy resistance (70% of maximum weight that can be moved in one repetition), and a low number of repetitions (five or fewer) will build strength. You can build endurance by doing sets of repetitions that are high in number (50 repetitions with a weight that is 50% of a 1-repetition maximum lift).

It also is good to simulate pummeling movements with your arms while holding dumbbells. A series of three 5-minute pummel sequences with a 1-minute rest between sets is advised.

Deltoid side raises work the anterior and medial parts of the deltoid muscles. Hold a dumbbell in each hand. Start with your hands at your sides. Raise the dumbbells in an arc out from your sides until they meet over your head. Return and repeat for the desired number of repetitions.

Technique for: Shoulders

Skill level: All wrestlers

Basic skill: Raising arms to side

Purpose: To strengthen the deltoid muscles

Prerequisite: Instruction in basic weight training

Bicep curls may be done together or alternately. The palms of your hands may be forward or facing each other. Your elbows are held tightly against your sides. Move the dumbbell from your thigh to your chin to accommodate a full range of motion. Do not swing the dumbbell to get it started.

Technique for: Biceps

Skill level: All wrestlers

Basic skill: Curling the dumbbells

Purpose: To strengthen the biceps

Prerequisite: Instruction in basic weight training

Triceps extensions are done by gripping the dumbbell and standing with it extended at arm's length directly overhead. Keep your upper arm and elbow stationary. Lower the dumbbell along a semicircular arc to the top of your shoulder, allowing only your forearm to move. Reverse the procedure and repeat the movement. You will feel stress in your triceps.

Wrist curls work the muscles on the insides of your forearms. Take an undergrip on the dumbbells and hold them in front of you shoulder-width apart. Place your forearms on a bench or table with your fists not supported by the bench. Allow your fists to bend as far down as possible; even roll the dumbbell down your fingers. Curl the dumbbells up as high as possible.

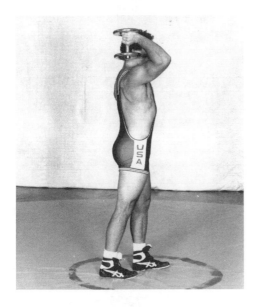

Technique for: Triceps

Skill level: All wrestlers

Basic skill: Moving a dumbbell in a manner that works the triceps muscles

Purpose: To strengthen the triceps

Prerequisite: Instruction in basic weight training

Technique for: Forearm

Skill level: All wrestlers

Basic skill: Wrist curl

Purpose: To strengthen the forearms

Prerequisite: Instruction in basic weight training

Large Muscle Groups

For the larger muscle groups of the body, strength is a primary concern in wrestling weight training. The total body endurance that wrestling demands can best be developed by very intense weight training sessions.

Having control of one's center of gravity and maintaining a correct wrestling posture in the standing position or on the mat is dependent on the wrestler's leg, abdominal, and neck strength. To strengthen these large compound muscle groups, lifts that use more than one muscle group are best. Because several muscle groups work together in such lifts, you can use heavier amounts of weight. The heavy training indicated here should occur in training sessions lasting no longer than 30 minutes. The exercises should be done in sets of six or fewer repetitions with weights that are 80% to 90% of a maximum one-repetition lift.

Toe raises are started by resting the bar across your shoulders. Raise up on your toes, working your calf muscles. Repeat the movement up and down.

Technique for: Calves

Skill level: All wrestlers

Basic skill: Raising a weight with your calf muscles

Purpose: To strengthen the calf muscles

Prerequisite: Instruction in basic weight training

Squats are the best all-around lower body exercise. Place the barbell in a comfortable position behind your head and across your shoulders. Place your feet a little more than shoulder-width apart with your toes slightly turned out. Position your body with your head up, your hips under your shoulders, and your vertebrae vertically aligned. Tighten your back and thigh muscles, and squat. Do not attempt to squat with more weight than you can handle, and do not bounce up at the bottom of the squat. Because it is possible to do squats with heavy weights, you should always use a squat rack and have two spotters working with you.

Technique for: Quadriceps

Skill level: High school and up

Basic skill: Raising a weight with your legs

Purpose: To strengthen the thighs

Prerequisite: Specific instruction in the correct form for squats

Lunges begin with the barbell in the same position as for the squat. Stand with your feet parallel and shoulder-width apart. Step forward with one foot as far as your balance will allow. Lower your center of gravity until the opposite knee barely touches the floor. Recover to the standing position and repeat with the other leg. In the extended position, your front knee should be ahead of your foot.

Leg curls can be done most efficiently on some form of leg apparatus. Lie facedown with your heels hooked under the top set of pads. Pull your heels up to your buttocks. Bend your knees as much as possible. Keep your body flat to the bench and work through a full range of motion.

Technique for: Hamstrings

Skill level: All wrestlers

Basic skill: Curling hamstring muscles

Purpose: To strengthen the hamstring muscles

Prerequisite: Instruction in basic weight training and the use of the universal gym

Technique for: Quadriceps

Skill level: High school and above

Basic skill: Stepping forward with a barbell on your shoulders

Purpose: To strengthen the hip and thigh muscles

Prerequisite: Specific instruction in the mechanics of the exercise

The power clean begins by standing with your feet shoulder-width apart and grasping the bar at about shoulder width with your palms toward your body. Dip your hips, flatten your back, and keep your head up. This is the basic position for pulling a weight from the floor. Start the lift with your leg muscles, then follow through with your back and then arm muscles. Raise the bar up to your chest with a slight knee dip, then catch the barbell on your chest. Keep your body erect and allow the bar to roll down your hips. Stop here. Then squat the barbell back to the floor and repeat the exercise. Because you are moving a heavy weight through space, balance is important, and this exercise should be done with a weight that you can handle.

Technique for: Back

Skill level: High school and above

Basic skill: Lifting a weight from the floor to your chest

Purpose: To strengthen the back

Prerequisite: Specific instruction in the mechanics of the lift

The snatch begins from the same position as the power clean but with your hands spread much further apart. Start the lift in the same sequence as the power clean. Pull the bar as high as possible and squat under the bar, catching it with your arms extended, locked, and straight. Complete the lift by standing up. Return the bar to the floor in the same manner as for the power clean. About 50% of the weight you used for your power clean should be about right for this exercise.

Technique for: Lower back

Skill level: Advanced weight trainer, serious wrestler

Basic skill: Lifting a weight from the floor to an overhead position in one movement

Purpose: To strengthen legs, back, and arms

Prerequisite: Advanced instruction in the mechanics of the lift

The dead lift starts when you assume the basic pulling-lifting position. Place your hands on the bar shoulder-width apart with one hand in an overgrip and one in an undergrip. Pull the bar up until your body is fully erect and your arms are extended, holding the bar close to your hips. Return the bar to the floor and repeat.

Technique for: Lower back

Skill level: Serious wrestler

Basic skill: Lifting a weight from the floor to your waist

Purpose: To strengthen the lower back

Prerequisite: Specific instruction in the mechanics of the lift

The bench press is executed by lying on your back on a bench and taking a barbell off the rack at arm's length directly above your chest. Any grip along the bar with the hands in an over-grip is acceptable. The varied grips will stress different areas of the muscles involved. Lower the bar straight down until it touches midchest, and press it up to arm's length. Repeat this action.

The incline press is a variation of the bench press done from an inclined surface. All the instructions for the bench press apply. You might have problems getting the bar to go up at first, but you will overcome that with practice.

Technique for: Chest

Skill level: All wrestlers

Basic skill: Pushing a weight up and away from your chest

Purpose: To strengthen the chest

Prerequisite: Specific instruction in the mechanics of the lift

Technique for: Chest

Skill level: All wrestlers

Basic skill: Pressing a weight away from the body at an angle

Purpose: To strengthen the upper pectoral muscles

Prerequisite: Instruction in basic weight training

The decline press is a bench press with the bench declined so that your head is below your feet. All of the mechanics are the same as for the bench press.

Technique for: Chest

Skill level: All wrestlers

Basic skill: Pushing a weight away from the body at an angle

Purpose: To strengthen the lower pectoral muscles

Prerequisite: Instruction in basic weight training

Coordinating Weight Training

Your weight training regimen must be coordinated with the yearly competition schedule. Obvious spaces between competitions (peaks) provide an opportunity for a specific program designed to meet the individual needs of each athlete. The training program must take place year-round to maximize the benefits and minimize reversibility of training. Training intensity will vary throughout the year. When you are preparing for a competition, success in that competition is the main goal. Your technical training will include the techniques and strategies

you plan to use against your likely opponents. This is a necessary focus. Your physical training will be designed to prepare you for a very specific degree of intensity for a very specific amount of time. This means that you must be in top physical shape. You must train hard and intelligently. When you reach top condition, you must allow for enough time between that point and the competition for your body and mind to be rested and focused on the competition.

After the competition, you will experience a natural emotional letdown. Your body will be fatigued, possibly injured, and most certainly sore. Your training will be in a recovery phase both physically and mentally. It is a time to restore relationships with your friends and loved ones who support you in your efforts. Give back to those who gave to you; reestablish the balance in your life.

After a short time you will evaluate your performance and make plans for improvement. You will regenerate your motivation and focus on new goals. At this stage you will begin to reactivate your work schedule. Weight training, technique and strategy improvement, running, and cross-training activities will fill your time. This is a logical period to seek out developmental competitions to test your new training and scout your competitors to see where you are in relation to them. You now begin your training program so you will peak mentally and physically at the next important competition.

The frequency of your training should vary only as competitions, injury, or needed rest periods dictate. Weight training must become part of your life as it fits in with your technical, physical, and psychological development to help you become a totally healthy athlete.

Running

Running is necessary for every athlete. The complete development of sound cardiovascular endurance is essentially impossible to achieve without running or an activity that closely approximates it. Running is the most natural and convenient method available. You can easily regulate and evaluate the intensity and length of exercise by applying the criteria of time, distance, and difficulty. There are almost unlimited running activities that you can do, such as jogging, aerobic exercise to music, obstacle courses, hill climbing, stair running, sprinting, interval running, and running against resistance as with a harness.

Begin with jogging and low- to medium-intensity distance running that will form a conditioning base and precede high-intensity anaerobic sprints. Begin jogging a half mile and increase to 2 miles a day, then increase the intensity of the activity by running a half mile for time. Increase the time running to 2 miles. When you can run 2 miles in 14 minutes, begin some sprint training. All times are adjustable up or down, depending on your size and weight. Take into account whether your running is already well or poorly developed. Now you can begin a run and sprint combination workout (see Chart 1).

Chart 1: Run and Sprint Workout
The run and sprint workout program is designed to prepare you during the weeks prior to a major competition. After the competition, rest and a readjustment of the training program are in order.

Day 1	Run 1 mile, rest 5 minutes, then sprint 4 × 100 yards with a 30-second rest between sprints.
Day 2	Run .5 mile, rest 2.5 minutes, then sprint 4 × 220 yards with a 30-second rest between sprints.
Day 3	Run 440 yards, rest 2 minutes, then sprint 8 × 200 yards with a 1-minute rest between sprints.
Day 4	Jog 2 miles.
Day 5	Run 1 mile for time.
Day 6	Jog .5 mile, run .5 mile.
Day 7	Sprint 8 × 100 yards with a 30-second rest between sprints.
Day 8	Jog .5 mile, run .5 mile.
Day 9	Run 1 mile for time.
Day 10	Run 1 mile.
Day 11	Run 2 miles.
Day 12	Sprint 8 × 220 yards with a 30-second rest between sprints.
Day 13	Sprint 6 × 220 yards with a 30-second rest between sprints.
Day 14	Sprint 8 × 100 yards with a 30-second rest between sprints.

Building up to running sprints should follow a pattern similar to that of the buildup of wrestling intensity that precedes a competition. When you are in the early stages of preparing for a competition and the degree of intensity in daily practice is nominal, distance running fits the workout plan. As the intensity of each practice increases and you focus more on actual match situations and match times, you should adjust your running program to sprint running and anaerobic conditioning. When the peaking segment of the practice plan begins, you should stop running because it is a major glycogen burner. Muscle glycogen, which is the major supplier of fuel during prolonged exercise, provides a very significant amount of the adenosine triphosphate (ATP) utilized in intense, short term exercise such as wrestling.

Resting immediately before competition is essential for the effect of your hard training to fully manifest itself in maximum wrestling performance.

After a difficult competition, a short rest period away from wrestling is a good idea. You can use jogging and low-intensity running to maintain your training during this period. Other activities such as basketball, soccer, or swimming may also be valuable.

As is the case with all training activities that vary from your main event, running must work in harmony with other nonwrestling training activities. Running must also work in harmony with all your wrestling training activities to supplement and expand your mastery of skills that make you a total, successful wrestler.

Cool-Down

Immediately after the day's practice, you should do a series of "cool-down" exercises to help the body return to normal. The activity should gradually return your heart rate to a normal resting state. The activity will shift the body from an anaerobic to an aerobic state of energy expenditure. You will maintain maximum oxygen intake while decreasing oxygen usage. Extend your muscles to the maximum range of motion as waste products move from intercellular tissue to the vascular system.

Cool-down can be divided into three phases. The first is control of respiration and heart rate. This phase lasts until the heart rate returns to 70% of age-adjusted maximum heart rate and respirations are below 20 per minute.

Activities for phase 1 are as follows:

Slow jogging

Fast walking

Arm circles while walking

Deep breathing while walking

Walking, (lunging, or striding)

Rhythmic limb movements while walking

Phase 2 should be about 5 minutes long and be designed to maintain the heart rate at 70% of the age-adjusted maximum. Waste products will move from the intercellular system to the vascular system during this phase.

Activities for this phase might include the following:

Running

Skipping rope

Cycling

Cooperative pummeling

Skipping

Fast walking

The third stage of the cool-down is designed to lengthen the muscles to their maximum range of motion. This segment should be 4 to 5 minutes long. You can use all accepted stretching exercises here.

Stretching activities include the following:

Hurdler's stretch

Prone press-ups

Arm and trunk rotation

Back and front bridging

Hip and thigh stretches

The stretches can be followed by a massage to end the training session.

This part of the daily practice is a cool-down, not a cool-off. Lead your body gradually from a state of high activity to a normal resting condition.

Putting It All Together

Structuring your overall training program allows you to not only prepare yourself to perform your very best at a particular meet, but also to surpass your best when situations demand it. Training should be an intelligent, orderly preparation with a definite structure and purpose for both team and individual goals. Using your time efficiently will best prepare you for success.

Tables 8.1 through 8.5 offer 1-week, 9-day, 5-month, and 1-year sample training plans that you can tailor to your needs and goals.

Table 8.1   Seven-Day Training Plan (Developmental Phase)

	Monday	Tuesday	Wednesday	Thursday	Friday	Saturday	Sunday
Early A.M.	Run 2 miles for time	Run 2 miles for time	Run 2 miles for time	Run 2 miles for time	Run 2 miles for time	Run 2 miles for time	
A.M. Training	Warm-up Gymnastics Select & analyze a specific standing technique; practice technique cooperatively Find the scoring positions for this skill Create opportunities to use the skill—drill on all the scoring situations Cool-down Weight training, upper body—30 min	Warm-up Cooperative technique Review previous day's lesson—emphasis on perfect form Wrestle a 5-min match immediately followed by technique drill when tired Cool-down Weight training, upper body—30 min	Warm-up Gymnastics Select & analyze a specific Par Terre technique (lifting); practice technique cooperatively Find the scoring positions for this skill Create opportunities to use this skill—drill on all the scoring situations Cool-down Weight training, upper body—30 min	Warm-up Cooperative technique Review previous day's lesson—emphasis on perfect form Wrestle a 5-min match immediately followed by technique drill when tired Cool-down Weight training, upper body—30 min	Warm-up Gymnastics Analyze the defense to the skills presented Drill cooperatively on the defense Drill full effort on attack & defense—emphasis on counterattack Cool-down Weight training, upper body—30 min	Warm-up Cooperative technique Review skills presented as they fit into attack, counterattack, & blocking Wrestle a series of cooperative 50%-effort technique matches Cool-down Weight training, upper body—30 min	R E S T
P.M. Training	Warm-up Cooperative technique Review A.M. technique Review scoring positions Drill on creating the scoring positions Wrestle—start from the scoring positions Wrestle a 5-min match—look for the technique of the day Cool-down	Warm-up Gymnastics Review previous day's lesson—emphasis on creating an opportunity to use the technique Wrestle a 5-min match immediately followed by technique drill when tired Cool-down	Warm-up Cooperative technique Review A.M. technique Review scoring positions Drill on creating the scoring positions Wrestle—start from the scoring positions Wrestle a 5-min match—look for the technique of the day Cool-down	Warm-up Gymnastics Review previous day's lesson—emphasis on creating an opportunity to score Wrestle a 5-min match immediately followed by technique drill when tired Cool-down	Warm-up Cooperative technique Review and drill cooperatively on the A.M. technique Wrestle a series of 5-min matches—emphasis on attack & counterattack Drill cooperatively on technique when tired—emphasis on perfect form Cool-down	Warm-up Gymnastics Wrestle a series of 5-min matches to test the use of skills presented After the matches, review all skills through cooperative mirror drilling Cool-down	R E S T
Late P.M.	Weight training, lower body—30 min	Weight training, lower body—30 min	Weight training, lower body—30 min	Weight training, lower body—30 min	Weight training, lower body—30 min	Weight training, lower body—30 min	

Table 8.2   Seven-Day Training Plan (Approaching Competition)

	Monday	Tuesday	Wednesday	Thursday	Friday	Saturday	Sunday
Early A.M.	Sprint series of 50 yd, 100 yd, 200 yd, 400 yd	Sprints	Sprints	Sprints	Sprints	Sprints	
A.M. Training	Warm-up Select the techniques to be used in competition Drill on these and the scoring positions Wrestle a 5-min simulated match using the selected techniques—emphasis on creating the scoring opportunity Wrestle a 5-min simulated match—emphasis on tactics & strategies in a specific situation Cool-down	Warm-up Put selected skills into a match format—think in terms of total matches Wrestle a series of 3-min matches that start from specific positions Finish with 5-min matches that put the total plan together Cool-down	Warm-up Work on creating situations for counter-wrestling—wrestle 3-min matches from specific positions Drill on head & hand control; slowing an opponent down; creating the desired tempo Cool-down	Warm-up Evaluate the previous day's training—emphasis on correcting errors Wrestle a series of simulated matches in which previous errors are corrected Cool-down	Warm-up Wrestle a series of 5-min matches—each with different tactics—slow pace; fast pace; low scoring; must pin; guts match; scoring early & protecting lead; preempting opponent's techniques Cool-down	Warm-up Wrestle a series of 5-min matches against different opponents using different tactics—have a referee & keep score Cool-down	R E S T
P.M. Training	Warm-up Cooperative technique Analyze and drill on the logical counters to selected techniques Wrestle simulated matches with specific situations to overcome Drill on specific strategies (e.g., at the edge of the mat, blocking an opponent, etc.) Cool-down	Warm-up Cooperative technique Drill on creating situations to trap opponent into doing what you want him to Wrestle a series of 3-min matches creating the desired scoring position Wrestle two 5-min all-out matches Cool-down	Warm-up Cooperative technique Wrestle a series of 3-min situation matches—having 2 min to score 3 pts; being 1 pt ahead with 30 sec to go; or cautioning opponent out Wrestle a 5-min match and then go into overtime Cool-down	Warm-up Cooperative technique Prepare for the unusual—near-pins; bad calls from the referee Wrestle matches designed to force maintained composure Cool-down	Warm-up Cooperative technique Study a scouting report and prepare a game plan Wrestle a 5-min match to put the plan into action; repeat the procedure and then evaluate the results Cool-down	Warm-up Cooperative technqiue Evaluate the morning matches—adjust tactics & strategies Wrestle cooperative, simulated, 5-min matches correcting the mistakes of the morning workout Cool-down	R E S T

Table 8.3   Nine-Day Peaking Plan (Prior to Competition)

	A.M. training	P.M. training	Weight hydrated	Diet
Day one	High intensity day—Four 5-min all-out matches; pulse at 30+ for 10 sec; burn glycogen	High intensity—Four 5-min all-out matches; pulse at 30+ for 10 sec; burn glycogen	5.5% over desired weight	Diet higher in complex carbohydrates than protein
Day two	Rest	Low intensity—volleyball or frisbee (active rest); pulse at 25 for 10 sec	5% over	
Day three	Medium intensity—Three 5-min technique matches; pulse at 27 for 10 sec	Medium intensity—Three 5-min technique matches; pulse at 27 for 10 sec	5% over	
Day four	High intensity—Four 5-min all-out matches; pulse at 30+ for 10 sec; burn glycogen	High intensity—Four 5-min all-out matches; pulse at 30+ for 10 sec; burn glycogen	4% over	
Day five	Rest	Low intensity—volleyball or basketball (active rest); pulse at 25 or less for 10 sec	4% over	
Day six	Medium intensity—Three 5-min technique matches; pulse at 27 for 10 sec	Medium intensity—Three 5-min technique matches; pulse at 27 for 10 sec	3.5% over	Diet balanced in protein and carbohydrates
Day seven	High intensity—sprint series of 50-m dashes; pulse at 30+ for 10 sec; burn glycogen	High intensity—sprint series of 50-m dashes; pulse at 30+ for 10 sec; burn glycogen	3% over	
Day eight	Rest—short walk; read	Rest	2.5% over	
Day nine	Sauna to make weight (do not burn glycogen)	Rest—sauna (do not burn glycogen)	Weigh in; rehydrate body	
Competition	Eat small meals three hours before competition begins and drink water between sessions			

Tables 8.4a-e   Five-Month Training Program

This training calendar is arranged around trials, camps, and competitions. It is designed to help a wrestler develop skill and strategy while balancing hard endurance practice with appropriate rest to accommodate peaking for competitions. The calendar allows for travel days as well.

The daily calendar is based on a 3:1 work ratio. Day 1 is a thinking practice devoted to discussion between coach and wrestler and physical programming of technique and strategy. Physically, it is a low-intensity day. Most of the technique and drill days present a specific problem to solve that day. Each practice must have a definite purpose. You should be active in discovering and solving behavior patterns that limit success both on and off the mat.

Day 2 focuses on active controlled situations, drilling of skills, and tactics presented on the previous day. Physically, it is a medium-intensity day.

Day 3 includes hard, intense wrestling under competition-like circumstances. Physically, it is a high-intensity day. Hard, intense activity will never last more than 30 minutes (six matches).

Day 4 is a low-intensity day consisting of a short session of basketball or other nonwrestling activity, film analysis, individual meetings with coaches, and rest. The cycle begins again the next day.

Table 8.4a   Month One of Five-Month Training Program

June	Intensity	Training
1	High	Four all-out matches; heavy weight training
2	Active rest	Run 2 miles
3	Low	Review results of last tournament; make a plan to solve problems
4	Medium	Wrestle situation matches; counter two-on-one arm bar
5	High	Four all-out matches; heavy weight training
6	Active rest	Run 2 miles
7	Low	Wrestle for the official; make it easy for him to make the call you want
8	Medium	Wrestle in groups of 3 people, change every 2 min—emphasis on mat position and regular scoring attempts throughout the match
9	High	Four all-out matches with a referee; heavy weight training
10	Active rest	Play 40 min of basketball
11	Low	Drill on 1-pt scoring techniques & the setups for them; arm drags
12	Medium	Simulated 5-min matches using only 1-pt scoring moves
13	High	Four all-out matches; heavy weight training
14	Active rest	40 min of volleyball or racquetball
15	Low	Par Terre technique—drill gut wrench & counters; defense on the mat
16	Medium	Live 1-min drills on the mat—emphasis on not getting turned
17	High	Four all-out matches with required 30-sec Par Terre every 1 min
18	Active rest	Sprints: 2 × 200 m, 4 × 100 m, 6 × 50 m
19	Low	Lifting technique—drill cooperatively on correct lifting form
20	Medium	Technique matches—emphasis on Par Terre lifting & countering the lift
21	High	Four all-out matches; heavy weight training
22	Active rest	Sprints: 2 × 200 m, 4 × 100 m, 6 × 50 m
23	Low	Wrestle pummel matches—emphasis on maintaining good position
24	Medium	Wrestle cooperative matches to create scoring opportunities
25	High	Four all-out matches; heavy weight training
26	Active rest	Sprints: 2 × 400 m, 4 × 100 m, 6 × 50 m
27	Low	Select a specific technique—work on the scoring positions for that technique
28	Medium	Wrestle cooperative matches using techniques from the previous day
29	High	Four all-out matches
30	Active rest	Rest

Table 8.4b   Month Two of Five-Month Training Program

July	Intensity	Training
1	Low	
2	Medium	
3	High	
4	Low	**Seven-Day Training Plan—Table 8.2**
5	Medium	
6	High	
7	Active rest	
8	High	
9	Active rest	
10	Medium	
11	High	
12	Active rest	**Nine-Day Peaking Plan—Table 8.3**
13	Medium	
14	High	
15	Active rest	
16	Active rest	
17	High	
18	High	**Major Competition**
19	High	
20	High	
21	Rest	
22	Rest	**Rest & Heal**
23	Rest	
24	Rest	
25	Low	Evaluate the past competition—view film, look for areas to improve
26	Low	Make a plan for improvement
27	Medium	Select specific areas of concentration in training
28	Medium	Begin working new technique into wrestling style
29	Medium	Start technique matches, get back to running & weight training
30	Medium	Wrestle simulated 5-min matches—emphasis on the new plan
31	Medium	Wrestle simulated 5-min matches—emphasis on counterattack & defense

Table 8.4c   Month Three of Five-Month Training Program

August	Intensity	Early A.M. (20 min)	A.M. Training (90 min)	P.M. Training (90 min)	Late P.M. (30 min)
1	Active rest	Run 2 mi	Basketball	Soccer	
2	Low		Drill bodylocks, cooperative 5-min matches	Drill bodylocks, cooperative 5-min matches	
3	Medium		3-min matches—start in over-under bodylock	Cooperative 5-min matches to get bodylocks	
4	High		Four 5-min all-out matches	Four 5-min all-out matches	
5	Active rest	Run 2 mi	Volleyball	Rest	Weight-train
6	Low		Drill headlocks & setups, cooperative 5-min matches	Drill headlocks & setups, counter headlocks	
7	Medium		3-min matches—start in pinch headlock position	Cooperative 5-min matches to practice headlocks	
8	High		Four 5-min all-out matches	Four 5-min all-out matches	
9	Active rest	Run 2 mi	Film study	Rest	Weight-train
10	Low		Drill gut wrench, cooperative 30-sec matches	Drill gut wrench & counter to gut wrench	
11	Medium		Cooperative 5-min matches—mandatory 30-sec Par Terre	Cooperative 5-min matches—mandatory 30-sec Par Terre	
12	High		Four 5-min matches—emphasis on controlling center of mat	Four 5-min matches—emphasis on controlling tempo of match	
13	Active rest	Run 2 mi	Film study	Rest	Weight-train
14	Low		Drill lifting, cooperative 30-sec lifting	Drill lifting & counters to the lift	
15	Medium		5-min simulated matches with Par Terre	Review lifting & counters	
16	High		Four 5-min matches—emphasis on the lift	Four 5-min matches—emphasis on lifting & counters	
17	Active rest	Run 2 mi	Rest	Rest	Weight-train
18	Low		Drill reverse bodylock & counters	1-min matches—emphasis on reverse bodylock	
19	Medium		Cooperative matches—3-min standing, 2-min Par Terre	Review reverse bodylock & counters, cooperative matches	
20	High		Four 5-min matches with referee	Four 5-min matches—emphasis on edge tactics	
21	Active rest	Run 2 mi	Basketball	Rest	Weight-train
22	Low		Drill pummeling & arm drags	5-min matches: one pummel & one cooperative for arm drags	
23	Medium		Drill combination—arm drag to bodylock	Drill bodylock to arm drag	
24	High		Four 5-min matches—emphasis on arm drags	Four 5-min matches—emphasis on arm drags	
25	Active rest	Run 2 mi	Film study	Rest	Weight-train
26	Low		Drill two-on-one armlock & counters to two-on-one	3-min situation matches—start in two-on-one position	
27	Medium		Drill combination—two-on-one to bodylock	Drill combination—two-on-one to arm throws	
28	High		Four 5-min matches—emphasis on two-on-one	Four 5-min matches—emphasis on over-under bodylock position	
29	Active rest	Run 2 mi	Volleyball	Rest	Weight-train
30	Low		Drill arm throws & counters	Situation matches—arm throw position	
31	Medium		Cooperative 5-min matches—emphasis on arm spin	Cooperative 5-min matches—arm spins & counters	

Table 8.4d　Month Four of Five-Month Training Program

September	Intensity	Early A.M. (20 min)	A.M. Training (90 min)	P.M. Training (90 min)	Late P.M. (30 min)
1	High		Four 5-min all-out matches	Four 5-min all-out matches	
2	Active rest	Sprints: 50-100, 200-400 m	Bicycle	Rest	Weight-train
3	Low		Drill creating a scoring position—arm throws	Situation matches for arm throws	
4	Medium		Cooperative 5-min matches for arm throws	Cooperative 5-min matches for arm throws & counters	
5	High		Four 5-min matches—plan for a whole match	Four 5-min matches—work on a specific game plan	
6	Active rest	Sprints: 2 x 400, 4 x 200, 6 x 100	Aerobic activity	Rest	Weight-train
7	Low		Create situations for 1-pt moves	Cooperative matches to set up 1-pt moves	
8	Medium		Cooperative 5-min matches for slide-bys	Cooperative 5-min matches for arm drags	
9	High		Four 5-min matches & overtime	Four 5-min matches & overtime	
10	Active rest	Sprints: 2 x 400, 4 x 200, 6 x 100	Rest	Rest	Weight-train
11	Low		Drill tactics & techniques to win a 2-1 match	Cooperative 5-min matches with low score	
12	Medium		Drill tactics & techniques to win with one throw	Cooperative 5-min matches to set up one throw	
13	High		Four 5-min matches	Four 5-min matches	
14	Active rest	Sprints: 2 x 400, 4 x 200, 6 x 100	Rest	Rest	Weight-train
15	Low		Identify the techniques for a low-scoring match	Cooperative 5-min matches to use these techniques	
16	Medium		Work on a specific 3-pt throw	Cooperative 5-min matches to get the throw	
17	High		Four 5-min matches	Four 5-min matches	
18	Active rest	Sprints: 2 x 400, 4 x 200, 6 x 100	Rest	Rest	Weight-train
19	Low		Define specific scoring positions & preventing them	Four 5-min co-op matches to preempt scoring positions	
20	Medium		Define specific scoring positions & countering them	Four 5-min co-op matches—counter wrestling to score	
21	High		Four 5-min matches	Four 5-min matches	
22	Active rest	Sprints: 2 x 400, 4 x 200, 6 x 100	Rest	Rest	Weight-train
23	Low		Define tactics & techniques for sudden death overtime	Cooperative 5-min overtime matches—specific techniques	
24	Medium		Drill tactics & techniques to catch up to a 4-pt lead	Cooperative 5-min matches to catch up	
25	High		Four 5-min matches	Four 5-min matches	
26	Active rest	Sprints: 2 x 400, 4 x 200, 6 x 100	Rest	Rest	Weight-train
27	Low		Drill techniques to use against specific opponents	Cooperative 5-min matches to counter opponent's moves	
28	Medium		Drill defense to use against specific opponents	Cooperative 5-min matches to counter opponent's moves	
29	High		Four 5-min matches	Four 5-min matches	
30	Active rest	Sprints: 2 x 400, 4 x 200, 6 x 100	Rest	Rest	Weight-train

Table 8.4e   Month Five of Five-Month Training Program

October	Intensity	Training
1	Low	
2	Medium	
3	High	
4	Low	**Seven-Day Training Plan—Table 8.2**
5	Medium	
6	High	
7	Active rest	
8	High	
9	Active rest	
10	Medium	
11	High	
12	Active rest	
13	Medium	**Nine-Day Peaking Plan—Table 8.3**
14	High	
15	Active rest	
16	Active rest	
17	High	
18	High	
19	High	**Major Competition**
20	High	
21	Rest	
22	Rest	
23	Rest	**Rest & Heal**
24	Rest	
25	Rest	
26		
27		
28		**Begin New Training Cycle**
29		
30		
31		

Table 8.5   One-Year Training Plan

January

a. Develop a new technique.
b. Build strength through heavy weight training for power.
c. Develop body awareness and flexibility through gymnastics.
d. Teach some youth wrestling to develop your analytical approach to wrestling.

February

a. Test technique and strategy in competitive matches in training.
b. Build strength through weight training.
c. Develop body awareness and flexibility through gymnastics.
d. Study films of yourself and opponents to test your analytical ability.
e. Simulate other wrestlers' styles, using what reinforces your strong points and what improves your weak points.

March

a. Work on creating openings to score.
b. Work on developing and following specific game plans.
c. Participate in local competitions.
d. Adjust your wrestling techniques as needed.

April

a. Prepare for a specific tournament (usually the national tournament).
b. Set specific goals for the tournament.
c. Go to the tournament.
d. Evaluate your performance and your opponents'.

May

a. Participate in competitions—domestic and foreign if possible.
b. Study the efficient scoring positions and the techniques that are effective from each position.

June

a. Rejuvenate yourself by taking a short break from wrestling.
b. Play other sports.
c. Develop aspects of yourself that do not directly relate to wrestling.

July

a. Evaluate the past 6 months and make a plan for the next 6 months.
b. Build strength through weight training.
c. Make a specific short-term list of things to accomplish.
d. Review fundamental positions and tactics.

August

a. Begin technique and strategy training.
b. Seek out and train good workout partners.
c. Study films of yourself and your opponents.
d. Critique your wrestling as an opponent would and strengthen your weak points.

September

a. Participate in a lot of matches designed to implement a specific strategy.
b. Compete in tournaments as much as possible.

October

a. Compete in tournaments.
b. Work on making your thought and your action one.
c. Think of total matches, not specific techniques.

November

a. Compete in as many matches as possible.
b. Push to a new level of endurance; work on technique and determination.
c. Push to the point of failure in everything you do.

December

a. Go cross-country skiing.
b. Enjoy family and the holidays.

Four-Year Training Plan

Creating a plan that will bring you to a desired position 4 years from now requires careful examination from numerous perspectives. You must recognize that things will not always go exactly as planned. You will experience setbacks and leaps forward, peaks and valleys, and variations of methods and goals as you improve and create a new vision of your abilities that will expand your motivation to succeed. Use your short-term objectives as bench marks to measure your improvement and progress toward your long-term goal.

For the purposes of this discussion, let's assume your goal is to win at the Olympic Games.

Arrange your training to allow segments for learning technique and strategy, building your body, developing an indomitable mental set, and bringing all of the training into focus as a total wrestling existence. You must periodically test your training in competitions. The competitions will give you an opportunity to evaluate yourself as well as your opponents. Each competition will provide new projects to work on.

The focus of year 1 is general (see Table 8.6). Examination of all aspects of your wrestling coupled with experimentation will highlight specific areas of needed development.

The next January begins year 2 of the 4-year plan. The focus of year 2 has its foundation in year 1, but is much more specific. While following the same general plan as in year 1, you should become involved in more competition. You must put the techniques developed in year 1 into logical, workable game plans that utilize your strengths effectively against all types of opponents. Several strategies exist that will aid your total wrestling development during this time.

I. Methods of attack
   A. Breaking balance
      All these methods can create openings: jerking, pulling, pushing, steady pressure, soft pressure, slow hand movement, rapid hand movment, changing levels, changing the angle of attack, movement at contact, movement after contact, and movement before contact.
   B. Controlling a specific part of your opponent's body, such as the hands, neck, elbow, head, or arm

This will limit your opponent's movement and opportunity to attack. It will make him conscious of freeing himself.
   C. Changing position and maneuvering
      Crowd your opponent, stay a little further away from him than he wants, get an angle on him, move him around the mat. Pull him and turn him.
   D. Fake attack
      For example, a threat to the head may open up the body.
   E. Repeated attack
      Make a move with less than full force. Your opponent will easily counter it. Then make the same attack with full force. Your opponent will be ready to counter the lesser effort.
   F. Double fake
      Do a form of repeated attack—for example, do an arm drag so that your opponent thinks it is a fake. Move to a bodylock (second technique) hard enough to make him think the first was a fake. Then go back to the arm drag (first technique) to score.
   G. Gambit
      Create a position that your opponent sees as an opportunity. When he makes his attack, you are prepared with a counter.
   H. Preempt
      Discover what your opponent does immediately before attempting a scoring move. Prevent this position, and do not let him get to his scoring move.
   I. Focus
      Be able to know what precise position or movement will allow a technique to work. When the situation occurs, immediately use a prepared technique or movement for a specific response.
II. Tactical combinations
   It is assumed that your opponent will answer any first attack or movement with defense or a counterattack. His defense or counterattack will create an opportunity for a second technique.
   This is why using moves in combinations is a valid way to create scoring opportunities.
   A. Combinations can be divided into three categories.
      1. Technique creates the opportunity for a second technique.

Table 8.6   Year One—Four-Year Training Plan

January

a. Develop a new technique and strategy.
b. Build strength through weight training.
c. Develop body awareness and flexibility through gymnastics.
d. Teach some youth wrestling to develop your analytical approach to wrestling.

February

a. Test technique and strategy in competitive matches in training.
b. Build strength through weight training.
c. Develop body awareness and flexibility through gymnastics.
d. Study films of opponents and great wrestlers.
e. Simulate other wrestlers' styles, using what reinforces your strong points and what improves your weak points.

March

a. Work on creating openings to score.
b. Work on specific game plans to beat a specific type of wrestler.
c. Participate in local competitions and evaluate your performance.
d. Adjust your wrestling techniques as needed.

April

a. Prepare for a specific tournament (usually the national tournament) and give an all-out effort to win.
b. Set a goal for the competition.
c. Go to the tournament.
d. Evaluate your performance and your opponents'.

May

a. Participate in as many competitions as possible.
b. Make every effort to participate in foreign competition.
c. Study the efficient scoring positions and the techniques that are effective from each position.

June

a. Rejuvenate yourself by taking a short break from wrestling.
b. Play other sports.
c. Develop aspects of yourself that do not directly relate to wrestling.

July

a. Evaluate the past 6 months and make a plan for the next 6 months.
b. Build strength through weight training.
c. Develop body awareness and flexibility through gymnastics.
d. Make a specific short-term list of things to accomplish.
e. Review fundamental positions and tactics.

August

a. Begin technique and strategy training.
b. Seek out and train good workout partners.
c. Study films of yourself and your opponents.
d. Critique your wrestling as an opponent would and strengthen your weak points.

September

a. Participate in a lot of matches designed to implement a specific strategy.
b. Compete in local tournaments.

October

a. Compete in tournaments.
b. Work on making your thought and your action one.
c. Think of total matches, not specific techniques.

November

a. Compete in as many hard matches as possible.
b. Push to a new level of endurance; work on technique and determination.
c. Push to the point of failure in everything you do.

December

a. Go cross-country skiing.
b. Enjoy family and the holidays.

2. A fake technique creates a defensive counter or movement that in turn creates an opening for a technique you have prepared for the situation.

3. The third category can be described as technique, countertechnique, and countertechnique to your opponent's counter.

   The first group of combinations requires strength and persistence.

   The second group requires quickness, initiative, and self-control.

   The third group requires a thorough knowledge of many techniques. Usually an experienced wrestler is able to see his opponent's mistakes. An alert wrestler can recognize favorable conditions for attack such as your opponent getting careless, complacent, depressed, distracted, timid, or out of synch.

III. Match tactics

Match tactics are aimed at achieving a predetermined goal by solving the problems your opponent presents during a match. All wrestlers have an individual style. This style is blended into a plan that accommodates the three general areas of tactics. They are attack, counterattack, and defense. These three strategies may be used in the following manner:

A. Attack

1. Seek initiative by the first attack. Set the tempo you want by attempting the first scoring move. Make your opponent defend.

2. Use nonstop attacks, spurt attacks, and single attacks.

   A nonstop series of attacks is based on one wrestler imposing his will, his pace, and his intensity on his opponent. This tactic requires endurance and willpower.

   A spurt attack is based on separate attacks carried out at a fast pace in bursts that last 15 to 20 seconds. This tactic allows you to vary the pace and catch your opponent off guard.

3. Counterattack

   You must create a situation that entices your opponent to act. You must be ready with a scoring coun-

tertechnique. You must have quick, precise reactions and a high degree of self-assurance.

4. Use defense

   This tactic is simply based on your opponent making gross mistakes and your taking advantage of those errors. The official is always a factor with this tactic as he may interpret your inactivity as stalling, and you will be penalized. Eventually you must attack. You can use defense for short time segments, such as 25 seconds.

You must prepare a tactical plan for a match beforehand. Set a goal and determine the means of achieving it. You must compare your qualities with those of your opponent. You must select tactics, the tempo of the match, and the stance and positions you want to wrestle from, and have confidence and determination in carrying out your plan. When the match starts you must be creative enough to adjust your plan. The plan cannot be too complicated. You must take care in preparing yourself mentally and emotionally to meet any unforeseen obstacle and still keep your focus on your goal. You must be realistic in your goals and have the audacity to beat the champion.

The 3rd and 4th years of the cycle should be virtually identical. Assuming the fourth year is the Olympic year, rehearse the entire program in a manner that closely approximates the time schedule of competitions leading up to the final Olympic team trials. focus on gaining specific results. Set definite goals for improvement and achievement. Apply all of your previous preparation to practical situations.

Year 4 should find you prepared to refine, adjust, and further develop your skills. Take care to prepare yourself for any physical, intellectual, emotional, or social obstacles that might occur. You have thought through your goals and the methods for achieving them so thoroughly that nothing can deter you. You should have a single-mindedness born of hard work and intelligent preparation. Your training plan must have defined peaks and rest periods that correspond to the major competitions you must win. Make certain that you do not leave your best efforts in the training room.

Glossary

American par terre—The style of mat wrestling common in United States colleges and high schools that emphasizes control of your opponent on the mat.

arm bar—Any armlock that uses an opponent's arm as a lever to turn him to his back.

arm drag—A method of pulling your opponent's arm in an attempt to throw him off balance and secure an advantage.

attack—Any movement against your opponent designed to score points.

backpedal—The act of moving backward in a small circle as you lift an opponent from the mat.

back-step hip punch—The foot and hip movement that precedes a hip throw. Your back is turned to your opponent and he is levered over your hip.

bear hug—A position where both your arms are around your opponent's trunk, with your hands locked while facing him.

blocking—A defensive pummeling the sole intent of which is to prevent your opponent from scoring. It is used when the score, time of match, or strategic situation dictates a posture to preserve a lead.

bridge over—To move from a front bridge position to a back bridge position (or from back to front) by kicking your feet over along the long axis of the body (the back).

butterfly lock—A lock where you lock your arms by hooking your hands on the wrist of your opposite arm.

collar elbow lock—A lock where you have one hand on the back of your opponent's neck (collar) and the other on his elbow.

counterattack—Movement after an opponent's attack that is designed to score points.

counterthrow—A throw to counter an opponent's attempted throw.

double-leg attack—An attack designed to secure both of your opponent's legs with both of your arms while you both are standing, allowing you to take him to the mat.

double overhook armlock—A lock where both your arms are over and around both of your opponent's arms, with your hands locked at his chest.

double underhook—A position where you have both of your arms under your opponent's shoulders around his trunk with your hands locked.

duck under—To move your head under your opponent's shoulder and between his upper arm and body to secure an advantage.

fireman's carry throw—A method of taking your opponent to the mat by means of an arm- and bodylock that utilizes a duck under.

folkstyle—The style of wrestling contested in any area or country that is part of a country's culture and is not governed by international rules. In Japan it refers to sumo wrestling, and in the United States, high school and collegiate wrestling are examples.

folkstyle standup—An escape maneuver used in American folkstyle wrestling where the man in the disadvantage position on the mat comes to his feet to secure a neutral position.

freestyle—One of the two styles of wrestling contested in the Olympic Games; a "catch-as-catch-can" style not limited in style of attack by clothing (judo) or an area of the body (Greco-Roman).

functional comfort zone—The wrestling position in which movement is most efficient or in which a particular wrestler is most comfortable.

Greco-Roman—The name given to one of the two styles of wrestling contested in the Olympic Games. It is a throwing sport that employs upper bodylocks and allows holds or grips only above the waist.

gut wrench—A par terre scoring maneuver where the attacker has his arms locked around his opponent's trunk. He turns his opponent's back to the mat by holding his opponent tight to his body and bridging over in a direction perpendicular to the long axis of both bodies.

hand-to-hand palms-down lock—A lock around your opponent's trunk where your hands are locked; with the palms of both hands toward the mat.

head and arm—A lock where both your arms are around your opponent's head and one arm.

headlock hip throw—A head- and armlock that allows your opponent to be thrown with a back-step hip punch maneuver.

head under arm bridge back—A maneuver where you throw your opponent to the mat from a standing position when your head is under his armpit.

high-crotch single leg—A single-leg attack that focuses on the point where the leg joins the body.

hook lock—A lock where the fingers of both hands are curled to form a hook. The hands are then hooked together, forming a lock.

inside position—A position where your arms are between your opponent's arms and his body.

lateral drop—A throw from standing that takes your opponent off balance to the side and pulls and turns him so that he hits the mat on his back.

lift—A maneuver where you lift your opponent from the mat.

mutual off balance—A position where you are locked up with your opponent and both of you are off balance.

Olympic styles—Freestyle and Greco-Roman wrestling are the common competitive styles whose rules govern world and Olympic championships. Freestyle is most like American folkstyle in that attacks are allowed on any part of the body. Greco-Roman is radically different in that attacks are allowed only above the waist. The legs are used only for support and balance.

one-half salto change—Refers to when a wrestler, after beginning a double armlock salto throw, changes to another technique halfway through the original move.

one-quarter nelson—A head- and armlock where the hand around your opponent's arm is locked to the wrist of your other hand, which is holding your opponent's head down.

over and under position—A lock with your opponent where one of your arms is under his arm and the other is over his other arm while you are standing chest to chest.

overhook—To lock an opponent's arm from the outside.

post—To cause a part of a wrestler's body to remain in a fixed position. Posting is most commonly applied to an opponent's leg, arm, or head.

primary attack areas—The areas of an opponent's body that are most vulnerable.

pummeling—Contacting and moving your opponent to secure a position of advantage.

ride—To control and keep your opponent on the mat in American folkstyle.

sagging bodylock—A front bodylock position common in Greco-Roman wrestling where one of your legs is between your opponent's legs, and you pull him to a position over your body before the throw.

salto position—A standing double armlock position performed while you are facing your opponent.

scramble—To move quickly while in a neutral position to secure a position of advantage.

secondary attack areas—Those areas of the body vulnerable to attack at the joints of the limbs.

secure a lock—To lock your arms around some portion of your opponent's body.

shuck by—To move your opponent quickly by your body, making him lose balance.

side roll—An American folkstyle technique where you roll your opponent from a position of advantage over your body to a position of disadvantage.

side whizzer—An armlock in which you are side by side with your opponent.

sit-through—An American folkstyle escape technique where the bottom man comes to a sitting position on the mat to throw his opponent off balance and escape.

slide by—To move to the side of your opponent while in contact and slide around him to a position of advantage.

snap down bear hug—A maneuver where you take your opponent directly to his back from a bear hug position.

step-around bodylock—A front bodylock throw where the thrower steps around his opponent after he has secured his lock to put his opponent offbalance and throw him.

two-on-one armlock—A position where two of your arms are holding one of your opponent's arms.

underhook—To have your arm deep between your opponent's upper arm and body with your hand over his shoulder.

wedge—The basic standing wrestling position.

Index

Targeting

Wellness

The Core

Acknowledgments

We gratefully acknowledge the expert advice and assistance of the following people, who by their careful reading and suggestions have helped to guide work on this book at various stages during its development:

Dale Anderson	California State University—Long Beach
Barbara Beier	University of New Mexico
John Bonaguro	Ohio University—Athens
Jerry Braza	Stress Management Resources
William Chen	University of Florida
Jacqueline Corn	Johns Hopkins University
Peter Cortese	California State University—Long Beach
Darrell Crase	Memphis State University
John Curtis	University of Wisconsin—La Crosse
Richard Detert	University of Wisconsin—La Crosse
Steve Dorman	University of Florida
Mal Goldsmith	Southern Illinois University—Edwardsville
Frederick Goldstein	Drug Interaction Services Corporation
Renee Guitierrez	Mayo Clinic
Marsha Hoagland	Modesto Junior College
Herbert Jones	Ball State University
David Lowing	Slippery Rock University
David Macrina	University of Alabama at Birmingham
Katherine Martin	North Carolina Baptist Hospital
Warren McNab	University of Nevada at Las Vegas
Jill Moore	University of North Carolina—Chapel Hill
Leslie Oganowski	University of Wisconsin—La Crosse
Woody Powell	Essex Community College
Martha Prince	Springfield College
Ruth Reese	Arizona State University
Donna Richards	Mountain View College
Judie Stepner	DeAnza College
Victor Strecher	University of North Carolina
Lucy Stroble	University of Maine—Presque Isle
Laurette Taylor	University of Oklahoma
Bill Wallace	University of Tennessee—Knoxville
David Weissman	Medical College of Wisconsin
Lawrence Wilson	L. D. Wilson Consultants, Inc.
Richard Wilson	Western Kentucky University
Mike Young	University of Arkansas—Fayetteville

Targeting

Wellness

The Core

Marvin R. Levy
Temple University

Mark Dignan
Bowman Gray School of Medicine, Wake Forest University

Janet H. Shirreffs
Arizona State University, West Campus

McGraw-Hill, Inc.
New York St. Louis San Francisco Auckland Bogotá
Caracas Lisbon London Madrid Mexico Milan
Montreal New Delhi Paris San Juan Singapore
Sydney Tokyo Toronto

Targeting Wellness: The Core

2 3 4 5 6 7 8 9 0   VNH   VNH   9 0 9 8 7 6 5 4 3 2

ISBN 0-07-037575-5

This book was set in New Baskerville by York Graphic Services, Inc.
The publisher was Barry Ross Fetterolf,
the editors were Frances A. Wiser, Bob Waterhouse, and Charles C. Roebuck,
the development staff included Carol Ciaston, Cheryl Morrison, Carol Klitzner, Mike Buchman, Lorraine Steefel, Cindy Mooney, Isabelle Tourneau, and Elaine Silverstein.
Teacher materials were edited by Frances A. Wiser and Jewel Moulthrop and written by Mary Bobbitt-Cooke and Lorraine Sintetos.
The production supervisor was Anita Crandall.
Drawings were done by Vantage Art, Inc.,
anatomical art by Paul Gioni,
photo research was done by Cindy Cappa.
Text design was done by Howard Petlack,
cover design was done by Ed Butler.
Von Hoffmann Press, Inc., was printer and binder.

Developed and produced by Visual Education Corporation, Princeton, New Jersey.

Library of Congress Catalog Card Number: 91-67937

Photo Credits

Cover Photo

G&J Images/The Image Bank

Chapter Opening Photos

1 Alan Oddie/PhotoEdit; **21** Melanie Carr/Zephyr Pictures; **41** Blair Seitz/Photo Researchers, Inc.; **60** Mary Kate Denny/PhotoEdit; **80** Renee Lynn/Photo Researchers, Inc.; **101** Ewing Galloway; **120** Tony Freeman/PhotoEdit; **141** Darryl Baird/Third Coast Stock Source; **161** Frances Roberts; **182** Blair Seitz/Photo Researchers, Inc.; **201** Tom Dunham; **220** MacDonald Photographers/Third Coast Stock House; **245** Tom McCarthy/Transparencies, Inc.; **268** Myrleen Ferguson/PhotoEdit; **290** David Young-Wolff/PhotoEdit; **312** Susan Kuklin/Photo Researchers, Inc.

Table of Contents Photos

v Alan Oddie/PhotoEdit; **v** Melanie Carr/Zephyr Pictures; **vi** Blair Seitz/Photo Researchers, Inc.; **vi** Mary Kate Kenny/PhotoEdit; **vii** Renee Lynn/Photo Researchers, Inc.; **vii** Ewing Galloway; **viii** Tony Freeman/PhotoEdit; **viii** Darryl Baird/Third Coast Stock Source; **ix** Frances Roberts; **ix** Blair Seitz/Photo Researchers, Inc.; **x** Tom Dunham; **x** MacDonald Photographers/Third Coast Stock House; **xi** Tom McCarthy/Transparencies, Inc.; **xi** Myrleen Ferguson/PhotoEdit; **xii** David Young-Wolff/PhotoEdit; **xii** Susan Kuklin/Photo Researchers, Inc.

Contents

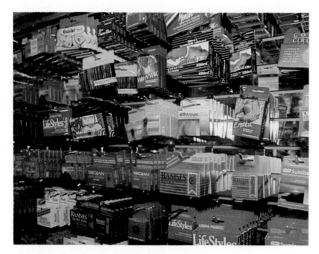

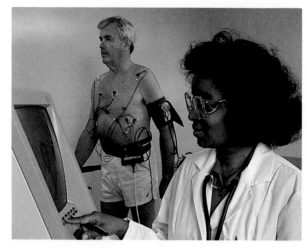

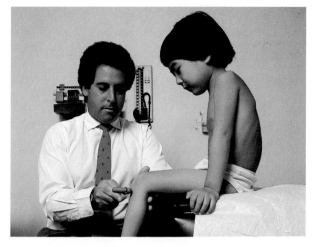

To The Student

Among all the subjects that you will study in college, health can be one of the most relevant to your life, one of the most interesting, and one of the most challenging.

Its relevance is hardly open to question: everyone can benefit from a basic knowledge of how the human body and mind work and how to lead a healthy lifestyle. Such knowledge can help us to function at our highest level from day to day. It can help us to maximize our potential for the future; to minimize our risks of disease and injury; and to develop our physical, emotional, intellectual, social, and spiritual resources for a longer, more productive, and more satisfying life.

Studying human health is also fascinating. The human body and human behavior are remarkable creations: though everyone has a personal and subjective understanding of them just through being alive, viewing them through the more objective eyes of science can bring home to one just how remarkable they are. Of all the subjects that can inspire awe and amazement—literature, art, music, geology, and astronomy are only a few examples—the study of the human body and mind are the nearest to us, and also in many ways the most amazing of all. Human beings are the most complex of all living things; understanding this complexity can deepen our appreciation of some of the mysteries of life.

Targeting Wellness: The Core is a new textbook published by McGraw-Hill, presenting current information for a person wishing to optimize his or her potential for wellness. It is based on *Life and Health: Targeting Wellness,* first edition. It is designed to convey an understanding of the subtlety and complexity of human life, to increase awareness of the challenges of health, and to help develop self-efficacy: a confidence that can inspire each individual to rise to those challenges and make progress toward a healthier lifestyle.

One challenge of health arises from the fact that health is a dynamic concept. The information that has been discovered about human health during the past 300 years—and especially during the last 25 years—is staggering. But the process of discovery has not stopped; if anything, it is accelerating. New insights are continually being generated by researchers, studied and checked by their colleagues, and published in scholarly journals and in the popular press. Thus, learning about the current state of health knowledge, as you will do in this course, is important not only because it gives you the best chance of making sound health decisions now, but also because it provides you with a basis for understanding new health discoveries and evaluating their implications for your health care in the future.

The second challenge of health lies in the fact that every person is unique and continues to change throughout life, both in terms of personal needs and of personal goals. For this reason, there is no single prescription for good health that will apply to everybody: the road to wellness involves a continuing process of self-discovery, of learning some general principles about life and health and then applying these principles to one's own particular changing situation.

This textbook has been designed to help you meet both of these challenges; key elements are specifically directed at one or the other of them:

- *Conclusions drawn from classic and recent studies* are presented not as rules, rather as recommendations which can be examined on the basis of evidence given.

- *End notes at the back of the book* familiarize you with scholarly and popular sources of up-to-the-minute health information, and allow you to evaluate specific topics from the text in more depth.

- *Straightforward language and illustrations* clarify significant ideas and important complexities of human health as it is understood by health experts today.

- *Technical terms of the health field,* are highlighted with bold-face type and defined where they first appear and in a glossary. This will help you to interpret and apply accounts of new discoveries in health that you may read about, and also to communicate with health professionals about these and other matters. Terms also appear in the margins next to their definitions in the text as an easy finding aide.

Targeting Wellness: The Core also includes many boxed features designed to help you to personalize the information presented in the book. There are five types of features:

- *"Thinking Critically"* features look at a significant health issue from two possible viewpoints. You are not expected necessarily to agree with either of them, but instead to ponder the issues being explored and to adopt a position that is consistent with the full range of your own understandings, values, and beliefs.
- *"Taking a Broader View"* features look at the wider implications of a particular health topic, presenting international implications, for example, and illustrating how research and actions designed to benefit individuals may have far-reaching global implications.
- *"Finding Your Comfort Level"* features explore a concept described earlier in this preface: the importance of applying health knowledge to your own life in a way that is in harmony

with your goals and values. In this way you can feel confident and comfortable with the actions and behaviors you adopt.

- *"Assessing"* features are brief self-tests designed to help you evaluate your present behaviors and beliefs and relate them to the health topic being discussed. Often based on diagnostic instruments prepared for health professionals, these questionnaires will give you important insights into your own needs and behaviors.
- Finally, *"Communicating About"* features are designed to guide you through some of the many pitfalls in communication associated with various health topics, and to encourage you to discuss some of these topics in a meaningful way.

As the authors of this book, we urge you to get involved in the topics presented. Strive to understand the major concepts and to incorporate them into your own lives as thoughtfully as possible. As you will read in the first chapter and throughout this book, personal health is an area in which each of us can really "make a difference," both for ourselves and for those around us.

MARVIN R. LEVY
MARK DIGNAN
JANET H. SHIRREFFS

The Concept of Health

Objectives

When you have studied this chapter, you should be able to:

- Define health in terms of a balance between five distinct dimensions.

- Analyze the importance to health of the components of lifestyle.

- Explain how health goals can be refined by relating them to needs and wants, personal goals, priorities, and trade-offs.

- Describe the process of setting health goals through realistic self-assessment.

- Distinguish between the immediate effects of active involvement in health-enhancing behaviors and the long-term benefits that can be gained by changing one's lifestyle.

Good health—what does it mean to you? Many people take health for granted, assuming that they are as healthy as they can be and will probably remain so. They accept their general level of health as a given. They do not think of their health as a matter of choices.

Yet many aspects of our health are affected by what we choose to do. With the right information, we can choose sensibly and improve both our health and our lives—for the healthier we are, the more vigor and enthusiasm we have to focus on, and achieve, important goals. By contrast, lack of knowledge can lead to significant limitations, caused by health problems.

Almost everyone has parts of their lives which seem quite healthy, and other parts which might be improved. Darlene, for example, is a 21-year-old star on the college swimming team. She follows a regular exercise routine and spends several hours every day in the pool. Darlene wants to earn good grades because she would like to go to medical school, and so she spends a lot of time studying. Darlene has almost no time for socializing. She sometimes wishes she had more friends, but she is very shy. She rarely dates.

Barry, who is 41 years old, is a very gregarious person with many close friends and acquaintances. He is involved in many activities, including playing trumpet in a jazz band. He often goes drinking with his fellow players. Barry earns a living as a taxi driver and appreciates the flexible work schedule, though he finds the job stressful and tiring. His doctor tells him he should stop drinking and get more sleep, but Barry does not feel motivated to do so. He enjoys smoking, too—he depends on cigarettes to keep him alert on the job.

A bright and energetic person in her middle thirties, Melissa has worked hard to support her children since the death of her husband. She is a stable and trustworthy individual. As a teenager Melissa smoked and experimented with illegal drugs, but she has found other outlets as she has grown older. Recently she enrolled part-time in a community college computer science program in order to earn a degree and get a better job. However, these activities have made it hard for Melissa to get regular exercise—she is 15 pounds overweight. Because of the history of heart disease in her family, she is trying to control her weight through diet but is finding it difficult.

Despite his arthritis, Luis, who is 68 years old, always seems to be in high spirits. He attributes much of his positive attitude to his religious faith. His wife, children, and grandchildren are also a source of support and joy. Because of his personality, people of all ages seem to come to Luis for advice. Luis goes to the doctor for a checkup every few months. So far he has had no major problems other than arthritis, although his blood pressure and total serum cholesterol are higher than they should be. He has managed to lower them somewhat by changing his diet and exercising more.

Darlene, Barry, Melissa, and Luis are typical Americans. None of them could be considered completely healthy or completely unhealthy; certain parts of their lives seem healthier than others. The question is: What is it about each of their lives that can be recognized as being healthy?

Health and Well-Being

Traditionally, different people have defined health in different ways. An athletic director might have said that health entails exercising regularly and eating carefully to maintain normal weight and good physical conditioning. A physician might have considered health to be the absence of disease.

Assessing Your Lifestyle

The following assessment is designed to help you explore your lifestyle choices and determine how they are affecting you.

Directions: Respond to each of the statements with one of the following designations: 5—definitely true; 4—mostly true; 3—not sure; 2—mostly false; 1—definitely false. Write the number that corresponds to your answer in the blank at the left.

_____ I am doing well in school.

_____ I am enjoying myself, not feeling bored or angry.

_____ I have satisfying relationships with other people.

_____ I express my emotions when I want to.

_____ I use my leisure time well and enjoy it.

_____ I am satisfied with my sexual relationships.

_____ I am satisfied with what I accomplish during the day.

_____ I am having fun.

_____ I am making use of the talents I have.

_____ I feel physically well and full of vitality.

_____ I am developing my skills and abilities.

_____ I am contributing to society.

_____ I am helpful to other people.

_____ I have a sense of freedom and adventure in my life.

_____ I feel joy or pleasure on most days.

_____ I feel that my body is fit enough to meet the demands made upon it.

_____ I feel rested and full of energy.

_____ I am able to relax most of the day.

_____ I enjoy a good night's sleep most nights.

_____ I usually go to bed feeling happy and satisfied about the day.

Scoring: Add up the numbers in your answers.

If your score was 90 to 100, you are making lifestyle choices that promote good health.

If your score was 80 to 89, many of your lifestyle choices are healthful ones. Look at the statements that you marked with a 1, 2, or 3 for areas that need improvement.

If your score was 61 to 79, there are aspects of your lifestyle that could use improvement. Statements to which you responded 1, 2, or 3 indicate areas where you could do better.

If your score was 60 or below, your lifestyle puts your health at high risk. Review the responses you marked with a 1 or 2 to decide how you can make better lifestyle choices.

Statements adapted from the Quality of Life Test in Robert Allen and Shirley Linde, *Lifegain* (Burlington, VT: Human Resources Institute, Inc., 1981): 25–26. Used with permission.

A psychologist might have argued that health includes the ability to cope with emotional problems and traumas. Today, however, most health professionals regard these and many other common definitions of health as incomplete. According to these professionals, the prevention and treatment of health problems requires a broader definition of the concept of health.

What Is Health?

The modern view is that health has several dimensions—emotional, intellectual, physical, social, and spiritual—each of which contributes to a person's well-being. To maintain good health, a person must examine each of these dimensions and make choices that enable him or her not only to live a long time but also to enjoy life to the fullest.

The word *health* originally meant "whole-th," or "wholeness."[1] When health professionals speak of health, they are acknowledging the original meaning. The World Health Organization stated in 1947 that health is "a state of complete physical, mental, and social well-being and not merely the absence of disease or infirmity."[2]

Health is a process in which all the parts of a person's life work together in an integrated way. No aspect of life functions by itself. Body, mind, spirit, family, community, country, job, education, and beliefs are all interrelated. The way in which these aspects jointly contribute to the richness of a person's life helps determine that individual's uniqueness as well as health.[3]

Perhaps the most important objective of this textbook is to help you realize your uniqueness and identify the ways in which you can sustain good health now and throughout your life.

The Dimensions of Health

Health includes more than a smoothly functioning body. It also involves the mind—emotions and intellect, social relationships, and spiritual values. To better understand health, then, it is necessary to examine more closely each of these dimensions, which together constitute overall health and well-being. The dimensions will only be introduced here (Figure 1.1). They will be dealt with in more detail throughout this book.

Emotional Health To a large extent the quality of a person's health reflects that person's emotions, the feelings he or she has toward self, situations, and other people. Emotional health includes understanding one's emotions and knowing how to cope with everyday problems and stress as well as being able to work, study, or pursue activities productively and with enjoyment.

While they are important in themselves, emotions can also influence physical health. Physicians frequently see demonstrations of the mind-body connection. For example, people with good emotional health have a low rate of stress-related diseases such as ulcers, migraine headaches, and asthma.[4] When stress or emotional turmoil continues for a long time, however, the immune system can shut down,[5] increasing the risk of developing these and other diseases.

In recent years some researchers have argued that a personality trait called hardiness may help strengthen the immune system against the damaging effects of stress.[6] **Hardiness** is defined as the possession of an optimistic and

hardiness

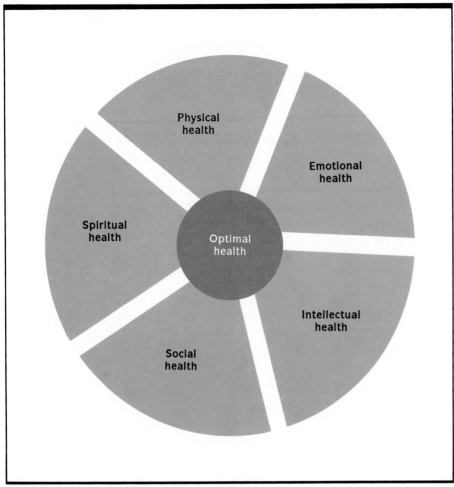

Figure 1.1 *Health is an inclusive concept comprised of several components. One person may choose to emphasize one component, whereas someone else may focus on a different one; but none of the components should be neglected. All are interrelated and can help to provide an overall balance in a person's life.*

committed approach to life, viewing problems, including disease, as challenges that can be handled.

Intellectual Health Intellect—the part of the mind which contributes to sound decision making—can play a crucial role in a person's overall health and well-being. Although intellectual capacity varies among individuals, all people are capable of learning how to acquire and evaluate information, choose between alternatives, and make decisions about different types of issues, including health.

Intellectual health is sometimes included with emotional health as a part of mental health. However, though closely interwoven with emotions, intellectual thought is distinct from them. Emotions can impair a person's ability to think and confused thinking can make emotional problems harder to deal with, but this relationship does not mean they are the same.

Physical Health   Physical health refers to the condition of the body and its responses to damage and disease. To stay in good physical health, it is important to behave in ways that enhance one's physical well-being. For example, avoiding cigarettes, drinking alcohol only in moderation, and eating breakfast daily are habits that promote good physical health. Adequate exercise, balanced rest and work, maintenance of normal weight, and intelligent choice of foods also help to keep the body healthy.[7]

Good physical health requires that a person pay attention to the messages the body sends about what it needs—more sleep or different foods, for example—and respond to those messages accordingly. Basic self-care skills can help people cope with small health problems on their own.[8] However, it is also important to take responsibility for receiving regular checkups and to know how to deal knowledgeably with health care providers such as doctors and hospitals if serious medical problems develop.

Social Health   Social health refers to the ability to perform one's role in life as a son or daughter, parent, spouse, friend, neighbor, or citizen effectively, comfortably, and with pleasure, without harming other people. Each of these roles entails different responsibilities and risks. All require the give-and-take of effective communication—healthy relationships are never one-way. The fulfillment of human needs for love, intimacy, and companionship is an important factor in social health. People who are deprived of these needs may develop behaviors that threaten their overall health and well-being.[9]

Spiritual Health   The final dimension of health is spiritual health, a feeling that one's behavior and basic values are in harmony. Many health professionals hold that spiritual forces affect and are affected by overall health. Spiritual health may include a sense of awe at nature's beauty and majesty, a deeply held religious faith, or a sense of inner peace with regard to one's life. It grows from the struggle to develop a meaningful relationship with the universe and with life itself.

A number of recent studies have indicated an association between religious affiliation and low rates of chronic disease and mortality. For example, Mormons and Seventh-Day Adventists have lower rates of certain kinds of cancer than does the general population.[10] Some people attribute these effects to religious rules, stating that religion can discourage behaviors that can lead to serious health problems. However, others have asserted that religious affiliation may contribute directly to health and general well-being.[11]

The Integration of Health

Each person assigns a different degree of importance to the five dimensions of health. Some people are more interested in emotional or intellectual health than in physical health. Others may derive their greatest satisfaction from their relationships with others or their involvement in working for religious ideals.

However, the dimensions of health are all integrated—each has an effect on the others. Suppose you feel that your work is in harmony with your basic values. This harmony may contribute to your spiritual health. Sound spiritual health in turn can have a profound effect on your emotional health. Sound emotional health can enhance your social relationships, and sound spiritual, emotional, and social health may enable your body to cope better with physical disease.

All the different dimensions of health—emotional, intellectual, physical, social, and spiritual—work together to determine how well you function and how much you enjoy life. The cultivation of any one dimension may also enhance the others. Similarly, the neglect of any single dimension may have serious consequences for one's overall health and well-being. To maintain your health, then, pay attention to all five dimensions, recognize the links among them, and attempt to keep them in balance so that they work best for you.

Health and Balance

Such balance is important because it affects the body's balance at a basic physiological level. The human body is a remarkably resilient organism. During our lives, we must respond to a variety of threats, including disease, physical injury, and stress. The body is capable of combating or adapting to many of these threats on its own, healing itself, and returning to a normal state.

To achieve this, the body continually seeks to maintain a balance between factors such as temperature, heart rate, blood pressure, water content, and blood sugar level. This natural equilibrium, or **homeostasis,** is achieved *homeostasis* through the functioning of automatic mechanisms within the body. For example, human beings tend to maintain a normal temperature of 98.6 degrees F (37 degrees C). In hot weather the body perspires to cool itself and prevent damage from overheating. In cold weather it shivers to increase muscle activity, thus burning nutrients and producing warmth.

Returning to a normal balanced state is also a key factor in healing or combating disease. The human body can automatically **regenerate,** or replace, *regenerate*

The deep breaths of a runner after a race illustrate homeostasis—the body's automatic effort to return its systems to balance. (Tony Freeman/PhotoEdit)

most damaged cells on a regular basis. When your skin is cut, new skin cells replace those damaged by the injury, and new blood cells replace those lost during bleeding. Having healed the wound and replaced the materials used in the healing process, the body is thus able to return to a homeostatic condition. Similarly, defenses against disease also work to take care of threats to health and restore the body to a state of balance.

Such defenses are not only a function of the body, however. As indicated earlier in this section, emotional states can have physiological effects, and can thus play an important part both in destroying and in restoring our physiological equilibrium. As a part of emotions, the brain produces various chemicals that enter the bloodstream and affect the body's homeostatic processes. Because emotions arise in response to all areas of life, a balance in all the dimensions of health is important for the proper functioning of the body.

Health and Lifestyle

The dimensions of health can be influenced by several factors. One obvious factor is the availability of competent medical care and sound health education, both of which can benefit an individual not only physically but mentally and socially as well. Other, more general environmental factors include the safety of homes and neighborhoods, the public services that are available, and negative factors such as the amount of toxic substances in the soil, air, and water. Several of these factors can be controlled to some extent by a person's choice of where to live, and others can be influenced through political action. However, for most people they are features of life that are given and can only be changed with difficulty.

genes   Even harder to control are hereditary factors, aspects of life which are driven by genes. **Genes** are inherited "code" chemicals found in every cell of the human body. They control many aspects of an individual's development and functioning, from gender to tendencies toward certain diseases. They affect physical health, emotions, intellect, and even social life. These are basic aspects of a person's life and health. Genetic factors cannot be controlled by the individual, though they often can be compensated for.

While all these factors are important in health, the most important influence in the developed world is lifestyle—and lifestyle is a factor a person *can* control.[12] An important message in this textbook and in every health course is that to a large extent you own your own health. While heredity and environment play a large role in your health status, the choices you make about your lifestyle affect your health even more (Figure 1.2).

lifestyle   **Lifestyle** refers to an overall way of living—the attitudes, habits, and behaviors of a person in daily life. According to the Centers for Disease Control (CDC), lifestyle contributes greatly to 7 of the 10 leading causes of death in the United States.[13] People who smoke cigarettes, for example, are far more likely than are nonsmokers to develop a wide range of diseases.

Though not all components of lifestyle are under an individual's control, all people encounter many lifestyle choices that directly affect their health and well-being. A third goal of this book is to help you identify alternatives when you are making decisions or setting goals that will have an impact on your short-term and long-term health.

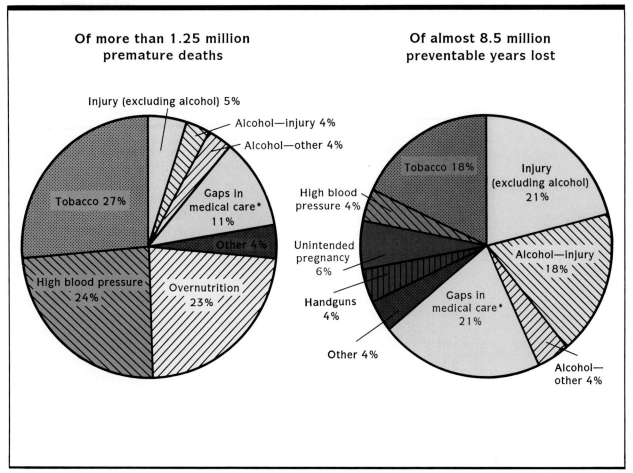

Of more than 1.25 million premature deaths

- Injury (excluding alcohol) 5%
- Alcohol—injury 4%
- Alcohol—other 4%
- Gaps in medical care* 11%
- Other 4%
- Overnutrition 23%
- High blood pressure 24%
- Tobacco 27%

Of almost 8.5 million preventable years lost

- Tobacco 18%
- High blood pressure 4%
- Unintended pregnancy 6%
- Handguns 4%
- Other 4%
- Gaps in medical care* 21%
- Alcohol—other 4%
- Alcohol—injury 18%
- Injury (excluding alcohol) 21%

Figure 1.2 *Compare these two charts showing precursors of premature, unnecessary deaths in the United States (estimated in a recent study to include more than three-fifths of all deaths). While more moderate use of alcohol could have prevented 8 percent of premature deaths, it might have saved 22 percent of the years lost because injuries due to alcohol kill a relatively large proportion of young people.*

*Gaps in medical care include inadequate access to care, mistaken diagnosis, and failed primary care.

Source: Adapted from Robert Amler and Donald Eddins, "Cross-Sectional Analysis: Precursors of Premature Death in the United States," in *Closing the Gap,* Robert Amler and H. Bruce Dull (eds.) (New York: Oxford University Press, 1987): 181–187. With permission.

The Components of Lifestyle

Lifestyle includes a number of different components that include the ways in which people carry out major parts of their lives such as working, playing, eating, coping, and so forth. The word *style* implies a pattern rather than an isolated event. The components of a lifestyle thus consist of general patterns of behavior. For example, going out with friends frequently indicates a highly social lifestyle.

Each individual develops a lifestyle largely through trial and error. People try different courses of action and generally adopt as habits those behaviors which are most successful and satisfying. These behaviors can be grouped into a number of overlapping patterns that make up the components of a lifestyle. Each component can have an effect on several dimensions of a person's health.

Working Style   The ways in which people produce, create, and study constitute their working styles. Some people are perfectionists who strive to make every aspect of their work perfect. Others may be more concerned with the quantity of work they produce than with the quality.

Traditional physical work has been linked with healthy longevity. For example, a very high proportion of the longest-lived Russians live in rural agricultural communities.[14] Other types of work stimulate the mind and help maintain intellectual health.

Recreational Style   How people spend their leisure time—their recreational style—also affects many dimensions of their health and well-being. People can engage in recreational activities that provide exercise, stimulate the mind, and nurture relationships with other people. Some recreational styles, however, can be harmful.

For example, too much emphasis on competition and aggression can harm one's social relationships or contribute to stress. People like Barry, whose recreational style focuses on the use of alcohol or other drugs, may be courting serious physical and social health problems.

Pleasuring Style   How does a person give pleasure to the important people in his or her life? How does that same person receive pleasure from others? The things people do to make themselves and others feel good and the ways in which they receive pleasure from others define their pleasuring style.

People like Luis are very unselfish in giving to others, while other people may be motivated more by self-interest. The ways in which people give and receive pleasure can influence their social, emotional, physical, and spiritual health.[15]

Coping Style   Stress is an unavoidable part of life. Stress can be positive when associated with growth (marriage, job promotion), or it can be negative when associated with loss (financial setbacks or a disagreement with relatives).

The way in which people cope with stressful events affects their health. One person may handle a family conflict by lashing out angrily, whereas a person like Melissa may try to mediate the dispute calmly and find a solution that is satisfactory to everyone.

Cognitive Style   Cognitive style refers to the ways in which people think, seek knowledge, and make decisions. Some people are very methodical in their approach to problem solving. They consider all the alternatives and carefully base their decisions on as much information as possible. Other people rely much more on intuition and tend to make quick decisions based on feelings, while still others may be fearful of making decisions at all and rely on others to tell them what to do. Cognitive style may be related to the conditions of a person's social and spiritual health. It also reflects one's intellectual health.

Communication Style   The ways in which people let others know what they need, want, feel, or think and the ways in which they respond to the thoughts and feelings of others are all part of their communication style. Some people use words to express their feelings, while others may be uncomfortable talking about their emotions. A person who does not express emotions may suffer social and emotional tensions, which could lead to physical problems as well.

Relating Style   Communication is only part of the way in which people relate to each other. An individual's relating style involves other types of interaction as well. Within a group, for example, some people may assume a leadership role while others are more comfortable letting someone else take the lead. Other aspects of relating style include the ways people approach others they would like to know better and the types of relationships people have with their families and friends.

Social health and emotional health depend in part on a person's ability to deal with interpersonal relationships in ways that satisfy his or her personal needs and desires.

Nutritional Style   A person's attitude toward and approach to food and eating constitute that person's nutritional style. For some people, food is a major source of pleasure; for others, it is merely a fuel required by the body.

A person's physical health depends to a large extent on what he or she eats. Food can also have an impact on one's intellectual health, and the way in which food is eaten—whether on the run or in a relaxed manner, alone or with other people—can affect one's social and emotional well-being.

Consuming Style   Another component of lifestyle consists of the ways in which people select and use products and services—their consuming style. A

The components of lifestyle are not always separate from each other: the role of consumer often contributes to people's pleasure and social life as well as nutrition. (Felicia Martinez/PhotoEdit)

person shopping for a home may be more concerned with either comfort or appearance. How pleasant a home is to live in may affect one's physical well-being, while the image the home presents may have an impact on one's social relationships and emotional satisfaction.

Ecological Style The decisions a consumer makes also affect ecological style—the way in which a person interacts with the physical environment. People's ecological style reflects the level of their concern for preserving a healthy environment. It involves decisions about whether they run errands by car, on foot, by bus, or by bicycle; how much heat or air-conditioning they use; how actively involved they are in recycling; and so forth.

Virtually every human action affects the environment. The way in which people treat the environment influences their own physical health as well as the physical health of others.

Lifestyle, Health, and Self-Efficacy

The multiple behaviors which make up a person's lifestyle indicate that lifestyle is affected by many variables and suggest that it is hard to control and change. However, in the United States people enjoy a high degree of individual freedom regarding the components of their lifestyles. People can make decisions about the work they do, where they live, how they spend their leisure time, and how they treat other people. They can decide what to eat, what to think, how to communicate with others, and how to treat the environment.

self-efficacy This freedom gives Americans the potential to develop a high level of self-efficacy, which is another important contributor to health. **Self-efficacy** means confidence in one's ability to plan and control one's own behaviors and one's lifestyle components.[16] No one can control every aspect of health, of course. However, people are free to make many important decisions that can affect their health and well-being.

Health Goals

To be effective, the health goals people set for themselves should be based on a sound understanding of health information and issues. Another purpose of this book is to provide such information. What are the usual outcomes of different types of behavior patterns? What techniques are most effective in changing these outcomes?

However, health goals cannot be based on health information alone; they must also be compatible with the broader goals that every individual has. One person may want to gain or lose weight in order to look more attractive. Another may need to lose weight to help control high blood pressure or diabetes. Objective information about weight control can be important in setting health goals, but people also need to examine goals in the context of their personal needs and wants.

Needs and Wants

Although most people have the same basic needs—food, shelter, safety, contact with other people, a sense of satisfaction in work and other activities—within these categories there is a wide range of possibilities that constitute people's wants. Neglecting universal human needs makes it difficult for a person to enjoy good health and a satisfying life, but neglecting particular wants may also have serious consequences.

Health professionals frequently cite the model of human needs formulated by psychologist Abraham Maslow.[17] According to Maslow, individuals progress through a *hierarchy of needs,* all of which must be met for a person to lead a satisfying and fulfilling life. The lower levels of Maslow's hierarchy consist of basic physiological and psychological needs such as water, food, shelter, sleep, health, human contact, safety and security, and love and acceptance. All these needs are "basic" in the sense that they are vital to positive human functioning (Figure 1.3).

Moving up Maslow's hierarchy, one finds growth needs, such as self-esteem, truth, goodness, justice, order, individuality, and self-sufficiency; self-actualization needs, which are basically drives to behave responsibly and morally toward oneself and others; and "transpersonal, transhuman, and transcendent" needs, which are experiences that allow people to transform their lives. As one moves higher in Maslow's model, individual wants play a greater part in achieving satisfaction and fulfillment. However, these higher-level needs and wants are also important aspects of overall human health.

Figure 1.3 Maslow's model of human needs has five levels. Lower-level needs such as exercise and a safe environment are the foundation of health, but a person cannot feel vibrant and whole without getting satisfaction from social life, achievement, and personal fulfillment.

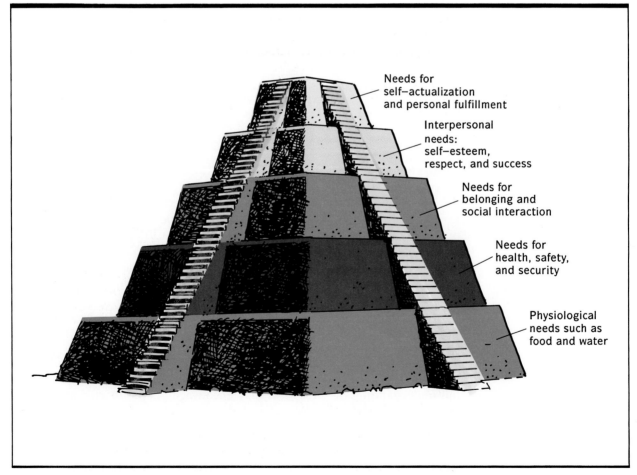

Needs for self-actualization and personal fulfillment

Interpersonal needs: self-esteem, respect, and success

Needs for belonging and social interaction

Needs for health, safety, and security

Physiological needs such as food and water

Defining Personal Goals

Defining personal goals is an important step in achieving the satisfaction and fulfillment described by Maslow. If needs and wants are not translated into specific goals, they may remain only ideas, awakening feelings of frustration rather than concrete plans for change.

Without goals, there is no way to measure progress or gauge success in meeting one's needs or satisfying one's wants. Goals are also important so that individuals can experience the satisfaction and sense of accomplishment that come with achieving them.

Effective goals must, of course, be realistic. Defining realistic goals that are appropriate to a person's needs, wants, and abilities provides opportunities for experiencing success and satisfaction, which help build self-esteem. Unrealistic goals may lead to failures that can undermine self-esteem and may even endanger one's physical health.

Long-Term and Short-Term Goals

The goals people set for themselves can be either long-term or short-term. Long-term goals, such as obtaining a graduate degree, may require years to achieve and are often closely connected to one's deepest needs and wants. Short-term goals, such as earning a good grade on a test, can be accomplished quickly. Short-term goals can, however, often be stepping-stones toward achieving long-term goals.

Since long-term goals may seem overwhelming even when they are realistic, it is easy to become pessimistic about the likelihood of accomplishing them. Short-term goals, by contrast, seem much more manageable to most people. Approaching a long-term goal as a series of short-term goals provides a way to experience a more immediate sense of achievement and helps make long-term goals easier to accomplish.

Priorities, Trade-Offs, and Comfort Levels

priority Most people who think about the goals they would like to achieve find that the list goes on and on. As goals are defined, people also need to establish **priorities** by deciding which needs, wants, and goals are most important. Many people try to do more than they can reasonably expect to accomplish given the time and resources available. As was mentioned at the start of this chapter, Melissa had difficulty finding time for the goal of daily exercise, and Darlene's social life also suffered because of a heavy schedule. Establishing priorities can help a person resolve such difficulties so that the most important needs and goals are taken care of first.

trade-off Equally important when there are many competing needs and goals are **trade-offs**—decisions that certain needs or wants have to be sacrificed or met in other ways. Some trade-offs are fairly obvious. For example, alcohol may seem an important part of someone's pleasuring style. Alcohol consumption, however, is not without major physical, emotional, and social health risks. A full understanding of these risks may encourage people to give up or limit alcohol consumption for the sake of their overall physical, emotional, and social health.

comfort level Making trade-offs involves determining individual **comfort levels**—the levels of compromise a person feels comfortable making among different goals in order to maximize overall benefits. People sometimes worry that they are slower, more intellectual, or less active sexually than their peers. Extreme differences *may* signal real problems, but there is a wide range of "normal" behaviors and conditions. If people could become more comfortable and accept their actual levels of behavior, they might find that they have fewer things to worry about. Then they could devote more time and energy to goals that are of greater importance to them. Establishing genuine comfort levels is a significant aspect of all health-related decisions.

Taking Stock of Your Health

The process of setting health goals that are realistic and appropriate starts with a thorough assessment of one's current health and capabilities. This self-assessment is a continuous process rather than a one-time task. It may be necessary to reconsider priorities, trade-offs, and comfort levels from time to time to accommodate changes in your body, wants or needs, and general circumstances. As some goals are reached, you may need to set new ones. Also, if a goal proves unattainable, it may have to be replaced with another, more realistic one with which you still feel comfortable.

Self-assessment includes eight important steps (Figure 1.4).

1. ***Clarify your health needs and wants.*** The first step in self-assessment is to focus on your current health status and on areas in which to consider change. It may be necessary to modify them as the assessment proceeds. Are there particular health goals that you already have or

Figure 1.4 Making changes in one's behavior patterns may be desirable, but do not expect it to be easy. There are often hidden pressures not to change—if you do not anticipate and deal with them, you will find that they block your progress. To be sure that the attempted behavior change really meets your needs, the change process should be spiral—as you evaluate your success, you should be thinking again about your needs: Is further action necessary?

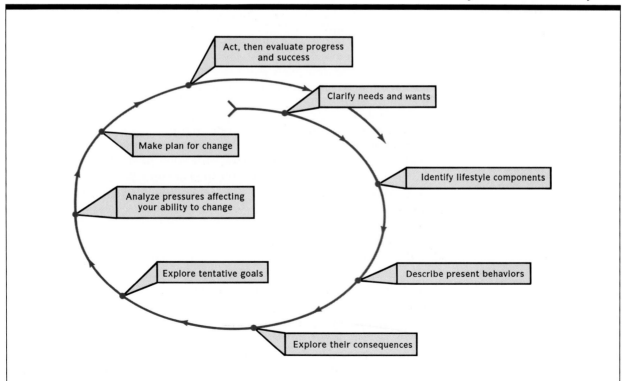

problems you wish to solve? Usually the two go together. If you want to improve your physique, it may be because you feel inadequate in some way. If you feel that your energy level is low, you may already have the general goal of becoming more active. Start by clarifying your areas of concern. For example, are you really overweight by objective standards? If so, what kind of action appeals to you? Do you favor a diet or an exercise program or both?

2. *Identify the lifestyle components involved.* Clarify to yourself which parts of your lifestyle are most closely related to each area of concern. Is it your nutritional style, your recreational style, or both that are important with regard to your physique? Perhaps your sedentary working style is a factor. With some concerns it may be relatively easy to make this decision. Others—for example, the problem of having low energy—may be harder to analyze.

3. *Describe your present behaviors with regard to these components.* What are your typical relating behaviors? Are you generally relaxed or tense with other people? How do you cope with these feelings? Does this make you withdraw into inactivity? Or do you feel socially at ease but still lacking in energy? Perhaps you are not eating right. What is your typical meal, and how often do you eat? These types of questions will help you explore the problem you are trying to deal with.

4. *Explore the consequences of these behaviors.* While a person's actions do not always have the same results, they can be typically successful or unsuccessful. Even if you suspect that irregular eating is the reason for your lack of energy, this eating pattern may have other consequences. Perhaps it allows you to stay involved in projects of interest to you or makes it easier to fit in spontaneously with your friends' activities. All behaviors have many consequences, some of which seem good and some bad. A few may make you wish to give up the behavior, but others probably encourage you to continue. You should try to understand your feelings about all these consequences, because they contribute both to your willingness to keep your behavior patterns and to your annoyance with them.

5. *Explore your tentative goals and other possible solutions.* So far you have considered the behavior patterns in your lifestyle that you want to change. You probably also have ideas about the changes you would like to make—perhaps you want to reevaluate the dreams or goals which led you to consider changing in the first place. Do you want to improve your physique? Now is the time to explore the possibilities. A changed behavior pattern will have both good points and bad points. If you sign up at a health club, you have an excellent chance of improving your physique, but it will take time and money. In fact, it is possible that the bad points of this solution outweigh the good so that you will give up your effort. Think about other ways you might improve your physique and also about whether a better physique is really the answer to your problem. Maybe your problem is really shyness and there are easier ways for you to impress people than by building your muscles. Explore these possibilities and their good points and bad points, and make a decision about which would be the best solution to try first.

6. *Analyze the forces and pressures that influence behavior.* After identifying the changes you want to make, think about why you have not made them already. This may give you ideas for strategies for changing behavior that are likely to work.

Various factors keep people from changing their lifestyle habits. Even when they know they should make changes, they often cling to old patterns of behavior. Sometimes, as suggested above, people do this because the existing behavior pattern is convenient or brings them pleasure. But maybe they do not know what to do instead or lack the self-confidence to try something new. Also, behaviors sometimes seem unavoidable, as when people knowingly expose themselves to hazards in order to earn a living.

It is possible, however, to lessen the effect of forces that block healthy change and strengthen those that promote it. If the benefits derived from an old behavior have kept you from changing it, think of other ways to obtain similar benefits. Have you resisted changing your diet because certain foods bring you pleasure? Be adventurous, and you may find healthful alternatives that you enjoy eating just as much or even more. Or try getting more pleasure from other things, such as activities, hobbies, and friendships. Also, find out what others have done to change similar behaviors and, if possible, get their support.

When you are trying to change a habit, it is important to reinforce the new behavior. Give yourself special rewards for successes along the way. These more immediate rewards can help provide the incentive needed for you to continue. Select as treats things that are meaningful to you, that you enjoy, and that you want to work toward.

7. *Make specific plans for change, including resources and a schedule.* Identifying a specific goal to aim for and useful strategies for change is only the first step in effecting real change in your life and health. You also need a detailed plan and a timetable you are likely to follow.

In their initial enthusiasm, people may set an unrealistic schedule for achieving their goals. This should be avoided. Spending 2 hours at a gym every day of the week may be difficult if you have a family and you work 10 hours a day. Failing to keep that schedule may result in feelings of failure and disappointment. Scheduling three 1-hour workouts a week would be more realistic and would still provide a significant amount of exercise. Following the less demanding schedule successfully would help build your self-esteem and support the overall effort to improve your health.

It is equally important to line up resources. There are usually many resources available that can help a person make and sustain a desired change in behavior. Arrange for the different types of resources you need and utilize them whenever possible. If your goal is to increase the amount you exercise, sign up at the gym or join the swimming club. Purchase a bicycle or a good pair of walking shoes.

Do not forget to consider human resources as well. The support, encouragement, and participation of family members and friends can help you change your behavior. Try to enlist their help. Tell them about your goals and let them know you would appreciate their help. Group support networks such as Weight Watchers and Alcoholics Anonymous are important resources for people who are trying to change certain behaviors.

8. *Evaluate your progress and success.* Once you have started your program for change, it is important to evaluate the progress being made from time to time. Satisfactory progress encourages a person to continue. Decide in advance how to measure or evaluate your level of success. Written records of efforts and actions may be helpful. For example, if your goal is to jog 2 or more miles three times a week, keep a log showing your days and distances. Visible evidence of

success may encourage you to continue jogging or to jog even more.

If there seems to be no progress, an evaluation can often help determine what is blocking success, and plans can then be adjusted accordingly. If the written records show that your goals are not being met, try to identify the reasons why. Think about how your goals could be adjusted to make them more attainable. Perhaps you would be more likely to run early in the morning than late in the afternoon.

Continue to keep records as you adjust the plan. This not only will help show you what works and what does not but also will help you find other ways of reinforcing your efforts.

Health and Your Future

Americans have begun to take a more active role in the pursuit of health and well-being. Half the participants in a study of health practices conducted by the National Center for Health Statistics reported that they are doing a good job taking care of their health; 15 percent said they are doing an excellent job.[18] According to a recent Harris survey, Americans are practicing more health and safety measures, including stress management, than ever before. Seventy percent of those polled reported that they take specific steps to manage stress, and 81 percent said they take steps to prevent accidental injury.[19] The 1989 Gallup Leisure Audit showed an increase in "back to nature" sports

Many human endeavors provide great short-term satisfactions, but the real benefits are felt throughout one's life. Health is no different: what you do today and tomorrow will affect your whole future. (Alan Oddie/PhotoEdit)

such as bicycle touring and racing, camping, hiking, and boating and a slight decline in "body image" activities such as weight lifting.[20]

Although many Americans are taking a more active role in their health, most people tend to focus on the immediate advantages and disadvantages of health-related behaviors rather than on long-term results. Most people, for example, concentrate on losing 5 pounds in 3 weeks rather than on developing a lifelong plan for maintaining ideal weight. Solving a current problem usually takes precedence over working to prevent problems that may occur later. People are more motivated to seek immediate benefits than to work toward goals that may be years or even decades ahead.

Many aspects of human behavior, however, affect long-range health even more than immediate, short-term health and conditions. The things you do today may not affect your health noticeably for years to come. A good example is cigarette smoking. In the beginning the negative health effects of smoking may seem slight or nonexistent. While some people may feel a little light-headed or nauseated, they do not feel the mucus clogging their breathing passages. Such damage is cumulative. It may take several years to develop smoker's cough, and lung cancer is most likely to strike people who have been smoking for years.

The positive effects of behavior on health can also be cumulative and subtle. Early environment and behavior—whether your mother avoided alcohol and other drugs while pregnant, what you ate as a child, whether you got enough sleep, how you learned to express or cope with feelings—have a lot to do with your health today. They play an important role in determining your physical characteristics, emotional and intellectual state, relationships with other people, and spirituality. Similarly, your environment and behaviors now are helping to determine the condition of your health during later life. The earlier you incorporate positive attitudes and behaviors into your life, the more apt you are to remain vigorous and energetic as you age.

Chapter Summary

- Health is a complex concept with several aspects, including emotional, intellectual, physical, social, and spiritual dimensions.

- Health involves more than the absence of disease; it is a process that contributes to enjoyment and well-being.

- Emotional health refers to the ability to express and cope with one's emotions in a productive way.

- Intellectual health includes the ability to evaluate information and make sound decisions.

- Physical health refers to the body's condition and its response to damage and disease.

- Social health is the ability to handle, enjoy, contribute to, and benefit from relationships with other people.

- Spiritual health refers to a sense of consistency, harmony, and tranquillity that appears to promote energy and nurture overall health.

- Although different people may focus on different dimensions of health, all these dimensions are interrelated. Positive effects in one dimension are likely to enhance other dimensions too, and negative influences in one dimension will probably cause problems in the other four.

- A balance between the dimensions of health is important. Balance is a key health concept—the body seeks homeostasis to maintain and restore itself.

- All the dimensions of health are affected by many factors, which can be grouped into health-care-system factors, general environmental factors, genetic factors, and lifestyle factors.

- Lifestyle factors are in many ways the most influential on overall health. They are also the factors that are most under the individual's control.

- Lifestyle includes sets of behavior patterns that affect different areas of one's life. The components of lifestyle are working style, recreational style, pleasuring style, coping style, cognitive style, communication style, relating style, nutritional style, consuming style, and ecological style.

- Although lifestyle is complex, it is under personal control and dictated by the ability to make wise choices that can benefit one's life and health.

- Making choices for health involves more than objective information; it also requires an understanding of the individual's overall goals in life.

- Human goals are in general based on human needs and wants.

- Defining realistic goals enables people to make specific efforts toward attainable objectives.

- Short-term goals can make it easier to reach long-term goals.

- When many goals are competing for one's attention, it is useful to consider priorities, trade-offs, and comfort levels.

- Goal setting can be handled on a rational basis through self-assessment. This is a continuous process of examining one's many needs and wants, exploring behavior patterns in one's lifestyle that facilitate or hinder those needs and wants, and then planning appropriate changes in behavior.

- Just as many health-threatening behaviors, such as smoking, are more damaging in the long term than they are in the near future, the development of health-enhancing behaviors has not only short-term benefits but long-term benefits.

Chapter 2

Activity, Exercise, and Physical Fitness

Objectives

When you have studied this chapter, you should be able to:

- Explain the difference between activity and exercise and discuss the benefits and dangers of exercise.

- Define 11 different components of fitness, distinguishing between those which are skill-related and those which are health-related.

- Explore the benefits of flexibility, strength, endurance, and cardiovascular fitness, indicating which types of exercises promote each one.

- Name four general principles that should underlie every exercise program.

- Describe important stages in developing a sound exercise plan to meet personal goals.

- Explain why an exercise plan should become a permanent part of a person's weekly routine.

Fitness is fashionable; the evidence is everywhere. Models, entertainers, and other popular idols are lean and fit, with trim, toned bodies that radiate good health. In recent years the trend toward fitness has taken hold: health clubs have sprung up everywhere, exercise books and videos have become best-sellers, and warm-up suits have become standard clothing. More Americans than ever are exercising regularly—running, swimming, doing aerobics, and walking their way to physical fitness. Regular exercise not only helps them look and feel better physically, it also helps them feel more relaxed and energetic and increases their sense of self-esteem. Physical fitness enables individuals to lead more productive, creative, healthy, and emotionally balanced lives.

Despite the interest in fitness and exercise, a recent survey by the National Sporting Goods Association (NSGA) showed that only about 20 percent of Americans get a significant amount of regular exercise and that 45 percent of American adults do not participate in any fitness or athletic activity.[1] This indicates that despite the emphasis on fitness, many Americans are still not exercising regularly or at all. Of course, everyone knows that exercise promotes weight loss and lowers one's chances of developing heart disease and other illnesses. Somehow, though, many people have missed the message that exercise is for everyone, not just for the young and the athletic. In fact, a lifelong commitment to regular exercise may be one of the most important factors in promoting health and longevity.

In its objectives for the year 2000, the United States Public Health Service (PHS) has made the goal of getting more people to exercise one of its top priorities.[2] While PHS objectives used to stress vigorous physical exercise for at least 20 minutes a day, recent research has indicated that fitness can be attained with considerably less exercise than was thought previously. Some studies have shown that people can improve their fitness significantly with just 12 minutes of exercise three times a week.[3] The PHS's newest guidelines recommend that almost everyone exercise on a regular basis. This exercise should include a moderately strenuous activity such as brisk walking in conjunction with warm-up, stretching, and cool-down activities.

When you consider the many benefits of exercise and the relatively small investment of time it requires, it is clear that a physical fitness program should be part of your health care plans. If you are already exercising regularly, this chapter can help you get the most out of your fitness program. If you are not exercising now, you can learn what you need to know to start and continue a physical fitness program that is right for you.

Physical Fitness and Health

The human body was designed to be used—to be kept in fairly constant motion. Until recently, the daily tasks of life required physical work. Even 100 years ago, most people spent their days getting strenuous exercise: working in the fields, operating machinery in factories, or scrubbing floors at home. Today, however, few people engage in daily activities that require physical exertion. Most people's waking hours are spent sitting at a desk, behind the wheel of a car, or in front of a television set. From the start, children do not get enough exercise. Many spend long hours watching TV or engaged in other passive activities.

Activity versus Exercise

Today, most people must make a special effort to get the amount of physical activity their bodies need for adequate health and fitness. Everyone engages in some **physical activity**—movement that uses energy. Physical activities include household tasks, work-related activities such as typing, walking across a parking lot, and even studying. However, few people get enough physical activity to meet the body's needs. Even people who are quite physically active may have periods of inactivity. As a result, almost everyone needs some **physical exercise**—planned, structured, repetitive activities designed to improve or maintain one or more components of physical fitness.[4]

physical activity

physical exercise

Physical Benefits of Exercise

Regular exercise is an important element in developing and maintaining overall physical health. Table 2.1 lists the physical benefits of regular exercise. There is mounting evidence that it reduces the risk of contracting many diseases, including heart disease.[5] In a landmark study of Harvard alumni whose health was followed for up to 40 years, the physically active men had much lower death rates. Men who burned as few as 500 calories a week through exercise and activity had death rates from all causes that were 15 to 20 percent

Table 2.1 The Physical Benefits of Regular Exercise

Major Benefit	Related Benefits
Improved cardiovascular fitness	Stronger heart muscle; lower heart rate; increased oxygen-carrying capacity of the blood; improved coronary circulation; possible improved peripheral circulation; reduced blood fat, including low-density lipoproteins (LDLs); increased protective high-density lipoproteins (HDLs); possible resistance to atherosclerosis; possible reduction in blood pressure; resistance to "emotional storm"; less chance of having a heart attack; greater chance of surviving a heart attack
Greater lean body mass and less body fat	Greater work efficiency; less susceptibility to disease; improved appearance; less incidence of self-concept problems related to obesity
Improved strength and muscular endurance	Greater work efficiency; less chance of muscle injury; decreased chance of low back problems; improved ability to meet emergencies; improved sports performance
Improved flexibility	Greater work efficiency; less chance of muscle injury; less chance of joint injury; decreased chance of low back problems; improved sports performance
Other benefits	Extended life; quicker recovery after hard work; decreased chance of adult-onset diabetes; less chance of osteoporosis; reduced risk of certain cancers

Source: Charles B. Corbin and Ruth Lindsey, *Concepts of Physical Fitness with Laboratories,* 7th ed. (Dubuque, Iowa: Brown, 1991). All rights reserved. Reprinted by permission.

lower than those of men who were more sedentary.[6] This finding was reinforced by a more recent study showing that death rates are inversely related to regular physical exertion, even in men at high risk for developing coronary heart disease. The decline in death rates was associated with a moderate increase in physical leisure-time activities such as gardening and home repairs.[7]

Exercise has also been shown to be related to the prevention and control of high blood pressure, osteoporosis, and even cancer. One study suggests that athletic women may cut their risk of developing breast and uterine cancer in half and the risk of developing the most common form of diabetes by two-thirds.[8] In addition, exercise can help prevent back pain.

Exercise and Psychological Health

Exercise promotes a feeling of mental and emotional well-being. People who walk, run, swim, or cycle regularly are familiar with the psychological and physical glow that often follows exercise. Exercise seems to reduce the tension that builds up when the body is under stress. After a strenuous workout, the body naturally relaxes, and this has beneficial effects on the mind as well (Table 2.2).

Physical exercise seems to reduce stress and help people manage it in at least two ways. First, exercise may use up the hormones and other by-products that stress produces in the body. Second, exercise seems to increase a person's tolerance for stressful situations.[9]

To get the full benefits of stress reduction, avoid activities that are highly competitive. Playing a competitive game of tennis or golf is not relaxing when a person's ego gets too involved. An individual activity such as walking or biking may be more relaxing and enjoyable.

Researchers have found that regular exercise can help reduce anxiety and depression. For many people, exercise increases self-esteem as well. As a result, most people who begin a regular exercise program can expect to sleep better, work more efficiently, cope better with stress, have more energy, and feel more relaxed and self-confident.

Table 2.2 The Psychological Health Benefits of Regular Exercise

Major Benefit	Related Benefits
Reduction in mental tension	Relief of depression; improved sleep habits; fewer stress symptoms; ability to enjoy leisure; possible work improvement
Opportunity for social interaction	Improved quality of life Increase in social support system
Resistance to fatigue	Ability to enjoy leisure; improved quality of life; improved ability to meet some stressors
Opportunity for successful experience	Improved self-concept; opportunity to recognize and accept personal limitations
Other benefits	Improved sense of well-being; improved self-concept; improved appearance

Source: Charles B. Corbin and Ruth Lindsey, *Concepts of Physical Fitness with Laboratories,* 7th ed. (Dubuque, Iowa: Brown, 1991). All rights reserved. Reprinted by permission.

Exercise and Physical Risks

Despite the benefits it brings, exercise contains an element of risk. Doctors, clinics, and emergency rooms handle an estimated 3 million to 5 million sports-related injuries a year. Millions of other aches, pains, and pulled muscles go unreported. Some people have to stop exercising because of pulled muscles or minor joint injuries. Others struggle on despite pain or discomfort, believing in the saying "no pain, no gain." Usually the cause of minor injuries or discomfort is exercising too hard and too long in the early stages of an exercise program. It is important to start slowly and build up the length and difficulty of the sessions gradually, particularly if a person has been inactive for some time.

Contrary to the saying, it is not necessary to feel real pain to improve fitness. Some soreness is to be expected when a person starts using muscles that have not been used recently. The soreness usually comes on gradually, and unless the exercise has been overdone, it is fairly mild. However, sudden or severe pain is always a signal to stop exercising. The body is warning you that something is wrong, and it is important to find out what it is. A person who experiences pain in the chest or repeated episodes of pain while exercising should stop and see a doctor.

While many people risk their health because they do not exercise enough, others become compulsive exercisers who may injure themselves by exercising too much. Sports medicine specialists suggest that excessive exercise is the primary cause of the increased number of sports injuries today.[10] Exercise addicts abuse exercise just as others abuse food, drugs, or alcohol. They risk injuries, and they continue exercising even when injured. For everyone, moderation is the key to proper exercise.

Physical Fitness and Its Components

Physical fitness is made up of several separate components. These can be grouped into two broad categories: skill-related and health-related.

Skill-Related Components   The skill-related components of fitness are the ones that athletes in particular try to improve with exercise. These components include the following:

- **Agility**—the ability to change the position of the whole body quickly while controlling its movement.   *agility*
- **Balance**—the ability to maintain or regain upright posture, or equilibrium, while moving or standing still.   *balance*
- **Coordination**—the ability to use the senses of vision and touch together with muscle sense to accomplish accurate, well-timed body movements.   *coordination*
- **Power**—the ability to do strength exercises quickly.   *power*
- **Reaction time**—the amount of time it takes to start moving once a person decides to do so.   *reaction time*
- **Speed**—the ability to perform a movement or cover a distance in a short time.[11]   *speed*

It is easy to see how each of these skill-related components is helpful to an athlete. To some extent, such skills are influenced by heredity. These components may not be important for your personal fitness goals. However, they may be helpful to you if you include a skill-related sport such as tennis in your physical fitness program.

Anyone can improve these components of fitness through exercise. Many types of exercise are very useful for improving coordination, agility, speed, and so on. If you are an athlete, you probably do these kinds of exercises as part of your regular sports training. When you work on developing skill-related fitness, you will probably improve only to a certain level, because the body has limits for speed, agility, coordination, power, and so on. This knowledge will help prevent frustration if you cease to improve.

Health-Related Components   The health-related components of fitness are the ones that all people need and should work to develop and improve. These components include the following:

flexibility

- **Flexibility**—the ability to use the joints fully and move them easily through their full range of motion.

muscular strength
muscular endurance

- **Muscular strength** and **muscular endurance**—the amount of external force the muscles which are attached to the bones can exert (strength) and the ability to use these muscles many times in succession without getting tired (endurance).

cardiovascular fitness

- **Cardiovascular fitness**—the ability to exercise the whole body for long periods and have the circulatory system work efficiently to supply the fuel—mostly oxygen—that keeps the body going.

body leanness

- **Body leanness**—the quality of having more than 75 to 80 percent of body composition as lean tissue (muscle and bone) and less than 20 to 25 percent as fat.

All the health-related components are linked. A certain amount of strength is necessary, for example, to develop cardiovascular fitness. However, it is possible for the body to exhibit one or more of these qualities without exhibiting all five. Yet to be healthy, a person must be at least minimally fit in each of these areas.

Developing Health-Related Fitness

Since the health-related components of physical fitness are particularly vital for health and well-being, it is important to look at each one in greater detail. (Body leanness is covered extensively in Chapter 4.)

Flexibility

Flexibility involves the range of motion possible at the many joints in the body (Figure 2.1). It is largely dependent on the various muscles associated with the joints. When these muscles are developed and lengthened through appropriate exercise, they allow the joints to move through a wider range of motion. Different joints have different ranges of motion. For example, the knee joint has a more limited range of motion than the shoulder joint does. At each joint, the connective tissue determines how far muscles can stretch and whether the joint can reach its full range of motion. Muscle tension can also affect a joint's range of motion. Relaxed muscles and elastic connective tissue allow one to achieve the greatest degree of flexibility.

Benefits   Flexibility is necessary for many routine daily tasks, such as reaching for a plate on a high shelf and pulling a sweater over your head. Good flexibility also helps prevent backaches. It is also vital in preventing injuries during exercise. Many athletes, even those whose sports require minimal flexibility, recognize the importance of flexibility and incorporate appropriate exercises in their conditioning programs.[12]

Stretching Exercises   Static stretching exercises are the best and safest way to improve flexibility. Regularity and relaxation are the keys to a good stretching program. The objective should be to reduce muscular tension in order to promote freer movement.[13] Stretching also can be a stress management technique that can break the tension–muscle pain cycle and foster more relaxed

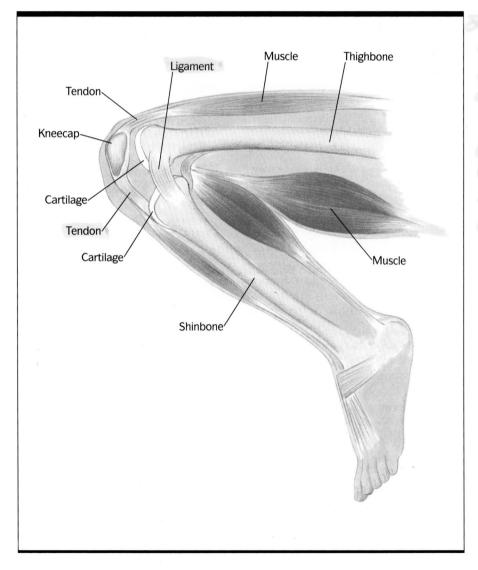

Figure 2.1 *The joints are highly complex systems. Powered by the muscles, they are surrounded by connective tissues. Tendons transfer movement from the muscles to the bones, ligaments hold the bones together, and cartilage cushions the bone ends. Warm-up and stretching increase the blood supply to the joint, making the muscles more efficient and making the other tissues softer, more flexible, and less likely to tighten or tear.*

Muscle Thighbone
Ligament
Tendon
Kneecap
Cartilage
Tendon
Cartilage
Muscle
Shinbone

muscles and a more relaxed state of mind. When engaging in a stretching program, you should follow these guidelines.

1. Do not start stretching without doing a warm-up first. When you increase the temperature of your muscles, they become more elastic so that stretching is safer and more effective. Walking is an ideal warm-up activity because it gets the muscles moving and the blood circulating.

2. After you have warmed up, begin stretching gradually and then increase the intensity. Do not stretch too hard at first. In all stretching exercises, a good rule is to stretch until you feel mild to moderate discomfort. Do not stretch to the point of pain.

3. When stretching, get into position and reach until you feel a mild amount of stretch. Hold this position for 10 to 30 seconds, until you feel your muscles relax. If this does not happen, ease up and find a more comfortable position. Deep, slow breathing helps increase flexibility.[14] As you breathe out, stretch a little farther and hold the position for 30 seconds more.

4. Stretch but do not strain. Do not bounce; the alternating tightening and stretching can pull your muscles too hard and too suddenly. Instead, relax into the stretch.

5. To improve flexibility in specific body areas, choose stretching activities designed especially for those areas. Try to do several exercises for each area.

6. To achieve the best results, stretch four or five times a week. While stretching can be done on its own, it should also be included in the general warm-up for other, more vigorous exercises.

Muscular Strength and Endurance

Muscular strength is the maximum amount of force a muscle can exert. It is often measured by how much weight a person can lift. Muscular endurance refers to the ability of a muscle to continue a prolonged or repetitive exertion without tiring. Many daily activities—washing windows, shoveling snow, even vacuuming—may make use of both endurance and strength. (But using muscles and developing them are not the same.)

When muscles are used, they burn, or metabolize, two kinds of chemicals provided by the body: carbohydrates and fats. They usually need oxygen for this process. These chemicals reach the muscle by way of the bloodstream.

To develop muscle, other chemicals are also needed, in particular proteins, from which the muscle fibers themselves are made. Proteins are also vital for the general repair of body tissue. In fact, muscle development is itself a special form of repair. Heavy work causes a slight breakdown of the tissue, which is then rebuilt larger and stronger. Unfortunately, if the muscle tissue is not used for a while, it will grow smaller again.

Benefits Building muscle strength and endurance is an important element in fitness that helps prevent muscle damage and fatigue. Although slight tissue breakdown is good for the muscles and causes growth and development, excessive muscle overload may cause long-term damage, resulting in considerable pain and stress. People who fail to keep their muscles properly toned often suffer unexpected and painful sprains.

Exercises for Muscular Strength and Endurance   Strength and endurance can be improved through exercises that require the muscles to lift, push, or pull against resistance.[15] When one does these exercises, the work load on the muscles is increased as they develop strength. Three kinds of programs are designed to develop muscular strength and endurance: isokinetic, isotonic, and isometric. They differ in the kinds of equipment used and the amount of resistance the muscles encounter at different points during a movement.

1. **Isokinetic** exercise relies on specialized machinery, such as Nautilus and Cybex equipment, that provides equal tension at all angles over the full range of a joint's motion. When properly used, this equipment is effective in increasing both muscular strength and endurance. Unfortunately, the special machinery needed for isokinetic training programs is usually available only at health clubs and gyms.

   isokinetic

2. **Isotonic** exercise involves lifting a constant weight through a full range of joint motion. Isotonic weight training, which involves the use of free weights such as barbells and dumbbells, can help increase muscular strength and endurance if it includes progressive resistance through a full range of motion. In other words, to execute a given exercise, you should warm up with a weight you can lift 10 times. For the next set, you should choose a weight you can lift only 8 times, and for the final set, you should select a weight you can lift only 6 times.

   isotonic

   Some experts believe that isotonic programs are superior to isokinetic exercises. When properly performed, they involve balancing a constant weight throughout the full range of movement, working many more muscles than isokinetic equipment does.

3. In **isometric** exercise, the individual pushes or pulls against an immovable object. Experts now consider this the least useful of these

   isometric

The three major approaches to developing muscular strength are isotonic exercises, such as weight lifting; isokinetic exercises, which require expensive equipment like that shown here; and isometric exercises, which involve pushing or pulling against a fixed resistance. Because they are designed to focus tension at all angles on a moving joint, isokinetic exercises require the use of specialized workout machines. (Burton McNeely; Robert Brenner/PhotoEdit; David Weinstein/Custom Medical Stock Photo)

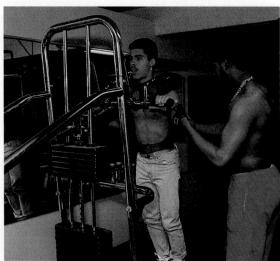

three methods. Because the range of motion is restricted, movement strengthens the muscle only at a particular angle.

Building Strength and Endurance   When properly designed and executed, weight-training programs build muscular endurance as well as strength. If the emphasis is on developing strength, a relatively small number of repetitions should be performed with a heavy load. If the goal is to develop endurance, each exercise should include a relatively large number of repetitions using a low to moderate weight load.

– Cardiovascular Fitness

Cardiovascular fitness is the quality that enables a person to exercise the whole body over an extended period. It requires that the heart be strong, the lungs healthy, and the blood vessels unobstructed. Since life depends on the capacity of these organs to deliver nutrients and oxygen to the tissues and remove wastes, it is essential that they function efficiently. Cardiovascular fitness is thus the most important component of physical health.

How does exercise aimed at cardiovascular fitness improve physical health? First, it makes the heart and lungs work more vigorously and the blood vessels carry more blood. The body becomes capable of handling future demands with less or no stress. In time, the muscles involved develop a more extensive network of blood vessels. This means that the blood has more routes for transporting the oxygen and nutrients it carries to all parts of the body. The body also develops more red blood cells (which carry oxygen) and a greater volume of blood. In addition, there is typically an increase in the amount of air the lungs can take in and breathe out at one time and in the amount of air the lungs can take in over a period of time.

Benefits   With improved cardiovascular fitness, the heart becomes stronger and more efficient. Although the heart does not increase much in size, it pumps an increased amount of blood on each beat and is emptied more completely. Between beats, it can slow down and rest more. The normal adult resting pulse rate is around 70 beats a minute, and 80 to 90 beats is not unusual in inactive individuals. In contrast, a physically fit adult usually has a resting pulse rate of only 55 to 60 beats a minute. Consequently, the heart makes thousands fewer beats per day, reducing wear and tear on heart valves and blood vessels.[16] Cardiovascular fitness may reduce some forms of hypertension (high blood pressure). Experts also believe that increased cardiovascular fitness may prevent coronary heart disease.

aerobic exercise   *Aerobic Exercise*   Cardiovascular fitness is usually improved through **aerobic exercise,** sustained exercise of the whole body that increases the heart rate for a significant period of time. Examples of this kind of exercise include vigorous walking, running, jumping rope, bicycling (including stationary bicycles), swimming, cross-country skiing, and aerobic dancing.

Every time the body performs an exercise, its oxygen needs increase. If the exercise is very strenuous, the heart and lungs cannot provide oxygen fast enough, so the effort cannot be sustained for long. Aerobic exercise is exercise done at a slightly lower level of intensity, allowing the body to keep going because it can meet its oxygen needs continuously.

Finding Your Comfort Level with Exercise

Many people who enjoy sports have no difficulty incorporating an exercise regime into their regular lifestyle. For many others, exercise turns out to be a short-term commitment if it becomes a commitment at all. They may work out when they have a goal to achieve—firmer muscles or weight loss—but either they reach their goal and then give up exercise or they just give up. These people miss out on the advantages of exercise which come only to those who persevere with regular physical workouts throughout their lives.

Exercise can help you reach important goals, such as building strength or stamina, becoming more flexible, and losing weight. But more important, exercise can help you maintain those goals and contribute to a lower likelihood of developing heart disease and other chronic problems in later life.

Any exercise program you set up for yourself should be designed to help you achieve your short-term physical goals. This will help keep you motivated. However, the program should also be fun; otherwise your willpower may fade early.

Fitness experts, who once advised people to choose a single strenuous activity as their main source of exercise, are now calling for exercise plans that include a variety of activities. You can run one day a week, do calisthenics or yoga on another day, and engage in a sport on a third.

An exercise plan that includes a variety of activities has several advantages. It is more fun, and so you are less likely to abandon the exercise routine out of boredom. Sports such as softball and racquetball, which require short bursts of movement, complement sustained strenuous activities such as swimming and jogging. Different activities also tone up different muscle groups. Even those which use the same muscles use them in different ways.

The benefits gained from one kind of exercise may make it easier to pursue another. For example, cycling strengthens the leg muscles so you can run long distances, and running develops calf and hamstring muscles that are important in cycling.

Your exercise routine can alternate long, slow workouts with short, more intense activities. For example, if you run 3 miles in 18 minutes one day, your next workout might consist of a softball game. Remember to include days of rest in your exercise routine, too, especially if you tend to squeeze a lot of activities into the day. Exhaustion leaves you prone to illness and injury.

For those who still find that they cannot abide exercise, studies indicate that physical activity can provide many advantages even if it is not strenuous enough to make you sweat. For example, a recent study of mail carriers led researchers to conclude that regular mild physical work provides many of the benefits of exercise. A job which involves walking appears to raise the body's level of "good" cholesterol.

There is no single fitness prescription that suits everybody, says a sports medicine specialist from New York. Instead, you should choose a mix of activities and be ready to change it periodically so that you stay challenged and interested.

Tailor your package to meet your goals and capabilities, but also be sure that you are comfortable with it and find it fun. That is the first step toward making exercise an integral part of your life.

Ideas based on Hal Higdon, "Base Fitness," *Walking* (February–March 1988): 38–43; "Mini Workouts Work," *East West* (August 1990); "Mix and Match" and "Smart Ways to Shape Up," *U.S. News and World Report* (July 18, 1988).

Exercise of this type also uses the large muscles and puts the joints through a wide range of motion. Thus, cardiovascular fitness and muscle endurance can develop together. As cardiovascular fitness improves, the muscles get the oxygen they need to perform longer.

Ideally, an aerobic exercise session should begin with a warm-up and stretching period at least 10 minutes long, followed by a period of aerobic exercising that lasts 20 to 30 minutes and ending with a cool-down period of 5 minutes or more to let the heart rate return to normal. The cool-down is not a period of inactivity but rather a time of very light activity, such as slow walking or a less vigorous version of the exercise you have been doing. Do not neglect this cool-down period. If you stop moving abruptly, blood can collect in the blood vessels in your legs and you may feel light-headed or dizzy.[17]

Low-impact aerobic exercise can be just as effective in improving cardiovascular fitness as is more vigorous exercise, and it is less likely to result in injury. The jarring impact of many exercise routines can cause or aggravate joint and muscle problems. There are many kinds of low-impact aerobic exercises. Race walking, for example, is lower-impact than jogging but can be just as effective. There are low-impact aerobic dance routines, and swimming is low-impact.

anaerobic exercise

Anaerobic Exercise   Exercise that causes the body's demand for oxygen to exceed the supply—producing "oxygen debt"—is called **anaerobic exercise.** An example of anaerobic exercise is sprinting 100 meters. The runner exercises so intensely that he or she can replace only part of the oxygen the body uses during the sprint and has to make up for the oxygen debt afterward. For a well-conditioned athlete, both aerobic and anaerobic exercises can be helpful in building cardiovascular fitness. For those who are not well conditioned, however, anaerobic exercise is a poor choice.

Principles of Exercise

To get the maximum benefit from any kind of exercise, it is necessary to understand four basic principles: specificity, overload, progression, and regularity.

Specificity

specificity

Specificity means simply that to develop a certain component of fitness, one must work on that particular component. For example, if you want to increase your flexibility, you should choose stretching exercises. If you want to develop cardiovascular endurance, you must select an activity that offers continuous aerobic exercise, such as running or swimming.

Overload

overload

As explained earlier in this chapter, for a muscle to become stronger, it must be **overloaded,** or worked against a greater load than usual. Systematic overloading can increase the strength, flexibility, and endurance of muscles. This does *not* mean starting out with an extremely strenuous routine, as this may cause a major injury. In the early stages of an exercise program, overloading a muscle can mean simply stretching it slightly, lifting a light weight, or moving slowly in an aerobic exercise routine. It is important to go at your own pace; what is easy for one person constitutes overload for another.

Progression

Progression refers to the fact that once muscles adapt to an overload, the load should be increased slowly and gradually. You should stretch farther, lift greater weights, and move more quickly and for a longer period of time. If you progressively and gradually increase your exercise load, your fitness level will improve over time. As your fitness improves, continue to increase the exercise load until you reach an optimum amount of exercise. Do not exercise at too high or too low a level. Exercising at too high a level can be dangerous, perhaps resulting in injury. Exercising at too low a level will not build fitness.

progression

Regularity

For exercise to be effective in developing fitness, it must follow the principle of **regularity.** That means it must be done frequently enough, with enough intensity, and for a sufficient period of time.

regularity

1. *Frequency.* Exercise must be performed regularly to be effective. Most fitness components require at least 3 exercise sessions a week.
2. *Intensity.* Exercise must be hard enough to require more exertion than normal, as measured by heart rate, in order to produce an improvement in fitness. Too little exercise will not improve fitness; too much may result in soreness or injury.
3. *Time.* An exercise period should be long enough to produce sustained, heightened activity in the muscles involved. For optimal fitness gains, 30 to 90 minutes is often recommended,[18] but several experts accept 20 minutes of vigorous exercise as a useful standard, and recent studies have suggested that exercise periods as short as 12 minutes can be beneficial.

Developing an Exercise Plan

When it comes to exercise, Americans often seem to do either too much or too little. They play football all Saturday afternoon and then get no exercise for the rest of the week. Regular exercise involving the whole body is essential for achieving lifelong fitness. Thus, a planned exercise program must take into account not only your present fitness level but also your fitness goals.

Evaluating General Fitness Goals

Exercise serves many purposes. A professional golfer may take up weight training to increase arm and upper body strength in order to put more force and speed into the golf swing. A senior citizen may undertake a series of exercises designed to improve back flexibility in order to relieve chronic low back pain. Someone in a weight-loss program may use aerobic exercise to help speed weight loss. Some people simply need a minimal exercise plan—a "fitness-for-health" plan.

One can benefit by deliberately exercising most of the muscles in one's body. However, one cannot directly exercise the heart, the muscle that ensures that oxygen and key nutrients reach all the other muscles. Prolonged repetitive exercise, especially vigorous exercise involving the long muscles of the legs and the other large muscles in the trunk and arms, ensures that the heart also gets a good workout.

A fitness-for-health plan suits the individual who wants the health benefits of basic fitness: flexibility, muscular strength and endurance, cardiovascular fitness, perhaps improved body composition (more muscle and less fat), relaxation, and improved emotional health.

Other people prefer a more ambitious plan—a fitness-for-its-own-sake or fitness-for-skill plan. A fitness-for-skill plan is geared to individuals who want to refine or improve skills, such as agility, speed, and coordination, which are needed in a specific sport or activity. Such a plan generally includes exercises that foster health-related benefits as well. A football player, for example, will follow a program of training with weights or other strength-training equipment. He will also engage in agility and cardiovascular exercises to improve his speed, strength, and endurance on the field.

Assessing Fitness Needs

Once your general fitness goals have been set, an essential part of planning a fitness program is finding your current fitness level. This can be done with professional help, particularly if you sign up at a professional fitness facility. If you plan to exercise by yourself, you can take the National Fitness Test developed by the President's Council on Physical Fitness and Sports. This consists of four separate tests: sit-ups, push-ups, sit and reach, and a walk/run test. These tests are used to assess, respectively, abdominal strength and endurance, upper body strength and endurance, flexibility, and cardiovascular endurance. Such tests will indicate the level at which you should begin your fitness program. Later, as your fitness improves, you can add to the pace or distance and increase the total time of workouts.

Planning the Program Yourself

After evaluating your general fitness goals, assessing your present fitness level, and choosing the exercises you will use, you are almost ready to begin. Before starting, however, you must decide how often to exercise, what exercises to do, how hard to work, and how much time to spend in each exercise session, as well as when and where to exercise.

How Often Should You Exercise?   As was noted earlier in this chapter, researchers have found that exercising at least 3 days a week provides the greatest cardiovascular benefits; 2 days a week or less is not adequate. Furthermore, if more than 2 days pass between exercise sessions, the beneficial effects of earlier sessions are lost. The guidelines of the American College of Sports Medicine (ACSM) recommend exercising three to five times a week. The ACSM sets five as the upper limit because studies have shown that exercising beyond that level increases the chances of injury.[19]

What Exercises Should You Do?   The mix of activities chosen for an exercise program depends on one's current fitness level, goals, and personal likes and dislikes. For optimal results, a fitness-for-health program should be planned around an aerobic exercise that you enjoy. In addition, it is recommended that two of your exercise sessions include strength exercises for the major muscle groups.[20]

Other considerations include the skill needed, the intensity of the exercise, and the length of time needed per session to produce a conditioning effect. Running, for example, is a more intense activity than cycling, and so exercising with a bicycle will require pedaling longer and faster to achieve the same level of conditioning. Above all, it is important to choose activities that feel good and that you enjoy.

How Hard Should You Exercise?   Recent studies have suggested that it is not necessary to exercise at high intensity to get benefits from a workout. Major health benefits can be obtained from exercise that is the equivalent of walking briskly for about 3 hours a week. Other research has shown that low-intensity exercise improves cardiovascular fitness nearly as much as high-intensity exercise does.[21] Not all experts agree on these findings; some state that more strenuous workouts are necessary to produce a conditioning effect.

Of course, what is strenuous for one person may be easy for another person who is more physically fit. One way to measure the intensity of a workout is to take your pulse to determine your heart rate during exercise. During an exercise session, your pulse should not exceed your target heart rate. Traditionally, physical fitness experts have stated that a person's target heart rate during exercise should be 70 percent of the heart's maximum capacity for that person's age (Figure 2.2). Some recent findings have suggested that a target heart rate of only 50 percent of the heart's maximum capacity can still produce real benefits.[22] Perhaps the best approach is to try to work up gradually from a lower to a higher target heart rate as your fitness program progresses.

How Much Time Should You Spend Exercising?   The answer to this question depends partly on your comfort level about physical fitness. The ACSM recommends doing 20 to 60 minutes of continuous aerobic activity per exercise

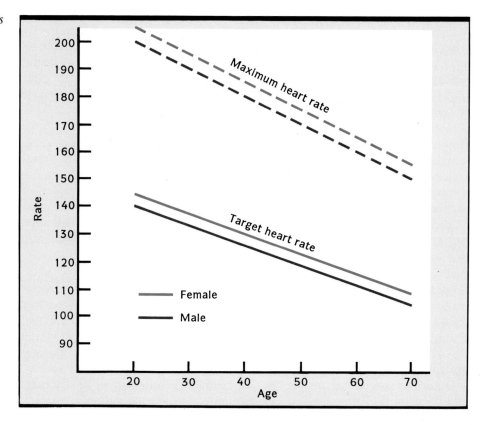

Figure 2.2 *The older adults become, the lower the maximum heart rate and therefore the lower the recommended target heart rate for an exercise session. Doctors calculate maximum heart rates in relation to one's age and sex and calculate the target rate on the basis of maximum heart rate and general fitness.*

session.[23] Studies mentioned earlier in this chapter indicate that even 12 minutes of exercise per session can produce benefits, but many exercise physiologists recommend 20 to 30 minutes per session.[24] Remember that extra time must be allowed for warm-up and cool-down and for stretching.

Playing It Safe: Getting Medical Approval

It is advisable to obtain medical clearance before beginning a fitness program, especially if you are inactive, over age 35, or under 35 and have documented or suspected coronary artery disease or significant risk factors. A number of medical conditions can be aggravated by physical exertion, and the possibility of your having such conditions should be ruled out by a medical examination before the exercise program begins. It is also a good idea to show the tentative fitness plan to a doctor who is familiar with your physical condition and medical history.

Deciding When and Where to Exercise

Once you have determined the type of exercise program you want to follow, you need to get down to the truly practical aspects: how can you fit the exercise into your weekly schedule, where do you plan to work out, and what alternatives do you have if the arrangements go wrong or you feel the need for a change? These are very important decisions, because people are more likely to stick with a fitness program if they have considered their options.

Fitting Exercise into Your Schedule   The time of day you choose to exercise depends on your schedule; no one particular time is best. Weather can pose problems, and you may need to consider this in planning a schedule. On an extremely hot, humid day, body temperature may rise much more than normal, resulting in heatstroke. In hot, humid weather, you may be able to do your jogging or cycling by exercising very early in the morning, when it is coolest. Extremely cold weather can also pose problems.

Selecting Places to Exercise   Another point to be considered in planning an exercise program is deciding where to exercise. This decision may be affected by various factors, such as the type of exercise program chosen, the equipment or facilities required, and personal motivation. Many good forms of exercise, such as walking and bicycling, can be done almost anywhere.

Even exercise that requires special facilities, such as swimming, can often be done at several different locations. Check out your school facilities, a community recreation center, a YWCA, or a similar organization. In the summer, consider a local park, a private swim club, or even a local quarry or lake.

For some people, exercise programs can be initiated quite easily at home. Even if equipment is required, it is often compact and possible to use at home. Before selecting equipment, though, consider personal fitness goals, the space available, and the cost.

There are exercise machines for aerobic conditioning and strength training. For aerobic conditioning, you can choose from stationary bicycles, rowing machines, treadmills, and cross-country skiing machines. Strength-training equipment includes a range of products from barbells to weight stack machines like those found in health clubs.

Most home exercise machines take up about 15 square feet. Some can be folded up and stored when not in use. Although treadmills and weight stack machines take up a good deal of space and are not easily stored, a set of dumbbell weights is quite small and can be put away easily.

Most exercise equipment costs several hundred dollars or more. Before buying a piece of equipment, check unbiased consumer ratings to be sure the equipment is safe, reliable, and effective. If possible, use the equipment at a gym first to make sure you will use it regularly.

The Health Club Option

People can usually design their own fitness-for-health programs by following some simple guidelines, including those already discussed in this chapter. However, there may be valid reasons for a person to prefer working in a setting with other like-minded people under professional supervision. Some people therefore begin an exercise program by joining a health club.

Reasons for Joining a Health Club   Many people feel that they cannot exercise properly on their own. They find that something always interferes with their plans to exercise at home. At a health facility, by contrast, the entire focus is on exercising and there are few distractions. Some people feel they need the help of professionals at a health club to plan an exercise program.

Many people enjoy the social atmosphere of a health club, finding exercise more pleasant when it is done in a group. There is less temptation to skip part of an exercise routine when it is done with others.

Choosing a Health Club Unfortunately, many people drop out of or rarely go to their health clubs after spending hundreds of dollars on membership. Generally, health clubs expect 50 to 60 percent of their members to drop out.[25] People are clearly not finding what they wanted when they joined. Before joining a health club, therefore, it is important to shop around, visiting several clubs and comparing them. At each club, you should do the following:

- Visit during the time of day or evening you plan to use the facilities to see how many people are there. See whether there are long waits for the equipment and facilities you plan to use. Find out whether the club sets limits on enrollment to prevent overcrowding.
- Observe the facilities to see whether the atmosphere is comfortable or is too intense or too social for your taste. Judge whether the equipment is well maintained and the club is clean and well ventilated. Ask people who belong to the club what their experience has been.
- Assess the convenience of the club. It is best to find a club close to home or work. A person is more likely to go to a club if it is convenient. People with children should check whether the club offers baby-sitting services.
- Determine the credentials of the instructors and find out what kind of instruction is offered. See whether the instructors are required to have a degree in exercise physiology or physical education and if they are certified by the ACSM as fitness professionals. Instructors should be certified in cardiopulmonary resuscitation (CPR). Be wary of a health club that requires only in-house training for its instructors.
- Find out what fitness-testing procedures the club uses. The club should take a health history and recommend that its members get medical approval before beginning an exercise program. Some clubs do fitness assessment testing to find a member's fitness level. After the initial assessments, the club should then set up a personalized exercise program to meet the individual's needs and goals.
- Find out the cost of membership and compare it to that at other clubs.

Staying with Your Plan and Modifying It

Many studies have shown that 60 to 70 percent of adults who start exercising drop out within the first month.[26] Once you have begun a fitness plan, how can you avoid being one of those who give up? Thinking ahead and anticipating pitfalls can help. Be sure to set realistic goals for improvement and know how much improvement to expect. Do not expect too much too soon. It may take a few months before the improvement is noticeable. If your goals are unrealistic, you may become discouraged and quit. Finally, be prepared to modify your exercise plan, change your activities, or revise your schedule if you have trouble sticking to the original plan.

How Fast and How Much Can Fitness Improve? During the first few weeks of exercise sessions, you can expect a period of soreness and fatigue. This will abate as the program proceeds. After 2 or 3 months you will probably reach a plateau. Improvement beyond that point may be minimal if you stay at the same level of activity.[27] While this can be discouraging, you should keep your original fitness goals in mind. If you have been following a fitness-for-health plan, you will have improved your overall endurance and cardiovascular fit-

Table 2.3 Amount of Exercise Needed to Maintain Conditioning after One Builds up to Optimal Fitness Level

Type of Exercise	Frequency (times per week)	Distance	Time (minutes)
Walking	3	4 miles	48–58
	5	3 miles	36–43
Running	3	2 miles	13–16
	5	1.5 miles	12–15
Cycling	3	8 miles	24–32
	5	6 miles	18–24
Swimming	3	1,000 yards	16–25
	4	800 yards	13–20

Source: Adapted from K. Cooper, *The New Aerobics* (New York: Bantam, 1983). Copyright by Kenneth H. Cooper. Used by permission of Bantam Books, a division of Bantam Doubleday, Dell Publishing Group.

ness and probably will have lost some pounds or inches as well. To improve beyond this plateau, you will have to work harder. The more fit you are, the harder it is to improve. Once you are really fit, however, maintaining that fitness is easier (Table 2.3).

How Quickly Can Fitness Deteriorate? Experts think that people get out of shape about as fast as they got into shape in the first place. So if it takes 3 months to attain a certain level of fitness, it will probably take 3 months to lose that fitness if you stop exercising. This is true even for people who have trained hard for a long time.

Modifying Your Plan It is important to evaluate your fitness program periodically and modify it as necessary. As was emphasized at the beginning of this chapter, exercise is not a temporary measure—it should be a part of your permanent routine throughout life. As you grow older, you may find that your overall fitness goals change. In addition, your interests may change. To be of maximum benefit throughout your life, your program should reflect your current schedule, needs, and interests. It should be flexible enough to change as your life changes.

Is Fitness Worth the Effort?

Physical fitness is definitely worth the effort. When you exercise regularly, you feel better and look better. At the same time, you probably will also feel more relaxed and energetic. Even when you are tired or unenthusiastic about things, exercise will help turn those feelings around and give you more energy. Perhaps most important, the long-term benefits to your health from exercise are enormous. Exercise not only can improve your life expectancy, especially by reducing the risk of developing heart disease,[28] it also can slow the aging process and keep you fit and healthy longer. Few things in life are as beneficial to physical and mental well-being as a regular program of exercise and physical fitness.

Chapter Summary

- Interest in fitness is at an all-time high in the United States. However, only 20 percent of Americans get adequate exercise.

- The vast majority of Americans today need more physical exercise than their jobs and lifestyles provide. They need planned and structured exercise.

- Exercise provides many health benefits, including a reduced risk of developing heart disease and protection against osteoporosis.

- Exercise also provides psychological benefits, including stronger defenses against stress, anxiety, and depression.

- Because exercise carries a risk of injury, it is important to follow sound guidelines in creating and following an exercise program.

- Exercise contributes to many physical skills. It also contributes to basic physical health, which is vital for everyone.

- Basic physical health includes flexibility, muscular strength and endurance, cardiovascular fitness, and body leanness.

- Flexibility refers to the range of motion in the joints. It is determined by the elasticity of connective tissue and the ability of muscle fibers to relax.

- A good exercise program begins with a basic warm-up routine that starts with simple muscle movement and ends with stretching exercises for flexibility.

- Strength and endurance are two qualities of muscles that are important in overall health. Besides the quality of the muscle tissue itself, optimal muscle fitness requires a good supply of chemicals from the blood.

- There are three basic types of exercises for muscle strength and endurance: isokinetic (weight machine exercises), isotonic (barbell exercises), and isometric (stationary pressure exercises).

- Cardiovascular fitness refers to fitness of the circulatory system, including the lungs, heart, and blood vessels. The heart muscle is vital to cardiovascular fitness.

- Aerobic exercise is recommended for cardiovascular fitness. It lasts long enough to increase the heart rate significantly but does not starve the muscles of oxygen.

- To be effective, an exercise program should be designed for specific muscles and purposes and should slightly overload the muscles at which it is directed. The exercises should become progressively harder until the desired level of fitness is reached. Regular times should be set aside for exercise every week.

- To design a personal fitness program for oneself, one must consider one's fitness goals.

- One must also assess one's current fitness, select appropriate exercises at an appropriate level, get a medical checkup, plan a workable schedule, and decide where to exercise.

- Staying with a fitness program is easier if your expectations are realistic, you periodically modify the program, and you are aware of the benefits of exercise to your life.

Diet and Nutrition

Objectives

When you have studied this chapter, you should be able to:

- Define nutrition and explain the importance of diet and proper nutrition to health.

- List seven different classes of components in food and give examples of foods which are good sources for each component.

- Explain some of the important functions of the major components and nutrients in food.

- Describe the two classic systems for determining a proper diet and discuss the drawbacks of each one.

- Discuss the basic principles of a positive food strategy.

- Explain some of the strategies for buying and preparing food that can help ensure a nutritious diet.

- Identify the universal principles that can provide guidance for everyone in developing a healthy diet.

Americans are more interested in food and nutrition than ever before. Proper nutrition has come to be recognized as a major factor in achieving and maintaining a healthy lifestyle. As a result, people are much more concerned about making dietary choices that promote health. They realize that food not only provides the fuel for muscular activity and exercise, but also supplies energy for all the other functions of the body.

Americans have more food choices than any people in history. The quantity and variety of foods available are amazing. What were once mainly regional or seasonal foods can be found almost everywhere at any time. People expect high-quality foods that taste good, look good, and are free of hazards. For the most part, such food is available, but the American food market does not guarantee adequate nutrition. Alongside fresh fruits and vegetables in the market there are junk foods and other foods of questionable value.

Thus, even with the great variety of American food products, a healthy and satisfying diet is not guaranteed. You need to learn about the nutritive substances in foods and use that knowledge to guide your choice of foods.

What Is Nutrition?

Nutrition is the science of food—how the body uses it and its relationship to good health. Nutrition includes the study of the major food components: proteins, carbohydrates, fats, vitamins, minerals, water, and fiber. It is concerned with how the body uses these nutrients and the effect of this process on health.

Food is vital to the good health of all people of all ages. The body uses food for energy, growth, and the repair of damaged tissues. Food can also help strengthen the body against the effects of future stress and disease.

Before food can be used by the body, it must be broken down into substances the body can absorb. The process by which the nutrients in food are *metabolism* converted into body tissue and energy is called **metabolism.**

The conversion of food into body tissue is a very complex process (Figure 3.1). Nutrients are chemically changed before they are used. For example, the protein in steak has to be metabolized into human protein. Another process of metabolism takes place as nutrients are converted into energy.

calorie The energy potential of food is measured in units called **calories.** (A calorie is the amount of heat needed to raise 1 kilogram of water 1 degree Celsius.) Foods differ in the amount of calories they contain per unit weight and thus differ in their energy potential. An individual's caloric needs depend on age, weight, height, sex, and activity level.

Too little or too much food—or, worse, too much low-nutrient food—leads to poor health. According to a 1988 report from the surgeon general on nutrition and health, poor dietary habits play a key role in 5 of the nation's top 10 causes of death.[1]

The Basic Components of Food

All foods are composed of various chemical compounds, or nutrients. There are two general classes of nutrients: macronutrients and micronutrients. The *macronutrient* **macronutrients**—nutrients the body needs in large amounts—consist of pro- *micronutrient* teins, carbohydrates, and fats. The **micronutrients,** which are needed in

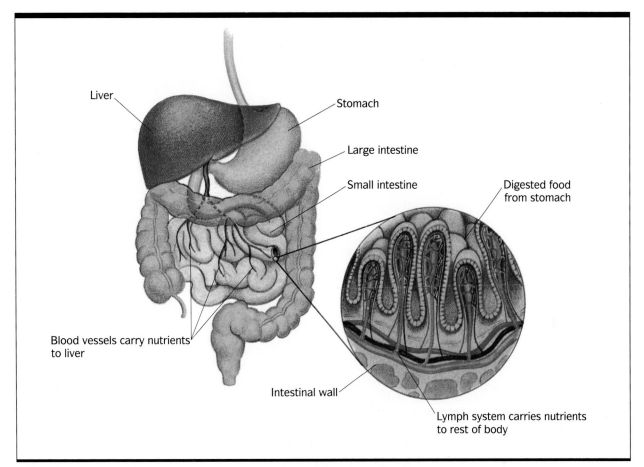

Figure 3.1 *Most people think of the stomach as the main organ in the digestive system. The stomach continues a process that begins in the mouth, physically and chemically breaking down the food into separate nutrients, but it ingests very little. Most nutrients are absorbed through the complex tissue of the intestinal wall, which carefully sorts them to travel to different parts of the body. There the nutrients are used to create human fluids and tissues. Much of this metabolism takes place in the liver.*

smaller amounts, include minerals and vitamins. In addition to the macronutrients and micronutrients, foods also contain two essential nonnutritives: fiber and water.

Proteins

Proteins are essential for the growth and repair of body tissues. The body uses proteins in muscle, hair, teeth, nails, bones, hemoglobin, and many other important components. Special proteins known as nucleic acids are found in the nuclei of all cells in the body. The job of these nucleic acids is to transmit hereditary characteristics. Another type of protein—**enzymes**—plays an important role in chemical reactions that build up and break down cellular material in the body. Each human cell contains several thousand kinds of enzymes.

protein

enzyme

Proteins and Metabolism Proteins are made up of different amino acids, chemicals that are the building blocks of the body. Twenty-two amino acids are used to build human proteins. Of these, nine are called **essential amino acids** because the body cannot manufacture enough of them—they must be present in food. The body can manufacture the other 13 amino acids from other substances in one's diet.

essential amino acid

The body assembles the forms of protein it needs by chemically linking amino acids in a specific order. For this to occur, however, all the amino acids must be available at the same time. Since amino acids cannot be stored in the body, you must supply the nine essential amino acids through your food choices at least twice a day.

One way to get protein is to eat foods of animal origin (meat, fish, poultry, eggs, dairy products). The proteins in these foods are known as **complete proteins** because they contain all nine essential amino acids.

complete protein

You can also get protein from plant foods. However, proteins of plant origin (vegetables, seeds, grains, and nuts) almost always lack one or more of the nine essential amino acids. They are called **incomplete proteins.** As a result, vegetarians must combine plant proteins either with each other in specific combinations or with animal proteins such as milk to get all nine essential amino acids.

incomplete protein

How Much Protein Do You Need? Clearly, it is vital to consume adequate amounts of protein every day. Getting too little protein can be dangerous. Even minor protein deficiencies eventually cause fatigue and irritability and reduce the body's production of antibodies, resulting in greater susceptibility to infection and slower recovery from disease. A continued protein deficiency may lead eventually to anemia and liver disorders.

However, it is desirable not to eat too much protein. If necessary, the body can convert protein to **glucose,** a fuel vital for energy, but excess proteins usually are stored in fat tissue.

glucose

Most Americans take in far more protein than is needed. The average daily consumption is about 100 grams, yet most young men need only about 56 grams and most young women about 45 grams. As people age they generally need less.[2] A daily protein need of 50 grams is roughly the amount of protein found in two 2- to 3-ounce servings of lean cooked meat, poultry, or fish. (These are considerably smaller portions than most people eat.)

Carbohydrates

Carbohydrates are found in abundance in all forms of plant life. They play an important role in metabolism as the body's chief source of energy. There are two basic types of carbohydrates: the simpler forms are sugars of various types, found in fruit and milk as well as in table sugar, and the more complex forms are starches and dietary fiber. (Fiber, however, cannot be converted into energy; its importance in the diet will be discussed later in this chapter.)

carbohydrate

Carbohydrates and Metabolism While all the macronutrients can be converted to energy, carbohydrates are the most economical energy source. The American Heart Association recommends that carbohydrates constitute 50 percent or more of total calories, with an emphasis on complex carbohydrates.[3]

Carbohydrates are metabolized in several stages by the digestive system and the liver and converted into a simple sugar called *glucose.* Sugars can thus enter the bloodstream rapidly, providing a quick burst of energy. Starches, by contrast, take longer to convert to usable energy. As a result, energy is released over a longer period of time. Some glucose remains stored in the liver and muscles, ready for release into the bloodstream if blood glucose levels fall too low. The remainder of the glucose goes right into the bloodstream and is used directly by all the cells in the body for energy. Excess glucose is converted to fat.

Besides providing energy directly, carbohydrates play an important role in the metabolism of fat stores. To utilize fat stores efficiently, the body needs at least some dietary carbohydrate.

How Much Carbohydrate Do You Need? As with all food components, the ideal amount of carbohydrate in the diet depends on a person's size, activity level, and metabolic rate. The National Research Council recommends five or more daily servings of vegetables and fruits in addition to six or more daily servings of starches such as rice and potatoes and other complex carbohydrates, including pasta, whole-grain breads and cereals, and legumes. A single serving is one-half cup of vegetables, a medium-size piece of fruit, or a slice of bread.[4] Foods rich in carbohydrates include grains (rice, wheat, rye, millet, barley, and corn), tubers (potatoes, yams, and sweet potatoes), and a variety of processed foods (pasta, cereal, and whole-grain breads). Most fruits and vegetables also contain carbohydrates.

Found in foods such as pasta and rice, carbohydrates should provide more than 50 percent of the body's energy needs; they are metabolized more efficiently than are fats and proteins. (Tony Freeman/PhotoEdit)

Fats

Fats are the only macronutrients that the body can store in large amounts. They serve as an important source of reserve energy. The energy they provide, however, is more limited than energy from carbohydrates. It is easily used in aerobic exercise but is much less useful for other types of activity. For example, fats cannot maintain brain function if carbohydrates are lacking in the diet.

In addition to storing and providing energy, fats are an important ingredient in the walls of every cell. They contribute to blood clotting and hormone synthesis, help store and carry important vitamins (A, D, E, and K), and insulate the body and protect vital organs from injury.

Fats and Metabolism There are many kinds of fats in the human body. Also known as **lipids,** each type of fat fulfills a specific function. Most fats are combinations of fatty acids called **triglycerides,** but there are other types, such as **cholesterol,** a fat which is thought to play a role in the development of heart disease. The fats that people eat are easily converted into the forms of fat that the body needs.

lipids
triglycerides
cholesterol

How Much Fat Do You Need? Because fats are easily manufactured from the other macronutrients, they are not a vital part of most diets. There are, however, particular types of fat which must be included in what people eat, but these fats are needed only in very small amounts, and they are present in many foods.

unsaturated fat

Most dietary fats (the fats in food) can be classified as either unsaturated or saturated (Table 3.1). **Unsaturated fats** include most vegetable oils. They are usually liquid at room temperature. They can be divided into polyunsaturated fats, such as corn, soya, sunflower, and cottonseed oil, and monounsaturated fats, such as olive oil. Polyunsaturated fats tend to lower blood cholesterol; monounsaturated fats do this to a lesser degree. The essential fats are unsaturated.

saturated fat

Saturated fats are found in meat, butter, coconut oil, palm oil, and whole milk. They are usually solid at room temperature. They tend to raise blood cholesterol. Saturated fats are associated with an increased risk of developing cardiovascular disease, so their consumption should be restricted.

The American Heart Association recommends a diet in which total fat intake is less than 30 percent of total calories. At least one-third of this fat should be monounsaturated—saturated fat intake should be less than 10 percent of total calories, and polyunsaturated fat intake should not exceed 10 percent.

There is some controversy over whether these guidelines are applicable to children. Some experts maintain that children need more fat in their diets to meet the added nutritional needs of growth, especially during adolescence. The Committee on Nutrition of the American Academy of Pediatrics recommends a diet of 30 to 40 percent fat for most children, except for those with highly elevated cholesterol levels. The American Heart Association recommends its figure of 30 percent or less for all persons over age 2.[5]

Minerals

minerals

Minerals are inorganic elements that the body needs daily to help form tissues and various chemical substances. They assist in nerve transmission and muscle contraction and help regulate fluid levels and the acid-base balance of the body. Since minerals are absorbed, used, and excreted by the body, they must be replaced continuously.

Table 3.1   Calories in Common Dietary Fats

Food	Measure (tablespoons)	Saturated Fat (calories)	Monounsaturated Fat (calories)	Polyunsaturated Fat (calories)
Butter	1	65	30	4
Corn oil	1	16	31	74
Lard	1	46	53	14
Margarine				
Hard	1	20	46	33
Soft	1	18	36	44
Olive oil	1	17	93	11
Peanut oil	1	22	59	41
Safflower oil	1	12	15	94
Soybean oil	1	19	54	48
Sunflower oil	1	13	24	83

Source: Eleanor Whitney and Eva Hamilton, *Understanding Human Nutrition,* 4th ed. (St. Paul, Minn.: West, 1987): H10–H12. All rights reserved. Reprinted by permission.

Different minerals are needed in different amounts. The body requires fairly large quantities of calcium, phosphorus, potassium, sodium, and magnesium. Iron, zinc, selenium, copper, cobalt, and manganese are needed in only tiny amounts daily.

Minerals are contained in almost every food, and most people can obtain sufficient quantities of essential minerals by eating a variety of foods, particularly fruits and vegetables. Although there are many different minerals, this chapter will discuss only calcium, potassium, sodium, and iron in detail.

Calcium **Calcium** is the most abundant mineral in the body. It is essential for many bodily functions, including building bones and teeth and ensuring normal growth. A calcium deficiency during childhood will cause bone deformities. Throughout adulthood, calcium is needed to maintain a strong, hard skeleton. If calcium is not replaced by calcium-rich foods or calcium supplements, one's bones can become increasingly thin, brittle, and fragile, particularly with inactivity. Many older people are afflicted with osteoporosis, a painful and crippling bone disease. A diet rich in calcium can help prevent this condition. Since osteoporosis is eight times as common in women as it is in men, women should make sure they get enough calcium.

calcium

Almost three-quarters of the calcium in the average American's diet comes from milk and milk products (cheese, yogurt, ice cream). The remaining one-fourth is supplied by foods such as leafy vegetables, salmon, and sardines with bones.

Potassium and Sodium A proper balance of **potassium** and **sodium** is essential for normal functioning of muscle tissue, proper conduction of nerve impulses, and maintenance of the body's acid-alkaline balance. Together, these two minerals are the primary **electrolytes**—substances that carry the electrical charges needed by cells to carry on their work.

potassium
sodium

electrolytes

Potassium is found in the highest quantities in beans, fruits (especially bananas), vegetables, whole grains, ocean fish, lean meat, and potatoes. It is more effective when consumed with vitamin B and moderate amounts of sodium. However, an excessive intake of sodium can decrease the body's supply of potassium, as can an excessive intake of sugar, aspirin, coffee, or alcohol.

Sodium is one of the most overconsumed nutrients. It is most commonly found in table salt but is a hidden ingredient in almost all processed foods and occurs naturally in many foods. In recent years there has been a great deal of concern about the relationship of sodium to high blood pressure. A high sodium intake is thought to be a contributing factor in this disorder. As a result, nutritionists and health authorities now recommend that all people limit their sodium intake.[6]

Iron Although it is needed only in small amounts, **iron** is one of the most important nutrients, essential for the production of hemoglobin in red blood cells. However, it is also the most frequently deficient nutrient in the diet. Since about 80 percent of the iron in the body is found in the blood, iron losses are greatest whenever blood is lost. Iron-deficiency anemia is a fairly widespread health problem in the United States, particularly among women of childbearing age, who regularly lose considerable amounts of iron through the menstrual process. A woman's iron requirement is almost twice that of a man, and this is the one nutrient that frequently requires supplementation.

iron

Table 3.2 Vitamins and What They Do

Vitamin	A	B₁[a] (Thiamin)	B₂ (Riboflavin)	Niacin	B₆ (Pyridoxine)
Found in	Milk and other dairy products, green vegetables, carrots, animal liver	Whole-grain or enriched cereals, liver, yeast, nuts, legumes, wheat germ	Liver, green leafy vegetables, milk, cheese, eggs, fish, whole-grain or enriched cereals	Yeast, liver, wheat germ, organ meats, eggs, fish; can be synthesized from the essential amino acid tryptophan	Yeast, wheat bran and germ, liver, kidneys, meat, whole grains, fish, vegetables
Benefits	Helps maintain skin and tooth enamel, bone formation, and vision	Helps convert glucose to energy or fat; helps nervous system and appetite	Vital to all major nutrient metabolism; keeps skin in good condition	Hydrogen transport; maintenance of all body tissues; energy production	Essential to amino acid and carbohydrate metabolism
Recommended daily allowance (RDA)	Men: 1,000 RE[b] Women: 800 RE	Men: 1.4 mg Women: 1.1 mg	Men: 1.7 mg Women: 1.3 mg	Men: 16–19 mg Women: 13–14 mg	Men: 2.2 mg Women: 2.0 mg
Deficiency causes	Night blindness, decrease in growth, lack of tears	*Beriberi:* numbness in feet and toes, tingling legs, weak muscles, heart irregularities	*Ariboflavinosis:* sore skin, cracking of corners of mouth, bloodshot eyes, sensitivity to light	*Pellagra:* diarrhea, skin rash, mental disorders	Greasy scaliness around eyes, nose, mouth; mental depression
Excess causes	Swollen feet and ankles, weight loss, tiredness, eye bleeding	Excess of water-soluble vitamins is rare	Excess of water-soluble vitamins is rare	Excess of water-soluble vitamins is rare	Excess of water-soluble vitamins is rare

[a] The vitamins listed in the blue columns are water-soluble.
[b] RE = retinol equivalents, the standard measure for vitamin A.

Everyone should try to include some iron-rich foods in the diet—meat and poultry, dried beans, dried fruits, dark-green leafy vegetables, and cereal that has been fortified with iron.

Vitamins

vitamins As you read earlier in this chapter, **vitamins,** along with minerals, are often referred to as micronutrients. Although they are needed only in small amounts, these substances are needed to trigger vital bodily functions. Vitamins do not form new compounds in the body as proteins, carbohydrates, and fats do. Rather, they help other chemical reactions and other bodily processes take place. For example, vitamin D helps calcium form strong bone structure.

Table 3.2 shows the specific functions, or benefits, of each vitamin, its food sources, its recommended daily allowance (RDA), and the specific effects of

Folacin (Folic acid)	B$_{12}$ (Cyanocobalamin)	C (Ascorbic acid)	D	E	K
Liver, nuts, green vegetables, orange juice	Meat, liver, eggs, milk	Citrus fruits, tomatoes, cabbage, broccoli, potatoes, peppers	Fish oils, beef, butter, eggs, milk; produced in skin on exposure to ultraviolet rays in sunlight	Widely distributed in foods: yellow vegetables, vegetable oils, and wheat germ	Spinach, eggs, liver, cabbage, tomatoes; produced by intestinal bacteria
Necessary for production of RNA and DNA and red blood cells	Necessary for production of red blood cells and normal growth	Collagen formation and maintenance; protects against infection	Promotes absorption and utilization of calcium and phosphorus; essential for normal bone and tooth development	May relate to oxidation and longevity; may protect against red blood cell destruction	Shortens blood-clotting time
Men: 0.4 mg Women: 0.4 mg	Men: 0.003 mg Women: 0.003 mg	Men: 60 mg Women: 60 mg	Men: 0.005–0.0075 mg Women: 0.005–0.0075 mg	Men: 10 mg Women: 8 mg	Men: 0.07–0.14 mg Women: 0.07–0.14 mg
Anemia yielding immature red blood cells; smooth, red tongue; diarrhea	*Pernicious anemia:* drop in number of red blood cells; irritability; drowsiness; depression	*Scurvy:* rough, scaly, skin; anemia; gum eruptions; pain in extremities; retarded healing	*Rickets:* a softening of bones causing bow legs or other bone deformities	Increased red blood cell destruction	Poor blood-clotting (hemorrhage)
Excess of water-soluble vitamins is rare	Excess of water-soluble vitamins is rare	Excess of water-soluble vitamins is rare	Thirst, nausea, vomiting; loss of weight; calcium deposits in kidneys or heart		Jaundice in infants

deficiency and excess. Recently much attention has been paid to vitamins A and C.

Vitamin A and Beta-Carotene   Vitamin A strengthens the body's protective mechanisms and contributes to bone formation. One of the richest sources of vitamin A is fish liver oil. In addition, a substance called beta-carotene, which occurs in many vegetables, is converted into vitamin A by the body. Beta-carotene is found in most yellow, orange, and dark-green leafy vegetables such as carrots, broccoli, and kale.

Vitamin A and beta-carotene improve the growth, repairability, elasticity, strength, and resistance of internal and external tissues. A deficiency of vitamin A or beta-carotene can harm the structure and function of these tissues.[7]

Vitamin C and Bioflavonoids   Numerous studies have suggested that vitamin C improves the immune system and counteracts radiation and chemical toxins. It is now generally recognized that it plays a role in cancer prevention as well.

There is considerable controversy over the recommended doses of vitamin C. Nobel Prizewinner Dr. Linus Pauling, who stated that vitamin C can prevent and cure the common cold, recommended that the minimum daily intake for adults should be between 2,000 to 10,000 milligrams. The possible side effects of such massive doses are a matter of concern. Toxicity is rare because vitamin C is one of the **water-soluble vitamins**—this means that the body can excrete the amounts it cannot use. Nevertheless, regular daily megadoses of 5,000 to 10,000 milligrams may lead to a buildup that can result in diarrhea, kidney or bladder stones, skin rashes, and gout.

water-soluble vitamins

Bioflavonoids are water-soluble substances that often occur in fruits and vegetables as complements to vitamin C. When ingested together, vitamin C and bioflavonoids are more effective than vitamin C is when ingested alone. Bioflavonoids appear to be completely nontoxic. Foods high in vitamin C and bioflavonoids include cherries, rose hips, sweet and hot peppers, strawberries, spinach and other dark-green leafy vegetables, and citrus fruits.

Are Vitamin Supplements Necessary? Most people can get all the vitamins they need by eating a healthy, varied diet. Some, however, feel the need to take daily vitamin supplements to maintain health and ward off illness. Experts disagree about the need to supplement a varied diet with additional vitamins. Several factors suggest, however, that moderate supplementation may improve health and probably does not diminish overall well-being.

The current state of nutrition seems to favor supplementation to ensure that individuals receive sufficient vitamins and minerals. Vitamin needs increase in the presence of stressors such as illness, physical activity, and psychological pressures.[8] In addition, poor diets, including those aimed at quick weight loss (below 1,500 calories), call for multivitamin supplementation, as do chronic problems such as alcoholism and chronic diarrhea.[9] However, most individuals can get the vitamins they need by eating a varied and balanced diet rich in an assortment of vitamins and other micronutrients.

Potential Hazards of Vitamin Megadoses People who take vitamin supplements in megadoses—amounts far above the RDAs—may be adversely affecting their health. When consumed in large doses, vitamins are properly considered drugs. Overdoses of vitamins A, D, E, and K—the **fat-soluble vitamins**—can cause illness or even death.[10] These vitamins cannot be excreted but are stored in the fatty tissues, where they may build to toxic levels.

fat-soluble vitamins

Fiber

Fiber is a nonnutritive carbohydrate. Also known as roughage or bulk, fiber is found in fruits, vegetables, and grains. Bran and fruit skins are a common source.

Humans cannot digest the cellulose found in fiber. As a result, fiber is not technically a nutrient. However, it plays an essential role in the digestive process. In the large intestine (colon), it binds other waste products with large amounts of water, forming an easily passed soft, large stool. Since fiber passes through the digestive system unchanged, it helps move food quickly through the intestines and out of the body. This in turn helps prevent constipation and

Thinking Critically about Food Additives

Food additives have been part of the food system for many years. Over the past several decades they have become a controversial topic. Two sides of the issue are presented below.

Without Additives, Foods Would Be More Limited — and More Expensive

The bounty of America's harvests today is maximized and prices are minimized when as few foods as possible go to waste. This is ensured if items are purchased and consumed soon after they arrive at the market. Foods move faster from the store if people find they taste good, look good, and are good for them. Additives—flavors, food colorings, and nutrients—can contribute to all these qualities.

Waste is also minimized when foods are slow to spoil. Many traditional preservatives— for example, salt and sugar—are now recognized as carrying considerable health hazards. If modern chemical preservatives carry any risk, it is considerably less.

In fact, testing procedures ensure that additives are used with a margin of safety larger than that for many substances that occur naturally in foods. Allergenic foods such as shellfish cause considerably more negative reactions than do additives.

The overall effect of food technology in the United States has been to improve the food supply. More people eat better now than before the food industry began to use additives. And the technology is also continually improving. Preservatives are beginning to be replaced by food irradiation, which kills many insects and bacteria but leaves no residue. (Although radioactive materials are used, the food is not made radioactive.) Modern food technology provides a net gain, and an increasing gain, to our lives.

Additives Are Potentially Dangerous and Are Also Unnecessary

Even if food irradiation proves completely harmless to food, it leads to the risk of transporting and disposing of radioactive materials. But its effects on health—like the effects of food additives—take a long time to show up. While only a few additives, such as cyclamates and Red Dye No. 2, have actually been withdrawn after being approved, they certainly cast doubt on the others.

True, tests are required and performed, but no testing can be perfect, and tests for toxic risks to humans are particularly difficult. Such tests cannot be performed on humans. In addition, the danger of additives in food may be long term, but the tests must be done in the short term, so they often use high concentrations. Third, tests cannot cover all the possible effects of an additive. Some hazards may not be discovered. Finally, the tests are usually done by the firms that produce the additives. These are all major imperfections in the testing procedure.

If the use of additives and similar procedures were the only way to ensure safe, nutritious foods in the market, it would be one thing. But some additives are used for color and flavor, hardly vital qualities of food. Furthermore, nutritional additives are frequently used to replace nutrients destroyed by poor processing techniques or to overload foods with many more nutrients than would be needed in a balanced diet. Finally, in recent years the health food industry has shown that natural foods can be successfully brought to the market at not too much added cost.

What is your opinion? Do you agree that food additives are safe and a beneficial part of our food production system? Or do you think that consumers should demand additive-free foods? How do the arguments above apply to food irradiation?

Information drawn from Geri Harrington, *Real Food, Fake Food, and Everything in Between* (New York: Macmillan, 1987); "Food Irradiation: Is the Time Ripe?" *Nutrition Action Letter* (November 1986).

diverticulitis, a physiological problem in which the wall of the large intestine weakens and balloons out.

There is some evidence that dietary fiber may also affect blood cholesterol levels.[11] It may help lower blood cholesterol levels by reducing the amount of time cholesterol-containing foods stay in the digestive tract.[12] Some researchers have suggested that fiber (found in foods such as oat bran, dried beans and peas, raw carrots, barley, and certain fruits) can directly reduce cholesterol levels.[13] The most recent evidence, however, suggests that this is not the case.

There are other documented benefits of dietary fiber. A high-fiber diet has been associated with a reduced risk of developing diabetes, colon cancer, and obesity. In addition, since fiber can act as a dietary "filler" without adding calories, a high-fiber diet can help people manage their weight.

Unfortunately, the diets of many Americans are lacking in adequate fiber. These diets consist predominantly of processed foods in which most of the fiber has been either milled out or peeled away. As a result, many traditional sources of fiber have disappeared from the diet. Moreover, Americans are not consuming enough fruits, vegetables, and whole-grain cereals, which are important sources of dietary fiber.

The National Cancer Institute recommends that people increase their dietary fiber intake to 20 to 30 grams daily, keeping it below 35 grams.[14] One's daily diet should include a variety of fruits and vegetables as well as whole-grain breads and cereals.

Water

Like fiber, water has no nutritional value yet is a very important food component. It is used to transport nutrients to the cells and to remove cellular waste products. In addition, it acts as a medium for digestion, regulates body temperature, and helps cushion the vital organs. An inadequate water intake will restrict the function of all body systems. Finally, water and some of the chemicals it carries are responsible for bodily structure. The cells in the body contain fluid, and there is fluid around the cells, too. As much as 80 percent of body weight may be water, although the average is closer to 60 percent.

While the body can survive for long periods without food, it can exist for only a few days without water. The actual amount of water the body requires per day depends on environment, physical activity, the season of the year, and the type of food eaten. Most people should drink six to eight glasses of water a day to maintain optimal health.

Toward a Balanced Diet

Knowing about the basic components of food is only the first step toward eating well. Virtually all foods contain nutrients, and most nutrients are so chemically complex that their effects on the body are not fully understood. In fact, most nutritionists would agree that it is not possible to create an "ideal" diet based on a balance of macronutrients and micronutrients. How, then, can people choose the right foods, achieve a balanced diet, and develop healthy dietary habits?

The Basic Four Food Groups

The most widely known set of guidelines for determining proper diet is the basic four food groups system. This system groups food into four basic groups: meat, milk products, fruits and vegetables, and breads and cereals. The system was based on the RDAs established by the National Academy of Sciences–National Research Council.[15] The RDAs, which are reviewed for possible revision every 5 years, are estimates of the optimal quantity of each nutrient that a person is likely to need.

The four food groups plan specifies that a recommended number of servings from each group be consumed daily. However, this system has recently been seen to have certain deficiencies. One problem is that the average energy content of a diet based on the basic four food groups is 2,200 calories daily, which is high for people who are concerned about weight control. This means that a person whose calorie allowance is less than 2,200 finds few if any options for food choices in this plan.[16]

Another problem with the basic four food groups is that a person can follow the guidelines and still fail to meet the day's needs for certain nutrients, especially vitamin B_6, iron, magnesium, and zinc.

Finally, two of the four food groups are milk and meat. This gives many people the mistaken idea that half the amount of food consumed daily should consist of milk and meat, leading to a high fat consumption. In reality, the system recommends only two milk and two meat servings plus eight servings from the plant-food groups daily.

The Exchange System

Another method of determining diet is the exchange system. Unlike the basic four food groups system, which classifies foods by the nutrients they provide, the exchange system groups foods by the calorie content of their carbohydrate, fat, and protein components and by serving size.

Each food group in the exchange system identifies a typical food of that group and specifies a serving size. Each of these typical foods heads a group of other foods that may be exchanged for the "standard" food. Eaten in the specified serving size, each exchange food provides the same number of calories—in the form of protein, carbohydrate, and fat—as does the standard food in its group.

The exchange system is a complicated approach to developing a healthy diet. It takes time and interest to compute dietary intake according to its careful rules. Therefore, this system, like the basic four food groups system, is confusing for most people.

A Positive Food Strategy

Unlike these complicated approaches to diet, there is a simple strategy for choosing foods that provide maximum energy, vitality, and health. This strategy requires a basic understanding of foods that are preferred sources of nutrients and those that should be limited. You need guidelines for consuming the proper ratios of these foods. This positive food strategy should be the basis of a lifelong commitment to new and better eating habits.

The average American's diet contains far too much protein. It is much more healthy to prepare meals with large amounts of vegetables. (Richard Hutchings/InfoEdit)

The positive food strategy includes four basic principles.[17]

1. Daily caloric intake should support normal growth in children and a desirable weight in adults. Eating just enough to maintain an ideal consistent weight is considered the key to increased length of life and an improved quality of life.

2. The daily intake of food should include a relative ratio of five times as much complex carbohydrates as protein. The key here is that protein should never constitute more than one-fifth of a meal. Servings of protein should be limited to 3- or 4-ounce portions.

3. The basic goal of a positive food strategy is to increase the intake of complex carbohydrates, decrease the intake of protein, and limit the intake of fat.

4. Limit the intake of foods of poor nutritional quality, such as refined grain products, processed meats, high-fat dairy products, canned vegetables, TV dinners, salt, coffee, tea, and liquor. Increase the intake of high-quality foods, such as whole-grain products, lean meat, fish, poultry, low-fat dairy products, and fresh fruits and vegetables.

Using this positive food strategy will help you become leaner and more energetic and will provide protection against diseases related to a poor diet. It will also enable you to enjoy all the foods you like. Although you have to limit the consumption of certain foods, you do not have to give them up entirely.

Meeting Special Needs

A diet based on the positive food strategy will meet the nutritional needs of most people. Some individuals and some situations, however, require special attention and certain changes in food choices.

Food Choices for Vegetarians   Vegetarianism has become more common among Americans. The vegetarian faces a special problem in diet planning— obtaining the needed nutrients from fewer food groups.

There are two major classes of vegetarians: ovolactovegetarians and vegans. Ovolactovegetarians eat eggs (*ovo-*) and dairy products (*lacto-*) as well as plant foods. Vegans eat plant foods only—no eggs, cheese, or milk.

Although either vegetarian diet can be adequate for health, it is far easier to obtain the necessary nutrients from the ovolacto diet than from the vegan diet. Since proteins from eggs and dairy products are complete, ovolactovegetarians can meet their basic nutritional needs even after giving up meat. Proteins from plant sources, however, are usually incomplete. They do not contain all the amino acids the body needs. Therefore, vegans must plan meals that combine incomplete proteins so as to form complete ones. Typically, this means a combination of grains and legumes, such as rice and beans, bread and peanut butter, or corn muffins and pea soup. By selecting appropriate food combinations and a wide variety of foods, a vegan can consume enough complete protein.

The real problem in the vegan diet is a lack of vitamin B_{12}, which is most often found in animal foods. Vegans must consume a source of B_{12} or suffer a deficiency. The nonmeat source may be a special form of yeast, soybean milk, or a B_{12} supplement. Besides vitamin B_{12}, iron may be a problem for vegans, since its best sources are animal foods. Vegans should make a special effort to eat plant foods high in iron (beans, spinach, prunes, tofu) and iron-enriched foods or take an iron supplement.

Food Choices for People under Stress   Prolonged stress can damage the immune system, providing fertile ground for a wide range of ailments. Eating patterns are often disrupted during periods of stress, and as a result, the body begins to lose a number of important nutrients, including potassium, glucose, protein, fat, and calcium. This can be prevented if nutrients are stored in the body.

Most people know the importance of eating a balanced and varied diet, but many are unaware that many nutrients literally go in one end and out the other if exercise is not used to make them "stick." Only muscles that are called on to work are able to grow and accumulate protein. The same is true of bones, which must be active to absorb additional calcium. Regular exercise is the most effective means of retaining nourishment.

Stress can have a significant effect on the appetite. Many people do not feel much like eating when they are under stress. This can be dangerous, because

the weaker a person becomes, the harder it is to combat the stressor. It is important to eat whatever you can, eat small amounts, and drink fluids. Some experts also recommend that a vitamin-mineral supplement be taken every day to replenish important nutrients.

Other people may overeat in response to stress. For them, the best solution is exercise. Exercise fuels the body by building muscle and bone and prevents excess calories from being stored as fat.[18]

The consumption of some foods can add to stress by stimulating the body's stress response. The most common of these substances is caffeine, which is found in coffee, tea, cola drinks, cocoa, and chocolate. It is advisable to limit the consumption of such foods.

Another connection between diet and stress is a phenomenon known as *vitamin depletion.* Excessive stress over prolonged periods can deplete the body of certain vitamins, such as vitamin C and the vitamin B complex. Such depletion can cause improper functioning of the endocrine and nervous systems. Sugar and sugar products have also been implicated as a factor in vitamin B complex depletion, and their consumption should be limited during periods of stress.

Putting Nutritional Principles to Work

Once you know the nutritional value of foods and the best dietary strategies, you need to develop the skills that will enable you to purchase and prepare the foods you need.

Buying Food

A key to shopping for food is to spend less time shopping in the center aisles of supermarkets and grocery stores. The majority of preferred foods are found along the outer walls of most food stores. On these walls there are fresh fruits and vegetables; fresh fish, poultry, and meats; dairy products; and bread. The middle aisles are filled primarily with low-quality processed foods, although there are some exceptions, such as grains, pasta, cereals, and frozen and canned goods. As a general rule, therefore, shop from the outer walls to get the foods that will best meet your nutritional needs.

Of course, almost everyone buys processed or packaged foods from time to time. When you buy these foods, assess what you are buying and know the contents of the products. You can do this by learning how to read the fine print on product packages.

Misleading Packaging　Companies often design product packages to appeal to health concerns. Thus, words associated with good health—*organic, natural, bran, oat,* and *fruit,* for example—often appear in product names and claims. Claims about the healthfulness of foods can be deceiving. Some products that claim to be nutritious may actually contain many low-quality nutrients, including sugars, fats, and salt. An example of misleading words is the term *natural,* which by law can be used to describe sugar, since sugar is a product of nature. It is possible to determine the contents and nutritional value of most processed or packaged foods by reading their labels.

Although vegetarian diets are considered healthful by many nutrition experts, a completely meat-free diet can lead to serious vitamin and iron deficiencies. Therefore, vegetarians must make informed choices to ensure good health. (Tony Freeman/ PhotoEdit)

Nutrition Labeling   Except for a few standard products, the law requires that every processed food list its ingredients in the order of the quantity used, by weight. In addition, nutrition labeling is required for every food that has been enriched with additional nutrients or makes a specific nutritional claim. Such food labels must show the following:

1. Serving size
2. Number of servings per container
3. Per-serving amount of calories, protein, carbohydrates, and fat
4. Percentage of U.S. RDAs per serving for certain essential nutrients—protein, vitamins A and D, thiamin, riboflavin, niacin, calcium, and iron—calculated by weight

Fats, Oils, and Shortening   An area of labeling to be aware of concerns the fat, oil, and shortening in processed foods. Although cooking oils and shortenings provide an analysis of saturated fats on their labels, the ingredient lists on processed foods mention only the fats in question without specifying how much is saturated or unsaturated. Many labels are quite vague, stating only what the food "may" contain. A consumer may read that the product contains corn oil, palm oil, and coconut oil but is not told how much is saturated or unsaturated. Worse, a vague term such as *vegetable oil* can refer to saturated fats such as palm kernel, palm, or coconut oil as well as polyunsaturated fats such as corn or safflower oil.

The habit of reading labels helps consumers get the right foods into their kitchens—and keep the wrong ones out. You can tolerate some low-quality foods and some less-preferred ingredients as long as most of your shopping basket is filled with preferred foods.

Avoiding Food Hazards

Americans in general have access to a great variety of safe high-quality food products. Even so, there are some potential hazards that consumers should recognize, understand, and guard against. The improper storage and handling of food may be hazardous to your health. For example, as many as one American in six may fall prey to food poisoning every year. Caused by bacteria, most of these cases are mild but some require lengthy recuperation and may be life-threatening.

There are ways to protect yourself against food poisoning and other similar hazards.

- Never buy, keep, or use canned goods if the can is swollen or badly dented. Damaged cans may allow air to enter, contributing to bacterial growth.
- Keep all perishable food refrigerated or chilled at all times. Do not let foods sit out for extended periods. The growth of harmful bacteria is slowed by refrigeration.
- Wash your hands frequently while preparing food. Do not prepare food if you are ill or have a cut or infection.
- Scrub vegetables intended to be eaten raw to remove parasites or germs that have survived from the growing fields or retailer.
- Always keep foods either hot (over 140 degrees F) or cold (below 45 degrees F).

Nutrition Information Per Serving	
Serving Size	½ Cup
Servings Per Container Approx. 3	
Calories	100
Protein	2 Grams
Carbohydrates	25 Grams
Fat	1 Gram
Sodium	300 Milligrams

Percentage of U.S. Recommended Daily Allowances (U.S. RDA)

Protein	2	Riboflavin	2
Vitamin A	2	Niacin	4
Vitamin C	8	Calcium	*
Thiamine	2	Iron	2

*Contains Less Than 2% Of The U.S. RDA Of These Nutrients.
Ingredients: Whole Kernel Golden Corn, Water, Sugar, Salt.

The nutrition label from this can of kerneled corn reveals that the product contains a significant amount of sodium. This is a serious concern for people with hypertension. (Tom Dunham)

Preparing Food

One of the keys to eating nutritiously is knowing the best ways to prepare and cook food. Here are some basic guidelines for preparing nutritious low-fat, low-salt, low-sugar meals.

1. Use water, defatted stock, juice, or wine instead of butter or oil to prevent food from sticking to the pan and burning while braising and sautéing it. Another technique is to use chopped onions and cook them slowly so that they release moisture, which will prevent sticking and burning.

2. Use vanilla extract, cinnamon, or concentrated fruit juice in place of sugar or artificial sweeteners. If you must use sugar, use one-half the amount called for in the recipe.

3. Use herbs and spices to replace salt. They contain no calories and add greatly to the flavor and enjoyment of food. Use two to three times as many herbs and spices as you would normally use.

4. Whenever possible, steam or stir-fry vegetables. Broiling and baking are other healthful cooking techniques.

5. When preparing poultry, meat, and fish, remove all visible fat before cooking. Remove the skin of poultry either before cooking or before serving. Broil or bake meat products and avoid meat products that are high in fat.

6. Use oils sparingly and select those which are low in saturated fats. Monounsaturates such as olive oil may be best for frying, since heat can saturate polyunsaturated oils.[19]

Eating Right in Today's Fast-Paced World

Every year Americans spend billions of dollars eating out in restaurants and fast-food outlets. The foods in these places sometimes present a health hazard. How can you make good food choices in these eating environments? The simplest advice is to follow a few basic universal principles that can provide guidance for everyone in developing a healthy diet.[20]

- **Eat moderately.** Eating too much at one meal or in one's total diet is stressful to the body. It may lead to poor digestion and can force the body to expend excess energy to digest large quantities of food. A meal should leave you feeling light and energized.

- **Eat early in the day.** Eating too close to bedtime can lead to poor digestion. Late-night snacks can easily turn to fat. Eat the majority of your dietary intake early in the day and taper off as evening approaches. Ideally, the evening meal should be the lightest, smallest meal of the day.

- **Eat natural foods.** Foods in the natural state have their original nutrients. Food processing, refining, preserving, aging, and cooking deplete these nutrients. Raw or lightly steamed fresh vegetables have more nutritional value than do those that have been overcooked; so do fresh, unprocessed fruits.

- **Eat quality foods and avoid junk foods.** Eat foods that provide the best-quality fuel and nutrients. Avoid cookies, cakes, and highly refined foods, plus heavily salted foods, such as potato chips.

- **Eat a wide variety of different types of foods.** This will help ensure that your nutritional needs are met.

Some additional strategies for life on the run include the following: Do not skip meals. If you eat between meals, choose snacks that are healthy. When eating out, select foods that are good for you. Ask how foods are prepared and make requests about the food you are served. For example, request broiled, baked, steamed, or poached meat, fish, or poultry or specify that sauces or salad dressings be served on the side.

Ideas about diet and nutrition are continually changing. New nutritional research will undoubtedly suggest additional strategies for healthy eating. Good nutrition and better eating habits play a very important role in the improvement of personal health.

Chapter Summary

- Proper nutrition is a major factor in developing and maintaining good health.

- Nutrition is the science of foods and how they are used in the body for energy, growth, and the repair of damaged tissues.

- There are several basic groups of nutrients in food—proteins, carbohydrates, fats, vitamins, and minerals. There are also two essential nonnutritive substances—fiber and water.

- Protein is composed of different amino acids, the building blocks of the body. Protein is essential for growth and the repair of body tissues. It is found in foods of animal origin (complete protein) and plant origin (incomplete protein).

- Carbohydrates are found in all forms of plant life and are the body's chief source of energy.

- A certain amount of fat is essential. Fat insulates the body, cushions the vital organs, and contributes to other bodily functions.

- Vitamins are essential for triggering vital bodily functions, such as helping chemical reactions take place. Different types of vitamins play different roles.

- Minerals help in the formation of body tissue and various chemical substances needed for nerve transmission and regulation of the body's fluid levels. The body requires different amounts of the different types of minerals.

- Fiber plays an essential role in the digestive process. A diet high in fiber has been associated with a reduced risk of developing diabetes, colon cancer, and obesity.

- Humans cannot live without water; it acts as a medium for transporting nutrients to the cells and removing waste products. It also aids in digestion, helps regulate body temperature, and cushions the vital organs.

- An important factor in proper nutrition is knowing how to buy the best-quality foods and prepare them in safe and nutritious ways.

- Foods must be stored and handled properly to ensure safety. Improperly stored or handled food may be dangerous.

- A few universal nutritional principles, such as eating high-quality, natural foods in moderate amounts, can provide guidance for everyone in developing a healthy diet.

Weight Management and Body Composition

When you have studied this chapter, you should be able to:

- Describe the relationship among weight, appearance, and body composition.

- Explain the different uses of fats in the human body.

- Identify and comment on at least four different techniques Americans use to control and manage appearance and body composition.

- Describe two theories that explain body composition problems.

- Explain how people can use natural management techniques for body composition.

- Name and describe three extreme conditions that occasionally affect body composition.

Weight is one of the most talked about and written about topics in the United States. Television shows, books, videotapes, spas, restaurants, and even manufacturers of frozen dinners cater to Americans who wish to lose, or sometimes gain, pounds. Weight control has become a major industry; $74 billion is spent each year on low-calorie foods. Millions more are spent on diet books, diet aids, and equipment designed to help people shed pounds.[1]

For most people the scales may be the measuring tool, but the mirror is a more important test. People have an idea of what they want to look like; and many make great efforts to achieve that look, even if only for a short time.

However, there is another element of even greater significance. Overweight and underweight have been linked with chronic long-term medical problems, some of which are serious and even life-threatening.[2] This is especially true when a weight problem begins in childhood or adolescence[3] or lasts for a long time. Several life insurance companies publish tables which indicate ideal weights for men and women of different heights. These tables are compiled to help insurers assess the risk that a given person may die early, because the insurers have observed that, on average, people who are overweight have a shorter life span.

Because weight is simple to measure, it has been the main focus of attention. However, actuarial predictions from weight alone are not ideal. The more elaborate insurance tables include other factors—for example, age and body frame type—acknowledging that the relationship between weight and life expectancy is not simple. The real issue for health—and for appearance too— is not weight but body composition.

Body composition refers to the proportion of different substances within the body, in particular the proportion of body fat to other body tissues. It is the body's fat content that poses the main health problem. While weight can be an indicator of the amount of fat, it can be misleading because of the variable weight of other tissues, such as bone and muscle.

body composition

Weight, Body Composition, and Health

Body composition, particularly the proportion of fat in the body, can affect a person's total well-being. Physically, it affects cardiovascular fitness for the long term, and it also affects energy levels, stamina, and endurance in the present. Psychologically, it may affect self-image and self-esteem. Socially, it affects a person's relationships with others.

Body Composition and Physical Health

One of the best documented health risks of excessive fat in body composition is heart disease. In the Framingham study, a classic long-term study of the health of the residents of a town in Massachusetts, death from heart disease was found to occur more often among overweight people.[4] (For simplicity, the terms *weight, overweight,* and *underweight* will be used in this chapter, but they should be understood to indicate proportion of fat rather than weight alone.)

Obese persons (defined as 20 percent or more over ideal body weight) are also at increased risk for developing hypertension (high blood pressure), cancer, stroke, and adult-onset diabetes. Together, these four conditions account for 70 percent of all deaths in the United States every year.[5] Extreme underweight can also be a threat to health. The Framingham study found that the thinnest subjects had a lower life expectancy than those who were overweight.

In addition to the health risks noted above, both overweight and underweight can impair the body's stamina and endurance. This frequently leads to reduced participation in physical activities and sports. Such inaction can aggravate health risks because exercise is an important component of weight control.

Body Composition and Emotional Health

There is a two-way relationship between emotional problems and problems of body composition. For years experts have observed that people who are depressed often have depressed appetites or eat excessively to comfort themselves. Researchers have also found that problems of body composition can contribute to emotional and psychological problems.

The principal factor here is body image—how a person views his or her body—rather than the amount of fat itself. For example, a negative body image may result in problems such as depression and feelings of low self-esteem. These emotional problems can be compounded if a person attempts to lose or gain weight and fails.

Paradoxically, the bad feelings people have as a result of body composition and body image often make it harder for them to deal with a body composition problem. Self-acceptance may be necessary *before* the problem is addressed. Such self-acceptance, combined with a desire to improve, creates a positive emotional attitude. This can enable an individual to achieve easier and more effective body composition management.

Body Composition and Social Health

Social health is closely related to emotional health. People often fear that their bodies announce to others who they are and what they are and are not doing. As a result, a person's weight and body image may influence that person's social interactions. People with a positive self-image can project a friendly, outgoing, and confident personality that helps them in social situations. Those with a more negative self-image may feel shy, aloof, or withdrawn, feelings that obviously inhibit social interaction.

If a person can temporarily accept his or her weight and be at ease with other people, other facets of character—kindness, humor, enthusiasm—are more likely to be revealed, making for a richer and more rewarding social life. This in turn helps a person develop a more positive self-image, which makes it easier to succeed in a program of body composition management.

Body Composition and Fat

Fat is unique among the major nutrients: proteins and carbohydrates are used in the body only to cover immediate metabolic needs, but fats are available as an energy reserve for the future. This means that the fat content of the human body can vary far more readily than can that of other tissues. In fact, when other nutrients are not required for the body's needs, they can be converted to fat for additional energy storage.

Getting involved in active pursuits can bring any person benefits besides weight loss. Social life and self-esteem may also improve. (Kevin Beebe/Custom Medical Stock Photo)

However, stores of fat are maintained at a price. Not only does additional fat make exertion more difficult, but it also requires more blood vessels to keep it nourished, putting a greater strain on vital organs such as the heart. Understanding and knowing how to measure fat therefore provides important background knowledge for weight control.

The Nature and Types of Fat

The human body is made up of many tissues, including muscle, bone, cartilage, connective tissue, skin, and the nerves. There is also fatty tissue, which includes fat cells and various other tissues.

The body needs some fat for survival. One type, called **essential fat,** forms part of the chain of chemical reactions by which the body stores nutrients from food and burns, or metabolizes, those nutrients to get energy. Essential fat is stored in the bone marrow, heart, lungs, spleen, and kidneys. A certain amount of essential fat is necessary for optimal health. Without it, the body would be unable to metabolize nutrients effectively. The minimum proportion of essential fat for men is about 3 percent of total body weight. For women, it is about 12 percent.[6]

essential fat

Another type of fat in the body is called **storage fat.** Some of this fat is brown and seems to be used for heat production, but most is white storage fat and is used for energy. This fat is found underneath the skin and around the internal organs. It helps cushion the body and protect the internal organs from injury.

storage fat

Women have an extra layer of fat under the skin and greater fat deposits on the breasts and lower body. This extra fat is probably important for healthy childbearing and other functions that rely on hormones, such as estrogen, stored in fatty tissue. However, recent evidence has suggested that the distribution of storage fat in the body may be related to disease. In overweight men,

Assessing Body Composition

Body composition is an important measure of health. The most direct way of assessing it would seem to be appearance—do you look too fat or thin?—but people's judgments are often distorted by ideas about fashion and other concerns. For years the objective method involved a simple ratio between weight and height, but this relationship can be misleading. Many other factors should be considered, including frame size and muscular development.

The most accurate measures come from hydrostatic weighing, bioelectrical impedance, and skinfold tests, as described in this chapter. However, these tests all require specialized equipment.

Medical researchers have recently focused attention on other body ratios that may provide more accurate clues than the weight-height ratio does. One is the waist-hip ratio. Because fat in the upper body is associated with greater health risks than is fat lower down, a simple comparison of waist and hip circumference provides an easy reckoning tool. Divide your waist measurement at the navel by your hip measurement at the hipbone. For women, the ratio should be 0.8 or less; for men, it should be 1.0 or less. If it is greater, you might consider a diet and exercise regimen or at least try some other tests.

Two other ratios that fit rather well with the waist-hip ratio are the weight-waist ratio for men and the hip-height ratio for women. The two charts included here provide a simple way of using these measures to estimate body composition. Lay a straightedge across the appropriate chart, from your weight to your waist girth if you are a man or from your hip girth to your height if you are a woman. Read off your percentage of fat on the center scale.

A healthy range for men is 12 to 15 percent; for women, 22 to 25 percent. If you are outside your healthy range in either direction, consider the benefits of weight management through exercise, diet, or both. If you "failed" one of the ratio reckoner tests presented here, watch your weight. If you failed two, it may be wise to consult a physician.

Adapted from "Win the Weight War," *Prevention* (June 1990): 46; David Higdon, "Lean Measure: Estimating Body Fat," *American Health Magazine* 6, no. 6 (July 1987).

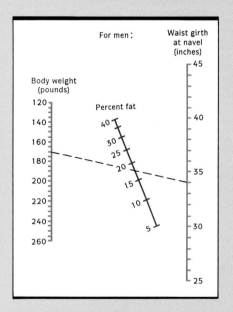
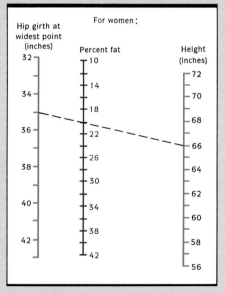

Source: David J. Higdon, *American Health* (1987). Used with permission.

for example, excess fat often is distributed primarily in the abdominal area, and this has been associated with an increased risk of developing high blood pressure and heart disease. In women, abdominal fat distribution has been associated with diabetes.[7]

It is clear that too much fat in the body can be unhealthy. The average American woman carries 25 to 28 percent of her body weight as fat, and the average man carries 15 to 18 percent. Health and medical experts suggest reducing this to 22 to 25 percent for women and 12 to 15 percent for men.[8]

Measuring Fat and Body Composition

Calculating actual body composition can help people determine whether they really need to change their weight. There are several ways to measure body composition, or the percentage of body fat. However, the three most popular methods—hydrostatic weighing, bioelectrical impedance, and skinfold measurement—all have limitations.

Hydrostatic Weighing   In the **hydrostatic weighing method,** also called underwater weighing, a person is weighed on a scale and then reweighed while totally submerged in water. This method is based on the principle that fat is lighter and more buoyant than lean tissue, so a person who is fatter will tend to float and appear less heavy when weighed underwater. After the dry and underwater weights are measured, technicians can calculate the body's density and determine the proportion of fat to lean tissue.

hydrostatic weighing method

However, studies have shown that the results of hydrostatic weighing can be in error by as much as 5 percent because of the buoyancy of some parts of the body. For example, although people are told to exhale the air from their lungs, there will always be some air remaining—different amounts in different people—which adds to their buoyancy. Measurements may also be more inaccurate among older people because their bones sometimes are more porous and therefore more buoyant.[9]

Bioelectrical Impedance   Another method of determining body composition is **bioelectrical impedance,** in which a weak electric current is used to measure the body's water content. This method is based on the fact that water can conduct electricity and that fat contains almost no water whereas lean tissue does. Small electrodes are clipped to a person's wrist and ankles, and a small electric current is sent through the person's body. A computer measures the amount of electric current that is lost and uses that measurement to calculate the percentages of lean and fat body weight. This method may, however, also produce inaccurate results because of the size and content of recent meals and the level of body dehydration.

bioelectrical impedance

Skinfold Measurement   A third method, **skinfold measurement,** uses calipers to measure the fat under the skin, where about half the body's fat is located. Measurements are taken on areas of the body such as the front of the thigh, the shoulder blade, the abdomen, the calf, and the back of the upper arm. From these measurements, the ratio of body fat to other tissues can be estimated. The primary limitation of this method is that the measurements must be very precise to yield reliable results.

skinfold measurement

Common Approaches to Body Composition Management

Despite the time, money, and effort spent on body composition control, studies show that Americans lose and then regain weight with predictable regularity. While this may help their social lives and self-esteem for a while, it does little for their long-term health and life expectancy. In fact, continual weight change has been shown to be harmful.[10] To achieve the kind of permanent weight management that can benefit health, a permanent change is usually needed in a person's lifestyle. Steps must be taken that people can feel comfortable with and feel they can maintain.

Diets

Almost certainly, the most common approach to controlling body composition is to go on a diet. Most people think of a diet as consisting of eating smaller portions and cutting out particular foods, such as foods laden with high-calorie fats and sugars. There are, however, a great many different types of diets, some of which are highly unusual in their approach.

The average American goes on one and a half diets a year—and also goes off them. Most often people are looking for a diet that is fast, because they want to lose weight for a specific occasion, and easy, because they have found from previous experience that dieting is difficult. Therefore, people are lured by diets that offer fast and painless results.

Unfortunately, this goes against the standard advice of dietitians, who state that a 1- to 2-pound weight loss per week is realistic and healthy. Anything faster is unlikely to work and may cause health problems.

Diet Concerns   Diets that may be harmful to your health and promote only temporary weight loss often involve a very low caloric intake, extreme restriction of one or more of the macronutrients (protein, carbohydrate, and fat), and reliance on formulas or special products.[11]

Concern about widespread dieting prompted the American College of Sports Medicine (ACSM) to issue a paper titled "Position Statement on Proper and Improper Weight Loss Programs."[12] In particular, the ACSM said that a person on a very low calorie diet may lose a great deal of water and minerals from the body and suffer dehydration, weakness, faintness, anemia, and a number of other medical problems as a result. Ironically, such a diet does not generally help a person shed fat. Most of the weight lost is water from bodily fluids such as blood.

Several diets involve cutting back not on fats but on carbohydrates and protein. Low-carbohydrate fad diets are not recommended. They cause your energy level to be lowered and will make you feel weak, light-headed, and fatigued. These conditions will not keep you operating at peak performance. Like low-calorie diets, they cause more water loss than fat loss. As a result, they do not promote true weight loss and may be dangerous. In addition to making the body use fats for energy, they also force it to deplete its supplies of protein, because the energy from fats cannot be used to power the brain.

Low-protein modified fasts that allow dieters to take in less than 800 calories a day may cause serious physical and psychological health problems and are intended only for those who are seriously obese and under a doctor's supervision. It is also possible to consume too much protein while dieting. People who wish to lose weight may be handicapped in their efforts if they consume too much protein, because it is likely that fruits, vegetables, and grains will be crowded out of the diet.[13] The key to good nutrition is to balance the amount of protein consumed with the other important foods.

Finally, many formula diets involve limiting one's intake to a specially prepared product. These diets usually seek to provide all the essential nutrients, a minimum of calories, and something to satisfy the appetite. Although such diets may promote weight loss, they are usually followed by rapid weight gain and are associated with the same health risks as very low calorie diets. Formula diet products have also been promoted for use in addition to one's regular eating to help a person gain weight. Weight gain can be achieved, however, through increasing one's intake of any kind of food and is also enhanced if exercise is increased.

Criteria for Evaluating Diets   To help people choose wisely from the wide variety of weight control programs available, the California Dietetic Association has issued guidelines for evaluating the health and safety of diets. According to these findings, a diet should meet the following criteria:[14]

- It should satisfy all nutrient needs except energy.
- It should be tailored to individual tastes and habits.
- It should be sufficient to minimize hunger and fatigue.
- It should be readily obtainable and socially acceptable.
- It should lead toward the establishment of a changed eating pattern.
- It should be conducive to the improvement of overall health.

Exercise

Exercise plays an important role in physical health because it contributes to control of one's body composition. However, some researchers believe that not all exercise is equally good for controlling body composition. Specifically, they argue that anaerobic exercise, which is defined as strenuous exertion that uses up energy faster than the blood's oxygen can supply it, may cause a considerable increase in appetite. Aerobic exercise—regular repetitive motions such as walking, swimming, and running—tends to consume fat to produce the needed energy, creating less of a craving for food.[15]

This is not to say that exercise is undesirable for body composition control. On the contrary, it is vital to a successful program. However, according to these researchers, aerobic exercise may be better for weight loss, and anaerobic exercise may be helpful to a person who seeks to gain weight.

Drugs

Every year Americans spend over $75 million on appetite suppressant drugs in an attempt to lose weight. These drugs are designed to reduce an individual's appetite by increasing the feeling of fullness.

Laxatives and diuretics are also used to help regulate body functions. One desirable side effect is weight loss. However, their use can result in serious

Commercial diet foods are nutritional and low-calorie, but if you eat more than the recommended servings, they will contribute little to weight loss. (Tom Dunham)

dehydration, electrolyte abnormalities, and organ dysfunction. None of these drugs provide a long-term solution to weight problems because they do not address the need to change one's basic eating behaviors.

One group of drugs sometimes used by people in an attempt to gain weight is steroid drugs. Used primarily by athletes, though now banned by many athletic organizations—including the Olympic committee—these drugs contain special hormones that can help a person develop bulkier muscles.[16] Steroids are not safe. They can cause impaired liver function, permanent changes in the reproductive system, and possibly a higher risk of developing heart disease.[17]

Surgery

liposuction
While surgical procedures for body composition change are less popular than other approaches, they are becoming increasingly available. The most common surgical approach today is **liposuction,** in which unwanted fat is sucked through a hollow tube after a surgical incision has been made. Liposuction was introduced in the United States several years ago and has become one of the most popular and controversial forms of cosmetic surgery. About 100,000 Americans undergo liposuction every year.[18] While liposuction may remove some unwanted fat, it does not cure obesity or deal with the underlying causes of a weight problem.

A variation of liposuction aimed at changing body proportions is called fat recycling, or fat grafting. In this procedure fat is sucked from one part of the body and put back somewhere else, often on the breasts. Done primarily for cosmetic purposes, fat grafting is an unproven and perhaps dangerous method of redistributing body composition.

Another surgical approach to the management of body composition involves stomach stapling. While stapling the stomach may result in weight loss, it carries a risk of complications. Stomach tissue is often damaged, and scar tissue may form. In addition, the resultant weight loss depends on the individual's ability to limit food consumption after surgery.

Group Weight-Loss Programs

Group weight-loss programs are big business. Each week over 1 million people participate in such programs, most of which include a dietary component and many of which encourage dieters to exercise. Although rapid weight gain may result once these programs are discontinued, they have enabled many people to achieve a permanent change in their nutritional style and thus their body composition.

A key element in these programs is the external support provided by the group leader and the other participants. Other important features include exposure to successful role models, peer pressure, group solidarity, and healthy competition among participants. One of the best-known group programs, Weight Watchers, combines diet, exercise, and behavior modification and offers some of the latest techniques for controlling body composition. Nutrition experts agree that group programs are helpful for some people, particularly those who are only moderately overweight.[19]

Other commercial weight-loss programs are the Diet Center and Nutri/System. These programs differ from Weight Watchers in that individuals are counseled on a one-to-one basis rather than exclusively in group sessions.

Understanding Body Composition Problems

With all the approaches offered for managing body composition, it seems odd that so few people succeed in losing weight and then keeping it off. A recent study reported that only 12 percent of the people in weight-loss programs lost as much as 20 pounds and that only 17 percent of that group kept the weight off for 2 years.[20]

There is no single theory or set of factors that can fully explain why some people gain or lose weight more readily than do others. There are, however, two general schools of thought for explaining body composition problems.[21] One approach, called the pull school, sees weight problems as being greatly influenced by physiological factors. The other, known as the push school, sees such problems as being more the result of psychological or social factors.

The Pull School: Physiological Bases for Body Composition Problems

The pull school argues that overeating results at least in part from physical metabolic factors that generate false signals to the body. The desire to overeat is stimulated by the "pull" of these factors. The eating response in turn leads to behaviors that increase eating and sustain excess weight. Overeating behaviors are developed as a result of physiological stimuli rather than psychological needs. A number of physiological factors are known or thought to contribute to body composition problems.

Genetic Factors   It is taken for granted that hair and eye color, facial features and height are inherited traits. No one is surprised when a 6 foot, 2 inch father has a taller-than-average son or daughter. Evidence suggests that the genes a person inherits may influence that person's body composition just as they influence other physical traits. Data from genetic analyses strongly indicate that patterns of fat distribution within the body may be inherited. In addition, data on the body weight and body composition of adopted children and their biological parents show an impressive correlation, indicating a strong genetic influence rather than an environmental one. To some extent, therefore, body composition problems may be inherited.[22]

Regulatory Factors   Body composition problems are thought to be caused in part by disorders of certain regulatory mechanisms in the body. The body's need for food is caused by the interaction of two regulatory mechanisms, one short term and the other long term. The short-term regulatory mechanism signals the body when to eat and when to stop eating. The long-term regulatory mechanism monitors the body's nutrient levels over extended periods and controls food intake so that body weight is maintained within a relatively narrow range.

When existing fat cells reach their maximum size, new fat cells are produced. The tendency for fat cells to enlarge and increase in number may result not only in a permanent increase in weight but also in maintenance of that weight. The phenomenon known as the *yo-yo effect*, which occurs when people who have reached a certain weight seem fated to return to that weight, is now thought to be a result of this physiological mechanism. The setpoint theory described below helps explain this phenomenon.

Setpoint Theory   Many people have had the frustrating experience of going on a diet, losing a few pounds in a week or two, and then hitting a plateau at which their weight seems to stay the same no matter how little they eat. The
setpoint theory
setpoint theory has suggested an explanation for this phenomenon. The basis of this theory is that each person has a given weight range—the setpoint—that is natural to his or her body.[23] Depending on their setpoints, some people stay thin and others stay fat regardless of what they eat. People who have a high setpoint are going to have problems trying to lose weight.
basal metabolism
The number of calories burned at rest (but not while sleeping) is called **basal metabolism.** Setpoint theorists argue that the body can change its basal metabolism to keep weight at the setpoint. The body reacts to a strict diet as if preparing for a prolonged famine: it hoards fat reserves to keep from starving to death. Suppose a person with a high setpoint tries to lose weight by means of strict dieting. Setpoint theorists hypothesize that this person's brain "senses" what is happening and the body responds by slowing its metabolism—burning food more slowly—to keep its weight stable. If the setpoint theory is correct, dieting will always be difficult because no matter how hard a person tries to cut back on food, that person's body will fight back by burning food more efficiently.

Although this theory makes a good deal of sense, there is not much scientific evidence to support it. Even if the theory is ultimately confirmed, this does not mean that people cannot lose weight. There are ways to speed the basal metabolism and thus lower the setpoint. The safest way to raise the body's overall metabolic rate is to increase physical activity.

The Push School: Psychological Bases for Body Composition Problems

Although most people accept the idea that body composition is affected by a variety of factors related to behavior, attitudes, and values, the push school argues that obesity is primarily a behavioral disorder. The urge to eat is caused not so much by physiological signals from the digestive and metabolic systems but more by psychological needs. In effect, people are driven by behavioral habit to "push" food into their digestive systems.

Proponents of the push school feel that people need to change their attitudes and behaviors about food in order to change their body composition. Such an approach can be difficult, as anyone who has tried to change an attitude or behavior can attest. Nevertheless, it remains an important approach to body composition management.

Behavioral Factors   One of the earliest approaches to the relationship of behavior to obesity was called the **externality theory.** Proponents of this theory argued that overweight people eat primarily in response to external food-related cues. Thus, it is the sight and smell of a steak more than internal hunger caused by metabolic needs that make such people eager to eat.

externality theory

Several studies have suggested that overweight persons do not in the long run eat much more per unit of lean body mass than do nonoverweight persons.[24] (This is to be expected given the ideas of setpoint theory.) However, many experts maintain that the eating behaviors of people with body composition problems are different from the behaviors of people who do not have these problems. One researcher has identified four behavioral differences between thin and fat people.[25]

1. Thin people do not think about food and hardly ever eat unless they are hungry. Their lives do not revolve around food, nor do they relate food to depression or sadness or use it to replace love, comfort, or companionship.
2. Thin people eat exactly what and when they want. They eat not just to be eating but because a particular food appeals to them at a particular moment.
3. Thin people eat consciously. They know what and how much they are eating and eat only enough food to satisfy hunger.
4. Thin people stop eating when the body is no longer hungry. They will ignore food, leave it on the plate, and even throw it away if they do not want it.

The Impact of Habits, Ideas, and Values   Push school theory emphasizes that the ways in which people think and behave in regard to food are rooted in a variety of habits, ideas, and values developed throughout their lifetimes. The quality of food you eat, how often you eat, and how much you eat are all based on simple habits. These habits are learned and then generated by the subconscious. Rather than the brain determining the body's *need* for food from internal physiological signals, life experiences have shaped the mind's *desire* for food.

Many body composition problems result at least partially from the ways in which such habits direct people's behavior and affect the way they use food. A

Obesity is known to have a genetic component, but learned eating habits also contribute to excessive weight. (Van Bucher/Photo Researchers, Inc.)

person cannot achieve and maintain a desirable weight and body composition without replacing habits that encourage overweight or underweight with other, more appropriate habits and behaviors.

Ideas and values formed early in life may also contribute to body composition problems. As children, people learn values, attitudes, and beliefs from their experiences and their parents, teachers, friends, and other role models. Attitudes often teach people to eat for reasons other than hunger and bodily requirements. Many people retain into adulthood views which continue to affect their eating behaviors. When people can recognize the views, attitudes, and behaviors that lead them to gain weight, they are in a better position to alter those habits and change their body composition.

Some of these attitudes and beliefs may have a great impact on a person's ability to achieve and maintain ideal weight and body composition. They may relate to a person's body image and attitudes toward proper nutrition and exercise. For many people, achieving and maintaining ideal body composition requires replacing health-destructive ideas, attitudes, and self-images with positive, health-enhancing ones.

Compensatory Overeating   Many scientists have suggested that people may overeat to compensate for something missing in their lives.[26] Eating gives them a feeling of satisfaction that cannot be obtained in any other way. The question people should ask themselves in such cases is: What do I really need that I am substituting this food for? By identifying the real need, a person can strive to fulfill it rather than to compensate for it.

Successful Control of Body Composition

Unfortunately, it is not advisable to try to alter quickly what took months or years to develop. Techniques for weight change that promise quick and easy results are usually ineffective and can be dangerous. The most successful programs for body composition management promote long-term changes in lifestyle—modifying unhealthy attitudes, beliefs, and habits—that lead to effective weight control. Body composition problems can best be overcome by combining proper nutrition, appropriate exercise, and appropriate eating behaviors.

Regulating Body Composition

Before looking at the components of a successful program for body composition management, it is useful to understand how the body regulates weight. The basic principle of weight regulation is the energy-balance equation:

Change in energy stores   = energy intake − energy expenditure
(body composition change)   (food/drink)   (activity/exercise)

The energy-balance equation suggests that body weight can be maintained at a stable level when the energy intake (calories from food and drink) equals the amount of energy expended (calories burned as a result of metabolism, activity, and exercise). If energy intake and expenditure are not equal, the result will be a gain or a loss of weight. For each 3,500 calories consumed in excess of energy expenditure, the body stores an additional pound of fat. Each time 3,500 calories are eaten below the level expended, the body loses a pound of fat.

The body adheres strictly to the energy-balance equation. While it can apparently (in setpoint theory) change the amount of calories that a particular exercise will burn, it *never* loses track of the excess calories consumed. As a result, weight gain often results from a slow and subtle process in which the body gradually accumulates excess calories and stores them as fat.

Natural Body Composition Management

Since the body regulates energy intake and expenditure so carefully, it is not realistic to try to lose weight by dieting for a while and then going back to old eating habits. Excess calories will accumulate again and lead to weight gain. Nearly everyone who goes on periodic diets gains back all the weight lost. Effective body composition management requires a long-range program that includes behavioral change, proper nutrition, sensible eating, and exercise.

Exercising Right for Body Composition Management   Over the long term exercise is an essential tool in an effective weight management program. Even if one's eating habits remain the same, beginning a program of regular physical exercise will start to shrink the body's fat tissues. A pound of fat can be lost in 7 to 12 exercise sessions.

Reducing the consumption of high-fat foods will also lead to a substantial loss of fat over time. One expert has estimated that an exercise program consisting of a brisk 1-hour walk three times a week plus a reduction of 100 calories a day in food consumed will produce a weight loss of 20 to 30 pounds in a year.[27]

Some people may wonder whether an increase in physical activity is likely to make an individual eat more. While vigorous exercise may cause a person to consume more calories over the long run, the calories consumed do not equal the calories burned while exercising.

People might also question whether the muscle mass developed through exercise will result in regaining lost weight. While some pounds may come back, exercise helps ensure that they are pounds of muscle, not fat. Remember that muscle is heavier than fat. When a person gets heavier because the body has more muscle, that person is still leaner and thinner (and healthier) than he or she was when the body weighed less but had more fat.

What is the best exercise program for successful body composition management? The ACSM recommends the following program:[28]

- Exercise at least 3 days a week, although 4 or 5 is even better.
- Exercise for at least 20 minutes at each session.
- Exercise should be a continuous and rhythmic aerobic type, such as walking, jogging, swimming, or bicycling.
- People over age 35 should not start a strenuous exercise program without first getting a checkup from a doctor.

People of any age can hurt themselves by starting a vigorous exercise program too quickly, especially if they have not previously been active. Therefore, an exercise program should start out slowly and include lighter, less strenuous

Junk foods are appetizing for the same reasons that they are not recommended: they contain considerable amounts of salt and fat. But people also eat them because they fit in with their lifestyle habits—always in a hurry and with no time to prepare meals. (Felicia Martinez/ PhotoEdit)

exercise at first. As the exercise program progresses, it can gradually include more strenuous activities. The important goal, however, is not to exercise strenuously but to exercise regularly.

Eating Right for Body Composition Management   A successful weight management program must also deal with what one eats. The key to achieving and maintaining a desired weight loss is a high-carbohydrate, adequate-protein, low-fat diet. The term *diet* here does not mean a temporary change in how a person eats. It means a lifelong commitment, taken one day at a time, to eating more whole grains, fresh fruits, vegetables, and fewer fast foods, processed foods, fatty meats, and rich desserts. Similarly, permanent changes in eating as well as exercise habits are required to achieve weight gain. An important step in any program for body composition management is to change the quality but not necessarily the quantity of the food consumed. Eating more low-fat, high-carbohydrate foods will decrease the number of calories consumed, since fats have more than twice the calories of carbohydrates and proteins.[29]

The body metabolizes carbohydrates faster than it does fats, which are burned slowly and stored in the body until needed. Thus, when the consumption of high-fat foods is decreased, there is a reduced accumulation of excess fat in the body. Recent studies have reinforced the idea that low-fat diets are an effective approach to body composition management.[30]

Since the body needs proper nutrition, care must be taken if a person decides to decrease the quantity of food consumed. Nutrition surveys suggest that the American people, especially women, young children, and teenage girls, already are at the low end (less than 80 percent) of the estimated daily requirements of calcium, magnesium, iron, zinc, and manganese.[31] For this reason, it is important to improve the overall quality of food consumed before reducing the size of portions. Most people can accomplish their weight-loss goals through a combined program of increased exercise and improved diet. Improving the quality of the diet not only ensures better nutrition but also results in caloric reduction without decreasing the size of the portions eaten.

One way to fulfill your nutritional requirements is to eat high-quality snacks throughout the day. Frequent eating of nutritious foods also promotes feelings of fullness that help control the appetite. As a general rule, eating five smaller meals a day is better than eating two or three large ones.

Surprisingly, eating frequent small meals that include starchy foods such as corn, rice, and potatoes will also help people who are underweight. For these people, the problem is to *increase* caloric intake, which may be difficult if they are unused to eating large meals. Ideally, they should consume 1,000 to 1,500 calories more than they use each day, at the same time exercising so that these calories do not turn to fat.

Proper nutrition is the cornerstone of a successful program for body composition management. The following guidelines should be considered when you are developing or evaluating a nutritionally sound food plan for weight management.[32]

- Eat a quantity of food that will help you achieve a safe, progressive weight loss of 1 to 2 pounds a week.
- Consume macronutrients (proteins and carbohydrates) in the amounts recommended in the U.S. Dietary Goals.
- Consume micronutrients (vitamins and minerals) in amounts recommended in the RDAs.

Make exercise enjoyable and it will be much easier to maintain it as part of your weight management program. (Michael Philip Manheim/Southern Light)

- Be aware of and avoid excessive amounts of cholesterol, sodium, and fat.
- Eat a wide variety of high-quality foods in moderation.
- Be sure to include in your diet foods that can provide fiber—fruits, vegetables, or breads—and at least 4 pints of water.

Weight Disorders and Eating Disorders

In addition to the body composition problems experienced by so many Americans, there are specific weight and eating disorders that afflict smaller proportions of the population. Before you embark on a program for weight gain or loss, it is wise to consider whether you have a more atypical problem.

Extreme Obesity

Although most people who become obese do so as a result of the eating and exercise habits of American society, there are a few whose excess weight seems to have been caused by other factors. Most frequently blamed is the thyroid gland, which controls the rate and efficiency of the metabolism, but research seems to show that malfunctioning of this gland is only rarely responsible for obesity. In some cases extreme obesity may in fact be caused by lesions in the brain, particularly in the hypothalamus, the part which receives energy signals from the body and controls hunger. Perhaps more common is obesity that is associated with diabetes. While some theorists maintain that obesity causes diabetes, others argue that diabetes and obesity may both be caused by the same insulin abnormality.

Cases of extreme obesity are best treated with a slow, deliberate weight loss rather than a crash diet. Exercise is clearly more of a problem, but it is still recommended.

Anorexia Nervosa

At the other extreme is a disorder in which people severely limit the amount they eat, in effect starving themselves. This condition is called **anorexia** (loss of appetite) **nervosa** (nervous or psychogenic). The great majority of people with anorexia are teenage girls and young women; only about 10 percent are men. Most people with anorexia come from upper-class or middle-class homes and often seemed like model children before developing the disorder.

anorexia nervosa

Description   In a typical case of anorexia, the victim mysteriously becomes increasingly obsessed with the idea that he or she is fat. This leads to continuous and extreme dieting in an attempt to lose weight.

About one-third of those suffering from anorexia are mildly overweight before developing the disorder. Simple dieting to lose weight leads to a life characterized by a repetition of the same meal day after day, coupled with exhausting exercise, personal isolation, and social withdrawal. For some reason, a person with anorexia feels fat even after losing weight and continues dieting to the point of starvation.

In the United States 1 in every 250 women aged 12 to 18 develops anorexia nervosa. An estimated 9 percent of these women die of starvation; between 2 and 5 percent more commit suicide.[33] According to the *Diagnostic and Statisti-*

It is hard to believe that someone this thin can believe that she is overweight, but victims of anorexia nervosa not only believe it, they diet to lose still more weight. (Visual Education Corporation Archives)

cal Manual of Mental Disorders, a diagnosis of anorexia nervosa requires evidence of the following:

- An intense fear of becoming obese that does not diminish as weight loss progresses
- A disturbance of body image (for example, claiming to "feel fat" even when emaciated)
- A loss of at least 25 percent of original body weight
- A refusal to maintain normal body weight[34]

Some experts have suggested that young women with anorexia may have abnormal fears of approaching womanhood. In losing so much weight, they lose their feminine curves, stop menstruating, and begin to look like little girls again. Specialists in treating anorexia feel strongly that both psychological counseling and medical treatment are necessary.

Medical Effects   In addition to loss of menstruation, the most common medical consequence of anorexia in women is estrogen deficiency. This deficiency may contribute to osteoporosis. In men with anorexia, testosterone levels may diminish, and this can contribute to impotence.[35]

Anorexia can also cause a slowed heart rate, slowed reflexes and respiratory rate, kidney problems, and cardiac arrest. The general malnutrition resulting from anorexia may cause lethargy, memory lapses, and even hallucinations and feelings of paranoia.

Bulimia

bulimia   **Bulimia,** a disorder characterized by eating binges followed by vomiting, may occur with anorexia nervosa or as a separate illness with different psychological roots. According to the U.S. Food and Drug Administration, the symptoms of bulimia are found in 40 to 50 percent of people with anorexia nervosa.[36] As with anorexia, the majority of bulimia victims are women, typically in their early twenties, college-educated, single, and white. Unlike those with anorexia, the victims of bulimia tend to be of nearly normal weight and have healthy, outgoing personalities. The greatest difference is that a person with anorexia turns away from food while a person with bulimia is obsessively drawn to it.

Description   There is a distinct pattern to the eating binges of people with bulimia. An individual with this disorder typically eats secretly, consuming an enormous amount of food at one sitting. The urge that drives such eating is clearly something beyond simple hunger. After the eating binge comes the need to vomit or take laxatives to make sure the food does not stay in the body and produce a weight gain.

An occasional eating binge does not necessarily signal bulimia. Most people overeat to the point of discomfort at one time or another. However, the following signs may indicate that a person is suffering from bulimia:

- Recurrent eating binges that the person realizes are abnormal but cannot stop voluntarily
- Eating binges followed by abdominal pain, sleep, or self-induced vomiting
- Repeated attempts to lose weight by severe dieting, self-induced vomiting, or an excessive use of laxatives and/or diuretics
- Regular fluctuations of more than 10 pounds in weight because of binge-and-fast episodes
- Feelings of depression after binge eating[37]

Medical Effects   While fewer deaths result annually from bulimia than from anorexia nervosa, the characteristic binge eating can cause an enlarged stomach and even stomach rupture. Repeated vomiting can cause chronic swelling of the salivary glands, rashes, swelling around the ankles and feet, and inflammation of or tears in the esophagus.[38]

Causes of Anorexia and Bulimia

Current theories about the cause of these eating disorders fall into three categories: physiological, sociocultural, and psychological. Certain physiological factors linked to depression may contribute to the development of these disorders. Seven of 10 persons with anorexia and/or bulimia are prone to depression, as are many of their relatives.[39] The setpoint theory has also supplied a possible causal factor.

Sociocultural factors that contribute to these disorders may include the undue significance attached to slimness and physical appearance in American culture, particularly among adolescent girls.[40]

There is also evidence to support a psychological cause of anorexia and bulimia. A report in the *New England Journal of Medicine* indicated that many people with these conditions have distorted attitudes and concepts that affect most areas of their lives. These attitudes include the idea that one should strive for perfection, that thinness is admirable while fat is disgusting, and that weight gain is a sign of lack of control.[41]

Whatever their cause, anorexia nervosa and bulimia are difficult to treat. The patterns associated with them are not easily disrupted. Moreover, many people with anorexia deny having the illness and refuse treatment. Those with bulimia, though frequently more inclined to seek treatment, often become easily frustrated and drop out of treatment.

Achieving Your Goals

Even people who suffer from problems such as extreme obesity, anorexia, and bulimia can often make progress if they receive good advice and are able to make the effort. Body composition problems do require knowledge and determination, but in most cases they *can* be corrected.

An important part of a successful program for body composition management must involve identifying unproductive attitudes toward food and replacing them with positive, healthy, esteem-building thoughts and beliefs. This is an essential part of achieving successful weight management.

While short-term progress may result from either a change in diet or an increase in exercise, long-term success requires that psychological changes be made. Fortunately, short-term progress can increase one's feelings of self-efficacy, and such confidence can provide support in the long term.

Chapter Summary

- The American obsession with weight control could more accurately be described as a concern about appearance and health.
- Body composition, specifically the proportion of fat to other tissues in the human body, can have long-term as well as short-term physical effects. It is a major influence in the development of heart disease and other chronic complaints later in life.
- Because of the effects of body image on self-concept, the fat content of one's body composition can have a profound effect on one's emotional and social life.
- Fats, while vital for human health and activity, are easily stored in excessive quantities and may be distributed in ways that are harmful to health. Americans in general have too much fat in their body composition.
- Techniques used to estimate body fat include the hydrostatic weighing, bioelectrical impedance, and skinfold measurement methods.
- Diets are the most common approach to body composition management in the United States. There are many types of diets, some beneficial and others harmful.
- Appetite suppressant drugs, surgery, and group programs employing social pressure are other techniques for losing weight, but to keep weight off, diet and exercise are the most important factors.
- Altering body composition has proved to be difficult for most Americans.
- The pull school argues that there are compelling physiological reasons why people gain and maintain weight, including genetic factors, disorders of the regulatory systems, and the development of a setpoint for body composition.

- The push school maintains that ingrained psychological habits of eating and food choice help maintain harmful eating behaviors.

- Today the theories of both schools are accepted as valid. Successful body composition control involves understanding the physiological mechanisms of the appetite and personal psychological habits.

- The energy-balance equation of food and drink taken in versus energy consumed by exercise, activity, and basal metabolism is fundamental to all programs for the loss or gain of weight.

- Adequate exercise is the first requirement for body composition management.

- A change of diet to nutritious foods rich in vitamins and minerals is the second important step for control of body composition.

- Calorie-controlled diets may be necessary, but only if the other two steps have already been taken.

- Even in potentially destructive eating and weight disorders such as severe obesity, anorexia nervosa, and bulimia, the energy-balance equation is important. However, in these cases medical and psychological help are almost certainly indicated as well.

- If a person has understanding and a willingness to work, body composition problems can usually be controlled.

Emotional Health and Intellectual Well-Being

Objectives

When you have studied this chapter, you should be able to:

- Identify two basic dimensions of the human mind and explain how they have an impact on each other and on health.

- Describe six physiological responses that are linked to the emotions.

- Explain how emotional responses are learned and how people can deal with their negative emotional states to achieve emotional health.

- Name and describe several types of nonpsychotic disorders and psychotic disorders.

- Distinguish between the two main components of intellect and describe the activities for which they serve as a foundation.

- Explain how self-concept, different types of therapy, and individual attention can help people develop a healthy self-image and work on mental health problems.

As you read in Chapter 1, health has several different dimensions that can be viewed separately but are intricately interrelated. Even though health is most commonly considered a physical attribute, it can also be thought of in mental, social, and spiritual terms. Of these, the mental—emotional and intellectual—aspects can be viewed as a key to all the rest. In the end, the satisfactions that people gain from their health and their lives are perceived as thoughts and feelings.

It is in the mind that people decide about the trade-offs involving health comfort levels that they make. Are you willing to put up with being above your ideal weight because you prefer to devote more time to painting than to physical exercise? Should you put off dealing with your social problems and watch television or play a video game? Decisions such as these are made in the mind.

Even at the unconscious level, the mind is a key to health. The brain coordinates the rest of the body. Physical health and social and spiritual health do affect mental functioning, but it is the mind and brain that can control, and benefit from, decisions people make about health.

The human mind has two basic dimensions: affective (emotional) and cognitive (intellectual). The affective dimension allows people to experience a wide range of feelings—love, hate, anger, sadness, despair, hope, and so on. The cognitive dimension lets people store and recall an enormous amount of information. It also enables people to think abstractly.

There is a constant interaction between these two dimensions of consciousness. Recalling an event or a person can make a person feel sad, happy, or angry. Pondering an idea can elicit feelings of frustration, joy, or despair. In addition, emotion and intellect have a significant impact on health, as does the interaction between them.

Emotions

Emotions are powerful forces within people's lives. They represent the feeling, nonrational side of the mind and provide the emotional ups and downs that everyone experiences. Emotions are also related to physical health—feeling bad emotionally may cause a person to feel bad physically as well. A person facing a difficult problem may get a tension headache; someone whose lifestyle includes habitual stress may develop a **psychosomatic disease** (a physical problem caused by the mind).

psychosomatic disease

Conversely, feeling well emotionally can help a person feel better physically. Surgeons routinely evaluate their patients' emotional state before operating on them because it has been learned that these emotional states can have an important effect on a patient's chances for recovery. Improving one's emotional health can thus be a powerful tool in the treatment of physical disease.

The Physiology of Emotion

Although most people think of an emotion as something which takes place solely in the mind, there are actually physical components to the emotions. When a person experiences an emotion, the body reacts with certain physical changes. The person perceives and interprets these changes as feelings of happiness, sadness, fear, and so on. An emotion is a complex combination of mental perceptions and physiological changes.

Figure 5.1 *Although much remains to be discovered, scientists have made considerable progress in determining the functions of different areas of the central nervous system. The part of the brain involved with emotions (the limbic system) is in the center of the underside of the brain. It includes the hypothalamus and is connected with the autonomic (sympathetic and parasympathetic) nervous system.*

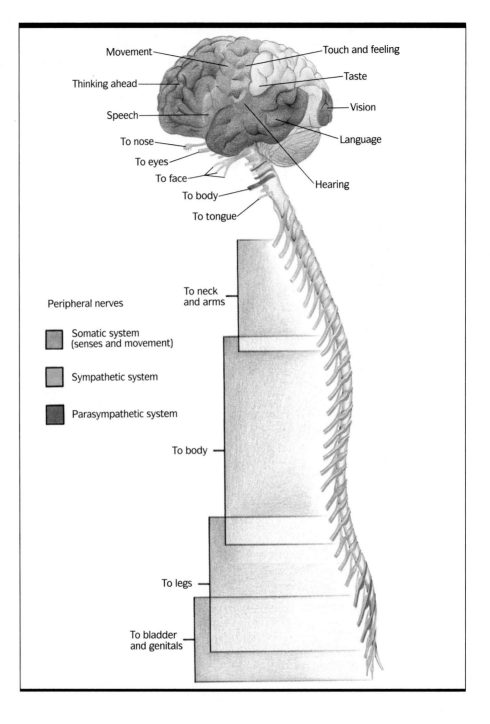

Movement

Touch and feeling

Thinking ahead

Taste

Speech

Vision

To nose

Language

To eyes

To face

Hearing

To body

To tongue

To neck and arms

Peripheral nerves

- Somatic system (senses and movement)
- Sympathetic system
- Parasympathetic system

To body

To legs

To bladder and genitals

How does the intricate relationship between emotions and physiological changes work? The answer lies in the organization of the nervous system (Figure 5.1). The nervous system has two levels: the **central nervous system (CNS),** which includes the brain and spinal cord, and the **peripheral nervous system (PNS),** which includes all the other nerves in the body.

The CNS is the command post of the body. It regulates and integrates all bodily functions, receiving and processing information and directing body

central nervous system (CNS)
peripheral nervous system (PNS)

movements. The spinal cord is responsible for receiving and transmitting tactile and motor information.

The PNS is divided into two distinct systems: the **somatic nervous system (SNS),** which is connected to the voluntary muscles and consists of nerves that run between the sensory and motor organs, and the **autonomic nervous system (ANS),** which is linked to the involuntary muscles, for example, the heart, arteries, and glands. The ANS is the part of the nervous system involved most directly with the emotions. It is through the ANS that the physical expression of emotion is controlled.

somatic nervous system (SNS)

autonomic nervous system (ANS)

Scientists commonly look at six physiological responses linked to the emotions: heart rate, blood volume, blood pressure, electrodermal responses, muscle potential, and brain wave patterns (electroencephalograms). All are controlled by the nervous system.

Heart Rate   This is the physiological response people think of first in connection with emotional situations, because it is easy to recognize a thumping heart. Heart rate can fluctuate a great deal depending on a person's emotional state and other factors.

Blood Volume   Blood vessels constrict and dilate (expand), altering the rate at which blood flows through them. When someone grows pale with fear, the flow of blood to the face has been restricted.

Blood Pressure   This term refers to the force exerted by the heart as it contracts to push blood out of the arteries and then relaxes. During highly charged emotional states, blood pressure can change drastically.

Electrodermal Responses   The skin, like the rest of the body, can conduct electricity. People sweat during strongly emotional states, and the added moisture makes the skin better able to conduct electricity than it is at other times.

Muscle Potential   Muscles often give visible signs of emotion, such as the tightening of the jaw during anger.

Electroencephalogram   The brain emits electric waves that can be measured by placing electrodes on the skull. The resulting pattern of waves is called an **electroencephalogram (EEG).**

electroencephalogram (EEG)

The Psychology of Emotion

The responses just described are physiological changes connected with all emotions. They are related to psychological feelings in a complex way. The process begins with an environmental stimulus such as the sudden noise of a balloon popping. This is relayed to the brain, causing an immediate reaction in the autonomic nervous system, leading to symptoms such as increased heart rate and blood pressure.

The person experiencing such physical reactions interprets them as an emotion, but what determines whether a person interprets particular physical reactions as fear, amusement, annoyance, or another emotion? It depends greatly on what the person has experienced in the past. People learn over their lifetimes how to interpret their experiences and emotional sensations. They learn emotional responses by association and by observing the experiences of others.

Learning by Association   The process that underlies learning by association is classical conditioning, which is mentioned later in this chapter. Most psychologists agree that emotional responses are particularly susceptible to classical conditioning.[1] A student who experiences fear and discomfort during an exam for which he or she is not prepared may experience the same feelings as soon as another exam is mentioned. This student has learned to associate the painful emotions of a particular experience with a whole category of objects and events—a process known as **generalization.**

generalization

Learning by Observation   People also learn emotional responses by observing the experiences of others. Consider the first experiences of a small child at the circus. Circus clowns often move wildly, wear aggressively colored clothes, and run through the audience. When a little child is first confronted with a clown, the first reaction may be to cry or even feel terror. However, the child hears the laughter of others, realizes that the clown is harmless, and is able to convert the feelings of fear into joyous amusement.

Negative Emotions and Emotional Conflict

Happiness, affection, excitement—these and other pleasant emotions make life seem wonderful. Everyone wants his or her life to be filled with such good feelings. But people's lives are not filled with positive emotions all the time. Many events in life are stressful and produce unpleasant, negative feelings. Such emotions can be triggered by a wide variety of events. The negative feelings that result can disrupt a person's emotional well-being.

An important part of emotional health involves learning to cope with negative emotions. Coping represents an attempt to remove or resolve a stressful situation or insulate oneself from the negative emotions that it can cause.

Negative feelings may result directly from unhappy situations such as fear of harm and sadness at loss. Everyone's life includes situations which give rise to such emotions, and they must generally be accepted and lived through. If a person is able to cope with a situation successfully, he or she will return to a normal state of emotional well-being.

Other negative feelings may arise from conflicts between different emotions, and in these cases it can be helpful to understand what is happening. Anger, for example, can be a positive force for doing good, but open displays of anger are disapproved of in most societies. This makes people feel conflicted about being angry. Other negative feelings also often result from feelings that people do not wish to acknowledge.

Anger   Anger is a natural human response. Some people, however, feel angry and frustrated much of the time. They may be more vulnerable to external stressors. They may need to desensitize themselves or learn to filter out the hurts the world throws in their direction. They may also need to look behind their anger to find out what other feelings it may be covering up and try to deal with those feelings.

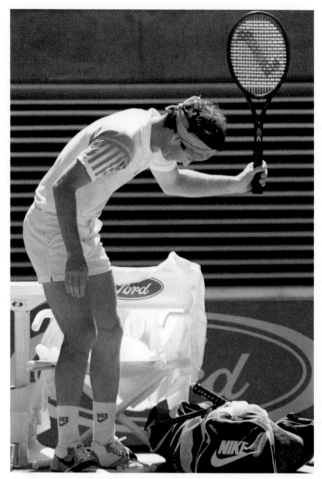

Anger is a natural human reaction to unpleasant moments and frustrating circumstances. Sometimes expressing the emotion can spur one to higher achievement; at other times it merely releases the tension. (left: Reuters/Bettman; right: Ron Grishaber/PhotoEdit)

If you feel that you are reacting with anger too often, try some of these techniques to cope with your angry feelings.

- Practice stress management techniques (Chapter 6) and work to develop feelings of security and self-esteem.
- Try to reduce competitive feelings so that you are not constantly under stress at work, at play, or with other people. This will help you ignore what might seem to be painful challenges in your environment.
- Figure out why you are reacting so strongly to a particular situation. Avoid situations and people who make you angry or see if you can change the way you perceive the situation.
- Sometimes anger is caused by frustration. Look at the situation and try to figure out what is frustrating you—and then do something about it.
- Anger can get even worse if you express it. This is particularly true if you feel helpless to cause change. In some situations it is better to deal with the underlying difficulties or let the matter drop rather than risk increasing feelings of anxiety and hostility by yelling.[2]

Anxiety   Anxiety usually occurs when a person feels fear that is related to an expected loss or hurt. Occasionally people feel "free-floating" anxiety, in which they cannot identify the reason for their fear. It does not matter whether the expectation is real or imagined; the fear is very real. In most cases the fear is over some loss or hurt that may occur in the future. People often feel that things are out of their control, and thus the anxiety is heightened.

The most effective way to deal with anxiety is to work toward regaining a feeling of *self-efficacy*—the feeling that you can control the events in your life or at least your reactions to them. Start by admitting to yourself that you are afraid of being hurt or losing someone or something important to you. Sometimes simply admitting that you are vulnerable to a loss or hurt can help relieve the anxiety.

Once the sources of anxiety are brought out into the open, they can be examined objectively. Imaginary fears can be seen for what they are, and real threats to your well-being or self-esteem can be better understood.

Minor Depression   Minor depression is sometimes referred to as the common cold of emotional disorders. Most people feel depressed at times. *Depression* is a "down" feeling that is usually associated with loss of self-esteem. It also may be due to anger that is directed inward.

To get over depression, start by directing energy away from yourself. Exercise, gardening, reading, and other distracting activities can often help break a depressed mood. Make a daily schedule so that you can structure your activities toward a productive end. Also, try to identify any sources of anger and allow your trapped feelings to escape.

While it is common to feel depressed, some people are more likely to become depressed and stay depressed longer than others are. If a depression is unusually severe or lasts more than a few weeks, the condition may be serious enough to require treatment.

The Use of Defense Mechanisms   Finding ways to cope with painful emotions is one of the most critical ongoing efforts of people's lives. Change is an inevitable part of the human condition: a family breaks up, a child leaves home, a mother or wife returns to work, a person finds a new job or goes to a new school. People are forced to adapt to all these changes. Luckily, the mind and body are adaptable. People may work through such adaptations by using **defense mechanisms**—mental strategies for preserving one's sense of self by protecting oneself from the anxiety associated with painful emotions.[3]

defense mechanism

Defense mechanisms can lead to problems if they become a person's primary or only way of dealing with painful emotions. However, they can also be used to help an individual adjust temporarily to stressful situations. People use several common defense mechanisms.

repression   • **Repression** is considered the most basic defense mechanism. A person who is repressing denies any awareness of thoughts, feelings, memories, or wishes that are threatening. He or she refuses to acknowledge a response that would ordinarily be expected in specific circumstances. For example, a child who displays no anger or distress during his or her parents' divorce may be repressing fears and anxieties.

rationalization   • **Rationalization** is a defense mechanism in which people assure themselves and others that they acted from better motives than was probably the case. A student who claims that her poor performance doesn't matter because she was too busy helping others may be rationalizing negligence of responsibility for schoolwork.

- **Denial** is a defense mechanism in which a person covers up truths about the outer world, ignoring those which threaten self-esteem or create anxiety. Thus, a person may not hear an insulting remark even though it is spoken clearly and within hearing distance. *denial*

- **Projection** is an attempt to attribute one's undesirable feelings, wishes, and motives to other people or even inanimate objects. A man who is about to be married, for instance, may claim that his roommate is interested in every good-looking woman who walks down the street. He may be projecting onto his roommate the unacceptable feelings he has about other women. *projection*

- **Psychic contactlessness** refers to an inability to communicate with or become intimate with others. A person who is deeply afraid of being hurt by intimacy, perhaps because he or she has been hurt in the past, is suffering from psychic contactlessness. Such persons keep their self-esteem intact: nobody can hurt them because nobody is allowed to get close enough to do so. *psychic contactlessness*

- A person who does not acknowledge that other people are fully human, with human feelings and emotions, is using a defense mechanism called **depersonalization.** Racial prejudice often contains strong elements of depersonalization: "That person doesn't experience the same needs or desires that I do, so it doesn't matter if he or she suffers socially or economically." Depersonalization has been used to justify slavery, pogroms, and other acts of violence against entire groups of people. *depersonalization*

- **Sublimation** refers to the substitution of socially acceptable behavior for unacceptable impulses such as hostility and aggression. Some people, for example, may become workaholics who work compulsively long hours each day rather than face the angry feelings they have about their home lives. *sublimation*

Many emotions bring people in a society together. If the emotions were unexpressed, people would feel more isolated from each other. (Robert Brenner/PhotoEdit)

The use of these various defense mechanisms is normal. Everyone resorts to them to one degree or another. They are not necessarily negative. They can serve as a moderating force in people's lives when change is too stressful, giving people time to marshal their resources and gain the strength to face new challenges.[4] Many defense mechanisms thus serve important positive purposes. In one study, university students who used defense mechanisms were found to have reduced their tension and anxiety significantly.[5] A mentally healthy person uses a variety of defense mechanisms when necessary in order to adjust successfully to stress and problems.

What Is Emotional Health?

What are the basic qualities associated with emotionally healthy people? Most authorities agree that emotionally healthy people exhibit the following characteristics.

- They are able to understand reality and deal with it constructively.
- They can adapt to reasonable demands for change.
- They have a reasonable degree of self-efficacy.
- They can cope with stress.
- They are concerned about other people.
- They have the ability to love.
- They are able to work productively.
- They act in ways that meet their basic needs.

Emotional health is a complex quality. It is not a static condition but a dynamic process, and it does not imply total control over one's emotions. A person's emotional state varies day by day. All people have days when they feel good about themselves and the world around them and days when most things seem to go wrong and they feel bad about themselves. Emotional health implies a balance among the emotions.

A person who is emotionally healthy is not a person who has no problems but a person who has learned to adjust and cope successfully with the problems he or she encounters. Such a person feels capable of living with emotional ups and downs.

From time to time, however, people are unable to cope effectively with their emotions. The result may be a temporary state of painful emotions or a long-term disruption of emotional health.

Emotional Disorders

Human behavior is far too complex to be easily categorized. It is sometimes very difficult to distinguish between a disorder and a behavior that is just "different." Most health practitioners and researchers have come to accept the categories suggested by the American Psychiatric Association in its *Diagnostic and Statistical Manual of Mental Disorders* (DSM).[6]

The third edition of this manual, DSM-III, which was published in 1980, raised a storm of controversy because it eliminated or revised many standard classifications. The term *neurosis*, for example, was replaced by terms such as *anxiety* and *personality disorder.* DSM-IIIR, a revised edition of the manual published in 1987, further refined some of the classifications.

The categories discussed in this chapter all come from DSM-IIIR, although only a few of the main disorders are covered. It should be noted that although such a categorization is useful, one should not assume that each disorder is a separate, sharply defined condition. Sometimes an individual may suffer from more than one disorder.

Nonpsychotic Disorders

Emotional and mental problems can range in intensity from minor disturbances to incapacitating mental illness. **Nonpsychotic disorders** are disorders that inhibit a person's full functioning, but that do not distort thoughts and emotions so much that the person loses contact with reality. A person suffering from a nonpsychotic disorder recognizes and is disturbed by the symptoms. Moreover, that person is aware of how distressing his or her behavior is. In a sense, people with nonpsychotic disorders have a double anxiety: the anxiety associated with the disorder itself and the anxiety of knowing that something is wrong.

nonpsychotic disorder

Nonpsychotic disorders often respond to treatment; *getting help is therefore essential.* Without treatment, a disorder may endure for the rest of a person's life. It is important to recognize this fact, since so many people experience at least mild nonpsychotic symptoms at some point in their lives.

The causes of nonpsychotic disorders are not always clear. They appear to have no genetic basis. In response to an extremely stressful and painful life situation, an individual sometimes develops an **adjustment disorder**—a response "in excess of a normal and expected reaction to the stressor." Other nonpsychotic disorders may be caused in part by faulty emotional development. However, in some cases no causes can be identified.

adjustment disorder

Anxiety Disorders   Unlike the type of anxiety most people experience, **anxiety disorders** involve a severe and persistent level of fear or worry that can be almost as damaging to an individual's everyday functioning as a serious mental illness is. Two important types of anxiety disorders are phobias and panic disorders.

anxiety disorder

Phobias are characterized by a persistent and irrational fear of a specific object, activity, or situation that leads to a compelling desire to avoid it. Many people experience unreasonable fear when confronted by a harmless stimulus such as a tiny spider. The fear is considered a phobia only if it becomes a significant source of distress or interferes with normal functioning. It is estimated that one in nine adult Americans suffers from some kind of phobia.[7]

phobia

Panic disorders are often characterized by recurrent attacks that may occur unpredictably or as a result of a specific situation. They are a common type of disorder, often starting in adolescence. These attacks may be confined to a period of several weeks or months or may become chronic. They involve sudden and intense fear that often is accompanied by chest pain, dizziness, sweating, faintness, and trembling. Some people suffer few of these physical symptoms but feel more muscular tension and mental anxiety instead.[8]

panic disorder

Personality Disorders   All people have distinct personality traits—patterns of perceiving, relating to, and thinking about their environment and themselves.

In some cases these traits impair an individual's ability to function and cope with his or her environment. Such styles of coping are termed **personality disorders.** People with these disorders may suffer from a continuing sense of failure, a feeling of resentment, or a sense of being exploited. Their usual emotional state is suppressed anger, and they have a rigid and repetitive style of interacting with others.[9]

personality disorder

There are a variety of different personality disorders. **Schizoid personality disorder** refers to a lack of desire to have social relationships. This can even include a total disinterest in sexual experiences with another person. **Narcissistic personality disorder** is typified by an exaggerated sense of self-worth, a constant need for praise and attention, and a tendency to exploit others. **Antisocial personality disorder** is marked by tantrums and behaviors which violate the rights of others, such as vandalism, aggressive actions, and theft. The treatment of personality disorders is difficult and time-consuming and may achieve only limited success.

schizoid personality disorder

narcissistic personality disorder

antisocial personality disorder

somatoform disorder

Somatoform Disorders   The **somatoform disorders** are a group of mental disorders that are manifested as physiological symptoms. An individual may suffer from recurrent and long-term ailments that have no physical basis. The individual does not consciously invent these complaints. He or she actually feels ill but is unaware of the process by which the symptoms develop. One well-known somatoform disorder is **hypochondriasis,** in which a person imagines that every minor physical complaint is the first sign of a major illness.

hypochondriasis

Psychotic Disorders

psychotic disorder

Among the most serious mental problems are the **psychotic disorders.** Psychotic disorders may be defined as those in which the individual has significantly lost contact with reality. Two of the most common psychotic disorders—major depression and schizophrenia—are affective disorders.

affective disorder

major depression

Affective Disorders   **Affective disorders** are serious disorders of mood or feeling. Some people develop **major depression.** This is much more serious than minor depression, which, as you read earlier, is quite common. People who suffer from major depression experience a profound unhappiness and a loss of interest in all aspects of life, even their favorite activities. This persistent unhappy mood may be accompanied by appetite disturbance, change in weight, sleep disturbance, decreased energy, difficulty in concentrating, feelings of worthlessness or guilt, and thoughts of death or suicide.

bipolar disorder

mania

In **bipolar disorder,** a less common affective disorder, the person who is affected exhibits **mania,** a mood of extreme excitement. Depressive episodes are likely to occur as well. Mania usually impairs social and occupational functioning to a serious degree. When a person is manic, he or she is hyperactive, often planning and participating in several activities at once. The person becomes extremely sociable, optimistic, and reckless and is likely to show poor and hasty judgment. For example, he or she may spend a great amount of money on unnecessary things. The manic individual feels inflated self-esteem, often accompanied by grand delusions. There is a decreased need for sleep. The mania may shift rapidly to depression, which can last for minutes, hours, or longer periods.

People suffering from major depression, schizophrenia, and other serious psychotic disorders require hospitalization; specialized psychiatric care may include occupational therapy. (Bill Aron/PhotoEdit)

Schizophrenia   By contrast to these mood disorders, **schizophrenia** is primarily a disorder in a person's thinking processes. The term *schizophrenia* refers to a group of disorders that share certain features:

- Duration of at least 6 months
- Failure to achieve an expected level of social development
- A marked lack of initiative, interests, or energy
- Disturbances in thought, perception, sense of self, relationship to the outside world, and psychomotor activity[10]

Schizophrenia appears to run in families, although nongenetic factors such as stress and socioeconomic status are also involved.

Schizophrenia is among the most serious psychotic disorders. Because those suffering from it seem to be totally removed from reality, it can be frightening both to the patients and to those around them. People with schizophrenia may hear voices, believe that electronic devices are monitoring their activities, and laugh and talk at inappropriate times.

These people's thoughts are connected in random order, with little or no meaning. When speaking, they may ramble, become increasingly vague, or repeat words. Often, others have difficulty responding to people who suffer from schizophrenia with the sympathy and rationality that are needed.

Antipsychotic drugs have stabilized many people with schizophrenia to the extent that they can be released from the hospital permanently or for long periods. The relative calm that these drugs bring to the disordered life of many people with schizophrenia enables these people to benefit from family, group, or individual therapy as well as social and vocational rehabilitation.

Although schizophrenia is a grave disease, the outlook is not completely discouraging. Most patients do require hospitalization and drug treatment during the acute phases of the disorder, but the rest of the time they may live at home, interact socially, perhaps hold a job, and require only low maintenance doses of drugs for years at a time.

The Intellect

intellect

The other dimension of the human mind identified at the start of this chapter is **intellect**—the thinking, rational side of human consciousness. If emotions and emotional conflicts are often the cause of mental disorders, intellect can often be a part of the solution.

Intellect can be thought of as being composed of memory and cognition. *Memory* is the ability to learn and recall associated actions, ideas, and information. The term *cognition* describes the several processes by which knowledge and action can be examined and improved upon. Together, memory and cognition are the foundation on which people learn, create, solve problems, and make decisions.

Learning and Memory

The ability to learn is essential for human survival and is also a sign of health. People who fail to learn by their mistakes are unlikely to survive very long, let alone be happy. Individuals, societies, and the human race as a whole depend on remembering what has been learned about health and satisfaction.

By studying animals, psychologists have discovered a great deal about the simpler aspects of learning. Much of what they have found can be applied to people as well. Out of their research have come various theories about how human beings learn. Two are briefly outlined below.

conditioned response theory

classical conditioning theory

operant conditioning theory

Conditioned Response Theories **Conditioned response theories** are very basic accounts of how animals learn to perceive simple stimuli and react with consistent responses. **Classical conditioning theory,** which was developed in Russia in the early 1900s by Ivan Pavlov, explores how sets of different objects or events (stimuli) become grouped, or associated, in an animal's mind and are evidenced by its behavior. If two different stimuli are experienced together consistently, the animal soon reacts as though they were different aspects of the same thing. **Operant conditioning theory,** which was developed by American psychologists such as Edward Thorndike, John Watson, and B. F. Skinner, examines the conditions under which behaviors are learned. This theory explores the idea that an action is likely to be repeated if it is followed by a reward or pleasurable stimulus (positive reinforcement) and discouraged if it is followed by an unpleasant stimulus (punishment).[11] Although these are very simple ideas, conditioning theorists have been able to examine the phenomena in detail, finding, for example, that positive reinforcement is almost always more effective in encouraging desired behavior.

This is relevant not only to discipline in child rearing; it also helps people understand better ways to discipline themselves when they want to change their behavior. Blaming oneself for failure is not a very helpful course of action; it is far better to congratulate oneself on the positive things one manages to accomplish—or even to promise oneself a reward if one succeeds.

social learning theory

Social Learning Psychologist Albert Bandura has formulated a different learning model, based on the notion that children learn a great deal by imitating the adults around them. This model is called **social learning theory.**[12] It suggests that people acquire strategies, outlooks, and behaviors by listening to others and observing their actions. For Bandura, learning is a process which can take place independently of rewards or punishments.

Social learning theory is also a crucial model for understanding health-related behaviors. People's attitudes toward exercise, diet and nutrition, sexual behavior, and drug use are formed primarily as a result of social learning. For example, people may have a poor eating pattern because that was all they knew as children.

According to Bandura, reinforcement is more important in getting people to exhibit a newly learned behavior than in teaching that behavior in the first place. Thus, people may know how to exercise and understand that exercise is good, but that is often not enough. The reinforcement of being with friends may be needed to encourage a person to act on that knowledge.

Memory A healthy person can recall a vast number and variety of things. People's memory of information, events, and life experiences affects their current behaviors and reactions to situations. As such, memory is a factor in good health. It allows people to remember healthy behaviors and repeat them. It also allows them to review information that can have an important impact on their health, such as the nutritional value of food, the danger of using certain drugs, and techniques for relieving stress.

People often assess the mental health of the elderly by noting how sharp their memory is. In fact, memory is an important factor in all aspects of health. For example, the decline of memory in some elderly people may contribute to their overall declining health if they forget to eat the proper foods or take adequate precautions against disease and accidents.

Social learning theory argues that children tend to imitate bad as well as good behaviors from the adults they adopt as models. (Richard Hutchings/InfoEdit)

Cognition, Problem Solving, and Decision Making

Learning and remembering are not the full story of intellect, of course; intellect also includes what one does with one's knowledge. *Cognition* is the creative part of mental activity. It involves thinking, judging, reasoning, imagining, synthesizing, making decisions, and solving problems. While these activities may seem quite different, they are all instances of creative thought and depend on the application of knowledge.

Everyone encounters numerous problems during his or her daily life and must make hundreds of decisions every day. The ability to solve such problems and make decisions is an important aspect of effective intellectual functioning and is essential to promoting and maintaining optimum health.[13]

Understanding the Problem   The first stage in problem solving is understanding the problem. This involves interpreting the problem and viewing it in a way that makes it more easily understood. Suppose you are trying to deal with the anger that you feel at someone for the way that person treats you. If you see the problem as "How can I get them to change their behavior?" a solution may be difficult. However, if you see the problem in terms of your own behavior ("What is it that is making me so angry?" or even "Why am I staying in this situation and getting hurt?") you may be much closer to finding a solution that you can control. In other words, if you are having trouble solving a problem, go back and look at the problem in a different way.

Selecting Suitable Strategies   When you attempt to solve a problem, it is important to select a suitable strategy for reaching the solution. The best approach is to consider the options available and select the strategy most appropriate to the problem. For example, in dealing with depression caused by anger, a person might try to think a problem through, talk with friends or loved ones, or seek professional therapy.

As a person tries to solve a problem, it is often necessary to reevaluate potential solutions and try others if the first ones prove ineffective. When trying to lose weight, a person may find that a low-calorie diet without exercise is less effective than is a moderate-calorie diet coupled with a daily exercise program. Rather than give up when one solution does not work, a person should try other possible solutions.

Making Decisions   Considering possibilities and selecting an appropriate strategy are useless unless decisive action is finally taken. However, the better able you are to understand a problem and evaluate different alternatives, the better your ultimate decision will be.

Toward a Healthy Personality

Emotional difficulties and disorders can make it hard to perceive or define problems and devise effective solutions. This chapter has already suggested strategies for controlling some negative feelings, but handling feelings is not easy. They can change very abruptly and can affect the way people look at things. What follows is a more general description of how one can "work on" mental health problems.

Concepts, Self-Concept, and Self-Esteem

In addition to initiating actions and making decisions, the intellect learns, examines, and explores ideas and concepts. A *concept* is a group of associated perceptions and thoughts about an object or something less tangible, such as an event or a theory. The human intellect works with many ideas and concepts, creating and changing them and exploring the relationships between them. A person's self-concept is central to the whole structure of ideas that that person has. **Self-concept** refers to all the perceptions a person has about himself or herself—strengths and weaknesses, the potential for growth, and ways of acting. It is the result of thinking about oneself and evaluating what others think. The self-concept evolves throughout life as people reevaluate their beliefs, attitudes, and values.

self-concept

Self-concept is important not only because it is central to the ideas that a person has but also because it is very basic to a person's overall mental health. Self-concept is focused on knowing oneself. A well-developed, realistic self-concept is vital to one's **self-esteem,** the feelings of worth and dignity which constitute an important part of overall health and well-being. In turn, a high level of self-esteem is vital to self-efficacy, the confidence that one can take care of important aspects of one's life and health. For example, a person who has high self-esteem is often better able to control the behaviors that contribute to being overweight than is someone whose self-esteem is low. Conversely, low self-esteem can be very damaging to health. There is much evidence that self-esteem and a sense of self-efficacy are lower in depressed people than they are in healthy people.[14]

self-esteem

The relationship between self-concept and self-esteem is important. Self-esteem is an emotional matter that is affected by the events of the day and the opinions of others. Self-concept, however, can be a stabilizing influence. People can review their self-concepts and remind themselves of their strengths as well as the weaknesses which are causing emotional problems.

Getting Help

In the past people were often reluctant to seek help for emotional problems. Today, however, many people realize that it makes sense to get help dealing with problems they are having trouble coping with on their own. Research has shown that people with low self-esteem have a greater chance of developing mental disorders than do those with high self-esteem.[15] As a result, many methods for coping with emotional problems and mental disorders are aimed at helping people achieve greater self-esteem and increased self-efficacy. They are designed to help give people more control of their lives by removing or managing the symptoms that prevent them from functioning normally.

Individuals who realize they need help have a variety of options. The choice is largely dependent on the individual's needs and the nature of his or her problem. The most common options are behavior therapy, psychotherapy, family and group therapy, and organic therapy.

Behavior Therapy **Behavior therapy** attempts to alter a person's behavior without attempting to discover its causes. It is based on the idea that a person acquires behaviors under specific conditions and then transfers the feelings and attitudes associated with those conditions to other, inappropriate situations.

behavior therapy

Assessing Your Self-Esteem

As this chapter stresses, self-esteem is critical to psychological health. The following exercise will help you evaluate your level of self-esteem. If you identify readily with a statement, check "Like Me." If you rarely or never feel that way, check "Unlike Me."

	Like Me	Unlike Me
1. I often wish I were someone else.	_____	_____
2. There is much I would change about myself if I could.	_____	_____
3. I am generally quite decisive.	_____	_____
4. I am a lot of fun to be with.	_____	_____
5. I get upset easily at home.	_____	_____
6. It takes me a long time to get used to anything new.	_____	_____
7. I am popular with people my own age.	_____	_____
8. My family expects too much of me.	_____	_____
9. I do not give in very easily.	_____	_____
10. Things are all mixed up in my life.	_____	_____
11. Other people usually follow my ideas.	_____	_____
12. I have a high opinion of myself.	_____	_____
13. There are many times when I would like to leave home.	_____	_____
14. I am not as nice-looking as most people.	_____	_____
15. If I have something to say, I usually say it.	_____	_____
16. My family understands me.	_____	_____
17. Most people are more popular than I am.	_____	_____
18. I seldom get discouraged at what I am doing.	_____	_____
19. Things usually do not bother me.	_____	_____
20. I am pretty happy.	_____	_____

Score your evaluation by giving yourself a point for each of these checks: "Like Me" for statements 3, 4, 7, 9, 11, 12, 15, 16, 18, 19, and 20 and "Unlike Me" for statements 1, 2, 5, 6, 8, 10, 13, 14, and 17. A score from 15 to 20 indicates that you have a high level of self-esteem; a score from 10 to 14 shows that you have doubts about yourself; a score below 10 indicates low self-esteem, and you might consider counseling.

Based on S. Coopersmith, *Self-Esteem Inventory* (New York: W H Freeman, 1967). With permission.

A behavior therapist tries to help a client get rid of troublesome behavior by creating learning situations in which the client can unlearn an unwanted response or learn an alternative response.

A behavior therapist may also try to teach new behavior by changing the environment so that the client is rewarded for developing the desired responses. The behavior of some individuals has been changed considerably through positive reinforcement of desired behaviors. Some behaviorists practice cognitive behavior therapy, which seeks to alter patients' self-concepts and thought patterns by persuading them to look at themselves and their situations in new ways which can be linked to healthier behaviors. In treating depression, the therapist attempts to show the patient that his or her negative thoughts that contribute to the unhappiness can be changed.

Psychotherapy Psychotherapy is based on the idea that people need to understand their problems. A psychotherapist meets regularly with a client to talk, listen carefully to that person's problems, and provide emotional support and acceptance. The therapist analyzes the patient's situation and suggests new ways of looking at problems. The goal of psychotherapy is to help the patient find insight into his or her problems and ways to function more comfortably and effectively.

Psychotherapy is changing in response to the changing needs of society.[16] For example, since many people do not have the time or money for long-term traditional psychotherapy, there has been an increase in the use of short-term therapy geared toward dealing with a specific set of symptoms. Specific forms of psychotherapy have also been developed to target the problems of groups within the population, such as the elderly, children, people with chronic pain, and so on.

Family and Group Therapies It is sometimes useful for a psychotherapist to work with a couple or an entire family as a unit so that the relationships that have contributed to a person's problems can be more easily untangled. Other people who are having problems in their lives can benefit from group therapy, which can give them the support and guidance of others who have similar problems. Group members learn to see themselves as others see them. They learn to understand other people's motivations and personality styles.

Today there is also a tremendous variety of nontherapeutic groups, such as "12-step groups," assertiveness training groups, support groups, and marriage encounter groups. Such groups focus on helping their members develop better skills in human relationships and thereby help them gain more satisfaction from life.

Self-help groups organized by laypeople who share common problems can be very effective in providing emotional support and reducing the emotional distress of their members. For example, there are self-help groups for single fathers, alcoholics (Alcoholics Anonymous), widows, and cancer patients.

Organic Therapies **Organic therapy** attempts to treat a person in a physical way rather than through learning or talking. The most common type of organic therapy involves the use of medications. Drug or medication therapy is increasingly used to treat a variety of mental disorders.

Three basic categories of medications used to treat mental disorders are antipsychotics, antidepressants, and anxiolytics. Each of these categories in-

organic therapy

cludes many different drugs, the use of which depends on an individual's emotional and physical condition.

The way in which antipsychotic drugs work is not clear. It has been found, however, that they are very powerful substances that can alter mental processes and thus benefit psychotic patients. These medications have potentially serious side effects, including drowsiness, irregular heartbeat, and persistent muscle twitching.

Antidepressants relieve depression by mechanisms that are also not well understood. They are most effective for depression that is not brought on by an outside event, such as a death in the family. Potentially serious side effects from antidepressants include dangerously low blood pressure, disorientation, and confusion.

The anxiolytics, sometimes known as minor tranquilizers, are the most commonly prescribed medications for mental disorders of all types. They reduce anxiety, induce sedation, and sometimes stimulate the appetite. They may also produce drowsiness, lack of muscular coordination, and confusion.

electroconvulsive therapy (ECT)
psychosurgery

Other organic therapy approaches include **electroconvulsive therapy** (**ECT;** shock treatment) and **psychosurgery.** In ECT, an electric current is applied to the patient's brain to induce a convulsion. The patient experiences very little discomfort. Before treatment he or she is given a sedative and injected with a muscle relaxant. In psychosurgery, small amounts of brain tissue are destroyed using sophisticated laser surgery techniques. These forms of treatment are risky and controversial and are usually reserved for cases in which all other types of treatment have been unsuccessful.

Helping Others

Individuals can sometimes play an important part in helping others deal with emotional problems. A person who has a problem will often find it helpful to talk about it with another person who will listen empathetically and uncritically. Verbalizing the problem can be an important step in resolving it. The most helpful approach is to acknowledge the person's feelings with responses such as "I can tell you are very worried" and "I've been down and unhappy, too." It is best to then let the person work out a strategy for resolving the problem independently rather than rush in with advice. It is appropriate, however, to encourage and reassure the person.

If it becomes apparent that the person is not feeling better, it is time to seek outside help. It is better to get help too early than too late. In many cases tragic outcomes might have been prevented if people who knew about the problems had sought outside help sooner.

A good first contact might be a campus counseling service, a member of the clergy, a family physician, or another professional the person with the problem can trust. Most communities have mental health associations, clinics, and medical societies that can provide referrals and advice. If the person seems uninterested in seeking help, a friend or family member might investigate how to get help and arrange the first contact.

Crisis Intervention If an emotionally disturbed person poses a danger to himself or herself or to others, those nearby must get professional help even against the person's expressed wishes. One source of help is a hospital emergency room. If the person is too upset to be taken there without help, another source is the police, who in most communities are trained to intervene humanely and effectively.

Many communities have a crisis hot line for helping people deal with emergency situations. People can telephone at any time and receive immediate counseling, sympathy, and comfort. Hot lines have been set up for suicidal persons, rape victims, and runaway children. Hot lines also provide information about other community services.

Recognizing a Potential Suicide   Every year some 30,000 Americans are officially reported as having committed suicide. The true number of suicides, however, may be as high as 100,000 a year, and there may be 8 to 10 suicide attempts for every one that results in death. Suicide attempts among teenagers and young adults have increased dramatically in recent years. The rate of death by suicide is second only to death by accidents among young adults.[17]

Many people who are thinking about committing suicide, particularly young people, are reluctant to seek professional help. Instead, they turn to peers when they are in distress or in need of emotional support.[18] To prevent tragedy, it is important to recognize the warning signs of a potential suicide.

- *Severe depression.* Suicidal people may be hopelessly depressed and so withdrawn or agitated that they cannot eat or sleep. Suicide is 500 times more likely among severely depressed people than it is among the general population.
- *Extreme mood swings.* A person who is severely depressed one day, elated the next, and depressed again the day after may be struggling with the desire to live and the even stronger desire to die.
- *Giving away precious possessions.* The suicidal person may do this to indicate that he or she no longer has any reason to live.
- *A crisis that may lead to a suicide attempt.* When suicidal individuals feel overwhelmed by external events, they may feel that they cannot cope with life. With young people, the suicide of someone they know or one reported in the media may act as a precipitating event and increase the chance of suicide.[19]
- *Talk of death or suicide.* Suicidal people often talk about their death wish long before they try to kill themselves.

Only a phone call away, 24-hour suicide hot lines offer immediate support for people undergoing major emotional crises. (Mary Kate Denny/PhotoEdit)

In addition to recognizing these warning signs, it is important to take every suicide attempt or threat seriously no matter how ineffective it may seem. People who quickly bounce back from a suicide attempt and act as if nothing happened may soon try to kill themselves again unless they receive help.

Helping others deal with their emotional problems can benefit both the person receiving help and the person giving it. A concern for others and an ability to help others are characteristic of an emotionally healthy person.

Like all areas of health, mental health results from a careful balance of interrelated factors: helping and being helped, thinking and feeling, physical and psychological states, and positive and negative emotions. Mental health is also closely related to other components of health—helping to promote them but also benefiting from them. For example, not only do productive attitudes and a sound self-concept help a person who wants to improve his or her physical health, but physical health can also contribute to a person's mental stability and satisfaction.

Chapter Summary

- The human mind has an affective (emotional) dimension and a cognitive (intellectual) one.

- Emotions occur in the mind, but they have an important physical component as well.

- Physiological responses, which include changes in heart rate, blood pressure, and brain waves, are controlled by the autonomic nervous system.

- People learn the meaning of their emotional responses by association and by observing the experiences of others.

- Negative emotional states are experienced by all people at times. Most people are able to deal with these feelings effectively.

- An important part of emotional health is learning how to cope with negative emotions. People employ a variety of defense mechanisms in their coping strategies.

- Sound emotional health allows a person to cope more effectively with the ups and downs of daily life.

- Some people experience nonpsychotic mental disorders, including anxiety, personality, and somatoform disorders. These disorders can seriously inhibit a person's ability to function.

- Psychotic disorders such as major depression, bipolar disorder, and schizophrenia are among the most serious mental problems. An individual with one of these disorders has lost contact with reality; professional treatment is essential.

- Intellect is the thinking side of the mind. Its two components are memory and cognition.

- Conditioned response theory and social learning theory attempt to explain aspects of how people learn.

- Memory is an important factor in good health.

- Cognition is the process of knowing that includes mental activities.

- The ability to solve problems and make decisions is an important element in effective intellectual functioning and is essential to promoting and maintaining good health.

- A healthy self-concept and sense of self-esteem and self-efficacy are vital parts of overall health and well-being.

- Many types of help are available for emotional problems, including behavior therapy, psychotherapy, group therapy, and organic therapies. The therapy that is chosen depends on the individual's needs and the nature of the problem.

- Individuals can help others deal with emotional problems by listening empathetically, encouraging them to seek outside help, and referring them to appropriate sources of help.

- Suicide is a significant problem in the United States, particularly among teenagers and young adults. Everyone should recognize the warning signs of a potential suicide and be available to help prevent it.

Stress and Its Management

When you have studied this
chapter, you should be able to:

- Define stress as the body's
  response to perceived challenges
  or stressors.

- Explain how the nervous system
  and chemicals in the
  bloodstream cause specific stress-
  related effects in the body.

- List some of the effects that
  stress can have on an
  individual's life.

- Describe different strategies that
  can be used to manage stress.

Do you remember how you felt when you were about to speak before a group of people for the first time? No doubt your heart was racing and pounding, your breathing was rapid, and you felt nauseated or had an ache in your stomach. As you began to make your opening remarks, you found that your mouth was dry, your palms were sweating, and your hands were shaking. Anyone who has experienced sensations like these has experienced stress.

People encounter a variety of stress-producing situations throughout their lives. For very young children, it may be the first time their parents leave them alone with a baby-sitter. For students, it may be the thought of impending exams. For parents, it may be the demands of combining career and family. For older people, it may be the approach of retirement.

Stress is a normal and necessary part of life from which people cannot escape. It can cause temporary discomfort and can also have long-term consequences. Yet while too much stress can threaten an individual's health and well-being, a certain amount of stress is needed to survive. Stress may result in a reduction of normal functioning or illness, but it can also help a person in danger and contribute to heightened achievement. Although some people feel burned out by stress, others respond to it positively.

The Nature of Stress

stress

stressor

To some experts, stress is an event that produces tension or worry. Others regard stress as an individual's perception of an event—how a person interprets it in his or her mind. Most experts, however, define **stress** as the psychological and physiological response to any stimuli that an individual perceives as threatening.[1] Such threatening events or stimuli are called **stressors.**

People perceive situations very differently. One person may dread flying in an airplane (a stressor) because he or she perceives it as threatening. Another person, however, may look forward to flying because he or she enjoys it. A person's perception of a stimulus or event is often linked with thoughts and feelings that have been learned, often in childhood. For example, a student rejected by a graduate school may feel devastated because of subconscious associations with unhappy experiences of rejection during childhood. A student with less unpleasant experiences of rejection as a child may view the rejection as a challenge instead of as a failure. Although the stressor is the same for both students, their perceptions and responses to it are quite different.

The Sources of Stress

Stress can be brought on by a variety of situations or events, ranging from the death of a spouse, parent, or child to a change in sleeping or eating habits. The amount of stress brought on by these stressors depends not only on an individual's perception but also on factors such as the type of stressor and its intensity and duration.

Types of Stressors   There are three general categories of stressors. *Cataclysmic stressors* are sudden disastrous events, such as the earthquake centered near San Francisco, California, in October 1989. Such events often disrupt a person's life and may cause that person to feel dazed initially. Since cataclysmic events usually affect many people at the same time, large support networks tend to form to help people deal with stress. *Personal stressors* are events such as the death of a parent or the breakup of a marriage. These stressors are powerful enough to challenge a person's ability to adapt. However, there are fewer and smaller support networks for dealing with them, because such stressors affect individuals rather than groups. *Background stressors* are persistent, repetitive, almost routine events that are part of everyday lifestyle. Although less potent than cataclysmic or personal stressors, these daily hassles may pose an equally serious threat. For example, a high-pressure job or caring for young children may, over time, overtax a person's adaptive abilities.[2]

Situational Stressors Cataclysmic stressors generally arise *outside* a person's normal life. Personal and background stressors, however, can arise from a variety of situations *within* a person's everyday life. Such stressors might include the physical environment, emotional conflicts, intellectual challenges, relationships with other people, and ethical or moral dilemmas.

Stressors that make people physically uncomfortable and force their bodies to adapt are called *physical stressors*. Loud noise, glaring lights, sickness, chronic headaches, and extremes of temperature and humidity are a few common examples. These and other physical stressors can hamper a person's performance and productivity as well as that person's health and well-being.

Disturbing or upsetting feelings and emotions are another source of stress. Such *emotional stressors*, including arguments with parents or loved ones, the beginning or ending of a love affair, and worry over a friend's illness, can cause a great deal of emotional upset. Emotional stressors may even affect people's physical well-being by causing them to eat improperly, neglect their physical health, or behave in ways that can lead to injury.

Stressors that challenge the intellect or affect one's ability to think and reason are referred to as *intellectual stressors*. Studying for exams, calculating income tax, and making quick decisions in dangerous situations can all induce stress. Feelings of being overwhelmed by intellectual stressors often result when a person worries more about being unable to solve a problem than about how to solve it.

Demands placed on an individual by family members, friends, or other people are called *social stressors*. For example, a boss who will not or cannot communicate effectively with subordinates can be a major source of stress. It is very frustrating when the person in charge does not effectively explain to others what is expected of them.

Spiritual stressors are conflicts in personal, ethical, and moral beliefs. A person whose religious beliefs are challenged by new ideas may feel stress because of a conflict between what he or she has been taught to believe and the new ideas. Philosophical issues that challenge individual beliefs, such as animal protection, euthanasia, abortion, apartheid, capital punishment, nuclear war, and pollution, are significant spiritual stressors.

Acute and Chronic Stressors Several factors affect the impact that stressors have on an individual. One factor is the intensity of the stressor—whether it is mild or severe. Another is the stressor's duration—how long it lasts. Intense stimuli of relatively short duration are called *acute stressors*. Examples are the shock of a loud explosion and a fall off a ladder. Stimuli that persist over an

Job-related stress is as often generated by physical factors such as noise as it is by emotional ones. (Tony Freeman/PhotoEdit)

extended period are called *chronic stressors*. These stressors are often milder than acute stressors, but their effects may be quite severe.

The type of prolonged stress brought on by chronic stressors can be particularly injurious. Chronic stress often erodes an individual's ability to adapt and may lead to serious health problems. Although chronic stress may be difficult to manage, its effects can be reduced somewhat if a person has a strong social support network of people to rely on. Several studies have shown that these networks can help improve unhealthy mental states such as depression and conditions associated with increased risk of illness such as elevated blood pressure and a high cholesterol level.[3]

Bad Stress versus Good Stress

Stress challenges a person's ability to adapt. Some people are able to adapt rather well; a stressor may encourage them to achieve more and can make their lives more interesting. Many people, for example, study and learn better under the stress of an impending exam. Getting married or leaving a job, although stressful, may lead to rewarding relationships and greater happiness.

Other people do not adapt well to stress, and this may result not only in poor performance and low productivity but also in illness. Employees who have too much work or responsibility not only may perform inadequately but also may become ill. A person who is unable to deal with the death of a spouse

The anticipation and excitement of the most joyful times in life can be major stressors. (Alan Oddie/PhotoEdit)

may sink into depression, neglect work, and do things that endanger his or her health.

Stress can thus have either a positive or a negative effect. Stress that has a positive effect—**eustress**—can help a person meet challenges more effectively. Stress that has a negative effect—**distress**—can take a heavy toll on the mind and body.

eustress
distress

Evaluating Stressors

Certain stressors have been shown to play a significant role in illness. In the early 1970s Thomas H. Holmes at the University of Washington in Seattle and Richard H. Rahe at the San Diego Naval Health Research Center attempted to quantify stressful major life events. The scale they developed—the Social Readjustment Rating Scale, or Holmes-Rahe scale—gives a numerical value to events in a person's life that have occurred within a given period of time. To determine his or her stress level for that period of time, a person could add up the number of life change units (LCUs) that correspond to the events listed on the scale. According to Holmes and Rahe, a high stress score—the result of several life changes within a relatively short time—indicates an increased susceptibility to illness.[4]

Until recently the Holmes-Rahe scale was widely used to assess the effects of stress on health. Recent research, however, has suggested that everyday stressors, or hassles, are more significant than are major life events.[5]

Studies contrasting life events and hassles have generally revealed that *hassles*—the persistent, repetitive, and almost routine events of everyday life—are better predictors of health outcomes than are major life events.[6] High on the "Hassle Scale" are such things as concern about weight, concern over the health of a family member, concern about rising prices, and having too much to do. These small daily worries seem to erode emotional and physical health more than major life events do. When such hassles are chronic and long-term, their effects on health are even more pronounced.[7]

The General Adaptation Syndrome

While the nature of stressors and a person's perception of them are important factors in stress, stress is also defined as a physiological response to a stressor. Stress researcher Hans Selye observed certain similarities in human physiological responses to stress. He determined that the body reacts to any stressor with the same series of responses: pale skin, rapid breathing, quickened heart rate, elevated blood pressure, and often extreme mental alertness, muscle tension, nausea, vomiting, and diarrhea. This is the body's way of mobilizing itself to do battle with stressors. Selye and other researchers identified a three-stage process, called the **general adaptation syndrome (GAS),** that the human body goes through in adapting to stress.

general adaptation syndrome (GAS)

The GAS begins with the *alarm stage,* in which physiological adjustments take place as the body reacts to a stressor. Next comes the *resistance stage,* in which the mind and body struggle to combat the stressor—to learn to live with it. Finally, if the stressor is not removed or if the individual is unable to overcome it, the body reaches the *stage of exhaustion,* in which the body can no longer adapt and the person may actually die.[8]

The GAS clearly indicates that stress can lead to physiological damage.[9] The body's ability to deal with stress is limited. If it cannot return to a state of balance, or homeostasis, the damaging effects of stress may build up, leading to uncomfortable symptoms (such as stomachaches) or disease (such as stomach ulcers).

When Selye proposed the GAS, he thought that the physiological reactions to stress are the same in all stressful situations. The body, in other words, does not differentiate between different kinds of stress. Instead, it responds with the GAS regardless of whether a stressor is "good" or "bad." Critics of Selye, however, contend that he failed to recognize that an individual's interpretation of an event may have much to do with whether that event is perceived as a threat. Richard Lazarus and other researchers dispute Selye's contention that the stress response is automatic in a potentially stressful situation. Lazarus suggested that unless the person consciously views a situation as threatening, he or she will not experience stress.[10]

The Stress Response

When a person reacts to a stressor, whether good or bad, an intricate physiological stress mechanism that upsets the body's balance is set in motion. One of the earliest descriptions of this mechanism characterized stress as the body's reaction to a perceived threat and called it the fight-or-flight response.[11] This response was needed in the early days of the human race, when a typical stressor was the sight of an enemy or a menacing animal. Stress would gear the body to defend itself by either fighting or fleeing the stressor. It may have also caused the body to freeze and be unable to move in any direction—but even this would have been a successful outcome if the predator thought the individual was dead and left the person alone.

How the Stress Mechanism Works

When confronted by a stressor, a person must decide how to cope with it. In effect, the stressor represents a problem that must be solved. Some scientists believe that stress generates an increased blood flow to the problem-solving parts of the brain. The brain's arousal level increases, putting the rest of the body on red alert. Meanwhile, it also activates two interrelated physiological systems: the autonomic nervous system (ANS) and the endocrine system.

The Autonomic Nervous System   The ANS is primarily concerned with controlling the inner workings of the body. It is divided into the sympathetic nervous system and the parasympathetic nervous system. In general, the sympathetic system mobilizes the body for action and the parasympathetic system reduces the level of output and conserves resources.

In highly emotional or stressful situations, the sympathetic system is activated and causes the following reactions:

- Blood pressure rises, and the pulse quickens
- Blood races toward the brain and skeletal muscles for fast action
- Digestion slows so that energy can be devoted to combating the stressor
- The pupils enlarge to take in more information

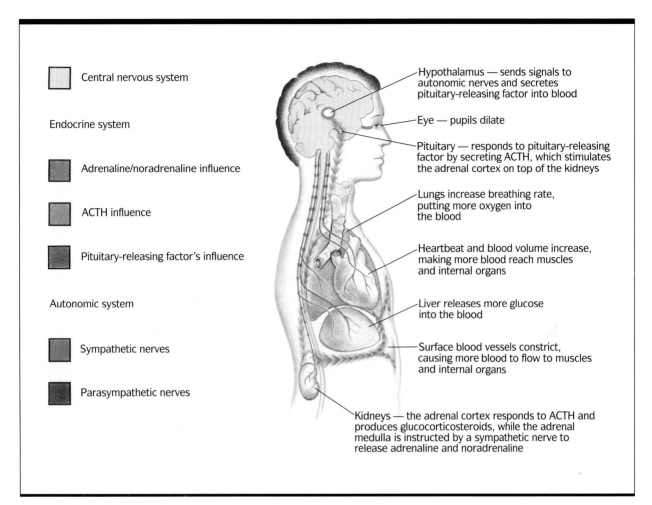

Central nervous system

Endocrine system

Adrenaline/noradrenaline influence

ACTH influence

Pituitary-releasing factor's influence

Autonomic system

Sympathetic nerves

Parasympathetic nerves

Hypothalamus — sends signals to autonomic nerves and secretes pituitary-releasing factor into blood

Eye — pupils dilate

Pituitary — responds to pituitary-releasing factor by secreting ACTH, which stimulates the adrenal cortex on top of the kidneys

Lungs increase breathing rate, putting more oxygen into the blood

Heartbeat and blood volume increase, making more blood reach muscles and internal organs

Liver releases more glucose into the blood

Surface blood vessels constrict, causing more blood to flow to muscles and internal organs

Kidneys — the adrenal cortex responds to ACTH and produces glucocorticosteroids, while the adrenal medulla is instructed by a sympathetic nerve to release adrenaline and noradrenaline

These reactions help the individual cope with short-term stress, such as running to catch a plane. Once the crisis has passed, the parasympathetic system—responsible for nonemergency functions such as digestion and respiration—takes over and helps the body return to normal.

The Endocrine System   A mechanism involving the endocrine system is also activated by stress, especially long-term stress. This system includes a collection of structures known as **endocrine glands,** which release a variety of chemical substances called **hormones** directly into the bloodstream. Hormones act as messengers within the body and help regulate the body's responses. They play an important role in many bodily functions in addition to the stress alert. The two main types of stress-activated hormones are adrenal hormones and pituitary hormones (Figure 6.1).

One of the key glands in the stress-alert reaction is the *adrenal medulla,* the inner portion of the paired adrenal glands. In response to a stress signal from the brain, the adrenal medulla secretes the hormones epinephrine (adrenaline) and norepinephrine (noradrenaline) into the bloodstream. Norepinephrine increases the heart rate, constricts blood vessels, inhibits gastrointestinal activity, and speeds up a number of other bodily functions. Epinephrine pro-

Figure 6.1 *Stress activates the endocrine system to increase its output of both adrenal and pituitary hormones. It also works directly through the autonomic nervous system. Both processes prepare the body for emergency action.*

endocrine glands

hormones

duces similar effects, although it is more effective in stimulating the heart and less effective in constricting blood vessels.

At the same time that the brain sends signals to the adrenal glands, it sends signals to the pituitary gland, a tiny "master control gland" at the base of the brain. In response, the pituitary gland secretes hormones that travel through the bloodstream to the adrenal, thyroid, and other glands.

The Stress Mechanism's Effects on the Body

The fight-or-flight response is useful if a physical reaction such as dodging a speeding car is called for or if a person has to meet a short-term psychological challenge such as giving a speech or taking an exam. The body is equipped to handle such stress without damage *if* it is able to relax afterwards. After the stressful situation has passed, the body must have a chance to regain its original homeostasis, returning to a normal blood pressure and normal hormone levels.

Trouble arises when one arousal reaction is piled on top of another and the body does not get a chance to return to normal. Today people are continually bombarded with a host of different stressors, from physical disease to emotional distress to value conflicts. As a result, the body is often unable to return to normal. Thus, stress tends to build up and disrupt the body's functioning, particularly through the action of hormones released under stress. Epinephrine, for example, may keep the muscles tense and the blood pressure and heart rate high for several days or even longer. It also may interfere with the immune system, lowering a person's resistance to disease.

The Role of Personality

Personality often affects the way people respond to stress and therefore affects the impact of stress on the body. Some people seem to invite stress into their lives. Everyone has seen people like this, impatiently blowing their car horns and glancing nervously at their watches all the time. People who behave this way are exhibiting Type A behavior, a pattern of behavior characterized by impatience, competitiveness, and a work-against-the-clock style. In contrast, a person who exhibits Type B behavior is generally low-key, contemplative, and relaxed.

In many ways Type A behavior resembles the traditional goal-directed orientation so common in American society. If kept within limits, such behavior may be viewed as adaptive. Many success-oriented middle-class college students are competitive and show other Type A behavior patterns.[12] In excess, however, Type A behavior has been linked to high levels of stress and thus may lead to health-related problems. In one study of women, those with Type A behavior were found to be four times more likely to have heart disease than were their Type B counterparts.[13] In another study it was found that people exhibiting Type A behavior are more likely to suffer from minor illnesses and have more severe symptoms than are those who are more relaxed.[14]

Not all stress experts agree that Type A and Type B behavior patterns by themselves can be linked with the presence or absence of health-related problems. Some experts have identified a personality trait called hardiness that may help alleviate the effects of stress.[15] Hardy individuals show three basic personality traits: they tend to become deeply involved in what they are doing, usually act in the belief that their work will make a difference, and view the majority of life changes as normal and beneficial for personal growth.[16]

Because of their greater feeling of self-efficacy, people with hardy personalities seem able to withstand the impact of stress.[17] Some researchers also contend that hardiness acts as a buffer against illness. Personality hardiness appears to be related to lower blood pressure, lower levels of fatty acids in the blood, less psychological distress, and increased happiness.[18]

The Impact of Stress

People may think they are adapting successfully to stress, but in resisting or becoming adjusted to a stressor, they are often unaware of the compromises they are making. They may not consciously recognize the stress caused by situations such as being late for an important meeting or doing heavy physical labor in extreme heat. They may think that they have become accustomed to poor eyesight, insufficient light, loud noise, or continuing family conflict.

In the short term stress can have a negative effect on a person's behavior, resulting in an inability to act in ways that promote good health. In the long term stress may have a serious effect on a person's vulnerability to illness and disease.

Stress and Behavior

Stress can have an impact on a person's behavior in a variety of ways. As was mentioned earlier, stress can affect the way a person deals with disease and responds to discomfort. Stress may also make a person irritable, withdrawn, cautious, energetic, outgoing, or optimistic, depending on whether the stress is perceived as positive or negative. While eustress can have a beneficial effect, distress can be detrimental if it leads to behaviors such as drug abuse and under- or overeating or to behaviors that can lead to injury. These and similar behaviors represent negative ways of coping with stress.

Many people turn to drugs, including tobacco, alcohol, and illegal substances, to relieve stress. Stress does not necessarily lead to abuse, however. It used to be argued that there is a link between stress and the onset of or an increase in drinking among the elderly. Drinking was considered a reaction to or a means of coping with stressful major life events typical of that age group, such as retirement or the death of a spouse. Recent research, however, has suggested that elderly persons who are generally successful at coping do not resort to such strategies for dealing with stress.[19]

Stress may also affect a person's eating behaviors. Some people tend to eat less when they feel stressed, while others eat more. In the short term this may not be a problem, but chronic stress can contribute to weight problems and problems associated with poor diet and nutrition. Research has shown that some foods trigger the production of natural painkillers (called *endorphins*) in the brain that ease stress and discomfort. Researchers have noted that the more stress a person is under, the higher the endorphin level in the blood.[20] The nature of these connections is unclear, but they suggest possible links between endorphins and a craving for certain foods.

Stress may also affect behavior in ways that can increase the risk of suffering an injury. For example, a person's driving ability may be impaired if that person is under severe stress. Similarly, a lack of concentration may be dangerous if it causes a person to disregard risk factors within his or her environment.

Suicidal behavior may also be linked to stress. Researchers at the New York Psychiatric Institute have concluded that most suicides in young people are preceded by stressful events such as getting into trouble with the law, breaking up with a girlfriend or boyfriend, and problems at home or school.[21]

Stress and Disease

If an individual already has a disease such as heart disease or diabetes, the increased muscle tension and elevated blood sugar caused by stress can aggravate the condition. Research has shown that prolonged stress may also be linked to the onset of illness and disease.[22] The degree to which stress contributes to the development of disease and the specific diseases it can contribute to are still unclear; researchers continue to study these questions.[23]

While research has demonstrated a strong correlation between stress and certain physical and psychological responses, it has not yet proved a direct cause-and-effect relationship. Thus, it cannot be concluded that stress in itself actually causes any specific disease. There is growing evidence, however, that stress can depress the ability of the immune system to fight diseases such as viral infections, autoimmune diseases (disorders in which the immune system seems to go out of control and attack body tissues), and some forms of cancer.[24] Furthermore, it is known that stress may affect the way in which people deal with disease, such as making them slower or faster in recognizing that something is wrong or altering the way they react to discomfort. With these

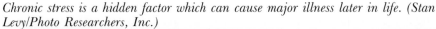

Chronic stress is a hidden factor which can cause major illness later in life. (Stan Levy/Photo Researchers, Inc.)

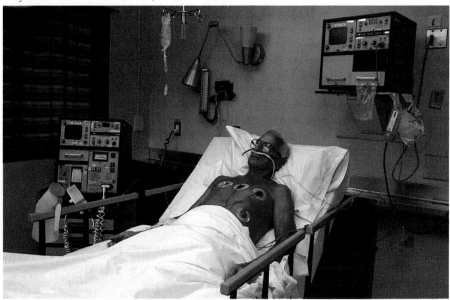

cautions in mind, consider some of the connections between stress and diseases that have been suggested.

Hypertension   Since an individual's blood pressure rises temporarily in reaction to a stressor, researchers have come to suspect a possible connection between stress and hypertension. Chronic hypertension—a condition of sustained abnormally high blood pressure that can lead to cardiovascular disease—is believed to be stress-related. A number of studies have revealed that people who work under great psychological pressure (such as airplane pilots) and those who are subjected to sustained environmental stress (such as people who work in places with high noise levels) are more likely to develop high blood pressure than are people who live and work in a less tension-filled atmosphere.[25]

Once again it should be remembered that perception plays an important role in stress. One study of a group of people with hypertension found that they rated their stress levels as high during the period preceding illness. The researchers concluded that a person's *subjective* rating of overall stress may be more meaningful than an *objective* measure of actual events.[26]

Heart Disease   Many researchers believe that stress is a contributing factor in heart disease. A Duke University study found links between heart disease and certain Type A behaviors that already were associated with high levels of stress. According to the study, a coronary-prone personality is one who mistrusts the motives of others, feels anger frequently, and expresses hostility toward others with no regard for their feelings.[27]

Other researchers, however, are not convinced that there is a link between Type A behavior and heart disease. One study suggests that the risk factors for heart disease seem to relate not to Type A behavior and aggression but to emotional problems such as an inability to perceive and verbalize negative emotions (expressing anger, for example) and to cope effectively.[28] At this point the consensus seems to be that although stress may be a secondary factor in the incidence of heart disease, it should not be considered a primary factor.

Cancer   The role of stress in the development of cancer is much debated. Nevertheless, there are indications that tensions may play a role in the onset of cancer in certain individuals who may be predisposed to contract the disease. Although the National Cancer Institute (NCI) states that there is as yet "no convincing evidence that certain emotions or personality traits might increase a person's risk for cancer," it adds that the possibility of such a relationship is still under study.[29] In contrast, researchers at the Memorial Sloan-Kettering Cancer Center in New York City have concluded that psychological states and traits can affect the transformation of normal cells into cancer cells. They have identified three types of risk factors: stress, personality traits (or coping styles), and personal habits (for example, smoking).[30]

It is more widely accepted that once an individual is diagnosed as having cancer, his or her emotional state will be one of the factors that determine the success of treatment. Medical records are full of reports of patients who believed they would get well again or discovered something to live for and went into *remission* (a state in which the disease's symptoms disappear) or recovered completely. Conversely, severe emotional traumas have been associated with the reappearance of cancer in patients who had been in remission.[31]

Infectious Disease and the Immune System   By altering the body's hormonal and nervous systems, persistent stress somehow creates a fertile climate for disease—researchers do not know exactly how. Stress can have a direct effect on the immune system—the group of mechanisms in the body that work together to fight infection—by reducing its ability to function effectively.[32] Stress can also act indirectly on the body's resistance to infection if it causes a person to eat poorly, neglect exercise, lose sleep, smoke or drink too much, or behave in other ways that may be harmful to health.

Many people who experience long-term psychological distress as a result of stressful life events appear to have adverse immunologic changes that can lead to infections as well as malignant disease. Indeed, several human and animal studies have suggested a relationship between exposure to stress and an impaired immunologic system.[33] Whether someone actually does become ill, however, also depends on the harmful agents to which he or she has been exposed and the health of the person prior to the stressful life event.[34]

Diabetes and Peptic Ulcers   Both diabetes and peptic ulcers have been linked more directly with stress.[35] In the case of diabetes, when stress causes the glucose (sugar) level of the blood to increase, cells in the pancreas react by producing insulin, a hormone that helps regulate blood sugar levels. Chronic stress can exhaust these cells, which cannot be replaced, seriously diminishing the ability of the pancreas to make the insulin needed to control the blood sugar level. The result is a higher risk for the onset of diabetes, especially among individuals who have a genetic predisposition for the disease.

A peptic ulcer is a sore in the lining of the stomach that is thought to be caused by excessive secretion of gastric acid (a digestive aid). A peptic ulcer often produces severe stomach pain and can cause internal bleeding if it makes a hole in the stomach wall. Although the cause of peptic ulcers is not known, it is generally accepted that stress can aggravate the condition.[36]

Asthma and Allergies   Since stress affects the body's immunologic response, it has been linked to asthma and other allergies, such as hay fever. These conditions often result from the reaction of the body's immune system to an invader. The invading organism causes a chain of events in which the body produces substances called antibodies. The antibodies in turn stimulate the release of chemicals that cause physiological changes, many of which may be more irritating and harmful than the original invader.

Skin Disorders   Stress is believed to aggravate several skin conditions, the most severe of which is eczema. This inflammatory condition is characterized by redness, itching, and oozing lesions that become scaly, crusted, or hardened. Eczema can recur and persist for months or even years. Many physicians have found that when stress is reduced in a person's life, eczema and other skin disorders often improve.[37]

Mental Disorders   Stress causes emotional upset, which can aggravate an existing emotional disturbance. It is difficult to ascertain, however, the role stress plays in causing emotional and mental disorders.

Mental health practitioners have developed a number of theories about the possible relationship between stress and mental dysfunction. Studies have noted a high incidence of stressful major life events shortly before the onset of schizophrenia, depression, and nonpsychotic disorders. According to one theory, some individuals are born with a predisposition to mental disorders, which may surface under unusual stress.[38]

The Economic and Social Costs of Stress

In addition to its potential effects on the health and well-being of individuals, stress has economic and societal impacts. Stress can lower job performance and productivity and thus affect the economic well-being of businesses and, ultimately, the economy as a whole. It may also contribute to societal tensions that manifest themselves in frustrations toward leaders and other authorities as well as impatience toward and intolerance of others.

Economic Cost Occupational stress is an increasingly common complaint in the United States. Its causes include having little input in decision making, doing too much or too little work, unclear work objectives, and facing conflicting demands.[39]

It has been estimated that occupational stress costs American industry about $150 billion a year. On any given workday, an average of a million workers are absent from their jobs because of such stress-related disorders as backaches, headaches, ulcers, insomnia, anxiety, depression, heart problems, hypertension, and gastrointestinal complaints.

Particularly troublesome in today's workplace is *job burnout,* a syndrome characterized by physiological and emotional exhaustion and often caused by chronic frustration with a job coupled with having too much work to do. The symptoms include:

* Increased use of drugs and alcohol
* Depression, low self-esteem, pessimism, and loneliness
* Increased lateness and absenteeism
* Fatigue, irritability, muscle tension, and stomach complaints
* A loss of one's sense of humor and an increase in feelings of guilt[40]

Job-related stress is not necessarily bad. If the tension and stress associated with a job are used constructively, the businesses and individuals involved can benefit. Some job-related stress can stimulate creative thinking, enhance performance, and increase productivity. Few companies, however, attempt to harness job-related stress in this way.[41]

Social Cost Stress has not only an economic cost but also a social cost. American society contains a diversity of individuals and groups of people whose needs and wants, attitudes, beliefs, and ways of living differ and sometimes compete. The society's stability depends in part on maintaining an acceptable equilibrium among these groups. Stress, however, may upset this balance. People under stress sometimes take out their frustrations on others, and their impatience and anger may contribute to greater intolerance of people different from themselves. If stress becomes chronic, these effects may harm the delicate fabric of society, leading to greater disharmony among people and increased frustration at the nation's authorities and institutions.

Many different occupations can lead to job burnout. The stress caused by a class of primary school students can be as great as the stress from making million-dollar business decisions. (John Moss/The Stock Shop)

Managing Stress

Stress is an inevitable part of people's lives. Learning to manage stress effectively is therefore the best defense against the discomfort or harm it can cause.

Some of the ways in which people attempt to manage stress—using alcohol and drugs, for example—not only are potentially dangerous but usually offer only a temporary escape from stress and often take away a person's sense of control. There are other, more healthful ways of relieving stress that are longer-lasting and reinforce an individual's sense of self-efficacy.

Keep in mind that the objective is not to eliminate all stress from your life. Stress, after all, not only is inevitable but also may be beneficial in some instances. Rather, you should try to evaluate the nature of stress in your life. Determine your personal comfort level where stress is concerned, then use eustressors to enhance the quality of your life and try to reduce the negative effects of the distressors you experience.

A number of stress management techniques may help you cope with stress. They range from various relaxation techniques to psychological approaches to changes in attitude and behavior.

Relaxation Techniques

Relaxation involves more than just reducing tension. It is a positive and satisfying peace of mind.[42] A person can achieve a state of relaxation through the use of various techniques, including progressive relaxation, meditation, autogenic training, and biofeedback. Table 6.1 includes a number of other stress management techniques.

progressive relaxation

Progressive Relaxation   More than 50 years ago, long before the scientific study of stress, Edmond Jacobson, a physiologist, developed a technique he called **progressive relaxation** for relieving muscle tension. This technique requires that the individual deliberately tense and then relax his or her muscles in order to learn the sensations of tensing and letting go. It is "progressive" because it moves through the various muscle groups in the body—from the hands and arms to the head, eyes, mouth, neck, shoulders, back, chest,

---

Table 6.1   Other Stress Management Techniques

There are a number of other things people can do to manage and alleviate stress.

Do not overload your schedule with too many things to do; students, for example, should avoid overloading their schedules with too many courses.

Take time to meet new people and develop new friendships and try out new activities.

Spend a little time regularly in self-talk or self-evaluation of your concerns and stressors.

Get help from a relative, friend, counselor, or other sympathetic person if you feel that stress is becoming unmanageable.

Get involved in a regular exercise program, even if it involves only walking briskly for 30 minutes every other day.

Pursue a hobby or do some light, enjoyable reading a few hours each week.

Set realistic goals based on your interests, strengths, and weaknesses.

---

abdomen, buttocks, thighs, calves, and feet. Jacobson extended his system to exercises for mental relaxation as well: the individual alternately imagines sensory experiences—sights, sounds, smells, shapes, and tactile sensations—and then lets go of the images.[43]

Meditation   Meditation is not a single, easily defined technique; rather, it encompasses a variety of diverse methods. The aim of the different meditative techniques is to focus attention on an image or thought with the goal of clearing one's mind and producing inner peace. Effective meditation produces a state of deep physiological and mental repose by reducing blood pressure, muscle tension, the pulse rate, and the level of stress hormones in the blood.

One well-known meditation method, developed by Dr. Herbert Benson of Harvard University, is called the **relaxation response.** Practicing this method for at least 20 minutes daily is said to increase the alpha brain waves associated with relaxation and well-being. The relaxation response can also help lower blood pressure in people with hypertension and discourage body tissues from responding to stress hormones as strongly as they would otherwise.[44] This method involves the following steps:

relaxation response

- Sit quietly in a comfortable position and close your eyes.
- Deeply relax all your muscles, beginning at the feet and progressing up to the face. Keep them relaxed.
- Breathe easily and naturally through your nose. Become aware of your breathing. As you breathe out, say the word *one* silently to yourself.
- Continue for 10 to 20 minutes. You may open your eyes to check the time, but do not use an alarm. When you finish, sit quietly for several minutes, at first with your eyes closed and later with your eyes open. Wait several minutes before standing up.
- Do not worry about whether you are successful in achieving a deep level of relaxation. Maintain a passive attitude and permit relaxation to occur at its own pace. When distracting thoughts occur, try to ignore them by not dwelling on them, and return to repeating *one*. With practice, the response should come with little effort.
- It is recommended that this be done twice a day, but not within 2 hours after any meal (an active digestive system interferes with meditation).

Autogenic Training   **Autogenic training** is based on the premise that the mind can compel the body to relax and return to a homeostatic balance by consciously focusing on sensations such as heaviness and warmth. A key principle of autogenic training is that the body will naturally balance itself when it is directed into a relaxed state. With practice, a person can learn to induce this relaxed state when necessary. Autogenic training has been shown to be effective in medical case studies of people with peptic ulcers, high blood pressure, migraine headaches, asthma, sleep disturbances, and other conditions.[45] The typical instructions for performing autogenic imagery are as follows:[46]

autogenic training

- Begin the exercise in a comfortable and relaxed sitting or reclining position with your eyes closed. Distractions should be kept to a minimum.
- Imagine that you have just completed a long walk and are feeling very tired; your legs are especially tired. Try to feel the heaviness in your legs. Let them weigh themselves down.

- Now imagine that your legs feel very warm and then try to feel that warmth. Keep your legs relaxed and feel how heavy and warm they are.
- Enjoy the feeling of heaviness and warmth in your legs and try to retain it as long as possible.
- As you end the exercise, imagine that you are refreshed and alert. Take a deep breath and stretch.

Biofeedback   In progressive relaxation, meditation, and autogenic training, a state of relaxation is verified by the individual's subjective evaluation. A more objective measure can be attained through biofeedback.

biofeedback **Biofeedback** is a technique for developing conscious control over involuntary body processes such as blood pressure and heartbeat. This technique has helped some people cope with various problems, including hypertension, headaches, menstrual cramps, and gastrointestinal disorders.[47]

In most biofeedback training sessions a person listens to tape-recorded relaxation instructions while receiving auditory or visual feedback about what is happening to various physiological functions, such as heart rate, skin temperature, and muscle tension. Gradually the person becomes aware of the state of mind, attitudes, or thoughts associated with these functions and can summon them at will without the biofeedback machine.[48]

Many of the skills of biofeedback are difficult to master alone, and biofeedback devices are not always available to the public. People who are interested in the technique should seek the help of a professional.

Psychological Approaches to Stress Management

Some methods of coping effectively with stress are primarily psychological. These methods focus on helping people learn healthier ways of looking at things. As you learned earlier, the amount of stress a situation evokes relates to the way in which a person perceives that situation. One psychological technique for learning different ways of perceiving situations is called **cognitive appraisal.**

Cognitive appraisal teaches people to consider less threatening explanations for any situation that is construed as harmful, threatening, or challenging. The cognitive appraisal approach is consistent with the time-honored advice "Don't take it personally."

Such an approach to stress management can be tried independently. It can also be undertaken with professional guidance. Such psychotherapy has been well worth the cost to the many people it has helped. A psychologist, psychiatrist, or social worker can help a person develop healthier ways of perceiving and dealing with anxiety-provoking situations as well as gain insight into his or her responses to particular situations.

Changing Behavior to Avoid or Reduce Stress

Researchers studying the relationship between poor health habits, stress, and illness have found that people may become ill after experiencing a stressor partially because they do not maintain good health behaviors.[49] Changing poor health habits therefore may make a difference between stress and illness and relaxation and good health. Four areas in which a person can readily

Thinking Critically About Stress

Stress is a part of everyone's life, yet there are many different ways to view stressors and their effect on a healthy lifestyle. Health experts agree that a person's attitude toward stressful events has an effect on how that person will react. Two ways of coping with stress are presented below. The first point of view suggests making lifestyle changes to avoid some stressors and lessen the effect of others. The second point of view recommends viewing stress as a source of energy that can be channeled to help a person accomplish individual goals.

Find Ways to Avoid or Reduce the Effects of Stress

High levels of stress have been correlated with health problems. Stress has been suspected as a contributing factor in such illnesses as high blood pressure, heart disease, and ulcers. Too much stress may also compromise the immune system and make a person more susceptible to infection.

Coping with stress successfully means avoiding the damaging effects of stressors in one's life. One way to do this is to discover how certain stressors can be avoided. Suppose a student knows that sitting in traffic on his route to school makes him tense and irritable. Perhaps he can avoid this problem by finding an alternate route to school.

If stressors cannot be avoided, it is possible to lessen their negative effects by making other changes in one's life. Plenty of sleep and regular exercise are important. Eating a balanced diet and cutting down on alcohol and caffeine may also help. Many people find that meditative and relaxation techniques help counteract the effects of stress. A network of positive relationships can also provide support and encouragement.

Overall, there are many ways to alleviate the stresses of modern life. Individuals must identify the causes of stress and find ways to avoid or reduce it.

Make Stress Work for You

Most people think of stress as a negative, damaging thing. Yet there is another way of looking at stress—as a form of energy.

Looked at in this way, stress is a challenge to be managed and used to enhance one's life. Dr. Robert Ritvo, dean of the University of New Hampshire's School of Health and Human Services, points out that stress can drive people to reach their goals. Dr. Peter G. Hanson notes that "students maximize their learning curves with the stress of an upcoming exam. Athletes set world records only with the stress of stiff competition."

In other words, stress can make people perform better. The key lies in a person's attitude toward stressful events. Is the end of a romantic relationship merely a loss? Or is it an opportunity to examine one's values and renew relationships that may have been neglected?

Stress can have its most devastating consequences when a person feels a sense of helplessness. Instead of identifying sources of stress as problems, individuals should strive to see them as challenges to be met. Finding ways to use stress to one's advantage gives a person more control over stressful situations, and this success boosts self-esteem and helps the individual face life's events with courage and confidence.

Which method do you think is better for handling stressful situations? List some current sources of stress in your life and decide how you might resolve them. Would you try to reduce or avoid the stressor, or could you use the stress to your advantage? Do you think that one of the strategies discussed above might work more successfully than the other for certain individuals or under different conditions? Why?

Based on ideas in Paul Martin, "The Power of Positive Stress," *Better Homes and Gardens*, March 1990 and in Peter G. Hanson, *Stress for Success* (New York: Doubleday, 1989).

make changes to avoid or reduce stress and increase health are exercise, nutrition, time management, and mental outlook.

Exercise   Runners have frequently reported a sense of well-being related to their exercise. Not only does running strengthen their bodies, it also may raise their endorphin levels. Current studies strongly suggest that individuals who exercise regularly are less susceptible to stress-induced health problems than are those who exercise less frequently.[50] Researchers are also finding that even brief periods of low-level exercise have a positive effect on a person's mood.[51] The real benefit of exercise is that it enables the body to rid itself of the by-products of stress, and because it helps reduce fatigue, exercise increases the body's capacity to cope with stress.

Nutrition   Although diet is obviously a factor that affects health, the specific role of nutrition in stress management is controversial. High levels of vitamin C and certain B-complex vitamins are said to be necessary during times of stress to keep the body's nervous and endocrine systems functioning properly, but there is no consensus on this. It is generally accepted, however, that a person who exercises regularly, is physically fit, and eats well-balanced meals is better able to handle stress.[52]

Time Management   For many people, the fast pace of modern life and the numerous demands placed upon their time lead to highly stressed lives. Reducing that stress and becoming more productive in the time available require that a person learn to manage time better.

Successful time management requires that you plan everything you do carefully, putting aside nonessential tasks and doing essential things *now*. It also requires that you stop thinking that you have to do everything at the same time. Some things can wait. It is also important to realize that you cannot be the center of all activities.

A good start in learning how to manage time is to assess your goals and values, decide which ones really matter, and proceed from there. An organized checklist of priorities will help you work toward achieving one thing at a time with a minimum of stress.

You should, of course, bear in mind that priorities are flexible and subject to revision if emergencies or conflicts arise. It would be self-defeating to use time-management techniques to lock yourself into a pattern that imposes more stress. The idea is to learn to manage time, not to let time manage you.

A positive outlook is a key factor in reducing stress. (David Young-Wolff/ PhotoEdit)

Developing a Healthy Mental Outlook   Personal attitude is an important element in coping with stressful events and a stressful lifestyle. People who develop a positive, healthy outlook toward life and its problems can minimize the effects of stress on their health and well-being.

Learning to manage stress in your life can bring great health benefits. Try to be open to change and to view it as a challenge rather than a defeat. Develop a sense of involvement in your life by controlling and influencing life events. Draw on sources of strength such as friendships, physical fitness, and positive, flexible attitudes. The sense of self-efficacy and confidence these sources bring will help you make desired changes in your life and lifestyle, changes that can affect your overall health, well-being, and longevity.

Chapter Summary

- Stress is the psychological and physiological response to a stimulus (or stressor) an individual *perceives* as threatening.
- The three general categories of stressors are cataclysmic stressors, personal stressors, and background stressors.
- The five general sources of stress within a person's life are physical, emotional, intellectual, social, and spiritual stressors.
- Stress that has a negative effect on a person is called distress. Stress that has a positive effect is called eustress.
- The Holmes-Rahe scale, a measure of major life events, has been used to assess the effects of stress on health.
- Major life events are powerful personal stressors—for example, the death of a spouse or a major illness. Hassles are persistent, repetitive, and almost routine events that cause stress.
- The general adaptation syndrome (GAS) is a three-stage process the body goes through in adapting to stress. It includes the alarm stage, the resistance stage, and the stage of exhaustion. The GAS helps explain how stress can cause physiological damage.
- When it is under stress, the body reacts with a specific physiological response that represents its attempt to cope with a stressor. This response is regulated by the autonomic nervous system and the endocrine system.
- Certain types of behaviors seem to be linked to high levels of stress and stress-related problems. Hardy personalities seem to experience less stress.
- Stress can affect a person's behavior as well as physical well-being.
- Research shows a correlation between stress and certain diseases, such as hypertension, heart disease, cancer, and infectious diseases. While a causal relationship has not been demonstrated scientifically, stress may aggravate these diseases.
- Stress has a direct effect on the immune system, reducing its ability to function effectively.
- Job-related stress can reduce a person's performance and productivity.
- Stress costs American industry millions of dollars each year in lost productivity, absenteeism, and accidents. It may also lead to disharmony within American society.
- Some people attempt to manage stress in ways that may be harmful, such as taking illegal drugs.
- A positive strategy for managing stress is to use one of a variety of relaxation techniques, including progressive relaxation, meditation, autogenic training, and biofeedback.
- Cognitive appraisal techniques, which usually require the assistance of a health professional, help teach people to perceive events in less threatening ways so that they are less stressful.
- Changes in behavior, such as better nutrition, exercise, and time management, can help a person manage stress better.

Marriage, Intimate Relationships, and Sexuality

When you have studied this chapter, you should be able to:

- Explain the importance of marriage and other intimate relationships.

- Identify and describe alternatives to marriage.

- Explain why the divorce rate remains high and discuss some of its potential effects on couples and their children.

- Distinguish between sex and sexuality and discuss the basis of sexuality and sexual behavior.

- Discuss the origin of attitudes toward sex and explain how those attitudes may change over time.

- Name the main structures of the male reproductive system and describe their functions.

- Name the main structures of the female reproductive system and describe their functions.

- Explain the various forms of sexual expression and discuss why responsible sexual expression is important.

Although American popular culture has always valued "rugged individualism" and "going it alone," most people develop and maintain intimate relationships with parents, children, relatives, friends, and sex partners. Such close ties help an individual develop a sense of worth as a human being and help satisfy a number of human needs.

Forming and maintaining successful long-term relationships is not always easy. At times it requires skill in coping with misunderstandings and other problems. Nevertheless, the learning and changing that are necessary to make a relationship work can foster personal growth, and people become healthier as they strive to achieve stronger ties with others.

Because intimate relationships involve varying expressions of sex and sexuality, this chapter will also focus on these subjects, including sexual anatomy and reproduction, and forms of sexual expression. The chapter concludes with a section on approaching sex responsibly.

Marriage and Its Alternatives

Marriage is one of the basic institutions of society. Most people still choose to marry, but the institution of marriage is facing a greater challenge than ever before. No longer does everyone assume that heterosexual marriage is the only natural and vital adult lifestyle. Some people acknowledge other alternatives, many of which are becoming increasingly accepted as a normal part of American life. Yet whether a person chooses to marry or to pursue an alternative to marriage, the goal is to develop a strong intimate relationship with another person.

The Need for Intimate Relationships

Close relationships with others satisfy a number of emotional needs. Everyone needs *intimacy*—a close, loving relationship that allows two people to share their deepest feelings and thoughts in an atmosphere of trust and acceptance. A close relationship can also help by providing *reassurance of worth*—the feeling that individuals are valued and considered special by the important people in their lives. Such a relationship can provide a sense of *support*—the knowledge that there are people one can turn to for help—and *nurturance*—the feeling that one can care for and be cared for by others. The lack of an intimate relationship, by contrast, can lead to feelings of loneliness and distress which can contribute to more severe problems.

As people grow from childhood to adulthood, their emotional needs are met through different types of relationships. Young children's most intimate relationships are with their parents. Children are dependent on their parents for their very survival. The support they get from their parents also gives them the security they need to take the first steps toward independence, and parental love gives them a sense of self-worth as well. As children grow, other close relationships become important. At first children develop intimate relationships with their siblings and friends. Then, as adolescents and young adults, they begin to form romantic relationships as well. For many adults, marriage becomes the most important intimate relationship.

A person's ability to form intimate relationships depends on several factors, including self-knowledge, self-esteem, self-efficacy, and feelings of caring, commitment, and tenderness toward another person. Honesty and empathy are also essential components of interpersonal intimacy, and effective communication is important in establishing intimacy and helping it to grow.[1]

The fact that some people do not develop intimate relationships suggests that certain barriers prevent them from doing so. One study identified several barriers to the start of intimate heterosexual relationships, including physical unattractiveness, fear of rejection, shyness, and clinging to traditional sex roles.[2] The study also suggested, however, that such barriers can be overcome. People can deal with unattractiveness by altering their appearance. Learning effective social skills and better means of communication can help people overcome shyness and fear of rejection, as can efforts to boost their self-esteem. Finally, although traditional sex roles are more difficult to alter, people can become more aware of their attitudes and attempt to learn new behaviors that will help them develop intimate relationships.

The Decision to Marry

Marriage is an institution that is changing. Traditionally, marriage has been an economic arrangement in which husbands have worked outside the home to provide financial security for their families, while wives have cared for the children and run the home. Today, however, this arrangement is changing. The roles of husband and wife are not as clearly defined as in the past, especially when both partners work and earn money for the family. Many people today expect and get more from marriage than economic benefits. They look to their spouses for sharing, emotional support, and intimacy. Happily married people often identify the spouse as their best friend.

Since antiquity, the marriage ceremony has provided a formal setting in which a couple can publicly affirm their love for and commitment to each other. (Tony Freeman/PhotoEdit)

Why Do People Marry?   The pressures for a couple to marry can be enormous. This pressure often comes from parents and other relatives as well as from the media. Sometimes the members of a family, ethnic group, or religious group may pressure individuals to marry so that a new generation can be raised in the teachings and values of the group.

Aside from these pressures, people marry for a variety of reasons. Some still marry for economic reasons. For others, marriage is viewed as the only acceptable framework in which to enjoy sex freely. Some people marry to escape from an unhappy home life, on the rebound from another relationship, or to avoid loneliness.

Researchers have identified several patterns in "high-quality," or well-balanced, marriages. Some of these married people tend to focus their energies on joint activities. Their strongest wish is to spend time together, yet they also strike a balance between privacy and togetherness. Other couples focus their energies on being parents and on raising their children. Some dual-career couples, although they spend much of their energy on their individual careers, develop intimacy by sharing what is going on in their work.[3] It thus seems that the desire to spend time together, raise children, and share other aspects of life and career are all healthy reasons for marrying.

Love and Romance   A basic element in most marriages is the love one person feels for another. There are many different types of love between persons, including parental love, fraternal love, and romantic love. Each requires caring and respect. Romantic love includes the qualities of deep intimacy and passion and begins with a feeling of intense attraction between two people.[4]

Although most marriages are based on romantic love, few couples sustain that romance as the years go by. Romantic love often develops into a less intense and all-consuming type of love known as companionate love.[5] A companionate love relationship is steadier than romantic love and is based on trust, sharing, affection, and togetherness. Maintaining the love in a marriage requires considerable effort and commitment. Married partners who succeed in communicating, giving physical warmth, and sharing interests and responsibilities are more likely to remain in love.[6]

Assessing Compatibility   When people are looking for a mate, they tend to be attracted to potential partners whose ethnic, religious, economic, and educational background is similar to their own. Certain physical attributes are also significant factors.[7] They are least likely to match up with a similar person in the area of compatibility of personality. Personality factors are not always easy to observe. Sometimes people do not reveal their true selves during courtship. Moreover, people with opposite personality types often attract each other, perhaps because one personality rounds out the other.

Unfortunately, great differences in personality can often lead to conflict later on. One study found that a source of marital dissatisfaction among husbands was a feeling that their wives were too possessive, neglectful, and openly admiring of other men. Dissatisfied wives complained that their husbands were possessive, moody, and openly attracted to other women. The study also found that sex is a source of great difficulties for unhappy married men and women. It found that women see sex as following from emotional intimacy, while men see it as a road to intimacy. As a result, men complain that their wives withhold sex from them and women complain that their husbands are too sexually aggressive.[8]

How can people be sure they are marrying people with whom they are truly compatible? One way is by taking plenty of time to get to know the other person. Researchers have found that couples seem to go through three stages in this process. First, each person tries to measure his or her good and bad qualities against those of the other person. People tend to be drawn to others who seem to have about the same assets and liabilities they themselves possess. Second, people look for compatible beliefs, attitudes, and interests to support the initial attraction. It is not until the third stage that people reveal to each other how they handle responsibility, react to disappointment, and cope with a wide variety of situations.[9] The key to compatibility is for the couple to be sure that they have arrived at this last stage before they think seriously about marriage. Such people are less likely to be unpleasantly surprised than are those who marry quickly.

Alternatives to Marriage

Since the 1960s there have been real changes in society's views on marriage, divorce, parenting, gender roles, and premarital sex.[10] While most young men and women still expect to marry, society no longer demands that people marry, stay married, or have children. Remaining single is now a widely accepted option. The restrictions and disadvantages of marriage are also an increasing concern for many people. In addition, there is a trend among both men and women toward marrying later in life.[11]

Finding Your Comfort Level with Sex Roles

People's self-esteem is very much affected by their success in measuring up to role expectations—their view of how others think they should behave. Some of the strongest role expectations are connected with sexuality. People want others to admire them as sexual beings and members of their gender— however members of their gender are expected to be.

For example, people often think they are supposed to feel strong attractions to others. The fact is, however, that people of both genders have varied levels of interest in sex: some people put a high priority on sex for its own sake, others value sex primarily for its emotional associations, and some people have relatively less interest in sex. Role expectations are nearly always narrower than the range of real human behavior.

People whose real nature fails to match sex-role expectations often suffer greatly. Having a low interest in sex may cause them to worry that they are homosexual; effeminate behavior in a man or aggressive behavior in a woman may also lead to fears of homosexuality. Homosexuality still carries a major stigma in American society. People not only tend to view it as opposite to their expectations about sexual preference, they also associate it with confusion involving other aspects of sexuality.

Is a man with feminine interests or a woman whose behavior is masculine necessarily homosexual? Certainly not. Some extremely macho men are gay, and some ultrafeminine women are lesbians. In a study of homosexual and heterosexual men by the Kinsey Institute, 18 percent of the gay men said they had been "very masculine" children. Most had not enjoyed typical girls' games as children. By contrast, 11 percent of the straight men said they had enjoyed feminine childhood activities such as playing with dolls.

The way in which parents raise children has little effect on how masculine or feminine the children are or on whether they are straight or homosexual. However, stifling masculine or feminine traits in children may have the effect of narrowing and reinforcing the children's expectations about sex roles. When parents reject parts of a child's personality, the child may come to undervalue and try to hide those traits.

The roots of these expectations are doubtless complex, based in the history of society and its traditional division of labor. But such expectations survive so strongly because the popular media—television, movies, literature, and other sources— bombard people with information about masculine and feminine behavior. The message is that men and women should conform to opposite roles. Men should be aggressive, and women should be passive. Other expectations—for example, the intense part sex should play in people's lives—are also supported by the media.

However, sexuality is, after all, only one component of a full life. A person who has less interest in sex than others have may take greater pleasure in many other aspects of life. A relatively low sex drive is not a sign of emotional disturbance. Similarly, sexual orientation is only one part of the human personality. Both homosexual people and straight people can be valued for strengths and qualities that have little or nothing to do with sexual orientation.

All people need to know that other people can accept them and love them as they are, regardless of their sexual orientation or whether they conform to the sex-role stereotypes. More important, people need to accept themselves as they are and feel comfortable with their sexual personalities.

Includes ideas from David Bjorklund and Barbara Bjorklund, "Straight or Gay?" *Parents* (October 1988): 93–98; Elizabeth Allgeier and Albert Allgeier, *Sexual Interactions* (Lexington, Mass.: D C Heath, 1984): 431–484.

Single Living With increasing numbers of people choosing to remain single or becoming single through divorce, there is a new acceptance of singlehood as a fulfilling alternative to marriage. For example, studies have shown that negative attitudes toward remaining single declined dramatically between 1957 and 1976.[12] This seems to suggest that marriage is becoming less important as an institution for structuring intimate relationships.

Who are the people who choose to remain single? Some are men and women who value their freedom and independence. Among women especially, greater career opportunities have brought more economic independence, and so marriage is no longer seen as the only route to economic security. In addition, many women no longer feel that marriage is necessary to achieve sexual expression and satisfaction.

The single state can be comfortable and rewarding for many people. Single people earning a good income can buy houses or rent apartments and establish homes of their own without waiting for a partner to come along. Many singles also earn enough to be able to pay for vacations or buy luxury items and other products. Moreover, many people find that it is easier to meet the demands of a career when they do not have to consider another person's interests while scheduling their time and activities.

Singlehood is not without disadvantages, however. Single people may have more difficulty in meeting their emotional needs than married people do. It is often more difficult for those who live alone to satisfy their needs for intimacy, interdependence, sexual satisfaction, and parenthood.

Cohabitation **Cohabitation,** an arrangement in which two unrelated people live together in a sexual relationship without marrying, has become more common in American society. Although some groups still disapprove of cohabitation on moral or religious grounds, a majority of Americans now seem to accept the idea of two people living together without marriage.[13] *cohabitation*

Why do people choose to live together instead of marrying? Some young people who are aware of the complexities of marriage prefer to try living together first so that they can find out whether they are mature enough to engage in a lifelong caring relationship. Often they also want to find out whether they are truly compatible. However, there is no evidence that living together increases the likelihood of a successful marriage.

Cohabitation is not limited to young people. A number of senior citizens live together but avoid formal marriage ties, often for economic reasons. Single, divorced, or widowed people who are retired sometimes lose their pensions or Social Security benefits if they marry or remarry. For these people, cohabitation makes good sense.

Couples who live together tend to face a number of problems, some of which are similar to the types of problems that confront married couples. In addition to the possibility of family disapproval and legal difficulties, cohabiting couples sometimes have conflicts over the purpose of the relationship.

Studies have suggested that the similarities between cohabitation and marriage are far more striking than the differences.[14] Cohabiting couples are not significantly different in regard to sex roles and division of labor. The way they divide tasks closely mirrors the behavior of married couples of a similar age. Cohabiting couples also appear to be no less monogamous than married couples are. People who live together, however, are more likely to end an unsatisfactory relationship than married couples are to seek a divorce. This makes sense, because many cohabiting couples live together as a trial to see whether they are truly compatible. Cohabitation has not displaced or eroded the institution of marriage, as many critics feared it might. Rather, it seems to be a part of the courtship phase of a relationship for many young people, most of whom expect to get married eventually.

Divorce

One of the greatest changes that has occurred in interpersonal relationships during the last few decades has been the increasing unwillingness of people to remain in an unsatisfactory marriage. In part this reflects people's changing expectations of what marriage should be and what it should provide. For example, people today expect greater personal fulfillment in marriage than did the people of a few generations ago. Along with changing expectations have come changing attitudes toward divorce. The great majority of Americans now feel that married people should not stay together, even for the sake of the children, if they are not getting along.[15] The increase in divorce is also a reflection of the changing status of women. As women have become less economically dependent on their husbands, divorce rates have increased.[16]

Divorce Today   Between 1962 and 1981 the number of divorces per year in the United States tripled. Although the rate has decreased slightly since then, the number of divorces each year remains quite high. About one marriage in three now ends in divorce.[17]

Divorce is often financially difficult. To ease problems concerning the division of property, child custody and support, and alimony, all but two states have some sort of provision for "no-fault" divorce, substantially reducing court costs. These divorce laws have backfired for many women, however. The provisions for the distribution of resources do not take into account the fact that most children live with the mother after a divorce. As a result, the income of women and their children one year after divorce is only about 67 percent of the predivorce income, while the income of divorced men is about 90 percent of the predivorce level.[18]

Changes have also taken place in the area of child custody, which is currently determined according to the best interests of the children. The laws in most states have been rewritten so that fathers now have a better opportunity to gain custody of their children.

The Effects of Divorce   Even though current divorce laws ease some of the problems of divorce, the ending of a marriage is painful for everyone involved. Divorced people have to deal with feelings of loneliness, anger, rejection, failure, panic, and self-doubt. Despite these negative feelings, there is optimism as well. Divorce can represent a new beginning, a chance to rebuild one's life, and an opportunity to seek a more fulfilling relationship than the one left behind. Most people who divorce do eventually remarry. Some studies have shown that remarried people report high levels of satisfaction, love, and trust in their new relationships. Children from a previous marriage, however, may place added strains on the new relationship.

What effect does divorce have on the children? For most children, the separation of their parents is a very painful experience. Extreme anger, regression

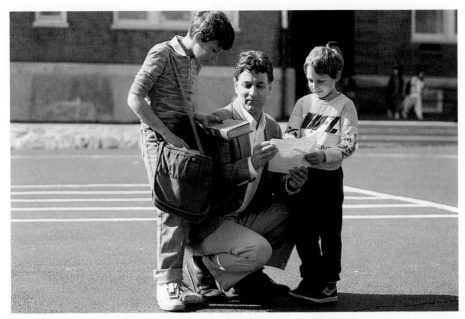

Parents who do not gain custody are usually given visitation rights not only for their own benefit but for the sake of the children, who will know that both parents are always there to provide care and support. (Richard Hutchings/InfoEdit)

to earlier forms of behavior, and physical symptoms such as asthma are not uncommon. For the first few months most children wish the couple could get back together so that the father or mother could rejoin the household. Children often feel that they did something to divide their parents. Younger children especially seem to blame themselves for the divorce. Older adolescents, by contrast, are more often angry or ashamed.[19] It helps if parents explain to the children that they are not at fault and that the problems are between the mother and father. Although children do suffer from the divorce of their parents, most of them adjust as time goes by.

Sex and Sexuality

Intimate relationships—whether between married couples, cohabiting couples, or dating couples—involve varying expressions of sex and sexuality. The way people think and feel about sex and sexuality is woven into the fabric of their daily lives. It has a profound impact on their personalities and their relationships with other people.

What exactly is the difference between sex and sexuality? Essentially, **sex** refers to either gender or the way in which people physically express affection or erotic feelings. **Sexuality** refers to the ways in which people's gender is part of their emotional, intellectual, social, and spiritual lives. In other words, sexuality is what it means to be a man or woman in society.

sex

sexuality

Sexuality includes not only actions and attitudes directly connected with sex but also other behaviors, such as assertiveness or submissiveness in work or other activities. Gender is not the only factor in sexuality. Sexuality also comes from what people have been taught to think and feel about being male or female and how they react to the expectations of others.

The Basis of Sexuality

People tend to act in certain ways because of a variety of factors, some biological and others learned. In men, the sex hormone testosterone may be a factor in a competitiveness toward other men. However, men may act in certain other ways because of what they have learned since childhood. Men may also behave in a certain way because of social pressure, such as following certain masculine roles.

These types of behavior reflect parts of men's personalities that are related to gender. It is often difficult, however, to tell whether a particular "male" behavior comes from a man's biological makeup, childhood upbringing, or response to societal expectations.

Similarly, women may act in certain ways because of the sex hormones estrogen and progesterone, because of so-called feminine behaviors learned since childhood, and because of societal expectations. Once again, it may be difficult to determine whether an aspect of women's sexuality is a result of being "born that way," being brought up that way, or feeling pressured by other people to act in a certain manner. For example, the traditional view is that women do not express anger through physical aggression, but there is still disagreement about how much of this is biological, how much is learned, and how much results from cultural expectations.

Some inborn differences in the way male and female babies behave are noticeable shortly after birth, although these differences are not as great as people once assumed.[20] Such sexual differences, which begin during prenatal development, are largely controlled by genes and hormones.[21] But then, from the first announcement of a baby's gender, society has different expectations depending on which gender the baby is. The baby gets a girl's name or a boy's name, a pink blanket or a blue one. The parents tend to talk more with a baby girl and roughhouse more with a baby boy. In most instances the fundamental sense of oneself as a male or female is established by age 3, and children behave in ways appropriate to their sex.[22]

Sexuality should not be thought of as something which is set unchangeably when people are young. Teenagers express their sexuality very differently from people who are middle-aged, and the sexuality expressed in middle age is different from the sexuality of older individuals.

Today the social conditioning that shaped the "typical" man and woman of the past has changed. More mothers are working outside the home, and they provide different role models from those provided by the homemakers of several decades ago. Children can now see that women have careers, and many little girls are encouraged to become physically active, assertive, and achievement-oriented. Many children also see that their fathers often help with the running of the house and are loving and tender.

These changes have affected the approach of many Americans not only to work and family but also to sexual experience. Some women now feel more free to be sexually assertive, and some men feel more free to express their emotional needs in a relationship. Men and women are also becoming better able to communicate their needs and desires to each other.

Such changes, however, are also leading to tensions both within society and for individuals. While some people feel at ease with changing gender roles, others feel very uncomfortable. People must decide for themselves what they feel comfortable with and act accordingly. Sexual expression can be an enriching and fulfilling experience, but only if people are fully aware of their attitudes toward sex and sexuality and can make choices based on their individual needs.

Attitudes toward Sex

Like all human behavior, sexual responses are not based on biology alone. The way people feel about themselves and their sexuality also influences how they relate to other people through sex. Thus, sexual behavior is shaped by what people have learned—starting as young children and continuing throughout life.

A major source of sexual learning is sex education classes in school (Figure 7.1). Although still controversial, sex education is generally accepted by a majority of the population, and courses are offered in over three-quarters of the nation's school districts. Recent investigation has shown that such programs do *not*, as once feared, promote early sexual behavior. In fact, the number of teenage pregnancies in some school districts with sex education programs has decreased.[23]

Source: Alan Guttmacher Institute, *Risk and Responsibility: Teaching Sex Education in America's Schools Today*, 1989. With permission.

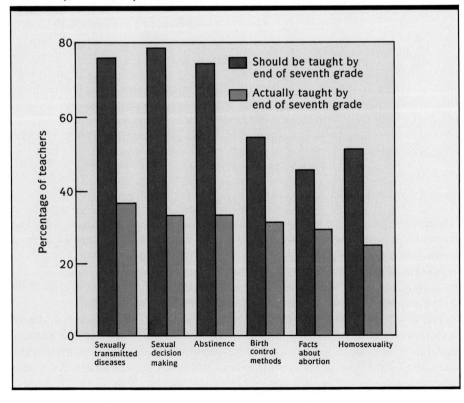

Figure 7.1 There is still quite a gap between the content of today's sex education curriculum and what teachers feel ought to be included. This graph compares the percentage of teachers who think particular topics should be taught by the end of the seventh grade and the percentage who are in school districts where the topics actually are taught at that level. Overall, however, sex education is gaining support. Eighty-five percent of Americans now approve of having sex education taught in schools, up from 69 percent 25 years ago.

So far as feelings are concerned, however, most people do not learn about sex or sexuality directly. Instead, they receive indirect messages from other people—starting with their parents—while observing the way those people act toward each other and the way they feel about their own sexuality.

Using what they have learned, people begin to shape their own ideas about how men and women should behave sexually, what is right and wrong, and the correct and incorrect way to handle sexual encounters and sexual feelings. Rarely, however, do people talk about how they feel about their bodies and about sex and sexuality. Despite the fact that feelings play a crucial role in sexual activity, people often ignore them. This may be based on a conflict between sexual activity and feelings and deeply held beliefs and values.

Feelings of guilt cause some people to be uncomfortable about having sex, preventing them from enjoying the experience. Others may deal with this conflict by repressing sexual behavior or feelings completely. Some people reduce their guilt by attributing sex to being "carried away at the time" and not really being responsible for one's behavior. Such an attitude may lead people to engage in hazardous sexual behaviors, such as risking pregnancy or disease by not planning for or using appropriate methods of contraception.

Sexual guilt and inner conflicts are poor reasons for people to take major risks involving sexual matters. Knowledge, rational thought, and self-appraisal can help people make decisions about these matters that are both comfortable for them and sensible in regard to their lives and futures.

Sexual Anatomy and Reproduction

An essential factor in developing a healthy sexuality is an understanding of sexual anatomy and physiology. This will contribute to a person's body awareness and to enhanced communication between sexual partners.

Basically, of course, the sexual anatomy enables human beings to reproduce. However, the reproductive aspect of sex is only one part of human sexual activity. Another aspect involves the intense sensations and feelings that people experience during sexual activity. These sensations and feelings are part of the erotic qualities associated with the sexual anatomy. This chapter will focus on the sexual organs and explain how sexual intercourse can lead to reproduction.

The Male Sexual Anatomy and Reproductive System

The male reproductive system has two basic functions: to produce sperm and to transport sperm to the site of conception. These two functions are carried out by specialized organs in the male reproductive system.

Several parts of the male sexual anatomy function not only reproductively but also as zones that can produce pleasure during sexual arousal (Figure 7.2). These sexual structures normally respond readily to stimulation.

penis
urethra
sperm

The most visible male sexual structure is the **penis,** the external organ of sexual intercourse (and urination). It is the outlet for the **urethra,** the passage through which male reproductive cells—**sperm**—and urine are discharged from the body. The penis is limp except when sexually aroused. As a man becomes sexually excited, blood rushes to the arteries that supply the penis and the surrounding tissue. The increased blood flow and pressure in the area cause the penis to become erect. Immediately before **orgasm**—the stage of sexual response referred to as the climax—physical reactions reach their most intense level.

orgasm

The **scrotum** is the loose pouch of skin that hangs behind and under the penis. The **testes,** or **testicles,** are two walnut-shaped organs located in the scrotum. The sperm are produced in the testes. Men's bodies produce new sperm cells every day, at the rate of about 200 million daily in a normal man. This process of continual sperm production begins at puberty and can continue well into old age. The testes also produce the male sex hormone testosterone, which stimulates the development of the sexual organs in a human fetus and the secondary sexual characteristics in an adult male.

scrotum

testes (testicles)

After sperm are produced in the testes, they mature while traveling through a network of several tubes—the **epididymis**—located in the scrotum behind each testicle. The sperm are stored and nourished in the epididymis before **ejaculation**—the process in which semen is forced out of the tip of the penis. During ejaculation the walls of each epididymis contract, pushing the sperm

epididymis

ejaculation

Figure 7.2 These are the anatomical features of the male sex organs. The testes, the male sex glands, are outside the main abdomen. This maintains a lower temperature which seems to favor sperm production.

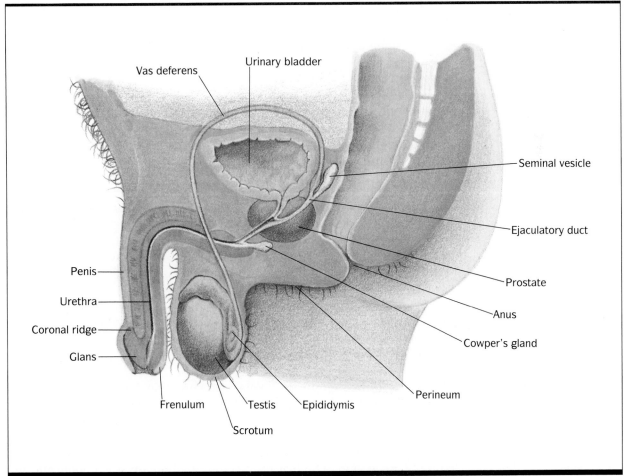

vas deferens into a pair of tubes called the **vas deferens,** which lead up into the man's body toward the seminal vesicles and the prostate gland. In the vas deferens sperm become capable of moving spontaneously in preparation for their journey into the female reproductive system.

seminal vesicles The **seminal vesicles** and **prostate gland,** which are located behind the
prostate gland urinary bladder, play an important role in the male reproductive system. Both
semen glands secrete fluids that combine with sperm to form a mixture called **semen,** the liquid that leaves the penis during ejaculation. This fluid provides the means for sperm to travel outside the body.

After linking with the seminal vesicles, each vas deferens constricts to form
ejaculatory ducts the **ejaculatory ducts,** which then join the urethra within the prostate gland. The urethra, which is the passageway for urine from the bladder, continues on to the opening of the penis. During ejaculation semen containing several hundred million sperm is discharged through the urethra and out the tip of the penis.

The Female Sexual Anatomy and Reproductive System

The female sexual anatomy also functions as both a reproductive system and a source of pleasure during sexual arousal (Figure 7.3). The female reproductive system has three main functions:

* To produce egg cells
* To position an egg cell where it can meet incoming sperm
* To provide an environment where, if fertilized, the egg cell can develop into a fetus

All these functions are carried out in a woman's body by organs in a process governed by a fairly regular monthly cycle in women of reproductive age. The external sex organs are more involved in sexual arousal. They include the vulva, the clitoris, and the vagina.

vulva *The Vulva* Most of a woman's most sensitive sexual areas are located in the external genital region called the **vulva** (which means "covering"). The two soft, sensitive folds of skin at either side of the opening of the vaginal area are
labia called the **labia.** These structures provide protection for the urethra (the tube from the urinary bladder through which urine passes out of the body) and the vagina.

clitoris *The Clitoris* The labia meet to form a hood over the **clitoris,** one of a woman's most sensitive sexual organs. For many women the clitoris is the primary focus of sexual arousal.

vagina *The Vagina* The **vagina** is a canallike structure that extends from the vulva inward to the internal sex organs. The vagina receives the penis during sexual intercourse and also acts as a passageway for a baby during birth.

ovaries *The Ovaries* This and the following internal organs make up the female reproductive system. The **ovaries** are two small organs, each about the size and shape of an almond. Each ovary is positioned close to the end of a Fallo-

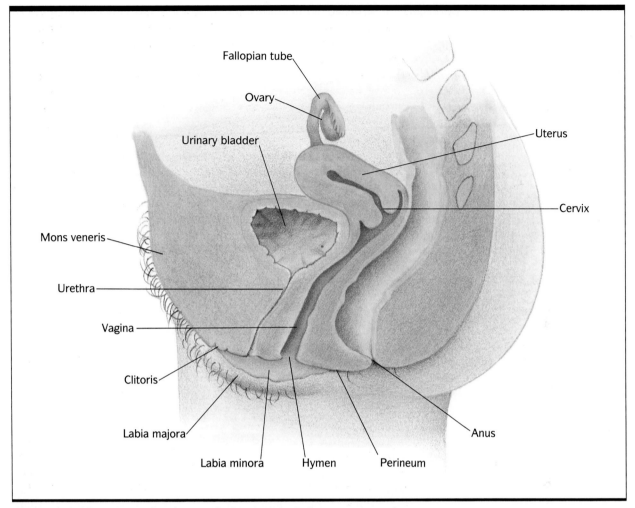

Figure 7.3 The primary female sexual structures include many external sensory zones as well as the internal reproductive organs, such as the female sex glands (the ovaries).

pian tube, which is the route the ovum takes when it leaves the ovary. Every normal woman is born with hundreds of thousands of unripened **ova** (singular: **ovum**) already present in her ovaries, but only about 400 will mature.

ovum (plural: ova)

At a point during puberty called **menarche,** a woman's ova begin to mature periodically and leave the ovaries in a process known as **ovulation.** This generally takes place at about the midpoint of a woman's menstrual cycle. In normal cycles ovulation occurs approximately 13 to 15 days before the first day of menstrual flow.

menarche

ovulation

The Fallopian Tubes The **Fallopian tubes** are tiny muscular tunnels that connect the ovaries and the uterus. When a mature ovum enters one of the Fallopian tubes, it travels slowly down the tube toward the uterus. Fertilization usually takes place in the Fallopian tubes.

Fallopian tubes

The Uterus The **uterus,** or womb, is pear-shaped in appearance and rests on its small end (the **cervix**) in the center of a woman's pelvis. It protects and

uterus

cervix

nourishes the fertilized ovum, allowing it to develop into a fetus. During pregnancy the uterus expands tremendously—from the size of a woman's fist into a large muscular pouch that almost entirely fills the woman's abdomen.

The Menstrual Cycle   Every month, if a woman is not pregnant, the inner lining of the uterus goes through a process of renewal and preparation known *menstrual cycle* as the **menstrual cycle.** Basically, the menstrual cycle is the way in which a woman's uterus prepares to receive and nourish a fertilized ovum.

The menstrual cycle begins when the pituitary gland secretes follicle-stimulating hormone (FSH). This hormone signals the ovary to ripen an ovum. If an ovum in one of the Fallopian tubes becomes fertilized, it travels down to the uterus and implants itself in the uterine lining, which develops further and nourishes the growing fetus. If pregnancy does not occur, the uterus sloughs off the lining entirely and prepares a new one. The blood and tissues of the *menstruation* old lining pass through the cervix and vagina in a discharge known as **menstruation.** A woman's menstrual flow generally lasts 3 to 6 days, and the typical menstrual cycle lasts 27 to 34 days.

Menopause: Myths and Reality

menopause **Menopause** is the gradual, permanent ending of a woman's menstruation and cyclic reproductive activity. It is brought on by decreased production of female sex hormones. On the average menopause begins at about age 51, but it may begin as late as age 55.[24] At that time a woman's menstrual periods usually weaken for a few months and then stop altogether. This change marks the end of the reproductive phase of a woman's life.

During menopause the ovaries, after 30 or 40 years of activity, lose their ability to produce mature eggs. While a woman may welcome the end of fertility, the reduced production of female hormones in her body can create problems. Subtle changes may occur in the body as a result of hormone deficiency. The skin may gradually become drier and more wrinkled. The vagina may become drier, and its lining thinner and more tender. Throughout the body bones may lose calcium and become more brittle.

It is not true, however, that a woman's sexual interest and activity decline after menopause. In fact, many menopausal and postmenopausal women, no longer concerned about becoming pregnant, actually feel more sexual desire and satisfaction.

Forms of Sexual Expression

People's knowledge and attitudes about sex influence and are reflected in the ways in which they express their sexuality. Sexual expression can take many forms, from sexual fantasies to sexual intercourse to a variety of other types of sexual expression and behavior.

Sexual Fantasies

Sexual fantasies arouse people just as much as the real thing does. People spend time wondering about, hoping for, wishing for, and even fearing different kinds of sexual experiences. It is not unusual to wish for a passionate love affair with a friend or a mysterious stranger. Sexual fantasies are usually harmless—in fact, healthy—even when they involve what might be considered bizarre behavior. For most people sexual fantasies are a safe way of working out fears, anxieties, or forbidden desires.

It is quite normal for fantasies to pop into a person's consciousness in the midst of daily chores and then vanish. Sharing these sexual fantasies with a partner may strengthen intimacy and enrich the sexual experience. Fantasies may be a problem, however, if they take up too much time and interfere with normal behavior.

Masturbation

Attitudes toward **masturbation**—sexual self-stimulation—have changed in recent years. For centuries people were discouraged from masturbating because of myths surrounding the activity. One myth was that masturbation is harmful to the body. Today, however, authorities on sexual behavior recognize masturbation as a legitimate way of exploring the body and finding out how it works. People start masturbating when they are infants, touching themselves all over to find out what feels good. In the same way, some adults find that masturbation can provide a release for sexual feelings or can help them learn what is sexually pleasurable. Many people reach orgasm more quickly and easily during masturbation than during intercourse.

masturbation

In excess, masturbation may be a symptom of dissatisfaction or anxiety, a signal that other areas of one's sex life need fulfillment. However, unless it interferes with daily life, masturbation can be considered a normal sexual behavior.

Petting and Foreplay

There are many ways of showing affection and enjoying sex with another person besides sexual intercourse. Most people start out kissing and stroking each other and then move on to other types of petting as they get more ex-

Good communication is an essential part of sexual expression between partners. (Harriet Gans/The Image Works)

cited. As they hug and kiss, a couple may explore each other's bodies, fondling and caressing genital areas, the breasts, and other sensitive areas. Petting techniques vary from person to person and from partner to partner depending on what the lovers enjoy and feel comfortable with. Many couples enjoy petting as much as intercourse and use it as a substitute when they want to feel close but intercourse is impossible or inconvenient. Quite often petting is also a

foreplay

form of **foreplay**—sexual activity leading to intercourse.

American society tends to emphasize intercourse as the most important sexual act, and many people behave as if all emotional and moral issues connected with sexual behavior were linked to that single act. However, petting is where most people first encounter the emotional issues and conflicts that arise in sexual relationships.

Sexual Intercourse

The act of sexual intercourse is regarded by most people in most cultures as the highest point of a sexual relationship. Sexual intercourse can be passionate, the expression of the deepest love between two people, but it can also be awkward, playful, or even dull depending on the two people involved, their feelings for each other, and the circumstances.

Although there are many parallels between the sexual responses of men and those of women, there are also some significant differences in regard to sexual intercourse. Men are usually more easily aroused and can engage in sexual intercourse more rapidly than women can. The average woman requires more psychological and physical stimulation before she begins to respond. Men also tend to depend less on circumstances—such as romantic settings—to become aroused. Yet the differences between the sexes are not nearly as great as those between different individuals.

Oral Sex

Oral stimulation of the female genitals (*cunnilingus*) or the male genitals (*fellatio*) by a sexual partner is a matter on which people—and even cultures—differ markedly. In some cultures oral sex is prevalent; in others it is rare. In the United States oral-genital contact is common, practiced by more than half of all married couples.[25] The religious beliefs of some communities and families, however, forbid any type of sexual activity except intercourse.

There are a wide variety of attitudes toward oral sex, ranging from pleasurable anticipation to disgust. In many ways oral sex is one of the most intimate types of lovemaking because it involves exposing private parts of the body that many feel most shy about to another person's view and touch. While oral sex is pleasurable for some people, not everyone enjoys it. As with any kind of sexual activity, it is best for each individual to decide whether to engage in oral sex.

Homosexuality

homosexuality

Homosexuality is a sexual or emotional preference for persons of one's own sex. Few areas of human behavior have produced more theories or provoked more controversy than the sexual tendencies and behaviors of gay men and lesbian women.

A number of ancient societies and some contemporary ones have approved of homosexual behavior and at times even made it an established practice. A comprehensive study of various cultures conducted several decades ago revealed that 49 of 76 preliterate societies either accepted or actually prescribed homosexual activity, although none practiced it exclusively.[26] Modern Western cultures, however, have encouraged only the expression of **heterosexuality**—a sexual or emotional preference for persons of the opposite sex. As a result, many men and women may repress their homosexual tendencies.

heterosexuality

No one knows for certain what factors cause a person to pursue a homosexual behavior pattern. Previously accepted explanations, such as family environment or seduction by older individuals, have not withstood scientific scrutiny. The idea of a genetic basis for homosexuality is also inconclusive, although research has indicated that genes may have an indirect effect on sexual orientation.

Whatever the factors that lead to homosexuality, an awareness of sexual orientation (homosexual or heterosexual) generally occurs during late childhood and adolescence.[27] Moreover, researchers agree that experimental homosexual activity is rather common, especially in adolescence.

Contrary to some stereotypes, homosexuality does not constitute proof of emotional or mental illness. In fact, the American Psychiatric Association in its *Diagnostic and Statistical Manual of Mental Disorders* (DSM-III) removed homosexuality from its mental illness categories in 1980.

In recent years, homosexuals have formed organizations to help fight for equal rights, and society has become somewhat more accepting of homosexuality. Discrimination still persists and appears to have increased in some places as a response to the acquired immune deficiency syndrome (AIDS) epidemic. However, this epidemic has also brought public sympathy, and people increasingly recognize that gay individuals should have the opportunity to live openly.

Coercive Sexual Behavior

Sexual behavior is a very private affair, and what is considered acceptable or unacceptable depends a great deal on the people involved. What some people consider abnormal may be perfectly normal and acceptable to others, but certain behaviors can certainly be considered deviant and undesirable. Many of these behaviors involve sex as a result of coercion rather than a mutual act between willing and consenting individuals. One example of such behavior is rape. Another is the sexual abuse of children, including incest.

Rape Rape occurs when a person—usually a woman—is forced to have sex against his or her will. According to the FBI, rape continues to be one of the fastest rising crimes. Rape is also more common than many people realize. In recent studies of women on college campuses, one in six said they were the victim of rape or attempted rape during the preceding year.[28] Often it is not a stranger who is the offender but a man the woman knows—so-called acquaintance or date rape.

A recent report revealed the disquieting fact that among males and females in the same college, only 25 percent of the men reported using sexually aggressive behaviors (including rape), whereas 54 percent of the women reported being sexually victimized. While it might be thought that many of the men, or many of the women, simply lied, the questionnaire was designed and

Female activists take a powerful stand against violence directed at women. Self-defense programs for women are representative of their efforts. (David Brownell)

tested in a way that minimized the likelihood of this occurring. Instead, the researchers suggest that the men did not perceive accurately the amount of force and coercion they used and failed to respect, or to interpret correctly, a woman's resistance.

In addition to the thousands of rapes reported each year, official estimates suggest that there may be 3 to 10 times as many cases that are committed but not reported.[29] This suggests a problem of overwhelming proportions for women. The problem has been worsened by the fact that rape is an area where the victim has sometimes been blamed for instigating the crime because of the clothes she wears, her actions, or even because she has walked alone late at night. Many times the law has looked at the behavior and reputation of the victim when putting a rapist on trial.

Conventional preventive measures have also been directed largely at women. They are advised to take extra caution in potentially dangerous situations. For example, when taking car trips alone, women are urged to have a good supply of gas, to lock the vehicle when leaving it, and to check both the front and the back before getting in. They are advised to drive with friends and not to pick up hitchhikers or hitchhike themselves. They are also warned that an empty home or apartment can be a potential danger, that they should take care to identify strangers before opening the door to them, that they should avoid entering themselves if they suspect someone is inside, and that they should avoid going to a date's home unless they know him well.[30]

All this is sound advice, but it still has the effect of suggesting that victims are responsible because they neglected to take care. However, society is slowly changing its views on rape. Rape hot lines are being made available to victims. Hospitals and police departments have specially trained personnel, often women, to help. Education is being used to teach women the psychological and physical skills needed to help them take care of themselves, including how and when to fight an assailant.

Incest and Child Sexual Abuse A serious misuse of sex also occurs in the case of incest and other child sexual abuse. Sexual abuse of children cuts across all socioeconomic boundaries and leaves great emotional scars on those who are molested.[31] It is estimated that as many as 40 million Americans may have been sexually victimized as children. These numbers are disturbing, especially when one considers that children who are abused are more likely to become abusers when they reach adulthood.[32]

Studies have shown that most sexual abuse happens to children between the ages of 9 and 12. The vast majority of cases, from 85 to 90 percent, involve a person who is already known to the child.[33] Moreover, rather than being an isolated incident, most cases of sexual abuse involve a situation that develops gradually over a period of time, with repeated incidents. In most cases the abuser uses bribery or intimidation rather than force to get the child to do what he or she wants.[34]

Children who are sexually abused are frequently so embarrassed that they keep the painful experience to themselves. One newspaper poll reported that one-third of people who said that they had been sexually abused never told anyone about the experience.[35] Although experts have found that some victims of sexual abuse reach adulthood relatively unharmed, many others develop serious psychological problems. Women may be distrustful of men, feel unattractive, or be afraid of intimacy. Men may be confused about their sexual identity, deeply ashamed, or sexually aggressive. In general, people who were sexually abused as children have lower self-esteem than others and are often anxious, depressed, and guilt-ridden.[36]

An increasing number of groups and organizations are making people more aware of the problem of sexual abuse and giving parents guidelines for protecting their children from sexual abuse and dealing with it if it does occur. Special programs in schools teach young children what to do if they are threatened with any kind of sexual abuse. Books are available that explain sexual abuse to children in a nonfrightening manner. Parents should be alert to potential sources of danger and should take their children very seriously when they report an incident.

Approaching Sex Responsibly

Sexuality is a very powerful force that influences many of the ways in which people act and behave. If sex is misused and abused, it can result in a great deal of pain and suffering. Responsible and healthy sexuality involves a consideration of the feelings and needs of others as well as one's own.

When approached responsibly, sexual expression adds a new dimension to relationships—a dimension that can add greater intimacy and understanding. Approached irresponsibly, however, it can lead to greater risk. Partners who communicate poorly with each other or treat each other badly may not enjoy sex, and their relationship may be put in danger. Today, with AIDS and other sexually transmitted diseases, a greater responsibility between partners is also required to ensure that sex is safe and not harmful to health.

Most people feel awkward and uncomfortable about sex, especially in first or new sexual encounters. Sexual feelings are exciting and acting on them can conflict with what a person has been taught by parents, friends, and cultural or religious leaders. Some people feel pressured to keep up with the sexual experiences of friends even if they have personal reservations about engaging in sex. Such conflicts and pressures can be puzzling. There is nothing wrong with abstaining from sex if a person is not ready. Approaching sex responsibly and safely is a healthy approach to sexual behavior.

Sex as a means of intimate expression is only part of the story. The reproductive function of sex is another major concern not only for the creation of children but also for the additional hopes, feelings, and fears that it awakens in any relationship. Sexuality can, therefore, involve responsibility for life as well as for the needs and feelings of others.

Chapter Summary

- Intimate relationships satisfy a number of emotional needs, including intimacy, reassurance of worth, a sense of support, and nurturance.
- Barriers to intimate relationships include physical unattractiveness, a fear of rejection, shyness, and clinging to traditional sex roles.
- The roles of husband and wife are not as clearly defined as in the past.
- People today marry for a variety of reasons, such as financial security, an acceptable framework for sexual relations, escape from an unhappy home life, and avoidance of loneliness.

- In assessing compatibility, people try to measure their own qualities against those of the other person, look for compatible beliefs and interests, and evaluate how the other person handles responsibility, reacts to disappointment, and copes with problems.

- Some people choose to remain single because they value freedom and independence and do not view marriage as essential for financial security or sexual satisfaction.

- Cohabitation may help people discover whether they can handle a mature relationship and are compatible.

- Many people see divorce as a viable alternative to an unsatisfactory marriage, but divorce may be difficult for the family.

- Essentially, sex refers to a person's gender and to types of sexual expression, while sexuality refers to the way gender is integrated into all aspects of life.

- Attitudes toward sex and sexual behavior are shaped by the influence of other people and through experience and education.

- Major structures of the male anatomy include the penis and scrotum. The male reproductive system consists of the testes, which produce sperm; the epididymis and vas deferens, which store and nourish the sperm and transport them from the testes; and the seminal vesicles and prostate gland, which secrete fluids that combine with sperm to produce semen.

- Major structures of the female anatomy include the vulva, clitoris, and vagina. The female reproductive system consists of the ovaries, which contain the ova; the Fallopian tubes, which are the passages where fertilization takes place; and the uterus, which is where a fertilized ovum develops into a fetus.

- The menstrual cycle is a monthly process during which a woman's uterus prepares to receive and nourish a fertilized ovum.

- There are a great variety of types of sexual expression and behavior. Individuals may differ in the types of sexual expression with which they feel most comfortable and which they will accept and engage in.

- Certain sexual behaviors—those which result from coercion rather than mutual consent and caring—are considered unacceptable in society. Among these deviant behaviors are rape, incest, and child sexual abuse.

- Responsible sexual expression requires a consideration of the feelings and needs of others as well as one's own. It requires good communication and mutual respect and caring.

Chapter

8

Sexual Health and Reproduction

Objectives

When you have studied this chapter, you should be able to:

- Identify the various contraceptive methods, explaining the benefits and drawbacks of each.

- Discuss how the role of parenthood has changed in recent years and describe how parents can foster healthy development in their children.

- Discuss the importance of planning for pregnancy and describe the beginnings of pregnancy and the development of a fetus.

- Identify and explain various techniques for terminating a pregnancy and discuss attitudes toward abortion.

- Discuss the choices parents must make in preparing for childbirth and describe the stages of labor.

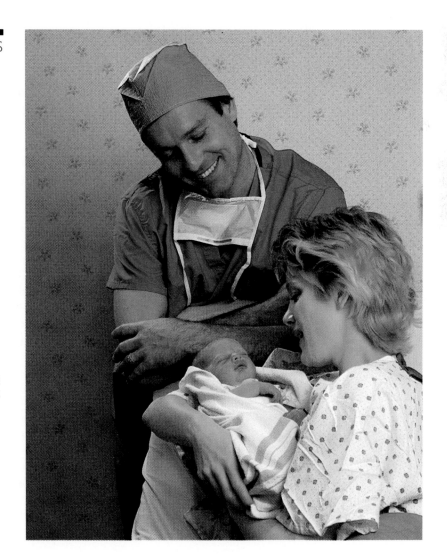

Sexual activity plays an important role in many close relationships, but it has a much greater significance. As the beginning of the process through which new lives are formed, it is intertwined with some of the most important questions people face. In regard to reproduction, at least three major issues touch on individual health and the health of society at large. The first is a fundamental concern—how to maximize the health and well-being of the child and the mother during the reproductive process.

The second issue concerns the dangers of infectious disease. Sexually transmitted diseases (STDs) have been very resistant to public health measures in the United States and throughout the world. These diseases include several types that can be transmitted from a mother to her developing fetus.

The third issue has to do with conflicting personal philosophies. For example, techniques for birth control have been a source of major disagreement in American society for some time. Some people believe that given the growing world population and the number of unwanted pregnancies, birth control is a viable and responsible course of action. Others believe that interrupting the natural link between sex and pregnancy or terminating a pregnancy once it has started goes against morality and ethical thought.

This chapter will address these three issues by exploring methods of birth control, decisions about parenthood, the process of pregnancy, techniques of abortion, and finally the birth event itself. It will not attempt to answer philosophical questions, because that is the responsibility of the individual.

Sexual Responsibility and Safer Sex

In sexual intercourse the male's penis deposits millions of sperm into the female's vagina. From there the sperm travel up into the uterus and then the Fallopian tubes, where they may encounter an ovum. If a sperm and ovum unite, the egg becomes fertilized and a few days later implants itself in the woman's uterine lining.

Frequently, however, a couple does not wish to conceive a child. They may be unable or unwilling to care for a child. Perhaps they are unmarried and do not want children or are married but wish to remain childless. In such cases they will want to avoid pregnancy.

In addition to pregnancy, another result of sexual intercourse may be the contraction of an STD. STDs can be very serious. They are covered in depth in Chapter 9. People who approach sex responsibly and safely are concerned about not spreading an STD to their partners.

There are a variety of methods for avoiding pregnancy and reducing the possibility of contracting an STD. Knowledge about the different possibilities, how to use them, and how effective they are is vital for a safer and more responsible sex life. Decisions about contraceptive methods should be based on reliable information about their safety and effectiveness. Another factor, of course, must be the individual's personal beliefs. If a person has inner doubts about using a contraceptive method, he or she may hesitate to use it.

In the past, workers in the field of family planning thought that the ultimate answer to effective birth control could be found in good, easy-to-obtain contraceptive methods, but this idea was only partly true. What these family-planning experts were ignoring was the human factor—the question of whether people would learn about contraceptive methods and then apply

Taking a Broader View of Birth Control

Science and technology have made it easier for people throughout the world to decide when and whether to have children. Still, in prosperous countries as well as poor ones, unwanted pregnancies occur, and the global population continues to soar. The solution—birth control and family planning—is unevenly successful throughout the world.

One reason is that not everyone believes that birth control is desirable. To farmers in some developing nations, the advantage of creating another pair of hands to work in the fields seems to compensate for the problem of having another mouth to feed. Resentment is also felt toward family-planning organizations from the West, which are sometimes perceived as trying to limit the growth of poorer nations.

In developed countries, many people believe that population growth is not necessarily going to cause economic decline. There are also many people who consider life an absolute value which should not be hindered by any means.

However, most nations at all levels of economic development perceive that fast-growing populations represent a real economic liability. Some, such as China, have instituted successful family-planning policies that even supporters of birth control find harsh. Many others, including Colombia in South America and Thailand in the Far East, have had surprising success in promoting family planning. Many nations in the West are getting close to zero population growth.

Ironically, one of the developed nations least successful at family planning is the United States, which has been a major advocate of birth control and is still the largest contributor to international programs. Its lack of success at home is particularly noticeable among teenagers. Almost all the developed nations of Europe, even those with similar patterns of adolescent sexual activity, have lower rates of teenage pregnancy. The higher success rate in other countries compared with the United States may result from the fact that contraceptive services in Europe are more widely available, free or inexpensive, and confidential. In addition, there are fewer methods of birth control available here than in other countries.

However, the failure of family planning and birth control is most severe in the developing nations, where, according to the World Health Organization, five of every six couples of reproductive age are still not using adequate methods of birth control. The problem is particularly severe in parts of Africa, Asia, and Latin America.

What are some of the reasons given for the limited success of birth control in the third world? The cost of birth control methods is one problem. Although many organizations make financial and other contributions, money is a major requirement for successful programs. Recently, the United States has been less willing to support family-planning organizations, especially those which have provided abortion services in developing countries.

Religious issues also play a large role in the availability of birth control programs. Ireland has a high pregnancy rate, doubtless because of its strong religious beliefs.

In addition to these fairly complex issues, there are three very simple ones. In both developing and developed countries family planning is most successful if contraceptive drugs and devices are available easily and inexpensively and if information is available about the advantages of using them and about methods for using them correctly.

Includes ideas from Peter Donaldson and Charles Keely, "Population and Family Planning: An International Perspective," *Family Planning Perspectives* (November–December 1988): 307ff; Philip J. Hilts, "Birth Control Backlash," *New York Times Magazine* (December 16, 1990): 41ff.

them correctly every time. It turns out that human error has a great deal to do with the effectiveness of any birth control method. With many contraceptive methods there is a significant difference between how effective the method is in theory and how effective it is when people actually use it.

Contraceptive Methods Requiring No Medical Supervision

Of the various contraceptive and birth control methods available, those which do not require medical supervision include abstinence; condoms; spermicidal jellies, creams, and foams; vaginal sponges; and withdrawal.

Abstinence The most effective means of avoiding pregnancy and controlling the spread of STDs (including AIDS) is abstinence from sexual intercourse. Abstinence, though unpopular, is possible. For some people it may mean avoiding all forms of sexual expression. For others it may mean engaging in alternative forms of sexual intimacy, such as petting and mutual masturbation.

condom

Condoms A **condom** is a thin latex or natural skin sheath that is placed over the erect penis just before intercourse. If used correctly, it captures and holds the man's semen so that sperm will not be deposited in the vagina.

The condom is an effective contraceptive device. It is also the second most effective method, after abstinence, for protection against AIDS and other STDs. To achieve the best protection against disease, however, latex condoms must be used. Natural skin condoms may have minute holes that allow some semen to pass through. Moreover, condoms must be applied at the appropriate time to ensure that sperm does not impregnate the woman during foreplay. Care must also be taken during withdrawal to prevent semen from touching the female genitals.

The condom has been widely used throughout the world for centuries. With no harmful physical side effects, it is the leading barrier method of birth control. When used in combination with vaginal foam, it is one of the most effective birth control devices. The fact that it provides a physical barrier between the partners makes it effective against disease too.

Jellies, Creams, and Foams Nonprescription jellies, creams, and foams are spermicides that the woman inserts before intercourse, deep in her vagina against the cervix, with a plastic applicator; they act by destroying sperm, and are effective as additional protection when used with barrier devices such as condoms and diaphragms. In addition to killing sperm, spermicides are also effective in reducing bacterial and virally caused STDs. In fact, researchers state that if spermicides are used in addition to condoms, the risk of contracting AIDS can be further reduced.[1] (Spermicides should not be used alone for this purpose, however.) In addition, women who use spermicides are only one-third as likely to develop cervical cancer and other diseases that are linked to sexual infection.[2]

The Vaginal Sponge In 1983 the U.S. Food and Drug Administration (FDA) approved the vaginal contraceptive sponge for over-the-counter sale. The sponge, which must be moistened to release its spermicidal chemical, fits into the vagina and covers the cervix. It must be left in place for at least 6 hours after intercourse and can work effectively for as long as 24 hours. A loop is attached to the sponge for easy removal.

The vaginal sponge does not provide protection against AIDS or other STDs. However, it appears to prevent pregnancy as reliably as the diaphragm, though not as dependably as the pill and the intrauterine device. In some women the sponge may cause irritation or an allergic reaction, and problems with removal have been reported.

Withdrawal **Withdrawal** is an ancient contraceptive method. The man withdraws his penis from the woman's vagina before he ejaculates. The idea is to prevent sperm from entering the vagina by ejaculating outside the woman's body. The apparent advantage of this method is that it is available to everyone and costs nothing, but it is one of the more unreliable techniques of birth control. Not only is there a risk of impregnation from sperm that is secreted before ejaculation, but it is also possible that the man will miscalculate the time for withdrawal or get carried away. Of course, there is no barrier to prevent contraction of AIDS or other STDs.

withdrawal

Contraceptive Methods Requiring Nonsurgical Medical Supervision

Among the available birth control methods that require some medical care and supervision are oral contraceptives, the intrauterine device, the diaphragm, and the cervical cap.

Oral Contraceptives Since 1960, when the FDA first approved **oral contraceptives (the pill)** for use with a doctor's prescription, millions of prescriptions for them have been written in the United States alone. Except for surgical sterilization, the pill is the most widely used form of contraception among

oral contraceptives (the pill)

When taken regularly, birth control pills prevent pregnancy by releasing hormones that prevent ovulation. (David Young-Wolff/PhotoEdit)

Although intrauterine devices are one of the most reliable forms of birth control, they can sometimes cause cramps and even injury. (Tony Freeman/PhotoEdit)

American women.[3] For the pill to be effective, the directions and schedule for taking it must be followed strictly. Missed days make a woman susceptible to pregnancy. On average, 2 of 100 women on the pill become pregnant, but the number is even lower when the regimen is followed carefully.[4] Unfortunately, the pill provides no protection against AIDS or other STDs.

Most forms of the pill introduce into the body certain synthetic equivalents of the natural sex hormones so that ovulation is prevented. Research has shown that ovulation can be effectively prevented with much smaller doses of hormones than were originally used; this is fortunate, because the likelihood of developing side effects is directly related to the amount of hormones in the pill. Most brands on the market today are "combination" pills; that is, each tablet contains both a synthetic form of progesterone and a synthetic form of estrogen.

For some women the pill does have side effects. The most serious are an increased risk of developing circulatory system disorders such as blood clots (usually in the legs), which can impair circulation; an increased risk of heart attacks; and a greater risk of death from a stroke. All these risks are increased if the woman smokes. The risk of pill use is greatest for women over 35 who smoke and for all women over 45.[5] Pill users also run a greater risk of developing gallbladder disease requiring surgery; benign liver tumors, which can be fatal if they rupture; and high blood pressure. If a woman takes oral contraceptives by mistake when she is pregnant, her baby may have birth defects involving the heart and the limbs.[6]

There are, however, some positive aspects of the pill. Recent studies have suggested that pill users have a decreased risk of contracting cancer of the ovaries and uterus.[7] The pill also regulates the menstrual cycle and reduces cramps and excessive blood loss. The likelihood of developing iron deficiency anemia, acne, pelvic inflammatory disease, ectopic pregnancies, noncancerous breast tumors, and ovarian cysts has also been shown to be reduced.

Whatever the risks and benefits of oral contraceptives, they are a very effective method of birth control, and the overall risk of death from their use is low—below that of pregnancy and childbirth itself—except among women who smoke. With all oral contraceptives, continuing medical supervision is necessary to minimize these risks and determine the appropriate pill for each woman.

intrauterine device (IUD)

The Intrauterine Device (IUD) **Intrauterine devices (IUDs)** are made of soft, flexible plastic molded into various sizes and shapes; some are coated with copper. They are inserted into the uterus by a physician. Some types of IUDs must be replaced every year or so. Other types can be left in place indefinitely.

Exactly how IUDs work is not completely understood, but it is thought that they interfere with the implantation of a fertilized egg in the lining of the uterus. It is also clear that they have no effect against the infectious agents of STDs and provide no protection against AIDS.

Some women select the IUD as a contraceptive method because it is long-lasting, need not be put in place before intercourse, and does not change body chemistry. IUDs are very effective, with a failure rate of 1 to 6 pregnancies per 100 women per year.[8]

IUDs do have disadvantages, however. About 15 percent have to be removed because of persistent uterine bleeding or cramps.[9] They have also been known to slip out of the uterus without the user's noticing. Finally, people have filed costly lawsuits charging that IUDs cause infections and infertility. These lawsuits caused the top U.S. manufacturer of IUDs to take its products off the market in early 1986.[10]

The Diaphragm   The **diaphragm** is a shallow rubber cup made of fine latex rubber stretched over a flexible, circular metal ring. The ring can be bent so that the entire device can easily be compressed and passed into the vagina. Upon release, it rests in the upper, large portion of the vagina, where it covers the cervix completely. The diaphragm must be fitted by a physician.

diaphragm

The diaphragm works as a mechanical barrier to prevent sperm from passing into the uterus. However, because it is not a complete barrier, it provides little protection against STDs. Spermicidal jelly or cream, which a woman must apply to the diaphragm before she inserts it, adds to its effectiveness as a contraceptive.

When a diaphragm is inserted properly, it causes no discomfort and neither partner notices it. The diaphragm does have a significant failure rate, but forgetfulness, improper insertion and use, or early removal—it should stay in place for at least 6 hours after intercourse—probably account for many of the pregnancies.

The Cervical Cap   The cervical cap is a soft rubber cap, smaller than a diaphragm, that fits snugly over the cervix. Variations on this device have been used by women throughout the world for centuries. The cervical cap must be fitted by a physician. Before intercourse, it is half filled with contraceptive cream or jelly and inserted. It is left in place for at least 6 hours afterward. The device remains effective for 1 to 3 days. A one-way valve lets menstrual blood and cervical mucus pass through. The cervical cap has a low failure rate, although it is sometimes dislodged during intercourse.

The cervical cap is classified by the FDA as a "significant-risk device" and should not be used by women who have diabetes mellitus, cardiovascular disease, liver or kidney disease, gonorrhea, active herpes simplex type 2 infection, an abnormal Pap smear, toxic shock syndrome, or a cervical or vaginal infection.[11] It also provides no protection against STDs.

Natural Methods of Contraception

Some people prefer not to use any methods of contraception that require medications or mechanical devices yet do not want to rely only on abstinence or withdrawal. Natural contraception requires careful planning and some initial guidance from a physician.

To use natural family planning, the couple avoids intercourse during the time when the woman may be ovulating. A number of variables are involved, including the length of time the sperm remain alive in the woman's reproductive tract and the length of time the released ovum is available for fertilization. Scientists do not know how to pinpoint these variables, and so there is about a 10 to 20 percent failure rate with natural family planning.[12] Moreover, these methods do not provide a barrier against the transmission of AIDS and other STDs.

A key variable in natural family planning is the timing of the woman's ovulation. This can be determined with fair accuracy in a number of ways, including the calendar method, the temperature method, the mucus evaluation method, and the sympto-thermal method.

The Calendar Method   This method is based on the observation that most women ovulate around the fourteenth day before the next menstrual period. A woman must keep about a 1-year record of her periods to be able to determine her fertile period with a reasonable degree of accuracy. Women vary considerably in the length of their menstrual cycles.

To use the calendar method effectively, the woman needs to get the advice of a doctor to learn how to chart her menstrual periods and calculate the days when it is "safe" and "unsafe" for her to have intercourse. Studies have shown that this method is the least reliable natural method.

The Temperature Method   With this method, a woman tries to pinpoint the time of ovulation by charting her basal body temperature every day. Ovulation will be followed by a slight rise in temperature (one-half degree Celsius) that will last until the start of the next menstrual cycle. This method is not foolproof. Although the temperature change provides a fairly good indication that ovulation has occurred, a slight rise in temperature can also be caused by minor colds and infections. The temperature and calendar methods, used together, are sometimes referred to as the rhythm method.

The Mucus Evaluation Method   A third method of natural family planning is known as mucus evaluation. It has long been known that the consistency of the mucus in the vagina changes with the menstrual cycle. At certain stages of the cycle this mucus becomes thicker and of a more gluey texture. It is possible to predict ovulation by examining the consistency of the cervical mucus. This technique has fairly high dependability, but it is complicated. Couples who wish to use it must obtain special training and information from a physician or other trained health care professional.

The Sympto-Thermal Method   The sympto-thermal method is essentially a combination of the temperature method and the mucus evaluation method. Temperature and mucus are both observed, and intercourse must be avoided if *either* of the two appears to indicate ovulation. Intercourse should not begin again until both variables indicate that sex is safe.

Contraceptive Methods Requiring Surgery

Millions of men and women have undergone surgical sterilization to prevent future pregnancy. Sterilization is virtually 100 percent effective. For individuals who are certain that they no longer wish to conceive, sterilization is the closest thing to an ideal method of contraception.

vasectomy   Every year in the United States, about 500,000 men have a **vasectomy.**[13] This simple and safe surgical procedure, which can be performed in a doctor's office, involves cutting and tying off the vas deferens, thus preventing sperm from exiting the testes. After a vasectomy the sperm are reabsorbed in the testes without harm. Many men are concerned about the effects of this operation on their masculinity, but the level of male hormones remains unchanged and there is no alteration in secondary sexual characteristics or sexual performance. Vasectomy is generally considered irreversible, although in some cases microsurgical techniques have restored fertility.

For women, the standard surgical technique is **tubal ligation**—dividing or tying off the Fallopian tubes—a procedure that may require hospitalization. As with a vasectomy, a tubal ligation does not affect sexual characteristics or performance. For the most part a tubal ligation should be considered permanent, although with certain techniques it is reversible.

tubal ligation

Before deciding on a vasectomy or tubal ligation, the individual should think the matter over carefully. The unforeseen death of a child may cause parents to rethink having more children. While adoption is always a possibility, it must be weighed against the desire to be the natural parents of children. The possibility of divorce and remarriage should also be considered. In general, voluntary sterilization should not be viewed as a solution to sexual or marital problems. Of course, it contributes nothing to the prevention of AIDS and other STDs.

A new surgical method that is reversible has been introduced into the United States after several years of use elsewhere in the world. This is the **contraceptive implant,** with the trade name *Norplant,* a chemical device inserted under the skin, usually on the upper arm or hip. Once implanted, it slowly releases chemicals that prevent menstruation. The effective life of Norplant is 5 years. After that it must be surgically removed and replaced. It can be removed earlier, however, if the woman wishes to become pregnant.[14]

contraceptive implant

The Decision to Have a Child

Reliable forms of contraception have made it possible for couples to delay parenthood or to choose to remain childless. Couples today can decide whether they want to have a child, and if so, when. However, they have many issues to consider when they make their decision about parenthood.

Important questions couples should ask themselves concern the effect that having a child will have on their lives and their situation. If they have a child now, how will it affect their education or career, their other children and home life, perhaps even their retirement plans? A child brings new financial pressures and demands a great deal of time, energy, and money. There are also emotional issues to consider: How will a new child affect a couple's relationship? Are the partners ready to give each other the emotional support and practical help they both need? There are still other aspects of parenthood to consider: How large a family does the couple want? How will the children be spaced in terms of age? All these questions should be considered when a couple is deciding whether to have a child. Careful planning can help ensure that a couple is prepared for the responsibilities of parenthood.

In the past the most common reason to marry was the creation of a family. In fact, every married couple was expected to have children. The reasons for having children varied. One was to carry on the family name. Another was to have someone to help in the house or in the field or to provide additional income for the family. Still another was to have someone to help care for the couple in their later years. Of course, many people became parents because they loved children.

In recent years attitudes have been changing. Today there is an increased recognition that although having children can be a wonderful experience, it can also have a negative and restricting effect on one's lifestyle. Certainly

For new parents, the birth of a child can be the embodiment of a dream. It is also the beginning of the most creative challenge of a couple's relationship. (Stephen McBrady/ PhotoEdit)

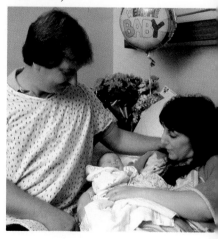

people are aware of the economic impact of having children. The cost of raising a child can be staggering. In addition to the financial strains of raising a child, parenthood may cause emotional and physical stress that sometimes results in depression, guilt, fatigue, and marital difficulties. Despite this new and perhaps more realistic assessment of parenthood, most people still expect to become parents, although they may have children somewhat later in life.[15]

What are some of the reasons people decide to have children today? Children provide love and companionship and can bring stimulation and happiness to their parents' lives. They may help fulfill a need to find a meaning and purpose in life. Watching children grow contributes to a feeling of accomplishment. Having children may also help parents feel more secure about their old age.

Many couples decide to become parents because they have developed a strong, secure relationship and would like to enrich it with children. If these people are willing to accept the responsibilities of parenthood and can meet a child's physical and emotional needs, they will probably be happy with their decision. However, if a couple decide to become parents to try to "save" a marriage or relationship, they may regret their decision.

Meeting Children's Health Needs

Parents are probably the most important single factor in determining whether a child is healthy at birth and will maintain healthy growth and development. They have a significant effect on all of the parts of a child's development.

- *Physical Development* Children have a better chance of enjoying good physical health if they receive optimal care beginning before birth and continuing throughout infancy, childhood, and adolescence. Good prenatal care of the expectant mother gives the newborn an excellent start. Providing a well-balanced diet, with restricted sugar and food additives, is important for ensuring healthy growth and development in the childhood and teenage years. To promote optimal physical health, parents need to be sure that their children have regular medical checkups and all necessary immunizations against disease. They also need to provide their children with chances for enough exercise, rest, and relaxation.

- *Emotional Development* Every child needs love and acceptance. If a child feels deeply loved and accepted, then his or her emotional development can proceed. To meet this need, parents should convey a sense of relaxation and enjoyment—rather than anxiety—as they feed and hold the baby. That way the baby will get the idea that the world is a friendly place and begin to feel that he or she can depend on the parents.[16] When early dependency needs are met, a child is free to grow toward security and independence.

- *Intellectual Development* Parental care is also a crucial factor in intellectual development and the key period is the child's first 5 years. Parents can help stimulate intellectual growth by singing and talking to an infant, offering choices (red or green shirt?) to even very young children, explaining family rules, answering questions, and encouraging children to try new experiences and tasks even though they may fail the first few times. The best type of home environment for intellectual development is one in which the parents are warm and loving, take time to explain their actions, encourage creativity and problem-solving, and show concern for the development of the children's competence.

- **Social Development** A child's ability to deal with other people develops primarily from his or her early relationship with the parents.[17] Parents have the main responsibility for teaching their children how to behave with other people. In part, children learn how to behave with others by watching how their parents act and then modeling their behavior on that of the parents. They also learn through *discipline*—the process by which parents communicate rules to them.

- **Spiritual Development** Parents also play an important role in a child's spiritual development. This may include various elements, such as the development of a child's value system, a sense of self-efficacy, and a feeling of purpose or meaningfulness in life. The people who are happiest and healthiest appear to be those who are connected to others by mutual need, who have a sense of identity and know and respect themselves, and, perhaps most important, who see a purpose in life and work actively toward it.[18]

Who Cares for Children?

In recent years there has been a dramatic increase in the number of mothers who work outside the home. While some of these women work for self-fulfillment, more often than not they work because their families need the income. This change in the number of mothers in the work force has affected the way child care tasks are divided between mothers and fathers and has meant that many children have care givers other than their parents at some time in their lives.

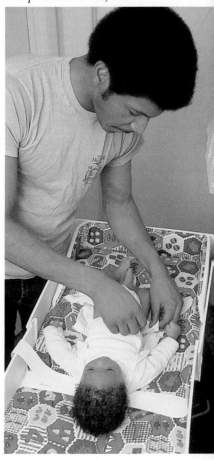

When the father participates actively in child care, both he and the child benefit. (Michal Heron/Woodfin Camp & Associates)

The Mother's Role Traditionally, mothers have provided the majority of child care. Even when mothers work, they usually still take primary responsibility for managing the work done by substitute care givers and for providing care when they are home. Mothers, more often than fathers, are also the ones who arrange their work schedules to meet their families' needs.[19]

Mothers who are employed often find balancing two major jobs—working and parenting—quite stressful and feel a conflict between the two responsibilities. However, working outside the home may have benefits, such as greater intellectual stimulation, more social contacts with adults, and, of course, greater income. These benefits may outweigh the negative effects of stress, particularly if a woman is working by choice and not by necessity.[20] Furthermore, being happier may make a woman a more effective mother when she is at home. Recent studies have shown that having a mother who works outside the home is not harmful even to young children. Children can form secure bonds both with their parents and with substitute care givers. Moreover, working outside the home does not appear to affect the commitment of either parent to parenting or to the children.[21]

The Father's Role Most fathers still consider their most important role to be that of providing financial security for their families.[22] However, while today's fathers do not share parenting equally with their wives, they are very different from the fathers of a generation ago. Fathers today are much more involved in the day-to-day responsibilities of child care than were fathers in the past. There is some evidence that men feel proud of these new child care responsibilities but guilty that they still do not do as much as they feel they should.[23]

Single Parenthood

Many people today find themselves raising children alone. While some of these single parents are fathers, the great majority are mothers.

Single parents face special stresses beyond those which married parents normally confront. Single-parent families usually have incomes lower than those of two-parent families. Since raising children is expensive, the reduced income of a single parent puts a great strain on the budget. As a result of these financial pressures, roughly half of all single mothers live below the poverty line.[24]

Single parents also face the stress of having to deal with changes and problems alone. They have to juggle work and child care responsibilities and must cope with the everyday problems of child rearing without the help and support of a spouse. Single parents must also try to make time to have a social life.

Although things can be difficult in a single-parent family, there is evidence that the situation is not necessarily harmful to the children. Some research has indicated that it is conflict between parents, not being raised by a single parent, that causes children to develop problems.[25]

Pregnancy

Becoming a parent involves the most profound changes the average person will ever experience. Parenthood is a lifelong responsibility, and it requires the same kind of planning as other major life decisions, such as selecting a career, getting married, and buying a house. No one can anticipate every difficulty, but there are important issues that should be considered when you are thinking about having a baby.

Planning for Pregnancy

Planning can be as useful when a couple decide to have a child as it is when they decide to avoid pregnancy. In fact, there are many more factors to consider. Some of the issues people should explore when deciding to have a child are whether they need genetic counseling and how to deal with problems of infertility.

Genetic Counseling   Genetic diseases, of which there are more than 2,000, affect 3 to 5 percent of all babies born in the United States.[26] Genetic counseling can provide prospective parents with information about whether they are likely to pass on a genetically linked disease to their child. For example, people who are carriers of Tay-Sachs disease may decide not to risk having children in order to avoid bearing a child who may have the disease and die early in life.

A genetic counselor can explain to prospective parents how a particular disorder is transmitted from generation to generation, what the odds are that the disease will recur in their family, and what the disease is like. If the risk of passing on a disease is slight or if an effective treatment is available, the potential parents may decide to go ahead with a pregnancy despite the risks. Otherwise, adoption may be an alternative.

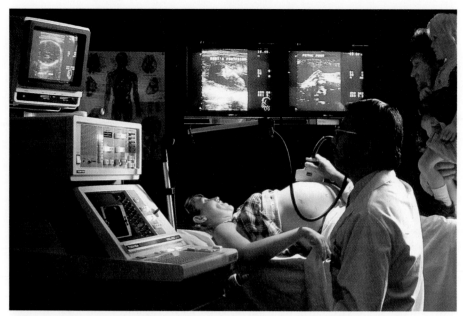

Physical disorders and other health problems sometimes can be detected through ultrasound. The ultrasound machine sends thousands of harmless vibrations into the womb each second, providing an in-depth image of the growing fetus. (Alexander Tsiaras/Science Source/Photo Researchers, Inc.)

Some genetic disorders cannot be identified before pregnancy, but many can be identified while the fetus is still in the uterus. It is now possible to test a fetus directly for about 100 genetic disorders as early as the fourth month of pregnancy. In a procedure called **amniocentesis,** a doctor can withdraw some of the amniotic fluid that surrounds a fetus in the womb. Laboratory tests of the fetal cells in this fluid can then determine whether the fetus has a genetic disorder. A newer technique, called **chorionic villi sampling,** is sometimes preferred over amniocentesis today. It takes only 2 days to get results, compared with about 3 weeks for amniocentesis.[27]

amniocentesis

chorionic villi sampling

Such tests usually are performed only if there is reason to suspect that the fetus has a particular disease, that is, if the couple have already had one diseased child or are known to be carriers of a defect. With a few of these diseases, treatments can begin before birth. Since certain disorders are more common as the age of the mother increases, doctors generally recommend that any pregnant woman over age 35 consider amniocentesis to test for genetic disorders.

Dealing with Infertility *Infertility,* or the inability of a couple to achieve pregnancy, is usually impossible to predict. A number of tests and procedures can be carried out by a physician to identify and correct many of the causes of infertility. Both the man and the woman must be involved in the process, and the procedures may take a great deal of time—often more than a year. Couples who start an infertility study should be prepared to go through the entire program.

The Beginnings of Pregnancy

placenta

A pregnancy officially begins when a fertilized egg implants itself in a woman's uterine lining. Soon afterward the woman's entire body undergoes general changes that can be detected by means of pregnancy tests. Meanwhile, specialized cells from the uterus and from the now-forming embryo begin to develop into a structure known as the **placenta.** The placenta is the physical link between mother and child. It is a mass of tissue attached to the uterine lining and to what will become the child's navel. For the next 9 months the placenta will absorb life-giving nutrients and oxygen from the woman's bloodstream and transfer them to the bloodstream of the developing fetus.

The events during the rest of the pregnancy constitute one of the truly amazing phenomena of life. What starts out as a single cell—a speck barely visible to the human eye—becomes, in the space of 9 months, a fully developed baby ready to be born.

prenatal

As an embryo, the organism is less than an inch long and looks a little like a curved fish. By 2 months, at which point it is called a fetus, it has developed arms and legs with fully shaped fingers and toes. By the end of the third month, although it is only about 3 inches long and weighs a mere ounce, the fetus can kick its legs, close its fingers, turn its head, and open and close its mouth. Also, by this time most of its internal organs are able to function, so that the rest of the **prenatal** period (the period before birth) can be spent in the process of growth and in putting on the finishing touches.

umbilical cord
amniotic sac

Throughout its prenatal life the fetus is attached to the placenta by the **umbilical cord** and is enclosed in a fluid-filled sac (the **amniotic sac**) which primarily provides protection. At birth, the average full-term infant weighs anywhere from 5 to 12 pounds and may be from 17 to 22 inches long.

Pregnancy: Diagnosis and Testing

Usually, the first sign of pregnancy is that an expected menstrual period does not occur. This is not, however, a definite sign of pregnancy, since it is not unusual for women's periods to be delayed 14 to 21 days, particularly in women who are normally somewhat irregular or are under stress. A pregnant woman may also notice breast congestion or tenderness, irritability, tenderness or a "heavy feeling" in her pelvis, and sometimes nausea.

If a woman misses her menstrual period, she may use an over-the-counter home pregnancy test. These tests should never be considered conclusive, however, since a negative reading can result from taking the test too early or using it improperly.

A physical exam by a qualified medical professional is necessary to confirm the diagnosis of pregnancy and begin prenatal planning and health care.[28] About 3 weeks after the missed period a physician can usually do a pelvic examination to determine pregnancy. The pelvic tissue will be slightly softened, the vaginal opening will be slightly purplish, and the uterus will have begun to enlarge.

Medical laboratory tests may be used to confirm pregnancy. A pregnant woman's system produces a hormone known as HCG. Tests of the woman's blood or urine can show whether this hormone is present.

Sometime during early pregnancy the woman should have a series of blood tests to check for anemia and rule out infection or other disorders. In addition, an Rh test must be done to assess the risk of Rh hemolytic disease, a genetically determined blood disorder. Most people have a substance known as the **Rh factor** in their red blood cells. If the mother lacks this substance and the baby inherits the factor from the father, the mother's blood can react against the baby's. The first pregnancy is usually not affected, but subsequent babies are at risk. Today, all mothers with the Rh condition can be immunized against this problem.

Rh factor

Prenatal Health

Pregnancy is not an illness. In ordinary circumstances a pregnant woman can do almost all the things she did before she became pregnant, including working, exercising, participating in recreational activities, and having sexual intercourse. She should, however, take extra care of her health. For 9 months a fetus will be depending on her for all its body-building materials. Ideally, she should be in excellent health *before* starting the pregnancy.

Proper Nutrition and Exercise   A pregnant woman should be sure to eat adequate quantities of milk and milk products, protein foods, fruits, vegetables, and grains and to drink plenty of liquids. Because she is eating for two, she should expect to gain a reasonable amount of weight, ideally about 25 pounds during the course of the pregnancy. The hormonal changes that occur with pregnancy account for the woman's increased appetite. This is nature's way of providing for the developing fetus. Women who are overweight before pregnancy should cease dieting while they are pregnant because continued dieting can have an adverse effect on the health of the fetus. Pregnant women should also get regular exercise to maintain their strength and endurance.

Avoiding Hazardous Substances   Since the mother-to-be largely controls the fetus's environment, she must protect the developing infant from as many environmental hazards as she can to ensure the health of her child. The most common threats to fetal health come from substances which the mother ingests and which pass directly through the placenta to the fetus. Among the most hazardous substances are alcohol, tobacco, caffeine, and drugs.[29]

A woman who drinks alcohol during pregnancy is in effect giving her fetus a drink too. However, the alcohol that crosses the placenta may do far more damage to the fetus than to the mother. Babies born to mothers who drink heavily are often born with **fetal alcohol syndrome (FAS).** Babies born with FAS have certain problems, including mental retardation and a wide range of physical defects.

fetal alcohol syndrome (FAS)

Tobacco is also known to affect fetal development. Women who smoke have a higher than normal rate of miscarriage and stillbirth. When their babies survive, they are smaller than average and are more likely to be irritable and hyperactive. Smoking has also been associated with a higher risk of cleft palate, crossed eyes, and hernias in the newborn.

Caffeine, which is present in coffee, tea, chocolate, and cola drinks, is another potential hazard to the fetus. A high caffeine intake has been associated with an increased risk of miscarriage and birth defects.

Prescription drugs, over-the-counter medications, and illegal drugs also pose a danger to a fetus. Since most prescription drugs have not been proved safe for pregnant women and many are known to cause birth defects, most physicians avoid prescribing any new medications for a pregnant woman. Several over-the-counter drugs often taken by pregnant women are also risky. According to current research, aspirin is dangerous to the fetus and may pose risks to the woman, particularly if she takes it near the time of labor and delivery. Aspirin decreases the blood's clotting ability and may cause either the mother or the baby to bleed excessively.

Guarding against Infectious Diseases   Some infectious diseases can cause problems for the developing fetus as well as the mother. One such hazard is rubella (German measles), a contagious viral disease. A woman who contracts this illness early in pregnancy—even a mild case—may have a multiply handicapped baby. Other diseases, particularly STDs, may also pose hazards to the developing fetus. AIDS, for example, is transmitted from an infected pregnant woman to her fetus.

Receiving Proper Medical Care   Prenatal care, or medical supervision of the pregnancy, is very important for both mother and baby to help ensure that problems will be detected early and treated. Prenatal examinations routinely include a test of blood pressure. Increased blood pressure may indicate danger or even toxemia, which can result in maternal or fetal death if left untreated. Urinalysis is another vital test conducted as part of prenatal care. It can detect kidney and bladder conditions and other disorders.

Prenatal care also includes measurement of the size of the woman's abdomen to determine the baby's growth. The baby's heartbeat is usually checked after the third or fourth month.

The first prenatal visit usually includes a vaginal examination, especially with a first pregnancy. The size of the birth canal is a crucial factor in safe delivery. Another examination closer to the due date helps predict when birth will occur by observing cervical softening, thinning, and dilation.

Regular medical checkups help ensure the health of the unborn baby and the mother-to-be. (Blair Seitz/Photo Researchers, Inc.)

Common Problems during Pregnancy

During pregnancy a woman may experience various problems or discomforts. While many of these problems pose little risk to the health of the mother or the fetus, a few may pose a significant threat.

- *Morning Sickness*   Some women may experience nausea or vomiting, often called *morning sickness,* during the first 3 months of pregnancy. There are some steps a woman can take to try to reduce the discomfort of morning sickness. Arising slowly and eating a few crackers, some dry cereal, or a piece of toast first thing in the morning may help reduce its effects, as may eating four or five small meals a day instead of going for long periods without food.
- *Constipation*   This may be caused by the position of the fetus. Other causes may include a decrease in exercise and a lack of adequate fiber or liquids in the diet. If constipation persists, the pregnant woman should consult her doctor.
- *Hemorrhoids*   This inflammation of rectal tissue may be brought on by persistent constipation or by the baby pressing on the veins of the rectum. Relieving constipation can help relieve hemorrhoids or reduce the possibility of their occurrence.

- **Heartburn**   Some women may experience heartburn during the last months of pregnancy. It is caused by pressure placed on the stomach as the fetus grows. Eating small meals four or five times a day may help reduce heartburn, as will avoiding fatty, fried, and spicy foods.
- **Back Pain**   This may be caused by carrying the extra weight of a fetus. Sharp leg pains and cramps may also be experienced during pregnancy. Varicose veins may develop because of the pressure the fetus places on the large veins of the legs. These conditions should all disappear after the birth of the baby.
- **Toxemia**   More serious conditions can also arise during pregnancy. One such condition is **toxemia,** the presence of toxins in the bloodstream. *toxemia* Toxemia may occur at any time during pregnancy, and about 6 percent of pregnant women develop it. The risks are greater in women's first pregnancies, especially in very young or older women. In its milder form, the symptoms include hypertension, swelling, and protein in the urine. A more severe form of toxemia may cause convulsions and coma.[30] The severity of the symptoms determines the type of treatment. For milder conditions, bed rest and sedation are prescribed and salt may be restricted to help reduce swelling. More serious symptoms require hospitalization.
- **Miscarriage**   In about one of six pregnancies a woman has a **spontaneous abortion,** commonly called a *miscarriage*. A spontaneous *spontaneous abortion* abortion happens either because the fertilized ovum was not implanted correctly in the uterine lining or because the egg or sperm was defective to begin with. In a miscarriage, a woman usually starts to have vaginal bleeding and cramps, which continue until the uterus expels the defective embryo or fetus.

Terminating a Pregnancy

The deliberate termination of pregnancy, also called **abortion,** means ending *abortion* a pregnancy before the embryo or fetus can survive on its own. This issue is at the center of one of the most heated controversies in American society today.

How a Pregnancy Is Terminated   During the first 12 weeks of pregnancy abortion is a relatively safe procedure when performed by a qualified physician. There are several techniques for terminating a pregnancy. One technique is the use of "morning-after" pills. These pills are normally used within 72 hours of intercourse and interfere with the development of fetal tissue.

A simple procedure for terminating a pregnancy, used during the first 2 weeks after a missed menstrual period, is *vacuum aspiration*. In this method, a small sterile tube is used to extract by suction the menstrual tissue, fetal tissue, and placenta. It is an inexpensive office procedure, requires little training, is easily performed, and poses minimal risk.

An operative procedure known as D and C—dilation of the cervix and curettage (scraping) of the uterine cavity—is also used up to about the twelfth week of pregnancy. These two techniques are frequently combined—the cervix is dilated, the uterine contents are removed with vacuum suction, and the procedure is followed by curettage to make sure that all the products of conception are removed.

After the twelfth week of pregnancy, abortion is performed in one of three ways: by *hysterotomy*, an operation which requires an abdominal incision; by introducing a salt solution into the uterus through the abdominal wall, a procedure called a *saline abortion*; or by the use of synthetic prostaglandins, either injected or administered in a vaginal suppository. Both the salt solution and the prostaglandins work by inducing contractions.

Attitudes toward Abortion   Despite its relative safety, abortion is vigorously opposed by many people in the United States, primarily on moral and religious grounds. These people wish to see abortion outlawed throughout the country. There are others who personally disapprove of abortion but believe that it should be a personal and private issue rather than a legal one decided by the government. They feel that women should have the right to make a choice about whether to have an abortion.

In 1973 the U.S. Supreme Court ruled in the case *Roe v. Wade* that a woman's right to choice should prevail and that in the first 3 months of pregnancy the decision to have an abortion should be left to the woman and her physician. The Court ruled further that in subsequent months of pregnancy, each individual state should be permitted to "regulate the abortion procedures" until 10 weeks before the child is due. From that point on, abortion should be prohibited except when necessary to preserve the woman's life or health.

Recent Supreme Court cases have begun to challenge *Roe v. Wade*. Although none have succeeded in overturning that decision, they have begun to limit the right to have an abortion. As Supreme Court justices age and retire, the philosophy of the Court may change, affecting the interpretation of the U.S. Constitution as it is applied to new laws regarding abortion. Whatever Court decisions are made, the issue will probably remain highly controversial in the future.

Though legalized in 1973 by the United States Supreme Court, abortion continues to be debated. Supporters argue that the decision to have an abortion should be a private choice, protected under the Constitution. People who are against abortion want to make it illegal, arguing that it is an immoral and criminal act. (Susan McCartney/Photo Researchers, Inc.; Bettye Lane/Photo Researchers, Inc.)

Childbirth

The birth of a child is one of the most amazing events in life. Witnessing the emergence of life gives a person a new perspective on what it means to be alive. In return, parents are given a tremendous responsibility as caretakers and guardians of a new human being.

How Birth Takes Place

Although birth involves hard work and pain, people come away from the experience awed by the wonder of it. A day or two before labor begins the woman may notice a small amount of vaginal bleeding. Then a clear fluid will normally drain from the vagina. This means that the amniotic sac has broken and labor is about to begin. At this point contractions can usually be felt, starting at intervals of 15 to 20 minutes and gradually becoming more frequent. In some cases, however, labor sets in abruptly, with the contractions coming every 3 to 5 minutes.

To understand what happens during a contraction, it helps to picture the uterus as a large muscular pouch that is upside down, with its open end leading into the vagina. Before labor, this opening is almost closed by an elastic ring, the cervix. As the walls of the pouch contract during labor, the baby's head is pressed firmly against the cervix, causing the cervix to dilate (get wider). As labor progresses, the cervix opens wide enough for the baby's head to pass through into the vagina.

When the baby's head has passed through the cervix and into the vagina, the woman feels a compulsion to bear down and push the baby out of her body. Typically, the top of the baby's head appears first. Then, with succeeding contractions, the head gradually slides out, usually facedown. Once the head is out, the shoulders emerge as the body rotates, and the rest of the body usually follows easily. After the baby has left the mother's body, an attendant ties off and cuts the umbilical cord, which connects the baby's navel to the placenta. Soon the uterus contracts again and expels the placenta.

After the birth the physician uses a suction apparatus to remove mucus from the infant's nose and mouth to make breathing easier. The newborn's breathing, muscle tone, heart rate, reflexes, irritability, and color are assessed immediately to determine whether the baby needs further medical help. If all is well, the baby is given to the mother and father, who can admire the miracle of life they have produced.

Chapter Summary

- People who approach sex responsibly and safely consider the consequences sexual activity may have on their lives, such as unplanned or unwanted children and the contraction of sexually transmitted diseases, and take precautions to avoid unplanned pregnancy and disease.

- A great variety of contraceptive methods and devices are available. Each method and device has benefits and drawbacks.

- Natural family planning does not require medications or contraceptive devices. It makes use of the timing of a woman's ovulation to determine when sexual intercourse should be avoided.

- In recent years more couples have chosen to remain childless, feeling that life can be rewarding and rich without children; nonetheless, most couples choose to have children.

- Parents have the primary responsibility for fostering their children's healthy development.

- Although mothers have traditionally provided the majority of child care, some fathers are taking increased responsibility in this area.

- Single parents often face financial pressures, have to deal with child problems alone, and must juggle work, child care, and their own emotional needs.

- Planning for pregnancy is important because of the great responsibility of parenthood.

- Pregnancy begins when a fertilized egg is implanted in the uterine lining. From that point on, cellular growth leads to the development of a fetus and tissues to nourish and protect the developing fetus. The fetus goes through tremendous changes from conception to birth.

- Routine testing for pregnancy includes tests to confirm pregnancy; blood tests to check for anemia, infections, and other disorders; and an Rh test to check for Rh hemolytic disease, a genetic blood disorder.

- Important factors in maximizing the health of the mother and child include getting proper nutrition and exercise, avoiding hazardous substances, guarding against infectious diseases, and receiving proper prenatal care.

- Pregnancy can be terminated by means of various techniques. However, there is a great controversy about the use of abortion in the United States. Some people are vigorously opposed to it. Others feel it is a private issue concerning a woman's control over her own body.

- During childbirth labor contractions force the baby's head against the cervix, causing it to dilate. As labor progresses, the baby passes through the cervix into the vagina, at which time the mother feels a compulsion to bear down and push the baby out of her body.

Communicable Diseases

Objectives

When you have studied this chapter, you should be able to:

- Explain the effects lifestyle, travel, and medical progress can have on patterns of diseases.

- Describe what an infection is and explain the role of agent, host, and environmental factors in a communicable disease.

- Identify the primary agents of a communicable disease.

- Describe how the body defends itself against infection, including first-line defenses, the inflammatory response, and immunity.

- List the major sexually transmitted diseases and describe their symptoms and potential effects.

- List the symptoms of HIV infection and full-blown AIDS; identify the primary modes of transmission of the HIV virus and the primary preventive measures for AIDS.

The word *disease* brings to mind a variety of ailments ranging from the common cold through measles to cancer. Diseases are different from one another in various ways. Some are *acute* conditions in which there is a sudden onset of illness that lasts for a relatively short period. The common cold is a familiar example. Others, such as heart disease, are *chronic* conditions that develop gradually over a relatively long period. Diseases may also be infectious or noninfectious. *Infectious* diseases are largely caused by infectious agents such as bacteria and viruses, while *noninfectious* diseases are caused by other factors, such as lifestyle and genetics. Finally, diseases may also be *communicable* or *noncommunicable*. That is, they can or cannot be spread from one person to another.

This chapter will focus on infectious, communicable diseases and will examine various agents of infection and the ways in which the body fights infection. Special attention will be given to sexually transmitted diseases because of their prevalence in the United States and the dangers associated with them.

The Changing Face of Disease

Disease is part of the human experience. Throughout their lives people are confronted with diseases that can affect their health and even shorten their life span. Some diseases, such as smallpox, have been wiped out and no longer pose a threat to humanity. However, new or previously unknown diseases, such as AIDS, have appeared. Thus, the patterns of diseases change over time. The risk of some diseases may be reduced, while the risk of others is increased. Three factors that are related to these changing patterns of disease are lifestyle, travel, and medical progress.

Lifestyle

American lifestyles are changing continually. Changing trends in work, diet, and activity not only influence the way people live but also affect the patterns of diseases to which people are susceptible.

As more women have entered the work force, larger numbers of young children now spend time at child care centers. At these centers, youngsters become exposed (and in turn expose others) to a greater number of diarrheal, respiratory, and other communicable diseases than they might encounter at home.

Changing diets and dietary fads also may influence the patterns of disease. For example, the increased consumption of high-fat, low-fiber foods over the past several decades may be linked to increases in cancer and heart disease among Americans.

Changing activity levels among Americans may affect the patterns of disease. For example, sedentary occupations and lifestyles seem to be linked to greater risks of developing cardiovascular disease. Leisure activities also may have an effect on the patterns of disease. For example, the risks of contracting tick-borne diseases such as Lyme disease and Rocky Mountain spotted fever increase as people spend more time hiking, camping, and engaging in outdoor activities in areas where ticks are abundant.

Travel

Americans are traveling with greater frequency and to more destinations around the world than ever before. This increased travel can be a factor in the patterns of disease. Travelers may bring back illnesses from their trips to foreign countries. For example, throughout the 1970s and early 1980s there was a steady increase in malaria among United States citizens who had acquired the disease while traveling abroad.[1] If you get sick after foreign travel, it is important to tell your doctor where you have been.

Medical Progress

Medicine has been making continuous progress in treating and preventing disease. As mentioned previously, smallpox has been eliminated throughout the world; the last case was reported in 1977. Similarly, medicine has made great progress in reducing the incidence of measles through the use of an effective vaccine although outbreaks of the disease still occur, especially in closed populations such as college students, which may include many unvaccinated people. Medical progress and technology have also helped identify previously unknown diseases, and future developments will no doubt reveal others, along with the means for treating them.

While medical progress has resulted in improved treatment, prevention, and identification of disease, it has had drawbacks. The use of antibiotics has been a great help in fighting bacterial infections. However, while these antibiotics inhibit the growth of certain bacteria, they may result in strains of bacteria resistant to the original antibiotic.

Medical progress and technology have also contributed to doctor-caused and hospital-caused problems such as adverse drug reactions, inappropriate treatments, surgical errors, and the spread of infections during hospital stays. For example, organ transplant patients face the problem of rejecting the new organ. While the use of immunosuppressant drugs has reduced the problem, the drugs also lessen the immune system's ability to fight infection.[2]

The Nature of Infectious Disease

An *infection* is the invasion of the body by disease-causing organisms and the reaction of the body to their presence. People with an infectious disease may have fever, nausea or vomiting, and general malaise.

Epidemiologists—the scientists who study human diseases as they affect populations—explain how people contract infectious diseases in terms of three components: host, causative agent, and environment. In the past the primary emphasis was placed on the role of the causative agent.[3] Today many epidemiologists prefer to view the interactions among the causative agent, host, and environment in a more balanced way. In this view, a change in one component does not necessarily result in illness. A parent, for example, who is exposed to a child with pneumonia will not necessarily contract the disease. Perhaps the parent is in optimal health or takes certain precautions to prevent contracting pneumonia.

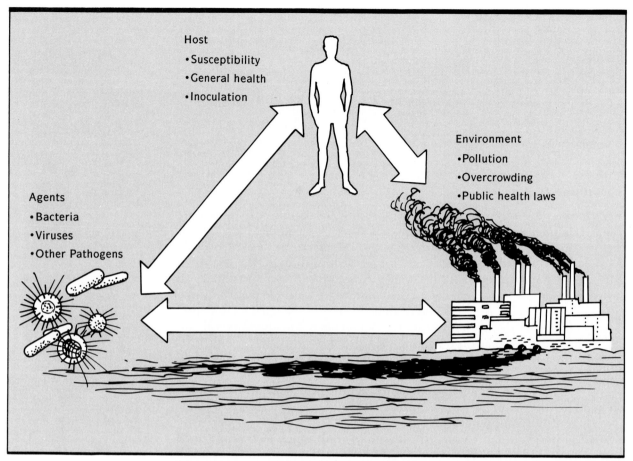

Figure 9.1 *Communicable disease results from a complex interaction which can be visualized as a triangle consisting of a disease agent (for example, bacteria or virus), a host, and the environment. Note that the environment may have an effect on the host (making the host more susceptible to disease) and also on the agents (causing them to grow and providing a means for them to reach the host). The agents also may affect a person's environment by creating an epidemic, surrounding that individual with people who are carriers of the disease.*

Agent, Host, and Environmental Factors

The agent-host-environment model (Figure 9.1) makes it clear that there is no single cause of an illness. Instead, an interaction of factors is responsible for the onset of disease.

agent factor **Agent factors** include the organisms that cause an infectious disease. These can be bacteria, viruses, rickettsiae, and fungi. In addition to the presence of such organisms, other agent factors include the disease-causing ability of the organism; the strength of the organism; the number of organisms necessary to cause an infection; and the ability of an organism to enter and move through living tissues.

host factor **Host factors** are attributes of individuals that may increase or decrease their susceptibility to certain diseases. They include genetic factors, immunity, health-related behaviors, and a person's general state of health. For example, a child who develops cystic fibrosis has inherited a genetic susceptibility to this disease. A person in poor general health is often much more susceptible to an infectious disease than is someone in excellent health. A host factor that offers special protection against disease is *immunity.*

Environmental factors are external biological, social, and physical factors *environmental factor* that influence the probability of developing an infection. Biological factors include the source of a causative agent (for example, soil, water, or animals) and its means of transmission (for example, through the air or through insect or animal bites). Social factors include customs, behaviors, and modes of cooking and dress. The kinds of food eaten and the thoroughness of cooking, for example, may be related to illnesses such as trichinosis, which is caused by parasites in undercooked pork. Physical factors include the quality of air, water, and living and working environments. The hospital environment, for example, can be a significant factor in the transmission of many infectious diseases.

The Course of Infectious Diseases

In all infectious diseases, foreign organisms invade the body, and the body reacts to them. After a person is infected, the course of the disease follows a common pattern marked by five specific phases. The first is the **incubation** *incubation period* **period,** in which the organisms invade and multiply in the host. The length of this phase varies with the disease and the individual. The second phase is called the **prodromal period.** This brief phase is characterized by general *prodromal period* symptoms such as headache, fever, runny nose, irritability, and general discomfort. A disease is highly communicable during the prodromal period. The third phase is called **clinical disease.** The illness is at its height during this *clinical disease* phase. Characteristic symptoms of the disease appear, and so a specific diagnosis can be made. During the fourth phase—the **decline stage**—symptoms *decline stage* begin to subside and the patient may feel well enough to become more active. The danger of relapse increases, however, if the patient becomes too active before achieving a full recovery. The final phase is **convalescence,** which is *convalescence* the recovery period. Although the patient is better, the disease may still be communicable. A patient who recovers but still gives off disease-causing organisms becomes a **carrier** of the disease. *carrier*

Most infectious diseases can be treated to relieve the symptoms and promote recovery. Bacterial infections can be treated with antibiotics, a group of drugs that help kill or disable infectious bacteria. Some antibiotics are effective against certain kinds of bacteria but not against others. Therefore, many different antibiotics have been developed. Some of the best-known antibiotics are penicillin, ampicillin, erythromycin, and tetracycline.

Agents of Infectious Diseases

Vast numbers of tiny microscopic organisms too small to be seen with the naked eye share the world with humans. Billions of these microorganisms normally live on or within the human body and are called **endogenous,** or *endogenous* "resident," microorganisms. Billions of others are **exogenous** microorgan- *exogenous* isms; that is, they normally live outside the human body. While some microorganisms are harmless, others can be **pathogens**—agents of infectious disease. *pathogens*

Bacteria

bacteria

The most plentiful microorganisms endogenous to humans are the various kinds of **bacteria** (singular: *bacterium*). Each of these tiny organisms consists of just one cell with a protective cell wall.

Endogenous Bacteria and Disease Most kinds of endogenous bacteria are not harmful. Some, in fact, are vital to human health. The *E. coli* bacterium lives in the intestines and is essential in the synthesis of the B vitamins. Other bacteria help kill foreign infectious organisms. However, endogenous bacteria can cause disease if they get out of hand. For example, skin bacteria may cause acne, and mouth bacteria may help cause pyorrhea, a serious gum disease.

Streptoccocal bacteria, which usually inhabit mucous membranes, may cause diseases such as strep throat (a severe throat infection), scarlet fever (an acute fever with sore throat and rash), or rheumatic fever (an infection that primarily affects the joints and the heart). While most streptoccocal bacteria are endogenous, others may be introduced from outside the body.

Staphylococcal bacteria, which are normally present on the skin, are usually harmless. Occasionally, however, if there is a scratch or other small opening in the skin, the staphylococci will enter the wound and produce a localized infection. Staphylococci also cause boils (infections of sweat glands and hair follicles) and sties (infections on the eyelids). An exception to the typical localized infections caused by staphylococci is the condition known as toxic shock syndrome (TSS). Women may contract an infection while using a particular type of tampon during menstruation. The symptoms of TSS include high fever, abdominal pain, diarrhea, vomiting, and a red skin rash. Sometimes blood pressure drops suddenly, causing death. TSS can be treated with antibiotics and can be prevented by changing tampons more frequently and using sanitary napkins when the menstrual flow is light.

Exogenous Bacteria and Disease Stepping on a rusty nail can be a painful experience. A worse scenario will occur, however, if the nail harbors disease-causing bacteria. Tetanus, which causes a serious infection known as lockjaw—the symptoms include muscle rigidity and convulsions—is a classic example of a disease resulting from a wound infected by an exogenous bacterium. Exogenous bacteria are responsible for a number of major diseases, including cholera, typhus, tuberculosis, gonorrhea, and syphilis.

A potentially serious exogenous bacterial disease that has recently come to public attention is *Lyme disease*. In this disease the bacteria are introduced into the human body by the bite of an infected deer tick. The first stage is usually marked by a raised red rash which develops and expands in circular fashion up to an average of 6 inches in diameter. The early symptoms may also include headache, fever, and muscle and joint pain. If left untreated, Lyme disease can progress to arthritis and heart and neurological problems. In its early stages, this disease can be treated with antibiotics.[4]

Viruses

A number of diseases, including mumps, measles, rubella (German measles), smallpox, and AIDS, are caused by viruses. A virus is a bit of nucleic acid within a protein coat. It is also a substance designed to duplicate itself. In fact, a **virus** is best defined as a microorganism that can reproduce only in living cells.

virus

Once inside a cell, a virus takes over and directs the cell to produce many hundreds of new viruses (Figure 9.2). However, body cells can protect themselves against some viruses. When exposed to certain viruses, they may produce a protective substance called **interferon,** which helps prevent the virus from infecting other cells.

interferon

Colds and Flu   The average person complains of cold symptoms at least twice a year. The common cold is really not so common, however. There are more than 100 viruses that can cause it. Rhinoviruses, named after the Greek word for "nose," are the major infectious agents of the common cold, especially in the fall. Over half of the other causal agents have not been identified.[5]

Cold viruses contaminate the air and the surfaces of objects. Breathing in these viruses or touching virus-laden hands to the eyes or the inside of the mouth or nose allows them to enter the body. Once inside the host, cold viruses reproduce during a short incubation period of 1 to 3 days. For the next 4 to 7 days the immune system battles them by releasing chemical substances that irritate the throat and prompt the nose and sinuses to produce fluid to soothe the irritated tissues. The results are a runny nose, watery eyes, and congestion.

Flu is rarely a serious disease unless it is complicated by a secondary infection. However, if bacteria become involved or if the virus spreads to the lungs, the condition may be fatal, particularly among the very young, the elderly, and those with heart or respiratory disease. Flu complications have killed more than half a million Americans in the last 25 years.[6]

There are three major varieties of flu virus—A (the strongest), B, and C—but also numerous changing strains within each major type. Immunity against one variety or strain of flu virus does not necessarily provide immunity against

Figure 9.2 *To reproduce itself, a virus must use the material in a living cell. (A) First the virus locks on to the wall of the host cell. (B) Viral DNA is injected into the cell. (C) The DNA takes over the host cell and begins to replicate. (D) New protein coats are formed around replicated viral DNA, creating new complete viruses within the host cell. Meanwhile, the attached cell may begin to release interferon. (E) The host cell bursts and releases the new viruses. (F) The new viruses attack neighboring cells. If enough interferon was created, these cells will have produced antiviral enzymes that help protect them from the virus and inhibit further viral reproduction.*

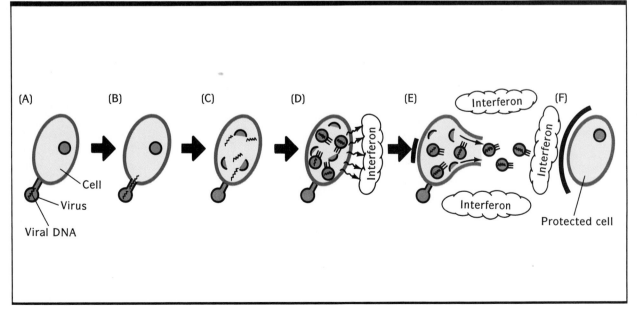

(A)   (B)   (C)   (D)   (E)   (F)

Cell
Virus
Viral DNA
Interferon
Interferon
Interferon
Protected cell

any other. Although there are vaccines against specific strains of flu virus, these vaccines are not effective against other strains. Also, since viral strains change, the vaccines are changed periodically, and individuals must be revaccinated every year.

Flu symptoms generally make a person feel tired, achy, and weak. In general, flu develops rapidly over a period of hours. A high fever usually appears within 12 hours of the first symptoms, and recovery may take 1 to 3 weeks.

Hepatitis Cases of hepatitis—a viral inflammation of the liver—have increased significantly in recent years, particularly among young people. At present there are four known viral causes of hepatitis in the United States. Experts suspect that there may be others as well. Of the four known types, the most common are hepatitis A, B, and C. Hepatitis A, or infectious hepatitis, is the most common type (and usually the least dangerous). Hepatitis B and hepatitis C are far more dangerous. Hepatitis A is caused by fecal contamination of food or the environment and can be prevented with proper hygiene. Hepatitis B and C are spread primarily through the exchange of body fluids during sexual activity or through blood transfusions.[7]

The different types of hepatitis have similar symptoms: fever, headache, nausea, loss of appetite, and pain in the upper right abdomen. The urine becomes deep yellow, and the patient may become jaundiced.

Hepatitis may be a prolonged illness and, if it causes serious damage to the liver, may be extremely dangerous. If liver failure is serious enough to cause a coma, the patient has only a 10 to 20 percent chance of surviving.[8] For unknown reasons, some people are healthy carriers of the virus and escape serious liver damage.[9]

Mononucleosis Infectious mononucleosis, or "mono," is common among high school and college students. Its short-term symptoms, which can be severe, may include fever, sore throat, nausea, chills, and general weakness. The individual may have a rash, enlarged and tender lymph glands, jaundice, and enlargement of the spleen. Mono can be diagnosed with a simple blood test.

The longer-term symptoms are the frustrating ones. Although permanent disability is unusual, the general weakness and feeling of fatigue can last for weeks or months. Fortunately, experts generally agree that people who have had the disease develop fairly long, if not permanent, immunity.[10]

A virus known as the Epstein-Barr virus is the cause of the most common form of infectious mononucleosis.[11] Although mono is sometimes referred to as the "kissing disease," kissing is only one of several ways it is spread. Strangely, it does not spread easily by ordinary contact. In fact, it is rare to have more than one case in a household.

Rickettsiae

rickettsiae **Rickettsiae** are organisms that are intermediate between bacteria and viruses. Most rickettsiae grow as parasites in the intestinal tract of insects and insectlike creatures, with which they frequently live in peaceful coexistence. Others are disease-causing agents that are transmitted to humans and other mammals through insect and tick bites. The insect serves as a carrier of the infectious agent, transferring the organism to a human host. Rocky Mountain spotted fever is transmitted to humans by ticks. Typhus fever is another major rickettsial disease that is transmitted by an insect vector—fleas, ticks, and lice.

Fungi

Fungi are infectious agents with which many people have had firsthand experience. Athlete's foot is caused by fungi, as are ringworm and yeast infections. Fungi are many-celled organisms that must obtain food from organic materials such as plants, animals, and, in some cases, humans. Fungi spread as bits of the organism are blown to new locations through the release of seedlike cells.

fungi

In humans, fungi tend to invade warm, moist areas such as the scalp, feet, and groin. Fungal infections are rarely serious and can be controlled with fungicides and proper hygiene.

Defense against Infectious Disease

If a pathogenic agent invades the body, what can the body do to fight off the pathogen and prevent it from causing disease? The body has three basic lines of defense: the skin and mucous membranes, the inflammatory response, and the immune system.

First-Line Defenses

The skin and mucous membranes are the body's first line of defense. An invading microorganism must find its way through the skin or the mucus-coated membranes that line the respiratory, digestive, and urogenital tracts. Secretions such as tears, perspiration, skin oils, and saliva, which contain chemicals that can kill bacteria, are part of this defense system. In addition, the respiratory passages are lined with fine, short moving hairs called *cilia* that spread a carpet of sticky mucus. The mucus traps inhaled microorganisms and foreign matter and carries them to the back of the throat, where they are removed by sneezing, coughing, or nose blowing or are swallowed and disposed of by digestive fluids.

Besides the cilia, other body hairs (the eyelashes, for example) may fend off invading microorganisms. Reflexes such as coughing, blinking, and vomiting are also part of the body's first line of defense, as are high acid levels in the stomach and vagina, which help destroy invaders.

The Inflammatory Response

Sometimes microorganisms get beyond the body's outer defenses—through a cut in the skin, for example. They then face a second line of defense in the blood and the tissues—**inflammation,** or the inflammatory response. The inflammatory response helps ward off any irritant or foreign matter.

inflammation

The white blood cells in the bloodstream form a vital part of the body's defense system. Some are of a type known as **phagocytes,** a term that literally means "cells that eat." A phagocyte can actually flow around a foreign substance, take it apart chemically, and digest it (Figure 9.3).

phagocytes

During the inflammatory response, the supply of blood to the endangered area increases while the flow of blood through the area slows down. As a result, some *blood plasma* leaks through the walls of the blood vessels into the spaces between the cells in the endangered area, bringing with it special proteins that help destroy pathogens. Meanwhile, phagocytes rush to the area to engulf bacteria and foreign particles.

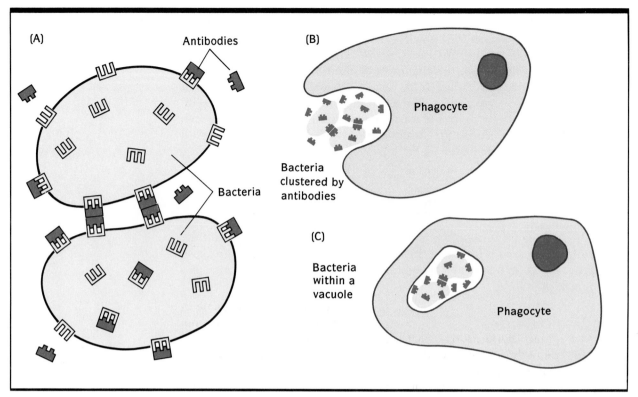

Figure 9.3 *(A) Antibodies may help neutralize bacteria by causing them to cluster together. (B) Large cells called phagocytes detect and engulf bacteria and other foreign substances. (C) The phagocyte isolates the foreign substances and destroys them. The remains are then eliminated through the lymphatic system.*

If the infection occurs in one part of the body, the patient usually shows the signs of inflammation only in that area. These signs include redness, local warmth, swelling, and pain. Such signs indicate that the invaders are being counterattacked. However, if the battle is being waged throughout the body, the patient usually has a fever. While higher temperatures may be harmful to normal body functions, fever can be helpful. It stimulates the body to produce more white blood cells and may kill the invading organism, since most pathogens cannot survive in above-normal body temperatures.

Whether the inflammatory response is sufficient to knock out the infection depends on how many invading organisms there are, how strong they are, and how well the body is able to defend itself. The struggle is resolved when enough invading organisms have been killed or inactivated to halt the infection. In more severe cases, this line of defense fails and the invading organisms begin to spread through the tissues and even into the bloodstream. The infection then spreads throughout the body and becomes highly dangerous.

Immunity

immunity   The body's third line of defense against disease is **immunity,** a group of mechanisms that help protect the body against specific diseases. Immunity is the body's most efficient disease-preventing weapon. It can help fight either a viral infection or a bacterial one.

The Role of Lymphocytes   In the immune mechanism, as in the inflammatory response, white blood cells become involved in fighting infection. Here the protective white blood cells are of a type known as **lymphocytes.**

When foreign or invading pathogens are present in the body, B lymphocytes, or B cells, help produce substances called **antibodies.** Antibodies react specifically to the parts of a pathogen that link up to human cells and cause damage. These parts, which are called **antigens,** are thus neutralized. If the invaders are viruses, the antibodies lock on to their antigens and prevent them from entering the target cells. If the invaders are bacteria, the antibodies lock on to them and cause them to clump together, making it easier for phagocytes to engulf and digest them. Antibodies can also lock on to bacterial toxins to make them less harmful to the body.

T lymphocytes, or T cells, fight infection in three major ways. First, some T lymphocytes spur the phagocytes to eat foreign substances faster. Second, some help stimulate the production of antibodies by B lymphocytes. Third, some can attack foreign cells, cells that have been killed by viruses, and possibly cancer cells.

Natural Immunity   As discussed earlier, when a virus attacks the body, it helps bring about its own destruction by triggering the production of interferon. Natural immunity works in somewhat the same way. When an invading antigen enters the body, it stimulates the body to produce certain antibodies that can inactivate it. As was mentioned above, antibodies work only on the specific antigens that trigger them: measles antibodies work only on the measles virus, mumps antibodies on the mumps virus, and so on. There are over a million different specific antibodies, each capable of fighting one antigen. That means that over a million different foreign antigens can stimulate the immune system to take action.

Acquired Immunity   In the past, having a disease was the only way to develop immunity to it. Today, however, immunity may be induced artifically by means of **vaccines,** which consist of killed or weakened viruses, taken orally or by injection. Several days or weeks after an individual receives a vaccination, the body starts to produce specific antibodies, which circulate in the bloodstream, ready to attack the antigen.

People who contract a disease or receive a vaccine for it usually develop **active immunity.** But what happens if a person is exposed to a serious disease and it is too dangerous to wait for the person's body to produce its own antibodies? In this instance a physician may offer **passive immunity** by giving the person antibodies from another person or an animal. These antibodies are found in certain proteins in the donor's blood.

In general, active immunity is long-term and in some cases lifelong, whereas passive immunity generally lasts only a few weeks or months. Babies have passive immunity at birth because antibodies that pass through the placental membrane become part of the fetus's immune system. Within 6 weeks after birth, however, passive immunity begins to weaken. The baby then needs to receive vaccinations to start the development of active immunity against certain diseases.

Maintaining Immunity   Vaccines have greatly limited the number of people who may be carrying certain infectious diseases and thus have reduced the risk of contracting these diseases in the United States and elsewhere. Effective and

lymphocytes

antibodies

antigens

vaccine

active immunity

passive immunity

Table 9.1   Recommended Schedule for Active Immunization

Age	Vaccines
2 months	Diphtheria-tetanus-pertussis (DTP), oral polio vaccine
4 months	DTP, oral polio vaccine
6 months	Oral polio vaccine (recommended for infants in areas where polio is endemic)
15 months	Measles, rubella, mumps
18 months	DTP, oral polio booster
4 to 6 years (school entry)	DTP booster, oral polio booster
14 to 16 years	Combined tetanus and diphtheria toxoid, adult type (repeat every 10 years)

Source: American Academy of Pediatrics.

safe vaccines are now available for many infectious diseases. Some vaccines have to be administered only once; others require periodic boosters to keep the level of antibodies high enough to give immunity. Because of vaccinations, American children today are avoiding many of the diseases their parents experienced during childhood.

Widespread regular immunizations (Table 9.1) not only defend individuals against disease, they lessen the presence of the disease organism itself. This benefits the whole population, including those who have not been vaccinated. Although it is not necessary for everyone in the population to be immune in order to prevent a disease from spreading, scientists do not know how far below 100 percent immunity the population can go without having new outbreaks of these diseases. That is one reason why school systems and colleges often require proof of immunizations before registration or for giving out grades.

Malfunction of the Immune System   Experts suspect that disorders of the immune system may be involved in many puzzling medical problems. At times the body's defenses seem to act against the body's best interests. This can be seen in allergies and connective tissue diseases.[12]

In response to dust, pollen, and certain other substances, some people produce antibodies in such large quantities that they cause harm. The overabundant antibodies attach themselves to *mast cells* which release toxins. That causes the individual to cough, produce large amounts of mucus, and suffer other allergic symptoms.

A number of mysterious diseases afflict the various kinds of connective tissue in the body, such as the cartilage that holds the joints together. In the disease known as lupus, the immune system somehow attacks the body's connective tissue. In rheumatoid arthritis, certain antibodies cause the body to put out other antibodies, which lock on to them and cause inflammation in the joints.

In addition to allergies and diseases of connective tissues, malfunction of the immune system can be seen most devastatingly in AIDS. This disease, which presents a major challenge to the immune system, will be discussed in detail later in this chapter.

Sexually Transmitted Diseases

Although AIDS has received a great deal of publicity recently, it is just one of a great number of diseases that can be transmitted sexually. In general, **sexually transmitted diseases (STDs)** are on the increase in the United States, with individuals under age 25 accounting for the majority of cases. In addition to young people, other groups at high risk for contracting STDs are minorities, the medically underserved, and people who partake in risky sexual behaviors.[13] These diseases pose a real problem to people's health and well-being. Some have serious consequences, including chronic pain, sterility, abnormal pregnancy, cancer, and, in the case of AIDS, disability and death.

sexually transmitted disease (STD)

Many STDs can be conquered or controlled with antibiotics. Some cannot always be cured, however. For example, resistant strains of the bacteria that cause gonorrhea have developed, making this disease less easily cured than it was in the past.[14] Other STDs are caused by viruses. Because there is no cure for viral infections, treatment of these diseases is aimed at controlling symptoms and reducing spread to others. With all STDs, the most important step in prevention is to avoid infection. One of the keys to this is knowledge about these diseases and safer sexual practices.

Genital Herpes

In recent years genital herpes, which is caused by the herpes simplex virus (HSV), has become one of the most prevalent STDs in the United States. There are two types of HSV: type 1 and type 2. Formerly, HSV type 1 (HSV-1) was associated with fever blisters and cold sores while HSV type 2 (HSV-2) was blamed for genital herpes. Today, however, it is known that genital herpes can be caused by either HSV-1 or HSV-2.

Symptoms of Genital Herpes   The symptoms of genital herpes include blister-like sores that appear anywhere on the genitalia about 6 days after sexual contact or other direct physical contact with herpes blisters. These sores rupture to form shallow ulcers that may be very painful. The first occurrence of these lesions lasts about 12 days. This is followed by a period during which the symptoms disappear. Subsequent, usually milder recurrences last about 4 days. Other symptoms of genital herpes may include difficult urination, swelling of the legs, watery eyes, fatigue, and a general feeling of illness. The symptoms usually respond well to treatment. The antiviral drug *acyclovir* has been helpful in reducing or suppressing symptoms.[15] Unfortunately, no cure has been found for the herpes simplex virus, which remains in the body indefinitely.

Herpes is a cyclical disease in which the virus retreats periodically to the base of the spine. During these periods the risk of transmitting the disease to a partner is low. Sometimes herpes lies dormant for years. When the symptoms recur, they are often activated by sexual intercourse. Exposure to the sun, lack of sleep, infections, and physical or emotional stress can also bring them on. In some women the symptoms tend to reappear just before the menstrual period. The disease can be spread any time during the recurrence of symptoms. Occasionally the symptoms are too mild to be noticeable, and a sexual partner may be infected without knowing it.

Taking a Broader View of a Killer Disease

Thanks to medical research and knowledge about disease transmission, communicable diseases no longer cause widespread sickness and death. Outbreaks still occur and cause great fear—especially outbreaks of newly discovered diseases such as AIDS—but the horror of communicable diseases in the Middle Ages is almost unthinkable now. Smallpox, cholera, tuberculosis, typhoid, and bubonic plague were all great killers until medical science began to develop and test techniques for their cure and prevention. Now they have been largely eliminated in the developed nations, and smallpox has been eradicated throughout the world.

Smallpox was the most feared disease—very contagious and deadly. Up to 40 percent of its many victims did not survive, especially the very old and the very young. Those who lived through severe cases suffered fever and pain for several weeks, were sometimes blinded, and were often left badly disfigured, with deep pockmarks all over the skin.

The tale of the end of smallpox begins in folk medicine. The crowded cities of eighteenth-century Europe and North America made smallpox dangerous among the wealthy and influential as well as the poor. Finding methods to combat it became a high priority. Fortunately, exploration and trade brought stories from all over the world about different folk methods for providing protection against this disease. One method, used in different forms in Africa, China, and Turkey, involved a preparation from the scabs of smallpox itself: the scabs were either blown into the patient's nose or applied to a scratch on the skin. It sounds very dangerous, but it met with some success both in London and in Boston.

In 1788, Edward Jenner found that the same effect could be produced with the harmless scabs of a related disease known as cowpox. He called the technique vaccination. It was the first form of immunization invented.

The technique underwent several improvements over the next century and a half. Methods were developed for producing the vaccine in large quantities and preserving it effectively under refrigeration. By 1940 compulsory vaccination programs had all but eliminated smallpox from many countries in Europe. In the United States the last case officially recorded occurred in 1949. Efforts to use mass vaccination in other nations met with only partial success, however. A 1950 drive to defeat smallpox in the Americas was successful in the Caribbean and Central America but failed in some South American countries.

In 1967 another approach was tried. Instead of relying only on mass vaccination, health workers would seek out reports of all cases of smallpox. Each would be investigated, and every contact would be tracked down, treated if necessary, and kept in quarantine until safe.

The last person to be diagnosed with smallpox was a Somalian named Ali Maalin in 1977. Maalin's illness began the last campaign to find people with smallpox. Maalin was a cook in a hospital. He had exposed 161 people to the disease, 41 of whom had never been vaccinated against it. Medical workers found all 41, vaccinated them, and monitored their health. None came down with smallpox.

Over the next 6 months medical teams scoured the villages near Maalin's hometown in search of others who might have been exposed. They investigated thousands of rash and fever cases, and the World Health Organization Smallpox Reference Center in Atlanta, Georgia, examined more than 500 specimens. No new cases of smallpox were found.

Based on Donald A. Henderson, "The History of Smallpox Eradication," in *Times, Places, and Persons: Aspects of the History of Epidemiology*, A. M. Lilienfeld (ed.) (Baltimore: Johns Hopkins University Press, 1980): 99–107. With permission.

While the physical symptoms of herpes can be painful, many victims find the emotional impact even more distressing. Herpes sufferers often feel isolated, angry, and ashamed. The disease can ruin relationships and make one's social life difficult. Since emotional stress can trigger an outbreak, it is important for herpes sufferers to learn how to live with the disease.

Dangers of Herpes   Genital herpes can pose a significant problem for pregnant women, whose miscarriage rate is more than three times that of all pregnant women in the general population.[16] When miscarriage does not occur, the birth process may expose the infant to the virus, causing death or brain damage. As a preventive measure, the baby may be delivered by cesarean section. If the child is delivered vaginally, there is about a 50 percent chance that it will contract the disease. Herpes is fatal for more than half of the infants who contract it.[17]

Research has also indicated a strong relationship between HSV-2 and cancer of the cervix and prostate. Women with HSV-2 are more likely to develop cancer of the cervix than are other women.[18] As a result, women with genital herpes should have Pap smears annually or more often to check for the early signs of cervical cancer.

One of the most notorious victims of syphilis was the Chicago gangster Al Capone, who died at the age of 48 after succumbing to the tertiary symptoms during his 9-year jail sentence. (UPI/Bettmann Newsphotos)

Syphilis

Syphilis, which is caused by a spiral bacterium (a spirochete), is an extremely dangerous STD. Without treatment, the disease remains in the body for years, moving through a number of stages. Fortunately, it can be cured with antibiotics during the first two stages. If left untreated, however, it can have serious consequences. Therefore, it is important for people who suspect they may have syphilis to seek medical diagnosis and treatment immediately.

First Stage   In the first stage of syphilis a spirochete enters a person's body through a small break in the skin. Syphilis usually enters through the warm, moist mucous membrane of the genital tract, rectum, or mouth. After 10 to 28 days a dime-sized moist lump appears where the spirochete entered the body. This painless *chancre* is sometimes invisible but always contagious. With or without treatment, the chancre disappears in a few weeks, deceiving many people into thinking they are cured. However, the disease is still present.

Second Stage   In the second stage the spirochetes travel through the bloodstream to all parts of the body. During this stage the symptoms appear any time from a few weeks to a year after the disappearance of the chancre. These symptoms may include a skin rash, small flat sores on moist areas of the skin, whitish patches in the mouth and throat, patches of temporary baldness, general discomfort, a low fever, headache, and swollen glands. Syphilis is more contagious during this stage than it is at any other time. The secondary stage lasts 3 to 6 months.

Latency Phase   After the second stage of syphilis, all signs and symptoms of the disease disappear. The disease has entered the latency phase, but it is not gone: spirochetes are invading various organs, including the heart and brain. This phase sometimes lasts only a few months, but it can last for 20 years or longer. A blood test will still reveal the presence of the disease.

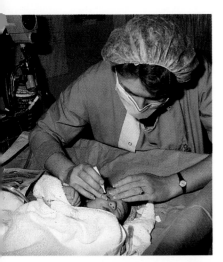

Application of a 1% silver nitrate solution to a newborn's eyes is a simple and effective precaution against gonococcal conjunctivitis, a form of blindness caused by the gonorrhea bacterium. (Susan Leavines/Photo Researchers, Inc.)

pelvic inflammatory disease (PID)

During the latency phase the individual is usually not infectious, but a pregnant woman can pass the infection to her unborn child. Early in pregnancy the infection may kill the fetus, produce various malformations, or result in an obviously diseased baby. A fetus infected late in pregnancy may seem healthy at birth, only to develop syphilis later. Treatment of an infected pregnant woman within the first 4 months of pregnancy halts the spread of the disease in her unborn child.

Tertiary Stage The tertiary stage generally begins 10 to 20 years after the beginning of the latency phase, but it sometimes occurs much earlier. With tertiary syphilis about one-fourth of all untreated patients become incapacitated.[19] Many develop serious cardiovascular disease. Some die of severe heart damage. Others have slowly progressive brain or spinal cord damage that leads to crippling, blindness, or insanity.

Gonorrhea

Gonorrhea is the most commonly reported communicable disease in the nation. Gonorrhea is caused by bacteria and is transmitted through sexual contact. It usually starts in the lower urinary and genital areas in both men and women. If left untreated, it can spread upward in the genital tract and cause sterility. It can also enter the bloodstream and cause severe arthritis and inflammation of the heart. Fortunately, it is easily treated with antibiotics such as penicillin if caught early.

Women may not even suspect that they have the disease at first. The early symptoms are frequently not pronounced, and most women never develop early symptoms. A few days after exposure they may notice a mild burning sensation in the genital region and perhaps a vaginal discharge. Later, after the disease has spread from the vagina up through the uterus and into the Fallopian tubes and ovaries, they may have pain and fever. These symptoms may be severe or mild. Sometimes a woman does not suspect she has gonorrhea until informed of the fact by a sexual partner.

Women who suspect that they have been exposed to gonorrhea or have a vaginal discharge of any sort should see a physician promptly for diagnosis and treatment. If left untreated, the symptoms of gonorrhea may diminish, but the disease will continue. The whole pelvis may eventually become inflamed by **pelvic inflammatory disease (PID),** a painful condition that can damage the reproductive organs and cause infertility. If gonorrhea organisms are present in a woman's birth canal, they may infect her baby's eyes during childbirth. To prevent blindness, most states require that silver nitrate solution be put in every baby's eyes shortly after birth.

The early symptoms of gonorrhea are more evident in men, although some men do not experience these symptoms. About 3 to 8 days after exposure men may notice a sharp, burning pain during urination. At about the same time pus begins oozing from the penis. This symptom causes many men to seek treatment.

If a man does not receive prompt treatment, the infection spreads to his prostate gland and testicles, where it can cause sterility. In time, the infection can cause the urethra to become narrowed, making it difficult to urinate. If the infection is severe, men can suffer arthritis and heart damage.

Condyloma

Condyloma, or genital warts, is the most commonly diagnosed viral STD in the United States.[20] The symptoms are warty growths around the anus and genitals. In women, the warts may develop inside the vagina and on the cervix. These growths can be painful. If they enlarge, they may destroy healthy tissue. In women, condyloma is suspected as a cause of cancer of the cervix. Early treatment of genital warts can prevent their spread. The warts may be removed surgically or with chemical ointments.

Chlamydia

While condyloma is the most commonly diagnosed viral STD, chlamydia is the most commonly occurring one. It strikes over 3 million American men, women, and children every year.[21] In men chlamydia causes infections of the urethra, epididymis, and prostate; in women it causes inflammation of the cervix and Fallopian tubes. Most women experience no symptoms from chlamydial infections, but if left untreated, these infections may spread throughout the pelvic area, causing PID. Untreated chlamydia also causes infections in pregnant women and in infants before and after birth. It is associated with higher rates of infant deaths and with eye, ear, and respiratory infections in newborns.

The symptoms of chlamydia include pain in the lower abdomen, vaginal discharge, and difficulty in urinating. A pelvic examination may show that a woman's cervix is swollen and inflamed and is discharging pus. Pain during this examination suggests inflammation of the Fallopian tubes.[22] Chlamydia is found most often among young, sexually active men and women. The more sexual partners a person has, the greater is the likelihood of contracting the disease.[23] In many cases, sexually active individuals suffer from chlamydia and other STDs simultaneously.

Because of the damage untreated chlamydia can cause, it is important that people with symptoms of the disease seek diagnosis and treatment promptly. Doctors usually prescribe a 7- to 10-day course of tetracycline or another antibiotic for both the patient and the patient's sexual partners. If a sexual partner is not treated, the infection is likely to be passed back. Fortunately, chlamydia responds well to antibiotic treatment, and people can protect themselves against contracting the disease (as well as other STDs) by using barrier methods of contraception such as condoms and diaphragms with spermicides.

AIDS

Acquired immune deficiency syndrome has increased rapidly throughout the world since it was first diagnosed in 1981. In the United States the Centers for Disease Control estimate that between 246,000 and 298,000 Americans will develop the disease by the end of 1993.[24] In this country about 93 percent of AIDS cases so far have occurred in men, mainly between ages 25 and 44 years. Although these cases have occurred primarily among homosexual men, the number of cases among heterosexuals is now increasing at a rate twice that for homosexual and bisexual men. Moreover, the disease is occurring more frequently among the young, the poor, women, and members of minority

The tragedy of AIDS was personified in the middle 1980s by Ryan White, a hemophiliac who contracted the disease from blood transfusions. Fearing for their children, the parents of some of his schoolmates tried to keep him out of classes even though the HIV virus does not spread by casual contact. (UPI/Bettmann)

groups. In some areas and in some age groups, AIDS is now the leading cause of death for women.[25]

AIDS is a collection of diseases caused by the human immunodeficiency virus (HIV). This virus invades and destroys the T cells (T lymphocytes), resulting in a defective immune system. Instead of recognizing and launching an immune response against foreign substances, the T cells actually begin producing HIV themselves. Without opposition from the T cells, HIV and other viruses multiply rapidly. The longer a person is infected with HIV, the more likely it is that his or her immune system will be impaired.

Initially, the majority of people infected with HIV exhibit no symptoms. About 2 to 5 weeks after infection, however, many suffer a viral syndrome similar to infectious mononucleosis, with fever, fatigue, or a variety of signs such as meningitis, a red rash on the face or trunk of the body, mild hepatitis, and swollen lymph glands. These symptoms pass, and a latency period of 5 to 10 years may occur. With the passage of time, people infected with HIV normally progress to a number of syndromes including generalized chronic swelling of the lymph glands, night sweats, fever, diarrhea, weight loss, fatigue, and rare infections.

AIDS is the most severe form of HIV infection. Twenty to 30 percent of HIV-infected persons develop AIDS within 5 years.[26] In the later stages of full-blown AIDS, the severely weakened immune system leaves the infected person vulnerable to a variety of diseases, including an unusual form of pneumonia, tuberculosis, and a rare form of skin cancer. Among those whose infection progresses to AIDS, 50 percent die within 18 months and 80 percent die within 3 years.[27]

Modes of Transmission

The human immunodeficiency virus is transmitted through the exchange of body fluids—principally blood and semen—during sexual contact and blood transfusions or by exchanging needles during intravenous (IV) drug use. During sexual contact, membranes in the vagina, cervix, mouth, rectum, and urethra can allow the virus to enter the body. Although HIV once was thought to be transmitted by saliva, urine, feces, and tears as well, the Centers for Disease Control no longer regard these as high-risk fluids unless they are contaminated with infected blood.[28] The virus can also pass from mother to child during the perinatal period, leading to an increasing number of newborns with HIV.[29] HIV is *not* spread through casual contact such as hugging and kissing. In addition, there is no evidence to suggest that the virus is spread by insects or in food or water.[30]

Preventive Measures for AIDS

At the present time prevention is the *only* way to control the spread of AIDS. People can take steps to protect themselves from contracting HIV. The primary step is knowing how HIV is transmitted and what precautions to take to avoid infection.

Because one of the primary modes of HIV transmission is sexual activity, knowledge about the safety of sexual behavior is essential. The safest sexual behavior is abstinence, since refraining from sexual activity ensures that a person will not be exposed to HIV sexually. The practice of mutual monogamy also helps control the spread of AIDS. A completely monogamous noninfected couple cannot contract the virus sexually.

No sexual activity involving direct contact with sexual secretions should be considered safe unless the people involved are known to be free of infection. Unfortunately, many people infected with HIV show no signs of the disease but can still transmit the infection to others. As a result, people need to be aware of and use safer sex practices.

Such practices include the use of chemical and physical barriers during sexual activity. These barriers include latex condoms used during vaginal intercourse and oral sex performed on a man, latex dental dams or plastic wrap used as a barrier to vaginal secretions during oral sex on a woman, and the use of more than one latex condom or an extra strong condom during anal intercourse (the form of intercourse which carries the highest risk of HIV infection). In all cases, the use of a lubricant containing the spermicide nonoxynol-9 is recommended to help reduce the risk further.

Besides sexual activity, HIV is transmitted by the sharing of needles used for the IV injection of drugs. Sharing needles when injecting cocaine or other drugs may be responsible for the increase in HIV infection among teenage addicts and their sexual partners. If an individual does inject drugs, needles, syringes, and other paraphernalia should never be shared.

Transfusion of blood and blood products is another known route of transmission of HIV infection. Although blood used for transfusions is routinely tested for HIV, about 1 in every 100,000 pints may be contaminated with the virus.[31] The safest type of transfusion involves the use of self-donated blood. With surgery, for example, if the timing and conditions allow it, patients can donate a pint of their own blood every week up to 6 weeks before the operation, ensuring that the blood used is free from infection.[32]

Because HIV infection is transmitted from mother to fetus, all women who may have been exposed to the virus should be tested before becoming pregnant. An HIV-infected woman should be counseled about the risk of transmitting the virus to her fetus if she becomes pregnant.

Current Treatment Options

Treatment of AIDS has involved attempts to treat complications such as infections and tumors, reestablish immune defenses, and control or destroy the virus.[33] Research to date has not been successful in developing a cure.

At present, the drug AZT remains the cornerstone of HIV therapy and continues to improve the prognosis of HIV-infected persons. While AZT does not cure AIDS, it has been found to prolong survival and reduce mortality in AIDS patients. The earlier the patient starts AZT therapy after the initial diagnosis of the disease, the better the chances are of long-term survival.[34]

In the future, AZT most likely will be used in combination with other drugs. Such combinations could lead to more complete suppression of the virus than can be achieved with any single drug.

Finally, the Centers for Disease Control advise HIV-infected individuals to remain as healthy as possible through proper nutrition, exercise, stress reduction, and avoidance of nonprescribed drugs, alcohol, and tobacco.

The Politics of AIDS

AIDS is not only a serious health threat but a political issue as well. One of the basic concerns has been the need to balance the rights and needs of AIDS-infected persons with those of the community. The U.S. Supreme Court, for example, has classified AIDS as a handicap protected under federal law in order to protect persons with AIDS from discrimination. The courts continue to debate whether an employer has the right to fire a person with AIDS if other employees are unduly afraid or if the place of employment will suffer as a result of the AIDS-infected person's employment.[35]

Another important politically related issue concerns where the money will come from to treat AIDS victims. The groups now hardest hit by the disease—drug abusers, blacks, and Hispanics—are the most difficult to reach with disease-prevention messages. These groups also have less access to health insurance and medical care. Government health care programs will not be able to absorb the rising cost of AIDS treatment easily, and help may come too late for many victims.

The Future of AIDS

Despite estimates by the Centers for Disease Control and other groups, no one knows for sure how many people are infected with HIV. What is certain, however, is that without a cure, the HIV epidemic and the AIDS problem will continue to expand.

Although unprecedented efforts have been made to find drugs that will decrease the transmission of the virus and halt the progression of the disease, the key issue is time: time to evaluate and test new drugs, time to continue research on the disease in hopes of finding a vaccine and/or a cure, and time to teach people how to prevent HIV infection as well as infection from other STDs. With education and time, not only AIDS but other STDs as well may eventually be conquered.

Chapter Summary

- Changing trends in work, diet, and activities may affect people's susceptibility to disease as they become exposed to infection or their bodies become less resistant to disease. Travel to other countries may also expose people to diseases. Medical progress has resulted in improved identification, prevention, and treatment of disease, but it also may contribute to other medical problems.

- An infection is the invasion of the body by disease-causing organisms and the reaction of the body to their presence. Agent, host, and environmental factors are responsible for the onset of disease.

- An infectious disease normally follows a common pattern marked by five phases: the incubation period, the prodromal period, clinical disease, the decline stage, and convalescence.

- The primary agents of infectious disease include bacteria, viruses, rickettsiae, and fungi.

- The skin and mucous membranes are the body's first line of defense against infection. Cilia in the respiratory passages also fend off invading microorganisms. If microorganisms get through the body's first-line defenses, the inflammatory response helps ward off and defeat them. White blood cells rush to infected areas to engulf and consume foreign organisms. Redness, local warmth, swelling, and pain are signs that the body is counterattacking invading organisms.

- In the immune system, B and T lymphocytes play a role in producing antibodies that help eliminate foreign antigens from the body. People may develop natural immunity when the body manufactures antibodies in response to disease, or acquired immunity through the use of vaccines that stimulate immunity before disease can strike.

- Some of the major sexually transmitted diseases include genital herpes, syphilis, gonorrhea, condyloma, and chlamydia. The symptoms of these diseases vary, but they all hold potential danger for people suffering from them.

- The symptoms of HIV infection include fever, fatigue, and a variety of neurological signs. The disease may then progress through a number of syndromes including generalized chronic swelling of the lymph glands, night sweats, fever, diarrhea, weight loss, fatigue, and the occurrence of rare infections. With full-blown AIDS, the patient's immune system is seriously impaired and the patient is susceptible to a variety of life-threatening diseases.

- The human immunodeficiency virus is transmitted through the exchange of body fluids—principally blood and semen—during sexual contact, blood transfusions, and the exchange of needles during intravenous drug use.

- At present AIDS cannot be cured. Prevention is the only way to control its spread. Preventive measures include safer sex practices along with the avoidance of shared intravenous drug paraphernalia. Current treatment options for persons with AIDS include the use of the drug AZT, established medical procedures to stem infections and tumors, and the maintenance of a healthy lifestyle.

- Two of the political issues surrounding AIDS are the rights of AIDS-infected persons and the availability of money to treat AIDS victims.

Cardiovascular Health and Disease

Objectives

When you have studied this chapter, you should be able to:

- Identify the components and structures of the heart and circulatory system and explain how they work.

- Define hypertension and atherosclerosis and discuss their cause and treatment.

- Explain how heart attacks and strokes occur and describe several treatments for them.

- Describe cardiovascular diseases other than heart attack and stroke.

- Identify several of the controllable risk factors for contracting a cardiovascular disease and discuss how they can be reduced.

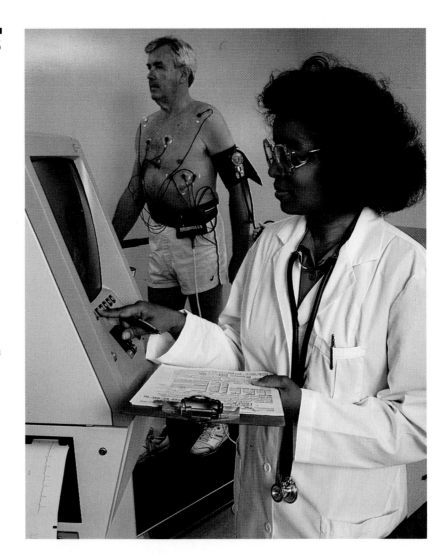

According to the American Heart Association, cardiovascular diseases claim more American lives—nearly 1 million people a year—than do all other causes of death combined. Cardiovascular disease (CVD) develops slowly and without noticeable symptoms over a number of years. It takes many forms, including high blood pressure, coronary artery disease (disease of the arteries that supply the heart muscle), stroke, abnormal heart rhythms, and rheumatic heart disease. More than one in four Americans has some form of CVD.[1]

People *can* protect themselves against CVD. Individuals who make an effort to control major risk factors can reduce their chances of developing CVD. In fact, death rates from heart attack, stroke, and other CVDs are declining. Advances in medical treatment and healthier lifestyles are contributing to this improvement.[2]

Although the situation is improving, a sizable percentage of the population is still at risk from CVD. As a result, it is important to know what causes CVD and what steps can be taken to help prevent it. First, however, it is necessary to know a few basic facts about the heart and circulatory system.

The Heart and Circulatory System

The major function of the heart is to pump blood into the lungs to pick up oxygen and then to pump that blood throughout the body to supply the tissues with fresh, oxygen-rich blood (Figure 10.1). This pumping process is carried out through a continuous series of contractions and relaxations of the heart. Blood is pushed out with each contraction and pulled in with each relaxation, over and over again.

Unlike organ systems such as the kidneys, which can shut down for a short time without causing permanent harm to the body, the heart must work non-stop. The only time it rests is during the split second between beats. The reason for this is that the cells of the body need a constant supply of oxygen—the fuel that keeps them alive. As oxygen is used up, it must be replenished constantly to prevent *oxygen starvation,* which causes destruction of body tissue, including the brain, the body's master control. Brain death, which results if the brain is deprived of oxygen, causes irreversible loss of consciousness.[3]

A Look at the Heart

The heart is a four-chambered muscular organ the size of an adult's fist that weighs less than 1 pound. It beats about 100,000 times a day, pumping about half a cup of blood with each beat. Divided down the center by a solid sheet of muscle, the heart consists of four distinct chambers. The top chambers are called the *atria* (singular: *atrium*). The lower chambers are called the *ventricles.* As the heart beats, the left atrium and ventricle work together to form one pump, while the right atrium and ventricle form another.

Blood enters the right atrium through the central veins of the body. It then passes through the right ventricle and into the *pulmonary artery,* which leads to the lung. In the lung there are millions of tiny air sacs at the ends of the branches of the respiratory tract. There the blood is cleaned of waste gas (carbon dioxide) and saturated with a fresh supply of oxygen. The blood then moves from the lungs back to the heart, passing first into the left atrium, then through the left ventricle, and finally out of the heart through the **aorta,** the   *aorta*

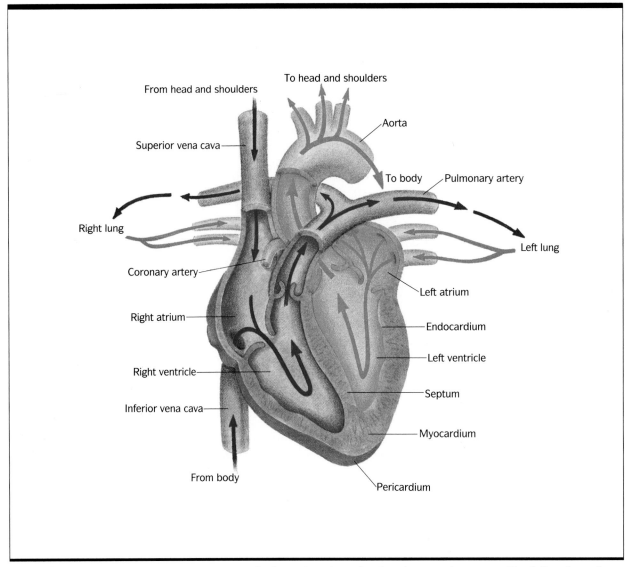

Figure 10.1 *The heart is a four-chambered pump that moves blood first through the lungs and then throughout the body.*

main artery of the circulatory system. Branching off from the aorta are the many smaller arteries that carry blood bearing oxygen and other nutrients to all the organs and tissues of the body.[4]

pacemaker This constant process of oxygenation is made possible by the heart's natural **pacemaker,** an electrical impulse center in the upper wall of the right atrium. This center regulates the heartbeat by stimulating the heart muscles to pump in a coordinated fashion. Valves separating the heart's chambers open and close to regulate the flow of blood through the heart and out into the body. These valves ensure that the blood always passes through the heart in the proper direction. Damage to any of the heart valves can result in backward movement of blood within the heart, causing reduced efficiency and even failure of the whole system.

The Circulatory System

The circulatory system consists of the heart and blood vessels (Figure 10.2). It takes approximately 10 to 15 seconds for blood to make a complete circuit of this system. Oxygenated blood leaving the heart through the aorta travels through a complex network of **arteries** to the head, the shoulders and arms, the digestive system, the legs, and the heart muscle itself. These arteries divide and subdivide into smaller and smaller branches until they finally become tiny **capillaries.** Capillaries have very thin walls through which nutrients and oxygen can pass directly from the blood into the tissues and waste matter and carbon dioxide can pass from the tissues into the blood. This deoxygenated blood then travels from the capillaries through a network of **veins** leading back to the heart, which then returns the blood to the lungs to receive a fresh supply of oxygen.

In contrast with the capillary walls and the walls of the veins, arterial walls are thick and muscular. When the powerful left ventricle contracts to pump blood throughout the body, the arteries receive more blood than can be moved instantly through the capillaries. Thus, the walls must stretch and then, using their own muscles, contract to squeeze the extra blood through the system.

arteries

capillaries

veins

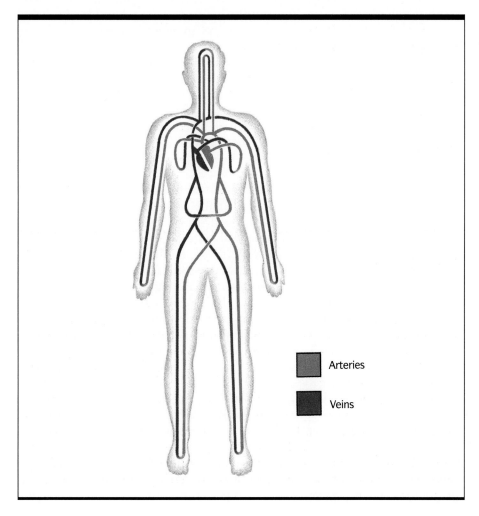

Arteries

Veins

Figure 10.2 The heart beats about 100,000 times a day, circulating the average person's 9 pints of blood 1,900 times. This stylized picture shows how blood is replenished in the lungs and digestive organs, and driven to nourish the brain and the rest of the body, all in less than half a minute.

Of vital importance among the arteries are the *coronary* arteries, which supply blood to the heart muscle, and the *carotid* and *vertebral* arteries, which bring blood to the brain. Sometimes branches of these arteries become blocked, cutting off the flow of blood from vital tissues. This is when heart attack and stroke, the major CVDs, occur.

The Causes of Cardiovascular Disease

Two important causes of blockage in the circulatory system are hypertension (high blood pressure) and atherosclerosis. In fact, because of the problems they lead to, these two conditions are usually considered dangerous types of CVD themselves.

Blood Pressure and Hypertension

blood pressure

Blood pressure is the force exerted by the blood on the walls of the arteries. It varies greatly during each heartbeat. When blood is being pumped out and the arteries are expanding, blood pressure is considerably higher than it is when the heart is refilling for the next beat. For this reason, a person's blood pressure is measured in two figures: the *systolic pressure,* when blood is being forced into the arteries from the heart, and the *diastolic pressure,* when the arteries are waiting for the next beat.

hypertension

Both of these figures can vary considerably in an individual, depending on activity and emotional state as well as many other factors, for example, infections, the use of nicotine and other drugs, and even the time of day. However, a person who is rested and relaxed yet has a systolic pressure above 140 or a diastolic above 90 is considered to have high blood pressure, or **hypertension.**

Hypertension is thought to be the root cause of many of the problems that plague the heart and blood vessels. The dangers of untreated high blood pressure cannot be overstated.

Who Gets High Blood Pressure?   Called the silent killer because it rarely produces noticeable symptoms, high blood pressure affects roughly one in four American adults and accounts for about 30,000 deaths annually.[5] It is rarely found in persons under 20 years of age, but by age 50 approximately one-half of the population has hypertension in some form. Until about age 50 to 55 men are far more likely than women to have high blood pressure. Some women, however, become hypertensive during pregnancy, and women who take oral contraceptives are more likely to develop high blood pressure than are those who do not. Also at risk are people who have a family history of high blood pressure, those who are overweight, smokers, and individuals with chronic conditions such as diabetes.[6]

How Can You Tell If You Have High Blood Pressure?   Advanced cases of hypertension may be accompanied by headaches (frequently at the back of the head), feelings of tension and irritability, dizziness, and fatigue. Generally, the only way to tell if you have high blood pressure is to have your blood pressure checked regularly. A single elevated reading does not necessarily mean that a person has hypertension. It is normal for blood pressure readings to vary from time to time. If your blood pressure is repeatedly above the normal range for your age, you should see a physician without delay and follow his or her instructions.

Treatment of High Blood Pressure   Most cases of hypertension, from the mildest to the most severe, can be treated effectively provided that the disorder is recognized. Treatment is often easy, is usually inexpensive, and protects against early disability or death from heart attack or stroke. While many medications help to lower high blood pressure, dietary change and improved exercise habits may control hypertension by themselves.

People can often reduce high blood pressure by decreasing the amount of salt in the diet, losing weight if they are obese, and restricting their intake of alcohol. Before prescribing drugs, doctors often recommend these methods, especially for people who have only mildly elevated blood pressure.[7]

If medications are indicated, there are several types to choose from. One group—the diuretics—rid the body of excess fluids and sodium. Others, known as beta blockers, reduce the heart rate and the heart's output of blood. Another type—the sympathetic nerve inhibitors—can inhibit the ability of sympathetic nerves in the brain to narrow blood vessels and cause blood pressure to rise. Still another type—the vasodilators—cause the muscles in arterial walls to relax, allowing the arteries to widen. Nitroglycerin is a vasodilator that is commonly prescribed for recovering heart attack patients.

In most cases, such drugs can help lower blood pressure. It is usually necessary, however, for patients to go through a trial period with a drug to determine its effectiveness and to monitor any side effects.

Dangers of High Blood Pressure   In a person with hypertension, the muscles of the arterial walls are constricted, causing the blood vessels to become narrower and less flexible. If the condition remains untreated, the heart must pump unnaturally hard to force blood through the network of constricted arteries. In severe cases, the heart may fail from the added strain.

Unrelieved high blood pressure also may cause arteries to become damaged as a result of blood pressing against their walls with added force. Fatty substances and other debris collect on the inner walls of the damaged arteries. This contributes to atherosclerosis, the other major cause of serious cardiovascular disease.

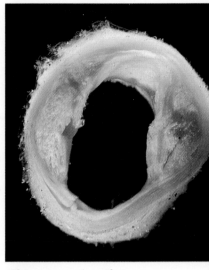

This cross-section of a human aorta reveals atherosclerosis, a partial obstruction created by fat deposits; when this occurs in smaller arteries, such as those in the heart and brain, it can lead to thrombosis, or total blockage. Part of the deposit may also break away and be carried by the blood to block a smaller artery, causing an embolism. (Richard Kirby, David Spears, Ltd./Science Photo Library/Photo Researchers, Inc.)

Atherosclerosis

In **atherosclerosis,** the arteries grow narrower as a result of fatty deposits on the inner lining of arterial walls. These deposits are called **plaque** and are composed of fatty substances, cholesterol, cellular waste products, calcium, and a clotting material in the blood.

atherosclerosis
plaque

The Cause of Atherosclerosis   Atherosclerosis is thought to begin as a result of damage to the inner lining of arterial walls. In addition to hypertension, other factors that are associated with damage to the arterial walls include high levels of fat and cholesterol in the blood, and cigarette smoking.[8]

Damage to an arterial wall triggers the body's usual healing mechanism. The blood thickens around the damaged area and forms a **thrombus,** or blood clot. Blood clots are a normal part of the healing process and usually dissolve harmlessly. In patients with atherosclerosis, however, the damaged arterial

thrombus

walls heal only partially. A jagged lesion remains, and as blood flows past the affected area, this rough surface attracts fatty debris and causes a buildup of plaque. In a final effort to heal the wound, scar tissue forms, creating a permanent deposit of plaque and a permanently narrowed artery.

The Role of Fats and Cholesterol The development of atherosclerosis has been linked to high levels of saturated fats and cholesterol in the blood.[9] Federal health officials therefore recommend that *all* Americans (not just those with high cholesterol levels) reduce the fat content of their diets to lower their risk of developing CVD.[10] The verdict on fats and cholesterol is not yet final, however, and many fundamental questions remain.

Dangers of Atherosclerosis Generally, the heart can continue pumping effectively even through arteries that have been reduced 60 percent in size. The narrowing of an artery in a person with atherosclerosis may first become noticeable when it is severe enough to cause inadequate blood circulation to the body cells that it supplies. This can take many years to develop or it can occur more suddenly. If the blood vessel sustains further damage, a blood clot may *thrombosis* develop in addition to the plaque. This type of clot is called a **thrombosis,** and it may block the vessel totally. Blockage can also occur if a blood clot or piece of plaque breaks off from an arterial wall and becomes wedged in the nar- *embolus* rowed vessel. Such a wedge is called an **embolus** (a Greek word meaning *embolism* "stopper"), and the condition is known as an **embolism.**

These complications of atherosclerosis can occur anywhere in the body. However, the most severe results of atherosclerosis occur when the damage is sustained in the blood vessels that supply the heart or the brain.

Major Cardiovascular Diseases

As was mentioned earlier, CVD takes many forms. The most catastrophic of these are heart attack and stroke. Together, these two diseases claim close to 700,000 lives a year.[11]

Heart Attack

heart attack Essentially, a **heart attack** is a loss of function in the heart. Most commonly, there is a total interruption in the supply of blood to a portion of the heart muscle, and that portion dies from lack of oxygen. This is known technically as *myocardial infarction* a **myocardial infarction.** Heart attacks result from blood vessel disease in the heart, usually referred to as coronary artery disease or coronary heart disease. This disease often results from atherosclerosis.

Prior to causing a full-fledged heart attack, coronary heart disease may lead to a condition called ischemic heart disease, in which a portion of the heart gets too little blood and oxygen. Ischemic heart disease is often accompanied *angina pectoris* by a chest pain called **angina pectoris,** which is felt during exertion but goes away if one rests. While angina can be a warning sign that a person is at risk for a heart attack, it does not always lead to a heart attack. Heart muscle can and often does recover from minor ischemic episodes, even those which result in pain. Some people have ischemia without experiencing any pain. This *silent ischemia* may lead to a sudden heart attack without any warning.

How a Heart Attack Happens   A heart attack occurs when a blockage forms in a branch of one of the coronary arteries, cutting off the blood supply to a portion of the heart. Thus deprived of oxygen and nourishment, the heart muscle that is fed by the affected artery dies. This may occur as a result of a **coronary thrombosis**—a blood clot that forms in a coronary artery. It can also occur as a result of a **coronary embolism,** in which a piece of clotted material breaks away from an arterial wall and travels with the bloodstream until it lodges in—and blocks—a coronary artery.

coronary thrombosis
coronary embolism

Whether the victim of a heart attack lives or dies depends in part on where the arterial blockage occurs. If the flow of blood through one of the main arteries is blocked, large portions of the heart muscle may die, irreparably damaging the heart's pumping mechanism. A total stoppage of the heart—called **cardiac arrest**—may result. When cardiac arrest occurs, immediate action is necessary or the patient will die. The brain can survive without damage for only about 4 minutes after the heart stops circulating blood. If, however, only a small arterial branch is blocked, other areas of the heart may be able to compensate for the loss and the attack will not be life-threatening.

cardiac arrest

What It Feels Like to Have a Heart Attack   Occasionally, heart attacks occur quietly and painlessly and are not discovered until months or even years later. Such "silent" heart attacks can be just as damaging to the heart muscle as painful ones and are extremely dangerous because the victim rarely seeks medical attention or takes steps to ward off further episodes.

In most heart attacks, however, the victim knows something is wrong, although he or she may initially think the sensations have been caused by indigestion or "heartburn." The typical symptoms of a heart attack vary from an uncomfortable feeling of pressure, fullness, and squeezing to a crushing pain in the center of the chest lasting 2 minutes or longer. The pain may then spread to the shoulders, neck, or arms. The victim may experience severe pain, dizziness, fainting, sweating, nausea, or shortness of breath. It is not uncommon to experience feelings of terror or a sense of impending doom. While these are some of the common signs of a heart attack, it is important to note that they may not be felt at all and may not be continuously present.[12]

Dealing with a Heart Attack   Heart attack can strike anyone at any time. Most victims can survive if they recognize what is happening and get help quickly. During a heart attack, the cardiac muscle does not die all at once. Prompt intervention—within 1 to 3 hours—can restore the flow of blood to the heart with a minimum of damage.

It is therefore critical that a person who experiences the warning signs of a heart attack take action promptly. If it is faster to get to a hospital than to call for help, the victim should be taken there immediately. Someone in cardiac arrest from a heart attack (or from drowning, electrocution, or strangulation) can be saved if cardiopulmonary resuscitation (CPR) is performed. When administered properly by a trained individual, CPR can help sustain the victim until medical help arrives. (A local American Heart Association or Red Cross chapter can provide information on CPR training.)

Recovery from a Heart Attack   After a heart attack, the patient must rest for a while to reduce the work load on the heart and allow it to heal. During the healing process, scar tissue forms around the area where the heart muscle died. This scar tissue cannot contract, but if the scar is small, the heart may continue to function well and the patient may recover. Eighty percent of people who survive heart attacks can return to work and their usual activities within 3 months.[13] In fact, physicians today are advising a shorter period of bed rest than they did in the past. In addition, they encourage patients to begin a planned program of exercise under medical supervision as soon as they are well enough.

After a heart attack, emotional recovery is as important as physical recovery. People who suffer the trauma of a heart attack become more aware of their mortality. A vital organ—the heart—has failed. As a result, most victims experience depression and fear. They may have the idea that it will be dangerous to put any strain on the heart. Thus, they may be afraid to exercise at all, even to get out of a chair and walk across the room.

Their families are also affected by the experience. Spouses may try to encourage recovering heart patients to avoid exercise, including sexual activity, and thus may reinforce the doubts the victim already has about his or her heart. The patient's fear of a recurrence of heart attack symptoms or even of sudden death may interfere with rehabilitation. Patients who continue to experience fear and depression after several months should probably seek professional counseling.

The first step toward emotional recovery is for heart attack patients to recognize that lifestyle changes can have a positive effect on their cardiovascular health and that they can help themselves return to a normal life. Patients must be reassured that an exercise program will not hurt them. In fact, moderate exercise not only will help improve overall health, it also can aid the process by which the heart develops **collateral circulation**—a system of smaller blood vessels that provide alternative routes for blood when a main artery is blocked.

collateral circulation

The affection of a loving relationship also aids a patient's recovery. Most people can return to their usual sexual activities after a brief recovery period.[14] As heart attack patients modify some aspects of their lifestyle and ease back into others, their confidence will grow and their lives will return to normal.

Stroke: When CVD Affects the Brain

stroke

A **stroke** is a sudden loss of brain function resulting from interference with the blood supply to part of the brain (Figure 10.3). Stroke is the third leading cause of death in the United States after heart attacks and cancer.[15]

cerebral thrombosis
cerebral embolism
cerebral hemorrhage

There are three types of stroke: cerebral thrombosis, cerebral embolism, and cerebral hemorrhage. A **cerebral thrombosis** is caused by a blood clot forming in a cerebral blood vessel. A **cerebral embolism** occurs when material from elsewhere in the body clogs a cerebral blood vessel. In a **cerebral hemorrhage,** blood flow to the brain is impaired by the rupture of a cerebral blood vessel. In all three cases, the flow of oxygen to parts of the brain is impaired, resulting in the death of some brain tissue.

Some strokes are so severe that they kill within minutes by destroying the part of the brain that regulates heart and lung functions. Others may be very mild, causing only temporary dizziness or slight weakness or numbness. Such strokes are called **transient ischemic attacks (TIAs)** and are often ignored.

transient ischemic attack (TIA)

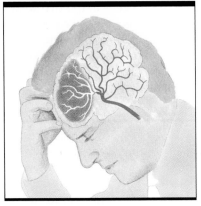 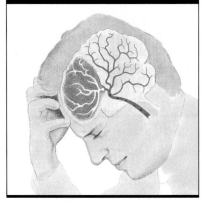 

(A) Cerebral thrombosis   (B) Cerebral embolism   (C) Cerebral hemorrhage

Figure 10.3 *Strokes usually occur as a result of localized blood loss in the brain. (A) In cerebral thrombosis, a blood clot forms within a cerebral blood vessel or in one of the arteries that supplies the brain. (B) A cerebral embolism occurs when a solid particle from elsewhere lodges in a cerebral artery. (C) Cerebral hemorrhage is a third cause of stroke. In this case, a diseased blood vessel ruptures and floods the brain tissue with blood that does not circulate.*

However, when a stroke, even a transient one, has occurred, the chances of having a second stroke are increased. This is one reason why it is a good idea to be alert to a possible TIA. The symptoms of a TIA may include:

- Brief unexplained numbness, tingling, unusual weakness, or paralysis of any part of the body
- Difficulty in swallowing, speaking, phrasing sentences, or thinking clearly
- Sudden dizziness, fainting, altered vision, or severe headaches

Such an attack may last anywhere from a few minutes to a few hours. A person who has clearly experienced the symptoms of a TIA should seek immediate medical attention.

In a stroke, the nearby brain cells, no longer fed by the blocked or ruptured artery, are deprived of oxygen and begin to die. Depending on what part of the body or mind was controlled by these cells, the victim may suffer partial paralysis and other crippling afflictions.

Recovery from Stroke The key factor determining the outcome of a stroke is the part of the brain affected by the stroke. Many stroke victims suffer from loss of memory and many exhibit general confusion. They become tired easily, and their ability to concentrate may be impaired. Sudden and extreme mood fluctuations and inappropriate emotional reactions are fairly common.

Many stroke victims are left with permanent physical impairment, yet in many cases there is hope for at least a partial recovery. Although brain cells do not regenerate (unlike most other body tissues), one area of the brain can learn to take over the functions of another area after brain damage has occurred. With appropriate physical therapy, it is often possible for a stroke victim to relearn basic self-care skills and sometimes other skills as well.

Recovery from a severe stroke is a slow, painstaking process. It requires enormous effort, patience, and strength on the part of the victim and those

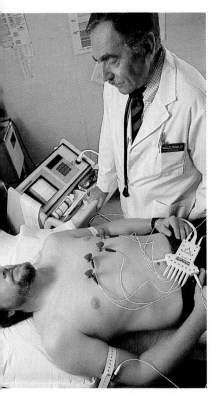

Doctors can gather a large amount of cardiovascular data with an electrocardiogram (ECG). This is done using electrodes to record electrical activity from the heart at several locations in the body. The electroencephalogram (EEG) measures similar impulses from the brain. (Doug Plummer/Photo Researchers, Inc.)

around him or her. The most dramatic improvements occur in the first weeks and months after the incident. Subsequent progress may be extremely slow. Physical therapists and others who help in the rehabilitation of stroke victims stress the importance of encouraging patients to do as much as possible for themselves, helping them regain confidence in their abilities, and try to prevent them from becoming too dependent on friends and relatives.[16]

Early Diagnosis of Major Cardiovascular Disease

Since CVD sometimes is not accompanied by obvious symptoms, it is important for people, especially those over age 40, to get regular checkups and periodic blood and blood pressure tests to detect potential problems. Of course, anyone who experiences severe chest pains or the symptoms of stroke should immediately consult a physician.

Tests for CVD fall into three categories: imaging, measuring electrical activity, and charting blood flow. The tests are painless and can be done on an outpatient basis.[17]

Imaging tests include computerized axial tomographic scanning (CAT scan), magnetic resonance imaging (MRI), and nuclear scan. Each of these tests can be used to create pictures of the heart and brain to identify areas of damage or potential blockage.

Physicians measure electrical activity with electroencephalograms (EEGs)—tests that chart the electrical activity of the brain so as to assess the damage caused by a stroke—and electrocardiograms (ECGs)—tests that chart the electrical activity of the heart to reveal cardiovascular abnormalities. ECGs may be done while the patient is at rest or on a treadmill.

A variety of tests are available to chart blood flow. One of the most common is cardiac catheterization, or *angiography*, a procedure in which x-ray pictures are taken of different areas in the cardiovascular system. A catheter, or small tube, is inserted into an artery in the leg or elsewhere and guided to the area to be studied. A dye is injected through the catheter, and x-ray pictures are then taken to detect the dye. With this process, doctors can get detailed pictures of narrowed arteries and potentially dangerous blood clots. Generally, the use of catheters is a safe procedure, but there are some risks, including an allergic reaction to the dye, disturbances of heart rhythm, arterial damage, blood clots, and bleeding.[18] Another procedure—the thallium radioactive isotope x-ray—is used today as a safer method.

Treatment of Major Cardiovascular Disease

In many instances lifestyle changes and "healthier living" alone can prevent or reduce the risk of a recurrence of major cardiovascular episodes. Sometimes, however, other steps must be taken to control the conditions that lead to CVD or to treat the victims.

Using Drugs to Control CVD Drugs offer doctors and patients a means of combating many of the conditions that lead to cardiovascular episodes. Several drugs are available for lowering the high cholesterol levels associated with atherosclerosis. Bile acid sequestrants, one commonly used type of medication, act by causing the body to produce extra bile acids for the digestive system. Body cholesterol is used up to produce these bile acids. Another type of medication, lovastatin, an enzyme inhibitor, limits production of an enzyme that controls the synthesis of body cholesterol and thus stimulates the removal of substances that carry fat throughout the body. Another drug, gemfibrizol, has also shown positive results in lowering cholesterol.

Aspirin, long known as a painkiller and anti-inflammatory agent, has also proved useful in the treatment of CVD. It acts to slow the clotting of blood—a capability that suggests its use as a therapy for the prevention of heart attacks and strokes in which blood clotting is a factor. The results of a study on aspirin use seemed to suggest that it does reduce the risk of developing a heart attack. However, the evidence concerning stroke and total cardiovascular deaths was inconclusive. For this reason, people should not begin a regular therapeutic course of aspirin without consulting a physician.[19]

Other Types of Treatment   Certain other types of treatment are also available for dealing with CVD. Among these are angioplasty, bypass surgery, and the use of transplants and artificial hearts.

Angioplasty is the process of squeezing the plaque within a coronary artery to increase the flow of blood. A catheter is inserted into an artery in the leg or arm and guided to the site to be treated in the coronary artery. A second catheter with a balloon tip is then inserted inside the first. At the site of blockage, the balloon is inflated, causing the plaque to be flattened against the arterial wall. When the balloon is deflated, the blood can flow more freely through the widened passage created within the artery.

angioplasty

If a coronary artery is damaged beyond repair, a doctor may consider **bypass surgery.** A portion of a healthy blood vessel, usually from the patient's leg, is removed and then used to replace (or bypass) the section of the coronary artery that is blocked. One end of the vessel is attached to the artery above the blockage, and the other end is attached below it, restoring blood supply to that area of the heart.

bypass surgery

When a patient's heart is irreversibly damaged by heart disease and the patient is at risk of dying, sometimes the only treatment is heart, or cardiac, transplantation. Cardiac transplantation is now an accepted procedure for patients who have been adequately screened and for whom it represents the only hope for survival.

Other Cardiovascular Diseases

Although the greatest cardiovascular dangers are heart attack and stroke, a number of other cardiovascular conditions threaten the health of thousands of Americans. These include arrhythmias, rheumatic heart disease, congenital heart defects, and congestive heart failure.

Arrhythmias

As was mentioned earlier, the beating of the heart is timed by electrical impulses that originate in the pacemaker in the right atrium. Sometimes there is an irregularity, or **arrhythmia,** in the rhythm of the heartbeat. In one type of abnormal rhythm known as **ventricular fibrillation,** the ventricles beat irregularly at an extremely fast rate—hundreds of times a minute—and in an un-

arrhythmia
ventricular fibrillation

coordinated manner. When this happens, the heart is incapable of pumping blood. Unless the fibrillation can be stopped and normal circulation can be restored, the patient will die.

Arrhythmias can develop when the pacemaker develops an abnormal rate or rhythm, when the normal pathways of the pacemaker's electrical impulses are interrupted, or when another part of the heart takes over for a failed pacemaker. Irregularities in heartbeat can be precursors to heart attacks or may result from heart attacks.

Arrhythmias can usually be treated with drugs, but if the drugs fail, an artificial pacemaker can be implanted in the chest. An artificial pacemaker is a small battery-operated device that produces electrical impulses and transmits them through tiny wires to the heart. These impulses prompt the heart to beat with a more normal rhythm.[20]

Rheumatic Heart Disease

rheumatic fever **Rheumatic fever** is an inflammatory disease that affects the connective tissues of the body, especially those of the brain, the joints, and the heart. When rheumatic fever permanently damages the heart, the damage is called *rheumatic heart disease.*

Rheumatic fever often begins with a streptococcal infection, usually of the throat (strep throat). It usually strikes children between ages 5 and 15, although it occurs in older people as well. While prompt treatment with antibiotics can prevent serious heart complications, approximately one-third of all victims of rheumatic fever are left with heart damage, particularly damage to the valves.[21]

The damage to the heart from the scarring of the heart muscle and valves is the greatest danger with this disease. Depending on the extent of scarring, rheumatic heart disease can interfere with the normal functioning of the heart and make it work much harder than normal. An attack of rheumatic fever does not necessarily leave a person with a damaged heart. The disease tends to recur, however, and with each episode the chance of permanent damage increases.

Congenital Heart Defects

Every year about 1 in every 100 infants is born with congenital heart defects—inborn defects or abnormalities of the heart.[22] Congenital heart defects vary in severity and can affect any part of the circulatory system. Most heart defects obstruct the flow of blood in the heart or in the blood vessels near it or cause blood to flow through the heart in an abnormal manner.

For the most part, scientists do not know why congenital heart defects occur. Some think that viral diseases or infections such as rubella (German measles) contracted during pregnancy may cause abnormal development of the baby's heart. Drinking too much alcohol or taking drugs during pregnancy may lead to a higher number of congenital defects.

Some congenital defects can be corrected surgically after the baby is born. Sometimes medications are used to prevent complications caused by the defect or to relieve symptoms. More recently, physicians have been trying to develop ways to detect and correct some congenital defects before birth, while the baby is still in the womb.

Congestive Heart Failure

Congestive heart failure is a condition sometimes caused by damage to the heart muscle. In a patient with congestive heart failure, the heart cannot keep the blood circulating normally throughout the body. The result is a congestion, or backing up, of blood in the body's tissues. As this fluid collects, it causes **edema,** or swelling, in various parts of the body, especially the legs and ankles. Fluid sometimes collects in the lungs as well, causing shortness of breath.

Almost every known type of CVD can produce congestive heart failure. Sometimes this condition can be aggravated by high blood pressure, which forces the heart to work harder to deliver an adequate supply of blood to the organs and tissues. It can also be caused by heart attack, defective heart valves, and weakening of the entire heart by disease or toxins. Finally, it can be caused by problems elsewhere in the circulatory system, for example, chronic lung disease.

Most cases of congestive heart failure are treatable. The treatment generally combines rest, proper diet, modified daily activities, and the use of certain drugs such as digitalis (to increase the heart's pumping action), diuretics (to help eliminate excess salt and water), and vasodilators (to expand blood vessels and allow blood to flow more easily). With proper medical supervision, people with congestive heart failure can live normal lives.[23]

congestive heart failure

edema

Preventing Cardiovascular Disease

While there are many medical treatments for the different types of cardiovascular disease, the most important approach remains prevention. Many deaths from CVD could be prevented if people had a better understanding of the associated risk factors and took steps to modify their behaviors and lifestyles accordingly.

Of course, some of the risk factors associated with CVD—age, gender, race, and heredity—are beyond the individual's control. For example, the risk of heart attack increases with advancing age. Before age 60, heart attack is more common among men than among women, although the difference decreases after menopause. Whites suffer heart attacks with greater frequency than do blacks and Asians. People with blood relatives who have had CVD are at greater risk of developing CVD.[24]

While there is nothing a person can do to reduce such risk factors, being aware of them can help an individual compensate for them in terms of lifestyle and medical treatment.

Controllable Risk Factors

Although some risk factors are uncontrollable, many can be controlled. Included among these are tobacco smoking, diet, lack of exercise, weight and obesity, hypertension, stress, and combinations of these and other factors.

A great deal of evidence has been gathered about the behaviors and habits associated with CVD.[25] Based on this evidence, the medical community has been able to make certain recommendations about lifestyle and behavior that can help prevent CVD. Real gains in preventing CVD could be made if people

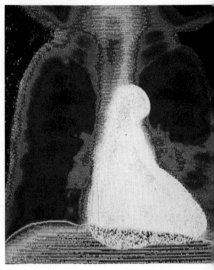

When the left side of the heart fails first, fluid is likely to back up into the lungs, causing breathing problems, especially at night. (SIU School of Medicine/Peter Arnold, Inc.)

Regular aerobic exercise, walking as well as running, helps maintain the body's stamina and reduces the threat of contracting cardiovascular disease. (David Young-Wolff/ PhotoEdit)

would modify the aspects of behavior and lifestyle that are within their control.

Tobacco Smoking   Tobacco smoking is very hard on the heart and circulatory system. It speeds the heart rate, raises blood pressure, and constricts blood vessels. It raises the fatty acid level in the blood and deprives red blood cells of oxygen.[26] It also contributes to atherosclerosis and therefore increases the risk of developing both stroke and heart disease. As a result, smokers have twice the risk of heart attack that nonsmokers have. In fact, tobacco smoking is the most important factor in sudden fatal heart attacks. A smoker who has a heart attack is more likely to die and to die suddenly (within an hour) than is a nonsmoker.[27]

In recent years these effects of tobacco smoking have been shown to be increased by oral contraceptive use. Women who smoke and use the pill have a higher risk of heart attack than do nonsmoking pill users and smoking nonpill users.[28] Smoking is also the greatest risk factor for the narrowing of the blood vessels that nourish the leg and arm muscles. In fact, this condition is confined almost exclusively to smokers.

The preventive value of *not* smoking has been clearly demonstrated. When people stop smoking, their risk of contracting heart disease decreases rapidly regardless of how long or how much they have smoked. Ten years after stopping smoking, a formerly moderate smoker's risk of death from heart disease is almost the same as that of a nonsmoker.[29]

Diet   People have become accustomed to the irony that the foods they like best—chocolate, hot dogs, French fries—are not good for them. Indeed, many specialists regard diet as the single most important factor in atherosclerosis, especially a diet high in fats and cholesterol.

As a result, experts recommend limiting the intake of saturated fats in one's diet and increasing the intake of complex carbohydrates. Eating a high-quality diet full of nutritious, natural foods is one of the best ways to reduce the risk of contracting a CVD.

Lack of Exercise   Although the value of exercise in preventing CVD has not been proved conclusively, recent studies have shown an association between regular moderate exercise and a reduced risk of contracting CVD.[30] People who are physically active seem to be less prone to heart attacks and to tolerate them better than are those who lead sedentary lives.

The *type* of physical activity undertaken is important. Certain forms of aerobic exercise, such as running, cycling, and swimming, enhance the development of an extensive collateral circulation. Thus, if a coronary artery is blocked, it can be immediately bypassed and circulation can be continued through these collateral arteries. This helps avert death and disability from heart attack.

If a person is already suffering from atherosclerosis, exercise may provide a warning signal that something is wrong. The reduced blood flow to the heart produced by narrowed coronary arteries may not be noticeable when the heart is beating routinely and is under little stress. However, when extra demands are made on the heart muscle—for example, when a person sprints or shovels snow—blood flow to the heart becomes insufficient and the individual may experience angina, an indicator of coronary heart disease.

Finding Your Comfort Level After a Heart Attack

In times not long past, a heart attack survivor often had to choose between living as an invalid and dying an early death. Today, thanks to medical technology and a better understanding of how diet and exercise contribute to coronary health, the outlook for heart attack victims is much brighter.

Some 10 million Americans who have survived heart attacks are living full, active lives today. While heart attack survivors need not restrict their activities completely, they generally need to make major changes in the way they live. Coronary patients face the challenge of learning new, healthier habits without taking the pleasure out of their lives or making themselves miserable.

Heart attacks illustrate an important fact about comfort level compromises: hard facts should not be ignored. Although there are modern medications and other products of technology to help the heart mend, the most important factor in recovery is patients' willingness to change their lives.

Risk factors that were present before are now more immediate; consequently, they require people to make a new arrangement. Smokers, for example, are at higher risk of suffering heart attacks than are other people. However, those who stop smoking after a heart attack are only half as likely to suffer another attack as are those who continue to smoke. In fact, giving up smoking is the most important step a patient can take toward establishing coronary health.

People with high cholesterol levels or high blood pressure are also at high risk for having heart attacks and repeat attacks. People can control their blood pressure and cholesterol levels with diet, exercise, and medication. Other risk factors that can be controlled include psychological stress, diabetes, obesity, and lack of exercise.

Although it is easy to identify the lifestyle changes that can improve a patient's chances of recovery, it is not easy to make them. For many people, exercising is not enjoyable or a priority. Others feel that smoking cigarettes, eating whatever they want, or succeeding in a stressful job makes life worth living. However, if coronary patients wish to maximize their chances of recovery, such behaviors need to be changed.

One's comfort level is an important element in making such changes. Recovering patients are often advised to alter their lifestyles bit by bit. Coronary patients who are willing to adopt healthier habits should make the changes gradually. Their new behavior is more likely to last if they make only one or two changes at a time. Suppose an overweight smoker with high blood pressure has just suffered a heart attack and knows she should make changes in her lifestyle. She begins by giving up smoking cigarettes and adopting a mild exercise program right away. Both changes will help reduce her blood pressure. For the time being she will not worry about losing weight.

While coronary patients need to exercise, they also may need to overcome their fear of exercise and activity after a heart attack. Medical professionals can help by working with them to develop exercise plans that are appropriate for their medical conditions. For instance, the best exercises are generally those that build endurance, such as hiking and ballroom dancing.

Recovery from a heart attack requires effort, but many survivors are healthier and happier than they were before their illnesses. New exercise routines may give them more stamina for the activities they enjoy. Diet and exercise may help them feel better about their looks. By learning new ways to handle stress, they may find that they can do their jobs more effectively and get along better with other people. At the very least, by developing new habits, they may live longer.

Regular aerobic exercise also tends to lower blood pressure, reduce stress, and help control obesity, all of which are potential risk factors for CVD. Before undertaking strenuous exercise, however, individuals over 35 years old should consult a physician to determine whether there are any cardiovascular irregularities that may suggest avoiding severe physical exertion.

Weight and Obesity   While the evidence linking obesity to coronary heart disease is unclear, excess weight does make the heart work harder. The link between weight and coronary heart disease is also based on the relationship between obesity and high blood pressure, high blood cholesterol levels, and possibly diabetes.[31]

Recent evidence has shown that the location of excess fat on the body can affect the risk of contracting heart disease. Studies have suggested that the waist-hip ratio is a possible factor in increased risk. In men, the waist measurement should not exceed the hip measurement. In women, the waist measurement should be no more than 80 percent of the hip measurement. Ratios greater than these may put a person at greater risk for CVD.[32]

Hypertension   As you learned earlier in this chapter, high blood pressure is an underlying condition in many heart attacks and strokes. Unfortunately, although hypertension is one of the most treatable disorders, only a minority of people with high blood pressure bring it under control.[33] Through regular blood pressure checks, the condition can usually be identified and damage can be avoided. People with high blood pressure can work with their doctors to control the condition through a program of diet, weight reduction, regular exercise, low salt intake, and medication.

Stress   While there is no proof that stress in itself helps cause CVD, some scientists have noted a relationship between the risk of developing CVD and certain types of stress. For example, it has been suggested that people with Type A personalities, with their competitive, fast-paced, and highly pressured lifestyle, may be more prone to heart attacks. It is unlikely that stress is as important a direct factor in heart disease as smoking, diet, and hypertension.

The Danger of Multiple Risks

One of the most troublesome aspects of CVD risk factors is the way they tend to reinforce one another. For instance, people often eat or smoke more when they are under stress, and overweight people tend to shun exercise. Separately, the risk factors represent a considerable threat. In combination, they are even more deadly.

Consider a fairly common combination of risk factors—obesity plus smoking. Obesity puts a strain on the cardiovascular system as a whole. For every pound gained, the body must circulate more blood to provide nourishment. Obese persons thus put much more stress on their hearts than do leaner people. If the obese person also smokes cigarettes, the risk is compounded. Smoking lessens the adaptability of the cardiovascular system as a whole. Consequently, a system that is already stressed by obesity is additionally stressed by smoking much more than it would be by nicotine alone. When uncontrollable risk factors such as age and heredity are added to the equation, the chance of an overweight smoker having a heart attack skyrockets.[34]

The Challenge of Changing Behavior

Although there are uncontrollable risk factors for CVD, the fact remains that more than any other major disease, CVD has its roots in lifestyle—the behaviors in which people choose to indulge and which they can choose to limit. The good news is that behaviors *can* be changed.

The bad news is that in the case of many risk factors for heart disease, such change is difficult. Smoking, for example, is a hard habit to break, and if one succeeds, other problems such as weight gain may become more severe.

However, with CVD the stakes are high—it is a matter of life or death. Of course, avoiding heart disease and stroke is not the only reward. Quitting smoking provides many other benefits, such as added stamina, a whole new world of smells and tastes, and protection from diseases such as cancer. A healthful diet and exercise can bring similar benefits, together with vibrant confidence born of new physical fitness and a new appearance.

The challenge of behavior change is not a matter of a sudden revolution. Habits are best changed little by little, with a carefully calculated plan. Reconsider the discussion of behavior change in Chapter 1. Then concentrate on the change you think is most necessary for you and perhaps also the change with which you think you will be most comfortable—these are the changes you will find most rewarding.

Above all, do not get discouraged and give up. There is no life without risk, so if you are aware of some of them, no great harm will result. You may even choose to accept a few, believing that the gains of living hard, for example, are worth the possible price. However, if you can lessen some of the other risks and thus lessen the possibility of having a heart attack or stroke, that is certainly worth some aggravation.

Chapter Summary

- The heart is a four-chambered muscular organ that pumps blood through the circulatory system, providing the cells of the body with oxygen and other nourishment. Along with the heart, the circulatory system consists of networks of arteries and veins which branch out to carry blood to all parts of the body.

- Hypertension is a condition in which blood pressure is sustained at a highly elevated level. High blood pressure can be reduced by reducing sodium intake, losing weight if one is obese, and restricting the intake of alcohol. It can also be treated with a variety of medications. Because it puts a strain on the blood vessels, chronic high blood pressure may cause arteries to become damaged and can lead to or accelerate atherosclerosis.

- Atherosclerosis is a condition characterized by a narrowing of the blood vessels. It is caused by the accumulation and hardening of fatty deposits on the inner walls of the arteries, possibly as a result of damage to the arterial wall. Evidence suggests that excess fats and cholesterol in the blood contribute to the development of atherosclerosis.

- Heart attacks occur when a blockage forms in one of the coronary arteries, cutting off the supply of blood to a portion of the heart. This blockage may result from a coronary thrombosis or coronary embolism. The symptoms of heart attack include pain in the center of the chest, which may then radiate to the shoulders, neck, or arms. The victim also may experience dizziness, fainting, sweating, nausea, or shortness of breath.

- A stroke is a sudden loss of brain function resulting from the blockage of blood to a portion of the brain. Strokes may be caused by a cerebral hemorrhage, cerebral thrombosis, or cerebral embolism.

- Early diagnosis of cardiovascular disease may be determined by imaging tests (including a CAT scan), tests to measure electrical activity (including EEGs, and ECGs), and tests to chart blood flow (including cardiac catheterization).

- Cardiovascular disease can sometimes be controlled with drugs, which can lower cholesterol levels or slow the clotting of blood. CVD can also be treated with angioplasty, bypass surgery, and heart transplants and artificial hearts.

- Other types of cardiovascular disease include arrhythmias, or irregular heartbeats; rheumatic heart disease, caused by rheumatic fever; congenital heart defects, inborn defects or abnormalities of the heart; and congestive heart failure, a backing up of blood in the tissues.

- Controllable risk factors for cardiovascular disease include tobacco smoking, diet, lack of exercise, obesity, hypertension, and stress. These risk factors can be reduced by modifying one's behavior and adopting a healthier lifestyle.

- The presence of multiple risk factors increases the danger of developing a cardiovascular disease because risk factors tend to reinforce one another.

Cancer: Some Cause for Hope

Objectives

When you have studied this chapter, you should be able to:

- Explain what cancer is, describe the process of metastasis, and identify various types of cancer.

- Discuss some of the psychological and social effects of cancer.

- Identify and discuss several risk factors associated with cancer.

- Explain the importance of early detection of cancer and describe procedures for self-examination and early diagnosis.

- Identify and discuss the primary treatments available for dealing with cancer.

- Discuss some of the ways in which people attempt to cope with cancer.

Although it once was talked about in hushed, fearful tones, cancer has become a much more openly acknowledged disease. Thanks to medical research, greater public knowledge, more open communication, and greater understanding, people today are better able to cope with this disease and their fear of it. However, while the fear of cancer has decreased in recent years, the disease is still a major health problem in the United States. One of every five deaths in this country is caused by cancer. Cancer is second only to heart disease as a cause of death.[1]

The death rate from cancer has increased from less than 6 percent of all deaths in 1900 to about 20 percent today. There are several reasons for this increase. First, today's technology and medical techniques permit earlier, more accurate diagnosis than was possible in the past, when many patients who had other disorders died without knowing that they also had cancer. Second, since the risk of getting cancer increases with age, the increasing life span of Americans has increased the prevalence of the disease. Third, the mortality rate from certain other diseases has decreased, resulting in a larger proportion of cancer deaths. Fourth, changing lifestyles have increased people's exposure to certain causative factors, such as tobacco and other cancer-producing agents.

Although the statistics on cancer and cancer deaths are troubling, the statistics on the long-term survival of cancer patients offer hope. In the early 1900s few cancer patients survived. Today, however, about 4 of every 10 cancer patients are still alive 5 years after diagnosis (Figure 11.1).[2]

What Is Cancer?

cancer **Cancer** is not a single disease. Rather, it is a group of more than 100 diseases, all characterized by the uncontrolled growth and spread of abnormal cells.

Cell Division, Growth, and Tumors

Cancer starts when one or a few cells undergo changes that leave them unable to perform their intended functions. These changed, or *mutant,* cells then begin to reproduce very rapidly. If cellular growth continues unchecked, the affected organs or body systems will be impaired and the victim will die.

tissue To understand the nature of cancer, it is necessary to know how cancerous tissues are distinguished from other kinds. The term **tissue** refers to a collection of specialized cells that perform a specific function. Muscle tissue is composed of cells that fulfill the function of muscles, nerve tissue is made up of cells that fulfill the function of nerves, and so on. The tissues of the body undergo constant change as cells die and new ones replace them.

mitosis Most cells in the body are continually reproducing. Normally, an individual cell divides to produce two new cells through a process known as **mitosis.** This process directs the body to replace worn cells when necessary or to produce additional cells for growth and the repair of damage.

tumor Sometimes the controls that govern cell reproduction break down, and the reproductive process goes out of control. Cells within a tissue that normally cooperate with one another in performing a useful function cease to do so. They begin to multiply independently, often rapidly, sometimes forming an *neoplasm* abnormal swelling or mass known as a **tumor** or **neoplasm.**

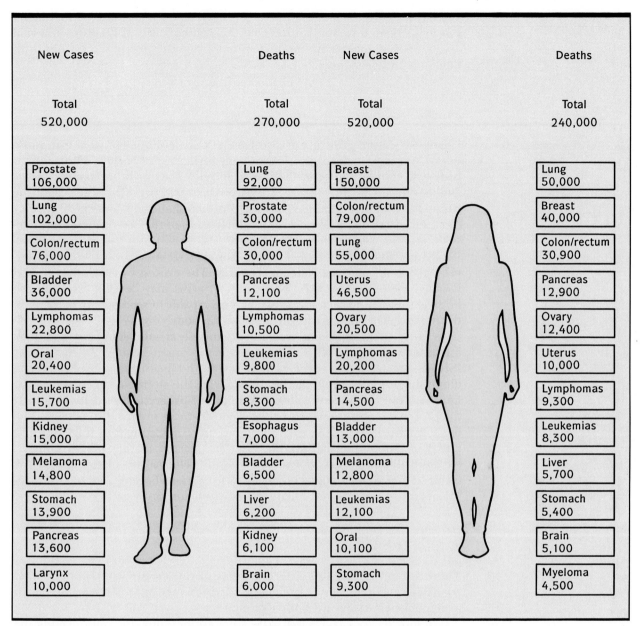

New Cases	Deaths	New Cases	Deaths
Total 520,000	Total 270,000	Total 520,000	Total 240,000
Prostate 106,000	Lung 92,000	Breast 150,000	Lung 50,000
Lung 102,000	Prostate 30,000	Colon/rectum 79,000	Breast 40,000
Colon/rectum 76,000	Colon/rectum 30,000	Lung 55,000	Colon/rectum 30,900
Bladder 36,000	Pancreas 12,100	Uterus 46,500	Pancreas 12,900
Lymphomas 22,800	Lymphomas 10,500	Ovary 20,500	Ovary 12,400
Oral 20,400	Leukemias 9,800	Lymphomas 20,200	Uterus 10,000
Leukemias 15,700	Stomach 8,300	Pancreas 14,500	Lymphomas 9,300
Kidney 15,000	Esophagus 7,000	Bladder 13,000	Leukemias 8,300
Melanoma 14,800	Bladder 6,500	Melanoma 12,800	Liver 5,700
Stomach 13,900	Liver 6,200	Leukemias 12,100	Stomach 5,400
Pancreas 13,600	Kidney 6,100	Oral 10,100	Brain 5,100
Larynx 10,000	Brain 6,000	Stomach 9,300	Myeloma 4,500

Figure 11.1 *1990 estimates: new cases of cancer and deaths. This graph gives estimates for each sex of the top 10 types of cancer identified in 1990 and the top 10 types that caused deaths in that year. Note that the lists do not correspond. For example, bladder cancer in men was diagnosed far more often than was stomach cancer but caused fewer deaths.*

Source: Adapted from American Cancer Society, *1990 Cancer Facts and Figures*, p. 12.

When this type of uncontrolled growth occurs, it does not mean that the individual has cancer. The person may have a **benign tumor**—a tumor that grows slowly and is localized. Benign tumors usually do not recur once they have been removed. However, they can do damage. They can cause pressure

benign tumor

and harm to surrounding structures and can rob normal tissues of their blood supply. A benign tumor can have serious consequences if it occurs in a vital organ such as the brain, but such tumors can be treated successfully with radiation and/or surgery.

Cancer and Metastatic Growth

malignant tumor

Uncontrolled cell growth can also lead to the development of a **malignant tumor,** or cancerous growth (*malignant* means "growing worse"). The cells that form a malignant tumor are of a special type. They grow in abnormal ways and may invade healthy tissues. Cancerous cells may break away and enter the lymphatic channels and blood vessels. The lymphatic and circulatory systems can then carry the cancerous cells to other parts of the body, where they may settle and form new malignant tumors.

metastases
metastatic growth

The new tumors that form when cancerous cells break away from the original malignant tumor are called **metastases.** The process by which they spread is called **metastatic growth.** These new growths may develop far from the original tumor, and each metastasis may be capable of seeding new tumors. In this way, cancer can spread throughout the body.

As cancer cells invade an organ or organ system and begin to spread, they act as disruptive elements in that organ or organ system. As the cancer spreads, the disruption becomes more severe and the functioning of the organ diminishes. For example, if the cancer is in the stomach, digestion will be impeded and the patient will lose weight and progress toward starvation. If the cancer involves the blood or the blood-forming organs (for example, the bone marrow), the patient may become more susceptible to infection, tire easily, or suffer internal bleeding. If the cancer is in the liver or kidneys, harmful substances that normally would be removed circulate through the blood to most body tissues. When such disruptions become severe, death results because the affected organs cannot function properly.

Types of Cancer

There are more than 100 different forms of cancer, most of them classified according to the tissues or organs from which they arise. About 30 types of malignant neoplasms are fairly common.[3]

carcinomas
epithelium

Carcinomas are cancers that arise from **epithelium**—the cells forming the skin, the glands, and the membranes that line the respiratory, urinary, and gastrointestinal tracts. Carcinomas tend to spread to other parts of the body through the lymphatic system. **Sarcomas** are cancers that arise from supporting or connective tissues, such as bone, cartilage, and the membranes that cover muscles and fat. Sarcomas tend to spread to other parts of the body through the bloodstream. The terms *carcinoma* and *sarcoma* are often modified to indicate more specifically the type or location of the disease.

sarcomas

lymphomas
leukemias
melanomas

Other major forms of cancer include **lymphomas,** cancers of lymphatic cells; **leukemias,** cancers of blood-forming cells; and **melanomas,** cancers of the pigment-carrying cells of the skin. There are also cancers whose cellular structure is so abnormal that they no longer resemble the cells of the tissues in which they originated. Such cancers are termed **anaplastic.**

anaplastic

Psychological and Social Aspects of Cancer

Cancer profoundly affects not only a person's body but also his or her psychological state and relationships with other people. Besides the physical changes that occur with cancer, the disease brings patients face to face with their own mortality. The way in which they and the people around them deal with the disease can mean the difference between confronting it with courage and hope and accepting it with depression, isolation, and despair.

The Psychic Pain of Cancer   Since cancer is not a single disease but a collection of illnesses that differ in terms of onset, prognosis, treatability, and other features, it is difficult to generalize about the kind of emotional turmoil and psychic pain each cancer patient feels.[4] However, most people would agree that a diagnosis of cancer is a powerful stressor.

Almost all cancer patients are initially concerned about dying as a result of the disease. While this concern is understandable, for some people it is unrealistic thanks to new methods of treating cancer and prolonging life or even curing the disease.

Most cancer patients are also concerned about the treatment of the disease. Many fear the effects of chemotherapy, radiation therapy, and surgery and the possibility of being unable to carry on normal activities. Medical personnel and people who have undergone treatment can be supportive and can reassure patients that many unpleasant side effects can be alleviated.

Such concerns can cause a great deal of emotional stress. Cancer patients must come to terms with a disabling illness that may result in the loss of a body part or death. Their usual methods of coping no longer work, and their emotional needs and defenses are knocked off balance. Anxious about whether they can continue meeting the ordinary demands of life, they often lose self-esteem, becoming more vulnerable to their own feelings and fears. Psychological problems may be particularly severe if the disease interrupts valued life activities and disturbs the patient's body image.

Feelings of Depression, Anxiety, and Anger   When they are confronted with cancer, many patients have to deal with depression, anxiety, or anger. Those accustomed to leading very active lives may feel depressed, especially on days when they do not feel well. Some develop anxieties about their bodies, feeling that they have become very fragile. Others believe that they have somehow brought the disease on themselves, and this makes them feel guilt-ridden.

Disruptions in Personal and Social Life   Being ill with cancer can sometimes disrupt a patient's personal and social life and lead to feelings of loneliness. Treatments are often time-consuming and exhausting, leaving little energy for interactions with family members and friends or for various activities. In addition, friends and some family members may avoid interactions with a cancer patient because they do not know what to say or do. For their part, patients often do not want to burden people with their concerns and feelings. Moreover, friends and family members, in an effort to maintain a positive attitude around the patient, often fail to share their true emotions. Faulty communication can lead to feelings of isolation that can hamper a person's ability to cope with the disease. By contrast, simple, direct, and supportive communication frequently provides much of what a patient needs.[5]

The more a person with cancer can join in normal social activities, the less likely it is that emotional stress will create additional problems related to the disease. (Tom Tracy/ MediChrome)

Cancer can also alter family dynamics as a result of changing roles. For example, the burden of certain responsibilities may shift to a healthy spouse or to children, who may resent the added responsibilities. This shift of responsibilities can cause feelings of guilt on the part of the patient.

Work-related problems can also disrupt the lives of cancer patients. Attitudes such as the idea that cancer is contagious or that cancer patients are unproductive, although false, can lead to a person's dismissal or demotion or to a reduction of work-related benefits. Some cancer patients also face problems maintaining adequate health insurance especially if they are not covered by group policies.

Fortunately, many of the psychological stresses associated with cancer are not inevitable. Accurate knowledge about cancer coupled with open communication, patience, and understanding on the part of the patient and others can help reduce the stress and anxiety associated with the disease. This sometimes contributes to a patient's recovery.

Understanding Risk Factors for Cancer

Over the years health professionals and researchers have identified a number of risk factors involved in the development of cancer. Some of these factors are hereditary and some are environmental, but several—for example, use of tobacco and alcohol and an inadequate diet—are directly related to individual lifestyles and behaviors. This means that, for many people, behavior changes may actually reduce the risk of developing cancer.

Hereditary and Genetic Risk Factors

As with any disease, the chances of developing cancer depend in part on the individual's genetic constitution. Many skin cancers, for example, are triggered by exposure to the ultraviolet rays of the sun. However, genetic "host" factors also appear to be involved—persons with fair complexions are more likely to develop skin cancer than are persons with heavy pigmentation.[6]

In a slowly developing disease such as cancer, it is often difficult to pinpoint genetic factors. For example, there is a high rate of stomach cancer among the Japanese. Does this mean that as an ethnic group the Japanese are at high risk, or could there be a typical element in the Japanese diet which adds to the likelihood of developing this type of cancer?

A few rare types of cancer, such as cancer of the retina, have been identified as definitely being hereditary. With other types of cancer, however, there is evidence that family members tend to inherit an increased risk of contracting a particular form of the disease. It is this predisposition to certain cancers, rather than a direct genetic link to a particular form of the disease, that is the most common type of hereditary risk factor. For example, women with female blood relatives who have had breast cancer are at higher risk of developing the disease than women with no breast cancer in their family.

Knowing one's family medical history is thus important when one is taking preventive measures against cancer. When a woman knows that there is a history of breast cancer in her family, for example, she can take special precautions and seek frequent screenings.

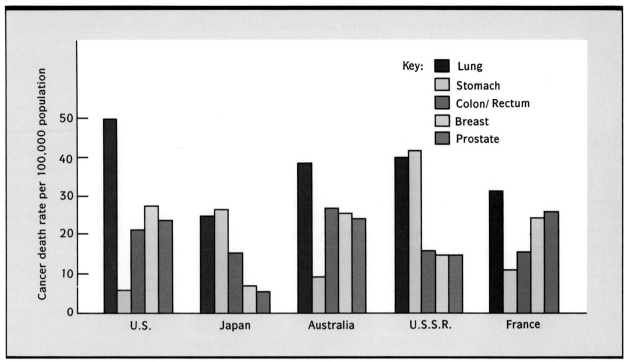

Source: American Cancer Society, *1990 Cancer Facts and Figures*, p. 30.

Figure 11.2 Cancer rates in different nations can tell investigators many things. Note the similarities between the United States, Australia, and France on the one hand and Japan and the Soviet Union on the other. However, this pattern does not appear in the lung cancer figures, suggesting that a different environmental factor may be operating.

Environmental Risk Factors

Although experts disagree about certain points, research strongly suggests a connection between environmental factors—such as chemicals and pollutants—and cancer (Figure 11.2). Animal studies have suggested that animals given high doses of certain chemicals tend to develop cancer. It is not clear, however, how closely these substances are connected with cancer in humans, because the conditions under which humans are exposed to them vary so widely. Among the chemicals suspected of being contributors to human cancer are nitrites (used in curing ham, bacon, frankfurters, salami, and other processed meats), saccharin, hair dyes, and certain pesticides.

The evidence is sometimes confusing, however. Cancer of the stomach, which might be thought to be related to chemical additives or preservatives in food, has been *decreasing* in the United States over the past 25 years. Furthermore, countries such as Poland and Czechoslovakia, which do not use American methods of food production or preservation, have cancer rates similar to or higher than those of the United States. Thus, connections between cancer and food additives and preservatives remain doubtful.[7]

What about the connection between cancer and environmental pollutants and chemicals in the workplace? It has been well established that lung cancer rates are higher in urban areas, even after smoking has been taken into account.[8] Studies on the role of water contaminants in causing cancer have generally been inconclusive. Such is not the case, however, with hazardous chemicals found in the workplace.

Evidence linking cancer to high-dose, long-term exposure to various work-place chemicals has been more conclusive. Chemicals such as asbestos (found in insulating and fireproofing), vinyl chloride (found in plastics), chromates (found in paint), benzene (found in rubber), and benzidine (found in dyes) have been shown to increase the risk of developing certain forms of cancer.

Unfortunately, it is not always easy to avoid chemicals in the environment and the workplace. People who are exposed to these agents have little choice but to change jobs or move. Perhaps a more appropriate alternative would be to reduce exposure as much as possible and become aware of, and perhaps involved in, efforts to change the laws regarding the use and disposal of hazardous chemicals.

Another environmental risk associated with cancer is ultraviolet radiation from sunlight. Excessive exposure to the sun's ultraviolet rays can lead to skin cancer. Sunbathing is therefore a risky behavior that most experts recommend reducing or eliminating. Exposure to other forms of radiation, such as x-rays, can increase the risk of developing other types of cancer. This does not mean that x-rays should never be used diagnostically, but they should be used with discretion, and exposure should be kept to a minimum.

Another environmental cancer risk is associated with radon, a naturally occurring radioactive gas found in many homes throughout the nation. Radon has been linked to lung cancer. Therefore, if people have their homes tested and discover high levels of radon, they should take steps to reduce those levels.[9]

Lifestyle and Behavioral Risk Factors

A high proportion of cancer in the United States is associated with people's personal habits and lifestyles. Smoking tobacco, drinking alcohol, and dietary factors are of major importance.

Smoking and Drinking Each year in the United States, many people die needlessly as a result of cigarette smoking. The incidence of this form of cancer has been rising among men and women. Among women, it is now the number one cancer killer.[10]

carcinogenic How is smoking related to lung cancer? Both the tar and the smoke from tobacco contain **carcinogenic,** or cancer-producing, chemicals. Evidence indicates that inhaling these chemicals over a period of time triggers the cancerous potential in lung tissue cells. When tobacco smoke is inhaled, it paralyzes the bronchial cilia, interfering with their natural cleansing mechanism. Carcinogenic agents can thus enter the lungs, irritate the lungs, and cause damage that can trigger cancerous growth.

Lung cancer is not the only type of cancer associated with tobacco. Cigarette, cigar, and pipe smoking and the use of smokeless tobacco are also risk factors in oral cancer, which can affect any part of the oral cavity, from the lips to the tongue to the mouth, throat, and jaws. Smoking is also one of the greatest risk factors in bladder and pancreatic cancers.[11] In the case of the bladder, the body attempts to excrete tobacco carcinogens through the urinary tract, irritating the bladder in the process.

Chronic excessive consumption of alcohol also seems to be associated with a higher risk of developing certain cancers. For example, oral cancer and cancers of the larynx, throat, esophagus, and liver occur more frequently among

Communicating with Your Doctor about Fears

When you have concerns about health, you need to communicate those concerns to your doctor. Good communication is the key to getting your fears addressed and getting good medical care.

Often people are reluctant to go to the doctor. Some hesitate because of the cost, some because they fear they will seem stupid or worried about nothing. Some are fearful of what they may learn that is bad, and some worry that they will not understand the doctor. However, with a serious illness such as cancer, early detection can mean the difference between life and death.

Doctors and patients use different languages to refer to the same symptoms. This can be a barrier to good communication. Many patients are reluctant to speak about intimate topics even to the doctor.

When you have fears about your health, remember that no matter how alarming something seems to you, you do not have the medical knowledge to make a diagnosis. For example, a lump that seems like cancer to you may be no more than a cyst. Only a doctor can diagnose such a problem. That is why it is so important that you do not withhold facts from the doctor. A doctor must have all the facts about your condition.

To communicate well with the doctor, be prepared by having the kind of information the doctor needs from you. Either get it clear in your mind or write it down ahead of time. First, be ready to tell the doctor what is wrong using simple, clear language. Give your symptoms, not a diagnosis. Do not say, "I've had this virus for a few days." Instead, say, "I've had diarrhea and a high fever for 2 days." Let the doctor interpret the cause and importance of each symptom. Do not fail to mention symptoms that seem intimate.

Then, for each symptom, try to pinpoint when it started. For instance, if the symptom is pain, what kind of pain is it? Where is it located? Is there a pattern to the symptom (time of day when it occurs, activities that bring it on, positions that make it worse, its relation to meals or sleeping)? When did it come on? Has the symptom gotten worse? Have you had it before? If so, how was it treated? In addition, provide a list of any drugs you are taking for this condition or any other conditions. You should also describe any other medical conditions you have.

Once you have told the doctor about your symptoms and answered any questions, the doctor will respond to you. At this point you should be ready to ask questions of the doctor. For instance, if the doctor asks you to have certain medical tests, ask about the costs, what the doctor is looking for in the tests, whether they are dangerous or painful, and when you will get the results.

When the doctor makes a diagnosis and recommends treatment, ask how you got the condition and what the usual course of the disease is. Request a definition of any terms you do not understand. You should also ask questions about the treatment the doctor has recommended. For example, what results can you expect and what kinds of things should you call the doctor about? You should ask about the reason for treatment and the risks, if any. If the doctor recommends surgery, ask about the chances of complete recovery and the length of your stay in the hospital and of your recovery at home afterward.

After a doctor has recommended treatment, you may want to get a second opinion. This is especially important if you question the doctor's judgment or have been diagnosed as having a serious disease such as cancer. Another doctor may help calm your fears or help you find alternative forms of treatment.

Based on J. Alfred Jones and Gerald M. Phillips, *Communicating with Your Doctor* (Carbondale and Edwardsville: Southern Illinois University Press, 1988).

heavy drinkers of alcohol, especially when accompanied by cigarette smoking or the use of smokeless tobacco.[12]

Avoiding tobacco and alcohol can reduce the risk of getting cancer, but quitting is often a problem. Tobacco contains nicotine, an addictive drug, and people can become physically and psychologically dependent on alcohol as well.

Dietary Factors   Evidence seems to link certain dietary factors with specific types of cancer. For example, individuals who are 40 percent or more overweight seem to have an increased risk of developing colon, breast, prostate, gallbladder, ovarian, and uterine cancers.[13] Some studies have linked breast, prostate, and colon cancers to a high dietary intake of fat, while others have found that foods high in fiber seem to have a protective effect against colon cancer.[14]

Extensive research is under way to evaluate the role diet and nutrition play in the development of cancer, but no direct cause-and-effect relationship has been proved. Nevertheless, most experts recommend that Americans reduce fat intake, increase fiber consumption, increase their intake of fruits and vegetables rich in vitamins A and C, and increase their consumption of cruciferous vegetables such as broccoli and cauliflower.

Other Lifestyle Risk Factors   While smoking, drinking, and diet may be the most common risk factors, other behaviors and lifestyles have been associated with cancer as well. A study by the American Cancer Society has suggested a correlation between exercise and cancer. The study, although far from conclusive, found that the more exercise a person gets, the lower is the incidence of death from cancer.[15]

Cancer of the cervix has been associated with factors such as sexual intercourse at an early age and sex with multiple partners. Women who have been infected with the herpes simplex 2 virus or the virus that causes genital warts are also at increased risk for developing cervical cancer. This does not mean that a woman with these viral infections will develop cancer of the cervix. It does mean, however, that the risk is higher, and women with these viruses should have more frequent medical examinations.[16]

The use of certain drugs may also increase a person's risk of getting cancer. Estrogen, birth control pills, and some drugs used in conjunction with organ transplants may be potentially carcinogenic. Estrogen, which sometimes is used in high doses to control menopausal symptoms, is associated with an increased risk of developing uterine cancer.

Researchers are unsure about the relationship between oral contraceptives and cancer of the cervix and have found no clear-cut evidence of an increased or decreased risk of breast cancer among women who use oral contraceptives. Research among women using the pill is ongoing. To date, cancer of the endometrium (the lining of the uterus) is the only form of the disease that has been linked to oral contraceptive use, and this may be limited to only one brand of oral contraceptive, Oracon.

In 1971 a very small but still unusual series of cases of a rare form of vaginal cancer were reported among women age 14 to 22 whose mothers had taken the drug DES (diethylstilbestrol) to prevent miscarriage. Recent research has shown that DES is associated with many kinds of cancer. Women who were exposed to DES before birth are now entering the age range when cancers of the cervix and breast begin to appear, and it will be a number of years before they reach the usual age for cancers of the endometrium and ovary. Men whose mothers took DES also may be at risk.

Certain drugs used during organ transplants to suppress the immune response and thus lessen the chances of the body's rejecting a new organ have been implicated as increasing the risk of developing cancer. Presumably, this increased risk is due to suppression of the immune system rather than to any carcinogenic properties of the drugs.

Early Detection of Cancer

Early detection of cancer can save a person's life. The American Cancer Society continually emphasizes this message in the hope that people will take appropriate steps to reduce the risks of contracting the disease. The more people take action to ensure early detection, the greater the chances of finding cancer early enough to treat it effectively.

The Importance of Early Detection

Case histories of cancer survivors indicate that early detection often saves lives. The more time that elapses between the beginning of the disease and its detection and treatment, the greater the chances of the cancer spreading to other sites, where it can damage or destroy vital organs.

A look at the statistics provides proof that time is of the utmost importance. For example, when the disease is detected early and treated promptly, over 75 percent of people with cancer of the colon and rectum can be cured.[17] When breast cancer is caught in the earliest stage—that is, when there is just a small localized tumor—the survival rate approaches 100 percent. A woman's options for treatment of breast cancer also depend on how far the disease has progressed. With surgical treatment, for example, it may mean the difference between the removal of just the tumor and the surrounding tissue and removal of the entire breast.[18]

Further evidence of the value of early detection can be seen by looking at the cure rates for cancers which are more easily detectable versus the rates for those which are not. Skin cancers are visible to the trained eye. As a result, they frequently receive early attention and treatment. Except for *melanoma*, a form of skin cancer particularly resistant to treatment, the cure rate for other skin cancers is 95 percent.[19] Lung cancer, by contrast, is difficult to detect early. It often does not produce obvious symptoms until it has gotten out of control. As a result, only 13 percent of lung cancer patients live 5 or more years after diagnosis.

Self-Examination and Seeking Further Advice

Most important in the early detection of cancer is a thorough familiarity with the warning signs of the disease (Figure 11.3). Some of these signs can be detected by means of a simple, painless self-examination. Others are often found during routine medical checkups. While these symptoms do not necessarily indicate that a person has cancer, they should not be ignored.

CANCER'S SEVEN WARNING SIGNALS

1. Change in bowel or bladder habits

2. A sore that does not heal

3. Unusual bleeding or discharge

4. Thickening or lump in breast or elsewhere

5. Indigestion or difficulty swallowing

6. Obvious change in wart or mole

7. Nagging cough or hoarseness

Source: American Cancer Society, *1990 Cancer Facts and Figures,* p. 18.

The most curable cancers are those which are detected early, and most tumors are first discovered by the patients themselves. For that reason, women are advised to examine their breasts for lumps every month to detect breast cancer (Figure 11.4). In addition to breast self-examination, regular pelvic examinations and Pap smears (microscopic examination of cells scraped from the cervix and uterus) are also recommended for detecting cervical and uterine cancers. Men are urged to spend 3 minutes once a month on a testicular self-examination; testicular lumps or abnormalities call for prompt medical attention (Figure 11.5).

Recommended for both men and women are monthly self-exams of the skin to detect growths, unusual discolorations, sores or lumps, and changes in the appearance of warts or moles—signs that skin cancer may be developing. A skin self-examination should include a survey of all the surfaces of the skin, using a mirror for hard-to-see areas.

To detect colon and rectal cancers, it is recommended that as part of a regular physical exam individuals obtain a stool sample at home and return it to the physician or clinic to be tested for hidden blood. New self-tests allow people to get instant test results themselves. A positive result from this type of screening, however, does not necessarily indicate cancer. Further testing is needed to make that determination. A rectal exam and proctoscopic exam are also recommended as part of regular periodic checkups.

Dangers Associated with Delay and Denial

It was discussed earlier how cancer can affect a person's psychological state. Among the most common initial reactions is fear. This fear may cause a person to deny that there is a problem and thus delay doing anything about it. One study found that delay in seeking medical help seems to be a conscious, deliberate act.

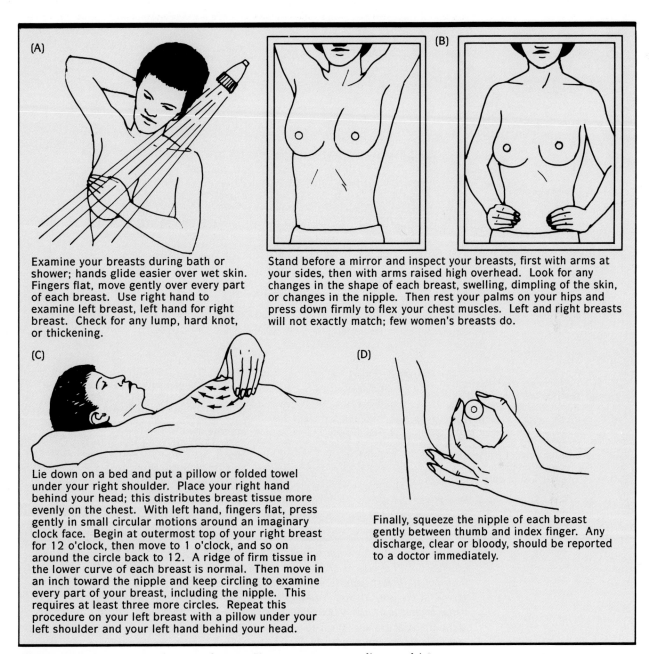

(A) Examine your breasts during bath or shower; hands glide easier over wet skin. Fingers flat, move gently over every part of each breast. Use right hand to examine left breast, left hand for right breast. Check for any lump, hard knot, or thickening.

(B) Stand before a mirror and inspect your breasts, first with arms at your sides, then with arms raised high overhead. Look for any changes in the shape of each breast, swelling, dimpling of the skin, or changes in the nipple. Then rest your palms on your hips and press down firmly to flex your chest muscles. Left and right breasts will not exactly match; few women's breasts do.

(C) Lie down on a bed and put a pillow or folded towel under your right shoulder. Place your right hand behind your head; this distributes breast tissue more evenly on the chest. With left hand, fingers flat, press gently in small circular motions around an imaginary clock face. Begin at outermost top of your right breast for 12 o'clock, then move to 1 o'clock, and so on around the circle back to 12. A ridge of firm tissue in the lower curve of each breast is normal. Then move in an inch toward the nipple and keep circling to examine every part of your breast, including the nipple. This requires at least three more circles. Repeat this procedure on your left breast with a pillow under your left shoulder and your left hand behind your head.

(D) Finally, squeeze the nipple of each breast gently between thumb and index finger. Any discharge, clear or bloody, should be reported to a doctor immediately.

Figure 11.4 *How to examine your breasts. Breast cancers were diagnosed in 150,000 women in 1990. Many were first discovered through monthly self-examinations for unusual lumps and other changes. Even though many of these changes are due to other causes, it is vital to see a doctor as soon as possible. The best time to perform the examination is a week after menstruation.*

When people are overcome with fear, the latest knowledge about cancer prevention, causes, and cures is of little value. What people *think* will happen during the course of the disease can produce so much anxiety that they delay seeing a doctor. Since survival often depends on early detection and treatment, delay can result in a progression of the disease to the point where it becomes irreversible and life-threatening.

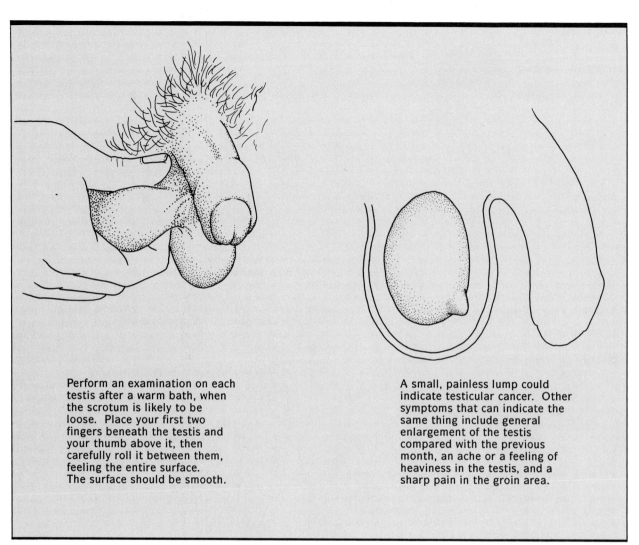

Perform an examination on each testis after a warm bath, when the scrotum is likely to be loose. Place your first two fingers beneath the testis and your thumb above it, then carefully roll it between them, feeling the entire surface. The surface should be smooth.

A small, painless lump could indicate testicular cancer. Other symptoms that can indicate the same thing include general enlargement of the testis compared with the previous month, an ache or a feeling of heaviness in the testis, and a sharp pain in the groin area.

Figure 11.5 *How to examine your testes. Men are encouraged to do monthly self-examinations for cancer of the testes. Although this is a much less common cancer than female breast cancer, it can still cause fatalities. If it metastasizes, it can spread to the lung tissues. Although lumps may be found in the epididymis—the soft tissue behind the testis—lumps on the testis itself are the main danger signal.*

Source: Dept. of Biomedical Communications, Bowman Gray School of Medicine of Wake Forest University, Winston-Salem, N.C.

Treating Cancer

Some people fear cancer because they are afraid of what will happen during treatment. Will it be painful? Will it disable them or make it hard for them to live a normal life? Will it help them or merely prolong and intensify their suffering? These are all valid concerns. While the outlook for many cancer patients is improving, the disease *can* be disabling or fatal, and treatment may involve pain or discomfort. However, modern cancer treatments can prolong survival and make a patient's life far more comfortable than in the past.

Types of Cancer Treatment

The number of treatable types of cancer is increasing, and treatment has become increasingly individualized. The basic goals of treatment for cancer include cure, prolongation of life, and the control of symptoms. After the disease has been detected, physicians use a procedure known as *staging* to assess treatment options. In staging, physicians evaluate factors such as the type of cancer, the size of the tumor, the degree to which the cancer has spread, and the health and condition of the patient. This type of evaluation helps determine the type of treatment that will be most effective and appropriate for the individual patient.[20]

Physicians often use a combination of treatments, which may include surgery, radiation therapy, and/or chemotherapy together with psychological, nursing, and nutritional support services. In many cases it is possible to cure cancer with some of these treatment approaches. If a total cure is not realistic, treatment can often extend the life of the patient and make the symptoms less severe.

Surgery   Medical thinking about the use of surgery to treat cancer has evolved, and some specialists are now challenging the use of some surgical operations. Nevertheless, for many forms of cancer, surgical removal of cancerous tissue remains the most effective method of treatment.[21]

Because of improved diagnostic equipment and laser instruments, cancer surgery has become more precise. It has proved very successful against various malignancies, especially tumors involving the lung, colon, stomach, bowel, liver, and skin. However, when surgery involves removing entire organs, it can mean more physical problems for the patient, sometimes with profound psychological effects. Some specialists question whether it is necessary to perform a radical mastectomy (surgical removal of the entire breast and the neighboring lymph nodes) in patients with breast cancer. If results can be achieved without such surgery, some of the emotional and physical trauma associated with losing a breast can be eliminated.

Radiation   Radiation therapy uses energy in very high, concentrated doses to destroy cancer cells. Once the location and extent of cancerous growths are determined, health professionals deliver radiation treatments in an attempt to cure patients or make them more comfortable. The decision to use radiation treatment depends on the type of tumor, evaluations by physicians, and the wishes of the patient.

The rate of success with some cancers can be improved by combining radiation therapy and surgery. For example, radiation is sometimes given before surgery to shrink a tumor before it is removed. Postoperative radiation—given after a surgical wound has healed—is used to destroy the microscopic cancerous growths that may remain.

Many patients with incurable cancer receive radiation therapy to shrink tumors and reduce their level of pain. Although such use of radiation treatment sometimes increases the duration of survival, the main object is to improve the quality of life by relieving symptoms without adding the side effects of chemotherapy.

With any radiation treatment, of course, it is impossible to avoid exposing some normal tissue to radiation. As a result, side effects such as skin redness, hair loss, loss of appetite, and fatigue can and do occur, depending on the site treated and the dose of radiation. Some of these side effects become apparent within weeks of treatment. Others may not become noticeable for months or even years. A few of these late side effects, such as damage to arteries, can result in major complications. Most of the early side effects clear up shortly after treatment has been stopped.

Although such problems do exist, radiation therapy today is more effective, less dangerous, and far more predictable than it was in the past. It results in fewer ill effects and long-term complications.

Chemotherapy   The use of chemicals to treat cancer is called *chemotherapy.* In recent years chemotherapy has become the major weapon against cancers that have metastasized. It is also used with surgery or radiation when it is likely that the cancer has not been cured by surgery or radiation alone.[22]

Chemotherapeutic drugs may be taken orally or injected, depending on the drug and the type of cancer. Intravenous injection is the most common method of administration. Sometimes the drugs are used in combinations to achieve a greater effect. Basically, chemotherapeutic drugs kill cancer cells because the drugs are toxic to cells that spend a great deal of time growing and dividing (as cancer cells do). Unfortunately, other fast-growing normal cells—such as those in the bone marrow, skin, hair, and stomach lining—also are affected by chemotherapeutic drugs. For this reason, chemotherapy often results in temporary side effects, including hair loss, nausea, diarrhea, and suppression of the ability of bone marrow to produce blood cells, thus increasing susceptibility to infection. Ways to decrease chemotherapy-induced side effects are being studied.

While traditional chemotherapy uses drugs that are toxic to cells, other chemicals are also used in the treatment of cancer. Among these are antihormones and hormones, which are used for the treatment of cancers of hormone-responsive organs such as the breast and prostate. Other chemicals used in chemotherapy are immune modifiers such as interferon, a chemical that the body normally produces in response to viral infections. When injected in large amounts, interferon may have some antitumor effects. Many cancer researchers believe that proper understanding and use of the immune system will ultimately provide the key to curing many forms of cancer.

Positive Developments in Treatment

Progress in cancer treatment is being made every day. An important example is the improvement in the survival rate of persons with acute lymphocytic leukemia, a cancer of the blood-forming tissues. Chemotherapy has proved to be quite effective in killing the abnormal cells produced by this disease. In addition, continuing research is yielding new and better drugs for treating leukemia patients.

Another sign of improvement has been seen in the management of testicular cancer in young men. The use of more precise diagnostic tools has allowed a better selection of treatment, and this has resulted in improved survival.

Meanwhile, scientists continue researching new and better treatments for cancer. Some are working on the theory that genetics can be used to enhance the tumor-fighting capacity of the immune system.[23] Another area of research involves cancer vaccines. Clinical trials performed with vaccines derived from tumor cells have indicated that they are safe and may be effective in some circumstances.

New approaches to drug therapy use combinations of chemotherapeutic drugs as well as chemotherapy combined with radiation and surgery. New substances are also being tested for their effectiveness in treating patients who are resistant to the drug therapies now in use.

New technologies are also proving helpful in fighting cancer. For example, high-technology diagnostic techniques have replaced exploratory surgery for some cancer patients. Advances in technology have also enabled physicians to locate tumors more precisely, making more accurate treatment possible. New technologies have also enabled doctors to use bone marrow transplantation as a treatment option in some cancer patients with leukemia.

The Dangers of Quackery

Unfortunately, some people fall prey to medical quackery. *Quackery* refers to incompetence in a licensed health professional or, more commonly, an unlicensed and unorthodox practitioner. Cancer quacks prosper because of patient ignorance and because patients are afraid and desperate for some type of cure. Quack treatments for cancer include the use of ineffective drugs, special diets, and other controversial methods.

Laetrile, also known as vitamin B_{17} or aprikern, is one of the most notorious quack cancer treatments. There is no such vitamin as B_{17}. The substance is an extract of apricot pits that costs about 2 cents a pill to produce and sells for $1.25 or more. Studies at reputable cancer and medical research institutes have not found any evidence that laetrile can cure or prevent any form of cancer. Nevertheless, advocates of laetrile as well as other quack treatments often claim success and offer testimonials by "cured" patients. What they do not say is that the cure may well result from a naturally occurring improvement (*remission*) or a standard medical treatment such as chemotherapy.

The greatest tragedy of any type of cancer quackery is that a patient who might be cured often delays making a trip to the doctor and instead relies on useless drugs and treatments. When he or she does finally seek appropriate treatment, it may be too late to curb the disease.

The love of friends and family members can be very important to cancer patients, who need the warmth of human contact and communication to help them get through difficult times. (Werner Bertsch/Medical Images, Inc.)

Living with Cancer

There are over 6 million Americans living who have a history of cancer; nearly 3 million of these people are considered cured of the disease. ("Cured" means that a person is free of the disease 5 years or more after the initial diagnosis and treatment.[24]) Thanks to earlier detection and new methods of treatment, many of these cancer survivors will have the same life expectancy as people who never had the disease. Others will live a longer time while continuing to battle the disease from day to day.

Making Each Day Count

For many long-term survivors, cancer is a chronic disease that must be dealt with over a long period. Just like people with chronic conditions such as hypertension and diabetes, cancer survivors need to take special care of themselves on a daily basis. They may or may not have to adhere to medication regimens or follow special diets, but they will need routine periodic health exams throughout their lives.

Living with cancer means trying to focus on living rather than dying, but it also means working through one's feelings about death, fear, and isolation. A program sponsored by the American Cancer Society called Make Today Count helps cancer patients and their families learn to live each day as fully and completely as possible. Groups such as this, along with other efforts to keep cancer patients active and involved, help improve a patient's outlook. This in turn promotes a patient's overall health and well-being.

Coping with Cancer

Cancer patients and survivors have to cope with a great deal. Many must deal with fears of disease recurrence and possible death. Disabilities resulting from the disease or its treatment may remain a source of ongoing distress. Anxiety, fear, and panic attacks can develop after cancer treatments have been completed. The experience of having had cancer produces a continuing concern about one's mortality and a lasting sense of vulnerability.[25]

People with cancer use various types of coping behavior to help them deal with the disease. They may use denial as a temporary protection against being overwhelmed by the experience. They may intellectualize the problem. They may suppress their feelings, project them onto others, or displace feelings such as anger to less threatening targets (such as a spouse rather than a physician) or more socially acceptable ones (such as an adult rather than a child). They may also search for a meaning for the illness and for their lives. For some people, faith in God may offer consolation.[26]

With the number of cancer survivors increasing and with those survivors living longer, it is important for cancer patients as well as their families and friends to learn how to define and live with their feelings about the disease. Since people's sense of control over their lives can be affected by cancer, attempts to increase personal control are beneficial in helping them cope with the disease.

Some people are able to cope with cancer by themselves or with the help of their families and friends. For others, support programs such as those offered by the American Cancer Society can provide information and counseling services. Through their own efforts and with the help of others, most cancer patients are able to lead normal, active lives filled with hope for the future.

Chapter Summary

- Cancer is a group of more than 100 diseases characterized by the uncontrolled growth and spread of abnormal cells. Sometimes these cells form an abnormal mass of tissue known as a malignant tumor. Sometimes new tumors form when cancerous cells break away and spread to other parts of the body. This process is known as metastatic growth.

- Some of the more common types of cancer are carcinomas, sarcomas, lymphomas, leukemias, and melanomas.

- Cancer brings people face to face with their own mortality and often causes a great deal of psychological pain and emotional distress. Cancer patients often fear dying, the possible pain and side effects associated with treatment, and not being able to lead a normal life. They may also face disruptions in their personal and social life that can lead to loneliness and depression. Family dynamics may change as roles and responsibilities shift as a result of dealing with the disease.

- A number of risk factors have been associated with the development of cancer. Certain cancers seem to be more strongly associated with some of these risk factors than with others.

- To help reduce the possibility of developing cancer, it is often suggested that people change their lifestyles and behaviors so as to avoid the risk factors associated with the disease. This includes avoiding tobacco smoking and excessive alcohol consumption, eating a nutritious diet, exercising, avoiding hazardous chemicals and other environmental pollutants, and avoiding exposure to the sun's ultraviolet rays.

- Early detection of cancer can save a person's life. The earlier the disease is detected, the better the prognosis for treatment, longer survival, and even complete recovery.

- Regular self-examinations should be performed to ensure early diagnosis of breast cancer and testicular cancer.

- The primary treatments for cancer are surgery, radiation therapy, and chemotherapy. The choice of treatment depends on the nature of the cancer, its spread, the health of the patient, and other factors.

- Since early detection of cancer is crucial to a patient's survival, medical quackery is particularly dangerous in regard to this disease.

- New developments in the treatment and diagnosis of cancer include the use of more precise diagnostic tools, combined drug therapies, and the potential for developing vaccines for some forms of the disease.

- Cancer patients must cope with the fears associated with the disease. To do this, they use many of the normal coping mechanisms, such as denial, intellectualizing the problem, suppressing feelings, projecting feelings onto others, and searching for meaning in their lives. While some cancer patients cope well with the disease by themselves, family members and friends can be crucial. Organized support groups can help provide information and counseling.

12

Drug Use and Abuse

When you have studied this chapter, you should be able to:

- Explain what drugs are, provide some reasons for their use and abuse, and describe how drug addiction can develop.

- Describe patterns of drug use and explain the relevance of the agent-host-environment model to drug dependence.

- Summarize the main effects of drugs and describe the different ways in which drugs are administered.

- List, describe, and give examples of the main types of psychoactive drugs.

- Identify programs that help drug abusers and discuss societal efforts to combat the drug problem.

An enormous variety of chemical substances—available both legally and illegally—play a significant role in the lives of millions of Americans. Drugs are used as a part of most medical regimens. Americans also use drugs to ease uncomfortable social occasions, give themselves a lift, help themselves relax, or simply out of habit. People seem to believe that drugs can provide easy solutions to many of their problems. However, drugs have been implicated in a host of problems, including accidents, crime, illness, violence, and family and community disintegration.

The issues people should be concerned about include the purposes for which drugs are used and the benefits, risks, and consequences of drug use for themselves and for society. The challenge is to maximize the benefits of drugs while reducing the associated risks. This is the basis for responsible drug use.

Drugs and Why People Use Them

Drugs include an enormous number of substances. Since the dawn of recorded history people have used and abused these substances for a variety of reasons.

Sometimes people experience little difficulty with the use of a drug. Most people, for example, can control their use of alcoholic beverages. At other times, however, drugs may cause serious problems both for users and for society.

What Are Drugs?

The term **drug,** as defined in this book, refers to any nonnutritional substance that is *deliberately* introduced into the body to produce a physiological and/or psychological effect. Drugs that act primarily on the brain, producing altered states of mood, perception, consciousness, and central nervous system activity, are called **psychoactive drugs.**

Psychoactive drugs, such as marijuana or cocaine, have the potential for abuse, while nonpsychoactive drugs, such as penicillin and other antibiotics, do not. Two psychoactive drugs that affect the health of millions of people are alcohol and tobacco. Because they are so widely used and cause such pervasive problems, they will be considered separately in Chapter 13.

drug

psychoactive drug

The Use of Drugs

Most people who take drugs do so legally, using them to prevent or treat health disorders, not to get high or feed an addiction. Nearly everyone takes aspirin, cold remedies, and other over-the-counter (OTC) drugs now and then to treat common ailments. In addition, most people occasionally use drugs that require a doctor's prescription. For many people with chronic diseases such as heart disease, daily life includes taking an assortment of prescription drugs to treat their illnesses.[1]

When prescribing a drug, a doctor must prescribe the right medicine for a particular problem *and* for a particular patient, given that some people have allergic reactions to certain drugs. Doctors can choose from a huge assortment of drugs, each with its own specific effects on the body. Prescription drugs are available to

- **Relieve symptoms,** for example, analgesics to control pain such as a headache
- **Prevent illness,** for example, vaccines to prevent diseases such as polio
- **Control chronic conditions,** for example, diuretics to control hypertension
- **Treat diseases,** for example, antibiotics to treat infectious diseases

Any drug can be harmful if a person ingests enough of it, but some drugs have much more potential for harm than do others. In addition, certain combinations of drugs can be lethal even when taken in small quantities. For example, even a small amount of certain sedatives can cause death if taken in combination with alcohol or other depressant drugs.

The drugs with the greatest potential for harm are regulated by federal and state laws. This is why certain drugs can be obtained legally only with a prescription. Some drugs offer so little medical benefit compared with the harm they can cause that they are rarely or never prescribed and can be obtained only illegally; examples are heroin, crack, LSD, and marijuana.

Drug Tolerance, Dependence, and Addiction

Among the factors that must be considered when one is making decisions about using drugs is the risk of becoming too accustomed to a drug—of becoming tolerant of, dependent on, or addicted to it.

tolerance

Tolerance In many cases it is possible to develop a dangerous tolerance to a drug. **Tolerance** means that the body becomes adapted to the drug so that increasingly larger dosages are needed to produce the desired effect. This increases the hazard of any undesired effects the drug may have as well. In this book, *tolerance* refers to both legal and illegal psychoactive drugs that some people use to alter their mental state.

dependence

Dependence There is often a very fine line between tolerance and **dependence**—a condition in which individuals become so accustomed to a drug that they cannot, or feel they cannot, function without it. Dependence may refer to psychic dependence or physical dependence.

Psychic dependence involves compulsive drug use for the sense of well-being it gives the user. With psychic dependence, a user deprived of the drug may feel restless, irritable, or anxious but does not become physically ill.

withdrawal syndrome

With *physical dependence*, the body's systems have been altered, and the continuous presence of the drug has become the norm. If a physically dependent person is deprived of the drug, he or she experiences the **withdrawal syndrome**—an unpleasant and possibly painful experience that may be life-threatening.

addiction

Addiction The term **addiction** has come to imply criminality and other socially value-laden ideas. Some experts use the term to emphasize a compulsive quality in a person's drug use. This pattern is marked both by tolerance and by psychic and physical dependence.[2]

Gambling is a type of compulsive behavior that can be explained by the theory of psychic addiction; gamblers often have the sense that the hopeless aspects of their lives can be eliminated by success in gambling. (PhotoEdit)

How People Become Dependent on Drugs

Dependence can develop both with drugs used medically and with those, such as alcohol and marijuana, used for recreational or social purposes. In either case, a person can become dependent in essentially the same way.

Relief of Discomfort   People sometimes take drugs, with or without a prescription, to relieve discomfort such as physical pain or anxiety. If a person follows the instructions of a physician or those indicated on the drug label, there should be no problem. However, a person may deviate from these instructions in two ways, each of which can lead to drug dependence.

- If the drug acts quickly to ease pain, the person may start taking the medication to achieve lower and lower pain levels. Such a pattern is less likely to develop with a drug that acts slowly.
- Since the drug eliminates pain, a person may reason that it is better to *anticipate* the pain and take the drug ahead of time, thus avoiding discomfort entirely. This can lead to regular but unnecessary use of the drug and can greatly increase the chance of developing psychic and/or physical dependence.

Replace the word *pain* in the description above with *anxiety, depression,* or even *nervousness,* and it is clear how dependence can develop with the use of any substance that promises relief from unpleasant feelings.

Levels of Drug Use   Not everyone who uses a drug a few times is destined for dependence. There are actually several levels of nonmedical drug use.

Whether a person is likely to develop a drug dependence depends in part on which level of use that person follows. The following are the major levels of drug use in roughly chronological order.

1. *Experimental use.* At this level the individual "samples" a drug, typically in social situations, but uses it very infrequently. The risk of dependence is usually low, though it *may* occur.

2. *Recreational use.* The individual uses modest amounts of a drug in social settings where such use is accepted or expected. The individual's level of use reflects that of his or her social group. The widespread use of alcohol and marijuana typify recreational use. Risk of dependence is still relatively low.

3. *Situational use.* The individual uses a drug in order to experience effects that he or she considers beneficial in a particular situation or in certain circumstances. An example of a situational user is a salesperson who typically takes a stiff drink before visiting a customer. At this level, the risk of dependence may be considerable, depending on the situation, frequency, and particular drug used.

4. *Intensified use.* The individual uses a drug regularly to reduce perceived physical, psychological, or social discomfort. The frequency of use generally increases and the amount of the drug the individual uses may increase. The risk of developing dependence is usually high at this level of use.

5. *Compulsive use.* The individual is preoccupied with obtaining and using a drug. Tolerance has often developed, and the drug has become less able to produce the anticipated effect. Normal functioning is impaired; the individual's social relationships are superficial; he or she usually develops some degree of physical weakness; and vocational or academic pursuits are endangered or abandoned. The individual's health is at risk.

The Agent-Host-Environment Model   The levels of drug use just described are primarily from the perspective of the individual, but it is important to view drug dependence as more than an individual problem. Since many of the pressures to take drugs and the availability of drugs come from outside the individual, the role of society and other factors must also be considered (Figure 12.1).

The agent-host-environment model can be helpful in explaining drug dependence. In terms of drug use, agent factors include the characteristics of a drug—dose, purity, toxicity, interaction with other drugs, and method of administration. Clearly, these factors can influence the potential for drug dependence. Host factors involve the physical, emotional, intellectual, social, and spiritual characteristics of the individual drug user. Emotional problems and physical illness, for example, can be factors in increased drug use and thus may play a role in drug dependence. Environmental factors include peer pressure, family patterns and behaviors, cultural mores, religious practices and beliefs, and laws. Pressures from family members, friends, and society may inhibit or encourage drug use and thus can be a factor in drug dependence as well.

There is no such thing as a "safe" or "unsafe" drug. What determines a drug's safety is the interaction of agent, host, and environment. Drug dependence should not be seen as just a function of the individual drug user but as

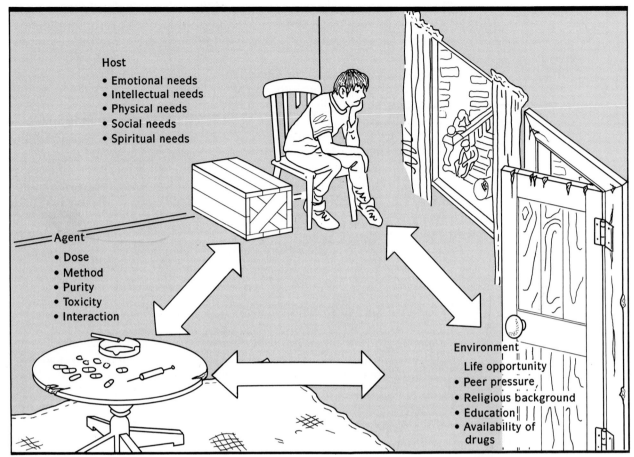

Host
- Emotional needs
- Intellectual needs
- Physical needs
- Social needs
- Spiritual needs

Agent
- Dose
- Method
- Purity
- Toxicity
- Interaction

Environment
Life opportunity
- Peer pressure
- Religious background
- Education
- Availability of drugs

Figure 12.1 The agent-host-environment model. Three complex sets of factors interact to determine drug use and abuse. Potential hosts bring their individual needs to social interactions. The social environment influences individual decisions by encouraging or discouraging drug use. As agents, drugs can change the characteristics of a host, and hosts select agents with different characteristics.

a result of the interplay among the individual (the host), a particular drug (the agent), and the setting in which the drug is taken (the environment).

Trends in Drug Use

The most frequently used illegal drug in the United States today is marijuana, although its popularity is nowhere near that of alcohol. A 1989 survey of 1,200 college students found that 16.3 percent had used marijuana in the past month, 2.8 percent had used cocaine, and 76 percent had drunk alcohol. Compared with previous studies, the survey showed a decline in the use of all three drugs through the 1980s.[3]

According to a recent survey by the National Parents Resource Institute for Drug Education (PRIDE), drug use is declining among younger students as well. This survey of students in junior and senior high schools found that 4.6 percent had tried cocaine—down from 6.4 percent in a similar survey done two years earlier.[4]

Despite the decline in drug use among students, drug abuse has become a critical national problem among other segments of the population. According to the National Institute on Drug Abuse, the number of people addicted to cocaine increased at least 33 percent between 1985 and 1989.[5] The term *co-*

caine as used in this book also includes cocaine derivatives such as crack. These derivatives are less expensive than cocaine and have quicker, more intense, and more dangerous effects. Their lower price has been a factor in their increased use.

The American Council for Drug Education has reported that women between ages 18 and 34 constitute one of the groups in which cocaine addiction is spreading most rapidly. This situation is especially lamentable because pregnant women can pass the addiction on to their babies. One-tenth of all babies born in 1988 had illegal drugs—usually cocaine—in their bodies and faced the prospect of severe health problems.[6] In New York City alone, an estimated 10,000 mothers were addicted to crack at the beginning of 1990—a threefold increase over 1988.[7] In Philadelphia, doctors at Temple University Hospital reported in 1989 that 16 percent of the women delivering babies had used cocaine—four times more than in 1987—and the University of Pennsylvania Hospital reported that one-fifth of the women giving birth had used cocaine or cocaine derivatives just before going into labor.[8]

The Effects of Drugs

Drugs can produce a wide range of effects, desirable and undesirable, on the body as well as the mind. Whether a drug affects a person physically, mentally, or both, it produces its effects by interacting with specific parts of the body.

How Drugs Interact with Body Cells

receptor sites

How does a particular drug act on a specific problem? Why does one drug act on the blood vessels and another on nerves? One explanation is the idea that a drug affects only specific **receptor sites** on cells where the drug molecules "fit." (A *molecule* is the smallest functional unit of a chemical substance.) Drug molecules do not act on the whole cell—only on the receptor sites. A drug acts only on cells that have receptor sites compatible with its molecules (Figure 12.2). To determine whether a drug will act on a given type of cell, it is necessary to find out *how much* compatibility there is between the drug molecules and the receptor sites in the cell.

side effects

Side Effects of Drugs   If a drug acted on only one site in the body—the place where there is a problem—the physician's task would be relatively simple. Unfortunately, drugs cannot be counted on to act this way in all circumstances. All drugs have **side effects**—effects that are unwanted and unrelated to the essential purpose of a drug. Some side effects may occur immediately, and some over a period of time; some are short-lived, and some permanent; some are mildly annoying, and some much worse—perhaps even life-threatening. Even aspirin can have the side effect of upsetting one's stomach.

What causes the side effects of drugs? Basically, some drugs are much less selective than others about the receptor sites with which they interact. Certain drugs used to treat bacterial infections, for example, go on a search and destroy mission that requires them to interlock with invading bacteria and combat those harmful organisms. Unfortunately, these drugs may interlock with

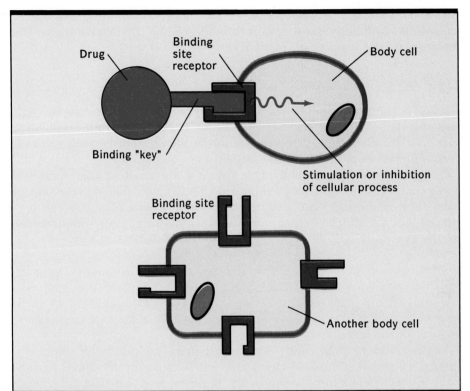

Figure 12.2 *Cells in the body have receptors in their membranes that can affect their functioning. Drugs stimulate these receptors when their chemical "keys" fit into, or bind with, the receptor "locks." Since receptors in different cells may be similar, drugs can affect several types of tissues. However, the effects on these tissues can be very different, depending on the number of receptors and their function in a particular cell. Opiates, for instance, inhibit muscle contractions in the intestine and create euphoria when they bind with receptors in the brain.*

and destroy healthy blood cells or glandular cells housing the bacteria, resulting in damage to the blood, glands, or vital organs.[9] Medical descriptions of drugs sometimes include terms that denote hazards to specific organs.

Drug use can pose greater risks for some people than it does for others because of variations in host factors or characteristics such as a compromised immune system, damaged organs, and pregnancy. A recent study found that a combination of health problems and the physiological decline that comes with age may make elderly people more apt to have adverse reactions to drugs.[10] Certain OTC antacids contain large amounts of sodium. For most people these drugs pose virtually no risk, but for people with hypertension they can cause medical complications. Other drugs pose little risk except when taken by a pregnant woman; while unlikely to injure the woman, they can cause birth defects.

When giving or prescribing *any* drug, especially if there is a possibility of injury, a physician must always take into account the risk-versus-benefit ratio. That is, the physician must weigh the good the drug can provide against any potential threat to the patient.

Drug Allergies An **allergy** is an overreaction to a specific substance by the immune system. Allergies to drugs can produce many reactions, ranging from mild rashes to life-threatening shock, in which blood pressure can drop so low that the person dies. Allergy to drugs can represent a major difficulty. This is especially true when a patient has an infection and is allergic to the antibiotic that is known to fight it most effectively. Fortunately, alternative medications

allergy

are often available. In some instances, an allergy to one drug will warn a person of possible similar reactions to other, chemically related drugs. This situation is known as **cross-sensitivity.**

cross-sensitivity

How Drugs Are Administered

There are two fundamental principles of responsible drug use: take the right drug for the specific effect needed and be aware of the other effects the drug can have. Another important principle is that the way a drug is administered can influence its effect.

route of administration

The way a drug enters the body is known as the **route of administration.** Drugs may be swallowed, injected, inhaled, implanted, applied to the skin, or administered through body orifices. The route of administration can be a crucial factor in a drug's effect. The most common routes of administration are by mouth, by injection, and by inhalation.

Oral Administration   Most medicinal drugs are taken by mouth. Drugs designed to be taken orally dissolve in the stomach and mix with the contents of the stomach and small intestine. Thus, they can pass through the walls of the gastrointestinal (GI) tract into the bloodstream, where they are circulated to the rest of the body.

A drug administered orally is absorbed more rapidly if the stomach is empty. Therefore, if rapid absorption is desired, a doctor may direct that the drug be taken before meals. Some drugs, however, tend to irritate the stomach and are best taken *with* or *after meals*.

Sometimes drugs cannot be taken orally. Some drugs are destroyed by digestive juices in the stomach. A person may be so nauseated that he or she cannot keep down anything taken orally. Some people have difficulty swallowing a pill.

parenteral

subcutaneous
intramuscular
intravenous

Injections   A drug that is administered **parenterally** goes into the body in a manner other than through the digestive tract. The most common means of parenteral administration is injection—either **subcutaneously** (under the skin), **intramuscularly** (into a muscle), or **intravenously** (into a vein). Intravenous injection, which places drugs directly into the blood, is the quickest way of getting a drug into the bloodstream. In life-threatening situations this time advantage can be crucial. Another advantage is that the walls of blood vessels are relatively insensitive and can tolerate certain irritating substances better than the stomach can tolerate them. A disadvantage of intravenous injection is that it requires special equipment and skill and thus should be attempted only by trained medical personnel.

Inhalation   Breathing a drug into the lungs allows the drug to be absorbed rapidly into the bloodstream without the paraphernalia required for injections. A drug that is inhaled comes into direct contact with the rich supply of capillaries (tiny blood vessels) in the nose, throat, bronchi, and lungs and is absorbed into the bloodstream through the alveoli and the capillary walls.

Inhalation has disadvantages. For example, dose levels are more difficult to regulate, and certain drugs do not spread through the lung tissues to reach the bloodstream. Moreover, the inhalation of some drugs can injure the body and irritate the delicate tissues that line the respiratory system.

The Time-Response Relationship

Another important factor in the effect of a drug is the time-response relation-ship—how much time it takes for the drug to produce the desired effect and how long that effect will last (Figure 12.3). If there is a possibility of side effects, it is important to know how long it will take for the body to transform the drug chemically, excrete it, or both.

Distribution and Speed of Effect   Different drugs have different ways of spreading through the body. Most drugs affect the parts of the body that are the most richly supplied with blood vessels (the brain, heart, liver, and kid-neys) before moving on to other internal organs and to the muscles, fat tissue, and skin. Some drugs, however, gravitate toward specific places in the body. Iodine, for example, usually winds up in the thyroid gland.

The speed with which drugs take effect can vary, depending in part on the way a drug is distributed. Some drugs react with the body almost immediately (alcohol moves quickly through the bloodstream to the brain), whereas others act more slowly. The duration of a drug's effect also depends in part on the way in which it is stored in the body. Drugs stored in fat tissues, for example, remain in the body longer than do drugs stored in muscle tissues.

Chemical Alteration and Duration of Effect   Certain reactions inside the body may chemically alter a drug so that it is a very different compound by the time

Figure 12.3 *Routes of administration and time response. The time it takes the body to begin responding to a drug and the time the drug's effect lasts vary with the size of the dose and the route by which the drug is administered. For example, a drug administered intravenously (by injection into a vein) reaches a high level in the bloodstream quite rapidly, and its effects wear off relatively soon. The same drug administered orally takes longer to reach the bloodstream and begin having an effect, and its action lasts longer.*

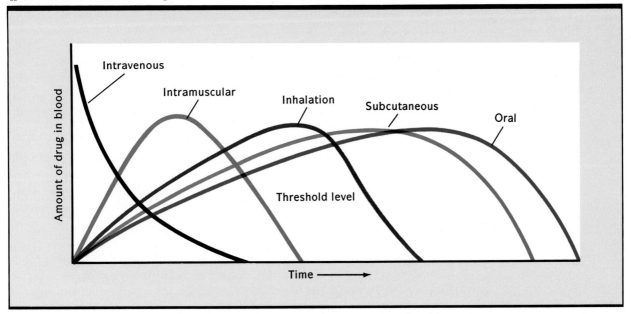

it leaves the bloodstream. Some drugs combine with body proteins in the bloodstream. Others are broken down into smaller chemical components by the liver, kidneys, and GI tract.

A drug that is chemically altered is less likely to linger in the body in active form after it is needed or wanted. Drugs that are not chemically altered are excreted more slowly and can continue to be active in the body for days. For example, small amounts of diazepam (Valium) may remain in the body for as long as 8 days. Certain substances, such as marijuana, are actually stored by body tissues and are retained long after absorption.

Excreting Drugs from the Body   Drugs are eliminated from the body in various ways. The kidneys do most of the work in eliminating drugs by excreting them in the urine, but other means of excretion include feces, respiration, tears, sweat, and saliva.

An often overlooked route of excretion is mother's milk. When drugs are taken by a nursing mother, they are often excreted in breast milk, sometimes in concentrated form. Since this can pose a danger to an infant, nursing mothers should take drugs only under medical supervision.

The Dose-Response Relationship

The least amount of a drug needed to produce a particular effect—known as the *threshold dose*—varies from person to person. Some tranquilizers, for example, are used in doses of 2 to 50 milligrams.

Effective Dose and Lethal Dose   As a reference point, doctors refer to the dose that causes the desired effect in 50 percent of the population. This is called the effective dose 50 (ED 50). Obviously, the effective dose for a particular individual is not necessarily the same as ED 50. Depending on factors such as weight, sex, health, overall metabolism, and other drugs being used, one person may need to take more or less of a particular drug than someone else does to receive the same therapeutic effect.

Every drug also has a lethal dose (LD) level. Statistical studies have helped establish the dose that can cause death in 50 percent of those exposed (LD 50). This is crucial because doctors need a reasonable margin of safety between the effective dose and the lethal dose. They refer to this safety margin as the *therapeutic index* **therapeutic index.** Obviously, a drug with a high therapeutic index (a large difference between the effective dose and the lethal dose) is safer than one with a low index.

With many drugs, the potential to cause harm is specifically related to the amount taken. Moreover, overdose is less likely to occur with some drugs than it is with others. Many deaths have occurred, accidently and otherwise, from overdoses of sleeping pills, alcohol, and powerful stimulants such as amphetamines.

Drug Interactions   A serious and often unpredictable risk of drug use is interaction between two or more drugs. An interaction problem occurs when one drug blocks or counteracts the effects of another. For example, an antacid may prevent an antibiotic from effectively battling an infection by decreasing its absorbability.[11]

A second interaction problem concerns increasing side effects. One drug may heighten the side effects of another drug. One effect of aspirin is that it interferes with blood clotting, resulting in an increased tendency to bleed.[12] If alcohol is taken at the same time as aspirin, the effect may be additive. That is, the anticoagulant effect of aspirin may be increased.

A third drug interaction problem occurs when two drugs, both with similar effects, are taken together or in rapid sequence. The end result may be not simply additive but much more extreme. A potentially lethal combination is that of alcohol with sedatives.

The Use of Psychoactive Drugs

Although all drugs can cause problems, the psychoactive drugs have the greatest potential for abuse. These substances affect different structures in the brain that are thought to control mood, consciousness, and behavior (Figure 12.4). Two important psychoactive drugs—alcohol and nicotine—are associated with such widespread problems that a separate chapter has been devoted to them. Among the remaining types of psychoactive drugs, some are prescription medications subject to abuse by patients or others who obtain them legally, and some are illegally marketed versions of those drugs. Others are strictly "street drugs" that are not used medically. Their sale and use are wholly outside the law.

The groups of psychoactive drugs to be discussed in this chapter are sedatives/hypnotics, stimulants (including cocaine), marijuana, volatile solvents, opiate narcotics, and psychedelics/hallucinogens.

Sedatives/Hypnotics

The **sedatives/hypnotics** are drugs that have either sedative (calming) or hypnotic (sleep-inducing) effects. The difference between these effects is just a matter of dosage. Technically, these drugs, more commonly known as "downers," are depressants—they slow the activity of the central nervous system. This group of drugs includes barbiturates and antianxiety drugs.

sedatives/hypnotics

Barbiturates The **barbiturates** range from short-acting drugs with effects lasting less than 6 hours such as Amytal, Nembutal, Seconal, and Tuinal to longer-acting ones such as Butisol and Luminal. The barbiturates are used primarily to treat insomnia or, less often, for daytime sedation. Certain barbiturates also have anticonvulsant properties.

barbiturates

Antianxiety Drugs The antianxiety drugs include Equanil and Miltown, Atarax, Librium, Valium, Tranzene, Serax, Xanax, and Halcion. These drugs are widely used to reduce anxiety. Some have muscle-relaxant properties as well, and a few have proved useful in controlling specific types of convulsive seizures.

Potential Risks A variety of side effects may occur with sedatives/hypnotics, including hangovers, nausea, headaches, dizziness, and drowsiness. Users may be at risk for accidents at home, at work, and while driving. Furthermore, these drugs are all potential killers through overdose.

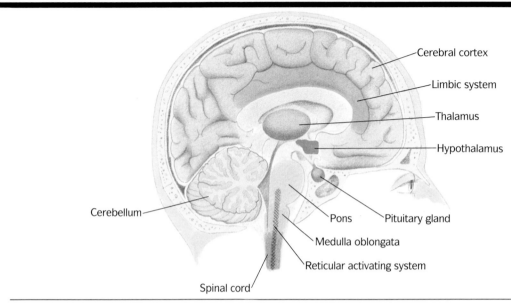

Labels on figure:
- Cerebral cortex
- Limbic system
- Thalamus
- Hypothalamus
- Pituitary gland
- Pons
- Medulla oblongata
- Reticular activating system
- Spinal cord
- Cerebellum

Brain Structure	Function	Drug Effects
1. Medulla oblongata	Monitors respiration and cardiac activity	Alcohol, analgesics, and sedatives/hypnotics can cause cardiovascular or respiratory failure
2. Reticular activating system (RAS)	Alerts brain to stimuli or blocks out certain stimuli; activates other parts of the brain	Sedatives/hypnotics dampen RAS activity, and stimulants overcome RAS underactivity; psychedelics distort perception and stimuli from different parts of the body from being correctly processed by the brain
3. Cerebellum	Controls the senses, motor coordination, balance, and agility	Alcohol and sedatives/hypnotics can produce uncoordinated movements and impair sensory perception, hearing, smell, taste, and touch; psychedelics can evoke vision distortion and alter time and space perception; marijuana can cause disoriented behavior
4. Thalamus	Communication center; directs messages to and from brain	Alcohol and sedatives/hypnotics can cause slurred speech and distortion of communication patterns; psychedelics can disrupt the transmission of impulses controlling cognitive, sensory, and motor functions
5. Hypothalamus	Control center for autonomic nervous system; regulates hormone production, temperature, fluid balance, feelings of hunger and fullness, thirst, pleasure, pain	Analgesics and sedatives/hypnotics can alter the pleasure-pain response; marijuana may affect testosterone production and feelings of hunger and fullness
6. Cerebral cortex	Controls learning, memory, thinking, integration of sensory impressions, inhibitions and emotions, time and space orientation, vision and hearing, speech and motor skills	Volatile solvents alter thought processes and behaviors; alcohol dulls discrimination, memory, concentration, and insight and disrupts motor processes while causing quick mood shifts; long-term marijuana use has been linked to apathy, disturbed self-awareness, and confusion; LSD may cause perceptual alterations and in large doses can produce paranoia and other psychotic reactions; PCP often induces psychosis, coma, or a comatose state
7. Limbic system	Connects cerebral cortex, thalamus and hypothalamus; involved with emotions and short-term memory	Antianxiety drugs alter physiological responses to emotions; opiates affect memory, spatial orientation, and emotions

Figure 12.4 *Different structures of the brain are affected by different drugs. This view through the middle of the brain shows the major structures which drugs may affect.*

A special danger exists with the interaction of these drugs—the use of one sedative/hypnotic with another or with a different type of depressant. In fact, aside from the problem of dependence, the most serious danger with sedatives/hypnotics is combining the drug with another depressant—especially alcohol. Young people have been known to combine sedatives/hypnotics with alcohol to achieve heightened intoxication. The depressant effects of both drugs on the central nervous system can cause critical conditions, including coma and death. People taking these drugs should be aware of the lethal potential and should heed warnings about not drinking while taking them.

Another risk with sedatives/hypnotics is the potential for dependence. Users can rapidly develop a tolerance for up to 15 times the normal dose.[13]

The withdrawal symptoms experienced by people dependent on these drugs are very severe. These symptoms begin with nervousness, trembling, and weakness. If they are not treated, the users of these drugs can suffer epileptic-like seizures or a toxic psychosis with delusions and hallucinations and can lose consciousness. The most severe symptoms of untreated withdrawal last about 4 days *and can be fatal.* If a pregnant woman is dependent on sedatives/hypnotics, her baby will have to suffer through the withdrawal syndrome shortly after birth.

Stimulants

The most widely used stimulant in the United States is caffeine. Drinking large amounts of beverages that contain caffeine, such as coffee and cola, *can* cause harm. Two other kinds of stimulants—amphetamines and cocaine—can be extremely dangerous.

Basically, **stimulants** rev up the sympathetic nervous system, the part of the autonomic nervous system that prepares the body to cope with stress in what is known as the fight-or-flight response. Stimulants start up this mechanism inappropriately, when it may not be needed. While caffeine does this on a relatively low level, more powerful stimulants do so on a larger scale.

stimulants

Caffeine Few people realize how potent caffeine is or how fast it can act. In less than 5 minutes after you drink a cup of coffee, caffeine has raced to every part of your body. It increases the flow of urine and stomach acid, relaxes involuntary muscles, steps up the intake of oxygen, and speeds the basal metabolic rate. It also increases the pumping strength of the heart, but too much caffeine can lead to an irregular heartbeat.

Amphetamines The **amphetamines,** sometimes known as pep pills or uppers, are synthetic drugs that include Benzedrine, or "bennies," Dexedrine, or "dexies," and Methedrine, or "meth" or "speed." The word *speed* is often used to refer to this group of drugs.

amphetamines

People have been using and misusing amphetamines since they were introduced 50 years ago. Amphetamines have some legitimate medical uses. They can be used to treat an extremely rare condition called *narcolepsy* (an uncontrollable need for short periods of deep sleep) and to treat *hyperkinetic* (uncontrollably overactive) children. Interestingly, the effects of amphetamines are paradoxical in hyperkinetic children: they seem to calm these children rather than stimulate them.

In addition to those uses, some amphetamines have been combined with others or with barbiturates or tranquilizers in a variety of products aimed at achieving weight control. It is unwise to use amphetamines as appetite suppressants. After 2 to 4 weeks they are no longer effective, and the risks are hardly worth it—many people who become dependent on amphetamines started out by using them as weight-loss aids.

Recently a new form of methamphetamine has become available on the illegal drug market. Called "ice," "glass," "freeze," or "quartz," it looks like rock candy and is inhaled after being heated in a glass pipe. The immediate result is a lengthy high with euphoria, and feelings of alertness and confidence, but the withdrawal causes an intense depression, and irritability and insomnia are also frequent effects. More serious psychotic effects have also occurred.

Potential Risks   People can become physically dependent on both caffeine and amphetamines, and these drugs pose other risks as well. For most people, about three to four cups of coffee can cause irritability, headaches, tremors, and nervousness. Double that amount can cause hallucinations and convulsions. People who drink at least five cups of coffee a day can suffer several days of withdrawal symptoms—including nausea, headaches, irritability, and fatigue—when they kick the habit. People who drink a lot of coffee regularly can experience rapid breathing, heart palpitations, agitation, and mood changes.

Caffeine may pose other dangers as well. Studies have linked it to heart disease, benign and malignant tumors, pancreatic cancer, and birth defects. Other studies, however, have refuted these links.[14] Nevertheless, it is a good idea for pregnant women to avoid caffeine as they would avoid any other drug. Recently, there has been increased concern about children who get too much caffeine. Even one cola drink gives an 8-year-old a hefty jolt of the drug, and many children consume much more than that every day.

Amphetamines often bring on unwanted side effects such as nervousness, elevated blood pressure, and headache with just one small dose. If the drug is used on a single occasion (to help a student study for an exam, for example), there may be no further detrimental effects. However, if the drug is taken in a situation that is inherently risky, such as by a trucker traveling a superhighway, there is an additional peril. The effects of amphetamines often cease abruptly and unpredictably, and sleep or even death can result.[15]

In large doses or over prolonged periods, amphetamines have unpredictable effects, including insomnia, dizziness, agitation, confusion, delirium, and malnutrition. A user may develop wildly exaggerated feelings of confidence and power which can lead to errors of judgment. For some people, prolonged use of amphetamines can lead to psychosis. In other instances the elevated blood pressure caused by continued amphetamine use can put a strain on blood vessels. Intravenous use of amphetamines can lead to death from ruptured blood vessels such as in a stroke.

As a rule, amphetamines are not used recreationally. They tend to be taken by individuals who want them or think they need them rather than shared in social situations. Thus, the first two levels of drug dependence—experimental use and recreational use—are often omitted. Individuals may proceed fairly quickly to situational, intensified, and compulsive use. Once they are into this pattern of use, users may find that they need increased amounts of the drug.

Thinking Critically about Legalizing Drugs

One of the most serious problems in the United States in the late twentieth century is the widespread use of illegal drugs. Drug use is largely responsible for the epidemic of violent crime that has swept through the cities and for the spread of AIDS and other serious diseases. By the early 1990s the problem had become so serious that for the first time, serious discussion of legalizing drugs began to enter the public debate. Following are the arguments on both sides of the legalization debate.

Pro-Legalization: Weighing the Costs of Drug Use

For over 100 years this society has made the use of certain drugs illegal and has penalized illegal drug use. But during that time the use of marijuana, heroin and other opiates, and cocaine has become an epidemic. Most recently, Americans have spent billions of dollars on arresting and imprisoning sellers and importers of crack cocaine, with almost no effect on the supply or street price of the drug.

The societal costs of illegal drugs are immense. They include the costs of law enforcement, criminal proceedings against those arrested, and jails and prisons. They also include the spread of deadly diseases such as AIDS and hepatitis through the use of shared needles; the cost to society of raising "crack babies," children poisoned by drugs even before birth; and the cost of raising a generation of young people who see illegal drug selling and violence as their only escape from poverty and desperation. Finally, the societal costs include the emotional cost of the violence that no one can now escape.

Legalizing drug use in this country would eliminate many of these costs. Billions of dollars would be saved. This money could be spent on treatment of addicts, job training, and education programs to help many disadvantaged young people assume valuable roles in society. The government could make drug use legal for adults but impose severe penalties on anyone who sells drugs to young people. Drug sales could be heavily taxed, thus deterring drug purchases and giving society the benefit of tax revenues that could be used for drug treatment and education.

Anti-Legalization: Providing a Positive Role Model

Certain drugs are illegal because they are dangerous and deadly and provide no societal value. To make their possession or use legal would send a message to young people that using drugs is acceptable and that drugs are not treacherous or life-destroying.

Making drugs illegal has not increased the number of drug users or sellers, just as making alcohol legal after Prohibition did not reduce the number of people who drank. Recent law enforcement efforts have indeed made a difference. Over the past few years, as law enforcement efforts have sent more and more people to jail, the number of young people who use illegal drugs has steadily declined. Furthermore, education about the ill effects of drug use has begun to deter people from buying and using illegal drugs.

Recently, the incidence of drug-related deaths and violence has begun to level off even in the areas of the most hard-core drug use. This is proof that strict law enforcement is working. This country has begun to turn the corner on this drug epidemic.

Which position do you favor? Do you think that legalizing drug use in this country would eliminate the societal costs of illegal drugs? Would legalizing drugs simply send a message to young people that using drugs is acceptable?

Based on information from *Atlantic Monthly* (November 1990); Richard Schlaad and Peter Shannon, *Drugs of Choice: Current Perspectives on Drug Use*, 2d ed. (Englewood Cliffs, N.J.: Prentice-Hall, 1982).

Tolerance does develop, and psychic dependence is strong.[16] Although the potential for physical dependence is not as great as with sedatives/hypnotics and opiate narcotics, there is often *some* degree of physical dependence as evidenced by depression, an increased appetite, and an increased need for sleep when the drug is stopped.

Cocaine

cocaine Among the most popular illicit drugs in use today, **cocaine** may also be the most dangerous.[17] Extracted from the leaves of the South American coca plant, cocaine is a stimulant closely related to caffeine, although it is much more potent. Cocaine initially decreases appetite and produces feelings of well-being, confidence, and alertness that last 20 to 90 minutes, depending on the form in which the drug is taken.[18] As these effects wear off, users experience feelings of anxiety which can last several hours.

Uses of Cocaine Medically, cocaine is used as a local anesthetic in certain types of surgery. It numbs tissues and constricts blood vessels, helping to reduce bleeding. Recreationally, cocaine is inhaled ("snorted") through the nostrils, injected, or smoked. Cocaine users inhale a powdery form of the drug, commonly known as coke, blow, toot, or flake. This powder can also be mixed with water and injected. This causes a faster high. Some users seek more intense highs by injecting cocaine with heroin, an extremely dangerous combination known as a speedball.

Cocaine users also smoke a form of cocaine known as freebase or a form known as crack. Smoking the drug produces a quicker high than does snorting or injecting it, although the high is shorter-lived.[19] While snorted cocaine is only 20 to 50 percent pure, freebase cocaine is nearly 100 percent pure, and so the smoker gets an extremely concentrated dose of the drug. Crack, a "rock" form of the drug, is 25 to 90 percent pure freebase cocaine. The introduction of prepackaged crack pellets has increased the availability of cocaine to lower-income people and adolescents because of the lower cost.[20]

Potential Risks According to the National Institute on Drug Abuse, cocaine is the illicit drug that currently poses the greatest threat to public health in the United States. It has been estimated that 2 million people are addicted to cocaine.[21]

Although it was once thought that cocaine use does not lead to dependence, animal experiments have demonstrated its addictiveness. In these experiments, monkeys that were allowed unlimited access to cocaine continued ingesting the drug until they died from exhaustion and malnutrition. This type of behavior is reflected in human users, who often pursue the drug without regard for their own health, safety, or welfare.[22] Most experts believe that crack is very addictive and that addiction may occur after relatively few experiences with the drug.[23]

Cocaine has been implicated in cardiovascular problems, including heart attacks and abnormal heart beat *(arrhythmia),* and in pulmonary problems and strokes.[24] Regular use of cocaine can lead to tolerance and dependence and is often accompanied by increased anxiety and depression, paranoid delusions, and malnutrition.[25] While cocaine may produce heightened sexual performance at first, long-term use can cause sexual dysfunction in both men and

Coca leaves produce a numbing effect when they are chewed, but when the leaves are refined into cocaine powder and then inhaled, the effect is dangerously enhanced. (Jose Azel/Contact Stock; James Prince/Photo Researchers, Inc.)

women.[26] Heavy, prolonged use of cocaine can also produce tremors and convulsions as a result of loss of motor coordination. Repeated inhalation of cocaine can cause the mucous membranes in the nostrils to degenerate and in rare instances can lead to perforation of the membrane between the nostrils.[27] Yet another danger associated with cocaine and other illicit drugs is related to the purity of the drug. Users can never be sure about what they are buying and what additives have been used.

Pregnant women who use cocaine are at higher risk for having miscarriages and premature deliveries than are women who do not use the drug. Moreover, babies born to users are likely to show signs of underdevelopment, including short bodies, lower birth weights, and small heads, along with neurological impairment. Cocaine use by pregnant women has been linked with other birth defects, including malformations of the heart, skull, and genitourinary tract. The babies of users may also be at greater risk for developing sudden infant death syndrome (SIDS).[28]

Marijuana

Marijuana—also called pot or grass—is the third most popular recreational drug in the United States (after alcohol and nicotine) and is possibly the most widely used of all controlled substances. *Cannabis sativa* (the botanical name for the hemp plant) is the source of **marijuana** and **hashish,** a concentrated and more potent resin from the plant. The chief psychoactive ingredient is THC. The amount of this chemical in a given quantity of marijuana determines its potency.

marijuana
hashish

Cannabis has a 5,000-year history of medical use, mostly as an analgesic, or pain reliever. Largely superseded by aspirin and other pain-relieving drugs for that purpose, cannabis appears to have a therapeutic potential for treating glaucoma and some of the side effects of cancer chemotherapy.

Short-Term and Long-Term Effects When it is taken in average doses, the effects of marijuana are not much different from those of moderate quantities of alcohol, with the addition of distortion of time perception, an increase in heart rate, dilation of blood vessels in the eyes, increased appetite and thirst, and some muscular weakness. These effects can last for as long as 8 hours.[29]

Other effects vary with the individual and the setting and may sometimes be like those of a mild sedative or, conversely, a mild stimulant. Marijuana may also intensify the effects of alcohol, caffeine, and barbiturates.[30] A marijuana user who is emotionally unstable may react in an exaggerated manner in almost any direction, including severe panic or paranoia. Higher doses may bring on significant sensory distortion. The ability to think clearly and learn is usually reduced by marijuana.

While long-term marijuana users can develop a tolerance to the drug, the reverse also occurs. An experienced user may require less of the drug to experience its effects. Although the risk of physical dependence is probably insignificant, psychic dependence is entirely possible.

Potential Risks Short-term marijuana use can endanger individuals in situations that require fully functioning perceptual ability and motor coordination, such as driving. The combination of marijuana and alcohol can be especially hazardous when one is driving.

With long-term use, the major risk of marijuana is respiratory damage. Like tobacco, marijuana may decrease the efficiency of the lungs. There is also evidence that marijuana smoke impairs defense systems within the lungs, posing an increased risk of developing an infection.[31] Although there is no direct proof that marijuana smoking is correlated with lung cancer, smoke residuals (like the "tar" in tobacco smoke) have been found to produce tumors in experimental animals. A known cancer-causing chemical in tobacco smoke is found at higher levels in marijuana smoke.

Another serious concern with long-term marijuana use is its effect on the reproductive system. A number of studies have found lowered testosterone levels in men who are heavy marijuana smokers, along with two abnormalities in sperm. It is believed that these effects are reversible when the drug is discontinued.[32] In women, marijuana use has been associated with disruption of the menstrual cycle and possibly with miscarriage.[33]

A third concern with marijuana use is its impact on a person's mind. Although delusional thinking, paranoia, and hallucinations have been attributed to the drug's use, it is unclear whether it causes these problems or precipitates an underlying predisposition to them.[34] It has also been suggested that long-term marijuana use leads to decreased drive and ambition, loss of motivation, apathy, inactivity, self-neglect, and lack of concern about the future. Studies have failed to prove such a connection.

Volatile Solvents

inhalants Substances containing volatile chemical solvents that have psychoactive and other effects when breathed into the lungs are called **inhalants.** Substances that have been inhaled for a quick high include gasoline, furniture polish, insecticides, transmission fluid, paint thinners, aerosols, cleaning and lighter fluids, and model airplane glue. All these substances can damage vital organs such as the lungs, kidneys, liver, and brain and can cause death.

Nitrous Oxide   Used by dentists as an anesthetic since the 1840s, nitrous oxide (laughing gas) is among the least toxic inhalants. Death can occur, however, if it is inhaled with insufficient oxygen. Furthermore, repeated long-term use can result in nerve damage, muscle weakness, hearing loss, changes in heart rate, impotence, and life-threatening anemia.

Amyl Nitrite and Butyl Nitrite   **Amyl nitrite** is a prescription drug used to treat angina (severe chest pain due to insufficient blood and oxygen supply to the heart). A similar drug, **butyl nitrite,** has never been used medically to any significant extent. Both drugs have been used recreationally as sexual stimulants. A related substance, isobutyl alcohol, produces similar but less powerful effects than those of butyl nitrite.

amyl nitrite

butyl nitrite

The immediate effects of nitrite inhalation include headache, dizziness, flushing, muscle relaxation, heightened heart rate, and lowered blood pressure, with possible nausea, vomiting, and fainting. These effects may be especially dangerous for people with low blood pressure or glaucoma. Users can develop tolerance to nitrites, although physical dependence has not been reported. Inhaling substantial amounts over time can lead to a condition in which normal hemoglobin can no longer carry oxygen. There is also a long-term risk of developing heart and blood vessel damage.[35]

Opiate Narcotics

The opiate narcotics make the user numb in both mind and body (Figure 12.5). They act as an analgesic on the central nervous system, relieving pain without causing a loss of consciousness. They also have a strong potential to create physical and psychological dependence.

The **opiate narcotics** include the **opiates**—opium, morphine, and heroin—and the **opioids**—a group of synthetic drugs that are chemically similar to the opiates. **Opium,** the parent substance, comes from the opium poppy, which is native to Asia Minor; its active ingredient is **morphine. Heroin,** a derivative of morphine, is more than twice as potent as morphine.

opiate narcotics
opiates
opioids
opium
morphine
heroin

A recent variant of heroin is "tango and cash," which combines heroin with a tranquilizer. A dangerous effect results, which caused several deaths during the first months that the drug was out on the street.

Medical Uses   The opiate narcotics are useful medically to relieve pain, control diarrhea, and suppress coughs. While most people who take these drugs under a prescription do not become dependent on them, a few do. If morphine is prescribed to relieve the severe pain of an injury, the individual taking it may develop a dependence by the time the injury has healed and the drug is no longer needed.

Potential Risks   Until the increase in cocaine use in the 1980s, heroin represented the nation's most prevalent illicit drug problem. Heroin is typically injected intravenously, although it is also sometimes injected subcutaneously (a practice known as skin popping) or sniffed (snorted). A person who uses heroin is at great risk of becoming physically dependent on the drug.

Typically, a heroin user seeks the drug's mind-numbing effect, its blurring of thought and feeling, which can include feelings of ecstasy similar to sexual orgasm. When a user has become dependent, the drug is also needed to avoid

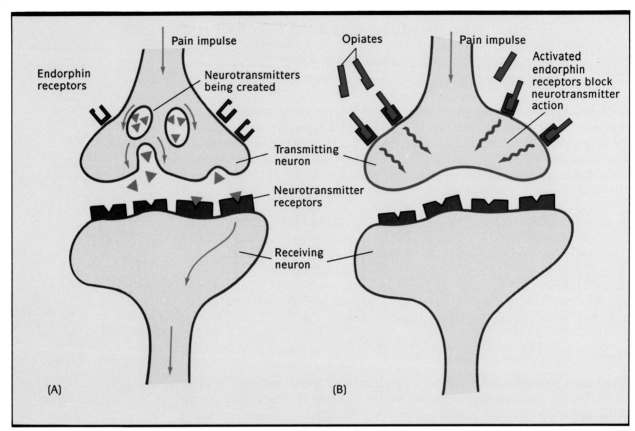

Figure 12.5 *Pain relief from opiates. (A) Normal nerve transmission involves electrical transmission within a nerve cell, and chemical (neurotransmitter) transmission from one cell to the next. (B) Opiates mimic the effect of natural endorphins by attaching to endorphin receptors and thus blocking the action of neurotransmitters between the nerve cells. While endorphins are rapidly dispersed, however, opiates linger at the receptor sites, causing tolerance and addiction.*

withdrawal. As the user becomes dependent, he or she is also likely to develop a tolerance.

Psychedelics/Hallucinogens

psychedelics/hallucinogens The **psychedelics/hallucinogens** are drugs that create illusions, distorting the user's mind by creating moods, thoughts, and perceptions that would otherwise take place only in a dream state. The earliest forms of these substances were derived from plants and have been employed in folk medicine and as part of religious rituals. Other forms have been developed in recent years.

LSD The well-known hallucinogen **LSD** ("acid") was developed in the late 1940s. In addition to LSD, this group of drugs includes a variety of substances, some natural plant derivatives and others created in chemistry labs. Among them *PCP* are **PCP** (an animal tranquilizer), **mescaline** (derived from the peyote cactus), *mescaline* **psilocybin** (a mushroom derivative), and other substances known by abbrevia-*psilocybin* tions of their chemical names.

None of these drugs causes physical dependence, and there is little if any psychic dependence, although tolerance can develop with frequent use. The real dangers of the psychedelics/hallucinogens lie in their unpredictable effects during use and occasionally long afterward.

LSD   An average dose of LSD produces slight dizziness, weakness, dilation of the pupils, and perceptual alterations such as intensive visual experiences, a distorted time sense, sharpened hearing, and **synesthesia**—a blending of the senses in which a person "hears" colors or "sees" sounds. The psychological symptoms include a flood of thoughts in new combinations, rapid mood changes, and a feeling of body distortion.[36]

synesthesia

PCP   Phencyclidine, also known as PCP, "angel dust," and other nicknames, was originally developed as an anesthetic for humans, but when its unpredictable properties became known, its use was restricted to veterinary applications. No longer manufactured for that purpose, PCP is now made illegally and can be combined with or represented as any of a number of other illegal substances (notably THC, the main psychoactive ingredient in marijuana). It is available as water-soluble powder, liquid, or tablet and is taken orally, sniffed, injected, or sprinkled on marijuana, kitchen herbs, or tobacco and smoked.[37]

Mescaline and Psilocybin   Mescaline is used in the religious ceremonies of Native Americans. Psilocybin has also played a part in Native American religious lore since the days of the ancient Aztecs. When taken in connection with traditional rituals and under the supervision of experienced users, these substances probably do no lasting harm. Outside such highly controlled settings, however, the effects can be unpredictable and hazardous.[38]

Potential Risks   Both PCP and LSD can cause strong adverse reactions, including death. LSD users sometimes experience "bad trips," complete with monstrous perceptions, extreme delusions, and severe panic. Such reactions are common with high doses and impure batches of the drug, although they can occur for no apparent reason. In some people LSD can trigger serious depression, paranoia, and chronic psychoses. Even occasional users of LSD can experience **flashbacks**—brief, sudden perceptual distortions and bizarre thoughts that can occur as long as 5 years after the user's last experience with the drug.

flashbacks

PCP is a perplexing and alarming drug with conflicting properties. It can act not only as a deliriant but also as a stimulant, a depressant, and an analgesic. Its effects can vary from person to person and from one time to another in the same person. Low doses may produce a feeling of intoxication, euphoria, overall numbness, thought disorganization, slurring of speech, hostile and bizarre behavior, or any combination of these effects.[39] Somewhat larger doses may cause nausea and vomiting, fever, loss of muscle control, or coma. Still larger doses may lead to any of these conditions plus large increases in blood pressure and heart rate, psychotic behavior (including violence), convulsions, and coma. PCP has been known to cause a psychosis similar to schizophrenia and occasionally an inability to move.[40]

Designer Drugs

A new class of drugs called *designer drugs* began to appear during the 1980s. These substances were created in underground labs with slight variations from controlled drugs, so that they mimicked the effects of those drugs. However, mistakes were sometimes made with serious consequences, such as the development of a Parkinson's-like condition. These drugs are illegal, due to a law passed by the U.S. Congress in 1986.

Dealing with Drug Use and Abuse

Many drugs can and do save lives and improve human health. Some people, however, use drugs to solve life's problems, and in this way, drugs become a problem. Substances, both legal and illegal, that can ease pain, reduce tension, or make life seem more pleasant may quickly turn a person's life into a nightmare of physical illness, psychic or physical dependence, or both.

Drugs themselves are only one factor in the agent-host-environmental model. The individual (the host) and the setting (environment) are also significant factors that must be considered. An individual's need for drugs can be tackled through treatment and rehabilitation. Environmental factors can be addressed through laws and social policy. The overall goal should be responsible drug use.

Dealing with People's Need for Drugs

Individuals must ultimately make their own decisions about drug use. The effectiveness of programs to treat dependence and abuse depends a great deal on these decisions and on the individual's willingness to kick the habit.

Treatment and Rehabilitation   For many drug users, treatment and rehabilitation are difficult tasks that require personal strength, conviction, and support from other individuals or groups.[41] Overcoming drug dependence can be one of the most difficult tasks a user ever faces, and some people do not succeed.[42]

There is little agreement about what constitutes success in treating drug dependence. Some people believe that recovery requires total abstinence. Others define recovery as using drugs in a controlled way or being able to function well without drugs.

People seeking help for drug dependence may be treated on an inpatient or outpatient basis, depending on the drugs used and the severity of the symptoms. In either case, the treatment may include participation in self-help groups such as Narcotics Anonymous. It may also involve individual or group counseling and may include the user's family.[43]

People whose drug abuse is fairly recent or who are not greatly dependent on drugs are often treated on an outpatient basis. Drug users with a serious dependence are more likely to be treated on an inpatient basis, which involves spending a period of time in a treatment center. Some inpatients require *detoxification* gradual **detoxification,** or medically supervised withdrawal from drugs. Sudden withdrawal from some drugs, including heroin and alcohol, can be dangerous, and so the treatment may include carefully monitored doses of the drug to help wean the patient from physical dependence. For heroin users, this may include the use of **methadone,** a synthetic drug that removes the desire for heroin and produces tolerance to its effects. Methadone, however, produces its own physical dependence, although without the serious side effects of heroin.

People who seek treatment for drug dependence often have other serious physiological, psychological, or social problems as well.[44] Some experts estimate that up to one-third of people dependent on drugs have psychiatric or personality disorders.

Some drug users also face the problem of multiple drug dependence; this is becoming the norm among people enrolled in treatment programs.[45] As a result, the trend is toward more general treatment of "substance abuse" rather than treatment for the abuse of a specific drug.[46]

Finding Alternatives to Drug Use   There are other ways to obtain relief from anxiety, become more alert, feel excitement, and experience some of the effects offered by psychoactive drugs.

The use of psychoactive drugs usually masks the symptoms of a problem without really solving it or provides only a short-term solution. A stimulant may help a person feel more energetic, but a lack of energy may stem from inadequate diet or insufficient sleep.

There are a number of alternatives to drug use that a person might consider. Stress-reducing methods can help relieve anxiety; psychotherapy and counseling can help with emotional problems; and vigorous exercise can provide a natural high. Since people turn to drugs for a variety of reasons, each person needs to discover alternatives that will meet his or her individual preferences and needs.

Societal Solutions to Drug Abuse

Although individuals must ultimately make their own decisions about drug use, the government and society must assume some responsibility for controlling the use of drugs and preventing abuse and addiction. Laws and societal attitudes are important environmental factors that have an impact on the availability and acceptability of drugs.

The greatest drug problem in recent years has been the marketing and use of illegal psychoactive drugs. Not only are these drugs ruining the lives of millions of Americans, they are also at the root of increasing rates of drug-related crimes. The federal, state, and local agencies responsible for enforcing laws against the possession and sale of these substances have stepped up their activities in recent years in response to the growing problem.

Law enforcement efforts are aimed at cutting off the supply of drugs and prosecuting those involved in illegal drug possession and trafficking. Although these efforts have had some notable successes, many experts feel that the real solution to the nation's drug problem lies in reducing the demand for drugs rather than cutting off the supply.

One aspect of reducing the demand for drugs is identifying drug users and making available to them opportunities for dealing with their drug use. Perhaps a more crucial component in reducing demand is education. Educating people about the dangers of drugs, why people use drugs, ways to avoid drug abuse, and ways to get help with drug abuse problems can reduce the demand for drugs and lead to healthier individuals and a healthier, safer society.

Exercise is a healthy alternative to drugs. People who maintain a regular exercise regimen are likely to live happier, healthier lives. (Robert Brenner/PhotoEdit)

Chapter Summary

- People use drugs for a variety of reasons, including to relieve pain and discomfort, escape boredom, escape problems, experience pleasure, and enhance performance.

- Prescription drugs are used to relieve symptoms, prevent illness, control chronic conditions, and treat disease.

- With tolerance, the body becomes adapted to a drug so that larger doses are needed to produce the desired effect. Dependence is a condition in which a person becomes so accustomed to a drug that he or she is unable to function without it. Addiction refers to compulsive use of a drug, including tolerance and psychic and physical dependence.

- The major levels of drug use, which affect the likelihood of dependence, are experimental use, recreational use, situational use, intensified use, and compulsive use.

- The agent-host-environment model views drug dependence as more than just an individual problem. Other factors also play an important role in drug use and dependence.

- Drugs produce a wide range of effects on the body. Basically, a drug acts only on cells that are compatible with chemical substances in that drug. Drugs can also produce side effects that are unrelated to their purpose. These side effects can be potentially hazardous.

- Drugs are administered orally, by injection, and by inhalation. The method of administration can be a determining factor in the effect of a drug.

- Effective dose is the standard that physicians use to determine the proper doses of a drug for individuals. This dose differs from one drug to another and from one person to another.

- Drug interactions are a serious and often unpredictable risk of drug use. Because of these interactions, one drug may block the effects of another, heighten potential side effects, or increase the effects of the drugs taken.

- The major categories of psychoactive drugs are sedatives/hypnotics (barbiturates and antianxiety drugs), stimulants (caffeine, amphetamines, and cocaine), marijuana, volatile solvents and other inhalants such as nitrous oxide and amyl nitrite, opiate narcotics (heroin, opium, and morphine), and psychedelics/hallucinogens (LSD, mescaline, psilocybin, and PCP). Each category of drugs entails potentially serious risks.

- Individuals who want to overcome a drug habit can seek help through outpatient or inpatient treatment. People can also seek alternatives to drug use, such as improvement in diet, exercise, social life, and emotional health.

- Societal responsibility for drug use and abuse includes laws to curb illegal drug use and distribution and educational efforts to teach people about the dangers of drugs.

13

Alcohol and Tobacco

Objectives

When you have studied this chapter, you should be able to:

- Explain alcohol's effects on the body and the factors which lead to alcohol dependence.

- Describe alcoholism, listing steps in its development and identifying signs of its presence.

- Discuss some of the major health consequences of alcohol abuse.

- Indicate the ways that you can guard against the development of alcoholism and the types of treatment available for problem drinkers.

- List the major substances found in tobacco and tobacco smoke and explain the effects of these substances on the body.

- Identify several major diseases associated with tobacco use and discuss the health risks involved.

- Discuss the factors that influence tobacco use and explain how tobacco can lead to dependence.

- Identify and describe several different types of programs aimed at helping people give up smoking.

Both alcohol and tobacco have played important, and in some ways disastrous, roles in the development of American society. Introduced to the country by early European settlers, the drinking of alcohol has been a popular American pastime ever since. From the beginning, its use has been associated with problems—from its role in the decline of various Native American cultures, to the violence and crime that accompanied its ban during the era of Prohibition (and which are sometimes linked to its use today), to its role in annual motor vehicle fatalities and its links to several serious health problems.

Tobacco has also had a long history in this country. Introduced to European explorers and settlers of North America by Native Americans, tobacco played an important role in early trade and commerce between America and Europe, ensuring the success of the American colonies and later the new nation of the United States. From the beginning, the use of tobacco also became a significant part of the American lifestyle. Unlike alcohol, however, which has been associated with certain problems from the start, tobacco was thought to be quite safe until only fairly recently. In recent years it has been shown to be a significant factor in several major health problems, most notably cancer and cardiovascular and lung disease.

Armed with information about the use of alcohol and tobacco and their harmful effects, individuals will be better able to determine what changes they should make in their attitudes and behaviors to ensure that these substances do not become a problem in their own lives. The first part of this chapter focuses on alcohol, and the second part on tobacco.

Alcohol Use and Its Effects on the Body

Because alcoholic beverages are so accepted and so common in our society, many people do not think of them as harmful substances. In reality, however, alcohol, especially when consumed in excess, carries a great risk for the health and well-being of people who use it and for other people around them.

Despite growing public awareness about the dangers, many Americans continue to drink excessively. It is estimated that between 9 and 10 million Americans are either alcoholics or problem drinkers.[1] A first step in saving oneself from a similar fate is to understand what alcohol does.

How Alcohol Works on the Body

Alcohol takes a rather direct route into an individual's system. After it is consumed, alcohol travels to the stomach and small intestine. From there it is absorbed directly into the bloodstream and distributed throughout the body. Its absorption can be quite rapid, especially on an empty stomach. Since the stomach can absorb fully one-fourth of the total dose (the rest is absorbed in the small intestine), when an alcoholic drink is taken on an empty stomach the maximum level of alcohol in the blood can be reached in as short a time as 30 minutes (Figure 13.1).

Dose Levels and Time Factors As the blood races through the body, the alcohol travels with it and is distributed fairly uniformly throughout the body tissues and fluids. The more the individual drinks, the more his or her entire body becomes saturated with alcohol, and the more its effects will be felt.

ethyl alcohol About 10 percent of absorbed **ethyl alcohol** (the active ingredient in alcoholic beverages) is eliminated unmetabolized through the kidneys, lungs, and

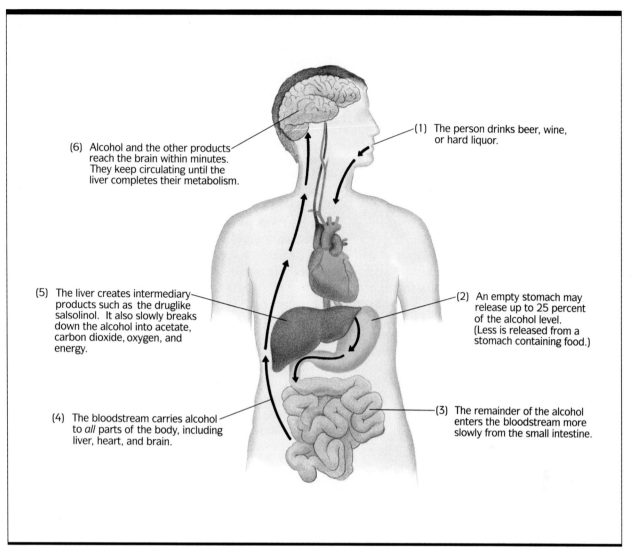

(1) The person drinks beer, wine, or hard liquor.

(6) Alcohol and the other products reach the brain within minutes. They keep circulating until the liver completes their metabolism.

(5) The liver creates intermediary products such as the druglike salsolinol. It also slowly breaks down the alcohol into acetate, carbon dioxide, oxygen, and energy.

(2) An empty stomach may release up to 25 percent of the alcohol level. (Less is released from a stomach containing food.)

(4) The bloodstream carries alcohol to *all* parts of the body, including liver, heart, and brain.

(3) The remainder of the alcohol enters the bloodstream more slowly from the small intestine.

Figure 13.1 *Alcohol enters a person's bloodstream through the stomach and small intestine. While it circulates through the bloodstream it affects a wide range of cells. These effects only wear off as the liver metabolizes the alcohol (at a rate of about 2/3 ounce per hour).*

Source: Scholastic Science World 39, no. 1 (September 3, 1982): 2.

sweat glands. The rest of the absorbed ethyl alcohol is metabolized by the liver to form a highly toxic substance.

The metabolism of alcohol occurs at a fairly constant rate. Depending on the individual, the liver metabolizes about 2/3 to 3/4 ounce of pure ethyl alcohol, or ethanol, per hour. If consumption exceeds this rate, alcohol levels in the bloodstream will rise. Since the brain is seriously affected by alcohol, judgment and motor activity are increasingly impaired as more is consumed.

The effects of alcohol vary from person to person depending on an individual's **blood alcohol level (BAL),** that is, the amount of alcohol that is in the blood at any one time. And the BAL can fluctuate depending on body weight, stress, the contents of the stomach, and other factors. For example, if an indi-

blood alcohol level (BAL)

vidual is drinking a lot of alcoholic beverages quickly and not eating, the alcohol will get into the bloodstream rapidly.

The amount of alcohol a large person can drink with little effect could cause intoxication in a smaller person. There are good reasons for the differences. A smaller, lighter person, with a correspondingly lower volume of blood and a smaller liver, would have a higher alcohol level in the blood that flows to the liver and possibly a higher level in the blood that leaves the liver too. Gender can make a difference as well. Males and females of the same weight have different levels of blood volume. The blood alcohol level also depends on how quickly the alcohol is *removed* from the body. This can vary according to a person's nutritional status, drinking history, and even the time of day he or she drinks.

Effects on the Central Nervous System   Alcohol is an anesthetic, a sedative, and a depressant. It is often valued at parties and other social occasions as a stimulant because its sedating action on the brain reduces social inhibitions. If enough alcohol is consumed, the result will be an easily measurable effect—a loss of motor coordination. The person will stagger, slur speech, and drop or spill things. An intoxicated person's vision may also be seriously affected by the alcohol, making it impossible to drive safely. Even small amounts of alcohol can make a drinker relatively blind in the face of bright lights at night and thus a serious hazard on the road.

The hangover that follows a few hours' intoxication is usually considered a state of mild withdrawal from alcohol. The sensations are caused, in part, by the drinker's allergic reaction to certain substances found in the drinks. But part of the hangover pain may also be caused by nerve cells in the brain, which become dehydrated by the alcohol. The severity of a hangover is related both to the amount and duration of the drinking and to the physical and mental condition of the drinker. Despite what has sometimes been written, there is no cure for a hangover except time. However, rest, the use of aspirin, and the intake of nonalcoholic liquids and solid food will help to relieve the symptoms.

One of the hidden problems with alcohol—as with other depressant drugs—is that while the user gets an initial "glow" of relaxation, an underlying feeling of edginess and agitation also builds up at the same time. This increased brain arousal lasts longer than the feeling of relaxed well-being, and it makes the user want another drink to calm down again. That next drink will have its own "edge," possibly setting in motion a vicious circle. Most drinkers simply stop after the second or third drink, so the buildup of brain arousal does not present a problem. But this feature of alcohol's effects may be a factor in alcoholism, discussed more fully later in the chapter.

Factors That Influence Alcohol Use

Despite its increasingly publicized potential for harming health and causing other problems, the use of alcohol remains widespread. People often continue using alcohol even when stopping could improve their physical, social, and emotional health. Alcohol's continued popularity rests on a complex web of physiological, psychological, and social factors.

Physical Addiction   One reason people continue to use alcohol is that they became addicted. Ethyl alcohol is a drug. As with other drugs, users can develop tolerance and become physically dependent. A person who develops a tolerance to alcohol must consume more and more to achieve the same effects.

Not everyone who develops a tolerance to alcohol develops a physical dependence on it. But it is not unusual for a person with a high tolerance also to have a physical need for alcohol, a chemical dependence that becomes evident when the person stops drinking. In such individuals an abrupt end to drinking will produce painful withdrawal symptoms—ranging from delirium tremens (often called the DTs or the "shakes") to seizures, hallucinations, and other signs of intense disturbance of the central nervous system.

Psychological Dependence   Many people become psychologically or emotionally dependent on alcohol even if they do not develop physical addictions. For example, since alcohol can help a person relax, some people come to depend on alcohol to relieve tension and anxiety rather than take other steps to relieve them. The alcohol makes people feel better without their having to expend any effort. This, in turn, reinforces the apparent value of alcohol for relieving unpleasant mood states. Over time, behavior patterns involving drinking become very familiar and comfortable and are quite difficult to change.

Social Pressures   Peer pressure and other social pressures also influence people to use alcohol. Many social events—parties, dining with friends, socializing at bars, and so on—may involve alcohol consumption. People who are drinking frequently urge others to join them. Although each person has the option of drinking or abstaining, social pressures to drink are often so strong that, for many individuals, it seems as if there is no choice.

When alcohol has entered the bloodstream, it affects vision and physical coordination in ways that are easily detected. (Van Bucher/Photo Researchers, Inc.)

Alcohol – Present Dangers and Long-Term Problems

A single bout of drinking may cause nothing more harmful than vomiting, a loss of coordination, or other unpleasant physical effects. These effects discourage most people from abusing alcohol. This is fortunate, because chronic heavy drinking can permanently damage the body. Even the occasional abuse of alcohol can have serious consequences for the people who drink, for those around them, and for the society as a whole.

Alcohol and Destructive Behavior

For some people, alcohol abuse can lead to a variety of destructive behaviors including the risk of injury from accidents, violence, and criminal behaviors. Such problems do not have to arise from alcohol dependency or addiction. They can be the result of any degree of alcohol use—from occasional drunkenness to chronic abuse.

Alcohol and Accidents   Drunkenness to the point that it endangers the drinker or others is not limited to people locked up in jail. In fact, most intoxication today occurs among men and women who live with their families, hold jobs, and maintain stable community ties. With alcohol such a widely used drug, most of these people have learned to mask the obvious signs of drunkenness.

Routine drinking has become more dangerous as life has become faster-paced and more technological. More and more jobs, such as jobs where the individual is required to operate machine tools, require exacting skill and judgment. Most people cannot avoid these everyday activities that are made impossible or at least extremely difficult by excessive drinking. Alcohol use can lead to serious accidents at work, as well as in the home or at play.

The most vivid evidence of the dangers of alcohol is the daily toll of men, women, and children on the nation's highways in alcohol-related accidents. Accidents are the fourth leading cause of deaths in the United States. Motor vehicle accidents account for over half of all these, and they are the highest cause of death among people younger than age 34.[2] Intoxicated drivers injure other people as well. One-third of all people who suffered the loss of arms or legs or other injuries can blame intoxicated drivers for their disability.[3]

In most states, a blood alcohol level of 0.10 percent defines legal drunkenness, and it is this figure that is usually used to determine if a person was driving while intoxicated. However, new evidence accumulated by the American Medical Association reveals that almost any measurable blood alcohol concentration interferes with the sharp judgment, coordination, vision, and reaction time necessary for safe driving.[4] Young drivers involved in car accidents are often found to have blood alcohol levels that are quite low, prompting some experts to suggest that even one drink is too much if a person intends to operate a motor vehicle.[5]

Alcohol and Violence While mild doses of alcohol may help people feel less inhibited, drinking does not generally promote social behavior. Quite often, drinkers act in antisocial and sometimes even violent ways.

It is generally agreed that alcohol plays a critical role in violent acts and criminal activity. Alcohol has been consistently correlated with a variety of actions, including disturbing the peace, robbery, rape, assault, and murder. One study of homicides, for example, revealed that alcohol had been used by the victim or the perpetrator, or both, in nearly two-thirds of the cases.[6] Overall, problem drinkers have higher incidence of criminal behavior than does the general population.

Alcoholism

While occasional drinking may itself be detrimental to the health and well-being of individuals and society, chronic, excessive drinking is an even more serious health threat. Drinking excessively to the point of damaging the body or seriously disrupting one's life is symptomatic of an underlying disease known as *alcoholism.* For someone with alcoholism, drinking may lead to physical or mental disorders, such as pancreatitis, malnutrition, anemia, cancer, depression, and psychosis.[7]

The Alcohol Continuum Alcoholism is a chronic disease characterized by preoccupation with alcohol and a loss of control over its consumption. With alcoholism, an individual becomes dependent on alcohol in a manner similar to other types of drug dependencies. Alcoholism is a progressive disease that develops as a series of stages through which any drinker may pass. At one end of the spectrum is occasional and moderate social drinking with family or friends on special occasions. At the other end is long-term, frequent, uncontrollable drinking with severe physical, psychological, and social complications. The full continuum can be summarized as follows:[8]

1. **Occasional drinker** drinks in small quantities only on special occasions to be sociable.
2. **Light drinker** drinks regularly in small and nonintoxicating quantities.
3. **Social drinker** drinks regularly in moderate and nonintoxicating quantities.
4. **Problem drinker** drinks to intoxication with no pattern to episodes, gets drunk without intending to or realizing it.
5. **Binge drinker** drinks heavily in recurrent episodes, often brought on by disturbances in work, home, or social life.
6. **Excessive drinker** experiences frequent episodes of uncontrollable drinking affecting work, family, and social relationships.
7. **Chronic alcoholic** is in serious trouble from long-term, frequent, and uncontrollable drinking; experiences physical complications including organic dysfunction, tolerance, and dependence; and develops severe work, home, and social problems.

As a person moves along the continuum toward chronic alcoholism, certain characteristics begin to emerge, including:

- The person drinks to achieve specific effects, such as reduced anxiety, guilt, boredom, tension, or depression.
- The person undergoes drastic personality and mood changes, such as weeping, picking fights, becoming sexually aggressive.
- Others notice and remark on the person's drinking habits; the person's friendships and family life change.
- The person experiences hangovers, stomach trouble, or blackouts. (A *blackout* is an episode of temporary amnesia, in which the drinker continues to function but later cannot remember what happened. This is not the same thing as "passing out" when drunk.)

Signs of Alcoholism The diagnosis of alcoholism is not something that can be precise, and it is often difficult for nonprofessionals to make. The disease carries such a stigma that the alcoholic, friends, and family often postpone seeking treatment. Meanwhile, it is not unusual for the alcoholic to deny the problem and rationalize continued drinking. Yet if the problem can be pinpointed and dealt with early, years of anguish can be saved for all concerned. Certain changes in behavior that warn of possible alcoholism include:[9]

- Surreptitious, secretive drinking
- Morning drinking (unless that behavior is not unusual in the person's peer group)
- Repeated, conscious attempts at abstinence
- Blatant, indiscriminate use of alcohol
- Changing beverages in an attempt to control drinking
- Having five or more drinks daily
- Having two or more blackouts while drinking

From left to right this picture shows: a normal liver; a fatty liver, which can indicate that cirrhosis is beginning; and a fully cirrhotic liver, with the liver swollen and scarred by excessive alcohol consumption. (A. Glauberman/Photo Researchers, Inc.)

Causes of Alcoholism   Most authorities now agree that alcoholism stems from a number of interrelated factors, ranging from family life to peer pressure to emotional upheavals. The significance of these factors may vary from person to person in determining whether that person will become an alcoholic.

Alcoholism definitely runs in families. Studies in the United States and Europe show that about 50 percent of the fathers, brothers, and sons of hospitalized alcoholics are also likely to become alcoholics. Yet researchers remain uncertain as to whether the family environment, heredity, or a combination of the two determines whether a person will develop alcoholism.[10]

A number of psychological traits have been closely associated with alcoholics. These drinkers tend to have more psychological problems than others, including deep-seated feelings of inadequacy, anxiety, and depression. Researchers also see drinking as a learned behavior that is reinforced by repetition. A person learns to take a drink to relax, for example, and then repeats the behavior in stressful situations until a pattern of heavy drinking has developed.[11]

Alcoholism in America   As many as 10 million American adults and 3 million children and adolescents are afflicted with alcoholism. All types of people can develop the disease, although genetic and environmental factors may make some people especially susceptible to it. For example, studies reveal that the incidence of alcoholism is higher for men than for women, although the number of female alcoholics is on the rise. The reason for this increase may be due, in part, to the fact that American women are increasingly adopting work and health-related behaviors more traditionally typical of men. As a result, they are experiencing similar problems and stresses that could contribute to alcoholism. The incidence of alcoholism also differs among religions and ethnic groups. Among Moslems and Mormons, whose religions forbid the use of alcohol, alcoholism is uncommon. Italians and Jews have relatively low rates of alcoholism, although the consumption of alcohol is an accepted practice among both groups. No group, however, is immune from alcoholism. It affects the very old as well as the very young. It affects people at all levels of education, in all occupational fields, and in all socioeconomic strata.[12]

Health Consequences of Alcohol Abuse

Chronic alcohol abuse is linked with many serious health problems that can destroy the body's most important organs and sometimes result in death.[13] Among the problems linked to alcohol abuse are gastrointestinal disorders, liver damage, cardiovascular disease, glandular disorders, damage to the central nervous system, and malnutrition. While chronic alcohol abuse can harm the health of the person who drinks, less excessive alcohol use by pregnant women is associated with birth defects and problems in pregnancy.

Gastrointestinal Disorders   Alcohol stimulates secretion of digestive acid throughout the gastrointestinal system, irritating the linings of the drinker's stomach, esophagus, and intestines. It is not unusual for alcoholics to develop bleeding ulcers in their stomachs and intestines and lesions in the esophagus. Alcohol can give "binge drinkers" diarrhea. It may inhibit the pancreas's production of enzymes that are crucial for the digestion of food. When heavily *pancreatitis* abused, alcohol can also lead to **pancreatitis** (inflammation of the pancreas).

Liver Damage   The liver is one of the organs most vulnerable to alcohol abuse. As much as 80 percent of liver disease deaths are alcohol-related.[14] Alcohol changes the way the liver processes important substances. It can also contribute to infections and other disorders. If the liver is disturbed or infected, the body's immune system and ability to flush out poisons are affected. Damage to the liver can also harm other organs because the liver is essential to the production and modification of many substances the body needs, such as a vast array of nutrients necessary for the building, maintenance, and repair of tissues.

Many alcoholics suffer **cirrhosis of the liver,** a chronic inflammatory disease in which healthy liver cells are replaced by scar tissue. Cirrhosis is a leading cause of death among heavy drinkers. Drinking can also cause **alcoholic hepatitis,** in which the liver becomes swollen and inflamed.

cirrhosis of the liver

alcoholic hepatitis

Cardiovascular Disease   There is debate in the medical community about whether small amounts of alcohol, such as one drink a day, may actually lower the rates of some heart diseases. There is no question, however, that *excessive* drinking takes a toll on the heart and circulatory system, even causing heart failure in some cases.

Moderate amounts of alcohol can affect the cardiovascular system by altering the heart rate and dilating blood vessels near the skin, which gives the drinker the illusion of feeling warmer. The truth is, however, that the person is actually losing heat from the body *more* rapidly than when alcohol is not present in the bloodstream. Drinking while exposed to cold for long periods of time can reduce a person's resistance to the common cold or even pneumonia.

Glandular (Endocrine) Disorders   Excessive drinking can damage the body's glandular system, which regulates such important functions as moods and sexuality. For example, men who drink too much may suffer impotence and reduced levels of the hormone testosterone. Women may also throw their hormonal systems out of balance through heavy drinking.

Central Nervous System Damage   Alcohol's most visible and measurable short-term effects are on the central nervous system. Even small amounts of alcohol can change the user's emotional state and physical behavior. Prolonged abuse can have even more damaging and sometimes permanent effects on the central nervous system. Recovering alcoholics have been found to have difficulty with memory, motor skills, and perception. A number of studies have estimated that 50 to 70 percent of alcoholics who seek treatment suffer problems with the central nervous system. Alcohol has literally killed some of their brain cells.

Alcohol abuse is also associated with severe emotional problems. Alcoholics consistently score higher on items measuring depression in psychological tests. And, according to some studies, the risk of suicide among alcoholics runs thirty times higher than in the general population.

Malnutrition   A common myth holds that alcohol, since it is made from fruit or grain, is food. It is not. Alcohol actually starves the body of essential nutrients. It does consist of calories, and so it produces energy. However, it contains none of the chemical substances the body needs to build and repair tissue. Alcohol abuse has been reported as the most common cause of vitamin

The effects of fetal alcohol syndrome continue long after birth, affecting a person's facial appearance, physical growth, and mental skills. (March of Dimes, Birth Defects Foundation)

deficiency in America. An alcoholic may undereat or, because the digestive system is disrupted, may be unable to process properly the nutrients that are eaten. Alcoholics may also suffer nutritional imbalances because of the diarrhea, loss of appetite, and vomiting that often accompany heavy drinking. In short, alcoholism can be a form of slow starvation.

Birth Defects   Even mild drinking by a pregnant woman can produce adverse effects on a fetus. Heavy drinking can cause fetal alcohol syndrome (FAS). Fetal alcohol syndrome consists of three main features—mental retardation; slow growth before and after birth; and a wide range of physical defects, ranging from cleft palate to hip dislocation. Mild to moderate mental retardation is characteristic of the syndrome. In fact, some researchers suggest that maternal alcoholism is the third leading cause of mental retardation in the United States.[15] The physical defects in babies born to alcoholic mothers are believed to be caused by a depletion of zinc in the mother's body, a depletion caused by alcohol.[16]

Some studies show that 74 percent of the infants born to mothers who drink more than ten drinks a day have the syndrome. Alcoholic women are also more likely to abort or give birth to stillborn children.[17]

There is no known safe level of alcohol that a woman can consume during pregnancy. The surgeon general recommends that women who are pregnant or considering pregnancy drink *no* alcoholic beverages and be aware of the alcohol content of certain foods and medicines.[18]

Dealing with Alcohol Abuse

Considering the tremendous harm that alcohol can do, few people knowingly become dependent on it. Many, however, develop alcohol dependency before they are aware of the dangers. Although numerous programs are available for treating this dependency, none can guarantee success.

Perhaps the only certain means of avoiding a dependency on alcohol is not to drink at all. Most people who use alcohol, however, are able to drink safely. For people who already have problems with alcohol, help is available.

Using Alcohol Responsibly

If you choose to drink alcohol, you must learn to drink responsibly. Doing so will help you guard against losing control and becoming dependent on alcohol, and abusing alcohol is known to be dangerous even if you are not dependent on it, since alcohol abuse can threaten your safety or that of others.

There are several good rules to follow in regard to alcohol:

- Know how much alcohol you can handle and do not exceed this limit, even on special occasions.
- Avoid drinking daily or at other regular intervals. Such habits are more likely to lead to dependency.
- Choose drinks that are mixed with nonalcoholic beverages, such as fruit juice or water, instead of drinks that use two or more kinds of alcohol.
- Drink slowly. The faster you drink, the drunker you will get.
- Since food slows the absorption of alcohol, eat before you drink or while you are drinking.

- Accept a drink only if you really want one. When you have had enough, stop drinking and refuse offers for more.
- Most importantly, don't mix drinking and driving.

If your drinking seems to be getting out of hand, or if a friend suggests that you may have a drinking problem, seriously consider the situation. If you even suspect that you may have a problem with alcohol, get help. The sooner you act, the more likely you are to overcome the problem.

The Treatment of Alcoholism

Society has had a difficult time dealing with the issue of whether alcoholism is an illness or simply a weakness and failure of willpower. And if alcoholism is an illness, is it a physical illness or an emotional problem? Treatment has usually approached alcoholism as both a physical and emotional disorder, dealing first with its physical aspects and then with its emotional ones.

Detoxification and Counseling

Treatment for alcoholism is likely to start with **detoxification,** the process of weaning the person from physical dependence and repairing the effects of alcohol in the body. In the early stages of treatment, the alcoholic's nutritional needs must also be addressed—as must other health problems created by drinking. After detoxification and attention to the alcoholic's medical needs, many treatment programs provide counseling to address the drinker's psychological and social problems.

detoxification

Alcoholics Anonymous (AA), founded in the 1930s, is among the most successful of treatment programs. AA members start by admitting that they have lost control over alcohol. They are then encouraged to think about the spiritual dimension of their lives and consider the idea that there is some power higher than themselves. Then they look closely at themselves, considering where alcohol has led them and what the future might hold.

Throughout the program, individuals receive support from fellow AA members, and eventually they themselves will work to help others through the process. AA's combination of group support, behavior modification, and spiritually oriented thinking has helped many alcoholics recover.

Developing Positive Alternatives to Alcohol Use

Alcohol problems can be prevented by taking responsibility for your drinking behavior *before* your judgment is impaired. Although the effects of alcohol are unpredictable, the fact is that even moderate amounts of alcohol may affect parts of the brain that control inhibitions, judgments, and feelings. The choices and decisions people make can be influenced by these alcohol-induced changes.

It is important to establish your own rules and limits for the use of alcohol and to respect an individual's decision not to drink alcohol. For example, if you are hosting a party, you might limit the amount of alcohol available or limit the time during which alcohol is served. Plan to serve nonalcoholic beverages as well as alcohol.

Finding Your Comfort Level with Alcohol

Social drinking is widely accepted in the United States; yet alcohol abuse is recognized as a major problem. Not only does abuse lead to violence and accidents; it can also lead to a crippling dependence on alcohol. But how can you tell if you abuse alcohol?

One measure of whether a person is drinking an acceptable amount is whether that person is free of any of the problems that result from drinking. If you are arrested for drunken driving, for example, or if hangovers are affecting your performance in school or on the job, you have been drinking abusively, not responsibly. A responsible social drinker is able to drink in a way that does not result in such problems.

Some experts on alcoholism define social drinking by the amount of alcohol the drinker consumes, but opinions differ as to what amounts are safe. The National Institute on Alcohol Abuse and Alcoholism (NIAAA) says that anyone who consumes at least five drinks on at least one occasion per week is a frequent, heavy drinker, not a social drinker. But other groups give different limits. A recent study concluded that daily consumption of five shots of liquor, three glasses of wine, or four cans of beer will have no harmful effects on someone who weighs 154 pounds (but nevertheless the person might not be sober enough to drive). Another study put the alcoholism cutoff point at four drinks per occasion—as long as the drinker partakes only three days per week.

People clearly differ both in their tolerance for alcohol and in their definition of what constitutes a problem. Everyone would be wise to think carefully about the issue, to be cautious with alcohol, and if they do intend to drink to establish a comfort level which they feel will enhance both their health and their lives. Questions to ask include the circumstances under which you drink and your reasons for using alcohol. As a rule, a social drinker consumes small amounts of alcohol in safe situations. Having a few beers with friends while watching a ball game may be "social." However, it ceases to be social if the drinking becomes more important than the game or the friends. It is also not social when it involves significant physical or social risk—drinking more than a minimal amount when you will be driving, for example.

You are not drinking socially when you

- Drink to steady your nerves
- Drink to resolve problems
- Understate the amount that you drink
- Drink when alcohol is likely to harm you
- Drink to the point of intoxication even though doing something that you know requires sober attention, such as driving.
- Do something while drinking that you would never have done while sober

Anyone who drinks may abuse alcohol on an isolated occasion, especially someone who is new to drinking and has not yet learned how much alcohol she or he can tolerate. A healthy response to such an episode is to drink more carefully so that it does not recur. However, some people have genetic backgrounds that may render them incapable of this response. People with alcoholic parents, for example, are far more likely than other people to develop alcoholism.

If your drinking ever results in a problem, drink less. If you continue to drink too much despite your efforts, you may be developing a dependency on alcohol and should seek counseling. If you can drink small amounts in safe circumstances, you may be able to enjoy a healthy life as a social drinker.

Based on V. M. Jackson et al., "Measurements of Social Drinking: The Need for Specific Guidelines," *Health Values* (January/February 1990): 25; Sandra Mull, "Help for the Children of Alcoholics," *Health Education* (September/October 1990): 42.

By developing positive alternatives to alcohol, you can make avoiding alcohol abuse easier for yourself and for others. The use of alcohol can be replaced by active pursuits such as walking, biking, tennis, or swimming; by quieter but still absorbing pursuits such as practicing a hobby or reading; and by using direct stress reduction techniques.

Tobacco Use and Its Effects on the Body

Unlike alcohol, which has ill effects that can be dramatic and immediate, tobacco's damage becomes apparent only after years of use. This makes it in many ways a more dangerous substance than alcohol. An estimated 390,000 deaths each year—one-fifth of all American deaths—have been attributed to smoking.[19]

How Tobacco Works on the Body

The chemical substance called **nicotine,** a toxic element found in tobacco, is responsible for much of the pleasure people experience while using tobacco. It causes a direct stimulation of the brain cells of the cerebral cortex, affecting brain chemistry and leading to feelings of increased alertness. It also causes muscle relaxation. And, perhaps most important, it has recently been positively identified as a pharmacologically addictive drug.[20]

nicotine

There are many other chemicals in tobacco which are toxic, causing lasting damage to the human body. And nicotine itself is responsible for many of the harmful effects linked to the use of tobacco.

When nicotine enters the body, it is absorbed into the bloodstream. One-fourth of it soon passes directly into the brain, where it causes the release of chemicals that stimulate the cardiovascular system.[21] As a result, the heart beats faster and blood pressure increases.

Meanwhile, the remainder of the nicotine in the bloodstream travels throughout the rest of the body, where it stimulates other nicotine receptor sites. Not only does nicotine stimulate the gastrointestinal tract, it also causes the adrenal gland to release hormones, which cause the body's fight-or-flight response. As a result, the heartbeat increases by 15 to 25 beats per minute, the pupils of the eyes dilate, and the blood vessels in the fingers and toes constrict.

Tobacco and Other Toxic Substances

In addition to the addictive drug nicotine, tobacco products contain a number of other toxic substances that can cause harm when they enter the body. Some of these substances are found in tobacco smoke, whereas others are found in tobacco itself.

Toxic Substances in Tobacco Smoke   When it burns, the average cigarette produces about 0.5 grams of smoke. To help determine what portions of tobacco smoke are responsible for the various diseases associated with cigarette smoking, chemists have broken down the smoke into its components. More than 80 major toxic substances have been identified in cigarette smoke.[22]

Of all the compounds in cigarette smoke, 92 percent are gaseous—and many of these are toxic. **Carbon monoxide,** one of the gases found in tobacco

carbon monoxide

The feeling of well-being that tobacco creates is greatly at variance with its actual effects on the body. (Margot Granitsas/The Image Works)

smoke, is considered to be one of the most hazardous. Carbon monoxide affects the human body in several ways, all of which are related to oxygen deprivation. Carbon monoxide impairs the blood's capacity to carry oxygen, causing serious problems for people suffering from cardiovascular diseases. Some researchers believe that carbon monoxide is partly responsible for the heightened risk of heart attack and stroke among cigarette smokers: it may be the *combination* of carbon monoxide and nicotine that is at fault.[23]

tar   The remaining 8 percent of tobacco smoke consists of solid (nongaseous) matter: ash, a tar-rich condensate, and a "wet particular matter" comprising hundreds of different substances. **Tar,** a sticky residue from burning tobacco, consists of more than 200 chemicals and can be separated into three parts: acidic, basic, and neutral.

benzopyrene   The neutral part of tar shows the highest carcinogenic, or cancer-causing, activity. It contains **benzopyrene,** one of the deadliest carcinogens known, and many other chemicals of the same family. The acidic part of the tarry condensate contains materials which may be carcinogenic themselves and which may activate "dormant" cancer cells so that they grow and spread. The basic part of tar contains the nicotine itself. It also contains other chemicals that are potent irritants to lung tissue and may play a role in such conditions as chronic bronchitis, chronic obstructive pulmonary disease, and emphysema.[24]

While nicotine affects the body primarily through the bloodstream, many of the other substances directly affect the body's respiratory system. The act of smoking impedes the respiratory system's ability to trap and eliminate air pollutants.[25] Normally, air pollutants are trapped in mucus secreted by membranes in the nasal cavity, trachea, and bronchi. These irritants are then either eliminated through the mouth or absorbed and eliminated by the lymphatic system. Both of these processes rely on the cilia, or fine hairs, that grow from cells lining the respiratory passages. The regular intake of smoke can flatten these cells, causing them to lose their cilia and produce excess mucus. This excess mucus may cause repeated cough reflexes—"smoker's cough"—that clear some of the mucus away. Or the mucus may stay where it is, blocking air passages and causing shortness of breath and wheezing (Figure 13.2).

Figure 13.2 *The lungs are a network of blood vessels and air passages, where oxygen from inhaled air is transferred to the blood through air sacs called* alveoli. *The air passages, or bronchial tubes, can become inflamed by tobacco smoke and narrowed by a defensive secretion of mucus. Normally mucus is transported from the lungs by tiny hairs called* cilia. *However, smoking can paralyze these, leaving the lungs with congestion (bronchitis) and reduced defenses against pollution and disease.*

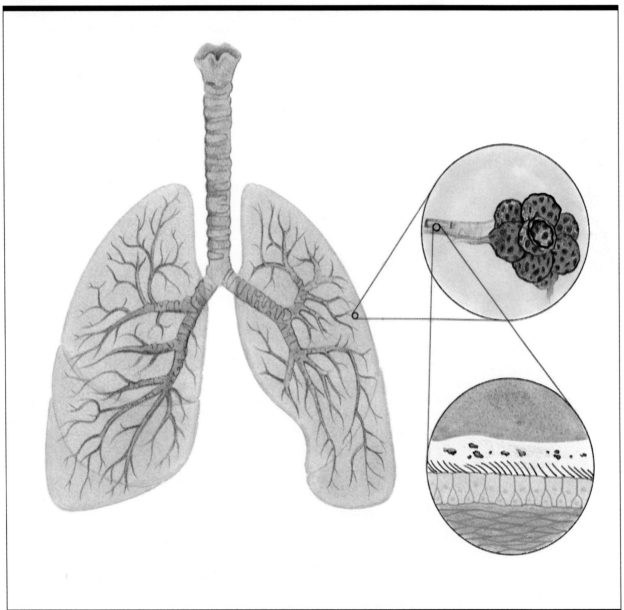

Toxic Substances in Smokeless Tobacco In addition to nicotine, the tobacco in snuff and chewing tobacco contains a number of potent chemicals. These include high concentrations of several chemicals known to be carcinogenic. In laboratory studies, animals exposed to some of these chemicals have been shown to develop an excess of a variety of cancerous tumors.[26] In humans, the use of chewing tobacco and snuff has been linked to cancer of the oral cavity, pharynx, larynx, and esophagus.[27]

Tobacco — Its Social and Health Consequences

As a result of the growing determination of health professionals and the growing public awareness about the dangers of tobacco, there has been a major shift in public attitude toward the smoking of tobacco. Smoking is less socially acceptable than it once was—and illegal in many public places. As a result, there has been a substantial decrease in the number of people who smoke. Today, about 29 percent of American adults smoke, compared with about 40 percent in 1965. And of some 50 million American men and women who still smoke, most have tried at least once to give up the habit.[28]

However, this means that there are still 50 million Americans who smoke cigarettes. And the recent decline in smoking has been accompanied by an increase in the use of smokeless tobacco (chewing tobacco and snuff), especially among young men. Smokeless tobacco users "dip" snuff or chew leaf tobacco. Snuff is a finely ground, moist tobacco that is usually placed between the lower lip and gum, where it is mixed with saliva and absorbed. Chewing tobacco is a rougher-cut tobacco that is placed between the cheek and gum, where the wad is sucked and occasionally chewed.

In 1986, an estimated 8.2 percent of males aged 17 to 19 were using smokeless tobacco. Some of this increase can be attributed to aggressive advertising campaigns. Despite evidence that these products can also cause deadly diseases, the number of people using smokeless tobacco products continues to increase.[29]

Tobacco and Major Diseases

Although a tobacco user is unlikely to notice any harmful effects from a single use of tobacco, any sustained use can lead to serious health problems. The facts about the relationship between tobacco and disease are grim, to say the least. About 35 percent of all smokers die prematurely as a result of their use of tobacco.[30] Smoking is associated with six of the ten leading causes of death.

The reduction in a person's life expectancy increases with the number of cigarettes smoked. For example, a man who smokes one pack a day loses 4.6 years of life expectancy; with two packs a day the time lost doubles. The earlier a person begins smoking, the more years of life are lost.

The range of diseases that are associated with tobacco use is wide. Smokers have been shown to have greatly increased risks of premature coronary heart disease, atherosclerosis, aortic aneurysms, cerebrovascular disease, chronic bronchitis and emphysema, asthma, gastric problems, and dental problems (including gingivitis, dental caries, and loss of teeth)—not to mention cancer of the oral cavity, esophagus, pancreas, larynx, lung, kidney, and bladder.

Although most of the research linking tobacco use to death and serious illness has focused on cigarette smoking, the studies that exist suggest that smokeless tobacco users often suffer consequences as well. These include decreased ability to taste and smell, gum and tooth devastation, high blood pressure, and cancer of the oral cavity and the esophagus.

Bronchitis and Emphysema   An earlier section of this chapter described how smoking can cause the cells of the respiratory system to flatten, causing them to produce excess mucus that can block air passages. If these cells are continuously assaulted as a result of chronic smoking, they can also become inflamed. This inflammation leads to chronic bronchitis, an inflammation of the mucous membranes that line the bronchial passages of the respiratory tract. Bronchitis is marked by coughing, spitting of saliva and mucus, and some difficulty in breathing.

Over time, chronic bronchitis may extend to other parts of the lungs and severely damage tissues. Breathing becomes more difficult as smooth muscle tissues enlarge and mucus becomes stuck in the passages. As a result, air is trapped in the air sacs in the lungs. The thin walls between the air sacs degenerate, which causes them to fuse and create enlarged air sacs. The resulting condition, in which air is taken in easily but is expelled only with great difficulty, is called emphysema, a potentially crippling condition that can result in death.

Cancer   The evidence linking smoking with various types of cancer is now overwhelming. According to the U.S. surgeon general, "Cigarette smoking is the major single cause of cancer mortality in the United States."[31] Of all cancer deaths, almost one-third can be linked to smoking.[32]

Even if an individual does not develop cancer after many years of smoking, the risks are still not eliminated. Death from lung diseases is six times more frequent among smokers. In addition, when an individual is exposed to tobacco and other carcinogens, the combined effect is greater than the effect of each on its own. For example, the risk of developing lung cancer increases sharply for those who smoke *and* work with asbestos. Blue-collar workers face the greatest danger, because they are the group that is most exposed to toxic agents *and* they also have the highest smoking rates, particularly among men.[33]

Once a rare disease, lung cancer is now considered to be an epidemic. In 1990 it was estimated to have killed 142,000 people. The American Cancer Society estimates that 83 percent of lung cancer is caused by smoking.[34]

The *way* an individual smokes affects the chances of developing lung cancer. The risk increases depending on how many cigarettes are smoked each day, how deeply the smoker inhales, and how much tar and nicotine are contained in the cigarettes smoked. People who started smoking early in their lives are also at greater risk than those who have only smoked for a few years.

If a person stops smoking, the chance of dying from lung cancer decreases. Over 10 to 15 years, the mortality rate drops steadily back to the nonsmoker's rate.[35]

Cardiovascular Disease   The risk of cardiovascular disease in cigarette smokers is one and one-half to two times greater than that of nonsmokers.[36] People who smoke and also have high blood pressure and/or a history of heart disease

WHY
START
A LIFE
UNDER
A CLOUD?

Smoking is harmful
to your baby's health.
Quit for both of you.
For help call your
American Cancer Society.

AMERICAN
CANCER
SOCIETY

Researchers have established a direct relationship between smoking during pregnancy and adverse effects on the health of the baby. (Courtesy American Cancer Society)

in their family are in an even higher risk category for having a heart attack at some time in their lives. The more they smoke, the greater the risk of having a heart attack—and at a younger age than nonsmokers. The risk of heart disease will decrease after a person quits smoking, and, as with lung cancer, declines steadily for 10 years after quitting to that of nonsmokers.[37] People who smoke also share a high risk of developing atherosclerosis, and those who have survived a heart attack face an increased possibility of suffering another one.

The combination of smoking and the use of birth control pills also increases the risk of cardiovascular disease. A woman who uses birth control pills and smokes as well is 10 times more likely to suffer a heart attack than a woman who neither smokes nor uses oral contraceptives.[38] According to the Food and Drug Administration, the risks increase further with age and with heavy smoking (15 or more cigarettes a day).[39]

Tobacco and the Lives of Others

The toxins in tobacco and tobacco smoke can harm the health not only of people who smoke, but of others as well. Children born to women who smoke during pregnancy are affected by it, and so are people of all ages who inhale tobacco smoke produced by others.

The Dangers of Tobacco Use during Pregnancy   A woman who smokes during pregnancy seriously endangers the health of her unborn child. Several large studies, involving tens of thousands of pregnancies, reveal that pregnant women who smoke have up to ten times as many miscarriages and stillbirths and two to three times as many premature babies as nonsmokers.[40]

Furthermore, babies born to women who smoke during pregnancy are, on average, nearly one-half pound lighter than babies born to nonsmokers.[41] The importance of birth weight cannot be overstated. A newborn's weight is an important index of mortality risk. The lower the weight, the greater the risk of death. While the minimum weight for a healthy newborn is 2,500 grams (5½ pounds), among the infants of mothers who smoke, twice as many weigh less than 2,500 grams at birth as do babies of nonsmoking mothers.

The effects of tobacco do not end when a baby leaves the hospital. Studies have found that smoking during pregnancy may affect the growth, mental development, and behavior of children at least up to the age of 11.[42] In one study, children were examined at birth and then at 7 and 11 years of age. In reading and math, the offspring of women who smoked at least ten cigarettes daily during pregnancy lagged an average of 3 to 5 months behind children born to nonsmokers.[43]

Because of the potential damage to children, both at birth and during their later development, it is recommended that all women stop smoking during pregnancy.

Passive Smoking and the Rights of Nonsmokers   Reports from the U.S. surgeon general's office suggest that tobacco smoke in enclosed indoor areas is an important air pollution problem. This has led to the controversy about *passive smoking* **passive smoking**—the breathing in of air polluted by the second-hand tobacco smoke of others. Carbon monoxide levels of sidestream smoke (smoke from the burning end of a cigarette) reach a dangerously high level. True, the smoke can be greatly diluted in freely circulating air, but the 1 to 5 percent carbon monoxide levels attained in smoke-filled rooms can be sufficient to harm the health of people with chronic bronchitis, other lung disease, or cardiovascular disease.[44]

Nicotine also builds up in the blood of nonsmokers exposed to cigarette smoke hour after hour. It has been estimated that passive smoking can give nonsmokers the equivalent in carbon monoxide and nicotine of one to ten cigarettes per day.[45]

Passive smoking has also been shown to be harmful to the children of smokers. Children whose parents smoke have a higher incidence of respiratory problems, such as bronchitis and pneumonia, than do children whose parents do not smoke. The effects of such problems may last a lifetime. Studies show that respiratory problems in adulthood may be related to early childhood respiratory conditions influenced by parental smoking.[46]

Nonsmokers are increasingly successful in campaigns for protection against passive smoking. In recent years, several cities have adopted laws that limit or ban smoking in enclosed public spaces such as restaurants. Many employers, too, have banned smoking in workplaces or have restricted it to designated areas. Moreover, smoking is now entirely forbidden on many airline flights.

Factors That Influence Tobacco Use

Despite the increasing opposition to smoking by nonsmokers, and despite the risks, many of which have been widely publicized, smokers continue to light up and tobacco use remains widespread. People addicted to nicotine have been known to continue using tobacco even while undergoing treatment for lung cancer or emphysema. As with alcohol, people appear to do this for a variety of reasons—social as well as physical and psychological.

Social Pressures   Certainly, people start smoking as a result of social pressures. New smokers are often led into smoking through direct peer pressure. Adults are influenced at work or social gatherings, as evidenced by the fact that people tend to adopt their boss's cigarette brand or the brand favored by their circle of friends. One study, for example, found that 68 percent of young female smokers had boyfriends or husbands who smoke.

For adolescents, of course, social pressure takes on another dimension. Children see many adults smoking, and yet it is illegal for them. This makes cigarettes a forbidden fruit and smoking seem like a rite of passage to adulthood. Smoking behind the barn and in the lavatory at school have been standard images of rebellious initiation throughout this century. Many smokers began their habit in this way, succumbing to social pressures from friends.

Tobacco and Physiological Dependence   One sign that nicotine is addictive is that it can produce a tolerance in the smoker, who must consume more and more to achieve the same effects. For example, people who smoke to relieve stress must gradually increase their daily intake to continue experiencing the same level of relief.

Another typical indication of physiological dependence on a chemical substance is the withdrawal syndrome. Smokers develop a craving for tobacco, and when they quit, or if they do not have a cigarette for a long time, they may become anxious, irritable, aggressive, and hostile, often experiencing head-

Vending machines make a hazardous, albeit legal, drug easily available to the public. (Tony Freeman/PhotoEdit)

aches, excessive hunger, nausea, and constipation or diarrhea. These symptoms appear while the body is going through more basic changes: after a person quits smoking, the heart rate and blood pressure drop, the level of adrenal hormones in the bloodstream drops, and the body's general arousal level decreases.

Tobacco and Psychological Dependence   The addictive effect of nicotine on the body is one reason that it is a habit-forming drug. The physiological need itself is also an important factor in creating psychological dependence. Psychological dependence is also created, however, by the pleasurable experiences or rewards that smokers associate with smoking as a result of the particular habits they develop.

Tobacco use can easily become linked with daily routines. The morning cup of coffee, the work break, and the drink at the end of the day can all be occasions for habitual smoking. Some people reward themselves with a cigarette after they accomplish a task. The chemical factors are made much more powerful because other secondary reinforcers—sights, smells, and agreeable surroundings—are also present.

In addition, the convenience of tobacco is another reason for its popularity. It comes in unusually handy forms. Cigarettes are convenient to carry, to light, and to hold, and moreover they give nervous people something easy to do with their hands. Smokeless tobacco is tucked into the mouth, leaving the hands totally free. Such ease of use provides very little discouragement, and makes the psychological habit that much easier to acquire.

Giving Up Smoking

Much of the decrease in the rate of smoking in recent years has occurred because of individual efforts to quit. For more than 20 years, increasing numbers of people have been successful in giving up smoking. According to a number of scientific reports, most people who have successfully quit have done so without professional help.[47] There are, however, a wide variety of treatment programs available for people who cannot quit smoking on their own.

There are many ways to break the smoking habit, ranging from simply quitting "cold turkey"—which some authorities consider the most effective method—to elaborate, highly structured (and sometimes expensive) group programs that attempt to reduce smoking over a period of many weeks.

- *Individual Programs* Products available to help people quit smoking on their own include books, records and cassettes, over-the-counter drugs, nicotine-containing chewing gum, and sets of graduated filters designed to reduce tar and nicotine intake over a period of time. Two drugs, clonidine and bispirone, have also been used to alleviate withdrawal symptoms.

- *Group Programs* Some group programs and clinics are sponsored by nonprofit health organizations such as the American Cancer Society, the American Heart Association, and the American Lung Association. Others are run as profit-making businesses. Group programs usually involve lectures, films, discussions, and practical tips on how to stop smoking.

- *Professional Therapy* Some programs to stop smoking involve hypnosis, where a professional practitioner induces a mild trance and then coaches the person about how to stop. Other programs rely on aversion techniques—such as using mild electric shocks or having the person breathe stale cigarette smoke or smoke extremely rapidly—in an effort to associate smoking with an unpleasant experience.

- *Behavior Modification and Learning Theory* Another approach applies the principles of behavior modification. The idea is simple. People who smoke generally do so at certain predictable times: with a cup of coffee, at a party, after a meal. Instead of smoking at those times, the person substitutes another behavior, such as taking a walk. Rewards and punishments can also be effective in learning to stop smoking. Researchers have reported good short-term results when people had to pay money every time they smoked.

Fostering a Smoke-Free Life

Smoking has become less tolerated in our society during the past few years. It is fast becoming a matter of where smokers will be allowed to smoke, rather than where their smoking will be restricted. Battle lines have been drawn between smokers who want to maintain the freedom to light up and nonsmokers who want the freedom to breathe air unpolluted by tobacco smoke.

The price of smoking is high for passive smokers. They are at increased risk of lung cancer and other diseases also, especially if they are exposed to tobacco smoke at home. But the price of smoking is even higher for smokers. It in-

Relaxing, sociable, and health-promoting rather than self-destructive, active exercise with friends is one of the best alternatives to tobacco use and social drinking. (Ron Grishaber/PhotoEdit)

cludes the cost of tobacco and health care—and life. A couple that forgoes a pack-a-day habit could each save over $1,000 a year.

Naturally, the best advice for those who smoke is to stop. If you are trying to quit, or have been successful in quitting, there may be actions you can take to help keep you off smoking. A brisk walk after meals will improve cardiovascular and pulmonary function as it diminishes tobacco craving. Gum chewing may help; so may a hobby or craft that is interesting and can occupy your hands. When you host a party, designate a smoking room, or allow smoking only outdoors. Limit contact with smokers and avoid places where people will be smoking. Try one of the individual or group programs mentioned in the chapter.

The best advice for those tempted to take their first puff is—don't. Abstaining from tobacco use is an individual choice that you can encourage in yourself and your friends. The benefits—keener senses of taste and smell, greater lung capacity, improved physical endurance, greater resistance to disease, and longer healthy life—speak for themselves.

Chapter Summary

- After it is consumed, alcohol is absorbed into the bloodstream and distributed throughout the body.

- Alcohol can impair judgment and motor activity, making it dangerous in certain situations, such as driving a car or using equipment.

- The use of alcohol can be attributed to a variety of factors, including physical and psychological dependence, and social pressures. These factors are often intertwined, making it difficult for a person to avoid alcohol use or stop once use has begun.

- Alcohol use has been linked to a variety of destructive behaviors, including an increased risk of accidents and violent acts and criminal activity.

- Alcoholism is a progressive condition marked by a series of stages, including occasional drinking, light drinking, social drinking, problem drinking, binge drinking, excessive drinking, and chronic alcoholism.

- Chronic, excessive drinking has been associated with a number of serious health problems, including gastrointestinal disorders, liver damage, cardiovascular disease, glandular disorders, central nervous system damage, malnutrition, and birth defects in children born to women who drank during pregnancy.

- People who choose to drink can attempt to use alcohol sensibly by knowing their limits and avoiding habits that may lead to dependency. In addition, people who even suspect they have a problem with alcohol use should seek help.

- The treatment of alcoholism normally begins with detoxification, in which a person is weaned from physical dependence, and proceeds to counseling programs designed to help a person deal with psychological dependence.

- People can often avoid the use of alcohol by substituting other, positive alternatives, such as walking, enjoying friends and family, limiting the use of alcohol in their home, and so on.

- Nicotine, the chemical substance found in tobacco, is absorbed into the bloodstream and passes directly into the brain, where it causes feelings of alertness and relaxation. However, it also releases chemicals that stimulate the cardiovascular system, resulting in a faster heartbeat and increased blood pressure.

- Tobacco and tobacco smoke contain a number of other toxic substances. These include carbon monoxide, which impairs the blood's capacity to carry oxygen; tar, a sticky residue that contains carcinogenic substances; and other carcinogenic substances. Smoking affects the respiratory system by irritating and damaging mucous membrances.

- Tobacco use has been linked to a number of serious diseases, including bronchitis and emphysema, various types of cancer, and cardiovascular disease. The use of tobacco can greatly increase the risk of dying from any of these diseases.

- Tobacco use during pregnancy seriously endangers the health of the unborn child. People who breathe in the smoke of others (passive smoking) are also adversely affected and are at increased risk for the same diseases as smokers.

- Tobacco use can lead to physical and psychological dependence.

- By giving up smoking, people can save money and extend their lives. Substituting healthy habits like exercise can help people stay free from tobacco.

Injuries and Their Prevention

Objectives

When you have studied this chapter, you should be able to:

- Summarize recent thinking about accidental and violent injuries, explaining how the agent-host-environment model is being applied to the occurrence of injuries.

- Identify the most common environments in which injuries occur, typical types of injury for each location, and the people who are likely to be injured.

- Discuss the major types of injuries in the United States.

- Explain basic strategies for the prevention and control of injuries.

- Describe important principles and procedures of emergency care which may be needed at any injury site before professional help arrives.

Injuries are one of the major public health problems facing the United States today. On an average day, more than 170,000 men, women, and children are seriously injured. Injuries have become the third most common cause of death in the United States after cardiovascular disease and cancer. For people between birth and age 45, they are the single greatest cause of death.[1]

People commonly hear the explanation "It was an accident" in many situations that have led to injury and death. Incidents such as motor vehicle crashes, falls, drownings, burns, and poisonings are often called accidents. However, the term *accident* is often inappropriate. Many of the situations in which injuries occur are predictable as well as preventable.

Injury and death also result from violence, which also may seem uncontrollable. However, violence too can result from predictable situations.

Injuries in Perspective

Although injuries represent a serious threat to public health, this need not be the case. Many injuries *can* be prevented. A better understanding of the factors that lead to injury can uncover ways to prevent many injuries or reduce the seriousness of the injuries that do occur.

Why Injuries Happen

For years researchers tried to explain why injuries occur by focusing on the shortcomings of the victims. They thought that most injuries happen to a few "accident-prone" people.[2] Most researchers, however, have rejected the theory of accident-proneness. Although some individuals may have higher injury rates than others do, current evidence indicates that this is a shifting group of individuals rather than a clearly defined accident-prone group.[3]

Today, investigators attempt to explain how injuries happen by looking at a variety of factors and the interactions among them. The current view is expressed by the threshold theory and the agent-host-environment model.

Threshold Theory According to this theory, injuries occur when a force or energy proves to be too great for a person to cope with. In other words, the energy exceeds the threshold of a person's skills and capabilities.

Five basic types of energy are responsible for all injuries: mechanical, thermal, chemical, electrical, and radiation. Mechanical energy includes motor vehicles, firearms, falls, and cuts. A person burned by a stove is injured as a result of thermal energy. Poisoning and injury from toxic substances are attributable to chemical energy. Shock from an exposed electrical wire is an example of an injury due to electrical energy. Injuries due to exposure to x-rays, the ultraviolet rays of the sun, and nuclear radiation result from radiation energy.[4]

Whatever the source of energy, injury occurs when the skills needed to handle a particular transfer of energy safely are beyond a person's abilities.[5] Different people vary enormously in their capabilities and therefore in their risk of sustaining injury. Young children, for example, are especially prone to receive certain types of injuries. Their inexperience and lack of knowledge, coupled with less developed physical skills, can be significant factors in this increased risk of injury. Individuals of any age or group are at increased risk if their knowledge, skills, and abilities fail them in times of need.

Figure 14.1 *The triangular agent-host-environment model can also be applied to injuries. People suffer accidental and violent injuries for a number of reasons, many of which can be controlled. In this one-car accident, the brakes on the car (agent) could have been made safer; the driver (the "host" who suffers the injury) should have been persuaded not to drive while intoxicated; and warning signs on the road (environment) could have been made more visible.*

The source of energy and the status of a person's skills are not the only factors that contribute to the risk of injury, however. Injuries also may happen because an object fails to function properly. Bicycles malfunction, toys break, and furniture collapses, injuring the people who are using them. Environmental factors also can contribute to injuries, for example, when children's toys are left on a staircase. Therefore, in determining the cause of injury, it is necessary to consider a variety of factors and the interactions among them. The interaction of all factors is best understood by applying the agent-host-environment model to the subject of injury causation.

Agent-Host-Environment Model   In the agent-host-environment model the agent, host, and environment are all seen as factors that interact over time to cause injury.[6] Agent factors include the energy source responsible for an injury and the mechanism by which that energy is transferred (an automobile is a mechanism through which mechanical energy can cause injury). Host factors include the person sustaining an injury and the skills, experience, and physical condition of that person. Environmental factors include the site at which an injury occurs and its condition as well as public attitudes and laws that affect the risk of sustaining an injury (Figure 14.1).

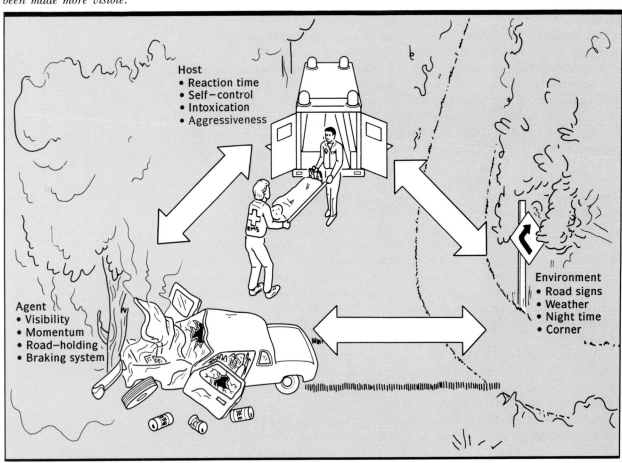

With the agent-host-environment model, personal responsibility for injury is only one of three factors that interact to increase or decrease the risk of injury. Therefore, a person (host) who takes drugs, is unable to cope with stress, is physically ill, or neglects to wear a seat belt while driving is only one factor affecting the risk of injury. Family and societal stressors, disease organisms, faulty car brakes, unsafe working conditions, and other agent and environmental factors are also important elements.

Of course, a potential change in any of these factors may not necessarily lead to injury if the other factors can compensate.[7] A person driving a car with worn brakes can avoid injury by stopping at the side of the road at the first sign of a problem. A major advantage of the agent-host-environment model is that by suggesting causal relationships, it provides a basis for developing strategies to prevent or reduce the risk of injury.[8]

Where Injuries Occur

The majority of injuries occur in familiar environments: at home, at work, and at recreational areas. A careful examination of these places can help identify ways to reduce or prevent the risk of serious injury. Certain types of injuries occur more frequently in particular environments primarily because of the types of hazards or safety features that are present.

Injuries at Home   People can be injured at home in a number of ways: falls, burns, poisoning, drowning, severe cuts, and so on. In 1987, 20,500 deaths resulted from injuries sustained at home and on home premises.

Home injuries occur more frequently among some groups than others. For example, 22 percent of children under age 6 and 18 percent of adults age 75 or older are injured in the home each year. More men than women die from home injuries, although adult women sustain more nonfatal injuries than do adult men.[9]

Certain home environments increase the risk of injury, and the kinds of injuries people suffer depend a great deal on environmental factors. Deteriorating homes in older neighborhoods may pose a greater risk of injury because of fire or structural hazards. The placement of potentially dangerous substances, including medications, may be a factor in the risk of poisoning and drug overdose.

The most dangerous room in the home is the kitchen. Hot stoves and boiling liquids are a danger to everyone, but especially to young children. However, all rooms may contain hazards, such as uncovered electrical outlets, loose rugs or carpeting, sharp or heavy objects, and potentially dangerous substances. The yard and its surroundings also contain numerous hazards, such as unguarded swimming pools and icy sidewalks.

The fact that knowledge and technology can easily help prevent many home injuries makes their occurrence especially tragic. The use of safety outlets, nonskid carpets, tamperproof bottle caps, and swimming pool enclosures can reduce the risk of certain types of injury greatly. Unfortunately, residential injuries continue to occur at an unacceptably high rate.

Injuries at Work   Every year in this country there are approximately 6,000 work-related deaths and 2.5 million to 11.3 million nonfatal occupational injuries.[10] Many occupations have particular associated injury risks. Sanitation

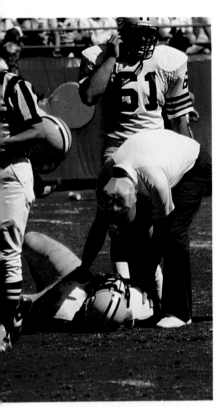

Among all competitive athletes, football players have the highest number of physical injuries annually. (Tony Freeman/PhotoEdit)

workers are at risk for sustaining lifting injuries, chronic joint conditions, and eye injuries. Fire fighters commonly sustain burns, cuts, sprains, broken bones, smoke inhalation, and eye injuries. Construction workers face a greater risk of having back injuries, cuts, and injuries from slips and falls.

Agriculture, now recognized as one of the nation's most dangerous industries, exposes its workers to risks of tractor rollovers, amputations by machinery, electrocutions, and pesticide poisonings. Workers in forestry, fishing, mining, construction, transportation, and public utilities are among those at greatest risk for sustaining occupational injuries.[11]

While people can be injured on the job in many ways, over 40 percent of all fatal occupational injuries are associated with motor vehicles. This includes highway vehicles and a variety of nonhighway vehicles, such as bulldozers, front-end loaders, cranes, forklifts, and tractors.

Age, sex, and race may be factors in the risk of sustaining occupational injuries. There is some evidence that young workers experience more injuries at work, possibly as a result of inexperience and lack of training. Minority group members also seem to be at greater risk for having occupational injuries. One study found that black workers were more likely to be engaged in hazardous jobs than were white workers. Although men predominate in some of the more hazardous occupations, women in occupations such as nursing and manufacturing frequently sustain serious injuries.[12]

Recreational Injuries Recreational activities such as swimming, boating, hiking, skiing, and tennis are an important part of the lives of many Americans. However, because they are "fun," many people forget that these activities can also be dangerous.

Many recreational injuries go unreported, and many activities are not studied in a systematic way. As a result, it is difficult to determine the full extent of the problem. It is safe to say, however, that hundreds of thousands of people are injured in recreational activities every year. Among recreation-related injuries, the highest incidence of death may come from drowning. In 1987, an estimated 4,400 people in the United States died as a result of drowning.[13] Other water-related injuries are associated with boating and diving.

Playgrounds are frequently the scene of injuries among young children. Although most playground-related injuries are minor, about one-quarter are more severe, involving concussions, crush wounds, fractures, and multiple injuries. A small number of deaths are caused by head injuries. Most playground-related injuries involve falls to the ground, collisions with playground equipment while running, and being struck by moving equipment such as swings.[14]

Competitive sports are another area in which recreational injuries frequently occur. Although serious and disabling injuries may result, the most prevalent injuries are sprains, especially of the limb joints; concussions; and abrasions. Among competitive sports, contact sports such as football and baseball have higher injury rates than do noncontact sports such as tennis.[15]

The Role of Violence in Injuries

Violence is defined broadly as the use of physical force with the intent of inflicting injury or death. Violence is a serious health problem because of the great toll it takes in lives, health, and quality of life. Violent actions are responsible for over 50,000 deaths a year. Information about nonfatal violence is less well reported, but it is estimated that each year at least 800,000 serious assaults result in injury.[16] Moreover, in many parts of the country the fear of violence has a powerful effect on people's lives, resulting in greater levels of stress, increased insecurity, and reduced enjoyment of life.

Injuries caused by interpersonal violence such as homicide and assault are sometimes characterized as "intentional," in contrast to the "unintentional" nature of most injuries. Whether intentional or unintentional, however, the result is the same—injury or death due to a combination of factors involving an agent, a host, and an environment.

Focusing on the injuries caused by violence allows public health practitioners to analyze violence from the perspective of causal factors (such as interpersonal relationships, stress, and availability of weapons). Their findings, combined with the efforts of law enforcement agencies and other groups, can lead to better means of preventing violence. Injury and death rates due to violence *can* be reduced. Indeed, public health officials do not consider violence an inevitable part of life but a concern to be addressed and remedied.[17]

Major Types of Injuries

Another way to analyze injuries is to look at the type of injuries that occur when people interact with the environment and with the agents and mechanisms that cause injury directly. The major types of injuries that occur every year are motor vehicle injuries, falls, burns, drownings, poisonings, and violence-related injuries.

Motor Vehicle Injuries

Every year in the United States, motor vehicles are responsible for almost 50,000 deaths and almost 2 million nonfatal disabling injuries. Among all fatal injuries, motor vehicle accidents are the most common cause of death for people age 1 to 34 and a major cause of death for people of all ages.[18]

Cars are especially dangerous in the hands of people who are intoxicated. Most states have defined a critical blood alcohol level which constitutes legal evidence that a person is driving while intoxicated (DWI) or driving under the influence (DUI). Depending on the state, this level ranges from 0.08 to 0.10 percent, as determined by a breath, blood, or urine test. However, even a blood alcohol level of 0.05 percent (which can occur with as few as three drinks in an hour) begins to affect a person's coordination and reflexes. Moreover, studies have shown that motor vehicle crashes in which alcohol plays a role tend to be much more severe than are nonalcohol-related crashes. The more severe the crash, the greater the likelihood that alcohol is involved.

Age, sex, and race are other factors in motor vehicle death rates. The death rate peaks in the late teenage years and early twenties and then begins to decline until about age 65, at which point it increases. Men, especially those in their early twenties, are more often fatally injured than are women. The highest death rates associated with motor vehicles are found among Native Americans. This may be partly attributable to the high incidence of alcohol use among Native American groups.[19]

A group of factors related to motor vehicle injury which are often over-looked involve the condition of automobiles and their safety features as well as the general safety of the driving environment. The presence of seat belts, padded dashboards, air bags, and other safety features can have a significant effect on the injuries sustained in motor vehicle crashes. Lower speed limits, well-lighted and well-constructed highways, and knowledge of safe driving practices also affect the risk of sustaining a motor vehicle injury.

Injury from Falls

Falls are second only to motor vehicles as a cause of nonviolent fatal injuries in the United States.[20] The group most at risk for fatal falls includes the elderly, especially people over age 75. More than half of all fatal falls occur among this group.

Children under age 5 are also at increased risk for falls. All children fall as they are learning to walk, and most of these falls do not result in injury. Some falls, however, can result in serious fractures or brain injuries. The incidence of falls is greatest in infancy and then declines throughout childhood.

While falls can occur in any environment, over 43 percent of all fatal falls occur in the home. Environmental factors such as overcrowded furniture, dangerous stairs, poor lighting, loose rugs, and slippery floor surfaces play a major role in the risk of falling among the elderly. Among children, common environmental hazards associated with falls include open windows, open staircases, and playground equipment.[21]

Another factor that contributes to the risk of falling among the elderly is the use of medications. Drugs such as sedatives and barbiturates are often associated with falls, especially in nursing homes, where a large percentage of elderly patients use such medications. Alcohol is also associated with an increased risk of falls among the elderly.

Fire and Burn Injuries

Burns are another significant cause of injury and death in the United States. Burn injuries result from a variety of sources, including fires, scaldings, electricity, chemicals, and ultraviolet radiation. The types of burns associated with each of these sources vary in severity and frequency and are linked to certain age- and sex-related factors.

About 75 percent of all deaths by fire result from house fires. The groups at greatest risk are young children and the elderly. Among the elderly, a large number of nonfatal fire-related burns are attributable to the burning of clothing, which often occurs while one is cooking. While clothing-related burns are somewhat common among children, improved flammability standards for children's clothing have resulted in a decreased risk in recent years.[22]

Burns sustained as a result of contact with hot objects (such as a stove) and scaldings from hot liquids are more common among young children. While such burns are seldom fatal, they can result in severe injury and pain. Flammable liquids such as gasoline are a lethal cause of burn injuries among boys from 6 to 16 years of age, and electrical burns are quite common among boys in this age group.[23]

Drownings and Near Drownings

Drowning, by definition, is a fatal injury. "Near drowning," in which a person is submerged long enough to suffer oxygen deprivation, can result in serious injury, including brain damage. As with other types of injuries, certain groups in the population are at greater risk of drowning than are others. For example, the rate of drownings among men is four times greater than that among women. Drowning rates are highest among children under age 5 and between ages 15 and 24.[24] Drowning often occurs among young children who lack proper supervision, because they are not familiar with the dangers of falling into deep water and do not usually call out for help. Among teenagers and young adults, increased risk taking can be a factor in the risk of drowning, as can the use of alcohol.[25]

Environmental factors play a role in the risk of drownings. Although between 50 and 75 percent of all drownings occur in lakes, rivers, and the ocean, a large percentage of drownings among young children occur in swimming pools.[26] This is particularly true where residential swimming pools are common. Proper supervision and safety features, such as fenced enclosures, are important factors in preventing residential drownings of young children.

Injury from Poisonings

In 1987 almost 5,500 deaths in the United States were attributed to poisoning. Poisoning is also responsible for a great number of the nonfatal injuries sustained each year.

Household cleaners and all other toxic substances should be placed in locked cabinets far out of the reach of children. (Barbara Burnes/Photo Researchers, Inc.)

As is the case with many other types of injury, young children and the elderly are at greatest risk for injury from poisoning. Young children are poisoned by a variety of substances found in the home, from medications to cleansing agents to personal-care products. Fortunately, the rate of ingestion of some potentially hazardous substances has decreased in recent years because of the use of child-resistant safety caps on many products.

In addition to poisoning from liquids and solids, poisoning from gases and vapors is a significant source of injury. The primary cause of such poisoning is carbon monoxide inhalation, most often from motor vehicle exhausts.

Violence-Related Injuries

In recent years the United States has experienced an increase in injuries and deaths resulting from interpersonal violence. The daily news recounts the latest incidents of homicides, assaults, rapes, and other violent acts. In 1987, for example, nearly 1.5 million violent acts were reported in the United States, a 36.7 percent increase from 1978.[27] This may represent only part of the problem, however, since assaults that are not fatal frequently go unreported.

Assaultive Injuries Every year hundreds of thousands of people in this country are victims of violent assault, from physical disputes among individuals to muggings—street assaults involving robbery—to rape.

Most acts of violence are committed by men. Age is another significant factor. During 1986, people under age 25 accounted for 48 percent of arrests for violent crime. Arrest statistics tell only part of the story, however. For every violent act leading to arrest, between 8 and 11 others are committed by juvenile offenders. Another factor associated with aggravated assault and rape is alcohol. Studies have shown that a large number of violent acts occur in places where alcohol is consumed. Another study found that over 50 percent of convicted rapists were under the influence of alcohol when they committed a crime.[28]

Race and socioeconomic status appear to be factors in determining who is victimized by assault and rape. The poor seem to be at greater risk for both assaultive injuries and rape, and blacks are at great risk as well. One study found that rape was 12 times more frequent among blacks than among whites. Age also seems to be a risk factor. Studies have revealed that the great majority of rape victims are between ages 13 and 25, predominantly between ages 13 and 19.[29]

Homicide The great majority of assaultive injuries are nonfatal. However, there were an estimated 21,500 homicides in 1989, a 29 percent increase from 1970.[30]

An increased risk of homicide is associated with various factors. Research has suggested that most homicide victims are young black males. For black males between ages 14 and 44, homicide is the leading cause of death.[31] Personal relationships are another factor in homicides. It has been estimated that almost half of all homicides are committed by persons either related to or acquainted with the victim.[32]

Homicides frequently arise from arguments rather than criminal activities and usually involve firearms. The use of alcohol and drugs is also frequently

Assessing Your Risk-Taking Behavior

This activity will help you find out how stimulating a life you want. If a statement is one that you might easily make, put a check mark in the space. If you would very rarely make the statement, leave the space blank.

_____   1. I would like a job that requires a lot of traveling.
    _____   2. I cannot wait to get indoors on a cold day.
    _____   3. I cannot understand people who risk their necks climbing mountains.
_____   4. I get bored seeing the same faces all the time.
    _____   5. I prefer having a guide when I am in a place I do not know well.
    _____   6. I would prefer living in an ideal society where everyone is safe, secure, and happy.
_____   7. I sometimes like to do things that are a little frightening.
    _____   8. I would *not* like to take up waterskiing.
    _____   9. When I go on a trip, I like to plan my route and timetable fairly carefully.
_____   10. I would like to learn to fly an airplane.
_____   11. I would like to have the experience of being hypnotized.
_____   12. I want to live life to the fullest and experience as much of it as I can.
    _____   13. I would never want to try parachute jumping.
    _____   14. I enter cold water gradually, giving myself time to get used to it.
_____   15. I prefer friends who are exciting and unpredictable.
_____   16. I would enjoy camping out on my vacation.
    _____   17. The essence of good art is its clarity and harmony of colors.
    _____   18. I prefer people who are calm and even-tempered.
_____   19. A good painting should shock or jolt the senses.
_____   20. I would like to drive or ride a motorcycle.

Score your responses. Begin with 100 points. *Add* 10 points for each check in the left-hand column. Then *subtract* 10 points for each check in the right-hand column. Find your score below to see what your ideal level of excitement is.

Scores	Your Ideal Level of Excitement
150 to 200	High
70 to 140	Moderate
0 to 60	Low

Interpretation: People who seek high levels of stimulation often accept higher risks than do those who seek predictable and moderate lifestyles.

Adapted with permission from Marvin Zuckerman et al., "Development of a Sensation-Seeking Scale," *Journal of Consulting Psychology* 28, no. 6 (1964): 477–482. Copyright 1964 by the American Psychological Association.

associated with homicides.[33] In recent years drug dealing has been linked increasingly to homicides that involve innocent children and bystanders.

Preventing and Controlling Injuries

Even though injuries pose a major public health problem, widespread misunderstanding of their causes has frequently led to inadequate efforts toward injury reduction and prevention. Successful prevention of injuries requires attention not only to host factors associated with individuals but to agent and environmental factors as well. Identifying all the factors that lead to injury and examining their interactions can result in more effective strategies on the part of individuals, organizations, public health professionals, and the government.

Approaches to Injury Control

There are several approaches to preventing and controlling injuries. One approach attempts to change individual behaviors to reduce the risk of injury. Such attempts include improving driving skills, curbing aggressive behaviors, and stopping the use of alcohol and other drugs. This approach is generally characterized as *persuasion* and includes elements such as education, rehabilitation, behavior modification, and social support systems.[34] Driver education classes, campaigns for stricter gun control, and counseling for drunk drivers are examples of efforts at persuasion. Unfortunately, since persuasive methods are aimed primarily at behaviors and attitudes, they are often the least effective method of injury prevention.

Another approach to injury prevention is through legislation. *Laws* approach the prevention of injuries more directly than persuasion can. Some laws are aimed at changing individual behavior, such as laws that require the use of seat belts, infant car seats, and motorcycle helmets. Other laws regulate the possession of handguns, require the installation of smoke detectors, and penalize people who drive while intoxicated.

While laws requiring behavioral change are generally more effective than educational methods of prevention, they are less effective than laws designed to provide automatic protection through changes in product and environmental design. Automatic protections such as built-in sprinkler systems, automatic seat belts, air bags, and childproof closures on containers have a great potential for preventing injuries and deaths because they require no action on the part of the individual.

Active and Passive Preventive Measures

active prevention

Preventive measures that require individuals to do something to reduce the risk of sustaining an injury are considered **active prevention.** Examples include the use of nonautomatic seat belts, the use of bicycle and motorcycle helmets, adherence to drunk driving laws, and voluntary compliance with gun laws. The greatest failing of active measures is that they depend on people to act in ways that will reduce their risk of sustaining injury. People forget to use seat belts and helmets, forget to put hazardous substances out of the reach of children, fail to follow the speed limit or comply with other laws, and are often

Passive injury prevention measures are designed to work without user participation. To benefit from automobile air bags, car owners need only buy cars that are equipped with them. (Courtesy Mercedes Benz)

careless or take risks. While education is an important means of changing unsafe behaviors and getting people to comply with the law, injury prevention can be achieved even more effectively through the use of passive prevention.

Preventive measures that require little or no individual action on the part of those being protected are characterized as **passive prevention.** These measures include seat belts that automatically engage when a person enters a car, automobile air bags, better street lighting, and built-in safety switches on power tools and electrical equipment. Since they require no action by individuals, these measures are directed at agent and environmental factors, modifying them so that they pose less of a risk.

passive prevention

Of course, the best prevention against injury involves a combination of passive and active prevention, of persuasive efforts and laws. Together, the combined efforts can eliminate or reduce many of the risk factors that can lead to serious injury or death.

Individual Strategies for Control and Prevention

Despite the progress that has been made in injury prevention in this country, there is still a long way to go. Few states have established comprehensive programs to prevent injury, governments have not always been forceful in legislating injury prevention measures, and some manufacturers have been slow in investigating passive safety features that are worthwhile and incorporating them into their products.

Until more passive prevention measures are legislated and incorporated into the design of all products and environments, it is largely up to the individual to act in ways that prevent injury. One should begin by examining one's own behaviors to see how they may contribute to the risk of injury. The next step is to identify potential hazards in products and in the environment. Then it is possible to take steps to reduce risky behaviors and eliminate hazards that may lead to injury.

The following are just a few of the many safety tips that can help reduce the risk of injury from motor vehicle crashes, falls, burns, drowning, and poisoning.[35]

Controlling Motor Vehicle Injuries   In addition to observing all traffic laws and driving carefully, people can reduce the risk of injury from motor vehicles by doing the following:

- Avoiding driving while under the influence of alcohol, illegal drugs, or medicines which carry a warning about drowsiness
- Wearing seat belts at all times, whether driving or riding as a passenger
- Using consumer-recommended car seats for infants and requiring older children to use seat belts
- Servicing vehicles regularly and keeping them in good working order
- Maintaining proper tire pressures and levels for gasoline, oil, and system coolants
- Wearing a helmet when riding a bicycle or motorcycle
- Teaching children to cross streets safely and keep away from roads and highways

Controlling Falls   Many falls can be avoided, especially those which result from environmental factors. The risk of injury from such falls can be reduced by doing the following:

- Keeping traffic areas in the home well lighted, especially stairs
- Installing stairway gates and window barriers to protect children
- Repairing loose floorboards and floor coverings
- Removing electrical cords from walkways
- Picking up small objects from the floor
- Placing nonskid mats under loose rugs and in bathtubs
- Cleaning up water and grease spills on the floor immediately

Controlling Burns   In addition to using smoke detectors in the home and knowing emergency procedures in case of a fire, people can reduce the risk of burn injuries by doing the following:

- Setting home water heaters no higher than 120 degrees F
- Using flame-retardant clothing for children
- Keeping matches out of the reach of children
- Not buying highly flammable solvents, or storing them in safe locations
- Taking care not to overload electrical circuits
- Repairing or replacing worn electrical wires
- Placing guards in front of fireplaces, open heaters, and radiators

- Keeping pots of hot liquids away from the front of the stove and turning pot handles to the rear

Controlling Drowning   While the ability to swim is very important in preventing drowning, people can reduce the risk of drowning or near drowning by doing the following:

- Enclosing pool areas or installing fences between the home and wells, ponds, streams, and other bodies of water
- Never leaving a child unattended in a bathtub, pool, or other body of water
- Keeping pails of liquid out of the reach of infants since infants can drown even in small pails
- Knowing and following water safety and boating rules

Controlling Poisoning   An important breakthrough in reducing the poisoning of children has been the use of safety closures on many bottled products and medications. Some other ways to reduce the risk of poisoning include the following:

- Keeping all medicines and caustic and poisonous household substances out of the reach of children
- Reading the labels on all substances carefully before using them
- Storing all substances, especially cleaning materials, in their original containers so that the contents are known
- Keeping the telephone number of the local poison control center in a visible and easily accessible location near the phone

Controlling Violence   As a cause of injuries, particularly in urban areas, violence continues to be a major problem. The major responsibility for violence obviously lies with those who perpetrate it, yet steps can be taken by potential victims that may lessen the likelihood of violence occurring. These steps include the following:

- Taking appropriate cautionary measures such as installing safety locks, avoiding dangerous areas, and traveling with friends rather than alone
- Reporting any violent incidents in the neighborhood and being willing to cooperate with official investigators
- Taking care not to escalate situations where there is a danger of violence occurring
- Being aware of potentially dangerous situations among one's acquaintances or family members and being ready and willing to get help from a trusted friend or professional if matters seem likely to get out of control

Providing Emergency Care

Despite efforts at prevention, injuries do happen. Therefore, it is important to know not only how to reduce the risk of injury but also how to deal with an injury when it does occur. Knowledge about basic emergency care procedures can be very helpful in dealing with injuries and other health-threatening conditions. It is also very important to know local medical emergency telephone numbers, such as 911, that provide assistance.

There is a great deal of information available on different types of emergency care procedures. Many communities also offer courses and training at the American Red Cross, American Heart Association, YMCAs and YWCAs, and other community centers on first-aid procedures such as cardiopulmonary resuscitation (CPR) and water safety or lifeguard training. Taking such courses can make you very valuable in an emergency.

Basic Principles of Emergency Care

There are three basic principles for giving emergency care.

1. Always begin by preventing further injury.
2. Do only what is absolutely necessary and get professional help as soon as possible. Certain situations, such as when a person has no heartbeat, is bleeding profusely, or has swallowed poison, require immediate help. Other situations are less life-threatening, even though they are frightening.
3. Know your limits. Offer help only when you are sure your actions will not cause further injury.

Basic Procedures for Emergency Care

To be helpful in an emergency, it is essential to act coolly and sensibly. The following sequence of steps applies to any medical emergency. Learning these steps will make you better equipped to use emergency care measures.

Try to Remain Calm Injuries and other medical emergencies can be very frightening, and fear can make people do irrational things that make matters worse. In dealing with an emergency, the first thing to do is make sure you are thinking straight. Keeping calm not only makes you more effective but also reassures the victim that someone sensible is going to try to help. Thus, the first thing to do in an emergency is to calm yourself before attending to the victim.

Find Out What Happened Finding out what happened to cause a medical emergency is extremely important. Make sure the scene is safe before approaching. In many instances there are good reasons to use or reject certain emergency care procedures. The only way to determine what to do is to ask what happened. (The method chosen for stopping bleeding from a serious wound, for example, depends on whether a foreign object is embedded in the wound.) While you are finding out what happened, let the victim know who you are and that you are trying to help.

Examine the Victim In some situations taking time to examine a victim is inappropriate. When the situation is beyond your capability, as with a serious head injury, arrange to have the victim transported to a hospital immediately. In other cases emergency care procedures should begin without delay.

When serious complications may be present, such as after a bad fall, make sure that you understand the nature of the injury. Careful examination in-

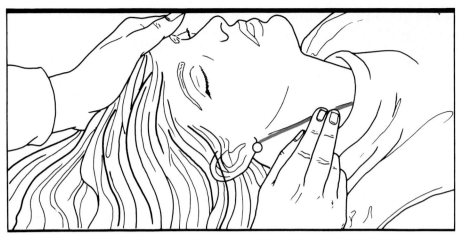

Figure 14.2 To take a pulse at the neck, place two fingers at the victim's Adam's apple and slide them down toward the back of the neck. About halfway down you will feel a groove. This is where the carotid artery runs, supplying blood to the head and brain. Its pulse, if present, will be very noticeable. Be careful not to press too hard or you will stop the flow of blood.

volves considering the injury in the context of the person's overall condition and includes checking the following:

- *Level of responsiveness.* Observe whether the person is conscious, responsive to what you say, and in pain.
- *Breathing.* Watch the person's chest rise and fall and put your ear close to the person's nose and mouth to listen and feel for breathing. Observe whether breathing is normal (about 12 to 18 breaths a minute) or shallow and rapid, gasping, or absent.
- *Pulse.* Feel for the pulse in the artery at the side of the neck or on the wrist below the base of the thumb (Figure 14.2). Observe whether the pulse is normal (about 70 to 90 beats a minute) or rapid, slow, weak, or absent.
- *Massive bleeding.* The loss of large amounts of blood can cause shock and death. Take immediate steps to control severe bleeding.
- *Pupils.* Check the pupils. They should be of equal size and should get slightly smaller when exposed to a bright light.
- *Deformity.* Compare one side of the body with the other. If one arm or leg is in an unnatural position, it may be fractured or dislocated.
- *Skin.* Look at the victim's face. Check the skin color (flushed, normal, or pale), texture (dry or moist, goose bumps), and temperature (hot, normal, or cool).
- *Neck or spinal cord injury.* Paralysis of the face, arms, or legs is a sign of a neck or spinal cord injury. Avoid moving the person to reduce the chance of causing further injury.

Administer Emergency Care   Assessing the victim's condition should take only a minute or two. During that time, you will get a clearer idea of the situation and the injured person will be calmed by your readiness to help. With a better idea of what may be wrong, you will be able to choose the appropriate emergency care procedure and begin applying it.

Common Situations Requiring First Aid

There are a number of situations in which emergency care procedures are required. It is essential for the person providing help to know the proper procedures for each particular situation. What that person does or does not do can sometimes mean the difference between life and death.

Heart Attack and Stroke   Cases of cardiac arrest, in which the heart has stopped completely, require CPR. CPR cannot be taught adequately in a brief overview like this, but it is not difficult or time-consuming to learn. A local Red Cross chapter or the local office of the American Heart Association can provide information about courses. Most heart attack victims, however, do not experience cardiac arrest. Emergency care procedures in such cases include the following:

- Arrange for transportation to the nearest hospital.
- Let the victim sit up or lie down as he or she prefers but not move around.
- Watch for nausea and make sure the victim has an open airway.

Choking   If a person who seems to be choking on food or a foreign object can speak, do not interfere with that individual's attempts to cough up the object. If the person is unable to speak, it is appropriate to provide emergency care by using the Heimlich maneuver (Figure 14.3). Stand behind the victim and place both arms around his or her waist. Grasp one fist with the other hand

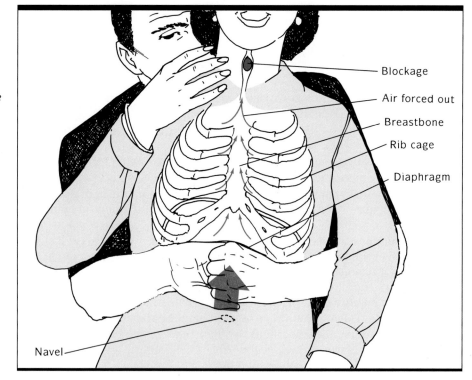

Figure 14.3 The Heimlich maneuver. Pressing inward on the diaphragm forces air out of the lungs, dislodging an object from the airway. Stand behind the victim. Position your fist between the navel and the rib cage to avoid breaking bones. Grasp your fist with your other hand. Pull both hands toward you with a quick upward and inward thrust.

Blockage

Air forced out

Breastbone

Rib cage

Diaphragm

Navel

and place the thumb side of the fist against the victim's abdomen, slightly above the navel and below the rib cage. Press your fist into the victim's abdomen with a quick inward and upward thrust. Repeat this procedure until the object is dislodged. The Heimlich maneuver should not be used with infants under 1 year of age.[36]

Shock   Serious injury, loss of blood, heart failure, severe burns, breathing impairment, and severe emotional upset can cause **shock**—a condition in which the body loses control of blood flow. In shock, the pattern of blood flow is interrupted and the heart cannot circulate blood effectively. Signs of shock include pale, cool, and clammy skin; shivering; a rapid and weak pulse; and shallow and rapid or deep and irregular breathing. A person suffering from shock may also be mentally confused, have drooping eyelids or dilated pupils, experience nausea and vomiting, or collapse.

shock

Shock is a life-threatening condition, and immediate attention is essential. Victims of serious injuries should always be treated for shock. With minor injuries, it is important for the person providing emergency care to watch for signs of shock. Procedures for dealing with shock include the following:

- **Warmth.** Make sure body heat is not lost. Place blankets or extra clothing over and under the victim if necessary.
- **Position.** Do not make the person lie down flat in cases of head and chest injuries, heart attack, and stroke. In these situations the victim may be more comfortable and able to breathe better in a semireclining position. If you are in doubt about these conditions and in all other cases (such as a suspected neck or back injury), keep the victim lying flat. Elevate the feet 6 to 12 inches if no neck, back, or leg injuries are suspected unless the victim is unconscious.

Severe Bleeding   Cuts, lacerations, and other wounds may involve damage to both surface and underlying tissue and can bleed profusely. It is always important to determine if foreign objects are embedded in a wound before proceeding with emergency care.

Three basic methods can be used to control severe bleeding.

1. **Direct pressure.** Pressure is applied directly on the open wound with a bare hand or a clean, lint-free cloth or towel. Use just enough pressure to stop the bleeding. Too much pressure may cause further injury. If a foreign object is embedded in the wound, do *not* use the direct pressure method and do *not* try to remove the object. Both can cause more damage.
2. **Elevation.** The injured site is raised so that it is higher than the heart, using gravity to slow or stop the bleeding. This method should be used in combination with direct pressure. Do *not* use elevation if it entails risking additional injury, as when a fracture is also present.
3. **Pressure points.** Pressure points are locations in the body where arteries pass over bones. If one presses down on a pressure point between the injury site and the heart, the artery can be closed enough to stem the flow of blood. The pressure point method is very useful when direct pressure and elevation cannot be used or do not suffice. All three techniques can be used in combination.

Unconsciousness Providing emergency care to an unconscious person presents some difficulties. Since the person cannot describe what happened, be particularly careful and conservative in taking action. For example, if there is any evidence that unconsciousness is a result of a severe electrical shock, do *not* touch the person until you have made sure that the electrical contact is broken by using a nonmetal object such as a dead tree branch or wooden handle. General rules to follow include the following:

- Check for breathing, pulse, and pupil size.
- Turn the person onto his or her side if you are sure there is no neck or spinal injury to help breathing and allow fluid to drain out of the mouth and nose so that the person does not choke.
- Help the injury victim maintain body heat by covering him or her with blankets or clothing.
- Never try to give food or liquid to an unconscious or dazed person.
- Arrange for professional medical attention as soon as possible.

Sprains and Fractures A *sprain* is an injury to a joint; a *fracture* is a break in a bone. When a bone is fractured or a joint is sprained, the surrounding tissues swell and sometimes become discolored, the limb may be visibly deformed, and there usually is pain. In addition, if the fracture is *open*, meaning that the skin is broken, there is an added risk of infection. In many cases the victim cannot move a fractured limb, but contrary to popular belief, the ability to move a limb does *not* necessarily mean that the limb is not fractured.

Since only an x-ray can establish whether an injury is a fracture or a sprain, all suspected fractures and sprains should be treated as if they were fractures. The emergency procedures that should be followed include the following:

- Urge the victim to remain still to avoid aggravating the injury.
- The basic rule for emergency care of fractures is to *immobilize the broken bone and both adjacent joints* (Figure 14.4). For example, a suspected fracture of the bone in the lower leg should be splinted so that the bone, the ankle joint below it, and the knee joint above it are immobilized. It is relatively easy to rig a splint for a suspected fracture. Anything rigid and long enough (such as a pair of skis) will do.
- After splinting, get medical attention for the victim. (*Note:* Special procedures are needed for immobilizing people with head and spinal injuries. Formal training in such procedures is necessary.)

Poisoning and Drug Overdose People can be exposed to a number of potentially dangerous substances, some poisonous and others nonpoisonous but harmful in large doses. As a result, information on the appropriate treatment for specific types of poisoning or substance overdose is often difficult to find. Specialized poison control centers have been established in most parts of the country. The telephone number of the nearest center should be accessible. General emergency procedures for poisonings and overdoses include the following:

- Keep the victim quiet, trying to prevent unnecessary movement.
- Try to identify the poison or substance and determine how much was ingested. If possible, have the container with you when you call the poison control center.

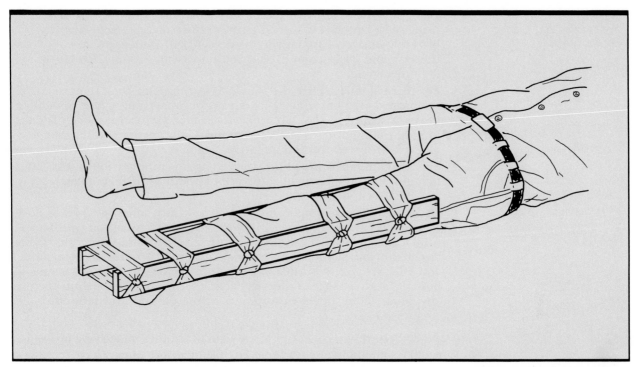

Figure 14.4 *When a bone appears to be broken, immobilize the broken bone including joints above and below the break, using any material at hand to make a splint. Here, both the ankle and knee are immobilized to treat a lower leg fracture. If a firm material is not available, you can bind a fractured leg to the victim's other leg.*

- Call the poison control center as soon as you are sure the victim has a pulse and is breathing. If the victim is not breathing, begin artificial respiration immediately. If the heart has stopped, begin CPR.
- Check for signs of the poison around the victim's mouth, such as burns or other indications that the poison is corrosive. Watch for nausea and vomiting. If the victim vomits, make sure he or she does not choke. Save a sample of the vomit for medical personnel. They may need to analyze it to identify the poisonous substance.
- If the victim is conscious, dilute the poison by having him or her drink water or milk. Try to induce vomiting *unless* there are burns around the mouth or the victim's breath smells like kerosene or gasoline. Such corrosive substances, if vomited, will burn the victim's throat and mouth a second time. If the victim becomes nauseated, discontinue giving fluids. Never try to give liquids to an unconscious or dazed person.

Burns   Burns are dangerous injuries that can cause extensive damage, and emergency care procedures can be very effective in limiting that damage. These procedures include the following:

- Get the victim away from the source of the burn. If the person's clothing is on fire, smother the flames with a coat or blanket or make the person roll on the ground. Restrain the person from running around in a panic. Movement fans the flames.
- Try to determine whether the burn is thermal or chemical. A *thermal burn* is caused by heat, such as fire or steam. The burning will continue as long as the heat remains in contact with the skin. A *chemical burn* is caused by a corrosive substance such as a strong acid or alkali. The burning will continue as long as the substance remains in contact with the skin.

- Determine the severity of the burn. *First-degree burns* involve surface tissue only; sunburn is a good example. *Second-degree burns* involve blistering, a sign of underlying tissue damage. *Third-degree burns* involve charring and destruction of skin and underlying tissue; such burns are life-threatening.
- For thermal burns, once the source of burning has been removed, cool the burned area immediately by means of immersion or the application of cloths soaked in cool tap water. (Ice water may cause shock.) Do not remove clothing that is stuck to the burn. For anything other than minor burns, seek medical attention promptly.
- For chemical burns, flood the affected area with water for at least 20 minutes, until the burning substance has been washed completely away, and then seek medical attention.
- Do not apply an ointment or cream to any burn unless advised to do so by medical personnel. One of the major dangers associated with burns is infection. Any burn can become infected, but those where the skin is blistered or burned away pose the greatest risk. To prevent both shock and infection, cover burned areas with material that will stick as little as possible, such as a clean sheet or tablecloth. Get medical help if there is any doubt about the extent of injury or the possibility of infection.

Seizures Seizures, or convulsions, are signs of another underlying problem, a signal that something else is wrong. For example, a child may have seizures as a result of a high fever. Seizures are also a sign of certain chronic diseases, such as epilepsy.

The most important objective of emergency care for seizures is to prevent further injury. Gently lower the person to the floor and do not try to restrain that person's movements. Try to keep the victim on his or her side. This helps keep the airway open by allowing fluid to drain out of the mouth. Do *not* put any object in the victim's mouth to prevent swallowing the tongue. The object itself can injure the victim. After a seizure has passed, consult a physician for instructions on what to do next.

Bruises, Minor Cuts, and Lacerations Bruises are closed wounds in which the skin is not broken but damage to tissues under the skin can cause invisible bleeding. The sign of such bleeding is the dark blue skin discoloration associated with a bruise.

If a person with a bruise develops a fever, becomes nauseated, or has red streaks on the skin near the bruise, get medical attention at once. Otherwise, the best procedure is to apply a cold compress to the area. Cold slows the underlying bleeding and reduces the size of the bruise.

While generally not serious, minor cuts and lacerations require emergency care to stop bleeding and prevent infection. The cut and the surrounding skin should first be washed thoroughly with soap and water. There is no need to apply alcohol or other antiseptics. Then blot the area dry and apply a clean bandage.

Infections Sometimes minor injuries become infected. Most infections can be treated successfully if they are recognized and attended to promptly. The main symptoms of infection are skin redness, swelling, fever, tenderness, and swollen lymph nodes. Emergency care involves immobilizing the affected part of the body, applying hot compresses, and getting medical attention.

When Professional Help Arrives

A person providing emergency care can safely give up his or her helping role when professional help arrives. At that point the person should explain the condition in which the victim was found, the emergency care measures already taken, when they were begun, and the victim's response to those measures. Any additional information that may help the professionals deal with the problem should also be discussed.

Chapter Summary

- Various factors contribute to the risk of injury. The threshold theory and the agent-host-environment model explain why injuries happen.

- All types of injuries can occur in the home. Home injuries frequently affect the very young and the very old.

- Many work-related injuries are associated with motor vehicles. Other significant work-related injuries include falls and burns.

- One of the most common recreational injuries is drowning. Among young children, falls are a common recreational injury, often occurring in playgrounds. Competitive sports can be quite hazardous.

- Violence is a significant health problem in terms of the number of people who are killed and injured every year. Violence-related injuries are often intentional and include such things as assaults, rape, and homicide.

- Motor vehicle injuries are a major cause of death. Young drivers and elderly drivers are at the highest risk for sustaining a motor vehicle injury. The young (under age 5) and old (over age 75) are at the highest risk for suffering injury from a fall. Environmental factors play a major role in the risk of falling. Burn injuries are also most prevalent among the young and the very old. With drownings, men are at greater risk, as are young children. Poisonings are also more common among the young and the old. Most violence-related injuries involve young men.

- Analyzing agent-host-environmental factors is essential in the prevention of injuries. When the various factors associated with injuries have been identified, steps can be taken to change behaviors, eliminate hazards, and design safer environments.

- The two major approaches to injury prevention are persuasion and legislation. Persuasion includes efforts to change people's behavior through education, rehabilitation, and social support systems. Laws are aimed at encouraging behavioral change and providing safer products and environments.

- Active prevention measures are measures that require individuals to do something to reduce the risk of injury. Passive prevention measures require little or no action on the part of the individual. The best form of prevention includes a combination of active and passive measures.

- In spite of the growing concentration on prevention measures, injuries still occur. A practical knowledge of emergency care procedures is therefore highly valuable.

- Important principles of emergency care include knowing one's own limitations, staying calm, and being able to follow appropriate care procedures until professional medical help arrives.

Lifestyle and Growing Older

When you have studied this chapter, you should be able to:

- Characterize the human life span in terms of healthy aging and pathological aging, and describe the common stages of growth and change in adult life.

- Comment on the concerns of people as they age.

- Clarify ways in which people can take actions to lessen the impact of aging on their own lives and on the lives of others close to them.

- Discuss the stages people may go through when confronting the fact that they are about to die.

- Explore ways that others may respond to the fact that a relative or friend is about to die, including practical considerations of medical and emotional care.

- Enumerate several preparations that people can make for their own deaths.

- Review the typical responses of those who are bereaved, the ways in which funeral ceremonies may help them, and other factors that may enable them to cope with and lessen their sadness over time.

Growing older is a fact of life. There is no fountain of youth that can stop or turn back the clock. Many people fear the aging process, believing that physical and mental decline is inevitable. Evidence suggests, however, that chronological age is a poor predictor of physical or mental health status and functional ability. While there are age-related changes in physical functioning, it is now thought that many of those changes are related to disuse and to destructive health habits rather than to age.[1] Developing and maintaining a healthy lifestyle throughout your life thus can have a significant effect on how you age.

The thoughts of most younger people are focused on schools, careers, and personal lives. Few think seriously about how they will spend their later years. The time to think about this, however, is now. Your health at age 64, 75, or older depends to a large extent on your current lifestyle. A healthy old age can be very rewarding, but if old age is marked by pain, disability, loneliness, and fear, it can be unbearable. Developing and maintaining a healthy lifestyle at all stages will increase the quality of your life not only today but throughout the years ahead.

This chapter explores the processes of aging. It looks at symptoms that people fear and often expect. And it explores what one can do to improve the experiences of growing older. Finally, the chapter will explore the issues of death and dying.

Growing Older and Aging

Aging is a lifelong process of physical, emotional, intellectual, social, and spiritual changes that occur from birth until death. There is, however, often confusion between normal aging and the aging that may occur during specific periods of one's life because of disease or poor health. **Normal aging** refers to certain biological processes that are time-related rather than being a function of disease, injury, or stress.[2] After age 40, for example, most people's vision and hearing begin a gradual deterioration which may become quite noticeable as the years go by. Although the rates of change differ from individual to individual, the process of normal aging is inevitable. **Pathological aging** refers to a decrease in functioning caused by illness, stress, injury, and other factors.[3] Some studies have shown that high levels of physical function in old age are associated with the absence of hypertension, a history of never smoking, maintenance of normal weight, and a limited consumption of alcohol.[4]

normal aging

pathological aging

Thus, the individual has the ability to control many of the factors that contribute to pathological aging; the human body itself has a great capacity for dealing with some of the other factors; and some health professionals believe that the mind can also contribute to lasting health.[5] However, the normal aging process is built into the human body, and no matter what people do, they cannot avoid the inevitable. They can only affect its course through the activities and habits they develop throughout life.

The study of aging—**gerontology**—attempts to shed light on the built-in normal aging process and also to explain other factors which affect how and why people age. Among the things gerontologists study are the human life span and the changes people experience at different stages throughout their lives, especially during old age.

gerontology

Human Life Spans

life span

The length of time a person lives is called the **life span.** Most scientists believe that the approximate limit to the potential human life span is about 120 years.[6] Indeed, very few people live past 100 years.

The life spans of individuals vary enormously. Some people die very young, while others reach very old ages. In American society today, most people are lucky to reach their eighties, though more and more are doing so. In fact, persons 85 years old and older currently constitute the most rapidly growing portion of the American population.[7]

life expectancy

The average predicted length of life is known as **life expectancy.** At present, the average life expectancy at birth in the United States is about 75 years.[8] This means that most children born today can expect to live to the age of 75. At the beginning of this century the average life expectancy at birth was only about 47.3 years.[9] Much of this increase can be attributed to a reduced infant mortality rate, the control of certain diseases, and other social and medical advances that have helped prolong people's lives. Changes in lifestyle, however, also figure significantly in this increase in average life expectancy.

Growth and Change

As people age, they change in various ways. Their appearance is altered, their physical strength increases and then declines, they can be more prone to injury and disease, and their behavior and concerns may change. Perhaps most important, they grow in terms of character as a result of meeting challenges and having new experiences.

Psychologist Erik Erikson described life as a series of eight psychosocial stages from infancy to old age, during which the individual encounters certain emotional crises that must be resolved. The resolution of these crises allows the individual to mature and move successfully to the next stage. Erikson's stages are useful in explaining the emotional changes that occur as a person grows older.[10] Consider the following stages, which are adapted from those of Erikson, and some of the characteristics of each stage.[11]

Preadult (Birth to Age 18) During early childhood and the teenage years, the most obvious form of growth is physical, as the individual reaches physical maturity during this stage. It is also a time, however, when individuals begin to develop the basis for emotional, intellectual, and spiritual development. Much of a person's energies at this stage are devoted to absorbing experiences and shaping a world view. Individuals begin to develop lifelong habits, attitudes, and behaviors which are shaped by their relationships with others.

Because of the changes that occur during these years, this period of life is usually broken down into several narrower stages, including infancy, childhood, and adolescence. At each of these stages the developing individual confronts very different experiences. During infancy the child learns basic physical skills and starts to develop trust and autonomy as a result of his or her relationship with the parents. In later childhood the person begins to experience a greater sense of duty and accomplishment. During puberty and adolescence the individual strengthens physically but also undergoes hormonal changes that upset his or her emotional equilibrium. Developing strong relationships with other people during this period helps a person develop a sense

The desire for greater independence from parents and closer bonds with peers is a well-known part of adolescence. (Robert Brenner/PhotoEdit)

of perspective as he or she faces a string of crises involving love, friendship, family, and school.

Adult Entry (Ages 19 to 24)   The late teens and early twenties are years when most people experiment with new roles. It is a time of transition when many people struggle with decisions about the future. During these years most people leave their parents' homes for college or to begin careers. They may select preferred sports and physical activities, or cease formal exercise habits. They begin to develop sexual love relationships and mature friendships. Some marry and have children. A person at this stage is secure enough in his or her identity to develop an intimate partnership in which he or she makes compromises for the benefit of another person.

While some people at this stage continue the struggle for individuality and independence that was begun in late childhood, others begin to assert their individuality and independence in a mature way. It is a time when intellectual challenges may be greatly expanding, social interactions are widening, and spiritual beliefs are facing serious challenge as they come into contact with other ideas and beliefs.

Young Adulthood (Ages 25 to 39)   By young adulthood many people have married or established a lifelong commitment. Most of them have children, households, and active careers. The timing of childbearing, education, and career is highly variable, however. A large number of people will have divorced and perhaps remarried; a few will be widowed.

In this stage of life individuals may find themselves surpassing their elders in some aspects of life or being surpassed by people younger than themselves. If they gave up exercise earlier, they may feel the need to start again. Some people at this stage are already the parents of grown children, and they will become conscious role models for these children and for other young people as well. People at this stage frequently begin to choose lifestyles that will shape their later years.

Middle Age (Ages 40 to 59)   By middle age most people are liberated by the end of parenting responsibilities. For better or worse, the children are gone. Parents who took primary responsibility for child rearing may return to the work force or seek additional training. Those who focused on a career may begin to assess their achievements.

Middle-aged people receive a variety of signals that remind them of advancing age. Society places subtle limits on different age groups in terms of acceptable dress, speech, and style. Since the middle-aged person shows outward signs of aging, dressing or behaving like a younger person may feel inappropriate. Middle-aged people are also reminded of their maturity by their generational relationships. They attend their children's weddings, become grandparents, and begin to take responsibility for their own parents.

During this stage of life people are also reminded of their mortality by the death of friends and family members. When someone dies, the grieving individual sees himself or herself in a new light. When parents die, a person feels like an orphan regardless of his or her age. Despite the increasing reminders of mortality, most people in middle age have reached only the halfway point of their life span. Health can remain strong, especially if people have followed sound health practices.

Older Adulthood (Ages 60 to 74)   Older adults usually face a number of role transitions. Spouses frequently die during these years, and some people face serious health crises. Most people retire from work during this stage, and with retirement come major changes in economic and personal status as well as lifestyle. While many older adults are financially well off, others have to manage their money very carefully. Those who have always seen themselves in terms of their work have to adjust their self-image.

Sporting activities, hobbies, and social relationships can become the new focus of daily living during older adulthood, but people generally find it difficult to begin entirely new pursuits and change long-standing habits. Retirement can also change the relationship between spouses. The additional time spent together causes relationships between some couples to flower, while other people encounter difficulties brought on by unaccustomed closeness.

Old Age (Ages 75 and Over)   Since the potential human life span is over 100 years, old age can represent the longest of life's stages. The quality of life in these later years depends a great deal on the characteristics of lifestyle during a person's earlier years. Your habits and behaviors play a significant role in shaping not only the person you are but the person you will become.

The Concerns of Growing Older

While some of the concerns people have about growing older are justifiable, a great deal can be done to maximize health and human potential in the later years of life. Lifestyle during the younger years plays an important part in determining whether old age will be productive and healthful or painful and limiting. There is no need for fears of deterioration, decline, and loneliness to overshadow positive thinking about growing older. Aging is a normal process. Disease and disability are not inevitable parts of the aging process.

Good exercise habits can help ensure a lifetime of physical activity, but physical neglect often leads to debilitating problems later in life. (Tom Davis/Photo Researchers, Inc.; Tony Freeman/PhotoEdit)

However, disease and disability can occur; and there are several other areas of concern about aging, including changes in appearance, decline in the immune system and in bodily functions, increased susceptibility to injury, and reduced mental functioning.

Appearance and Body Tissues

As adults grow older, their physical appearance gradually changes. Such change is inevitable, although the degree and rate of change vary among individuals. For example, two people of the same chronological age may appear to be of quite different ages.

One of the reasons for changes in appearance during the later aging process is the body's decreasing ability to produce new cells to replace dead or worn-out tissue. There is also a decrease in the efficiency of the processes by which cells burn fuel and use the energy produced. Not all tissues in the body appear to be equally subject to these changes. The liver and kidneys, for example, usually are not affected as early as are the skin and certain muscle tissue.

Research has suggested that up to 30 percent of the body's cells may disappear between the ages of 35 and 75.[12] This results in various changes in appearance. Most people shrink physically as they get older. Posture can become stooped because of bone and muscle deterioration. The skull tends to thicken, and nose cartilage tends to grow. Hair often thins and loses its color. The skin loses much of its elasticity and begins to stretch and wrinkle. Skin tissue may also thin and become translucent, especially in places that have been exposed to excessive sunlight, such as the back of the hand.

Older people generally have diminished physical strength. Muscle cells gradually die and are not replaced. The condition of the remaining muscle tissue deteriorates gradually. The ratio of fat to muscle also tends to increase with age—caused both by the built-in aging process and by lifestyle factors.

Generally, as people grow older, their bodies become stiffer. Most bones lose density, and joints become less lubricated and more prominent. Since these conditions are often accompanied by pain, older people become less active, and this can increase the deterioration.

Body Functions

With age, many of the body's basic functions slow down. The body's metabolism decreases, and less food is needed to supply energy. The body's ability to return to a state of homeostasis also slows, as does its ability to regenerate cells and fight disease.

In women, the onset of *menopause* (when ovulation and menstruation cease) is accompanied by hormonal changes that may affect the body's functions. A recent study showed that early natural menopause is associated with reduced life expectancy.[13] Aging also affects the body's sexual functioning. Women remain fertile only until menopause. As men age, their ability to produce viable sperm decreases, though it does not cease entirely. These changes need not interfere with the ability of older people to enjoy sex, however. While health problems or lack of a partner may detract from sexual functioning, research shows that many older men and women continue to lead active sex lives.[14]

As the body ages, internal organs also decrease in efficiency and lose some of their function. Heart rate and pumping capacity decrease, as does the ability of the kidneys to filter blood. The lungs lose some of their elasticity. Consequently, the ability to move air in and out decreases. The nervous system slows, resulting in slightly decreased reaction times.

Certain cognitive, or learning, functions may change as a person grows older, but these changes do not seem to be an inherent part of the aging process. In fact, most adults maintain *fluid intelligence*—the ability to solve abstract problems and generate new ideas—at normal levels throughout the life span. *Crystallized intelligence*—the ability to use accumulated knowledge and learning—actually increases throughout adulthood and declines only slightly in old age. Memory also continues relatively unchanged throughout the life span. Early memories usually remain intact, though some older people have difficulty recalling particular recent events.

Advanced age does seem to affect both the quality of sensory perception and the ability to receive, process, and act upon that information, leading to slower responses to various stimuli.[15] The functioning of the sensory organs usually fades with age. Taste and smell may become less acute. Hearing loss at higher sound frequencies commonly begins during the twenties or thirties and continues as a person becomes older. Visual impairment also increases. Older people need more time to adjust to changes in light and to change focus between near and far objects.

Injuries

Since people experience a gradual loss of various abilities as they age, older adults are generally more prone to sustain injuries than are young and middle-aged adults. Poor night vision, slower reflexes, and reduced strength may contribute to a fall down a poorly lit staircase, and damage from such an accident is likely to be more severe in an older person whose bones are more brittle. Furthermore, recovery from a serious injury, such as a broken hip, may be longer and more painful for an older person than it is for a younger one. Older adults can, however, minimize the risk of having accidents by exercising to keep in good condition and by improving the safety of the home.

Infectious Diseases

Everyone is subject to acute infections, but such infections may have more serious consequences in people of advanced age. An older person may be less attentive to sanitation and body cleanliness than he or she was in earlier years. Older people often contract digestive ailments by eating food contaminated by bacteria. Moreover, since older people are more prone to have accidents, they are more likely to get skin and mouth cuts, scrapes, and other abrasions that enable disease-carrying organisms to enter the body. Because the cleansing mechanisms in their respiratory and urogenital tracts no longer function as well, the consequences of these infections are likely to be more serious.

The body's ability to repair and renew itself lessens with age and the immune system becomes less efficient. As a result, older people have less resistance to attack by disease-producing organisms. This is why physicians routinely recommend that older people receive preventive inoculations against certain infections, particularly pneumonia and influenza.

Chronic Diseases

The greatest number of older people die from or are disabled by *chronic conditions*—disorders that persist or worsen gradually as the body's resist-and-repair capabilities decrease.[16] These conditions are frequently a delayed result of a person's lifestyle during earlier years. Some of the most common chronic diseases affecting older people are disorders of the cardiovascular system, cancer, osteoporosis, and diabetes.

Disorders of the Cardiovascular System   Cardiovascular disorders, including heart disease, stroke, hypertension, and atherosclerosis, rank first among chronic diseases of the aged, accounting for more than 60 percent of deaths in people over age 65. The primary cardiovascular disorder is atherosclerosis, which in turn may result in angina, myocardial infarction (heart attack), stroke, and kidney problems. While cardiovascular disorders are a great concern of older people, a recent study found only a tenuous relationship between aging and cardiovascular disease.[17] These disorders are much more dangerous if an older individual has certain other chronic conditions as well.

Cancer   The second most common chronic disease among older people is cancer. Cancer is actually many different diseases that vary widely in seriousness and treatability. Approximately half of all cancers are found in people over age 65. This may be due to a number of reasons. One is that certain cancers can be traced to long-term exposure to risk factors such as sunlight. A second reason may be that the immune systems of older people are less efficient. Other reasons include long-term use of alcohol and tobacco and exposure to various toxic substances.

Osteoporosis Another chronic condition common to older people, especially
women, is **osteoporosis,** a condition marked by thinning, brittle, easily fractured bones. In patients with osteoporosis, the bones most often affected are
the weight-bearing ones of the lower spine and hip and the ones in the wrist.
Twenty percent of women with hip fractures die of complications such as
pneumonia, making osteoporosis a leading cause of death among older
women in the United States.[18]

osteoporosis

Osteoporosis accelerates the normal process by which bone density and
mass decrease with age. Since women have smaller bones to begin with, its
effects are more severe for women. The condition rarely produces symptoms—
except for mild, chronic lower back pain—until the bones become so thin and
weak that they snap just from the weight of the body or break in a simple fall.
The vertebrae may disintegrate, resulting in severe back pain, loss of height,
and ultimately the classic "dowager's hump," characterized by a rounded spine
and a shortened chest area.

The cause of osteoporosis is unclear, but the loss of estrogen that accompanies menopause or surgical removal of the ovaries seems to be a factor. Other
contributing factors are inactivity (exercise builds bones as well as muscle),
cigarette smoking, excessive alcohol intake, and a family history of osteoporosis. The most likely reason for the loss of bone, however, is prolonged calcium
deficiency, a dietary problem which can be avoided.

diabetes

Diabetes **Diabetes** is a condition in which the body is unable to regulate the
level of sugar in the blood efficiently. The condition is caused by an insufficiency of insulin, a hormone produced in the pancreas. One form of diabetes—
type I—strikes early in life. However, another form—type II—generally does
not appear before age 40 and is more prevalent among older populations,
occurring in about 10 percent of people over age 65.[19] Diabetes poses a special
threat to older persons because it can result in blindness and loss of limbs (due
in part to poor circulation and nourishment of body cells). It can also lead to
neurological problems, kidney problems, heightened susceptibility to infection, stroke, and heart disease. Fortunately, diabetes can be controlled with
diet and medication.

Disability

A person's ability to perform personal-care activities is a common measure of
physical vitality. Among the typical activities that may be curtailed among
older people are walking, bathing, going outside, getting in and out of bed or
a chair, dressing, using the toilet, and eating. Among people who experience
disability, some have trouble with more than one of these activities. The total
number of disabled people over age 65 is not as great as one might expect.
Among the entire population 65 and over (not including those in institutions),
over 77 percent have no difficulties with personal-care activities. Furthermore, disability is more reversible than was previously thought. In a 2-year
study of approximately 4,000 older persons, 22 percent of those who were
severely disabled at the beginning of the study had improved 2 years later.[20]

arthritis

One condition that can be disabling for older people is **arthritis**. According
to some sources, it is the most common disease among older people; more
than 35 percent of men and 56 percent of women over age 65 suffer from
some form of this disease.[21] Arthritis is actually a collective term for several

diseases—including rheumatoid arthritis and osteoarthritis—that affect the tendons, ligaments, cartilage, and other tissues of the joints. The symptoms of arthritis include pain and stiffness in the joints. Sufferers often become less active, miss work, and lose sleep. Treatment usually focuses on reducing inflammation and pain.

Alzheimer's Disease

It is a myth that severe memory loss is an inevitable part of growing old. However, there is a condition that involves progressive deterioration of memory and other mental functions and is associated with advancing age. It is **Alzheimer's disease.**

In patients with Alzheimer's disease, the brain's medium-sized and small blood vessels degenerate. A common early symptom is severe difficulty with short-term memory. As the condition worsens, the patient may display personality changes, have difficulty reading or speaking, and become extremely disoriented. Ultimately, those suffering from Alzheimer's disease become completely helpless and dependent on the support of others.

Progressive, with no known cause or cure, Alzheimer's disease is now believed to have a gradual onset, beginning well before an individual grows old. Recent studies have linked the disorder with head injuries sustained earlier in life and with thyroid disease. Some experts think that it may be related to the individual's genetic background and may be associated with a specific biochemical defect (this would mean that it is potentially treatable).[22] Using the few clues that are available, researchers are trying to devise a test to identify Alzheimer's disease early and to develop a drug that will halt or reverse the mental deterioration that characterizes the condition.[23]

The proportion of older people who have Alzheimer's disease is quite low—only 6 to 8 percent. Memory loss, confusion, and other symptoms often displayed by older people may be caused by a wide range of disorders, many of which are treatable. Emotional problems such as depression can lead to symptoms that resemble those of Alzheimer's disease. So can overconsumption of alcohol, accidents, poor vision and hearing, and physical disorders such as malnutrition, glandular problems, drug toxicity, infection, dehydration, and atherosclerosis. Brain tumors, small strokes, epilepsy, and other cerebral disorders can also produce symptoms that mimic those of Alzheimer's disease.

People who suffer from Alzheimer's disease should be encouraged to maintain their daily routines, physical activities, and social contacts for as long as possible. Medication is available to relieve some symptoms, such as depression and severe agitation. Behavior therapy may slow the process of mental deterioration, and exercise and proper nourishment may help delay the loss of physical mobility.[24] The children of people with Alzheimer's disease seem to have an increased risk of developing the condition. Symptoms usually develop before age 65 in these people, and the progress of the disease is likely to be rapid and severe.[25]

Depression and Suicide in the Elderly

Depression and suicide are other potential threats to people as they grow older, although the risks are greater for some groups than they are for others. Rates of suicide among men increase with age, while the rates for women

Alzheimer's disease

Although most older people live happy lives, a small percentage of the elderly are plagued with severe depression. (Myrleen Ferguson/Photo Edit)

remain relatively unchanged. The risk of suicide is highest for white males. Suicide attempts among older persons are more likely to be fatal compared with attempts by adolescents, who succeed only about 1 percent of the time.[26] These statistics do not include "silent suicide," or the attempt to kill oneself by passive means such as refusing food or medical treatment. Silent suicide occurs not among the terminally ill but among otherwise healthy older people.[27]

Depression seems to be the leading cause of suicide, and it may be underdiagnosed among older persons because of the belief systems of family members and health care providers. People just do not want to believe that another human being, especially a respected elder, may have developed an emotional disorder such as depression.[28] Furthermore, the symptoms of depression can be confused with those of organic brain disorders such as Alzheimer's disease.

Making a Difference for Yourself

Everyone can shape a life that is longer and healthier as well as satisfying and rewarding. The key is to develop healthy behaviors now and maintain them throughout your life. Ultimately, individuals are responsible for their own health and well-being. The description of a healthy lifestyle that appears throughout this book offers guidance in shaping habits and behaviors which can maximize health, prolong life, and promote physical, mental, and social well-being.

To achieve long and healthy lives, people must assess their strengths and weaknesses and then adjust their life patterns accordingly. There are many options for improving health. Knowledge of these options coupled with sound planning can help each person make decisions that are best for himself or herself.

The eating habits that people develop when young affect their food choices and their health throughout life. (Benn Mitchell/The Image Bank)

Maintaining Physical Health

Exercise plays an important role in the maintenance of physical health as a person ages. Regular exercise can help reduce the loss of muscle mass that accompanies the aging process. Between the ages of 30 and 70 years, the average person loses 30 to 40 percent of the body's muscle mass. Exercise can retard these changes by as much as 20 years.[29] There is also substantial evidence to link exercise with a reduction in the risk of developing cardiovascular disease and with improved general well-being and morale.[30] One study showed that even among people age 80 or older, the most physically fit were the least likely to have health problems 2 years later.[31] A program of regular exercise would thus seem to be essential for maintaining physical health as one grows older.

Diet and nutrition also have an important impact on physical health. Research in nutrition has shown that lifelong dietary habits affect a person's health in old age. Dietary factors such as an excess caloric intake, a high salt intake, and a high fat intake can predispose individuals to various health-threatening conditions, including obesity, diabetes, hypertension, and atherosclerosis. Although the negative effects of a poor diet may become evident slowly, they accumulate with age. Thus, eating habits that contribute to a healthy old age must begin in youth and middle age.

Other factors that have an impact on physical health include the use of dangerous substances such as alcohol, tobacco, and drugs; the risk of accidents; and exposure to infectious diseases. All these factors have been discussed in detail throughout this book.

For people concerned about their physical health, regular visits to professional health practitioners can help point out potential problems early and prevent the complications that may accompany a neglected condition. Various types of checkups are recommended for different stages in a person's life, since the risk of developing certain conditions becomes greater with age.

Maintaining Intellectual and Emotional Health

Good physical health contributes to good intellectual and emotional health and vice versa. Developing an optimistic outlook toward life is an important factor in good health. A positive attitude can help guard against destructive behaviors that may threaten a person's health. The ability to put life crises in perspective can also improve an individual's decision-making ability. An active mind can improve the quality of life at all ages, especially in retirement or old age, when illness may deprive a person of stimulation.

The habits, general activity, and coping strategies associated with good intellectual and emotional health can help people adjust to the changes that come with age. A recent study showed that while older people tend to use fewer coping strategies, they adjust to the stresses of health problems better than do their younger counterparts.[32]

Intellectual and emotional health can have an important impact on stress, which affects a person's overall health and well-being. Attitude can greatly affect an individual's reaction to events that may be stressful. For example, people with so-called Type A personalities may be at greater risk for developing heart disease and stroke than are those who react to stress less intensely. Learning how to cope with stress and resolve feelings such as anger and frustration can thus help preserve health.

Intellectual and emotional well-being is also enhanced by keeping active. Hobbies and interests that provide stimulation throughout life by helping to balance rest and work cycles can be pursued during retirement as well. Some older persons stimulate their minds by going back to school. Others travel through educationally affiliated programs. Still others may begin new careers.

Another important factor in maintaining intellectual and emotional health is the development of strong family and social ties. The maintenance of active networks of family members and friends contributes to emotional health by providing emotional support and companionship.[33] The feeling of belonging that people get from these ties also makes them feel wanted, needed, and loved.

Good intellectual and emotional health can best be nurtured by keeping interested in the world and abreast of the times, caring about and reaching out to others, developing a sense of independence and self-efficacy, developing new interests and hobbies, and treating oneself with dignity.

Maintaining Social and Spiritual Health

A recent study showed that men and women both seek and maintain meaningful friendships in their later years.[34] Such relationships help maintain an individual's social health and well-being.

As people grow older, the social relationships provided by friends and family members play a more important role as other activities decrease. Women who have been central care givers in their families find that their roles change with age. People who retire must find replacements for the social interactions that were once part of their daily routine.

Generally, people feel better within networks of friends and loved ones. The loss of an intimate relationship can be devastating and is sometimes associated with declining health or a shortened life span. In one study, the immune systems of recently widowed men declined during the 2 months after the deaths of their wives and their recovery from this lost capacity was slow.[35] Stories of one spouse dying shortly after the death of the other are common.

People develop and maintain social relationships in various ways. Many people choose to live in retirement communities where they can enjoy the company of people with similar needs and perspectives. Since intimacy and companionship can enhance health, retirement communities may offer a health advantage to older adults. For some older people, community senior centers can be good places for meeting peers. Such centers usually offer programs that include recreation, entertainment, educational and fitness classes, and meals. Churches, synagogues, and many other community institutions often provide similar services for older people. Other older people find greater fulfillment within groups that are less age-restricted, allowing them to develop relationships with people of various ages.

As the number of older persons in American society grows, the focus may shift from the separation of age groups to intergenerational social arrangements. With their experience and wisdom, older persons can be an important resource for their communities. Volunteer organizations provide one way to help channel their talents toward the needs of the community. Participation in volunteer efforts can benefit older persons as well as the communities they serve. The volunteer can regain the status that once came from a job or a role within the family. Volunteerism also provides an opportunity to develop friendships and social relationships while serving others.

Spiritual health is a more elusive quality. It can come from formal or informal religious beliefs and affiliations or from a strongly held personal philosophy and world view. While spiritual health is an essential part of well-being, it may become more important as a person ages and begins to experience feelings of personal mortality. It brings an inner peace that helps the individual cope with the inevitability of death as well as with the challenges still left in life.

Dying and Death

thanatology   Death is, of course, a natural part of the life cycle. Increasingly, the subject of death is discussed more freely, and **thanatology,** a Greek word meaning "the study of death," has become an important field of research.

Modern changes in disease patterns and technological advancement have made research into death and its implications all the more essential. People in this country today are increasingly less likely to die from short, acute illnesses or injuries. While death was in the past considered to occur with absence of

clinical death   heartbeat and cessation of breathing, these are now only evidence of **clinical death:** a period during which—although these life signs have stopped—all the vital cells of the body may still survive. With quick medical intervention, a "clinically dead" person may be revived or put on a life-support system until treatment can be provided.

Such advances have led physicians, lawyers, and religious leaders to reconsider what death is. A concept has been developed, **brain death,** defined when an electroencephalogram (EEG) detects no brain activity for at least 24 hours, even though breathing and circulation are artificially maintained. But there is still uncertainty whether this can be accepted as evidence of true death. Thus, new philosophies of death are emerging, and new forms of care for people who are near death.

brain death

The problems of survivors are also a concern. For the first time, researchers are objectively studying how people react to the death of a loved one and how such a loss may upset people's emotional and physical well-being. While everyone must face death at some point, the study of death may, ironically, help people gain a greater perspective on the meaning of life.

The Process of Dying

It is difficult to define the point in time when a person begins to die. The exact moment that a disease becomes terminal can rarely be pinpointed, for illness is a process of gradual deterioration. Doctors cannot even easily agree on what constitutes a terminal illness, and the prognosis changes for certain illnesses as progress is made in treating them. For certain types of cancer, for example, early detection leads to more effective treatment than in the past.

Stages of Acceptance

Because the exact moment when the unalterable movement toward death begins is so elusive, dying arrives in several stages for most people. The initial news usually comes when a doctor or other health professional tells a patient that he or she is dying. With that news, the individual begins to move from the psychological position of a living person to that of a dying one. The process is rarely simple. It is not unusual for people to take some time to accept the news that they are dying. Some are not psychologically ready to hear such news, so they distort facts and information. At times, too, doctors are disturbed by having to relay unpleasant news, and so they may garble the message in clinical terms that are not readily understood. As a result, it often takes time for an individual to understand a terminal diagnosis and accept it. And many people slip in and out of accepting their fate.

The Stages of Kübler-Ross Based on interviews with hundreds of patients, psychiatrist Elisabeth Kübler-Ross concluded that many dying people go through five specific stages[36]:

1. There may be a *denial* of the diagnosis. A terminal patient will often assert that the news cannot be true.
2. The dying individual may grow *angry* at the world, asking "Why me?"
3. The person may try to *bargain* with fate, asking to be allowed to live long enough for an important event, such as a child's graduation or wedding.

4. He or she may grow *depressed,* drained by stress and physical suffering, and may withdraw from friends and family.

5. Finally, the dying person may *accept* fate. This final stage is rarely a happy or blissful one; but the individual does grow more peaceful and becomes resigned to a foreseeable death.

Kübler-Ross found that some people may not get to every stage: some stop along the way, never accepting their death. Some may go back and forth among various stages or may experience more than one stage at the same time.

Other Viewpoints The research of Kübler-Ross has been helpful for its compassionate exploration of what dying people experience, and she has offered useful strategies by which people can cope with their feelings when a loved one is dying.

However, as more studies have been made of death and dying, it has become clear that not every dying person goes through the stages described by Kübler-Ross. It has also become increasingly clear that no one facing death should feel that he or she necessarily *should* go through five stages—or any series of stages—to adapt to the situation. Indeed, researchers are finding that most often an individual's attitude and conduct during dying simply reflect his or her attitudes and conduct throughout life.[37]

Care of the Dying

Although dying is essentially an individual, personal experience, it can be affected by the actions and attitudes of others. The type of care a dying person receives and the responses of loved ones and care givers can make a great difference in the person's happiness and comfort during the time that remains.

Practical Issues of Care

In facing death, a terminally ill patient and his or her loved ones must not only adjust to emotions about dying, they must also deal with a number of practical issues. For example, should the patient be kept at home, be put in a hospital or nursing home, or receive a combination of home, hospital, and nursing care? Which environment offers the best care at a cost the family can afford?

Decisions on these issues are just as critical to the final experiences of the dying patient as the emotional adjustments he or she must make. They can play a significant role in making the last days more pleasant and comfortable for everyone. Although most people die in a hospital, in recent years there has been an increase in other alternatives to care for the terminally ill, including hospices and home care.

Hospices The word *hospice* refers as much to a philosophy of care for people who are dying as to a type of health care service. It encourages patients to take more control over the care they receive and to participate as fully as possible in life until death occurs.

One of the hardest tasks for any doctor is to tell a patient that an illness may be terminal. (Blair Seitz/Photo Researchers, Inc.)

Hospices offer a variety of services, including personal care for dying persons and emotional support for them and their families. Many also offer support services for the bereaved after the death of a hospice patient. Some hospices are affiliated with hospitals, some work with home health agencies, and others are independent. In addition to inpatient care, hospices arrange for their services to be brought to the patient's home through a system of professional and volunteer care providers.[38]

Hospice care is distinguished by its emphasis on meeting the needs of the dying patient and often the family of the patient. The primary goal is to allow patients to be as free from physical pain and discomfort as possible and to meet their psychological, social, and spiritual needs by providing a comfortable, caring environment in which loved ones can actively participate in the patient's care.

The highest priority of hospice care is to make the dying patient comfortable without using devices for prolonging life, such as respirators, intravenous feeding apparatus, and so on. Instead, pain and other distressing symptoms are controlled by the skillful use of medications.

Home Care Another common alternative to institutional care is home care (in which hospice care may or may not play a role). Home care for the dying is seen as a particularly good option if the family is able and willing to provide care. With the patient at home, family members can take active roles in providing care and can offer a level of emotional and psychological support that is not available in an institutional setting, such as a hospital. One study, for example, found that mutually responsive relationships had a positive effect on patients' length of survival.[39]

Studies show that home care can prove beneficial not only to the dying person but to the family as well. Patients generally experience more dignity and comfort at home than in the hospital, and families adjust with less difficulty. Home care costs the family a fraction of what a hospital stay would cost, and programs encouraging such care also benefit the community as a whole by freeing hospital beds for patients requiring acute care.[40]

Yet, while home care can provide a humane way to die, it can also create strain among family members. It is not unusual, for example, for several relatives to feel that they must take primary responsibility for the dying person. So the family members must sort through their various abilities and relationships to find an appropriate role for everyone. Some may be able to provide the dying person with intensive psychological support, while others may feel more comfortable attending to practical details, such as paying bills.

Preparing for Death

Since death is an emotional experience, the practical side of preparing for death and doing what needs to be done is often very difficult. Yet it is important to think ahead and consider critical issues such as the preparation of a will, the possibility of organ donation, and the decision at a certain point to employ life-sustaining measures. Early decisions about these issues can forestall future problems and can play a role in making the last days of life more pleasant, comfortable, and free of worry.

Communicating with Someone Who Is Dying

Communicating with a friend or relative who is dying can be a real service to a person one cares about. It can also be a comforting experience for you. Being with, talking with, hugging, and listening to someone who is dying can give you both a chance to say things you always meant to say, clear up unresolved issues, and begin to deal with your feelings.

Talking with someone who is terminally ill is disturbing to many people. It can seem awkward. You do not know what to say and are afraid of saying the wrong thing. In the face of something as serious as death, people often do not know how to behave. As a result, many people put off communicating with a dying friend or relative until it is too late. It is important to realize that a person who is sick or terminally ill does not expect or want you to be any different from the way you usually are.

Many people are afraid of expressing their sadness while talking to someone who is dying. Whether the person knows about his or her condition or not, you do not need to hide your feelings or stop yourself from crying. The person will see your tears as a sign of concern and love.

When you are faced with the reality that a friend or relative is dying, you need to face your own feelings honestly. Losing someone you care about is very hard, and dealing with someone else's death reminds everyone of his or her own mortality. Recognizing your own fear of death may help you communicate with a dying friend or relative more easily.

Some people are afraid that they will hurt a terminally ill person by reacting negatively to his or her appearance or behavior. It may be easier to be supportive if you are prepared in advance. Ask someone else what to expect— how does the person appear, what is his or her mood, how easily does he or she tire? You should also find out in advance how much the ill person knows about the true chances for recovery. You do not want to reveal information he or she is not aware of.

There are no real rules for communicating with someone who is dying, but there are guidelines you may find helpful. First of all, just be yourself. If you are naturally a very physically expressive person, hug or touch your relative as much as usual. If you have always joked with this person, do not lose your sense of humor now.

A large part of your role in communicating with a terminally ill person will probably be to listen. Let the person talk about whatever he or she wants to discuss. It may be about his or her illness or fears, or it may be about plans for family members after he or she is gone.

The person you are talking to may never bring up the subject of his or her impending death. Many people who are dying do not want to talk about death. Other people may not be aware that the sickness is terminal. Follow the person's lead. Do not feel you have to bring up the subject or offer reassurance. It is better to provide support with comments that tell the person you care about what he or she has to say. Comments such as "I'm sorry that's painful" and "It sounds as if you're lonely here in the hospital" tell the person you are willing to listen.

When you communicate with someone at the end of his or her life, it is a chance for you to say some of the things that have been left unsaid over the years. A simple statement such as "You know how much I have always loved you" can make both you and the person who is dying feel much better.

Based on Lynne Ann DeSpelder and Albert L. Strickland, *The Last Dance: Encountering Death and Dying* (Palo Alto, Calif.: Mayfield, 1983); Elisabeth Kübler-Ross, *On Death and Dying* (New York: Macmillan, 1970).

Making a Will

A *will* is a legal document that specifies how a person wishes his or her property to be distributed after death. Everyone should have a will. Without one, a person's property will be distributed not as he or she would want, but according to the laws of the state of residence. In addition, the absence of a will may provoke disputes among family members over claims to the person's possessions in the event of death.

Although a valid will can be written on a simple "do-it-yourself" form, it is usually wiser to seek the advice and assistance of an attorney. In either case, the following information may be helpful[41]:

- The *testator* (the person making the will) names an *executor* to supervise the distribution of property after death.
- One or more witnesses (the number depends on the testator's state of residence) must sign the will. To prevent coercion and fraud, witnesses may not be beneficiaries of the will.
- Upon death, the executor files the will as designated by the county or state (typically, in the office of the clerk of the probate court). The executor also has the witnesses called in to verify the deceased's signature and their own and to swear that they have witnessed the proper execution of the will.
- Property that is titled (such as a jointly owned home bearing the right of survivorship) and insurance benefits (where the surviving spouse or other individual has been designated as beneficiary) will be passed along automatically, independently of the will. If no additional property is bequeathed under the will, administration of the estate is unnecessary. However, the will may be filed and become a matter of public record, available if it is ever needed.
- A person who dies without a will is said to have died *intestate*. If the person owned any property, the court appoints an administrator to distribute it in accordance with the state's laws.
- A will should be kept in a place that is safe but readily available to spouse, parent, or other next of kin. A safe-deposit box may not be the best place. (In some jurisdictions, safe-deposit boxes must be sealed upon a person's death and are not released until audited by the tax authorities.)
- A will should be reviewed periodically to make sure that it is up to date. If the testator moves to a new state, the will must meet the legal requirements of the new place of residence.

Organ Donation

Modern medical technology and surgical techniques have made it possible to transplant a variety of body parts from dead donors to live patients. Donated organs can be used to save another person's life, as with a kidney or liver transplant, or to help the person live more productively, as with a corneal (the cornea of the eye) transplant.

Today, it is fairly widely accepted that an individual has a right to decide what will be done with his or her body after death. People may choose to bequeath their entire bodies or specific body parts for use in transplants, medical treatments, or medical research and education. While the right of organ donation is widely accepted, one study found that only about 3 percent of the respondents had actually made preparations for the use of their organs.[42] Those who have chosen to become donors often carry donor cards, which are legal documents stipulating what parts of the body may be used in the event of death.

All 50 states have enacted some form of legislation providing for the donation of the body or designated body parts upon the death of the donor. Despite this legislation and the legal decisions of donors, organ donations are sometimes not utilized because of objections by the deceased's family.

The Right to Die and Euthanasia

While the right of organ donation is quite widely accepted, there is less general acceptance of the idea that any means should be used to prolong the life of a person with a debilitating and terminal medical crisis. There is also much less acceptance of the idea that a person has the right to take steps to end his or her life should the pain and problems of a serious illness become unbearable. The basic question underlying these ideas is whether people have the right to control their own fate—whether they have the right to control how they die or when death will occur. This is known as **euthanasia**—allowing or helping a person to die.

euthanasia

The issue of euthanasia can be considered from several perspectives. **Passive euthanasia** refers to situations in which no action is taken to prolong life even though action might enable a person to live longer. An example of passive euthanasia would be *not* hooking up a respirator to a person who is unable to breathe unassisted. In contrast, **active euthanasia** refers to situations in which something is done to a patient to directly cause death. An example of active euthanasia would be the removal of an already functioning life-support system (such as a respirator or intravenous feeding tube) from a vegetative, comatose person.

passive euthanasia

active euthanasia

While many people might agree that people have the right to control their own fate, and might also agree that people should not have to endure unbearable pain and suffering, the issue of euthanasia is not that simple. Death affects not only the deceased, but also family, friends, and others. Their "right" to have the person live may be just as valid as the person's "right" to die. Therefore, while euthanasia might be merciful to a dying person, it places a difficult burden on others.

After Death: Responses of the Living

After someone dies, the impact of death is felt by the living. Survivors mourn the loss of parents, children, spouses, friends, and other loved ones. As difficult as it may be, these survivors can and do learn to cope with their loss. Among the first things that help in the coping process are funerals and mourning.

Funerals and Mourning

mourning

After death comes **mourning**—all those culturally reinforced patterns of thought, feelings, and behaviors that individuals experience as a result of losing a loved one. Part of mourning is the larger society's support for survivors and the rituals and expectations with which society responds to death.

When death finally arrives, it brings a need for a parting ceremony, a rite of passage, that can help friends and relatives absorb and comprehend their loss. This ritual occurs, in one form or another, in every human society and like other rituals, satisfies deep-seated human needs.

Funerals are of major psychological value to survivors. The funeral provides an important emotional release in the first few days after death, giving the survivors something concrete to do. It also helps confirm the reality of the death and provides a network of people who may be called on for support. Funerals also seem to fulfill several important societal functions, such as bringing families together, thus affirming the importance of family networks and helping reinforce the social order.

Postfuneral rituals are also helpful to survivors. Sending out acknowledgments for kindnesses expressed at the time of death and sorting out and disposing of the deceased's personal effects can be a healthy indication that the death is being accepted.[43]

War memorials not only serve as a patriotic memorial to those who died for their country, they also provide a tangible solace for every individual who mourns their loss. (Owen Franklen/Sygma)

bereavement

grief

Bereavement

The death of a loved one causes a great deal of stress, which can have a profound effect on the survivors. There is the stress that comes from **bereavement**—the loss of a loved or valued person—and from the change in one's own status (as from spouse to widowed person) that results from the death. Then there is the stress of **grief**—the subjective, emotional response to bereavement. When people grieve, they may experience symptoms of distress in both their minds and bodies. Grief can sometimes become so intense that it causes biochemical and physiological reactions that can result in physical illness and even death.[44] The psychological and behavioral responses to grief can cause loss of memory and difficulty in mental concentration—sometimes even to the point where the grieving person questions his or her sanity.

Many experts believe that survivors go through various stages as they attempt to deal with their loss and work through their grief. These stages are part of the process of mourning (Figure 15.1). The stages a bereaved person may experience include shock, a yearning for the deceased and protest that the death occurred, a period of disorganization and despair, and finally, an integration and adjustment to a realistic view of life without the deceased. People may progress through the stages in that order, regress to previous stages, skip stages, or experience different stages at the same time.[45]

No one can predict exactly how long a person will grieve for the loss of someone dear. "Normal" grief seems to begin with a period of acute mourning immediately following or soon after a death and then diminishes gradually over the course of 2 or more years.[46] Too little grieving soon after a death or too much grieving too long after, or both, are considered abnormal.

In order to cope with death, a grieving person has to come to terms with certain "tasks of bereavement," including the need to detach him- or herself from the deceased, maintain relationships with others who can be supportive, and hold on to a satisfactory self-image.[47] Researchers have also found that there are ways of coping with grief that can lessen the stress and help people come through the experience intact. Perhaps most important of all, studies show that it is crucial for people to "allow" themselves to grieve and to verbalize the feelings that accompany grief. The simple act of expressing feelings

Figure 15.1 *The grieving process. During the grieving process the mourner may pass through several stages characterized by different ranges of emotional expression. In Stage I denial may accompany the initial shock at the loss of a loved one. In Stage II the mourner yearns for an idealized loved one. Anger at abandonment may turn to guilt. In Stage III the mourner may be disorganized and depressed. Finally, in Stage IV the mourner integrates the loss. Love and support of friends help the mourner accept the loss and refocus his or her ongoing life.*

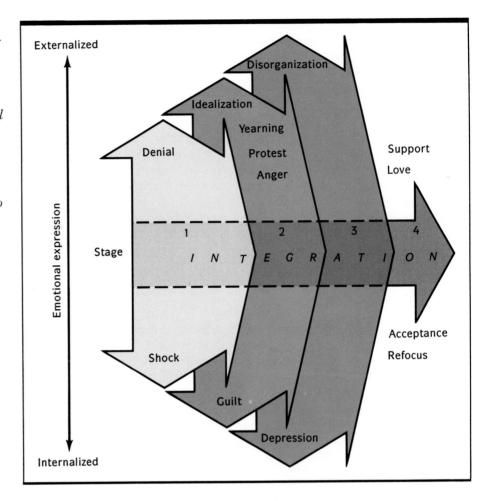

about oneself, the death, and the person who died can help a person survive the most desolate moments. Talking helps to release negative emotions such as hatred and guilt. If such feelings are left unattended, they can make a person feel desperate and confused. If discussed, they can help the bereaved come to understand that the feelings are the natural outgrowth of a sense of abandonment and loneliness. Grief is an expression of the conflict between the longing for the deceased and the recognition that the person is truly gone forever. Talking helps to bring the reality of death into focus. Talking also, however, helps to reinforce the feeling that, although a loved one may be gone forever, his or her memory will live on as a permanent part of those who remain.[48]

Chapter Summary

- Normal aging refers to a biological process that is time-related. Pathological aging refers to a decrease in functioning caused by illness, stress, injury, and other factors.

- The human life span seems to have a maximum limit based on biological evolution. Life expectancy varies considerably, depending on numerous factors.

- Successful growth and emotional development can be viewed as a positive progression through a series of emotional stages, each with unique characteristics. Stages discussed in this chapter are preadult, adult entry, young adulthood, middle age, older adulthood, and old age.

- As people grow older, they often are faced with concerns such as changing appearance and body functions, a greater risk of accidents, a higher susceptibility to certain infectious diseases and chronic conditions, and the threat of disability.

- Individuals can shape a longer and healthier life by developing a healthy lifestyle and maintaining it throughout their lives.

- There are various ways people can maintain their physical, intellectual, emotional, social, and spiritual health as they grow older. One of the main purposes of this book is to examine the ways in which people can improve their lifestyles.

- Kübler-Ross identified five stages of dying: denial, anger, bargaining with fate, depression, and acceptance.

- Hospice care encourages patients to take more control over their care and to participate fully in life until death occurs. Hospice care provides emotional support for patients and their families and tries to free the patient from pain without the use of life-sustaining devices. Home care can also be emotionally satisfying for patients because of the familiar environment and the presence of loved ones.

- Euthanasia—allowing or helping a person to die—is a controversial issue. In passive euthanasia, no actions are taken to prolong a person's life. In active euthanasia, something is done to cause death.

- Funerals provide an emotional release for survivors and confirm the reality of death.

- People in mourning often experience shock, a yearning for the deceased and a protest that the death occurred, a period of disorganization and despair, and finally, an integration and adjustment to a realistic view of life without the deceased.

- To cope with grief, a person has to come to terms with certain tasks of bereavement, including detachment from the deceased, maintaining other supportive relationships, and holding on to a satisfactory self-image. It is crucial for people to allow themselves to grieve and to verbalize their feelings with friends and other loved ones.

Medical Care in America

Objectives

When you have studied this chapter, you should be able to:

- Explain the importance of being health-activated and describe some of the basic attitudes, judgments, and behaviors characteristic of health-activation.

- Describe important information needed for medical self-care.

- Compare and contrast the different types of medical care available in the United States today.

- Discuss different ways in which health care is financed in the United States and analyze some of the advantages and disadvantages of the available systems.

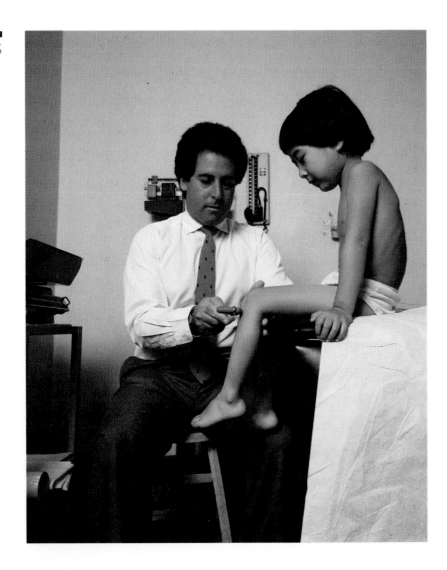

Today, people are taking greater responsibility for their own health and health care. This greater self-responsibility has come about in part because more and more Americans are beginning to understand the value of good health and realize that they can do a great deal to promote their own health and well-being. People realize that their own actions can play an important role in preventing many health problems and in dealing with the minor problems that may arise.

Becoming Health-Activated

Although many people still equate health care with health professionals, increasing numbers of individuals want to become more active participants in their own care and treatment. Health care is no longer seen as the exclusive domain of doctors, nurses, and dentists but rather as something that each person has an interest in.[1]

This trend toward more active participation, or health-activation, reflects a spirit of self-reliance. People are taking some of the responsibility for health care into their own hands. They are becoming more confident about their ability to take actions that affect their own lives and health.

While health-activated individuals assume more responsibility for their health, the goal is not to eliminate the role of health professionals. Rather, it is to know when to use those professionals, who to consult, and how to make the best use of medical advice and expertise.

Health-activated people want to learn what steps they should take to stay healthy, deal with medical problems that do not require professional attention, and manage small medical problems so that they do not become major problems. These people may regularly engage in aerobic exercise; eat low-fat and low-cholesterol foods; avoid tobacco; be careful not to abuse alcohol and drugs; and practice stress management techniques. They are aware of the risk factors associated with lung cancer and cardiovascular disease and modify their health behaviors to reduce those risks and to enhance the quality of their lives. Health-activated people understand that many of the factors that affect health are under their control and that a healthier lifestyle is often the most effective way to ensure good health.

Judging Health Care Problems

People could save substantial amounts of time and money if they were able to distinguish between medical problems that require professional care and problems that can be treated at home.

Consider the time and money spent on professional treatment of minor ailments such as headaches, stomachaches, diarrhea, muscle aches and pains, mild fevers, and the common cold. These ailments usually run their course within a short period of time despite what a doctor may prescribe. Furthermore, some of these problems are caused by viruses that cannot be killed by antibiotics or other medicines. Doctors cannot cure such problems. They can only tell a patient what to do for himself or herself, such as rest or drink plenty of fluids. Health-activated people know what they can do for themselves to deal with the symptoms of such minor illnesses.

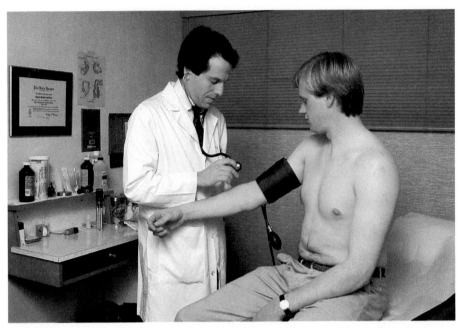

Health-activated people have regular physical examinations and seek the advice of a qualified doctor when health problems arise. (Hank Morgan/Science Source/Photo Researchers, Inc.)

Being health-activated also includes using one's judgment to determine when to seek professional help. When a medical problem exceeds a person's skills, the tools or information available, or the support to deal with it, it is time to consult a health professional.[2] For example, a person with occasional indigestion has a common health problem that can be treated at home with over-the-counter antacids. However, repeated indigestion over a long period and additional symptoms such as blood in the stool constitute a cause for concern. A health-activated person recognizes unusual, uncommon, or alarming symptoms and acts promptly to get professional treatment or advice.

Health-activated people know when to seek medical advice, but they are also aware that the final decision on health matters is their own. They understand health matters and are ready to question the recommendations of health professionals. If they are unsure about a doctor's opinion on a serious matter, they seek a second opinion from another practitioner.[3]

Judging Health Products and Treatments

Today's health-conscious consumer can be overwhelmed with all the information on health care issues. While this information is useful in helping people become health-activated, it may also cause confusion and indecision. Conflicting studies and opinions make it difficult to know what to believe about health care issues. A major goal of this text is to help provide insight into many of these issues.

The same is true regarding health care products and methods of treatment. When seeking an over-the-counter (OTC) drug to relieve cold symptoms, a consumer may feel overwhelmed by the vast array of medications for sale. People face similarly difficult choices when they consider alternative methods of treatment. In treating a backache, for example, a person can choose among rest, exercise, various medications, and relaxation techniques.

A health-activated individual considers the alternatives and chooses what seems to be most appropriate for his or her needs, based on as much information as possible. This may mean choosing among several OTC medications or taking no medications at all, treating oneself or seeing a doctor, and seeking a second opinion or getting advice from a practitioner of an alternative method of treatment.[4]

Selecting Medications   One area of choice for consumers concerns OTC medications. With so many brands and varieties available, the health-activated individual considers carefully before choosing a medication to relieve the symptoms of a minor illness. This means thinking about the symptoms to be relieved, reading labels on medications, and perhaps speaking to a pharmacist or consulting a reference book about drugs and medications. Taking these steps allows an individual to choose the OTC medication that is most likely to meet his or her needs.

Another area of choice concerns the use of prescription drugs, specifically the use of brand-name versus generic drugs. When a company develops a new drug, it is given the exclusive right to market that medication under its brand name for up to 14 years. During this time the drug is available only in the brand-name form. When this period ends, other companies can begin producing the drug under a **generic name**—the name of the chemical ingredient in the drug—or under their own brand names.

generic name

While generic drugs are supposed to meet the same federal standards for safety, purity, and effectiveness that apply to brand-name drugs, there have been recent controversies about whether this is always the case. Consumers should be wary of any drugs that are not produced under strict guidelines.

Since generic drugs are often less expensive than brand-name drugs, they can save consumers money. However, the decision whether to use them instead of brand-name drugs requires some research by the consumer. The primary resource, of course, is the physician who prescribes the drug, but health-activated individuals often take the time to gather information from other sources as well. Pharmacists are an excellent source of information and advice. Reference books on drugs and medications can provide the consumer with important information for making a decision. With this information in hand, the health-activated individual is better able to choose between a brand-name and a generic drug.

Avoiding Medical Quackery   Sometimes people's fear of pain, illness, or death leads them to seek help from unqualified practitioners who sell miracle cures or treatments that are painless and fully guaranteed. Driven by the desire for profit, these medical quacks urge patients to trust them rather than rely on competent health professionals.

Evaluating information about types of medical treatment can help people avoid quackery and save not only money but also their lives. While most quack cures are harmless, some of the products and treatments offered by quacks are harmful or deadly. All are expensive and represent a needless cost.

The best way for people to protect themselves against quackery is to learn what *does* work and to learn how quacks work, too. Quackery often follows certain patterns. People should beware of the following:

- A product or service that claims to be battling the medical profession
- A remedy sold door to door, advertised at public lectures, or promoted in magazines or by crusading organizations
- People who employ scare tactics in trying to promote their products or treatments
- The use of unsubstantiated "testimonials" that claim that a product or service has done wonders for others
- A product or service that claims to be good for a vast array of illnesses or is guaranteed to provide a quick cure

A health-activated person does not rely on such self-serving claims. Good and reliable information on products and types of treatment is available from the following sources:

- Licensed physicians
- The U.S. Food and Drug Administration (FDA), which was created to protect consumers against unsafe and ineffective products
- The Federal Trade Commission (FTC), which warns consumers about false advertising
- The U.S. Postal Service, which guards against the sale of fraudulent products by mail
- The Consumers Union, which impartially tests and rates consumer products

Medical Self-Care

In addition to judging health care problems and making choices about the use of medications and medical treatment, health-activated people are able to take care of some of their own medical needs. Through caring for themselves, people gain greater knowledge about their bodies and how they function. This helps them develop a sense of power over their bodies and makes them realize that health is largely a matter of how they care for themselves.[5]

Medical self-care allows people to utilize skills, information, and insight to deal with minor medical problems that do not require a physician. Carrying out medical self-care responsibly includes monitoring one's own health, being prepared to deal with minor problems at home, and knowing when to seek the help of a health professional.[6]

Measuring Your Body's Physiological Data

How does a person know when he or she has a medical problem? One indication is whether the person's condition seems different from "normal." This can be determined by measuring some basic physiological data. Each individual has certain normal, or baseline, measurements, including temperature, respiration, pulse, and blood pressure. When these measurements differ from what is normal, it is an indication that something may be wrong.

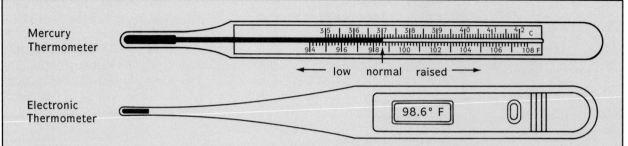

Figure 16.1 *Always compare temperatures taken by the same method. Axillary (under the arm) readings are lower than oral readings, which are lower than rectal readings. To measure oral temperature with a mercury thermometer, do the following: 1. Clean the thermometer. 2. Shake it down below 95°F (35°C). 3. Place it under the tongue and hold it in place with the tongue and lips. Allow 3 to 5 minutes to register. 4. With the light to your back, slowly turn the thermometer until the silver band of mercury is magnified against the white background. Read to the nearest 0.2°F or 0.1°C.*

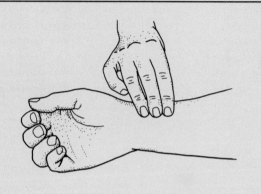

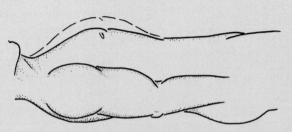

DESCRIBING ABNORMAL BREATHING

Unusually deep breathing
Unusually shallow breathing
Difficulty in breathing when lying down
Waking up unable to breathe
Excessive sighing and yawning
Noisy, wheezy, or bubbly breathing
Wheezing with difficulty exhaling (a sign of asthma)

Figure 16.2 *Measure pulse rates at rest. 1. Place the index and middle fingers along the line of the artery, on the thumb side of the wrist. (Never use your own thumb to measure someone else's pulse. You may feel your own pulse instead.) 2. Count the beats of the pulse for half a minute and multiply by two.*

Figure 16.3 *Respiration rate is the number of times the chest rises and falls in 1 minute. The normal adult rate is 12 to 19 breaths a minute. The normal infant rate is 30 to 40. Observe respiration rates at rest for consistency. Also note any abnormal breathing and be prepared to describe the condition and onset to your doctor.*

Temperature, Respiration, and Pulse The 98.6 degrees Fahrenheit (37 degrees Celsius) body temperature that is usually considered normal is only a statistical average. A person's normal temperature can vary a degree or two on either side, depending on the individual, the time of day, and other factors, such as a woman's menstrual cycle. A variation greater than that, however, usually suggests infection (Figure 16.1).

Pulse, or heartbeat, is affected by age, physical exertion, stress, and, of course, cardiovascular disease. The pulse rate also may be affected by emotions, pain, sex, and body composition. In nearly all people, the pulse rate tends to rise with fever. In a healthy adult at rest, the heart normally beats 60 to 90 times a minute. For athletes the rate may be as low as 40 to 60 beats a minute, and for young children it may be as high as 90 to 120 beats a minute (Figure 16.2).

The normal range for an adult's respiration is 12 to 19 breaths a minute. This rate can change as a result of strenuous activity or emotional tension as well as illness. It is also important to learn the *sound* of one's normal respiration. If respiration seems to be shallower or deeper than normal or if unusual noises are associated with it, this is an indication that something may be wrong (Figure 16.3).

Blood Pressure   Blood pressure is affected by several factors, including the strength and speed of the heartbeat, the total blood volume, and the condition of the arteries. Blood pressure measurements consist of two figures, the systolic and diastolic rates, which are expressed as a fraction, with the systolic pressure on top. (A reading of 120/80 is read as 120 over 80.)

Blood pressure can vary considerably depending on the individual and on age. Pressures generally increase as people age. Normal systolic pressure ranges from about 110 or lower to about 140 or higher; diastolic, from about 60 to 90. A reading of 120/80 would be considered ideal in an average, healthy young adult.

Blood pressure can also vary with the time of day and with circumstances. Tension, excitement, weight gain, kidney disease, hormonal malfunction, and other events may cause blood pressure to rise. Malnutrition, injury, extensive bleeding, shock, and a number of illnesses can cause it to fall.

The Home Medicine Chest

One aspect of medical self-care is administering OTC medications or employing simple treatments when one is dealing with minor illnesses or injuries. In these instances, people generally reach into the medicine chest to find what they need.

A properly stocked medicine chest should contain medical supplies for treating minor ills that do not require a doctor's care (Table 16.1). In stocking a medicine chest, however, it is important to consider individual health care needs as well. A person who has never had a problem with constipation probably has little need to keep a laxative on hand. Such considerations are especially important when one is purchasing medications that have an expiration date or may be hazardous to children. It makes little sense to purchase items that may lose their effectiveness before they are used or that may be dangerous.

The FDA recommends the following safety measures for the safe storage of medications:

- Date all OTC drugs to indicate when they were purchased.
- Buy medicines and health supplies in realistic quantities—only enough for your immediate needs.
- Store all drugs out of the reach of small children, locked up if necessary.
- Read labels carefully and observe all warnings and cautions.
- Do not use medicine from an unlabeled bottle. Transparent tape over a label will keep the label from wearing or washing off.

Table 16.1   Basics for the Home Medicine Chest

Nondrug Items	Drug Items
Adhesive bandages (assorted sizes)	Analgesic (aspirin, acetaminophen, ibuprofen); all reduce fever and pain, but only aspirin reduces inflammation
Sterile gauze (pads and a roll)	
Absorbent cotton	
Adhesive tape	Emetic to induce vomiting (syrup of ipecac and activated charcoal)
Elastic bandage	
Small, blunt-end scissors	Antacid for stomach upset
Tweezers	Antiseptic solution for cleaning minor wounds
Fever thermometer (rectal for young child)	Cortisone cream for skin inflammation and rash
Hot water bottle	Calamine lotion for poison ivy, insect bites, and other skin irritations
Heating pad	
Eye cup (for flushing objects out of the eye)	Petroleum jelly for dry skin and diaper rash
Ice bag	Antidiarrhetic
Dosage spoon (household teaspoons are rarely the correct size)	Cough syrup (nonsuppressant type)
	Decongestant
Vaporizer or humidifier	Burn ointment
First-aid manual	
Plus other supplies and medicines as common sense and family needs dictate	

Source: Adapted from *FDA Consumer.*

- Do not administer medicine in the dark. The label may be hard to read.
- Pay attention when measuring drugs.
- Do not take several drugs at the same time without consulting a physician or asking a pharmacist about possible drug interactions.
- Remove leftovers regularly, especially prescription drugs used for a prior illness.
- Flush discarded drugs down the toilet and dispose of their containers so that children will not have access to them.

Always take special care before administering drugs or other products from a medicine chest, especially to young children or elderly persons. A small mistake in dosage can be very harmful to a child or older adult. It is best to ask a doctor before giving medicine to young children or the elderly, a pregnant or nursing mother, or anyone who has a chronic health condition. Also, always ask a doctor or pharmacist about possible drug interactions with other medicines or foods before administering any type of medication to someone who is already taking another drug, whether prescription or nonprescription.

Physical Examinations

While "norms" such as temperature, pulse, and blood pressure can be monitored by individuals, other norms can be established only through physical examinations by a physician. Moreover, taking responsibility for scheduling regular physical examinations is an important activity done by health-activated individuals who monitor their health.

Physical examinations can vary considerably in complexity, from those involving extensive screening, questioning, and laboratory and monitoring tests to much simpler exams involving only a few key tests and observations. The nature of the exam depends on variables such as age, current health, and symptoms or problems. Periodic examinations are very important because of their greater potential for spotting adverse conditions before they become serious.

Frequency of Physical Examinations   There is little agreement among physicians and professional medical associations about the optimum frequency of physical examinations. A general rule of thumb is that as people grow older, regular physical examinations have a greater potential for detecting adverse health conditions. While young, people should have enough physical examinations to establish what is normal for them. The American Medical Association recommends an examination every year or two between ages 2 and 20. Between ages 20 and 30, routine annual examinations rarely reveal a new illness. In these age groups, it is probably better to wait until unusual symptoms appear and then respond promptly by visiting a physician. Exceptions include pregnant women and people with chronic diseases. At all ages, people who have abnormal symptoms, have existing medical problems, or are taking a prescribed medication should have physical examinations as often as recommended by their physicians.

What Is Tested   A basic part of a physical examination is a blood pressure test to check for hypertension. The physician may also request a urine sample to test for signs of bladder and kidney infection or diabetes and a blood test to determine the blood count and cholesterol, glucose, and triglyceride levels. In addition, during a physical examination the doctor will generally listen to the heart and lungs, look in the throat and check the thyroid and neck area for enlarged or tender lymph nodes, and feel the abdomen to detect tumors, enlargement of organs, or tender areas.

Beyond those basic procedures, the tests performed depend on factors such as sex, age, medical history, and risk factors for developing a particular disease. For example, a woman with a family history of breast cancer may be a candidate for an annual *mammogram* (breast x-ray), and a person who smokes may see a doctor more frequently for tests to detect lung cancer.

For people past age 40, an electrocardiogram may be included in examinations to diagnose heart problems. An ECG is also recommended for people who experience shortness of breath, chest pain, or faintness and people starting a strenuous exercise program.[7]

The American Cancer Society recommends that women age 20 to 40 with no abnormal symptoms have a breast exam by a physician every 3 years, a self-exam every month, and a baseline mammogram between ages 35 and 39. In addition to monthly self-exams, women age 40 and over and women who have had a hysterectomy and are taking estrogen supplementation should have a breast exam by a health professional every year and a mammogram every 1 to 2 years for those 40 to 49 and every year for those age 50 and over.[8]

Women who are or have been sexually active or have reached age 18 should have an annual pelvic exam and Pap test to check for cervical cancer. If a woman has had three or more consecutive satisfactory annual exams, the Pap test may be performed less often at the discretion of the physician.[9]

To help reduce the risk of prostate cancer, it is recommended that men receive an annual rectal exam beginning at age 40. These exams are also recommended for both men and women over age 40 to test for colon and rectal cancer. Men should also have a testicular exam as part of a regular physical examination in addition to monthly testicular self-exams.[10]

Apart from regular physical examinations, regular dental checkups and eye examinations are an important aspect of medical care. Dental exams are necessary to take care of routine dental concerns and detect gum disease and oral cancer. Regular eye exams, while important for testing vision, can also reduce the risk of developing *glaucoma,* a condition of increased pressure within the eyeball that can lead to blindness. The eyes should be checked for glaucoma every 2 years after age 35.

When to Seek Professional Help

The need for routine physical examinations varies, but people should not delay in seeking professional help if they experience persistent, severe, or unusual symptoms or medical problems. Greater self-reliance should *not* lead individuals to ignore such things or try to deal with them themselves. There are also certain symptoms that are associated with potentially serious problems, such as cardiovascular disease, stroke, and cancer. A health-activated person recognizes these symptoms and responds to them quickly by seeking professional medical help.

In addition to the symptoms associated with certain diseases, there are certain emergency situations in which a person should see a physician immediately. Aside from obvious situations such as massive bleeding that cannot be stopped, major burns, suspected broken bones, and suspected poisoning, the following conditions demand immediate medical help:

- Severe pain
- Cold sweats, particularly if combined with light-headedness or chest or abdominal pain
- Shortness of breath at rest (if not because of simple exertion)
- Unconsciousness or a stupor
- Disorientation to the point that the person cannot describe what has happened or say his or her name or whereabouts

Knowledge about when to see a physician and when and how to treat minor medical problems at home is an important aspect of medical self-care, but it is not the only one. Health-activated individuals are also very familiar with the professional health care system and are concerned about evaluating the health care providers and institutions they go to for help.

Health Care Providers and Institutions

The body is a resilient organism. In some situations it can gather all its resources to heal itself or set things right again. At other times individuals can help restore or maintain their own health through medical self-care. Sometimes, however, people and their bodies need the kind of help that only health care professionals or institutions can provide.

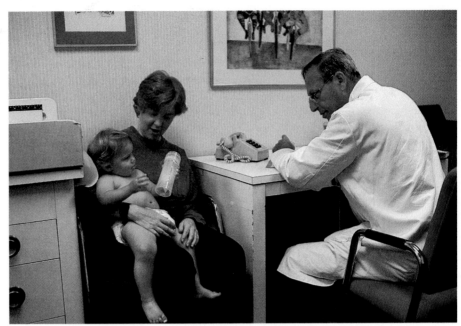

Found mostly in rural areas, single-doctor clinics can provide excellent basic medical care, though they do not provide the extensive medical services available at larger medical groups with several specialists. (Robert Brenner/PhotoEdit)

Physicians and Dentists

There has been a significant trend in the United States toward a decline in the number of physicians in general practice and a rise in the number specializing in a particular type of medicine. Most physicians today are specialists, such as allergists, pediatricians, gynecologists, obstetricians, cardiologists, surgeons, and gastroenterologists. The same trend is often true of dentists as well, with oral surgeons, orthodontists, periodontists, and endodontists. This trend has resulted in fewer medical professionals who are willing to deal with the general health of the population.

Another trend is an increasing lack of an adequate supply of health care workers in many rural and inner-city areas, where many physicians are hesitant to set up a practice. Recently, young health professionals have begun to spread out geographically because of increasing competition in major cities and as a result of federal incentive programs. However, until additional incentives are provided for moving into areas where the need is great, the uneven distribution of health services will be a problem for many Americans seeking access to quality health care.

Selecting a Physician or Dentist There are a number of avenues to explore when you are choosing a physician, dentist, or other medical specialist. The recommendations of others, including family members, friends, and other health professionals, can be very helpful. (Although family members and friends are not necessarily qualified to evaluate the competence of professionals, their suggestions can be useful.) When one is receiving the recommendations of another person, it is important to ask why that person has recommended a particular professional. What one person may consider a good quality in a physician or dentist is not necessarily something another person will find appealing.

In some places, free referral services offer the names of physicians on staff at affiliated medical centers. This can be an important source, especially for people who have already chosen a medical center to use in case of illness. Some referral services also provide information about the qualifications of particular doctors, including their medical education and number of years in practice.

Inquiries at the nearest accredited hospital or dental school can uncover a list of the names of qualified physicians and dentists who practice there, as can talking to the nurses and staff physicians (residents) at those institutions. County medical and dental societies often provide the names (but no evaluations) of local doctors or dentists.

Directories available in most libraries can be used to find out about a physician's educational background, training, and other credentials. The *Directory of Medical Specialists,* published by the American Medical Association, lists physicians, by state, who are certified by the professional boards of their specialties. The American Dental Association publishes a similar directory of dentists.

After you have compiled a list of possibilities, call the physicians' or dentists' offices and ask questions about fees, the average waiting period for a visit, board certification, and their availability in case of emergency.

The last step in selecting a health professional is to make an appointment. After that visit, a person can decide whether he or she would feel comfortable entrusting his or her health care to the medical professional. If the physician or dentist does not seem right, it is always possible to choose someone else.

Assessing Medical and Dental Care Health-activated people use professional medical advice as one of many sources of guidance.[11] If they are not satisfied with a physician's or dentist's performance or attitude, they consider finding another one. Health-activated people evaluate the care their medical professionals are providing, taking into account that a good physician or dentist should do the following:

- Emphasize preventive medicine, ask about lifestyle, and make suggestions for improvement
- Take a careful medical history, listen to complaints, and answer questions and explain procedures in nontechnical language
- Take the time to do a thorough exam
- Welcome a second opinion, especially if surgery or an extensive procedure may be necessary
- Not keep the patient waiting for a long period
- Maintain a courteous and nonjudgmental attitude

Communicating with Medical Professionals People naturally prefer medical professionals who communicate clearly and respectfully, avoid jargon, explain things well, and keep interruptions to a minimum. They want medical professionals to show respect by listening without interruption, making eye contact, and responding directly to spoken and implied questions.[12] Communication is a two-way street, however. The way in which a patient responds is also important in building a working relationship with a medical professional.

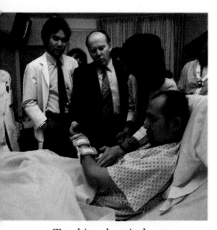

Teaching hospitals attract students and give them superior training, and so medical care in such hospitals is usually the best. (Tom Tracy/MediChrome)

Patients have a responsibility to provide accurate information and communicate clearly with their physician or dentist. For example, describing symptoms concisely and clearly is very important, as is providing information about allergies, medications being taken, and changes in habits or behaviors that may be associated with the health problem being investigated.

Patients also have a responsibility to ask questions so that they understand the diagnosis and treatment. This includes asking about the medications prescribed, how and when to take them, and what side effects may exist. It also includes asking what a particular treatment involves, why it may be necessary, and whether there are alternatives.

Be prepared for a meeting with a medical professional, perhaps with a list of detailed symptoms, current medications and allergies, and questions to ask. It is vital that patients understand what a medical professional has said before leaving the office, clinic, or hospital. However, do not hesitate to call back with other important information or questions at a later time.

Hospitals and Clinics

Hospitals and clinics play a crucial role in the health care system. With their large staffs, high-tech diagnostic equipment, advanced life-support systems, and great variety of services, most hospitals can provide every type of medical care. Medical centers and clinics, while usually not as well equipped as hospitals, can provide specialized care from same-day minor surgery to treatment of emergencies such as broken bones. However, since medical centers and clinics usually lack advanced life-support systems, high-risk patients are probably better off going to a hospital even for a minor procedure.[13]

Assessing Health Care Institutions   It makes good sense to evaluate a health care institution before using it. Brochures and other materials describing services, staff, and policies are available from many health care institutions. They can be an important source of information in making an evaluation. The opinions of personal doctors, family members, and friends can also be useful.

When you are trying to evaluate an institution, there are a number of issues to consider. The care received at a clinic, medical center, or hospital has much to do with the medical professionals who work there. Therefore, in selecting a health care facility, it is important to find out about the staff.

Another important consideration in selecting a health care facility is the fee structure. Some clinics require patients to pay for services and submit their own claims for insurance reimbursement. Others wait for insurance reimbursement and then bill for noncovered expenses.

One of the first things a person should find out about a hospital is whether it is accredited by the Joint Commission on Accreditation of Hospitals (JCAH). The JCAH is a professional group that sets minimum standards for hospital performance and confers accreditation only to institutions that meet those standards. There are a number of additional guidelines for choosing a good hospital, among which are the following:

• The best hospitals are often teaching hospitals that are affiliated with medical schools and have full "house staffs" of interns and residents.
• Good hospitals offer a wide range of services, including an x-ray laboratory, intensive care units, coronary care units, a postoperative

recovery room, an emergency room, an outpatient department, a blood bank, and a pathology laboratory.

- Good hospitals have board-certified physicians in a broad range of specialty areas, such as internists, surgeons, neurologists, and psychiatrists.
- Good hospitals regularly assess the quality of their own care. For example, a committee of physicians regularly reviews the hospital's surgical cases to make sure that all surgery performed is necessary and appropriate.

Dealing with Health Care Institutions   One major mistake a hospitalized patient can easily make is to give up control over his or her health care. The patient should be sure to maintain an active role in making decisions about hospital care. If the patient is unable to speak for himself or herself, a family member should act on his or her behalf.

Probably the most common complaint about the quality of medical care today concerns how medical staff interacts with patients. Patients have the right to be treated with respect. They also have the right to know about their condition, the procedures being used to diagnose it, or the risks involved in a certain course of treatment. These and many other aspects of patient care are set forth in a list the American Hospital Association has issued called the "patient's bill of rights."

Complementary Approaches to Health Care

What can a patient do when conventional medical techniques and procedures have not been successful? What can someone do to enhance the care received from a doctor? Some people turn to the use of nonconventional therapies such as osteopathy, chiropractic, homeopathy, and acupuncture. The trend is to use these therapies in partnership rather than in competition with conventional medicine; therefore, such therapies may be called complementary approaches to health care.[14]

Do such therapies work? This is a difficult question, since medical research is funded primarily by the government and the pharmaceutical industry, neither of which has invested in research on unconventional therapies. Some studies have shown that complementary medicine is at least as successful as conventional medicine for the short-term treatment of certain conditions. The few studies on long-term treatment of certain conditions have suggested that they may on occasion be more successful. For example, some studies have shown that acupuncture is as effective as painkillers in relieving pain and can be more effective in the long term.[15] This is not to say, however, that there are no complementary health practitioners who are fraudulent or who dupe their clients. The crucial issue is to separate the quacks from those who are competent and offer real possibilities for healing.[16]

Some people consider all complementary medicine to be quackery. As a result, the Coalition for Alternatives in Nutrition and Healthcare (CANAH) was founded in 1984 to defend complementary medicine and holistic health care. According to CANAH, many conventional health practitioners call complementary approaches quackery to discourage competition. CANAH is proposing a health care rights amendment to the U.S. Constitution, which would provide that no government can pass laws interfering with the people's right to choose the type of health care they prefer for themselves or their children for the prevention or treatment of disease, injury, or illness.[17]

While there are a variety of different complementary health care approaches, some of the most common and well-known are osteopathy, chiropractic, homeopathy, and acupuncture. There is little scientific evidence to support the effectiveness of most of these complementary approaches to medicine, and many conventional health practitioners question their use. They have proved helpful to some people, however. In general, people should not rely on a nonconventional approach *instead* of a conventional one, although they may wish to try such approaches *in conjunction with* conventional health care.

Osteopathy   Osteopaths are the most accepted alternative health care practitioners, largely because of the versatility of their training. The idea behind osteopathy is that the structure and function of the body are interdependent. If the structure of the body becomes altered or abnormal, the function is altered and illness results. Doctors of osteopathy (DOs) receive an education similar to that of doctors of medicine (MDs), but they also learn manipulative skills and may use them in their treatments, trying to manipulate the bones and muscles to bring the body back to normal. Because of their training, osteopaths are accepted by most institutions that accept MDs.[18]

Chiropractic   Chiropractors are concerned with the function of the muscles and bones. Chiropractic is the largest of the complementary healing professions. It is based on the theory that misalignments of the spinal vertebrae interfere with the proper functioning of the central nervous system and ultimately cause disease. Chiropractors treat patients by adjusting the vertebrae to restore proper alignment of the spine. In addition to their adjustment techniques, chiropractors may use exercise, advice, nutritional guidance, and changes in work position in their treatment.[19] Chiropractic is generally considered to be useful in treating problems such as stiffness and pain in the neck or back. However, its theory of disease causation is considered very controversial, as is the quality of chiropractic education.

Homeopathy   Homeopathy is an approach to healing that is based on the principle that "like is healed by like." Homeopathic practitioners hold that diseases and symptoms can be cured by treating the patient with tiny doses of the substance that is causing a problem. For example, a person suffering from nausea and vomiting may be treated with tiny doses of ipecac, a drug that *causes* vomiting. This is supposed to stimulate the body's natural defense mechanism to fight whatever is causing the ailment.

Acupuncture   Acupuncture is an ancient Chinese method of healing and relieving pain. Needles are inserted into the body at strategic points along invisible lines. The needles do not draw blood. Once the acupuncturist knows the nature of the complaint, the patient is examined to find the points that correspond to the problem. The needles are then inserted into those points for about 20 minutes. At times they are connected to an electrical current to produce further stimulation.

While the effectiveness of acupuncture in curing disease has not been documented, there is evidence to support its effectiveness in treating pain. Studies

Finding Your Comfort Level with a Medical Plan

The increasing costs of health care make medical coverage a necessity for everyone. Many people subscribe to a particular medical plan because their employer provides it as a fringe benefit. If that is your situation, it is helpful to understand as much as possible about your medical coverage.

In other companies employees are offered a choice between traditional health insurance, such as Blue Cross–Blue Shield, and a health maintenance organization (HMO). If you have to make a choice or if you have to secure your own coverage, you can make a better decision if you are well informed about both types of health insurance.

Traditional health insurance protects people from major medical expenses and loss of income caused by health-related problems. There are three basic kinds of policies that provide different types of coverage. The first— major medical policies—are the most comprehensive. They cover hospital stays and physicians' services in and out of the hospital. The second—hospital-surgical policies—cover only hospital services and surgical procedures. The third—hospital-indemnity and dread-disease policies—offer the most limited benefits. Hospital-indemnity policies pay a fixed amount each day you are in the hospital. Dread-disease policies pay benefits only if you contract a specific illness.

Most employers that offer traditional health insurance require employees to pay a deductible each year before benefits begin to be paid. It may be quite high.

Health maintenance organizations cover the same things traditional health insurance does but they operate differently. HMOs are prepaid health care plans with predetermined fixed benefits. An HMO requires that people enroll, become members, and agree to use only its services. In return, the HMO provides a defined set of services from participating health care professionals at a set price. Most HMOs require people to pay a small copayment fee when they use these services.

There are two types of HMOs. The most familiar type—the prepaid group practice— has physicians either on salary or working under contract. These plans often have their own outpatient facilities, which members must use except in extreme circumstances. Hospital admission is strictly controlled.

The other type of HMO—the independent practice association—contracts with physicians who maintain a private practice in addition to seeing HMO members. These plans usually use hospitals for inpatient services, and so their costs may be higher.

When a consumer compares specific plans, he or she needs to ask what each one covers. For example, many major medical and hospital-surgical policies do not cover routine prenatal care or routine deliveries. Subscribers have to buy a separate rider to pay the cost of routine maternity care.

The next question consumers need to ask is: How does the policy pay? For example, does it only pay the usual and customary fee? If that is the case, when a bill is greater than the insurance company's "usual" figure, subscribers may have to pay for part of it.

Finally, consumers need to ask how much the policy costs. What are the deductibles, premiums, or copayments? If two policies are comparable in every way but cost, it makes sense to choose the one that is less expensive.

Personal preferences are the main considerations in deciding which type of health insurance to choose. For some people, being able to stay with a particular physician is the most important factor. For other people, the benefits offered play the key role in this decision. No one plan will have everything you want, but you probably can find a plan that you feel comfortable with.

Based on *Choosing an HMO: An Evaluation Checklist* (Washington, D.C.: AARP Health Advocacy Services Program Department, 1986); "The Crisis in Health Insurance," *Consumer Reports* (August 1990): 533–547.

have shown that acupuncture eases pain by causing the release of endorphins, the naturally occurring opiatelike chemicals that suppress the transmission of pain signals in the brain. This success also seems to depend on changes in energy fields and electrical circuits that flow within the body.[20]

One of the most dramatic uses of acupuncture occurs during surgery. Acupuncturists can anesthetize a patient during major surgery, yet the patient remains awake and feels no pain. Acupuncture is also being used to treat addictive problems such as smoking, compulsive eating, and drug abuse.[21]

The Cost of Health Care

Every year in the United States an enormous amount of money is spent on health care—over $500 billion in 1987 (almost $2,000 per person.)[22] Soaring health costs caused by increasing hospital and doctor fees, expensive technology, and the increased use of medical services have put a tremendous strain on the medical system and have led to growing concern about the future of health care in this country (Figure 16.4). The nation may soon have to decide whether to provide adequate health care at any cost or to contain costs by rationing services. At stake is the health of all Americans, but especially those who cannot afford the high cost of health care or do not have health insurance.

Health Insurance

Most Americans have some form of health insurance, though the adequacy of coverage varies widely. However, almost 14 percent of Americans have no health insurance at all, a situation that is one of the most urgent health policy issues today. Most of the uninsured are working poor people whose job benefits do not include health insurance or who earn too much to qualify for government health insurance programs and cannot afford to pay insurance premiums themselves.[23]

Unlike most two-party transactions, in which a buyer purchases goods or services directly from a seller, most health care payments are handled by a third party—the insurance carrier. This insurer may be billed directly by a health care provider who either accepts the amount received as full payment or bills the patient for the difference. Alternatively, the patient may pay the health care provider first and then be reimbursed by the insurance carrier.

basic health insurance

Several kinds of health insurance coverage are available. **Basic health insurance** pays benefits for hospitalization and for medical and surgical expenses. This means that *part* of the hospital bill and *part* of the physician's and sur-

major medical insurance

geon's fees are paid by the insurance company. **Major medical insurance** is designed to protect a person from the high medical expenses that can accumulate if he or she is seriously injured or ill for a long time. Typically, major medical coverage is purchased for an extra fee to complement basic medical

disability insurance

coverage. **Disability insurance** pays benefits to a person who is unable to work because of injury or illness.

Private Insurance Plans   Most private health insurance is provided by nonprofit corporations such as Blue Cross–Blue Shield and by commercial insur-

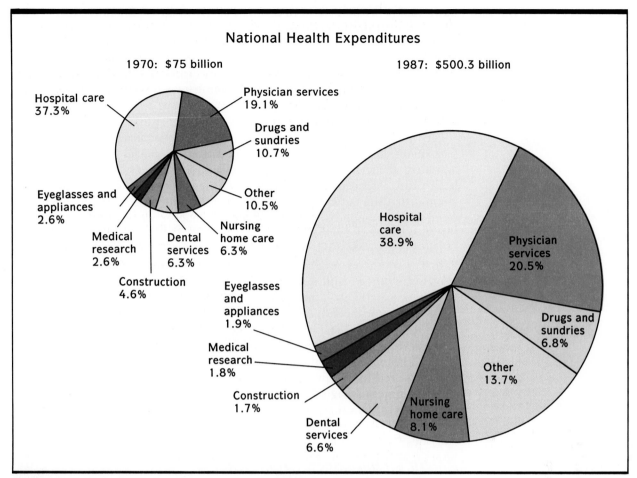

National Health Expenditures

1970: $75 billion

1987: $500.3 billion

Hospital care 37.3%
Physician services 19.1%
Drugs and sundries 10.7%
Eyeglasses and appliances 2.6%
Other 10.5%
Medical research 2.6%
Dental services 6.3%
Nursing home care 6.3%
Construction 4.6%

Hospital care 38.9%
Physician services 20.5%
Drugs and sundries 6.8%
Eyeglasses and appliances 1.9%
Other 13.7%
Medical research 1.8%
Construction 1.7%
Dental services 6.6%
Nursing home care 8.1%

Figure 16.4 *Since 1970 American spending for health care has risen nearly sevenfold. Spending for nursing home care, hospital care, physician services, and dental services has risen faster than has spending in other categories.*

Source: U.S. Bureau of the Census, *Statistical Abstracts of the United States, 1990,* 110th ed. (Washington, D.C.: U.S. Government Printing Office, 1990): Table 136.

ance companies. Since the mid-1970s, self-insured plans have been gaining in popularity, as have prepaid plans such as health maintenance organizations (HMOs). All these plans offer group and individual insurance policies.

Group policies account for the majority of private insurance plans. Most are offered by employers to groups of employees. These policies usually offer basic coverage for cheaper rates than are charged for individual policies. Some companies have begun taking steps to limit group health insurance coverage, something that would have been unthinkable several years ago. Some have given employees the choice of receiving health care through a company-designated network of doctors and hospitals or paying a greater share of the expenses out of their own pockets.[24] More and more group plans are including features to help manage costs, such as outpatient surgery and testing on an outpatient basis.

Individual policies are bought primarily by single persons, couples, and families who are self-employed and do not have access to group plans. With

group policy

individual policy

individual policies, the cost of comparable coverage is generally much higher than it is with group policies.

Government Insurance Programs   The government subsidizes some health coverage for the elderly, disabled, and poor through Medicare and Medicaid.

Medicare

Medicare, a federal health insurance program designed to benefit people age 65 or older and the disabled, is made up of Part A and Part B.

Part A Medicare is an insurance program for hospitalization. It pays a large part of the hospital bill when a senior citizen on Social Security has to be admitted. Alternatively, it may cover skilled nursing services, part-time home health care, or hospice care for the dying. There is, however, a deductible amount that the patient must pay for hospitalization. Also, if the illness lasts more than two months, patients or their families must begin to contribute to the costs.[25]

The main physician's charges are not covered. These can be lessened by Part B, a voluntary program that involves an additional monthly fee. Part B also covers other medical services not covered by Part A, but usually it pays only 80 percent of an "approved charge"—a charge that may often be considerably less than the full bill.[26] Currently, most private insurance companies sell "Medigap" policies, which cover costs Medicare does not pay.

Medicaid

Medicaid is a federal-state health insurance program to assist people of any age who cannot pay for medical care. Under Medicaid, patients are wholly or partly covered for hospital stays and other medical expenses. During the last decade, tightened eligibility rules have eliminated thousands of poor women and children from the program.[27]

Health Maintenance Organizations

Some critics of fee-for-service care believe that the traditional system of payment for services encourages physicians and hospitals to give more care (such as tests and surgery) than is really needed and to charge for that care. Partly in response to this problem, health maintenance organizations were developed. An HMO is a type of group practice plan in which consumers pay a set fee every month in return for health care at little or no additional cost.

More than 31 million Americans are currently enrolled in HMOs.[28] The two major types are group practice and individual practice plans. Group practice plans provide medical services at centers staffed by salaried physicians. Laboratories, x-ray facilities, and pharmacies are all on the premises, so members can obtain outpatient care at one location. Individual practice plans offer medical care in the private offices of doctors under contract to an HMO. In an individual plan, patients have a wider choice of physicians.

HMOs have some advantages over traditional health care systems. For one thing, they are structured in a way that encourages patients to "think preventive." Since various services are offered at one location and since most costs are covered, patients may be more likely to come for preemptive tests, which can help catch health problems early and prevent them from becoming more serious. Moreover, some studies have shown that HMO patients have less frequent hospitalizations, shorter periods of hospitalization, and less surgery than do patients under the care of fee-for-service practitioners.

Some people feel that there are disadvantages to HMOs. With an HMO, a patient gives up much of his or her freedom to choose physicians and can be shuffled between rotating doctors. Furthermore, HMO physicians are not independent professionals but employees of an HMO, with a duty to serve not only the interests of their patients but the demands of the HMO as well.[29]

Before deciding to join an HMO, it is important to find out what membership includes. Does it include prescription drugs or dental care? Are there any extra costs? How many of the HMO's physicians are board-certified? Can patients choose the physicians they prefer? How long does it take to get an appointment? Is the HMO affiliated with accredited hospitals? Who pays for emergency treatment by an unaffiliated physician? In addition to finding the answers to these questions, people investigating HMOs should evaluate their own health care needs to see if they are compatible with an HMO's services.

Controlling the Cost of Health Care

There are no simple ways to control the ever-increasing costs of health care. For its part, the government might try to regulate fees and provide incentives for quality care at a more reasonable cost (but without limiting patient care). Health care providers might do more to encourage preventive care and avoid the use of expensive and unnecessary testing and procedures. Most important, individuals can take steps to help keep their medical costs down and bring about changes in the health care system.

The best way for individuals to keep health care costs down is to become health-activated and health-conscious. By taking charge of their own health, people are better able to distinguish between medical problems that require professional help and those that can be dealt with less expensively through self-care. Health-activated people practice prevention by adopting the principles of a healthy lifestyle. By focusing on prevention, they can eliminate much of the need for expensive medical care and ensure optimal health and well-being.

Chapter Summary

- Becoming health-activated allows individuals to increase their sense of control over their health and assume basic responsibility for many of their health care needs.

- Health-activated people take steps to remain healthy, deal with medical problems that do not require professional attention, and manage small medical problems so that they do not become major ones. They judge health care problems and are able to decide when to care for themselves and when to seek professional help. They are also able to make informed choices regarding health care products and treatments.

- A home medicine chest is useful in dealing with minor injuries and medical problems. A well-maintained medicine chest includes medications and supplies to deal with emergency situations as well as the individual needs of family members. Safety measures for a medicine chest include maintenance of the freshness of all drugs, realistic amounts of all supplies, carefully labeled supplies and medications, storage out of the reach of children, and proper use of all supplies.

- Regular physical examinations allow medical problems to be detected early, before they become more serious. The frequency of examinations varies with age, sex, and medical history.

- A person should seek professional help if he or she experiences persistent, severe, or unusual symptoms or medical problems.

- In selecting a health professional, a person should consider the professional's qualifications, philosophy of care, credentials, and demeanor. Recommendations from family members, friends, and other medical professionals may be helpful in selecting a physician or dentist. Hospitals, referral services, and directories can also be useful in judging qualifications.

- In assessing health care institutions, a person should consider the services offered, the qualifications of the staff members, the fee structure, and accreditation.

- In addition to conventional methods of treatment, people may seek treatment with a variety of alternative, or complementary, approaches, including osteopathy, chiropractic, homeopathy, and acupuncture.

- The basic kinds of health insurance coverage are basic health insurance, major medical insurance, and disability insurance. All these types of insurance can be provided through private insurance plans (group or individual policies) or government-funded programs (Medicare and Medicaid).

- An HMO is a type of group health practice in which consumers pay a set fee every month for complete health care at little or no additional cost. One advantage HMOs have over traditional systems is that they encourage prevention. A disadvantage is that patients must choose among the participating physicians and thus lose some freedom of choice.

- The best way for individuals to control the cost of health care is to practice prevention and take steps to adopt a healthier lifestyle.

References

Chapter 1

1. M. L. Dolfman, "The Concept of Health: An Historic and Analytic Examination," *Journal of School Health* 48, no. 8 (1973): 491.
2. Constitution of the World Health Organization, *Chronicle of the WHO* 1 (1947): 1.
3. Carl A. Hammerschlag, *The Dancing Healers: A Doctor's Journey of Healing with Native Americans* (San Francisco: Harper & Row, 1988).
4. Emrika Padus, *The Complete Guide to Your Emotions and Your Health* (Emmaus, Pa.: Rodale Press, 1986); Larry A. Tucker et al., "Stress and Serum Cholesterol: A Study of 7,000 Adult Males," *Health Values* 11 (1987): 34–39.
5. Robert Ornstein and David Sobel, *The Healing Brain: A New Perspective on the Brain and Health* (New York: Simon & Schuster, 1987); Sally Squires, "The Power of Positive Imagery: Visions to Boost Immunity," *American Health* (July 1987).
6. Suzanne C. Kobasa, "Stressful Life Events, Personality, and Health: An Inquiry into Hardiness," *Journal of Personality and Social Psychology* 37, no. 1 (January 1979): 1–11.
7. N. B. Belloc and L. Breslow, "Relationship of Physical Health Status and Health Practices," *Preventive Medicine* 1 (August 1972): 409–421.
8. Lowell S. Levin, "The Layperson as the Primary Care Practioner," *Public Health Reports* 91(May–June 1976): 206–210.
9. G. M. Moss, *Illness, Immunity and Social Interaction* (New York: John Wiley, 1973); S. Gore, "The Effect of Social Support in Moderating Health," *Journal of Health and Social Behavior* 19 (1978): 157–165.
10. L. J. Lyon et al., "Cancer Incidence in Mormons and Non-Mormons in Utah during 1967–1975," *Journal of the National Cancer Institute* 65 (1980): 1055–1061; F. R. Lemon, R. T. Walden, and R. W. Woods, "Cancer of the Lung and Mouth in Seventh-Day Adventists: Preliminary Report on a Population Study," *Cancer* 4 (1964): 486–497.
11. Gordon W. Alport, *The Individual and His Religion* (New York: Macmillan, 1950); William James, *The Varieties of Religious Experience* (New York: New American Library, 1958).
12. M. Lelonde, *A New Perspective on the Health of Canadians: A Working Document* (Ottawa: Government of Canada, 1974); U.S. Department of Health, Education and Welfare, *Healthy People: The Surgeon General's Report on Health Promotion and Disease Control,* USPHS, DHEW (DHS) Pub. No. 79-55071 (1979); Mary Weisensee, "Evaluation of Health Promotion," *Occupational Health Nursing* (January 1985): 9–14.
13. DHEW, op. cit., pp. 2–3.
14. Bill Thomson, "In Search of Longevity," *East/West* (December 1989): 94–95.
15. Robert Ornstein and David Sobel, *Healthy Pleasures* (Menlo Park, Calif.: Addison-Wesley, 1989).
16. Albert Bandura, "Self-Efficacy: Toward a Unifying Theory of Behavioral Change," *Psychological Review* 84, no. 2 (1977): 191–215.
17. Gary F. Render and David Lemire, "A Consciousness/Spirituality Domain Based on an Elaboration of Maslow's Hierarchy," *Holistic Education Review* (Summer 1989): 29–33.
18. National Center for Health Statistics, "Basic Data from the National Survey of Personal Health Practices and Consequences," in *Vital and Health Statistics* 15 no. 2, DHHS Pub. No. (PHS) 81-1163, Public Health Service, Washington, D.C., USGPO (August 1981).
19. Louis Harris, Louis Harris Poll, "Prevention Index" (1989).
20. George Gallup and Frank Newport, "1989 Gallup Leisure Audit," *Gallup Poll Monthly,* no. 295 (April 1990).

Chapter 2

1. National Sporting Goods Association news release (October 1988).
2. United States Public Health Service, "Promoting Health/Preventing Diseases: Objectives for the Nation" (Washington, D.C.: U.S. Government Printing Office, 1980).
3. "12 Minutes Does It," *American Health* (June 1988): 41.
4. Carl J. Casperson et al., "Physical Activity, Exercise, and Physical Fitness: Definitions and Distinctions for Health-Related Research," *Public Health Reports* 100, no. 2 (March–April 1985): 126–130.
5. Robert J. McCunney, "Fitness, Heart Disease and High Density Lipoproteins: A Look at the Relationships," *The Physician and Sports Medicine* 15, no. 2 (February 1987): 67–75, 78–79.
6. R. S. Paffenbarger et al., "Physical Activity, All-Cause Mortality and Longevity of College Alumni," *New England Journal of Medicine* 314 (March 7, 1986): 605–613.
7. Arthur Leon et al., "Leisure-Time Physical Activity Levels and Risk of Coronary Heart Disease and Death," *Journal of the American Medical Association* 258, no. 17 (November 6, 1987): 2388–2395.
8. R. Rish, American Association for the Advancement of Science, reported in *Time* 131, no. 9 (February 29, 1988): 68.

9. D. Giordano et al., *Controlling Stress and Tension: A Holistic Approach* (Englewood Cliffs, N.J.: Prentice-Hall, 1990).
10. John Yacenda, "First Aid and Self-Care for Minor Sports Injuries," *Fitness Management* 4, no. 8 (October 1988): 56–57.
11. Charles Corbin and Ruth Lindsey, *The Ultimate Fitness Book* (New York: Leisure Press, 1990).
12. Katy Williams, "Crucial to Performance and Injury Prevention, Warm-Up, Warm-Down Is Simple, Practical, and Adaptable to Every Sport," *Sportscare and Fitness* (1988): 35.
13. Bob Anderson, *Stretching* (Bolinas, Calif.: Shelter Publications, 1980).
14. Barbara Brehm, "The Importance of Mind and Muscle," *Fitness Management* (September/October 1987): 16–17.
15. Charles Corbin and Ruth Lindsey, *Concepts of Physical Fitness,* 5th ed. (Dubuque, Iowa: Brown, 1985).
16. R. S. Paffenbarger et al., "A Natural History of Athleticism and Cardiovascular Health," *Journal of the American Medical Association* 252 (1984): 496.
17. Barbara Brehm, "Don't Forget to Cool Down," *Fitness Management* (September 1988): 15.
18. Corbin and Lindsey, *Concepts.*
19. Hal Higdon, "Base Fitness," *Walking Magazine* (February–March 1988): 38–43.
20. American College of Sports Medicine, "The Recommended Quantity and Quality of Exercise for Developing and Maintaining Cardiorespiratory and Muscular Fitness in Healthy Adults," pp. 265–274.
21. "New Rules of Exercise," *U.S. News and World Report* (August 11, 1986): 52–56.
22. Ibid.
23. American College of Sports Medicine, op. cit.
24. Higdon, op. cit.
25. *Consumers Digest* 26, no. 1 (January–February 1987): 60–65.
26. Kenneth E. Powell et al., "The Status of the 1996 Objectives for Physical Fitness and Exercise," *Public Health Reports* 101, no. 1 (January–February 1986): 15–20.
27. Higdon, op. cit.
28. "Physical Exercise: An Important Factor for Health," position paper of the International Federation of Sports Medicine, *The Physician and Sports Medicine* 18, no. 3 (March 1990): 155–156.

Chapter 3

1. *Surgeon General's Report on Nutrition and Health* (USDHHS [PHS] Pub. No. 88-50210, Washington, D.C.: U.S. Government Printing Office, 1988).
2. Food and Nutrition Board, National Research Council, *Recommended Dietary Allowances,* 9th ed. (Washington, D.C.: National Academy of Sciences, 1979).
3. Nutrition Committee, American Heart Association, "Dietary Guidelines for Healthy American Adults: A Statement for Physicians and Health Professionals," *Circulation* 77, no. 3 (March 1988): 721A–724A.
4. From "Diet and Health: Implications for Reducing Chronic Disease Risk," in "The Latest Word on What to Eat," *Time* (March 13, 1984): 51.
5. Ellen Ruppel Shell, "Kids, Catfish, and Cholesterol," *American Health* (January–February 1988): 56.
6. N. A. Boon and J. K. Aronson, "Dietary Salt and Hypertension: Treatment and Prevention," *British Medical Journal* 290, no. 6473 (1985): 949–950.
7. Eli Seifter, "Vitamin A and Beta-Carotene and Effects of Gamma Radiation," *Journal of National Cancer Institute* 73, no. 5 (Nov. 1984): 1167–1177.
8. D. Giordano et al., *Controlling Stress and Tension: A Holistic Approach* (Englewood Cliffs, N.J.: Prentice-Hall, 1990): 101.
9. Elaine Feldman, *Essentials of Clinical Nutrition* (Philadelphia: F A Davis, 1988): 334.
10. Ibid.
11. D. J. Fletcher and D. A. Rogers, "Diet and Coronary Heart Disease," *Postgraduate Medicine* 77, no. 5 (1985): 319–328.
12. Ibid.
13. Leslie Roberts, "Measuring Cholesterol Is as Tricky as Lowering It," *Science* 238, no. 4826 (October 1987): 482–483.
14. Elaine Lanza et al., "Dietary Fiber Intake in the U.S. Population," *American Journal of Clinical Nutrition* 46 (1987): 790–797.
15. Food and Nutrition Board, op. cit.
16. S. Chuck Clapp, "The Basic Four?" *Community Nutritionist* 2 (January–February 1983): 1–7.
17. Jeanne Jones, *Jet Fuel: The New Food Strategy for the High Performance Person* (New York: Villard Books, 1984).
18. Surgeon General's Report (1988).
19. Ibid.
20. Elson M. Haas, "Dieting with the Seasons," in *The New Holistic Health Handbook,* Shepherd Bliss (ed.), (Lexington, Mass.: Penguin Books, Stephen Green Press, 1985): 129–131.

Chapter 4

1. "A Nation of Healthy Worrywarts," *Time* (July 25, 1988): 66–67.
2. A. L. Stewart et al., "Conceptualization and Measurement of Health Habits for Adults in the Health Insurance Study: Vol. 11," in *Overweight* (Santa Monica, Calif.: Rand Corporation and HEWS, 1980); George E. Schauf, "Is the Caloric Theory Valid?" *Nutrition Today* (January–February 1979): 29–31.
3. Artemis P. Simopolous, "Characteristics of Obesity: An Overview," in *Human Obesity,* Richard J. Wurtman and Judith J. Wurtman (eds.), *Annals of the New York Academy of Sciences* (New York, 1987): 7.

4. W. B. Kannel and T. Gordon, "Obesity and Cardiovascular Disease: The Framingham Study," in *Obesity,* W. L. Burland, P. D. Samuel, and J. Yudkin (eds.) (London: Churchill-Livingstone, 1974): 24–51.

5. Simopolous, op. cit., p. 11.

6. Frank I. Katch and William D. McArdle, *Nutrition, Weight Control and Exercise,* 3d ed. (Philadelphia: Lea & Febiger, 1988).

7. Reva Frankle and Mei-Uih Yang, *Obesity and Weight Control: A Health Professional's Guide* (Rockville, Md.: Aspen, 1988): 7–8.

8. Trish Ratto, "The New Science of Weight Control," *Medical Self Care* 39 (March–April 1987): 25–30.

9. Alice Madar, "Heavy Facts about Body Fat," *Walking* (February–March 1988): 48.

10. Kelly Brownell, "The Yo-Yo Trap," *American Health* (March 1988): 82.

11. Cheryl Rock and Ann Coulston, "Weight Control Approaches: A Review by the California Dietetic Association," *Journal of the American Dietetic Association* 88, no. 1 (January 1988): 44–48.

12. American College of Sports Medicine, "Position Statement on Proper and Improper Weight Loss Programs," *Medicine and Science in Sports and Exercise* 15, no. 1 (1983): ix–xiii.

13. "Dietary Protein and Body Fat Distribution," *Nutrition Review* 40 (1982): 89–90.

14. Rock and Coulston, op. cit.

15. Martin Katahn, *The T-Factor Diet* (New York: W W Norton, 1989): 205–226.

16. Charles Yesalis, "Winning and Performance Enhancing Drugs—Our Dual Addiction," *The Physician and Sports Medicine* 18, no. 3 (March 1990): 161–167.

17. C. Everett Koop, *Anabolic Steroids* (Washington, D.C.: U.S. Public Health Service, Department of Health and Human Services, 1987).

18. Carrie Dolan, "Fat-Cutting Surgery Gains Wide Popularity but Can Be Dangerous," *Wall Street Journal* CCIX, no. 1245 (June 26, 1987): 1, 10.

19. Patricia Hodgson, "Review of Popular Diets," in *Nutrition and Exercise in Obesity Management,* J. Storlie and H. Jordan (eds.) (Laurel, Md.: Spectrum, 1984).

20. Paul Williamson et al., *International Journal of Obesity* (December 1988).

21. M. R. C. Greenwood and Virginia A. Pittman-Waller, "Weight Control: A Complex, Various and Controversial Problem," in Frankle and Yang (eds.), op. cit., pp. 4–5.

22. S. B. Roberts et al., "Energy Expenditures and Intake in Infants Born to Lean and Overweight Mothers," *New England Journal of Medicine* 318 (1988): 461–466.

23. R. E. Keesey et al., "The Role of the Lateral Hypothalamus in Determining the Body Weight Setpoint," in *Hunger: Basic Mechanisms and Clinical Implications,* D. Novin et al. (eds.) (New York: Raven Press, 1976).

24. E. Ravussin et al., "Reduced Rate of Energy Expenditure as a Risk-Factor for Body Weight Gain," *New England Journal of Medicine* 318 (1988): 467–472.

25. Joseph R. Vasselli and Carol A. Maggio, "Mechanisms of Appetite and Body Weight Regulation," in Frankle and Yang (eds.), op. cit., p. 19.

26. Clark Cameron, *How You Can Benefit Most from Permanent Weight Loss* (Chicago, Ill.: Nightingale Conant Corporation, 1982).

27. M. L. Pollack et al., *Health and Fitness through Physical Activity* (New York: Wiley, 1978): 28.

28. American College of Sports Medicine, op. cit., pp. vii–x.

29. Ratto, op. cit., p. 30.

30. Lauren Lissner et al., "Dietary Fat and the Regulation of Energy Intake in Human Subjects," *American Journal of Clinical Nutrition* 46 (1987): 886–892.

31. _____ , "Eating Management," in Frankle and Yang (eds.), op. cit., p. 169.

32. Reva T. Frankle, "Weight Control for the Adult and Elderly," in Frankle and Yang (eds.), op. cit., p. 376.

33. Karen Lehrman, "Anorexia and Bulimia: Causes and Cures," *Consumers Research Magazine* 70, no. 9 (September 1987): 29–32.

34. American Psychiatric Association, *Diagnostic and Statistical Manual of Mental Disorders,* 3d ed. revised (Washington, D.C.: American Psychiatric Association, 1987).

35. Lehrman, op. cit.

36. Ibid.

37. Craig Johnson et al., "Incidence and Correlates of Bulimic Behavior in a Female High School Population," *Journal of Youth and Adolescence* 13, no. 1 (February 1984): 15–26.

38. Ibid., p. 29.

39. Ibid.

40. Ibid.

41. Ibid.

Chapter 5

1. Camille Wortman and Elizabeth Loftus, *Psychology,* 3d ed. (New York: Knopf, 1988): 130.

2. Carol Tavris, *Anger: The Misunderstood Emotion* (New York: Simon & Schuster, 1983).

3. The discussion of defense mechanisms is based on Sidney M. Jourard and Ted Landsman, *Healthy Personality,* 4th ed. (New York: Macmillan, 1980): 214.

4. G. E. Vaillant, "Introduction: A Brief History of Empirical Assessment of Defense Mechanisms," in *Empirical Studies of Ego Mechanisms of Defense* (Washington, D.C.: American Psychiatric Press, 1986).

5. Sidney M. Jourard and Ted Landsman, *Healthy Personality,* 4th ed. (New York: Macmillan, 1980): 211–245.

6. American Psychiatric Association, *Diagnostic and Statistical Manual of Mental Disorders,* 3d ed. revised (Washington, D.C.: American Psychiatric Association, 1987).

7. A. T. Beck et al., *Anxiety Disorders and Phobias* (New York: Basic Books, 1985).

8. Rudolf Hoehn-Saric et al., "Symptoms and Treatment Responses of Generalized Anxiety Disorder Patients with High versus Low Levels of Cardiovascular Complaints," *American Journal of Psychiatry* 146, no. 7 (July 1989): 854–859.

9. F. Von Broembsen, "Role Identity in Personality Disorders: Validation, Valuation, and Agency in Identity Formation," *American Journal of Psychoanalysis* 49, no. 2 (1989): 115–125.

10. Kenneth S. Kendler et al., "Psychotic Disorders in DSM-III-R," *American Journal of Psychiatry* 146, no. 8 (August 1989): 953–955.

11. Wortman and Loftus, pp. 130–133.

12. Ibid., pp. 144–146.

13. The discussion of problem-solving steps is derived from Bootsin et al., *Psychology Today,* 6th ed. (New York: Random House, 1986): 259–265.

14. P. McC. Miller et al., "Self-Esteem, Life Stress and Psychiatric Disorder," *Journal of Affective Disorders* 17 (1989): 65–75.

15. Ibid.

16. T. Byram Karasu, "New Frontiers in Psychotherapy," *Journal of Clinical Psychiatry* 50, no. 2 (February 1989): 46–52.

17. James C. Overholser et al., "Suicide Awareness Programs in the Schools: Effects of Gender and Personal Experience," *Journal of American Academy of Child and Adolescent Psychiatry* 28, no. 6 (1989): 925–930.

18. Ann Garland et al., "A National Survey of School-Based, Adolescent Suicide Prevention Programs," *Journal of American Academy of Child and Adolescent Psychiatry* 28, no. 6 (1989): 931–934.

19. David A. Brent et al., "An Outbreak of Suicide and Suicidal Behavior in a High School," *Journal of American Academy of Child and Adolescent Psychiatry* 28, no. 6 (1989): 918–924.

Chapter 6

1. D. S. Jewell, "The Psychology of Stress: Run Silent, Run Deep," *Advances in Experimental Medicine and Biology* 245 (1988): 341–352.

2. Richard S. Lazarus and Joseph B. Cohen, "Environmental Stress," in *Human Behavior and the Environment: Current Theory and Research,* vol. 2, I. Attman and J. F. Wohlwill (eds.) (New York: Plenum, 1977).

3. S. Gore, "The Effects of Social Support in Moderating the Health Consequences of Unemployment," *Journal of Health and Social Behavior,* 19 (1978): 157–165; K. Nuckolls et al., "Psychosocial Assets, Life Crises, and the Prognosis of Pregnancy," *American Journal of Epidemiology* 95 (1972): 431–441.

4. Thomas H. Holmes and Richard H. Rahe, "The Social Readjustment Rating Scale," *Journal of Psychosomatic Research* 2 (1967): 213–218.

5. A. D. Kramer, J. C. Coyne, and R. S. Lazarus, "Comparison of Two Models of Stress Management: Daily Hassles and Uplifts versus Major Life Events," *Journal of Behavioral Medicine* 4, no. 1 (1981): 1–39.

6. R. S. Lazarus, "Puzzles in the Study of Daily Hassles," *Journal of Behavioral Medicine* 7, no. 4 (1984): 375–389; J. J. Zarski, "Hassles and Health: A Replication," *Health Psychology* 3, no. 3 (1984): 243–251.

7. Carolyn M. Aldwin, Michael R. Levenson Spiro III, and Raymond Bosse, "Does Emotionality Predict Stress? Findings from the Normative Aging Study," *Journal of Personality and Social Psychology* 56, no. 4 (1989): 618–623.

8. Hans Selye, *The Stress of Life* (New York: McGraw-Hill, 1976): 36–38.

9. Becky deVillier, "Physiology of Stress: Cellular Healing," *Critical Care Quarterly* (March 1984): 15–20.

10. James W. Mason, "A Historical Review of the Stress Field," *Journal of Human Stress* 1 (1975): 22–36.

11. Walter B. Cannon, *The Wisdom of the Body* (New York: W W Norton, 1932).

12. Alfred B. Heilbrun, Jr., and Eric B. Friedberg, "Type A Personality, Self-Control, and Vulnerability to Stress," *Journal of Personality Assessment* 52, no. 3 (1988): 420–433.

13. J. Howard et al., "Personality (Hardiness) as a Moderator of Job Stress and Coronary Risk in Type A Individuals: A Longitudinal Study," *Journal of Behavioral Medicine* 9 (1986): 229–244; K. M. Nowak, "Type A Hardiness and Psychological Distress," *Journal of Behavioral Medicine* 9 (1986): 537–548; Kevin McNeil et al., "Measurement of Psychological Hardiness in Older Adults," *Canadian Journal on Aging* 5 (1986): 43–48; Julian Barling, "Interrole Conflict and Marital Functioning amongst Employed Fathers," *Journal of Occupational Behavior* 7 (1986): 1–8.

14. Jerry Suls and Christine A. Marco, "Relationships between JAS—and FTAS—Type A Behavior and Non-CHD Illness: A Prospective Study Controlling for Negative Affectivity," *Health Psychology* 9, no. 4 (1990): 479–492.

15. Deborah J. Weibe and Debra Moehle McCallum, "Health Practices and Hardiness as Mediators in the Stress-Illness Relationship," *Health Psychology* 5, no. 5 (1986): 425–438.

16. Nowak, op. cit.

17. Thomas Ashby Wills, "Stress and Coping in Early Adolescence: Relationships to Substance Use in Urban School Samples," *Health Psychology* 5, no. 6 (1986): 503–529.

18. Howard et al., op. cit.; K. M. Nowak, op. cit.; McNeil et al., op. cit.; Barling, op. cit.

19. Anthony J. LaGreca, Ronald L. Akers, and

Jeffrey W. Dwyer, "Life Events and Alcohol Behavior among Older Adults," *The Gerontologist* 28, no. 4 (1988): 552–558.

20. Paul Raeburn, "Eater's High," *American Health* (December 1987): 42–43.

21. "Suicide," in *Injury Prevention: Meeting the Challenge,* National Committee for Injury Prevention and Control, *American Journal of Preventive Medicine* (1989): 252–260.

22. Richard H. Rahe, "Anxiety and Physical Illness," *Journal of Clinical Psychiatry* 49, no. 10 (suppl.) (October 1988): 26–29.

23. Roberta Gerry, "CME Update: Stress on the Rise," *Physicians' Travel and Meeting Guide* (October 1989): 26–27.

24. Ibid.

25. H. P. R. Smith, "Heart Rate of Pilots Flying Aircraft on Scheduled Airline Routes," *Aerospace Medicine* 38 (1967): 1117–1119; J. A. Roman, "Cardiorespiratory Functioning in Flight," *Aerospace Medicine* 34 (1963): 322–337; R. T. Rubin, "Biochemical and Endocrine Responses to Severe Psychological Stress," in *Life Stress and Illness,* E. K. E. Gunderson and R. H. Rahe (eds.) (Springfield, Ill.: Charles C. Thomas, 1974).

26. A. Jalowiec and M. Powers, "Stress and Coping in Hypertensive and Emergency Room Patients," *Nursing Research* 30, no. 1 (1981): 10–15.

27. Gerry, op. cit.

28. Liisa Keltikangas-Jarvinen and Jaana Jokinen, "Type A Behavior, Coping Mechanisms and Emotions Related to Somatic Risk Factors of Coronary Heart Disease in Adolescents," *Journal of Psychosomatic Research* 33, no. 1 (1989): 17–27.

29. Gerry, op. cit.

30. Ibid.

31. Gotthard Booth, "Psychobiological Aspects of 'Spontaneous' Regressions of Cancer," *Journal of the American Academy of Psychoanalysis* 1 (1973): 303–307; Theodore R. Miller, "Psychophysiologic Aspects of Cancer," *Cancer* 39 (1977): 413–418.

32. George F. Solomon, Alfred A. Amkraut, and Phyllis Kasper, "Immunity, Emotions and Stress," *Psychotherapy and Psychosomatics* 23 (1974): 209–217.

33. Robert Ornstein and David Sobel, *The Healing Brain: A New Perspective on the Brain and Health* (New York: Simon & Schuster, 1987).

34. J. K. Kiecoltk-Glaser and Ronald Glaser, "Psychological Influences on Immunity: Making Sense of the Relationship between Stressful Life Events and Health," *Advances in Experimental Medicine and Biology,* 245 (1988): 237–247.

35. S. Cobb and R. M. Rose, "Hypertension, Peptic Ulcer, and Diabetes in Air Traffic Controllers," *Journal of the American Medical Association* 244 (1973): 1357–1358.

36. Alexander L. Strasser, "Outside Stress Factors May Underlie Variations in Workplace Productivity," *Occupational Health & Safety* 58, no. 3 (March 1989): 20.

37. Dennis G. Brown, "Stress as a Precipitant Factor of Eczema," *Journal of Psychosomatic Research* 16 (1972): 321–327.

38. G. W. Brown et al., "Life Events and Psychiatric Disorders," parts 1 and 2, *Psychological Medicine* 3 (1973): 74–87, 159–176; B. Cooper and J. Sylph, "Life Events and the Onset of Neurotic Illness: An Investigation in General Practice," *Psychological Medicine* 3 (1973): 421–435; Arthur Schless et al., "The Role of Stress as a Precipitating Factor of Psychiatric Illness," *British Journal of Psychiatry* 130 (1977): 19–22.

39. Christopher T. Cory, "The Stress-Ridden Inspection Suite and Other Jittery Jobs," *Psychology Today* (January 1979): 13–14.

40. John W. Jones, "A Measure of Staff Burnout among Health Professionals," presented at American Psychological Association meeting, Montreal (September 1980).

41. Penelope Want, Karen Seringer, Tom Schmitz, and Mary Bruno, "A Cure for Stress?" *Newsweek* (October 12, 1987): 64–65.

42. Herbert Benson, with Miriam Z. Klipper, *The Relaxation Response* (New York: William Morrow, 1976).

43. Edmond Jacobson, *Progressive Relaxation,* 2d ed. (Chicago: University of Chicago Press, 1938).

44. Benson, op. cit.

45. Vera Fryling, "Autogenic Training," in *The New Holistic Health Handbook: Living Well in a New Age,* Shepherd Bliss (ed.) (Lexington, Mass.: Stephen Green Press, 1985).

46. Jerrold S. Greenberg, *Student-Centered Health Instruction* (Reading, Mass.: Addison-Wesley, 1978).

47. D. G. Danskin and M. A. Crow, *Biofeedback: An Introduction and Guide* (Palo Alto, Calif.: Mayfield, 1981); M. D. Litt, "Mediating Factors in Non-Medical Treatment for Migraine Headache: Toward an Interactional Model," *Journal of Psychosomatic Research* 30 (1986): 505–519.

48. Ruth Rosenbaum, "The Body's Inner Voices," *New Times* (June 26, 1978): 48.

49. Wiebe and McCallum, op. cit.

50. Jonathon D. Brown and Judith M. Siegel, "Exercise as a Buffer of Life Stress: A Prospective Study of Adolescent Health," *Health Psychology* 7, no. 4 (1988): 341–353.

51. Andrew Steptoe and Sarah Cox, "Acute Effects of Aerobic Exercise on Mood," *Health Psychology* 7, no. 4 (1988): 329–340.

52. Jewell, op. cit.

Chapter 7

1. James C. Coleman, *Intimate Relationships, Marriage and Family* (Indianapolis: Bobbs-Merrill, 1984).

2. Susan Sprecher and Kathleen McKinney, "Barriers in the Initiation of Intimate Heterosexual Relationships and Strategies for Intervention," *Journal of Social Work and Human Sexuality* 5, no. 2 (Spring–Summer 1987): 97–110.

3. Based on Stephen R. Marks, "Toward a Systems Theory of Marital Quality," *Journal of Marriage and the Family* 51 (February 1989): 15–26.
4. William H. Masters et al., *Human Sexuality*, 3d ed. (Glenview, Ill.: Scott, Foresman, 1988).
5. Ibid.
6. Ibid.
7. Bernard I. Murstein, "Mate Selection in the 1970s," *Journal of Marriage and the Family* 42, no. 4 (November 1980): 777–792.
8. Daniel Goleman, "Study Defines Major Sources of Conflict between Sexes: Differences Are Found in What Disturbs Men and Women," *New York Times* (June 13, 1989): C1, C14.
9. Bernard I. Murstein (ed.), *Theories of Attraction and Love* (New York: Springer, 1971).
10. Discussion of changing attitudes in this section taken from Arland Thornton, "Changing Attitudes toward Family Issues in the United States," *Journal of Marriage and the Family* 51 (May 1989): 873–893.
11. "Americans Are Marrying Later Than They Used To," *NCHS Monthly Vital Statistics Report* 38, no. 2 (Supplement) (April 3, 1990): 4.
12. Thornton, op. cit.
13. Thornton, op. cit.
14. Eleanor D. Macklin, "Nonmarital Heterosexual Cohabitation," in *Marriage: Creating a Partnership*, 2d ed., Chesser and Gray (eds.) (Dubuque, Iowa: Kendall-Hunt, 1979): 67.
15. Thornton, op. cit.
16. Katherine Trent and Scott J. South, "Structural Determinants of the Divorce Rate: A Cross-Societal Analysis," *Journal of Marriage and the Family* 51 (May 1989): 393.
17. National Center for Health Statistics, "Annual Summary of Births, Marriages, Divorces, and Deaths: United States, 1988," *Monthly Vital Statistics Report* 37, no. 13 (Hyattsville, Md.: U.S. Public Health Service, 1989).
18. Sara McLanahan and Karen Booth, "Mother-Only Families: Problems, Prospects, and Politics," *Journal of Marriage and the Family* 51 (August 1989): 557.
19. Judith Wallerstein and Joan Kelly, *Surviving the Breakup: How Children and Parents Cope with Divorce* (New York: Basic Books, 1980); Wallerstein and Kelly, "The Effects of Parental Divorce: Experiences of the Child in Later Latency," *American Journal of Orthopsychiatry* 48 (1979): 256–269; Wallerstein and Kelly, "The Effects of Parental Divorce: The Adolescent Experience," in *The Child in His Family: Children at Psychiatric Risk*, vol. 3, A. J. Koopernik (ed.) (New York: Wiley, 1974).
20. Elizabeth R. Allgeier and Albert R. Allgeier, *Sexual Interactions* (Lexington, Mass.: D C Heath, 1984): 155–156.
21. S. S. Wachtel, "H-V Antigen and Sexual Development," in *Genetic Mechanisms of Sexual Development*, H. Vallet and I. Porter (eds.)

(New York: Academic Press, 1979): 271–277; F. Haseltine and S. Ohno, "Mechanisms in Gonadal Differentiation," *Science* 211, no. 4488 (1981): 1272–1278.
22. W. Masters et al., *Human Sexuality*, 3d ed. (Boston: Scott, Foresman, 1988).
23. M. D. Perlman et al., "Sex Education in the Inner City," *Journal of the American Medical Association* 255 (1986): 43–47.
24. A. B. Little and R. B. Billiar, "Endocrinology," in *Obstetrics and Gynecology: The Health Care of Women*, 2d ed., S. L. Romney et. al. (eds.) (New York: McGraw-Hill, 1981): 122.
25. Allgeier and Allgeier, op. cit., pp. 209–215.
26. Clellan S. Ford and Frank A. Beach, *Patterns of Sexual Behavior* (New York: Harper & Row, 1951).
27. G. T. McDonald, "Individual Differences in the Coming Out Process for Gay Men: Implications for Theoretical Models," *Journal of Homosexuality* 8 (1982): 47–60.
28. Liz McMillen, "Colleges Urged to Set Up Efforts to Prevent Rape, a Major Menace to Students on Campuses," *Chronicle of Higher Education* 35 (September 1, 1988): 1.
29. Mary P. Koss et al., "The Scope of Rape: Incidence and Prevalence of Sexual Aggression and Victimization in a National Sample of Higher Education Students," *Journal of Consulting and Clinical Psychology* 55, no. 2 (1987): 162–170.
30. Domeena C. Renshaw, "Treatment of Sexual Exploitation," *Psychiatric Clinics of North America* 12, no. 2 (June 1989): 257–277.
31. Ibid.
32. Alfie Kohn, "Shattered Innocence: Childhood Sexual Abuse Is Yielding Its Dark Secrets to the Cold Light of Research," *Psychology Today* (February 1987): 54–58.
33. D. Schetky, "Emerging Issues in Child Sexual Abuse," *Journal of the American Academy of Child Psychiatry* 25 (1986): 490–492.
34. Kohn, op. cit.
35. Ibid.
36. Ibid.

Chapter 8

1. Daniel R. Mishell, "Medical Progress: Contraception," *New England Journal of Medicine* 320, no. 12 (March 23, 1989): 777–787.
2. Ibid.
3. Jacqueline Darroch Forrest and Stanley K. Henshaw, "What U.S. Women Think and Do about Contraception," *Family Planning Perspectives* 15, no. 4 (July–August 1983): 157.
4. "Facts about Methods of Contraception," Planned Parenthood Federation of America (April 1985).
5. Rochelle G. Kanell, "Oral Contraceptives: The Risks in Perspective," *Nurse Practitioner* (September 1984): 25.
6. H. W. Ory et al., "The Pill at 20: An Assessment," *Family Planning Perspectives* 12 (1980): 278.

7. D. A. Grimes, "Birth Control Pills: A Reappraisal of the Pros and Cons," *Medical Aspects of Human Sexuality* 16, no. 8 (August 1982): 32J–32Y.

8. W. H. Masters et al., *Human Sexuality* (Boston: Little, Brown, 1982): 128–129.

9. R. A. Hatcher et al., *Contraceptive Technology 1982–1983,* 11th ed. (New York: Irvington, 1982): 84.

10. "Searle Quits IUDs," *Newsweek* (February 10, 1986): 60.

11. Mary Alice Johnson, "The Cervical Cap as a Contraceptive Alternative," *Nurse Practitioner* 10, no. 1 (January 1985).

12. Masters et al., op. cit., p. 137.

13. "Vasectomy: Facts about Male Sterilization," (Patient Information Library, Daly City, Calif.: Krames Communication, 1987): 2.

14. Larry Wichman, "Twenty-First Century Birth Control," *Men's Fitness* 6, no. 3 (March 1990): 100–103.

15. Discussion of changing attitudes in this section taken from Arland Thornton, "Changing Attitudes toward Family Issues in the United States," *Journal of Marriage and the Family* 51 (May 1989): 873–893.

16. J. Evoy, *The Rejected: Psychological Consequences of Parental Rejection* (University Park: Pennsylvania State University Press, 1982).

17. Willard W. Hartup, "Social Relationships and Their Developmental Significance," *American Psychologist* 44, no. 2 (February 1989): 120–126.

18. Victor Frankl, *Man's Search for Meaning,* 3d ed. (New York: Touchstone, 1984).

19. Linda Thompson and Alexis J. Walker, "Gender in Families: Women and Men in Marriage, Work, and Parenthood," *Journal of Marriage and the Family* 51 (November 1989): 845–871.

20. Pamela Kotler and Deborah Lee Wingard, "The Effect of Occupations, Marital, and Parental Roles on Mortality: The Alameda County Study," *American Journal of Public Health* 79, no. 5 (May 1989): 607–612.

21. Ellen Greenberger and Wendy A. Goldberg, "Work, Parenting, and the Socialization of Children," *Developmental Psychology* 25, no. 1 (1989): 22–35.

22. Thompson and Walker, op. cit.

23. Ibid.

24. Sara McLanahan and Karen Booth, "Mother-Only Families: Problems, Prospects, and Politics," *Journal of Marriage and the Family* 51 (August 1989): 558–559.

25. McLanahan and Booth, op. cit., p. 563.

26. H. K. Nadler and B. D. Burton, "Genetics," in *Fetal and Maternal Medicine,* E. J. Quilligan and N. Kretchmer (eds.) (New York: Wiley, 1980): 59–107.

27. W. Hogge et al., "Chorionic Villus Sampling: Experiences of the First 1,000 Cases," *American Journal of Obstetrics and Gynecology* 154 (1986): 1249–1252.

28. Hatcher et al., "Pregnancy Testing and Management of Early Pregnancy," in *Contraceptive Technology 1988–1989,* 14th rev. ed. (New York: Irvington 1988): 380–387.

29. David W. Martin, "Alcohol and Drug Abuse in Pregnancy: Information for Patients," in *Pregnancy, Childbirth, and Parenthood,* Paul Ahmed (ed.) (New York: Elsevier, 1981): 141–142; G. D. Zike, "Maternal Alcohol Use and Its Effects on the Fetus," *Physician Assistant and Health Practitioner* (February 1981): 86–94, 140–151.

30. E. Braunwald et al. (eds.), *Harrison's Principles of Internal Medicine,* 11th ed. (New York: McGraw-Hill, 1987): 1204.

Chapter 9

1. Bennett Lorber, "Changing Patterns of Infectious Diseases," *American Journal of Medicine* 84, no. 3 (March 1988): 569–578.

2. Ibid.

3. Judith S. Mausner and Shira Kramer, *Epidemiology: An Introductory Text* (Philadelphia: W B Saunders, 1985).

4. Peter A. Schlesinger, "Lyme Disease: Prevention and Intervention," *Hospital Medicine* (October 1989): 92–119.

5. Joanne Silberner, "Best Ways to Fight That Cold," *U.S. News and World Report* (January 29, 1990): 54–60.

6. Lawrence K. Altman, "Infections Still a Big Threat," *New York Times* (July 20, 1982): C2.

7. Abram S. Benenson (ed.), *Control of Communicable Diseases in Man,* 13th ed. (Washington, D.C.: American Public Health Association, 1981): 161–169.

8. C. C. Boyd and H. Sheldon, *An Introduction to the Study of Disease,* 7th ed. (Philadelphia: Lea & Febiger, 1977): 304.

9. Lawrence K. Altman, "Quandary for Patients: Have Surgery, or Await Test for Hepatitis C?" *New York Times* (February 13, 1990): C3.

10. A. S. Evans et al., "Seroepidemiologic Studies of Infectious Mononucleosis with EB Virus," *New England Journal of Medicine* 297 (1968): 1121.

11. Ibid.

12. B. H. Park and R. H. Good, *Principles of Modern Immunology: Basic and Clinical* (Philadelphia: Lea & Febiger, 1974).

13. Hatcher et al., *Contraceptive Technology 1988–89,* 14th ed. (New York: Irvington, 1988): 14–45.

14. Ibid.

15. Ibid.

16. C. E. Campbell and R. J. Herten, "VD to STD: Redefining Venereal Disease," *American Journal of Nursing* 81, no. 9 (September 1981): 1629–1635.

17. L. B. Meeks and P. Heit, *Human Sexuality: Making Responsible Decisions* (Philadelphia: W B Saunders, 1982).

18. A. J. Nahmias et al., "Epidemiology of Cervical Cancer," in *Viral Infections of Man: Epidemiological Control,* A. S. Evans (ed.) (New York: Plenum, 1975).

19. Boyd and Sheldon, op. cit.
20. Hatcher et al., op. cit.
21. Mark Bricklin (ed.), "Making Chlamydia Detection Easier," *Medical Care Yearbook 1990* (Emmaus, Pa.: Rodale Press, 1990).
22. Neville Golden, "Treating the Adolescent with *Chlamydia trachomatis* Infection," *Medical Aspects of Human Sexuality* 19, no. 7 (July 1985): 80.
23. Centers for Disease Control, "*Chlamydia Trachomatis* Infections, "*Morbidity and Mortality Weekly Report* (January 29, 1990): 28.
24. Steven Findlay with Joanne Silberner, "The Worsening Spread of the AIDS Crisis," *U.S. News and World Report* 34, no. 3 (August 23, 1985): 53ff.
25. Lauren Poole, "HIV Infection in Women," in *The AIDS Knowledge Base*, P. T. Cohen et al. (eds.) (Waltham, Mass.: Medical Publishing Group, 1990): 4.2.9, p. 1.
26. Hatcher et al., op. cit., pp. 1–13.
27. Ibid.
28. Joseph E. Smith et al., "Everyday Ethics in AIDS Care," *AIDS Patient Care* (October 1989): 27–31.
29. P. Samuel Pegram, "Human Immunodeficiency Virus Infection," *North Carolina Medical Journal* 50, no. 3 (March 1989): 151–154.
30. Hatcher et al., op. cit., pp. 1–13.
31. Lawrence K. Altman, "Quandary," op. cit.
32. Ibid.
33. Pegram, op. cit.
34. Michael S. Gottlieb and Mark Katz, "A Clinician's Report from the AIDS Conference," *AIDS Patient Care* (October 1989): 9–12.
35. Smith et al., op. cit.

Chapter 10

1. American Heart Association, *1990 Heart and Stroke Facts* (Dallas: American Heart Association, 1989).
2. Ibid., p. 1.
3. Ibid.
4. L. M. Elston, *It's Your Body: An Explanatory Text in Basic Regional Anatomy with Functional and Clinical Considerations* (New York: McGraw-Hill, 1975): 485–486; Robert C. Schlandt et al., "Anatomy of the Heart," in *The Heart*, 7th ed., J. Willis Hurst et al. (eds.) (New York: McGraw-Hill, 1989).
5. American Heart Association, op. cit., p. 9.
6. Ibid., pp. 11–12; W. Boyd and H. Sheldon, *An Introduction to the Study of Disease*, 7th ed. (Philadelphia: Lea & Febiger, 1977); William C. Roberts, "The Hypertensive Disease," in *Topics in Hypertension*, J. H. Laragh (ed.) (New York: Dun Donelly, 1980).
7. American Heart Association, op. cit., p. 11.
8. Ibid., p. 6.
9. Ibid.
10. Gina Kolata, "Report Urges Low-Fat Diet for Everyone," *New York Times* (February 28, 1990): A-1, A-22.
11. Ibid., pp. 17–21.
12. Ibid., p. 17.
13. Ibid., p. 15.
14. American Heart Association, *Sex and Heart Disease* (Dallas: American Heart Association, 1983).
15. American Heart Association, *1990 Facts*, p. 2.
16. R. S. Fowler and W. E. Fordyce, *Stroke: Why Do They Behave That Way?* (Dallas: American Heart Association, n.d.); *Self-Care for the Hemiplegic* (Minneapolis: Sister Kenny Institute, 1977).
17. American Heart Association, *1990 Facts*, p. 150.
18. Frederic R. Kahl et al., *A Patient's Guide to Cardiac Catheterization* (Raleigh, N.C.: Bowman Gray School of Medicine, North Carolina Baptist Hospital, 1986).
19. Steering Committee of the Physicians' Health Study Research Group, "Final Report on the Aspirin Component of the Ongoing Physicians' Health Study," *New England Journal of Medicine* 321, no. 3 (July 20, 1989): 129–135; Valentin Fuster et al., "Aspirin in the Prevention of Coronary Disease," *New England Journal of Medicine* 321, no. 3 (July 20, 1989): 183–185.
20. American Heart Association, *1990 Facts*, p. 16.
21. Boyd and Sheldon, op. cit., pp. 228–234.
22. American Heart Association, *1990 Facts*, p. 29.
23. Ibid., pp. 33–34.
24. Ibid., p. 18.
25. S. P. Fortmann et al., "Effect of Long Term Community Health Education on Blood Pressure and Hypertension Control," *American Journal of Epidemiology* 132, no. 4 (1990): 629–646; J. A. Berlin and G. A. Colditz, "A Meta-Analysis of Physical Activity in the Prevention of Coronary Heart Disease," *American Journal of Epidemiology* 132, no. 4 (1990): 612–627.
26. *You and Your Heart* (South Deerfield, Mass.: Channing L. Bete, 1986): 12.
27. American Heart Association, *1990 Facts*, p. 18.
28. L. Rosenberg et al., "Oral Contraceptive Use in Relation to Non-Fatal Myocardial Infarction," *American Journal of Epidemiology* 111, no. 1 (1980): 59; D. E. Krueger et al., "Fatal Myocardial Infarction and the Role of Oral Contraceptives," *American Journal of Epidemiology* 111, no. 6 (1980): 655.
29. American Heart Association, *1990 Facts*, pp. 18–19.
30. R. S. Paffenbarger et al., "A Natural History of Athleticism and Cardiovascular Health," *Journal of the American Medical Association* 252 (1984): 491–495; J. N. Morris et al., "Incidence and Prediction of Ischaemic Heart Disease in London Busmen," *Lancet* ii (1966): 553–559; H. Blackburn, "Physical Activity and Coronary Heart Disease: A Brief Update and Population View," *Journal of Cardiac Rehabilitation* 3 (1983): 101–111, 171–174; K. E. Powell et al., "Physical Activity and the Incidence of Coronary Heart Disease," *Annual Review of Public Health* 8 (1987): 253–287.
31. American Heart Association, *1990 Facts*, p. 20.
32. Ibid.

33. Ibid., p. 3.
34. W. Windelstein and M. Maimot, "Primary Prevention of Ischemic Heart Disease: Evaluation of Community Intervention," *Annual Review of Public Health* 2 (1981): 253–273.

Chapter 11

1. American Cancer Society, *Cancer Facts and Figures—1990* (Atlanta, Ga.: American Cancer Society, 1990): 3.
2. Ibid.
3. G. R. Newell et al., "Epidemiology of Cancer," in *Cancer Principles and Practices of Oncology*, V. T. DeVita et al. (eds.) (Philadelphia: Lippincott, 1982): 3–32.
4. Bobbie M. Atwell, "Psychosocial Aspects of Cancer," in *Understanding Cancer*, Bobbie M. Atwell and Robert Michiellutte (eds.) (Winston-Salem, N.C.: Oncology Research Center, Bowman Gray School of Medicine, 1986): 196–206.
5. Rob Buckman, "Communicating with Cancer Patients," *The Practitioner* 233 (October 22, 1989): 1393–1396.
6. American Cancer Society, op. cit., p. 13.
7. D. Schottenfeld, "The Epidemiology of Cancer," *Cancer* 47 (1981): 1095–1108.
8. Norton Nelson, "Cancer Prevention: Environmental, Industrial, and Occupational Factors," *Cancer* 47 (1981): 1065–1070.
9. American Cancer Society, op. cit., p. 18.
10. Ibid., p. 9.
11. Ibid., p. 13.
12. Ibid., p. 18.
13. American Cancer Society, op. cit., p. 22.
14. Caryn Lerman et al., "Reducing Avoidable Cancer Mortality through Prevention and Early Detection Regimens," *Cancer Research* 49 (September 15, 1989): 4955–4962.
15. American Cancer Society, op. cit., p. 27.
16. Judy Bahnson, "What You Must Know about the Pap Smear and Cancer Prevention" (Winston-Salem, N.C.: Cervical Cancer Prevention Project at Bowman Gray School of Medicine).
17. American Cancer Society, "Colorectal Cancer: Go for Early Detection" (Atlanta, Ga.: American Cancer Society).
18. "Getting Good Care Means Knowing All the Choices," *U.S. News & World Report* (July 11, 1988): 56.
19. American Cancer Society, op. cit., p. 13.
20. J. Michael Sterchi, "Surgical Management of the Cancer Patient," Atwell and Michiellutte (eds.), op. cit., pp. 11–21.
21. Ibid.
22. Douglas R. White, "Chemotherapy," Atwell and Michiellutte (eds.), op. cit., pp. 35–51.
23. Barbara J. Culliton, "Fighting Cancer with Designer Cells," *Science* 244 (June 23, 1989): 1430–1433.
24. American Cancer Society, op. cit., p. 3.
25. Deborah Welch-McCaffrey et al., "Surviving Adult Cancers: Psychosocial Implications," *Annals of Internal Medicine* 111, no. 6 (September 15, 1989): 517–524.
26. Atwell, op. cit.

Chapter 12

1. Katie E. Cherry and Mark R. Morton, "Drug Sensitivity in Older Adults: The Role of Physiologic and Pharmacokinetic Factors," *International Journal of Aging and Human Development* 28, no. 3 (1989): 159–174.
2. Jerome H. Jaffe, "Drug Addiction and Drug Abuse," in *Goodman and Gilman's The Pharmacological Basis of Therapeutics*, 6th ed., A. G. Gilman et al. (eds.) (New York: Macmillan, 1980): 535–577.
3. Lloyd Johnston, *10th National Survey of Drug Usage among College Students* (Ann Arbor: University of Michigan, Institute of Social Research, February 1990).
4. Dan Sperling, "Teen Drug Use Drops, but Users Get Very High," *USA Today* (undated).
5. Amy Linn, "Of Motherhood," *Philadelphia Inquirer* (September 17, 1989).
6. Ibid.
7. Douglas Martin, "Big Bribe Helps Mothers Fend Off Allure of Crack," *New York Times* (March 7, 1990).
8. Jim Detjen, "Cocaine and Pregnancy: Experts Fear a Holocaust," *Philadelphia Inquirer* (December 15, 1989).
9. Brent Q. Hafen and Brenda Peterson, *Medicine and Drugs*, 2d ed. (Philadelphia: Lea & Febiger, 1978): 28.
10. Cherry and Morton, op. cit.
11. Brent Q. Hafen, *The Self-Health Handbook* (Englewood Cliffs, N.J.: Prentice-Hall, 1980): 77.
12. *FDA Consumer* (December 1980–January 1981): 14.
13. Robert Fink et al., "Sedative-Hypnotic Dependence," *American Family Physician* 11 (1974): 116.
14. *Harvard Medical School Health Letter* 7, no. 9 (July 1982): 1–2.
15. *Amphetamine Report*, HEW Series 28, no. 1 (Washington, D.C.: National Clearinghouse for Drug Abuse Information, 1974).
16. T. W. Rall, "Central Nervous System Stimulants," in A. G. Gilman et al. (eds.), op. cit., pp. 592–607.
17. Jill M. VanDette and Laura Cornish, "Medical Complications of Illicit Cocaine Use," *Clinical Pharmacy* 8 (June 1989): 401–411.
18. Frank H. Gawin, "Cocaine Abuse and Addiction," *Journal of Family Practice* 29, no. 2 (1989): 193–197; VanDette and Cornish, op. cit.
19. Norman S. Miller et al., "Cocaine: General Characteristics, Abuse, and Addiction," *New York State Journal of Medicine* (July 1989): 390–394; VanDette and Cornish, op. cit.

20. George R. Gay, "Cocaine," *New York State Journal of Medicine* (July 1989): 384–386.
21. Gawin, op. cit.
22. Miller et al., op. cit.
23. Mary E. Guinan, "Women and Crack Addiction," *Journal of the American Medical Women's Association* 44, no. 4 (July–August 1989): 129.
24. VanDette and Cornish, op. cit.
25. Miller et al., op. cit.
26. VanDette and Cornish, op. cit.
27. Ibid.
28. Ibid.
29. K. Solomons and V. N. Neppe, "Cannabis—Its Clinical Effects," *South African Medical Journal* 76 (August 5, 1989): 102–104.
30. Ibid.
31. AMA Council on Scientific Affairs, "Marijuana: Its Health Hazards and Therapeutic Potentials," *Journal of the American Medical Association* 246, no. 16 (October 15, 1981): 1823–1827.
32. NIDA, "Marijuana: Research Findings," op. cit.
33. AMA Council on Scientific Affairs, op. cit.
34. Solomons and Neppe, op. cit.
35. Sidney Cohen, "The Volatile Nitrites," *Journal of the American Medical Association* 241, no. 19 (May 11, 1979): 2077–2078.
36. S. Cohen, "Psychotomimetics (Hallucinogens) and Cannabis" in *Principles of Pharmacology*, 2d ed., W. G. Clark and J. delGiudice (eds.) (New York: Academic Press, 1978): 357–369.
37. R. C. Peterson, and R. C. Stillman, "Phencyclidine: An Overview," in *Phencyclidine (PCP) Abuse: An Appraisal*, R. C. Peterson and R. C. Stillman (eds.) (Washington, D.C.: NIDA, Research Monograph 21, Dept. HEW, 1978): 1–17.
38. Cohen, "Psychotomimetics."
39. Jerome H. Jaffe, "Drug Addiction and Drug Abuse," in A. G. Gilman et al. (eds.), op. cit., p. 567.
40. P. V. Luisada, "The Phencyclidine Psychosis: Phenomenology and Treatment," in Peterson and Stillman (eds.), op. cit., pp. 241–253.
41. Gay, op. cit.
42. Joan E. Zweben and James L. Sorensen, "Misunderstandings about Methadone," *Journal of Psychoactive Drugs* 20, no. 3 (July–September 1977): 275–281.
43. George W. Bailey, "Current Perspectives on Substance Abuse in Youth," *Journal of the American Academy of Childhood and Adolescent Psychiatry* 28, no. 2 (1989): 151–162.
44. Miller et al., op. cit.
45. Zweben and Sorensen, op. cit.
46. Zweben and Sorensen, op. cit.; Bailey, op. cit.

Chapter 13

1. National Institute on Alcohol Abuse and Alcoholism, *Facts about Alcohol and Alcoholism*, DHHS pub. no. (ADM) (1980): 30–31.
2. National Center for Health Statistics, *Monthly Vital Statistics Report* 34, no. 6, Supplement 2 (September 25, 1985): 5.
3. James T. Weston, "Alcohol's Impact on Man's Activities: Its Role in Unnatural Death," *American Journal of Clinical Pathology* 74, no. 15 (November 1980): 755–758.
4. Council on Scientific Affairs, "Alcohol and the Driver," *Journal of the American Medical Association* 255, no. 4 (January 24–31, 1986): 522–527.
5. Editorial, *Journal of the American Medical Association* 255, no. 4 (January 24–31, 1986): 529–530.
6. National Committee for Injury Prevention and Control, "Injury Prevention: Meeting the Challenge," *American Journal of Preventive Medicine* (1989): 197–198.
7. Roland E. Herrington et al. (eds.), *Alcohol and Drug Abuse Handbook* (St. Louis: Warren H. Green, 1987): 181–183.
8. Morris E. Chafetz, *The Alcoholic Patient: Diagnosis and Management* (Oradell, N.J.: Medical Economics Books, 1983).
9. N. J. Estes and M. E. Heinemann (eds.), *Alcoholism: Development, Consequences, and Interventions*, 2d ed. (St. Louis: Mosby, 1982); George Vaillant, *The Natural History of Alcoholism: Causes, Patterns, and Paths to Recovery* (Cambridge, Mass.: Harvard University Press, 1983.)
10. Marc A. Schuckit and Robert M. J. Haglund, "An Overview of the Etiological Theories on Alcoholism," in Estes and Heinemann, op. cit.
11. Jean Kinney and Gwen Leaton, *Loosening the Grip: A Handbook of Alcohol Information* (St. Louis: Mosby, 1978).
12. Herrington et al. (eds.), op. cit., pp. 181–182.
13. This discussion of the impact of alcohol on the body, organs, glands, and central nervous system is based on information and studies cited in Eckardt et al., "Health Hazards Associated with Alcohol Consumption," *Journal of the American Medical Association* 246, no. 6 (August 7, 1981): 648–661.
14. John R. Senior, "Digestive Diseases Information Fact Sheet," *Alcoholic Liver Disease*, vol. 2 (1983).
15. Clair Toutant and Steven Lippmann, "Fetal Alcohol Syndrome," *American Family Physician* 22, no. 1 (July 1980): 113–117.
16. Arthur Flynn et al., "Zinc Status of Pregnant Alcoholic Women: A Determinant of Fetal Outcome," *Lancet* (March 14, 1981): 572–574.
17. Toutant and Lippmann, op. cit.
18. *FDA Drug Bulletin* no. 11 (December 1981): 1.
19. Kenneth E. Warner, "Smoking and Health: A 25-Year Perspective," *American Journal of Public Health* 79, no. 2 (February 1989): 141–143.
20. U.S. Department of Health and Human Services, *The Health Consequences of Smoking: Nicotine Addiction. A Report of the Surgeon General* (Rockville, Md.: U.S. Department of Health and Human Services, 1988): 7–9.
21. *The Behavioral Aspects of Smoking*, NIDA Research

Monograph Series, U.S. Department of Health and Human Services pub. no. (ADM) 79-882 (1979): 12–13.

22. *The Changing Cigarette: Report of the Surgeon General* (1981): 33–34.

23. *The Behavioral Aspects of Smoking,* op. cit. p. 12.

24. *Smoking and Health: Report of the Surgeon General* (1979): I-15 to I-17.

25. J. F. Nunn, "Smoking," *Applied Respiratory Physiology* (London: Butterworths, 1987): 337.

26. U.S. Department of Health and Human Services, "The Health Consequences of Using Smokeless Tobacco," *A Report of the Advisory Committee to the Surgeon General,* NIH pub. no. 86-2874 (April 1986).

27. Elbert D. Glover et al., "Just a Pinch between the Cheek and Gum," *Journal of School Health* (August 1981): 415.

28. American Cancer Society, *Cancer Facts and Figures— 1990* (Atlanta: American Cancer Society, 1990): 20; Warner, op. cit.

29. U.S. Department of Health and Human Services, op. cit., pp. 5–20, 565–587.

30. American Cancer Society, *Cancer Facts and Figures— 1989* (Atlanta: American Cancer Society, 1989): 20.

31. *Cancer: Report of the Surgeon General* (Washington, D.C.: U.S. Government Printing Office, 1982).

32. *The Changing Cigarette: Report of the Surgeon General,* op. cit.

33. Ibid.

34. American Cancer Society, *Cancer Facts and Figures— 1990,* op. cit.

35. *Smoking and Health: Report of the Surgeon General,* op. cit., p. I-16.

36. *The Changing Cigarette: Report of the Surgeon General,* op. cit.

37. *Smoking and Health: Report of the Surgeon General,* op. cit., p. I-15.

38. Jonathan E. Fielding, "Smoking: Health Effects and Control," part 1, *New England Journal of Medicine* 313, no. 8 (August 22, 1985): 496.

39. *Smoking and Health: Report of the Surgeon General,* op. cit., p. I-18.

40. Ernest L. Abel, "Smoking during Pregnancy: A Review of Effects on Growth and Development of Offspring," *Human Biology* 52, no. 4 (December 1980): 593–625; Richard L. Naeye, "Influence of Maternal Cigarette Smoking during Pregnancy on Fetal and Childhood Growth," *Obstetrics & Gynecology* 57, no. 1 (January 1981): 18–21.

41. *Smoking and Health: Report of the Surgeon General,* op. cit., p. I-22.

42. Ibid.

43. Jean Seligmann et al., "Women Smokers: The Risk Factors," *Newsweek* (November 25, 1985): 78.

44. *The Behavioral Aspects of Smoking,* op. cit.

45. Fielding, op. cit., p. 495.

46. Steven L. Gortmaker et al., "Parental Smoking and the Risk of Childhood Asthma," *American Journal of Public Health* 72, no. 6 (June 1982): 574–

578; D. M. Fergusson et al., "Parental Smoking and Respiratory Illnesses in Infancy," *Archives of Diseases in Childhood* 55 (1980): 358–361; Fielding, op. cit., p. 495.

47. *Primary Care & Cancer* (November 1986): 22–31.

Chapter 14

1. Stuart T. Brown et al., "Injury Prevention and Control: Prospects for the 1990s," *Annual Review of Public Health* 11 (1990): 251–266.

2. J. A. Waller, " 'Accident' Proneness: Fact or Fiction?" in *Injury Control: A Guide to the Causes and Prevention of Trauma* (Lexington, Mass.: D C Heath, 1985): 467.

3. Frederick P. Rivara, "Epidemiology of Childhood Injuries," in J. D. Matarazzo et al., *Behavioral Health: A Handbook of Health Enhancement and Disease Prevention* (New York: Wiley, 1984): 1003– 1020.

4. Committee on Trauma Research, Commission on Life Sciences, National Research Council, and Institute of Medicine, *Injury in America* (Washington, D.C.: National Academy Press, 1985): 1–21.

5. Rivara, op. cit.

6. National Committee for Injury Prevention and Control, "Injury Prevention: Meeting the Challenge," *American Journal of Preventive Medicine* (1989): 4–18.

7. Judith S. Mausner and Shira Kramer, *Epidemiology— An Introductory Text,* 2d ed. (Philadelphia: W B Saunders, 1985): 26–41.

8. Frederick P. Rivara and Marsha E. Wold, "Injury Research: Where Should We Go from Here?" *Pediatrics* 84, no. 1 (July 1989): 180–181.

9. National Committee for Injury Prevention and Control, op. cit., pp. 145–162.

10. Ibid., pp. 177–191.

11. Ibid.

12. Ibid.

13. National Center for Health Statistics, *Vital Statistics of the United States, 1987,* Vol. 2A. (Washington, D.C.: Dept. of Health and Human Services, 1989. Pub. no. (PHS) 89-1101).

14. National Committee for Injury Prevention and Control, op. cit., pp. 153–176.

15. Ibid.

16. Ibid., pp. 192–203.

17. Ibid.

18. Ibid., pp. 115–144.

19. Ibid.

20. National Center for Health Statistics, op. cit.

21. National Committee for Injury Prevention and Control, op. cit., pp. 145–162.

22. National Committee for Injury Prevention and Control, op. cit., pp. 145–162.

23. Ibid.

24. Ibid., pp. 163–176.

25. Carol W. Runyan and Elizabeth A. Gerken, "Epidemiology and Prevention of Adolescent

Injury," *Journal of the American Medical Association* 262, no. 16 (October 27, 1989): 2273–2279.

26. National Committee for Injury Prevention and Control, op. cit., pp. 163–176.
27. John W. Wright (ed.), *The Universal Almanac— 1990* (Kansas City, Mo.: Andrews and McMeel, 1989): 202.
28. National Committee for Injury Prevention and Control, op. cit., pp. 205–212, 243–251.
29. Ibid.
30. Federal Bureau of Investigation, "Uniform Crime Reports for the United States, 1989." (Washington, D.C.: U.S. Dept. of Justice, 1990).
31. Runyan and Gerken, op. cit.
32. National Committee for Injury Prevention and Control, op. cit., pp. 204–221.
33. Ibid., pp. 192–203.
34. Leon S. Robertson, "Behavior and Injury Prevention: Whose Behavior?" in Matarazzo et al., op. cit., pp. 980–989.
35. Robert A. Dershewitz, "Childhood Household Safety," in Matarazzo et al., op. cit., pp. 1021–1036.
36. American Heart Association, "Management of the Obstructed Airway," in *American Heart Association Instructors' Manual for Basic Cardiac Life Support* (Dallas: American Heart Association, 1981).

Chapter 15

1. M. W. Riley and K. Bond, "Beyond Ageism: Postponing the Onset of Disability," in *Aging in Society: Selected Reviews of Recent Research,* M. W. Riley et al. (eds.) (Hillsdale, N.J.: Erlbaum, 1983).
2. Nancy L. Wilson and Rosanne Trost, "A Family Perspective on Aging and Health," *Health Values* II, no. 2 (March–April 1987): 53.
3. Wilson and Trost, op. cit.
4. J. M. Guralnik and G. A. Kaplan, "Predictors of Healthy Aging: Prospective Evidence from the Alameda County Study," *American Journal of Public Health* 79, no. 6 (June 1989): 703–709.
5. Bernie Siegel, "How to Heal Yourself! The Curing Power of Hope, Joy, and Inner Peace," *Redbook* (June 1989): 110–160.
6. Emily T. Smith et al., "Aging—Can It Be Slowed?" *Business Week* (February 8, 1988): 60.
7. Charles F. Longino, "Who Are the Oldest Americans?" *The Gerontologist* 28, no. 4 (1988): 515–523.
8. Population Reference Bureau, *1989 World Population Data Sheet* (Washington, D.C.: Population Reference Bureau, 1989).
9. U.S. Department of Commerce, Bureau of the Census, *Statistical Abstract of the U.S.* (Washington, D.C., 1966).
10. Sandra Scarr and James Vander Zanden, *Understanding Psychology* (New York: Random House, 1987): 377.
11. Ibid., p. 394.
12. E. Fritz Schmerl, *The Challenge of Age* (New York: Continuum, 1986): 6.

13. David A. Snowdon et al., "Is Early Natural Menopause a Biological Marker of Health and Aging?" *American Journal of Public Health* 79, no. 6 (1989): 709–714.
14. W. H. Masters, V. E. Johnson, and R. C. Kolodny, *Human Sexuality,* 3d ed. (Boston: Little, Brown, 1988).
15. Geri Maas Burdman, *Healthful Aging* (Englewood Cliffs, N.J.: Prentice-Hall, 1986).
16. The discussion is based on Howard C. Hopps, "Pathologic versus Nonpathologic Aspects of Senescence," in National Research Council, *Panel on Aging and the Geochemical Environment* (Washington, D.C.: National Academy Press, 1981): 25–41.
17. T. Bennett and S. M. Gardiner, "Physiological Aspects of the Aging Cardiovascular System," *Journal of Cardiovascular Pharmacology* 12 (suppl. 8) (1988): S1–S7.
18. "The Calcium Craze," *Newsweek* (January 27, 1986): 48–49.
19. Beth J. Soldo and Emily M. Agree, "America's Elderly," in *Population Bulletin* 43, no. 3 (Washington, D.C.: Population Reference Bureau, Inc., September 1988).
20. Kenneth G. Manton, "Planning Long-Term Care for Heterogeneous Older Populations," *Annual Review of Gerontology and Geriatric Psychiatry* (New York: Springer, in press), from Soldo and Agree, op. cit., "America's Elderly," p. 20.
21. Soldo and Agree, op. cit., p. 20.
22. John M. Last (ed.), *Maxcy-Rosenau's Public Health and Preventive Medicine,* 11th ed. (New York: Appleton-Century-Crofts, 1980): 1338.
23. James A. Mortimer et al., "Alzheimer's Disease: The Intersection of Diagnosis, Research and Long Term Care," *Bulletin of the New York Academy of Medicine* 61, no. 4 (1985): 334–337.
24. David A. Lindeman, *Alzheimer's Disease Handbook* (Washington, D.C.: U.S. Department of Health and Human Services, April 1984).
25. Marsha F. Goldsmith, "Steps toward Staging, Therapy of Dementia," *Journal of the American Medical Association* 251, no. 14 (April 13, 1984): 31.
26. Robert I. Simon, "Silent Suicide in the Elderly," *Bulletin of American Academic Psychiatry Law* 17, no. 1 (1989): 83–95.
27. Ibid.
28. Ibid.
29. Smith et al., op. cit.
30. Susan B. Gilbert, "Health Promotion for Older Americans," *Health Values* 10, no. 3 (May–June 1986): 38–46.
31. Tamara Harris et al., "Longitudinal Study of Physical Ability in the Oldest-Old," *American Journal of Public Health* 79, no. 6 (June 1989): 698ff.
32. Suzanne Meeks et al., "Age Differences in Coping: Does Less Mean Worse?" *International Journal of Aging and Human Development* 28, no. 2 (1989): 127–140.

33. Jay Meddin and Alan Vaux, "Subjective Well-Being among the Rural Elderly Population," *International Journal of Aging and Human Development* 27, no. 3 (1988): 193–206.

34. Karen A. Roberto and Priscilla J. Kimboko, "Friendships in Later Life: Definitions and Maintenance Patterns," *International Journal of Aging and Human Development* 28, no. 1 (1989): 9–19.

35. E. Fritz Schmerl, *The Challenge of Age* (New York: Continuum, 1986).

36. Elisabeth Kübler-Ross, *On Death and Dying* (New York: Macmillan, 1970).

37. R. J. Kastenbaum, *Death, Society and the Human Experience*, 2d ed. (St. Louis: Mosby, 1981): 191.

38. R. A. Kalish, *Death, Grief, and Caring Relationships*, 2d ed. (Belmont, Calif.: Brooks/Cole, 1985).

39. A. D. Weisman and J. Worden, "Psychosocial Analysis of Cancer Death," *Omega* 6, no. 61 (1975).

40. Barbara Ward, "Hospice Home Care Programs," *Nursing Outlook* (October 1978): 646–649; S. Malkin, "Care of the Terminally Ill at Home," *Canadian Medical Journal* 115 (July 1976): 129–130; Anthony Amado et al., "Cost of Terminal Care," *Nursing Outlook* (August 1979): 522–526; R. G. Benton, *Death and Dying: Principles and Practice in Patient Care* (New York: Van Nostrand Reinhold, 1978): 64–66.

41. Harry Hayman, "Some Legal Suggestions—Your Will," *Help Your Widow While She's Still Your Wife: A Guide to the Rights and Benefits of Widows* (Alexandria, Va.: Retired Officers Association, 1983).

42. R. A. Kalish and K. K. Reynolds, *Death and Ethnicity: A Psychocultural Study* (Farmingdale, N.Y.: Baywood, 1981).

43. Christopher Bolton and Delpha J. Camp, "The Post-Funeral Ritual in Bereavement Counseling and Grief Work," *Journal of Gerontological Social Work* 13, no. 3/4 (1989): 49–59.

44. G. L. Engel, "A Unified Concept of Health and Disease," in *Life and Disease*, D. Ingle (ed.) (New York: Basic Books, 1963); J. Frederick, "Grief as a Disease Process," *Omega* 7 (1976): 297–306; W. E. Rees and S. G. Lutkins, "The Mortality of Bereavement," *British Medical Journal* 4 (1967): 13–16.

45. Jan Van Der Wal, "The Aftermath of Suicide: A Review of Empirical Evidence," *Omega* 20, no. 2 (1989–1990): 149–171.

46. Sarah Brabant, "Old Pain or New Pain: A Social Psychological Approach to Recurrent Grief," *Omega* 20, no. 4 (1989–1990):273–279.

47. Van Der Wal, op. cit.

48. Charles E. Hollingworth and Robert O. Pashaw, *The Family in Mourning: A Guide for Health Professionals* (New York: Grune and Stratton, 1977): 145–147; Benton, op. cit.

Chapter 16

1. Tom Ferguson, "Self-Care in the Information Age," *Medical Self-Care* 39 (March–April 1987): 77, 80.

2. Tom Ferguson, "The Power of Self-Care," *East West* (October 1986): 58–60.

3. Tom Ferguson, "The Rise of the Medical Prosumer," *Medical Self-Care* 45 (March–April 1988): 52, 64.

4. Tom Ferguson, "Toward Self-Responsibility for Health, Part II," *Medical Self-Care* 38 (January–February 1987): 67, 72.

5. Kirk Johnson, "A Medical Lab in Every Home," *East West* (October 1986): 61–65.

6. Keith W. Sehnert, *Selfcare-Wellcare* (Minneapolis: Augsburg, 1985): 147.

7. "Road Signs," *Vim and Vigor* (Summer 1988): 71–72.

8. American Cancer Society, *Cancer Facts and Figures—1990* (Atlanta, Ga.: American Cancer Society, 1990): 18.

9. Ibid.

10. Ibid.

11. Bill Thomson, "Are You Your Own Best Doctor?" *East West* (October 1986): 54–57.

12. Ferguson, "The Rise of the Medical Prosumer," op. cit., pp. 52, 64.

13. Jon Hamilton, "Shopping Mall Medicine," *American Health* (March 1988): 106–110.

14. Stephen Fulder, "A New Interest in Complementary (Alternative) Medicine: Towards Pluralism in Medicine?" *Impact of Science on Society* 143, vol. 36, no. 3 (1986): 235–243.

15. Ibid.

16. Mark Blumenthal, "Crashing the Quackbusters," *East West* (November 1988): 81–84.

17. Michael Davis, "Medical Freedom Fighters," *East West* (November 1988): 65–68.

18. Material on osteopathy and homeopathy from Sehnert, op. cit., pp. 112–131.

19. Fulder, op. cit.

20. Sehnert, op. cit.

21. Fulder, op. cit.

22. U.S. Bureau of the Census, *Statistical Abstract of the United States: 1990*, 110th ed. (Washington, D.C., 1990): 92.

23. Ibid., p. 100.

24. Malcolm Gladwell, "Health-Insurance Rates to Rise 20%–30%, Experts Say," *Arizona Republic* (October 28, 1988): 1, 6.

25. *1990 Medicare and Medicaid Benefits* (Chicago: Commerce Clearing House, 1990): 6–12.

26. Ibid., pp. 13–16.

27. Donald Robinson, "Who Should Receive Medical Aid?" *Parade* (May 28, 1989): 4–5.

28. Donald Robinson, "How Well Do You Know Your HMO?" *Parade* (February 5, 1989): 17–18.

29. Nancy Gibbs, "Sick and Tired," *Time* (July 31, 1989): 48–51.

Glossary

abortion—the termination of a pregnancy by removal of the uterine contents before the embryo or fetus is developed enough to survive on its own.

active euthanasia—a situation in which something is done to a patient to cause death.

active immunity—long-lasting resistance to an infectious disease acquired through the production of antibodies as a result of having the disease or being vaccinated against it (compare with *passive immunity*).

active prevention—preventive measures that require individuals to do something to reduce the risk of injury, such as use a seat belt.

addiction—a compulsive pattern of drug use marked by tolerance and psychic and physical dependence.

adjustment disorder—a nonpsychotic disorder in which the individual's response to a painful event is more extreme than would ordinarily be expected or considered normal.

aerobic exercise—sustained exercise of the whole body that increases the heart rate for a significant period of time.

affective disorder—a serious disorder of mood or feeling.

agent factor—an organism that causes an infectious disease; includes bacteria, viruses, rickettsiae, and fungi.

agility—the ability to change the position of the whole body quickly while controlling its movement.

alcoholic hepatitis—an alcohol-related disease in which the liver becomes swollen and inflamed.

allergy—an overreaction to a specific substance by the immune system.

Alzheimer's disease—a progressive, irreversible loss of mental and physical capacity associated with advancing age; the symptoms include severe memory loss, confusion, and depression.

amniocentesis—a procedure in which a doctor withdraws amniotic fluid from a pregnant woman's uterus to test for certain genetic disorders in the fetus.

amniotic sac—a fluid-filled sac within the uterus that encloses and protects the developing baby.

amphetamines—a group of synthetic stimulant drugs; the word *speed* is often used to refer to this group of drugs.

amyl nitrite—a prescription drug used to treat angina; it sometimes is used recreationally as a sexual stimulant.

anaerobic exercise—exercise in which the body's demand for oxygen exceeds its supply, producing oxygen debt.

anaplastic—refers to cancers whose cellular structure is so abnormal that they no longer resemble the cells of the tissue from which they originated.

angina pectoris—tightness, pressure, and intense pain in the chest caused by insufficient blood flow through partially blocked coronary arteries.

angioplasty—the process of increasing the diameter of the opening in a narrowed artery by expanding a balloon-like device.

anorexia nervosa—an eating disorder in which people severely limit the amount they eat, in effect starving themselves.

antibodies—chemical substances produced in response to an invading microorganism (the *antigen*) that can inactivate that microorganism.

antigens—parts of an invading microorganism that stimulates the body to produce a chemical substance (*antibodies*) that can inactivate a microorganism.

antisocial personality disorder—a personality disorder marked by tantrums and behaviors which violate the rights of others; examples include vandalism, aggressive actions, and theft.

anxiety disorder—a nonpsychotic disorder involving a severe and persistent level of fear or worry that interferes with an individual's everyday functioning.

aorta—the main artery of the circulatory system; carries blood from the heart to the arteries.

arrhythmia—an irregularity in the rhythm of the heartbeat.

arteries—blood vessels that carry blood from the heart to the various parts of the body.

arthritis—name for several diseases that affect the connective tissues of the joints.

atherosclerosis—narrowing of the arteries caused by fatty deposits on the inner arterial walls.

autogenic training—a method of self-induced relaxation in which the person imagines certain relaxing sensations.

autonomic nervous system (ANS)—the part of the peripheral nervous system that coordinates involuntary muscles such as the heart.

bacteria (singular: **bacterium**)—a single-celled plantlike microorganism.

balance—the ability to maintain or regain upright posture, or equilibrium, while moving or standing still.

barbiturates—sedative/hypnotic drugs that are used primarily to treat insomnia and, less often, for daytime sedation; some also have anticonvulsant properties.

basal metabolism—the number of calories burned when the body is at rest but not sleeping.

basic health insurance—insurance that pays for hospitalization and for medical and surgical expenses.

behavior therapy—a therapy that attempts to alter a person's behavior without attempting to discover its causes.

benign tumor—a tumor that grows slowly and remains localized.

benzopyrene—a chemical found in tobacco smoke, one of the deadliest carcinogens known.

bereavement—the loss of a loved or valued person.

bioelectrical impedance—a method of determining body composition in which a weak current is used to measure the body's water content.

biofeedback—a technique for developing conscious control over involuntary body processes such as blood pressure and heartbeat.

bipolar disorder—an affective disorder in which an individual exhibits mania and, in some cases, depressive episodes.

blood alcohol level (BAL)—the concentration of alcohol in the blood at a given time.

blood pressure—the force exerted by the blood on the walls of the arteries. It is measured by two separate figures taken when the heart is pumping and when it is at rest.

body composition—the proportion of different substances within the body, in particular the proportion of body fat to other body tissues.

body leanness—the quality of having more than 75 to 80 percent of body composition as lean tissue (muscle and bone) and less than 20–25 percent as fat.

brain death—this occurs if an EEG (electroencephalogram) detects no brain activity for 24 hours, even though breathing and heart circulation are artificially maintained.

bulimia—an eating disorder characterized by eating binges followed by purges.

butyl nitrite—a drug similar to amyl nitrite that is used recreationally as a sexual stimulant.

bypass surgery—surgery during which a portion of a healthy blood vessel, usually from the patient's leg, is removed and used to replace (bypass) the section of the coronary artery that is blocked.

calcium—the most abundant mineral in the human body; essential for building bones and teeth and ensuring normal growth.

calorie—the amount of heat needed to raise 1 kilogram of water 1 degree Celsius; used to measure the energy potential of food.

cancer—a group of more than 100 diseases characterized by the uncontrolled growth and spread of abnormal cells.

capillaries—very small blood vessels that serve as a link between the smallest arteries and veins.

carbohydrate—a basic component of food that is found in all forms of plant life and is the body's chief source of energy.

carbon monoxide—one of the most hazardous gases in tobacco smoke. It impairs the blood's capacity to carry oxygen.

carcinogenic—cancer-producing.

carcinomas—cancers that arise from the epithelium.

cardiac arrest—a total stoppage of the heart.

cardiovascular fitness—the ability to exercise the whole body for long periods and have the circulatory system supply the fuel that keeps the body going.

carrier—a patient who has recovered from a disease but still gives off disease-causing organisms.

central nervous system (CNS)—the brain and spinal cord, which together regulate all bodily functions.

cerebral embolism—impaired blood flow to the brain caused by a mass of abnormal material clogging a cerebral blood vessel.

cerebral hemorrhage—impaired blood flow to the brain caused by rupture of a cerebral blood vessel.

cerebral thrombosis—impaired blood flow to the brain caused by a clot blocking a cerebral blood vessel.

cervix—the narrow lower end of the uterus; located at the upper end of the vagina.

cholesterol—a fat found in all foods from animal sources and also manufactured by the human body that is thought to play a role in the development of heart disease.

chorionic villi sampling—a technique to test for genetic disorders in a fetus.

cirrhosis of the liver—a chronic inflammatory disease in which healthy liver cells are replaced by scar tissue, impairing the liver's function.

classical conditioning theory—a theory that explores how sets of different objects or events (stimuli) become grouped, or associated, in an animal's mind and are evidenced by its behavior.

clinical death—the brief period after heartbeat and breathing have stopped, but before vital body cells decay irreversibly.

clinical disease—the phase in the pattern of a disease when characteristic symptoms appear and a specific diagnosis is possible.

clitoris—an extremely sensitive external female sexual organ located under a hood formed by the upper joining of the labia.

cocaine—a stimulant drug extracted from the leaves of the South American coca plant.

cognitive appraisal—a psychological and intellectual technique for analyzing stressors and learning different ways of responding to stress.

cohabitation—an arrangement in which two unrelated people live together in a sexual relationship without marrying.

collateral circulation—a system of smaller blood vessels which develop to provide alternative routes for blood when a main artery is blocked.

comfort level—the level of compromise a person feels comfortable making among different goals in order to maximize overall benefits.

complete protein—a protein of animal origin (meat, fish, poultry, eggs, dairy products) that contains all nine essential amino acids.

conditioned response theory—a basic account of how animals learn to perceive simple stimuli and react with consistent responses.

condom—a thin latex or natural skin sheath that is placed over the erect penis before intercourse to prevent conception and the spread of disease.

congestive heart failure—a condition in which the heart cannot pump enough blood, resulting in congestion, or backing up, of blood in the lungs and other body tissues.

contraceptive implant—a device implanted under the skin that slowly releases chemicals to prevent menstruation.

convalescence—the final phase of a disease; the recovery period.

coordination—the ability to use the senses of vision and touch together with muscle sense to accomplish accurate, well-timed body movements.

coronary embolism—blockage of a coronary artery that occurs when a piece of clotted material breaks away from the arterial wall and dams a narrowed coronary artery.

coronary thrombosis—a blood clot in a coronary artery.

cross-sensitivity—a situation in which an allergy to one drug warns the user of possible similar reactions to other, chemically related ones.

decline stage—the phase of a disease when symptoms begin to subside and the patient may feel well enough to become more active.

defense mechanism—a mental strategy for preserving one's sense of self by protecting oneself from the anxiety associated with painful emotions.

denial—a defense mechanism in which an individual covers up truths about the outer world, ignoring the things that threaten his or her self-esteem and create anxiety.

dependence—a condition in which individuals become so accustomed to a drug that they cannot, or feel they cannot, function without it; may be physical, psychic, or both.

depersonalization—a defense mechanism in which an individual refuses to recognize that other people are fully human, with human feelings and emotions, and thus protects himself or herself from feelings of guilt, disappointment, or obligation.

detoxification—the process of weaning a person from physical dependence on alcohol or some other drug and repairing the toxic effects of the drug in the body.

diabetes—a condition, caused by an insufficiency of insulin, in which the body is unable to regulate the level of sugar in the blood efficiently.

diaphragm—a shallow rubber cup that is inserted into the vagina, where it completely covers the cervix, forming a mechanical barrier that prevents sperm from entering the uterus.

disability insurance—insurance that pays benefits to a person unable to work because of injury or illness.

distress—stress that has a negative effect.

drug—any nonnutritional substance that is *deliberately* introduced into the body to produce a physiological and/or psychological effect.

edema—swelling caused by fluid collecting in the tissues.

ejaculation—the process in which semen is forced out of the tip of the penis.

ejaculatory ducts—two structures formed by the ends of the seminal vesicles and the vas deferens that in turn join the urethra.

electroconvulsive therapy (ECT)—an organic therapy, also known as shock treatment, in which an electric current is applied to the brain to induce convulsions.

electroencephalogram (EEG)—the pattern of electrical waves that can be measured by placing electrodes on the skull.

electrolytes—substances that carry the electrical charges needed by cells to carry on their work. Potassium and sodium are the body's primary electrolytes.

embolism—a sudden blockage of a blood vessel by a blood clot (*embolus*).

embolus—a blood clot that breaks off an arterial wall, flows through the circulatory system, and becomes lodged in a smaller artery, where it blocks the flow of blood.

endogenous—pertaining to microorganisms that normally live on or within the human body, usually causing it no harm and often contributing to its welfare but sometimes causing disease.

environmental factor—an external biological, social, or physical factor that influences the probability of developing an infection.

enzyme—a type of protein that plays an important role in chemical reactions that break down cellular material in the body.

epididymis—a highly coiled network of tubing in the back of each testicle through which sperm cells travel as they mature.

epithelium—the cells forming the skin, the glands, and the membranes that line the respiratory, urinary, and gastrointestinal tracts.

essential amino acid—one of the nine amino acids that the body cannot manufacture in adequate amounts and that therefore must be present in the diet.

essential fat—fat that is necessary for the body's normal physiological functioning; it is involved in the storage and use of nutrients.

ethyl alcohol—the active ingredient in alcoholic beverages (distilled spirits, wine, beer) prepared from natural plant products such as fruits and grains.

eustress—stress that has a positive effect.

euthanasia—allowing or helping a person to die.

exogenous—referring to microorganisms that normally live outside the human body; many of these organisms can cause disease if they enter the body.

externality theory—the theory that overweight people eat primarily in response to external food-related cues rather than only to internal hunger caused by metabolic needs.

Fallopian tubes—two tiny muscular tunnels that transport ova from ovaries to the uterus.

fat-soluble vitamins—vitamins that are stored in the fatty tissues and cannot be excreted.

fetal alcohol syndrome (FAS)—characteristic adverse effects (including mental retardation, slow growth before and after birth, and a wide range of physical defects) exhibited by children born to women who drink heavily during pregnancy.

flashbacks—brief, sudden, unexpected perceptual distortions and bizarre thoughts—similar to those experienced while on an LSD trip—that occur long after the immediate effects of a drug have worn off.

flexibility—the ability to use the joints fully and move them easily through the full range of motion.

foreplay—sexual activity leading to intercourse.

fungi—many-celled plantlike organisms that must obtain food from organic material, in some cases from humans.

general adaptation syndrome (GAS)—a three-stage process the body goes through in adapting to stress. The three stages are alarm, resistance, and exhaustion.

generalization—the association of the emotions involved in a particular experience with a whole category of objects and events.

generic name—the name of the chemical ingredient in a drug.

genes—inherited "code" chemicals found in every cell of the human body. They control many aspects of an individual's development and functioning.

gerontology—the study of aging.

glucose—a type of sugar that is readily used by the body; a fuel vital for energy.

grief—the subjective, emotional response to bereavement.

group policy—a kind of insurance policy offered by employers to groups of employees.

hardiness—a personality trait which gives a person an optimistic and committed approach to life, so that he or she is able to weather life's ups and downs.

hashish—a concentrated and potent resin of *Cannabis sativa* (the hemp plant).

heart attack—the death of a portion of the heart muscle from lack of oxygen.

heroin—a narcotic analgesic derived from morphine and more than twice as powerful.

heterosexuality—a sexual or emotional preference for persons of the opposite sex.

homeostasis—the body's natural equilibrium, achieved through automatic mechanisms that control temperature, heart rate, blood pressure, and so on.

homosexuality—a sexual or emotional preference for persons of one's own sex.

host factor—an attribute of an individual that may increase or decrease his or her susceptibility to certain diseases; includes genetics, immunity, and general state of health.

hydrostatic weighing method—underwater weighing; a technique for measuring the proportion of lean tissue to fat tissue in the body. It involves weighing a person out of the water and then in the water and then calculating body density.

hypertension—an elevation of blood pressure from the normal range; increases the risk of developing a cardiovascular disease.

hypochondriasis—a somatoform disorder in which a person imagines that every minor physical complaint is the first sign of a major illness.

immunity—a group of mechanisms that help protect the body against specific diseases.

incomplete protein—a protein of plant origin (vegetables, seeds, grains, and nuts) that lacks one or more of the nine essential amino acids.

incubation period—the time between the first exposure to a virus or other disease-causing organism and the appearance of symptoms.

individual policy—an insurance policy bought primarily by single persons, couples, and families who are self-employed and do not have access to group plans.

inflammation—a general defense mechanism in the blood and tissues to ward off an irritant or foreign body. Also called the *inflammatory response*.

inhalants—a group of substances containing volatile chemical solvents that have psychoactive and other effects when breathed into the lungs.

intellect—the thinking, problem-solving, rational side of human consciousness.

interferon—a substance produced by the body to help protect it against disease.

intramuscular—pertaining to the injection of a drug into a muscle.

intrauterine device (IUD)—a soft, flexible device that is inserted into the uterus to prevent pregnancy.

intravenous—pertaining to the injection of a drug into a vein.

iron—a trace mineral that is one of the most important nutrients; it is essential for the production of hemoglobin in red blood cells.

isokinetic—referring to the strength training of muscles through the use of special machinery that provides equal tension at all angles over the full range of a joint's motion.

isometric—referring to the strength training of muscles by pushing or pulling against a fixed or an immovable object through a relatively narrow range of motion.

isotonic—referring to the strength training of muscles through exercises that involve muscle contractions throughout a complete range of motion.

labia—soft, sensitive folds of skin at either end of the opening of the vagina.

leukemias—cancers of blood-forming cells.

life expectancy—the average predicted length of life from birth to death.

life span—the length of time a person lives.

lifestyle—a person's overall way of living—the attitudes, habits, and behaviors of a person in daily life.

lipids—fats.

liposuction—a surgical procedure in which unwanted fat is sucked from the body through a tube.

LSD—a synthetic psychedelic/hallucinogen used recreationally; also called acid.

lymphocytes—protective white blood cells in the immune system that fight infection.

lymphomas—cancers arising from lymphatic cells.

macronutrient—a nutrient the body needs in large amounts, such as proteins, carbohydrates, and fats.

major depression—an affective disorder in which an individual experiences a profound unhappiness, loses interest in all aspects of life, and may suffer from other incapacitating symptoms.

major medical insurance—medical insurance designed to protect against the high medical expenses that may accumulate if a person is seriously injured or ill for a long time.

malignant tumor—a tumor whose cells grow in abnormal ways and may break away and spread to other parts of the body.

mania—a mood of extreme excitement; an aspect of bipolar disorder.

marijuana—material from *Cannabis sativa* (the hemp plant) that is dried and prepared for smoking and has a variety of mind-altering and physiological effects.

masturbation—sexual self-stimulation.

Medicaid—a federal-state health insurance program to assist people of any age who cannot pay for medical insurance.

Medicare—a federal health insurance program for people 65 and older and those who are disabled.

melanomas—cancers of the pigment-carrying cells of the skin.

menarche—a point during puberty in which a woman's ova begin to mature and ovulation first takes place.

menopause—the gradual permanent ending of a woman's menstruation and therefore of the reproductive phase of her life.

menstrual cycle—the monthly cycle in which the lining of the uterus first thickens and prepares to receive a fertilized ovum, then is discharged during menstruation if a pregnancy does not occur.

menstruation—the discharge of blood and tissues from the vagina that results if an ovum is not fertilized in the uterus.

mescaline—a psychedelic/hallucinogen derived from the peyote cactus of the U.S. Southwest.

metabolism—the process by which the nutrients in food are converted into body tissue and energy.

metastases—secondary tumors that form when cancerous cells break away from the original malignant tumor and are transferred to a new location in the body.

metastatic growth—the process by which cancerous cells break away from the original malignant tumor and are transferred to a new location in the body.

methadone—a synthetic drug that removes the desire for heroin and produces tolerance to its effects; used in the treatment of heroin addiction.

micronutrient—a nutrient consisting of minerals and vitamins that the body needs in small amounts for its essential functions.

minerals—inorganic elements that the body needs daily to help form tissues and various chemical substances.

mitosis—the orderly division of a cell into two new cells.

morphine—a narcotic analgesic that is the active ingredient in opium.

mourning—all the culturally reinforced patterns of thought, feelings, and behaviors that individuals experience as a result of losing a loved one.

muscular endurance—the ability to use muscles continuously over a period of time without getting tired.

muscular strength—the amount of external force the skeletal muscles can exert.

myocardial infarction—the death of a section of the heart muscle caused by a reduction in the supply of blood to that area.

narcissistic personality disorder—a personality disorder typified by an exaggerated sense of self-worth, a constant need for praise and attention, and a tendency to exploit others.

neoplasm—a group of cells growing in an uncontrolled fashion to form an abnormal swelling or mass.

nicotine—a toxic element found in tobacco that acts as a stimulant and is responsible for many of the harmful effects of smoking.

nonpsychotic disorder—a mental disorder in which the individual's functioning is seriously inhibited but in which his or her thought processes are not so grossly distorted that the individual loses contact with reality.

normal aging—certain biological aging processes that are time-related rather than being a function of disease, injury, or stress.

operant conditioning theory—a theory that examines the conditions under which behaviors are learned.

opiate narcotics—a group of narcotics made from the opium poppy that includes the opiates and opioids.

opiates—a group of narcotic analgesics that includes opium, morphine, and heroin.

opioids—a group of synthetic drugs that are chemically similar to the opiates.

opium—a narcotic analgesic substance made from the opium poppy; it is the parent substance of the opiate narcotics.

oral contraceptives (the pill)—synthetic equivalents of natural sex hormones that are prescribed to prevent ovulation and thus prevent conception.

organic therapy—a therapy that attempts to treat a person who has emotional problems in a physical way rather than through learning or talking; the most common type of organic therapy involves the use of medications.

orgasm—the stage of sexual response referred to as the climax.

osteoporosis—a chronic condition, most common among older women, that is marked by thin, brittle, easily fractured bones.

ovaries—two small internal female sexual organs that produce ova and female hormones.

overload—to work against a greater load than usual.

ovulation—the process by which ova periodically ripen and leave the ovaries.

ovum (plural: **ova**)—a female reproductive cell.

pacemaker—an electrical impulse center in the upper wall of the right atrium that regulates heartbeat by stimulating the heart muscles to pump in a coordinated fashion.

pancreatitis—inflammation of the pancreas associated with heavy alcohol intake.

panic disorder—a type of anxiety disorder characterized by episodes of extreme anxiety that may occur unpredictably or result from a specific situation.

parenteral—pertaining to the introduction of a drug in a manner other than through the digestive tract.

passive euthanasia—a situation in which no action is taken to prolong life even though action might enable a person to live longer.

passive immunity—short-term resistance to infectious disease acquired through the administration of antibodies formed by another person or an animal (compare with *active immunity*).

passive prevention—preventive measures that require little or no individual action on the part of those being protected; examples are automobile air bags and better street lighting.

passive smoking—the breathing in of air polluted by the tobacco smoke of others.

pathogens—organisms, such as bacteria or viruses, that can be the agent of an infectious disease.

pathological aging—a decrease in functioning caused by illness, stress, injury, and other factors.

PCP—a psychedelic/hallucinogenic drug once used as an animal tranquilizer; also called angel dust.

pelvic inflammatory disease (PID)—inflammation of the pelvis; a painful condition that can damage the reproductive organs and cause infertility.

penis—the external male organ used in sexual intercourse and urination.

peripheral nervous system (PNS)—all the nerves in the body other than those in the central nervous system; divided into the somatic nervous system and the autonomic nervous system.

personality disorder—a trait that impairs an individual's ability to function and cope with his or her environment.

phagocytes—white blood cells that protect the body from infection by engulfing and digesting invading foreign substances.

phobia—a type of anxiety disorder characterized by a persistent and irrational fear of a specific object, activity, or situation, leading to a compelling desire to avoid it.

physical activity—any movement that uses energy.

physical exercise—planned, structured, repetitive physical activities designed to improve or maintain one or more components of physical fitness.

placenta—a mass of tissue attached to the uterine lining that during pregnancy absorbs nutrients from the mother's bloodstream and transfers them to the bloodstream of the developing baby.

plaque—fatty deposits made up largely of cholesterol that can build up on the inner walls of blood vessels, narrowing them and eventually closing them completely.

potassium—one of the two primary electrolytes in the body; found in beans, fruits, vegetables, whole grains, fish, lean meat, and potatoes.

power—the ability to do strength exercises quickly.

prenatal—before birth.

priority—a need, want, or goal that is more important than another.

prodromal period—the second phase in the pattern of a disease; characterized by general symptoms such as headache, fever, runny nose, irritability, and generalized discomfort.

progression—the principle that once muscles adapt to an overload, the load should be increased slowly and gradually.

progressive relaxation—a technique for relieving muscle tension in which the individual tenses and relaxes various muscle groups in turn.

projection—a defense mechanism in which an individual attributes his or her undesirable motives and feelings to other people or even to inanimate objects.

prostate gland—the male organ that surrounds the urethra and produces about 30 percent of the seminal fluid.

protein—a basic component of food that is essential for growth and the repair of body tissues.

psilocybin—a psychedelic/hallucinogenic drug derived from a Mexican mushroom.

psychedelics/hallucinogens—a group of drugs that create illusions, distorting the user's mind by creating moods, thoughts, and perceptions that would otherwise take place only during the dream state.

psychic contactlessness—a defense mechanism in which an individual is unable to communicate with or become intimate with others.

psychoactive drug—a drug that acts primarily on the brain, producing altered states of mood, perception, consciousness, and central nervous system activity.

psychosomatic disease—a physical problem caused by the mind.

psychosurgery—an organic therapy in which small amounts of brain tissue are destroyed using laser surgery techniques.

psychotic disorder—a mental disorder in which an individual has lost contact with reality.

rationalization—a defense mechanism in which an individual does not admit that his or her motives are anything but the highest.

reaction time—the amount of time it takes to start moving once a person has decided to do so.

receptor sites—specific spots on cells where the molecules of a specific drug "fit."

regenerate—to replace damaged cells on a regular basis.

regularity—the principle that exercise needs to be done frequently enough, with enough intensity, and for a sufficient period of time.

relaxation response—a method of stress management similar to meditation that involves muscular relaxation and conscious breathing.

repression—a defense mechanism in which an individual denies having threatening thoughts, feelings, memories, or wishes.

Rh factor—a substance in the red blood cells which, if lacking in the mother and inherited by the first baby from the father, can cause the mother's blood to produce antibodies that result in a blood disorder in second and later children.

rheumatic fever—an inflammatory disease that affects the connective tissues of the body, especially in the brain, the joints, and the heart.

rickettsiae—infectious organisms that grow in the intestinal tract of insects and insectlike creatures and can be transmitted to humans through insect bites.

route of administration—the way a drug enters the body.

sarcomas—cancers that arise from supporting or connective tissues, such as bone, cartilage, and the membranes covering muscles and fat.

saturated fat—a fat that is usually solid at room temperature; found in meat, butter, whole milk, and some oils.

schizoid personality disorder—a personality disorder that involves a lack of desire to have social relationships.

schizophrenia—a serious psychotic disorder of the thinking processes in which the individual seems to be totally removed from reality.

scrotum—the loose pouch of skin that hangs behind the penis and contains the testicles and the epididymis.

sedatives/hypnotics—drugs that have either sedative (calming) or hypnotic (sleep-inducing) effects.

self-concept—all the perceptions that a person has about himself or herself; the result of thinking about oneself and evaluating what others think of one.

self-efficacy—confidence in one's ability to plan and control one's behavior and lifestyle components.

self-esteem—a person's feelings of worth and dignity which constitute an important part of overall health and well-being.

semen—the sperm-carrying liquid expelled from the penis during ejaculation.

seminal vesicles—two small structures located at the base of the bladder that produce about 70% of the seminal fluid.

setpoint theory—a theory in which the basic idea is that each person has a given weight range, or setpoint, that is natural to his or her body. Depending on their setpoints, some people stay thin and others stay fat regardless of what they eat.

sex—gender (maleness or femaleness); the physical expression of affectionate or erotic feeling which sometimes culminates in sexual intercourse.

sexuality—masculinity or femininity; the ways in which gender—male or female—is integrated into a person's personality and behavior.

sexually transmitted disease (STD)—an infectious disease that is transmitted during sexual intercourse or other sexual activity.

side effects—effects of a drug that are unwanted and unrelated to its essential purpose.

skinfold measurement—a method of measuring body composition using calipers to measure the fat under the skin.

social learning theory—a learning model based on the notion that behavior is learned by observing the experiences and actions of others.

sodium—one of the two primary electrolytes in the body. It is found in table salt and in many processed foods and also occurs naturally in many foods.

somatic nervous system (SNS)—the part of the peripheral nervous system that controls the voluntary muscles; it consists of nerves that run between the sensory and motor organs.

somatoform disorder—a mental disorder that manifests itself in the form of physiological symptoms; hypochondriasis is a well-known example.

specificity—the principle that to develop a component of fitness, one must work on that particular component.

speed—the ability to perform a movement or cover a distance in a short time.

sperm—the male reproductive cells.

spontaneous abortion—the expulsion of an improperly implanted or defective embryo or fetus from the uterus; commonly called *miscarriage.*

stimulants—drugs that activate the sympathetic division of the autonomic nervous system, causing a person to feel restless, talkative, more lively, and often unable to sleep.

storage fat—fat deposited under the skin and around the internal organs to protect them; some storage fat is used for heat production and energy.

stress—an individual's psychological and physiological response to any stimulus that is perceived as threatening.

stressor—a threatening event or stimulus that causes stress.

stroke—a sudden loss of brain function resulting from interference with the blood supply to a part of the brain.

subcutaneous—pertaining to the injection of a drug under the skin.

sublimation—a defense mechanism in which an individual substitutes socially acceptable behavior for unacceptable impulses, for example, conformity for hostility.

synesthesia—a blending of the senses in which a person "hears" colors or "sees" sounds.

tar—a sticky residue from burning tobacco consisting of more than 200 chemicals, many of which are hazardous.

testes (testicles)—the male organs that produce sperm and male hormones.

thanatology—the study of death.

therapeutic index—the safety margin between the effective dose of a drug and the lethal dose.

thrombosis—the development of a blood clot within an artery that severely constricts or blocks the flow of blood.

thrombus—a blood clot.

tissue—a collection of specialized cells in the body that perform certain functions.

tolerance—a situation in which the body becomes adapted to a drug so that increasingly larger doses are needed to produce the desired effect.

toxemia—the presence of toxins in the bloodstream during pregnancy.

trade-off—a need, want, or goal that has to be delayed, postponed, or given up in order for a priority to be accomplished.

transient ischemic attack (TIA)—a mild stroke that causes only temporary dizziness or slight weakness or numbness; such a stroke is often ignored.

triglycerides—combinations of fatty acids found in the human body.

tubal ligation—a surgical sterilization technique for women in which the Fallopian tubes are severed or tied.

tumor—a swelling or mass formed by a group of cells within a tissue that grow to an abnormal size and shape and multiply in an uncontrolled fashion.

umbilical cord—a ropelike tissue that links the developing fetus to the placenta nourishing its blood supply.

unsaturated fat—a fat that is usually liquid at room temperature. Most vegetable oils are unsaturated fats.

urethra—the tube from the urinary bladder through which urine and male reproductive cells are passed out of the body.

uterus—the womb; a hollow muscular internal female sexual organ that contributes to sexual response and shelters and nourishes the fetus during pregnancy.

vaccines—killed or weakened viruses that are taken orally or by injection to stimulate the body to produce antibodies that give immunity to the specific disease caused by a virus.

vagina—the canallike structure of the female body that extends from the bottom of the uterus to the vulva; it receives the penis during sexual intercourse and acts as a passageway for a baby during birth.

vas deferens—long tubes that carry sperm from the epididymis to the seminal vesicles.

vasectomy—a surgical sterilization technique for men in which a section of each vas deferens is removed.

veins—blood vessels that carry blood from the body back to the heart.

ventricular fibrillation—an arrhythmia in which the ventricles beat irregularly at an extremely fast rate.

virus—a microorganism that can reproduce only in living cells.

vitamins—substances found in food; they are needed in only very small amounts but are essential for triggering vital bodily functions.

vulva—the external genital region surrounding the opening of the vagina.

water-soluble vitamins—vitamins that dissolve in water and that the body can excrete.

withdrawal—a method of contraception in which the man withdraws his penis from the woman's vagina before he ejaculates.

withdrawal syndrome—an unpleasant and possibly painful condition that an individual who is physically dependent on a drug experiences when deprived of that drug.

Index

Boldface page references refer to features text, figure captions, and tables.

President's Council on Physical
    Fitness and Sports, 34
Pressure points, 285
Pressures influencing behavior,
    analyzing, 16–17. *See also*
    Peer pressure
Pressure to control severe
    bleeding, 285
Prevention
    active, 278–79
    passive, 279
Priorities, 14
Private health insurance, 328–30
Problem drinker, 251
Problem solving, 94
Prodromal period, 165
Professional help
    communicating with medical
        professionals, **209**, 323–24
    judging when to seek, 313–14,
        321
Progesterone, 128
Progression in exercise, 33
Progressive relaxation, 114–15
Prohibition, era of, 246
Projection, 87
Prostaglandins, 158
Prostate gland, **131**, 132
Proteins, 28, 43–44, 54, 55
Psilocybin, 240, 241
Psychedelics/hallucinogens, 240–
    41
Psychic contactlessness, 87
Psychic dependence, 222, 223
    on alcohol, 249
    on tobacco, 264
Psychic pain of cancer, 205
Psychoactive drugs, 221, 231–42,
    243
    cocaine, 225–26, 236–37
    designer drugs, 242
    marijuana, 225, 237–38
    opiate narcotics, 239–40
    psychedelics/hallucinogens, 240–
        41
    sedatives/hypnotics, 231–33
    stimulants, 233–36
    volatile solvents, 238–39
    See also Alcohol; Tobacco
Psychological bases for body
    composition problems, 71–72
Psychological health, exercise and,
    24
Psychosocial stages of
    development, 292–94
Psychosomatic disease, 81

Psychosurgery, 98
Psychotherapy, 97, 116
Psychotic disorders, 90–91
Puberty, 131, 133, 292–93
Pull school approach to body
    composition problems, 69–70
Pulmonary artery, 183
Pulse rate, 30, 35
    first aid and checking for, 283
    measuring, **317**, 317–18
Punishment, 92
Pupils, checking person's, 283
Push school approach to body
    composition problems, 71–72
Pyridoxine, **48**

Quackery, 217, 315–16, 325

Race
    assaultive injuries and, 276
    motor vehicle death rate and,
        273
    occupational injuries and, 272
Racial prejudice, 87
Radiation, 208
Radiation energy, 269
Radiation therapy, 215–16
Radical mastectomy, 215
Radon, 208
Rahe, Richard H., 105
Rape, 137–38, 276
Rationalization, 86–87
Reaction time, 25
Reassurance of worth in intimate
    relationships, 121
Receptor sites on cells, 226, **227**
Recommended daily allowance
    (RDA) for vitamins, **48–49**,
    53
Recreational injuries, 272
Recreational style, 10
Recreational use of drugs, 224
Rectal cancer, 212
Rectal exam, 320–21
Red Dye No. 2, **51**
Reflexes, 169
Regeneration, 7–8
Regularity of exercise, 33
Regulation of body composition,
    70, 72–73
Rehabilitation for drug users, 242–
    43
Reinforcement, 93
    positive, 92

Relating style, 11
Relaxation response, 115
Relaxation techniques, 114–16
Relief of discomfort, dependence
    on drugs for, 223
Religious affiliation, 6
    alcoholism and, 252
    birth control and, **143**
Remarriage, 126
Remission, 111
Repression, 86
Reproduction, 149–59
    childbirth, 159
    decision to have children, 149–
        52
    pregnancy, 152–58
        substances to avoid during,
            155–56, 226, 227, 237,
            254, 262
Reproductive systems
    female, 132–34
    male, 130–32
    marijuana use and effect on,
        238
Residential injuries, 271
Resistance stage of general
    adaptation syndrome, 105
Resources for changing behavior,
    17
Respiration, measuring, **317**, 318
Response to stress, 106–9, **107**
Responsiveness, checking level of,
    283
Restaurants, eating out in, 58–59
Resuscitation, cardiopulmonary,
    189, 282, 284
Reticular activating system (RAS),
    232
Retirement communities, 302
Rheumatic fever, 194
Rheumatic heart disease, 194
Rheumatoid arthritis, 172
Rh factor, 155
Rh hemolytic disease, 155
Rhinoviruses, 167
Rhythm method, 148
Riboflavin, **48**
Rickettsiae, 168
Right to die, 308
Ringworm, 169
Risk(s)
    associated with cardiovascular
        disease, 195–98
    for cancer, 206–11
    of cocaine use, 236–37
    of exercise, 25

smokeless, 260, 261
toxic substances in, 257–60
Tolerance
alcohol, 249
drug, 222
Toxemia, 156, 157
Toxic shock syndrome (TSS), 166
Toxic substances in tobacco, 257–60
Trade-offs, 14
Training, autogenic, 115–16
Traits associated with alcoholics, 252. *See also* Personality
Transfusion of blood, HIV spread by, 179
Transient ischemic attacks (TIAs), 190–91
Transplants, organ, 193, 211
Travel, changing patterns of disease and, 163
Treatment(s)
of alcoholism, 255
of cancer, 214–17
judging health, 314–16
of major cardiovascular disease, 192–93
See also Therapy
Triglycerides, 45
Tubal ligation, 149
Tumor, 202
benign, 203–4
malignant, 204
Type A behavior, 108, 111, 198, 301
Type B behavior, 108
Typhus fever, 168

Ulcers, peptic, 112
Ultraviolet radiation, 208
Umbilical cord, 154, 159
Unconsciousness, emergency care and, 286
Underwater weighing, 65
University of Pennsylvania Hospital, 226
Unsaturated fats, 46
Uppers, 233–36
Urethra, 130, **131**
Urinalysis, 156
U.S. Food and Drug Administration (FDA), 76, 144, 147, 262, 316, 318

U.S. Postal Service, 316
U.S. Public Health Service (PHS), 22
U.S. Supreme Court, 158
Uterine cancer, 210
Uterus, **133**, 133–34

Vaccination, **174**
Vaccines, 171–72
cancer, 216–17
flu, 168
Vacuum aspiration, 157
Vagina, 132, **133**
Vaginal cancer, 210–11
Vaginal sponge, 144–45
Valium, 230
Values, body composition problems and, 71–72
Valves, heart, 184
Vas deferens, **131**, 132
Vasectomy, 148–49
Vasodilators, 187
Vegans, 55
Vegetarians, food choices for, 55, 56
Veins, 185
Ventricles, 183
Ventricular fibrillation, 193–94
Vertebral artery, 186
Vinyl chloride, 208
Violence
alcohol and, 250
controlling, 281
defined, 272
injuries and, 272–73, 276–78
Viral infections, 110
Viruses, 166–68, **167**, 173, 178, 179, 180
Vitamin depletion, 56
Vitamins, 48–50, 55, 56
Vitamin supplements, 50
Volatile solvents, 238–39
Volunteerism, 302
Vomiting, bulimia and, 76–77
Vulva, 132, **133**

Waist-hip ratio, **64**
Wants, 12–13
clarifying your health, 15–16

Water, 52
Water-soluble vitamins, 50
Watson, John, 92
Weather, exercise and, 37
Weight, 61–62
at birth, 262
management of, 66–75
common approaches to, 66–69
successful, 72–75
theories about problems in, 69–72
prevention of cardiovascular disease and, 198
See also Body composition
Weight disorders, 75–78
Weight gain, eating for, 74
Weight-waist ratio, **64**
Weight Watchers, 17, 69
Well-being, health and, 2–8
White, Ryan, 178
White blood cells, 169
Whitney, Eleanor, 46
Will, making a, 307
Withdrawal method of birth control, 145
Withdrawal syndrome, 222, 233, 234, 249, 263–64
Womb, 133–34
Women
alcoholism among, 252
body fat in, 63–65
divorce and, 126
with genital herpes, 175
iron requirements of, 47
Type A behavior in, 108
in work force, 151
Work, injuries at, 271–72
Work force, mothers in, 151
Working style, 10
Workplace, chemicals in, 207–8
World Health Organization, 4, **143**
Smallpox Reference Center, **174**

Yeast infections, 169
YMCAs and YWCAs, 282
Young adulthood, 293
Yo-yo effect, 70